# In the Eye of the Eagle

# In the Eye of
# the Eagle

Jean-François Lisée

HarperCollins*Publishers*Ltd

Published by
HarperCollins Publishers Ltd
Suite 2900, Hazelton Lanes
55 Avenue Road
Toronto, Ontario M5R 3L2

Cover photo: Elizabeth Zeschin
Cover illustration: Heather Harrison

**Canadian Cataloguing in Publication Data**

Lisée, Jean-François
    In the eye of the eagle

Translation of: Dans l'oeil de l'aigle.
Includes bibliographical references.
ISBN 0-00-637636-3

1. United States — Relations — Quebec (Province).
2. Quebec (Province) — Relations — United States.
3. Quebec (Province) — History — Autonomy and
independence movements. 4. Nationalism — Quebec
(Province). 5. Parti québécois. I. Title.

E183.8.C2L5713 1990    327.730714    C90-095300-4

90 91 92 93 94 95 RRD 5 4 3 2 1

# Table of Contents

# Acknowledgements

This book was born, survived crises, and reached maturity thanks to the patience, encouragement, and good graces of a large group of friends, relatives, and kind and competent strangers, who were ready to give their help to a project that was sometimes deemed useless, sometimes overly ambitious. Marci McDonald, one day during a depressing presidential campaign, served as the spark to revitalize an idea that was dormant. John Sawatsky inadvertently brought the project out of the doldrums by pointing out, by his own example, that one has to dig, dig, dig. Larry Black, in New York, and Fred Harrison, in Ottawa, applied their talent and patience to many drafts of the original proposal and opened their homes to me during my visits to conduct interviews and research. Juliet O'Neill, Denis Nadeau, and Lucie Lessard, in Ottawa, Marc Goulet, in Quebec City, and Mavor Sawtell, in Boston, were kind enough to pretend that I wasn't bothering them when I invaded their homes and monopolized their telephones. Caroline Jamet and Stéphan Bureau, in Montreal, were among my chief victims. Pierre Tourangeau not only pointed me toward some information but provided the electronic hardware on which these thousands of words were produced.

The Canada Council's Explorations program provided financial aid; I suspect that the recommendations of my three "sponsors"—Michel Roy, Pierre Nadeau, and Colin MacKenzie—were of help. In Quebec, an overworked and efficient civil servant, Hélène Latouche, and a motivated trainee, Suzanne Bergeron, allowed me access to important documents. In Montreal, Robert Tellier ruined his eyes reading microfilm and digging up old newspaper articles without which at least one of the chapters in this book would never have been conceived. Louise and Willis Armstrong and Cleveland Cram, in Washington, interceded for me with friends and contacts who otherwise would have remained beyond reach.

Jim Lesar, my nearly pro bono lawyer in Washington, undertook the legal guerrilla warfare necessary to obtain thousands of American government documents. Driven by his thirst for truth and openness, Jim put the litigation departments of half a dozen government agencies on the defensive. Robert Bowen, professor at Colby College in Maine, assisted in these legal skirmishes by informing us of requests that he himself had made regarding Quebec questions. In Montreal, Maître Claude Melançon also represented me in a number of important steps. He was among the believers. In Toronto, Helen Heller championed the project, inspiring passion with her serious, warm voice.

Robert Parks, at the Roosevelt Library, Maura Porter, at the Kennedy Library, Regina Greenwell, at the Johnson Library, Joan Howard, at the Nixon Project, and Paul Marsden and Karry Badgley, at the National Archives, were a great help in the search for documents, as was Jeff Marshall, at the University of Vermont in Burlington. The staff at the Library of Congress and at the Canadian Embassy's library in Washington, Denise Pélissier, at the Archives de l'Université de Montréal, and many others also lent their support. Others were kind enough to open their personal archives to me.

I want to mention the assistance I received from Lise Bissonnette, André Bouthillier, Robert Bureau, Suzanne Côté, Daniel Creuzot, Serge Délisle, Johanne Dupuis, Louis Falardeau, Lorraine Fillion, Jean-Claude Goulet, Paul-André Goulet, Robert Hepburn, Michèle Leroux, Marie-Josée Lorion, Pierre Lussier, Andrée Roy, Régent Thivierge, and, of course, Elizabeth Zeschin. The entire team at Éditions du Boréal, directed by Pascal Assathiany, played its role of wise literary muse with competence, enthusiasm, and a touch of frenzy. Stacy Schiff then cracked the whip for the speedy translation ordered by David Colbert, of Harper and Collins.

Andrée and Jean-Claude Lisée, my parents, silently endured weeks of the clatter of the computer and the printer, sometimes late into the night. Their hospitality allowed me an ideal place to write, for which a mere thank-you is not enough. Marie-Claude Lisée, my older sister, was attentive and critical and an ideal reader. Because she sometimes yawned over the manuscript, subsequent readers have less reason to fall asleep.

No one, however, helped me more, or lived and suffered more closely through this enterprise than my collaborator, companion, conspirator, spouse, and lover, Catherine Leconte. She provided the moral support in the cycles of mania and depression that seized me as I worked. She was a perfectionist in her transcription of interviews recorded on what were called, between us, the "damned tapes." An editor with long linguistic teeth, she excised abused metaphors and flat sentences, purged these pages of twisted turns of phrase, tightened up flabby passages, forbade wandering detours, and fixed disjointed structures. If this book is readable, it is largely thanks to Catherine. I claim responsibility for the obscure, tortured, and kitsch passages, since I did not always follow her advice.

# About the text

This volume seeks to cast light on hitherto hidden events, which it means to present as accurately as possible. To that end, I have made a conscious choice not to soften harsh uses of language. At the White House, as in the parliament of Quebec, politicians occasionally put things crudely.

All scenarios have been reconstructed using texts or oral accounts from one or more participants. Conversations have been recreated from 240 interviews and several thousand documents. When sources have provided conflicting accounts, I have favored the contemporary written source over the retrospective interview, and have attached more importance to the vivid recollections of certain speakers than to the dilute memories of others. When equivalent sources conflict, I have mentioned both. The reader with a detailed interest in these sources should consult the notes and references which follow the main text.

*In the Eye of the Eagle* covers some fifty years of history. Events are recounted as they unfold, rather than from a standpoint of historical omniscience. The reader should remember that certain descriptions are thus valid only for the period under scrutiny, and that what is true in 1963 may have proved false by 1976, ludicrous even by 1990.

— Jean-François Lisée

*To*

Clément Marchand,
Pierre Tourangeau,
Elisabeth Gillion,
Frances Madden,
Réal Pelletier,

*who, over the last eighteen years, have
each in turn opened doors for me I
hadn't known existed.*

# Prologue

The independence of Quebec?
"The United States has no imaginable reason to
frown on such a tardy but natural development."
René Lévesque
in *Foreign Affairs*, July 1976.

For the United States, the independence of
Quebec would be "much more grave than the
Cuban Missile Crisis," nothing less than "a crime
against the history of mankind."
Pierre Elliott Trudeau
Washington, February 1977.

"Mr President, if Quebec secedes from Canada,
would you favor US statehood for any of the
remaining provinces, should they desire it?"

"I always make a practice, whenever I have a
town hall meeting of this kind, to avoid answering
at least one question. I think I will choose your
question for that response."
Jimmy Carter
To Spokane voters, May 1978.

# 1
# René Lévesque and the Heart-Broken Lovers

*I was thus in the process of becoming a "Yankee-bécois."*
*The south of the border attracted me so strongly...*
RENÉ LÉVESQUE

The American consul general in Montreal rarely lost his composure. But there were, as they say in Quebec, "damned limits" to his patience.

In the spring of 1972, John Topping had been living in Montreal for two years. The notion of Quebec independence was central among his preoccupations; it had become a part of his life. After all, his neighbor and friend, Englishman James Richard Cross, had been held hostage for two months, beginning in October 1970, by a group of violent Québécois separatists, the Front de Libération du Québec, or FLQ.

Topping had met with the leaders of the legal independence movement, including René Lévesque. He often discussed the economic consequences of the separatist plan with businessmen, analysed the electoral progress of the movement in his diplomatic dispatches, listened to what his local acquaintances, separatist and federalist, had to say.

He didn't like what he was hearing.

"Entirely too often, when the subject of separatism comes up here, I find Canadians blandly assuming that the US would actively support a separatist Quebec, to the extent of offering special assistance and even a 'special relationship,'" Topping wrote to his superiors at the State Department in Washington.

"A particularly disturbing aspect is that those who so assume are both pro- and anti-separatist," the consul continued. Both groups "assume that that old imperialist to the south would take full advantage of any opportunity to establish closer associations (read "dominance") with any available parts of Canada."

The indignant Topping assured Washington he "somewhat vehemently" insisted in these conversations that his country in no way harbored such intentions. He noted that his acquaintances, whichever side they were on, frequently seemed "disappointed" by his disclaimers; disappointed and disbelieving.

## "This order must not change"

Separatists and federalists shared this penchant, a need almost, to project their hopes and fears about Canada's future on to their southern neighbor. Over more than twenty-five troubled years, all kinds of theories had circulated about what Washington wanted, what Washington was doing, what Washington was plotting, what Washington would do in the event of a separatist victory.

"I'll bet my bottom dollar that the CIA has a permanent presence behind the scenes," Lévesque wrote at the end of his career, a perfect example of the extent to which the absence of hard information on American activities in Quebec opened the door to speculation.

Topping's circle of acquaintances did not, as it turned out, represent the entire range of opinion. Certainly some separatists and federalists believed that the United States would greet an independent Quebec with joy, but the contrary opinion was also very popular, especially in the separatist camp.

The FLQ claimed to be at war with the Americans as much as, if not more than, with English Canadians. Even former FLQ thinkers, like Pierre Vallières, were pessimistic about Quebec's chances for independence because, he reasoned, the "old imperialist to the south," Wall Street, the Pentagon and the Trilateral Commission, would not permit it. "Canada is the largest colony of the United States," Vallières wrote in 1977, "and Quebec must stay in its place within it, a province like the others ... this order must not change." Pierre Trudeau could count on the American armed forces, the former senior FLQ theorist added, because they "share his point of view entirely."

Popular Liberal cabinet minister Claude Castonguay came to a similar conclusion when he left political life in 1973. Speaking two months after the military coup in Chile, Castonguay declared that "the United States has shown many times that it does not like instability." So, he asked, "What makes anyone think the United States would look passively on Quebec separation?" They would not even have to send in the Marines, he added. "The best way for the United States would be to aggravate instability. This is more or less what the US was accused of doing in Chile."

When a demonstration by Quebec's truck drivers paralysed traffic around the Quebec parliament building in 1977, several Parti Québécois cabinet ministers surveyed the mess from a window of the stately stone building. "You know what this reminds me of?" asked one above the chorus of car horns, only slightly muffled by the closed window. "Allende," replied another. The CIA had heavily subsidized a strike by teamsters in Chile to destabilize the local economy and weaken the power of Marxist President Salvador Allende.

But not all Parti Québécois ministers shared this paranoia. "Let's not overestimate our own importance," warned Energy Minister Guy Joron. "Quebec's plans don't rock Western civilization. They don't crack the columns of Wall Street's temples, and they probably don't change even the last decimal point on General Motors' sales projections."

No one, however, placed more hope in the vision of an America favorable to Quebec sovereignty than the man who embodied and served as the engine for the dream of independence, René Lévesque.

The hopeful father of a sovereign Quebec had come close, in his formative years, to adopting the United States as his home. In 1943, at the age of 21, having run aground in his law studies, he found himself threatened with conscription. "Anything to get overseas, but not in His Majesty's uniform," he decided. His childhood in a bilingual corner of the Gaspé region having afforded him a sound command of English, he signed up in New York with the American Army's information service, who assigned him the rank of sub-lieutenant. His vision of the United States then becomes confused with the benevolent image of G.I.'s liberating Europe from fascism, handing out chewing gum and nylon stockings and introducing jazz to the Old World — all under the enlightened authority of Franklin Delano Roosevelt.

The love affair with America was to last all his life.

Lévesque did not bridle in 1944 when an English daily, *The Star,* devoted a short article to "three young Americans" working for armed forces radio in London. Lévesque was described in the article as the one of the trio who "originally came from Canada and who spoke the French of his forefathers." The young US Army lieutenant sent the clipping to his mother and sprinkled his letters with contemptuous references to the Frenchmen he had met: "We are certainly as good as they are... only they have the knack for self-promotion."

Quite a contrast with the judgment he made toward the end of his life about "the average American, the most likeable 'foreigner' one can know, the guy in whom, more than any other, we recognize ourselves." The quotation marks in that sentence around the word "foreigner" say a good deal; they express better than all his speeches put together his barely-repressed feeling of belonging to the United States.

Once demobilized, Lévesque entered what he called his "American Period." Depressed by English Canada, in which he perceived nothing but a "dismal cold greyness," he was fascinated by everything that came from the south: the political values, the commitment to social issues and trade unions, the popular culture, the literary and journalistic standards — he loved Ernest Hemingway and Erskine Caldwell — and the foreign policy. Lévesque's fascination did not stop short of the Korean War, which he saw first-hand as a reporter for Radio-Canada. "In '45, and again in '52, on each return [from war], the temptation was strong to fall in step with my American friends, who were going back to New York or to Boston to find plum positions in the media organizations which were growing by leaps and bounds."

As a journalist, he closely followed the 1956 American presidential campaign. He developed a profound respect for "this sense of democracy, one might call it innate, which springs, as it does among us [in Quebec], from rough, simple people whom no class barrier divides." In particular, he applauded the courage of the American Senate, however belated, in muzzling Senator Joe McCarthy and in putting an end to his anti-communist witch-hunt.

The United States, he would write twenty years later, constitutes "the most viable of empires, of all the empires we have known until now." Rejecting the "facile anti-Americanism" fashionable in leftist Québécois circles, he avowed an "unparalleled admiration for some of the achievements" of this empire.

## An Idol, An Error

René Lévesque looked for his political heroes in American history. He was never at a loss for words to praise the founding fathers: Hamilton, Washington, Jefferson. His favorite, however, was a contemporary figure — the legendary FDR.

"To my knowledge one cannot find anywhere, in any era, somebody who might serve as a model for one's own life; but there are fairly close affinities which develop with people one admires," Lévesque wrote in his memoirs. "I took a great deal from FDR." Lévesque admired Franklin Roosevelt's gift for communication, his use of radio to touch his voters, and the capacity, above all, of "this aristocrat to hold in place for so long a coalition of minorities, blue-collar workers and the poor."

In 1932 Roosevelt's advisors handed him an enormous document outlining the economic renewal programs of the New Deal; he condensed it down to a brief manifesto. Lévesque used the same approach in 1968 to present, briefly but forcefully, the concept of sovereignty-association in his book *Option-Québec*. In the section dealing with "the country we can make," he even borrowed FDR's famous statement: "We have nothing to fear but fear itself." The connection to Roosevelt is evident in another document: the government White Paper on sovereignty-association which launched the referendum debate in 1979. Lévesque entitled it "Quebec-Canada: A New Deal."

In fact, Franklin Roosevelt had a few ideas of his own on how Québécois and English Canadians could forge a new deal. The idol of René Lévesque proposed a solution that was clear, clean and definitive: assimilation. He made this recommendation to his friend, Canadian Prime Minister Mackenzie King, in a letter sent during the Second World War.

The two Canadian solitudes had just been through one of their periodic crises, in which culture, language, religion and politics all become sources of division, exposing the depth of their differences. In 1939, Mackenzie King had won the electoral support of Quebec's voters by solemnly promising not to force them to take up arms in the global conflict. Three years later, it was to all Canadians that he turned, by way of a plebiscite, to be released from his promise. In the rest of the country, predominantly English-speaking and loyal to the imperilled British crown, no fewer than 80% of voters approved this breach of political contract. Quebec remained monolithic in its opposition, with 85% of French-speakers — urged on by, among a host of others, youthful Jean Drapeau and Pierre Trudeau — refusing to change their minds.

This vote, King wrote at the time to FDR, showed "the real situation, which was always there." The President's envoy in Ottawa — not yet called an ambassador — was Pierrepont Moffat; it was his opinion that "the problem of Canadian unity has not been solved, and it will pass over as a legacy from the war to plague Canada in the days of reconstruction. The bitterness will be slow to die down and although in the conscription issue the French Canadians have been wrong, the British Canadians have not helped matters by their attitude. They do not so much hate the French Canadians as despise them, and are increasingly talking of them as though they weren't even Canadians, merely a minority living in Canada."

Roosevelt had been hoping to see massive Canadian troops flanking his own and the English forces, which were being overwhelmed by Hitler. He had followed the conscription debate with considerable impatience toward the French Canadians, whom he saw as preventing full mobilization. Was this not the same bloodline that had produced the stubborn French minority of New England, which, time and again, despite its poverty, went on voting for the Republicans and against Roosevelt's own progressive agenda?

At his retreat at Hyde Park in New York State, Franklin Roosevelt devoted long minutes of his precious time to drawing up for his "Dear Mackenzie" (the friendship was no sham; far from it) one or two ideas which, he wrote, "may have some merit in these days of national planning."

"When I was a boy in the nineties, I used to see a good many French Canadians who had rather recently come into the New Bedford area near the old Delano place at Fair Haven. They seemed very much out of place in what was still an old New England community. They segregated themselves in the mill towns and had little to do with their neighbors. I can remember that the old generation used to say, 'This is a new element which will never be assimilated. We are assimilating the Irish, but these Quebec people won't even speak English. Their bodies are here, but their hearts and minds are in Quebec.'

"Today, 40 or 50 years later, the French Canadian elements in Maine, New Hampshire, Massachusetts and Rhode Island are at last becoming a part of the American melting pot. They no longer vote as their churches and their society tell them to. They are intermarrying with the original Anglo Saxon stock: they are good, peaceful citizens and most of them are speaking English in their homes.

"At a guess, I should say that in another two generations they will be completely Americanized and will have begun to distribute their stock into the middle west states, into the Middle states and into the far west.

"All of this leads me to wonder whether by some sort of planning Canada and the United States, working toward the same end, cannot do some planning — perhaps unwritten planning which need not even be a public policy — by which we can hasten the objective of assimilating the New England French Canadians and Canada's French Canadians into the whole of our respective bodies politic. There are, of course, many methods of doing this which depend on local circumstances. Wider opportunities can perhaps be given to them in other parts of Canada and the US: and at the same time, certain opportunities can probably be given to non-French Canadian stock to mingle more greatly with them in their own centers.

"In other words, after nearly two hundred years with you and after 75 years with us, there would seem to be no good reason for great differentials between the French Canadian population elements and the rest of the racial stocks."

Mackenzie King did not respond to Roosevelt's suggestions, about which he was entirely silent in his next letter. But the attitude of this most liberal of American presidents toward his own minorities (which was one thing) and toward the French-speaking population of Canada (which was quite another) denoted a way of thinking, an American logic with which the Québécois nationalist project had only just begun to collide.

## Thomas Jefferson or Jefferson Davis?

In Roosevelt, Lévesque thought he had discovered an ideological affinity with the universe of American politics far stronger than any he felt for trends of leftist French thought. From the very beginning he recognized his own people in the stubborn, democratic little nation which had fought for its independence behind George Washington. The founder of the Parti Québécois filled every page of his social democratic program with the spirit of the New Deal. Were there not obvious parallels between Quebec's slow awakening and the battle of the American black minority to gain access to education, politics and the economy? The reactions of John Kennedy and Lyndon Johnson to Martin Luther King seemed to portend a new open-mindedness in the American elite. Lévesque hoped one day to benefit from these changing attitudes.

Nor was Lévesque entirely unique in his attraction to the south. Many progressive Québécois quite naturally identified with the American Left, turning towards Boston and Berkeley rather than toward Paris. In 1979, a Toronto journalist was surprised to find a framed quotation by American black leader Whitney Young on the office wall of Jean Lavigne, one of the first administrators of the French Language Charter (Bill 101): "Some practical advice to white employers who want to be fair, but can't find enough qualified negroes." (It was at this time that the Sun Life Company had announced its plan to move its headquarters from Montreal to Toronto, alleging it could not find enough competent French people in Montreal who spoke English.)

The heroes worshipped by Lavigne and many Quebec nationalists of his generation were none other than Martin Luther King and John F. Kennedy. The guardian of Bill 101, which made French the only official language of Quebec, considered his language legislation a Quebec version of the affirmative action programs in the United States which help blacks and women overcome inequality and injustice.

In the United States, on the other hand, no one seemed aware of this parallel. Eugene Rostow, a senior official in the State Department and a professor at Yale University, remembered a Quebec student whom he befriended in the 1960s. "He talked a great deal about it; he was very sympathetic, originally at least, to the Quebec movement." Campuses, it goes without saying, were in a turmoil and any cause that took aim at the status quo and the establishment found automatic sympathy. The cause of the Québécois, curiously, failed to arouse much enthusiasm. "This was in the middle of the Vietnam uproar. He thought he would get a lot of sympathy for them among the students. You know, Thomas Jefferson and self-determination and so on. Instead of which, to a man and woman, they all identified the Quebec separatist movement not with Thomas Jefferson, but with Jefferson Davis." Davis was President of the Confederacy during the Civil War, the defender of slavery.

"The Civil War is a much stronger element in American history than anything else," Rostow explained. It was also a rather recent event: the Civil War, the most murderous conflict in all American history, had ended barely a century before. Politicians in the United States during the 1960s and 1970s were old enough to have heard their grandparents tell horror stories about the battle. The southern states had only really returned to the bosom of national politics in 1964 with Lyndon Johnson and 1976 with Jimmy Carter.

In the collective American imagination, the notion of separation, of secession, was associated with regression, tragedy and political myopia. The reaction was visceral and automatic. In 1976, when Quebec elected a separatist government, Americans immediately thought of civil war. In a letter overflowing with good wishes, *National Geographic* editorial writer Gilbert Grosvenor wrote, "We pray that the day will never come that a Canadian prime minister must decide, as Abraham Lincoln had to do, whether to preserve a country by force of arms." The respected review *Annals of The American Academy of Political and Social Sciences* also explored the idea in a lengthy comparative study entitled "Institution Design and the Separatist Impulse: Quebec and the Antebellum American South."

Melting pot and civil war: two ideological barricades separating Quebec nationalists from American society, even left-leaning, intellectual American society.

In 1974, a Quebec academic, Louis Balthazar, and a Louisiana native, Alfred Hero, two rare specialists in American-Québécois relations, diagnosed this serious misunderstanding: "With their messianic origins and their lively sense of having created a civilization suited to all humankind (a premise embraced by a multitude of immigrants), Americans seem fundamentally incapable of understanding nationalist impulses. What fascinates most American intellectuals," they wrote, "is the concept of integration. And integration, of course, often presupposes the assimilation of minority cultures into a larger whole, dominated by English-speaking culture." When you speak to Americans about Quebec ambitions, Balthazar and Hero noted, they display "an amused skepticism or incredulous indifference, if not downright opposition."

"For Americans, English is a heavenly gift," minister Claude Morin explained to a reporter from *The New York Times*. "They don't see why Québécois should not want to assimilate as fast as possible." Morin knew what he was talking about. The future *péquiste* strategist had already encountered the question. A young American, Mary Lynch, confronted him with it in the 1950s when he was studying at Columbia University. He had known how to convince Lynch; eventually he married her.

Melting pot and civil war: together they formed a conceptual padlock which Quebec separatists would have to spring open if they wanted to cultivate sympathy and understanding south of the border. René Lévesque and many members of his "Yankee-bécois" troop failed to understand these cultural differences or chose simply not to face them.

## Charming the Americans

"Lévesque really, sincerely thought he'd seduce them by saying, 'We're the Boston Tea Party' or whatever," says Louise Beaudoin, whose portfolio in the Lévesque government was French politics. She was reminded of as much by Lévesque:

"You stick to France. It's what you're familiar with," he told her. "Don't talk to me about the United States."

He demonstrated a similar territoriality with Claude Morin, his de facto foreign affairs minister. "Every time we spoke of the States," Morin claims, "Lévesque said only half-jokingly, 'Who here was in the American army?'"

The first journalist to become a Quebec television star, the first anti-politician to earn overwhelming popularity among the electorate, the first visionary to create a successful political movement in Quebec since the 1930s, Lévesque thought he possessed the magic formula, the secret weapon, the logic which would convince the Americans. He would speak to them honestly and calmly on television and convince them of the justice of his cause. He would delineate all the obvious parallels between Quebec independence and George Washington's battle. He would indeed speak of the Boston Tea Party, explain how the Québécois, far more than the English Canadian, was the American citizen's true twin.

"I asked René Lévesque, before there was even a gleam of hope for power in his eyes, how he would ever persuade Americans that a separate Quebec would not be a threat to them, to their investments or security," Gerald Clark of the now defunct *Montreal Star* explained. "The answer, he said, was simple. He would go to places like New York and speak to Americans — in person and on television. I think he meant it sincerely, that his message would be straightforward and reassuring, and that, because of his experience as a broadcaster, he could put it across."

In 1969 Lévesque indulged in a game of political fiction with biographer Pierre Desbarats. The head of the Parti Québécois placed himself in 1976 and ruminated on how Quebec's independence had been established. "There was more understanding than anyone had hoped for on the American side." According to his scenario American investors had indeed reacted strongly to the advent of independence, but their reaction was not what the pessimists had predicted. "The problem was to avoid being swamped by American investment," he continued.

With the Republic of Quebec thus created, Lévesque said he lost no time translating a long-cherished dream into reality: he became Quebec's first ambassador to Washington. (Lévesque's scenario seemed so reassuring that the Montreal daily, *The Gazette*, refused to print the commissioned article.)

In reality, only part of the separatist leader's strategy of charm would work. Many American diplomats and politicians with whom he rubbed shoulders over the years developed considerable respect for him. Richard Snelling, governor of Vermont, was to become a great friend; and Kenneth Curtis, an American ambassador hailing from Maine, was to claim, "René was one of probably the smartest politicians serving at any level whom I ever met in my political life." A diplomat in Washington, whose responsibilities included reading dispatches on the subject of the eminent Québécois sent to him from colleagues in the field, confessed, "I'd begun to feel extremely fond of him by the time I'd finished reading these documents."

Nevertheless, not one of these Lévesque admirers went so far as to support the separatist cause. Despite his skills as a communicator, Lévesque simply could not ignite a spark of sympathy for his cause in the United States, where a conceptual padlock remained firmly in place. The debate over the American role in the separatist battle would not center on the degree of support or understanding shown by neighbours south of the border. It would center on the degree of the opposition to the sovereignty option expressed in Washington and New York. When Lévesque finally awoke from his American dream, he admitted that a strong and loud American opposition could "delay" independence. It would destroy any margin of victory in a referendum. The task facing the Lévesque government was clear: they would have to contain pro-federalist American sentiment; they would have to try to manoeuvre it offside.

In his efforts, Lévesque would not even be able to count on the political confusion that seemed the rule in American foreign matters: for a quarter century, American politicians would close ranks, grouping tightly together behind the official pro-federalist position on the Quebec question. All, that is, except one. And he was one of gargantuan proportions.

# Part One

# The End of Indifference

*I have never talked to an intelligent French Canadian who*
*fundamentally believed in separation.*

A CIA official specializing in Canadian affairs.

# 2

# The Irishman and the Franco-American

*All politics is local politics.*
THOMAS "TIP" O'NEILL
Democratic Congressman from Massachusetts

Three ill-fated men are seated in the elegant restaurant of Parker House, Boston's most stylish hotel. Their names are Jack, Bob and Ted, diminutives which they will carry unabashedly from primary school all the way to Washington.

It will take the Kennedy brothers 16 years to engrave their names on the national conscience. A murderer in Dallas, another in Los Angeles and a drunken night at Chappaquidick will, each in its turn, put an end to their glory years.

In 1952, however, they still have everything before them. The Kennedy brothers are preparing the ground for future successes and sweet-talking a fourth person at their table, who wears a cassock and a Roman collar. Small and plump, Father Armand Morissette would — with another 15 kilos — make an excellent Friar Tuck. The 42-year-old oblate, seven years older than the future president, is a Franco-American, but one unlike most others.

When the French of America swore by Pétain, Morissette was among the first foreigners and Catholics to turn towards de Gaulle. He still kept a visiting card on which de Gaulle had scribbled a short note of thanks; he was proud to have been awarded a Légion d'honneur and a Croix de Lorraine. Ordained in an era when the Vatican was not known for its daring, Armand Morissette became the confidant and confessor of Jack Kerouac: the angst-ridden, talented godfather of the beatniks was one of Morissette's parishioners in the Little Canada district of Lowell, Massachusetts. Father Morissette also boasted the dubious status of official chaplain to the Rockettes, the dancers from Radio City Music Hall in New York City, better known for their long legs than their novenas.

A decade too late for Quebec Abbé Lionel Groulx's "We shall have our French state," and a decade too early for modern separatists Marcel Chaput and Pierre Bourgault, the good priest also cherished the curious, iconoclastic dream that the province of Quebec could, must and would become a sovereign state. Quebec would, according to this French Canadian descendant, have "representatives in the United Nations," the ultimate criterion of independence in the post-war years of decolonization. Father Morissette, mischievous and proud, cultivated and ambitious, eagerly shared his convictions with any open-minded person who happened along, provided the latter possessed sufficient intellectual curiosity to listen to the copious and, according to a rival, "very, very articulate" prose of the good man. Jack Kennedy.

Geography, migration patterns and politics conspired to make Morissette guardian of one of the first doors the Kennedy brothers had to pass through to get from Boston to the Oval Office.

"Among the voters of Massachusetts born outside the United States, the largest group by far was born in Canada," JFK would say in 1961 to Canadian members of Parliament and senators congregated in the Ottawa House of Commons. Kennedy had a good memory. He remembered that the voice of the Franco-Americans "is enough to determine the outcome of an election." If it wasn't possible to win a majority, they had to be neutralized, their votes rendered useless by dividing their allegiances. In short, the influential Franco-American priest from Lowell could boost Jack Kennedy into the Senate.

## Kennedy and Independence: First Contact

Father Morissette could not necessarily guarantee the votes of the French Canadians of Massachusetts. All the same, he was a master trump precisely because he was known to have ties with the enemy Republicans. And he was already very nearly part of the Kennedy fan club.

One day in 1937, his superior had said to him, "Armand, a 'bonne femme' from Boston is going to speak in French at a tea for students and sisters at the College," referring to a local Catholic institution. The superior had better things to do. Take care of it, Armand, he asked; "I have to go play golf with my cousin."

Armand was forced to accept the burden of the 'bonne femme' from Boston; she happened to be Rose Kennedy. Francophile to the marrow of her bones, she sought out any occasion to converse in the language of Molière. Young Father Morissette, who adored mixing with high society, was a willing volunteer. The Sunday following his first meeting with Rose, he was invited into the Kennedy lair.

"They were all there, all the Kennedys, boys and girls," Morissette recalled, his eyes going soft and dreamy. A dynasty in the making, still pimply or in short pants. Ted, the future senator, was only five. Sitting on Morissette's lap, he entertained himself by removing the priest's Roman collar. "Ted, don't touch!" Rose thundered. The clan was getting ready to move to London where Joseph, the father, had just been named ambassador. In 1939, he pulled a couple of strings and got his son Jack, then 22, a job in the American embassy in Paris, a stone's throw from the Champs-Elysées. JFK would draw a taste for France and the French language from this experience. In the spring of 1939, when the sound of the marching boots that would soon overrun the continent was just beginning, young Kennedy criss-crossed Poland, Turkey and Palestine. He even touched down in Bolshevik territory. A passion for foreign affairs was born.

After his return from the war, Kennedy the war hero made it into Congress. Once again, he ran into Morissette. The two men discussed domestic and foreign politics, exchanging views on de Gaulle, whom an ungrateful France had forced into early retirement. Morissette believed in Kennedy. He had known the energetic teenager and today he was meeting the reflective adult, shaped by study, travel and the war. Morissette decided that Kennedy was going places.

The good Father chose this moment to lay his obsession — the province of Quebec and its thirst for self-determination — before Kennedy for the first time. Morissette felt that the "Canayens" (who would call themselves Quebeckers only twenty years hence) had been wrong not to fight under the British flag when the future of liberty, and more importantly of France, demanded it. But this was no reason for Mackenzie King to impose a war on them of which they wanted no part. It was not cowardice but principle that had made them back off from the war in the beginning. At Dieppe they had certainly shown the Nazis their mettle.

If, as historian Mason Wade notes, "Never had the old dream of an independent, Catholic and French state, a *Laurentie*, been as popular as in the period immediately preceding the war," the years that followed confirmed the justice of this dream for Morissette. Kennedy, who knew Quebec only from the ski slopes of Mont Tremblant, listened quietly, filing arguments for future use. They would ferment with the heat of other nationalist causes.

This was not the first time in history that an American politician had unexpectedly encountered Quebec nationalism. A dozen years before, one of Quebec's premiers — either Maurice Duplessis or Adélard Godbout — had evidently asked George Aiken, then governor of Vermont, "If we were to separate from the rest of Canada, don't you think Quebec and New England would form a nice little country?" Aiken was left speechless.

Was it electoral strategy or pleasure that brought JFK around to see Morissette again? In 1950, the two men fell into a conversation about a particular political event in Quebec. Quebec's dictatorial premier, Duplessis, had just demonstrated the extent of his power by having the Vatican transfer Montreal's arch-bishop, Monseigneur Joseph Charbonneau, to Victoria — at the other end of Canada. According to Duplessis, the prelate had delivered an "inexcusable personal and political affront" by criticizing the government's brutal actions in a miners' strike the year before. The government had used truncheons to shatter the wills of striking miners in the cities of Asbestos and Thetford Mines.

This showdown between secular and religious powers sent a shock wave through American Catholic communities, also through the important Catholic center of Boston. Kennedy was a Catholic, and according to Fred Holborn, one of his advisors at the time, "I guess he enjoyed gossip like everyone else, there was a lot of it." This incident offended his most basic anti-totalitarian convictions, and according to Holborn, imparted to him "some sense of the undercurrents of Quebec nationalism."

## The Franco-American Stakes

In February 1952, while Kennedy was catching senatorial fever, he stopped by the town of Lowell, situated outside his congressional district. He wanted the French press to talk about him; he wanted to be seen with Morissette, who had become an influential local figure with close ties to Republican senator Henry Cabot Lodge. At the time, JFK had let circulate a false rumor that he intended to go after the state governorship. He was to get the support of Morissette, who would abandon the local Republican candidate without a moment's hesitation and latch onto the Kennedy star.

But JFK did not want to reach the White House via Boston, he wanted to go through the capitol, through the Senate, which seemed to him the antechamber to power. This strategy put Morissette in an awkward position. He was tied by a longstanding friendship to Cabot Lodge but tempted by Kennedy's future promise; he did not know which way to turn.

Invited by the Kennedy brothers to Parker House during the senatorial campaign, the priest listened to some astonishing confessions. "All three of them, Jack, Bob and Ted, told me that day that they wanted to be president. All three of them!" A staunch Republican like the majority of his French Catholic flock, he contemplated the notion of three successive Irish Democratic presidencies with a mixture of fear and amusement.

The Senate was not only the warm-up area for pretenders to the title, it was also a house of retirement for politicians who had had enough vigour, style and money to make it in but not enough to get them out the other end. Run by an iron-fisted Texan named Lyndon Johnson, it was also a place where everyone fought for his piece of turf. Kennedy would meet this political ogre of a Democrat at a later crossroads; for the moment, two all-powerful Republicans stood between him and his career plans.

The first of these was the general responsible for the biggest military operation in history, the Allied victory over the Germans. Dwight Eisenhower was powering towards the White House at an impressive clip. Local Republicans hung onto his political coat tails as if he were an express train — or a tank — heading for certain re-election. In Massachusetts, Democratic Governor Paul Dever felt his electoral pedestal give way beneath his feet.

As for the second Republican, he was so confident of victory he did not for a minute think he would need Eisenhower's wave of popularity to regain access to his padded Washington chair. Henry Cabot Lodge had been a good, competent and worthy Republican senator from Massachusetts since 1936, longer than one needed to be re-elected without having to wage a war.

The Kennedy-Lodge showdown had all the trappings of a family feud. Thirty-six years before, Grandfather Kennedy (John F. Fitzgerald) had fought against Grandfather Cabot Lodge for a Senate seat. The venerable Kennedy "only lost by 30,000 votes in a period when women didn't have the right to vote," according to his handsome grandson, who well knew the power of that vote.

Political observers in Massachusetts thought the young Kennedy had lost his mind. In 1948, he had proved that a golden childhood had in no way deprived him of the qualities necessary to unseat an old Democratic Party political chief in a largely blue collar district. He had wisely banked on his veteran's halo — the halo of a minor hero, but a hero nonetheless of the Pacific battle that was still so fresh in every memory. His great energy and ambition, and election funds provided by the coffers of the family fortune, did the rest. This time around, however, he seemed to have bitten off more than he could chew. Cabot Lodge was a name, a party, a veritable machine. His political record was as clean as a whistle; he had personal contact with Eisenhower, whom he had had the good sense to support from the start.

Cabot Lodge also spoke an elegant French. He had won over the important electoral block of the state's huge Franco-American community, constituents worth their weight in votes. Richard Donohue, a local Kennedy organizer, reminisces that "they basically were very diligent voters, I mean they were very active citizens. They tended to register in a higher proportion or at least as high as others."

Senator Lodge was convinced that the French vote was in the bag. His opponent was badly handicapped: on top of being a Democrat he was Irish, and thus congenitally antithetic to any Franco-American worth his prejudices. The rivalry between the Irish and the Franco-Americans was long-standing and as fierce as rivalries get at the bottom of the social ladder. As a political scientist from Boston explained, "The conflict with the Irish was part of the now familiar pattern of one immigrant group displacing another by accepting lower wages and harsher working conditions." In this case, social tensions had blossomed in the dusty air of the New England textile mills: blocks of red brick that were remarkable only for their dull monotony. It was here that the Little Canadas had risen up and begun to supplant the Little Irelands. What was more, the two Catholic communities shared the same church, which was dominated by the Irish.

It was entirely out of opposition to the Irish, who made their political nest with the Democrats, that the Franco-Americans opted, without much enthusiasm, for the Republican Party. While the Irish invaded the Democratic Party, gained control over it and used it to climb the social ladder, Franco-Americans were not interested in becoming party bosses. They displayed neither organization nor ambition.

When the Kennedy team attempted to supplant Cabot Lodge in the French community, it was moving against the tides of history. Eunice Kennedy, JFK's sister, discovered how much when she travelled to Worcester, a city about 100 kilometers west of Boston, to meet Wilfrid Beaulieu, owner and director of a small French daily, *Le Travailleur*.

Not satisfied with asking Beaulieu to print campaign ads for her brother, she enjoined him to pull all Cabot Lodge publicity and accept only that of the Kennedy clan. She was out of luck: in the 1920s, Wilfrid Beaulieu had been temporarily excommunicated by the Catholic hierarchy for protesting against a particularly unjust decision of the Irish bishop. Now, thirty years later, he faced Irish arrogance once again. With the heavy Quebec accent he had never managed to shed, Beaulieu told the intruder, "Madame, please leave ... there is the door." There would be no Kennedy ad in *Le Travailleur*.

## The Kennedy Offensive

"Believe me, there were many efforts made to get him to abandon his loyalty to Lodge," Donohue, Kennedy's man in Lowell, recalls. He remembers having seen Kennedy phone Morissette once or twice to try to convince him to change sides. "Morissette was extremely vain and Lodge played to that vanity," he says.

A friend of the priest remembers the Kennedy camp publishing some photographs showing Kennedy and Morissette standing side by side. Needless to say, they did not help Morisette's friendship with Lodge. But none of their carefully planned tactics seemed to win him over completely. Morissette's nickname was "Father Spike" because he tried to compensate for his diminutive height by standing very straight. The nickname suited him; he might waver a little, but he never broke. The Kennedy team ultimately ran out of ways to impress Morissette, and eventually had to resign itself to bypassing him.

Father Morissette wasn't the Kennedy clan's only French card. The importance of the French Canadian vote was no secret to Kennedy's head organizer, Larry O'Brien, whose wife Elva Brassard had Quebec roots. A campaign memo contained a list of subjects of interest to the French electorate: 1. Safeguarding French language and culture; 2. Favourable consideration vis-a-vis Canada; and 3. Continuation of the Marshall Plan, under which France was a beneficiary. Every ethnic group was noted in a "List of Issues Which Affect Nationality Groups in the United States." The list specified that in the case of Lithuanians, Hungarians, Czechs and Poles, "independence" of the mother country ought to be promoted.

One month from election day, an organizer suggested to Robert Kennedy — who was already managing his brother's political machine — that Rose Kennedy's flawless French might be exploited. Why not tape one of Rose's French speeches and broadcast it on French radio? "The fact that Mrs Kennedy would be talking French would naturally suggest," she wrote "that the whole family can do so." The suggestion was misleading, to say the least; the future American president spoke French "with a bad Cuban accent" according to one of his rare French interlocutors. "He apparently doesn't believe in French verbs," joked another.

All the same, Rose delivered a long pro-French manifesto. All her daughters had studied with French nuns; her children loved to ski in the Laurentians and owed Canadians "many hours of happiness and fun" on the snowy slopes. Rose recounted how Jack had worked for the American ambassador in Paris, where he was "instructed in the ways of government and diplomacy by officials of the French government." A rather hasty apprenticeship, it was, and in a lousy school — that of the ungovernable Third Republic: the diplomacy he learned was one of prostration before Hitler, the politics that of an ostrich hiding from the Spanish Civil War. Rose went on to shower Eisenhower with vinegar, a bottle of which he himself most graciously delivered into her hands. "I was very much dismayed, as were all the people of France, by comments of a United States representative, General Eisenhower. But I am sure the French do not feel that these remarks reflect the attitude of most Americans."

Eisenhower had made a serious gaffe. In front of a group of supporters in Nebraska that summer he had waxed eloquent on the theme of American Christian values. By contrast he cited the example of the French. "One of the ways in which France has gone astray is that they now brag that 50 percent of them are either agnostics or atheists." The French, he continued, "have reached the point where their moral fibre has disintegrated." The French reporters, visiting the United States to cover the presidential campaign, immediately seized upon the statement. The French consulate in Boston took it upon itself to inform the Kennedy camp (confidentially) that far from being atheistic, 37 of France's 41 million people were Catholic and 1.5 million were Protestant. Cabot Lodge was terribly bothered by Eisenhower's statement. He tried to explain his leader's deviation to a reporter from *Le Monde*, but his excuses sounded lame because he could not deny that the words had been spoken. "There certainly must have been some mistake. Anyone who has seen the confusion around here, and the tension under which people who haven't slept for two days are living, will understand that sometimes one says things one doesn't really mean."

After reminding the audience that the leader of the enemy camp harboured anti-French sentiments, Rose Kennedy concluded with this promise: "If elected to the Senate, [Jack] will always work for the rights of France and for the wishes of her children in this country."

Jacqueline Bouvier, JFK's fiancée since June, also put to use the French picked up in childhood, polished later at the Sorbonne and again in 1951 during a six-month stint at *Vogue's* Paris offices. After all, the Bouviers came from Pont-Saint-Esprit, a quiet village near the Rhone. Jackie made quite an impression in the living rooms of Little Canada.

## A Legion of Spies

During the down-to-earth campaign for the French electorate, family patriarch Joseph came up with an idea. What if France herself, the mother country, were to give Jack a boost in the right direction? Joseph Kennedy, who wielded considerable influence in Washington circles, began calling on his numerous connections, among them General Walter Bedell Smith, then director of the young and powerful CIA. Smith contacted Philippe de Vosjoli, the representative of the French secret service (SDECE) in Washington. Between puffs on the long Russian cigarettes for which he had developed a taste as ambassador in Moscow, Smith presented his petition to the dumbfounded Frenchman. "I have a friend you may have heard of — Joseph Kennedy, a member of our Intelligence Advisory Committee." (A body of prominent individuals appointed by the President to supervise intelligence work.) "His eldest son, Joe, was killed over France while piloting a bomber. Now his second son, John, is a candidate for the United States Senate in Massachusetts. Many people in that state are of French origin, and it would be helpful to his campaign to have the French government confer the Legion of Honor posthumously on his brother Joe. I would appreciate it very much if you could arrange it."

Légions d'honneur are a political currency with which France is generally not stingy, especially if the investment promises to be profitable. But the key word is *honneur*. In France's eyes, Kennedy's father simply was not made of the right stuff. Vosjoli passed Smith's request along to Henri Bonnet, the French ambassador in Washington, who leapt up indignantly. "You want me to request a Légion d'honneur for a Kennedy? Don't you know?" He explained to Vosjoli that while working as ambassador in London, Kennedy had been a great admirer of Hitler and the manner in which he had governed Germany. He had been much more worried about the Red Peril than the Nazi Menace, and had even gone so far as to suggest a Germano-British alliance. Of the many pre-war mistakes, those of Ambassador Kennedy had been of the first order. When France fell in 1940, Kennedy kept up his criticism of the French and never lifted a finger to help the French liberation. "It's very sad that his son was killed during the war," Bonnet continued, "but when it happened he was not on any specific mission to help the French. I cannot request a Légion d'honneur for everybody killed in action."

Vosjoli knew he could not refuse to help out the head of the CIA, however; his liaison work depended on good relations with the agency's director. Vosjoli used his own connections in the French bureaucracy and finally got what he wanted, but only after the election was over. The French had walked a fine line: they had not entirely refused General Smith's request, but neither had they given in to the older Kennedy's designs.

The night of the election, Eisenhower triumphantly took the presidency. Democrats lay strewn like so many corpses across the battlefield. In Massachusetts the General beat Adlai Stevenson, his Democratic opponent, by 209,000 votes. Even so, election night on November 4 finished late in Boston. The local fight for the position of senator was fraught with suspense. In the final count, Henry Cabot Lodge got 1,141,243 votes. His opponent, John F. Kennedy, won with 1,211,984: a majority of just three percent. He owed his victory largely to the splintered Franco-American vote.

At the end of the day, Morissette had cut the pie in half. To be more exact, he had cut it in thirds, with two pieces going to Lodge. "Vote according to your consciences," he told his flock. "I'm going to vote for Lodge." To Lodge, who had been hoping for more, he confided, "I'm voting for you, but I'm betting on Kennedy." Lodge, who already felt the winds shifting, answered, "I'm afraid you might be right."

Kennedy's victory didn't extend to the whole of Little Canada, but had Father Morissette's flock voted unanimously for Lodge, the young Irishman would not have made it into the Senate.

Cabot Lodge had not lost everything. Eisenhower named him ambassador to the United Nations, a position with all the importance and prestige of the new and still promising assembly of nations. Father Armand Morissette, by a turn of events that can hardly be called fortuitous, became "special advisor to French delegates" at the UN. A single trip to New York would now suffice to bless diplomats and Rockettes alike. Cabot Lodge wasn't angry over the priest's semi-defection: he showed up at his side in 1972, when Father Spike launched a late and stillborn political career as candidate from Lowell for the House of Representatives.

In a manner unlike any other post-war president, Kennedy had immersed himself in Franco-American culture. The special configuration of the election he had just won had sensitized him to a group that neither his predecessors nor successors knew much about.

## Birth of a Nationalist

In December 1953, Kennedy made a short stopover in Montreal. Returning from their honeymoon, he and his wife were guests of honor at a charity ball for Saint Mary's, Montreal's Irish hospital. Jackie was stunning in her white satin dress with a sash of red and pale orchid, according to the description in *La Presse*. The reporter called the assembly of over 700, 18 of whom were debutantes, a "soirée of exceptional refinement."

Several hours earlier, Kennedy had spoken before professors and students at the University of Montreal's English Literary Club. He preferred the French Catholic university to the more famous McGill University, which he found too Protestant for his taste. "Canadians aren't strangers to me," the young and barely-known Senator told his audience of fifty. He spoke at length on the subtleties of the constitution before broaching a more engaging topic: ethics and foreign policy. In the fight against Communism, he explained, the morality of a given tactic was secondary to the morality of one's overall strategy. Allying oneself with Communist Yugoslavia in order to thwart the Soviet Union's plans, for instance, violated the moral rule that one should not flirt with Communists. But since Tito was a thorn in Stalin's side, why not send him roses?

As for the classic dictum, "the end justifies the means," Kennedy put forward a thesis that he was to revisit and modify over the years: "If our foreign policy were based on moral grounds alone, it would be difficult to understand how we can reconcile our favoring freedom for the people behind the Iron Curtain with our opposition to freedom for the people of Morocco — merely because we have air bases there." Strict adherence to morality, he concluded, would push the United States "to work against their own best interests." The decade was still young; Kennedy had only scratched the surface of the matter.

He spent barely thirty-six hours in the French city and spoke English most of that time. But the future president was no ordinary tourist. He had a great capacity to soak up information, was a speed reader and had a rare interpreter in his wife. Did he take the time to notice that the distinct society Morissette kept talking about was still lying dormant? Did he ask Marcel Faribault, secretary general of the university, who welcomed him that day, about the social and political situation? Faribault believed in a strong Quebec within a unified Canada, but had not hesitated to tell Americans on other occasions all he thought was wrong with the current federal system.

His trip apparently made a lasting impression. Seven years later, when Cardinal Paul-Emile Léger, rector of the university, invited the new President to come back to Montreal to receive an honorary degree, Kennedy answered that he would love to do so if time permitted. The President hoped, according to Pierre Salinger, his press secretary, "to renew the acquaintances he made on his first visit" in 1953.

Back at his office in the capital, Kennedy decided to let his nationalist voice be heard. The first subject he tackled was Indochina. French troops equipped by Washington had not yet been thrashed at Dien Bien Phu. The more independence was delayed for the Vietnamese people, he claimed, the worse off Vietnam and its neighours would be when they finally obtained their liberty. At the time, he did not see the conflict in terms of a showdown between east and west, as it was to become a decade later. In 1957, he set another cat among the pigeons by demanding independence for Algeria. Booed in the State Department and the Elysée alike, he became a symbol of emancipation in northern Africa. A reporter who had taken his notebook deep into the Algerian interior came home with a tale of illiterate resistance fighters asking if it was true that their friend Kennedy might become president of the USA.

Several years before de Gaulle saw the light, Kennedy understood that the disintegration of colonial empires was inevitable and irreversible. It was important, he thought, to cultivate allies among the rebel chiefs who would be the ministers of tomorrow. If the United States supported decolonization in Morocco, he reasoned, the country that emerged would gratefully allow US Air Force planes to touch down on its territory. His confidant and advisor, Ted Sorensen, wrote, "On many subjects — Algeria, Indochina, Poland, Latin America and defence — Kennedy's speeches were well ahead of both his colleagues and the headlines."

JFK undoubtably understood before many others that strategic interests of the United States demanded greater sympathy for the colonies and less compromise with the metropolitan centers that ran them. Was this more political tactic and media-grabbing for this young senator frustrated by the back seat he was forced to take in the Senate, where his elders monopolized the spotlight? There are no obvious answers. Holborn, who worked with JFK on his Algerian speech, speaks of his former boss's "pretty reasonably firm convictions." He must have had at least that much faith in his convictions in order to turn diplomats in two countries — his own and France — completely against him.

## Vietnam, Algeria, Quebec

The senator did not forget Morissette. Discussions with the priest continued in both his Boston and Washington offices. The priest, more of a francophile than a decolonizer, reprimanded JFK for abandoning France in the Vietnamese conflict. As for Algeria, he understood and shared Kennedy's position. Father Spike tried to push ahead in the politician's thinking: if he believed in self-determination for Indochina and for Algeria, why not independence for Quebec?

If Kennedy had been any other American politician, the decolonization-of-Quebec idea would not have taken hold. The idea that a western country could split in two, or that an ethnic or linguistic group should want to break away, seemed repugnant. For Americans, the creation of a nation from a fusion of cultures is more than an ideal; it is dogma. Even those who regard decolonization as a step forward in human evolution condemn secession as regressive. But Kennedy was no ordinary politician. For one thing, he knew how to listen.

Charles Bohlen, one of the giants of American diplomacy who from the 1930s on helped six presidents develop the emerging superpower's foreign policy, noted that, "He was one of the most unprejudiced men that I have ever run into. In conversation with him I could detect no sign of bias one way or the other in his approach to any given question."

What was more, he was "100 percent pure Irish," as he put it. He accused his friend, journalist Ben Bradlee, of not being more open about his Irish origins.

Like every American politician with Irish roots, Kennedy was duty bound to cheer Ireland's independence. But his dedication went further than that. His support for the Irish cause was directed towards work yet to be done: from the floor of Congress in 1951 he demanded that Northern Ireland, still under British rule, be handed over to the young Irish Republic. "Ireland's fight for national unity and independence is over 700 years old. It is a fight that cannot be considered won until the six counties of the north are reunited with the 26 counties that comprise Eire." He demanded a "free, united, integrated Ireland."

This tie with Ireland and its independence movement was crucial. It taught Kennedy that a fight for secession in a democratic country where two groups share a common history and — at least in modern times — a language, is not always unjustified. The painful experience of the Civil War was not automatically transferrable abroad, even to another country in the western hemisphere. The conceptual padlock — secession equals disaster — was about to be sprung. When Morissette talked enticingly about a minority living for 100 years among a majority of a different language (as opposed to the 700 weighty years of Irish history), Kennedy listened. His sympathy for peoples who yearned for independence, his love of things French, sensitivity to the Franco-American reality, and a sixth sense for historical changes in the making helped.

Sometime between his election to the Senate in 1952 and his decision to make a bid for the Democratic nomination in 1960, Kennedy conceded to Father Morissette's way of thinking. "Quebec, like Algeria, will become a nation," he told him. The issue was not the responsibility of the United States, the senator believed, but he also thought that independence of this "special unity" so fiercely attached to "its language and traditions" would one day come to pass. "It will happen," he said.

Morissette wanted to spread his good news, but no one around him shared his anachronistic separatist views. Beside which, Kennedy was not popular in every corner of Little Canada. Gérard Arguin, a political columnist with *Le Travailleur*, wrote that the Algerian speech exposed the senator as a "little politician in need of publicity." In August 1960 Arguin added that "He'd say anything to get elected."

The 1960 presidential campaign was underway. During the course of the Democratic nomination, Jack had managed even to oust Lyndon Johnson and then offer him the lesser prize of the vice presidential candidacy. Father Spike disliked the Republican candidate, Richard Nixon, though he had had enough sense to choose Cabot Lodge as a running mate. Now the priest wanted to see Jack in the White House. He sang his praises while Jackie relaxed in the living room of one of Morissette's sisters, Jeanne Hardy. He tried to convince Abbot Richard Santerre, the stubborn secretary of the Saint Jean Baptiste Church in Lowell, of the Irishman's merits. But Santerre refused to join the fan club. In his eyes Kennedy was a "first class opportunist, interested only in getting elected, and totally lacking in moral values."

Morissette, running out of arguments, finally brought out the heavy artillery. JFK liked Franco-Americans. What was more, he supported the independence of Quebec. Santerre regarded Armand's words as premature to say the least. In Quebec, Raymond Barbeau's separatist Laurentian Alliance, formed three years previously, had attracted little attention. Jean Lesage, elected premier of Quebec in June of 1960, had barely launched his ambitious program of social and economic reforms known as the *Révolution tranquille*, and the RIN or *Rassemblement pour l'indépendance nationale*, the first genuine separatist party, would only be founded in September of that year.

Santerre may have been intrigued, but he was unconvinced. He voted for Richard Nixon.

## At the Summit

Once through the doors of power, ambitious people often leave their convictions hanging in the vestibule. In the Oval Office, Kennedy had neither the time nor the motivation to dwell on his Quebec sympathies. He would, however, return to them eventually, moved by his nationalist and francophile impulses.

Kennedy's ascension to the presidency did not quiet his anti-imperialist beliefs. His inauguration speech, in which he exhorted young countries "strongly to support their own freedom," marked the beginning of a race he would run against the Soviet Union to assure the friendship, if not the out-and-out allegiance, of the emerging nations. Early in 1961, to the chagrin of the

European powers, he told the State Department that new African nations no longer needed permission from their former European masters before requesting aid from Washington. When a member of his youthful administration was criticized in Europe for promoting "Africa for Africans," Kennedy had this to say: "I don't know who else Africa should be for."

He took up the cause of Angola's independence, at the time a Portuguese colony, despite Lisbon's threat to withdraw permission for the Pentagon to use a base in the Açores. Kennedy had done an about-face since his speech in Montreal. He let advisor Ted Sorensen know he would abandon the American military base in the Açores if need be rather than let the Portuguese despot, Salazar, dictate his African policy. He even allowed leaders of the Angolan independence movement into the White House when they visited the offices of his brother Robert, then Attorney General — a gesture tantamount to yelling "Vive l'Angola libre!" had it not been kept secret.

Kennedy's open-mindedness, including his tendency to converse with people who were not voters or campaign contributors or even influential, is illustrated in a story told by French diplomat Claude Cheysson about his visit to the Oval Office in May 1962. Ben Bradlee had mentioned the young Frenchman to JFK and spoken of his intimate knowledge of nationalist ferment in North Africa. Kennedy liked to meet people who lived "out there on the cutting edge." Cheysson was one such man.

Two minutes after the Frenchman entered the den of power, the discussion took flight. "I am interested in Africa," Kennedy told him. He was alone in the office, sitting comfortably in his rocking chair. "I know little about it."

Cheysson recounted what he knew, what he had seen and experienced. The President "was listening attentively, speaking very little, just to ask an additional question," according to the Frenchman. The telephone did not ring and no one bothered them. The President, it seemed, had nothing better to do for an entire hour than perfect his understanding of North Africa. The two men discussed newly independent Morocco and Tunisia as well as Algeria, which was still being bloodied by war. They did not for a moment question whether the French colony would one day achieve statehood; instead, they asked what they would do when it did become independent.

"Very seldom in my life have I been listened to so well," said Cheysson, Mitterrand's future foreign affairs minister. Years later it still surprised him that "the most powerful man in the world" took the time "to hear — from someone unknown and insignificant — news and impressions about a problem that was not urgent, but a problem which bore on the independence, on the liberty and the progress of countries and peoples."

## Kennedy in the Language of Molière

John Kennedy's attraction to France and its culture did not decrease with the exercise of power. His relationship with de Gaulle, whom he found at once insufferable and admirable, was fraught with the feelings of a frustrated francophile. If the august French leader had not been so pretentious, Kennedy would have been very happy to accomodate him. As it stood, the General demanded that his country be recognized as an equal rather than as an ally, throwing a sizeable wrench into the spokes of American foreign policy.

Why does this "bastard de Gaulle" take such pleasure in "trying to screw us," Kennedy asked. Yet he said he was "fascinated" by France's astonishing economic revival; its GNP boasted an annual growth of five-and-a-half percent as opposed to America's two-and-a-half percent. Kennedy sent a team of experts to France to study de Gaulle's magic; in May of 1962, he laid out the red carpets and lavishly welcomed André Malraux, France's minister of cultural affairs.

Over dinner Kennedy lamented that, unlike his wife and several of his guests, he was unable to converse with the writer in his mother tongue. (He did, however, speak it better than some. During a visit to Ottawa in 1961, after hearing Diefenbaker blunder his way through a few words in French, Kennedy announced that "having had a chance to listen to the Prime Minister," he felt perfectly comfortable saying a thing or two in French. The crowd erupted in laughter, much to Diefenbaker's discomfort.)

Kennedy also invited his children's French teacher to his office, as if his other responsibilities did not keep him busy enough. "Do you think I could manage to sound like a French person?" he asked her. Jacqueline Hirsh gave four lessons to the aspiring polyglot who said he "couldn't wait" to "surprise [his] wife and everyone" by unexpectedly holding forth, with the confidence and grace of a scholar, in the language of Molière.

As for Canada, he was preoccupied above all with John Diefenbaker. The Canadian Prime Minister had refused, among other things, to allow the Americans to install nuclear warheads on anti-aircraft Bomarc missiles based on Canadian soil. During his official visit to Ottawa, JFK misplaced a document on which he was falsely accused of having scrawled the letters S.O.B. in reference to Diefenbaker. The President later explained in private, "I couldn't have called him an S.O.B. — I didn't know he was one at that time."

Sorensen wrote that Kennedy "troubled himself to learn more about Canada than any previous American head of state." To prepare for his Ottawa trip, he scoured the famous presidential briefing book, a rather boring handbook on current affairs, with one lively chapter entitled "Scope Paper" prepared by the State Department and describing the characteristics of the populations of host countries.

"Some Canadians," it claimed, had a tendency "to believe that we are inclined to be dominated by a trigger-happy military, that we are not regardful of cultural values, that we are harsh and discriminatory in our attitude towards minorities, that we are inept and lacking in perception in our handling of relations with underdeveloped countries in both diplomacy and aid, and that we tend to be absentminded and neglectful of the interests of Canada." It was a well-known refrain, but one rarely so well put. For better or worse any attempt to rectify matters was doomed to failure. "The anti-American sentiment in Canada comes and goes, often without any identifiable connection with what the United States in fact does." A memo sent by Secretary of State Dean Rusk in February 1961 was even more brutal: Canadians suffer from an "inferiority complex which is reflected in a sensitivity to any real or fancied slight to Canadian sovereignty."

## Jack Kennedy and Réal Caouette

The President certainly never read the letters written by admiring Quebeckers, as nice as they were naive, asking if they might drop by the presidential residence on their trips through Washington en route to the Carolinas or to Florida. Likewise, he never saw the letter sent by one Brian Mulroney to his advisor Larry O'Brien. Was the young secretary to the Canadian minister of agriculture preparing for the future? He requested a copy of the Democratic presidential campaign organization manual from 1960, the year the Democrats reinvented the electoral art, emphasizing image at the expense of content.

One thing was certain. JFK had heard of Réal Caouette. Kennedy, who was eager to see Diefenbaker ousted, followed Canadian electoral forecasts with great interest. Willis Armstrong, the man in charge of Canadian affairs at the State Department, recalls that "Kennedy would have loved to get up there [Canada] to help liberal leader Lester B. Pearson campaign ... The State Department tried to get some restraint on it."At the start of 1963, Washington lent a good deal of support to Diefenbaker's political opponents, who lost no time in putting it to use.

One acerbic writer noted, "Do you think that [American] General Norstad, formerly commander-in-chief of the Allied forces in Europe, was merely sight-seeing when he came to Ottawa January 3 and publicly enjoined the Canadian government to respect its commitments" to install nuclear warheads on the Bomarcs. This polemist, called Pierre Trudeau, writing for the controversial left-wing Quebec magazine, *Cité Libre*, asked, "Do you think the State Department inadvertently leaked a communiqué to the papers on January 30, supporting Mr Pearson's position and crudely insinuating that Diefenbaker was a liar?"

The Kennedy team denied accusations made by Trudeau and others that they had orchestrated the fall of Diefenbaker's government on February 5, 1963, and the elections that followed. (McGeorge Bundy, Kennedy's national security advisor, would later admit having "knocked over the Diefenbaker government by one incautious press release." He suggested that in future there was a "need for being extra-polite to Canadians," whose governments are so fragile.)

Diplomats in the State Department specializing in Canadian affairs bridled at the thought of a new shower of criticism like the one that had followed the anti-Diefenbaker communiqué of January 30, and wanted to prevent any future American involvement in the Canadian elections. Canadians, they knew, were ultra-sensitive. If Kennedy could be convinced that voters would on their own relieve Diefenbaker of his responsibilities, he would be good enough to stay on the sidelines. "The White House was skeptical of our capacity to forecast the election," recalls Armstrong, the diplomat. At the INR, the Intelligence and Research Bureau of the State Department, an election specialist makes it his job to offer country-by-country forecasts based on local data. Armstrong, who spent four years at the embassy in Ottawa before assuming the direction of the Canadian desk, decided to become an electoral soothsayer. He read reports sent by consuls in the twelve American diplomatic posts in Canada, and relied in the network of connections he had cultivated during his stint north of the border.

Three days before polling day, McGeorge Bundy received his verdict. Following standard procedure, he sent it to the President. It was here that Réal Caouette made his appearance. According to the document, "Neither of the major parties has an able French leader who can compete with the oratory of the Social Credit leader Caouette, who is appealing to Quebec restlessness and French Canadian nationalism."

An exceptional politician from Quebec, full of verve and sophistry, delivered with disarming common sense, Caouette promised to teach a lesson to the "St. James Street sharks" — the finanicial elite. He vowed to print paper money equal to the gross national product and help ordinary people prosper. The right-wing, populist speech flattered and impressed the largely agricultural electorate, who would discover the economy and the Quebec Stock Savings Plan only 20 years later. As one rural Social Credit supporter explained, "Money is made of paper; paper is made of wood; and wood," he said, making a brisk gesture towards the forests bordering his field, "we have to spare!"

"The apparent success of the Social Credit campaign in Quebec," the State Department document continued, "which is expected to give that Party considerably more than their present 26 seats, will probably deny the Liberals a majority." Three days later Lester Pearson formed a minority government. But the State Department had overestimated what even one leader of the Social Credit Party called "the Social Credit scourge that was sweeping the province." Caouette lost six of his 26 Quebec seats. It was still enough for the "scourge" to prevent the Liberals from getting a majority. Kennedy was only semi-content. Without this blasted Caouette, his friend Pearson would have enjoyed a solid victory.

## Kennedy and the "Liberation of Quebec"

Had Kennedy gotten wind of "the loud separatist professions of faith that were attracting so much attention inside as well as outside the province in 1961 and 1962," as American historian Mason Wade put it? Marcel Chaput had sold 35,000 copies of his book, *Why I am a Separatist*, during this period. It was quite a sign of impatience while the government in Quebec City was already taking huge steps forward under the banner, "Maitres chez nous." Canadian Conservatives, whom JFK hated, were more than slightly responsible for the new surge of separatism. In 1958, just after they had been elected, Diefenbaker's lieutenant, Gordon Churchill, made it clear the Conservatives could govern without French Canada. Did Kennedy know that even the Canadian left included geniuses like Douglas Fisher, Member of Parliament for the New Democratic Party, who told students at the University of Laval in 1961 that English Canadians could easily dispense with their French compatriots? In his view they were fit only to become hockey players, night club singers, and irresponsible, good-for-nothing federal politicians.

Whether, as one CIA specialist in Canadian affairs put it, Kennedy was motivated by the Bomarc affair and a dislike for Diefenbaker, or whether he was propelled by his love of French and the anti-colonial sentiment of the day, or influenced by his 1963 trip to Ireland (during which he held forth on "the role of the little nations"), or was simply becoming more sympathetic to nationalist causes in general. He then privately declared himself supportive of Quebec independence once more.

This time the news travelled via a different route. Friends of Kennedy and Jackie shared their feelings with New York acquaintances sympathetic to the cause, who in turn passed the word along to Raymond Barbeau, founder of the *Alliance laurentienne*, a right-wing separatist group. The message that reached him described Kennedy as interested in "the political and economic liberation of Quebec," as a means "to protect the French culture" of a "nation that did not feel at ease within Confederation." Kennedy had told Morissette that the issue really did not concern the United States; Barbeau heard a slightly modified version of this statement. His New York informants told him that Kennedy envisioned independence "without ulterior motives or plans to lay a finger on Quebec."

Barbeau dropped his bombshell at a press conference on February 25, 1963, while launching a book about the "economic liberation" of Quebec. He said he had "proof" to back up his statements and announced he would reveal his source if pressed to. Some 25 years later Barbeau has not come forth either with documentation or a witness, but he still swears that his information about Kennedy's leanings is true. For his part, Father Morissette says that between 1960 and 1963, he spoke further with Kennedy about the future of a free Quebec. Morissette and Barbeau never met.

If he had had time, would Kennedy have turned a personal conviction into an official policy? Was he waiting, like de Gaulle, who supported independence as early as 1960 but remained quiet, for conditions to be ripe and the movement to become irreversible? If it turned out that independence was inevitable, was the new state's friendship worth securing at the risk of a temporary falling out with Ottawa? Would it be more costly than a military base in Morocco or the Açores?

Today, not one of Jack Kennedy's entourage can state that their illustrious friend defended Quebec independence in their presence. Then again, no one heard him take the contrary position. Fred Holborn, co-author of the Algerian speech, thinks now that Morissette "may be right." He adds that you have to watch out for "politicians who listen sympathetically to ethnic constituents." Ray Cline, assistant director of intelligence at the CIA since 1962, the man who furnished the White House with the last bits of information collected by the agency, recalled Kennedy's infatuation with everything French. Kennedy "was very romantic about France and I suspect that he, unlike most Americans, he would have thought that a greater French cultural input into Canada was a good thing." But it was a big jump from supporting French culture to advocating Quebec separatism. Another CIA official specializing in Canadian affairs who helped brief Kennedy before his meetings with Canadian prime ministers was less skeptical than Cline. He remembers having heard a rumour at the time, possibly regarding Babeau's press conference. "When I heard it, I found it quite credible that he [Kennedy] would have said that," he says.

Kennedy's silence with his subordinates is understandable. The Quebec issue got buried under the astonishing number of critical events that filled the 1000 days of Kennedy's presidency. Kennedy had to deal with the failed invasion of the Bay of Pigs and the Cuban missile crisis, the mess in Indochina, the launching of the Apollo. And there were Marilyn and Martin Luther King.

Richard Donohue, his organizer in Lowell, notes that Kennedy "all of a sudden talked to you about issues that were very close to you which was a reflection of his interest. But he wouldn't say the same thing to me, feeling that I wouldn't know anything about it anyway." Morissette was one of the only people in his entourage who was aware of the Quebec dream.

Secretary of State Dean Rusk recalls that he asked Kennedy about Quebec, even though he remembers only the general thrust of the discussion. According to Rusk, "As soon as the secession discussion took some hold in Quebec," Kennedy said "that it was contrary to the national interest of the United States that Canada split." The President did add, however, that it was important to "remain relatively quiet on the subject." Rusk adds that Kennedy could have held personal views of a different nature. Did he support Quebec independence? "He might have made a remark like that off the cuff because he liked to explore ideas. But whether he said something like that playing touch football in Hyannis Port or West Palm Beach or in the Rose Garden to somebody, I don't know."

His two closest friends reacted differently when told of testimony that John F. Kennedy harboured separatist sympathies. Ted Sorensen said he would be "astonished" to learn that Kennedy "seriously advanced such a position." Larry O'Brien, on the other hand, easily imagined his old buddy cheering on the Quebec fight for independence. "It's not out of character," he said.

It should be noted that O'Brien is Irish.

# 3

# The Americans Discover Quebec

*Calm and sovereign*
*Like an American*
PIERRE FLYNN
*On the Road*

The best intellects in the CIA tapped every source — diplomatic, economic, military and, needless to say, Intelligence — to prepare special National Intelligence Estimate (NIE) documents for their President. Their mandate was and remains to give the President an exact political report on the country under study, as well as a forecast of what the future might bring.

Judged against this mandate, National Intelligence Estimate #99-61, entitled "Trends in Canadian Foreign Policy" and issued for Kennedy in the spring of 1961, was an abject failure.

Estimate #99-61 was the first time the CIA officially confronted the Quebec problem, and it failed to detect the stormclouds in the distance. That omission stands out glaringly because the nine-page document was clairvoyant regarding the rest of Canada. Its emphasis was on Canadian policy and the United States, and it read like a retrospective on a decade that had barely begun. Paragraph 36, for instance, stated that "Canadian sensitivity to US cultural intrusion will probably continue to mount, particularly in intellectual circles. As a consequence, further steps will probably be taken to increase the 'Canadian content' of Canada's radio and television programs." Elsewhere, the document predicted that Ottawa would normalize relations with the People's Republic of China, maintain ties with Cuba despite US pressure, Canadianize the national economy, and drag its feet on cooperative nuclear ventures. All of which it did. It was like reading the political agendas of Diefenbaker, Liberal Prime Minister Pearson and his successor Pierre Trudeau before they could ever possibly have been drafted. American Intelligence had deciphered the rising tide of Canadian nationalism with uncanny accuracy.

But the document completely missed the second, critical factor that would shape and splinter Canada in the 1960s — nationalism in Quebec. Paragraph 11 of the NIE's "Basic Considerations" stated that Canada would hitherto enjoy "a sharpened sense of national unity, including an improved relationship between the major English- and French-speaking communities." In May of 1963, almost two years to the day after JFK first perused the document, Canadian army troops poured into the streets of Westmount. Terrorized citizens in the quiet residential neighbourhood approached their mailboxes with fear, expecting them to explode in their faces, thanks to the newborn Quebec terrorist group, the Front de Liberation du Quebec, or FLQ. Diefenbaker himself had narrowly escaped a bomb attempt on his life.

## Colonial Status

According to Paul Martin, Canadian minister of external affairs, his American counterpart, Dean Rusk, familiarized himself very quickly with the situation. Even Ray Cline of the CIA recalls discussing the Quebec question with the White House around 1963 or 1964. Without sounding any alarms, American diplomats were monitoring every step of Quebec's awakening. A diplomat posted in Montreal during the first half of the 1960s recalls that the separatist movement was a question "significant from the moment I was there ... We never thought of it as a minor development." On the contrary, during the Quiet Revolution, separatists were viewed as having "considerable potential," he reported. Especially the Liberal yet separatist-leaning René Lévesque, "such a compelling personality." What direction would he take? The diplomat remembered that in reports as well as conversations with the State Department, "we never said it [independence] would happen; we said it could happen." He also said he had "never accepted the idea that a separate Quebec would not be viable ... Had it happened, it would not have been a small nation."

Very few Americans were sympathetic to the goal of sovereignty, but French Canadian nationalism had its supporters. Willis Armstrong, right-hand man to the American ambassador in Ottawa, said, "I felt that to some extent Quebec had a colonial status and I am against colonial status."

In Quebec, Premier Jean Lesage was giving the "colonials" the means to fashion a Quebec state worthy of their long-buried defiance. Like many of his colleagues posted in Ottawa, Quebec and Montreal, Armstrong was impressed by Lesage and regarded the Quiet Revolution favorably. The nationalization of electricity companies, endorsed during the election-cum-referendum of 1962, was the most visible manifestation of this revolutionary fervor.

Willis Armstrong remembers that "We were more amused than anything else." He was later moved to the State Department in Washington where he was responsible for "northern Europe," a region whose peculiar geography included Canada. Occasionally Armstrong attended presidential briefings on Canadian affairs. Several Americans who held shares in the electricity companies that now fell within Quebec natural resources minister René Lévesque's portfolio were pestering the State Department about these Canucks; until recently they had seemed so timid. But the United States itself had dozens of nationalized power utilities. Quebec critics who feared their representatives would be treated like Bolsheviks if they ever stepped on Wall Street again were proven wrong. In fact, New York investment house Halsey Stuart offered to advance the $200 million needed to finance the Quebec project up front in the event that the province's banks proved too cautious to provide the funds.

"I was amused," Armstrong said, "by the fact that people talked it up as something that might get everybody angry, and you know our position had been, if you pay for it, you have the right to do it." He had other reasons to laugh. "US interest [Wall Street] was developing the money to pay for it and US interests [shareholders of electricity companies] were being bought out, which is fundamentally a vindication that in North America you have a financial common market anyhow."

After the creation of the RIN in 1962, Armstrong warned his colleagues to keep an eye on Quebec. He predicted "rough times ahead" and thought it might be a good idea to "alert the intelligence people to look at this and realize what's going on or what could be going on."

In Quebec City, consul general Richard Courtenaye worried about the heavy-handedness of the authorities. He reported a chilling discussion he'd had in 1963 with Brigadier J.A. Dextraze, whose soldiers were assisting police in eastern Quebec when things got rough. On the subject of FLQ suspects, Dextraze said, "Let them howl about their democratic rights ... If I have to break their arms to make them talk, I'll break them." The diplomat added that "On at least one occasion bones were broken and other serious injuries sustained by the demonstrators at the hands of his troops." These incidents were never reported, according to Courtenaye, because "Brigadier Dextraze professed to have an understanding with the press of Quebec City." The consul general concluded that this "disregard for legal or moral niceties" seemed "potentially dangerous in the emotionally charged atmosphere which exists in Quebec extremist circles." Men like Dextraze would leave martyrs in their wake and would "weaken public support for legally constituted authority as an instrument of justice."

Armstrong, who was responsible for naming American diplomats to Canada, made sure "always to have talented, competent senior officers" in Montreal and in Quebec City. "The personnel people in Washington [at the State Department] were always trying to unload hacks on me for consular posts in Canada and I kept fighting them off. But they never tried to send me any hacks for Montreal or Quebec City because they were aware of the fact that this was different." This said, postings to Montreal and Quebec City were not coveted by ambitious diplomats. Until the mid-1970s, they were given as consolation prizes to those who, while perfectly competent, were not up to ambassadorial standards; Montreal and Quebec were often used as end-of-career bonuses for those who had just not made the grade.

Most American diplomats posted to Quebec had at least a rudimentary knowledge of French. Some spoke it fluently. By and large the American diplomatic service in Ottawa was more at ease in French than the high-ranking federal civil servants. Many say they were shocked in the 1960s by the way English Canadians condescended to the French.

American representatives did not, however, always demonstrate sympathy themselves. Walt Butterworth, ambassador from 1962 to 1968, thought that French Canadians were just Cajuns of the north. According to one of his former subordinates,"He was a nouveau riche who played the aristocrat" and regarded the Québécois as "hewers of wood and drawers of water." In the mid-1960s, when the American Consulate in Montreal wondered whether to post a bilingual sign, Butterworth's office let it be known that English alone would suffice.

During the constitutional debate, reports of which he sent to Washington, Butterworth supported moderates like Pearson, those who wanted to make more room for Quebec. He feared that the failure of Canadian duality would nourish "French Canadian nationalists-racists." This, according to the diplomat, was a "burgeoning" phenomenon in Quebec, one which pushed English speakers in the province to "feel their position as a minority."

## On the Menu of an Indigestible Dinner: Quebec

Only two months after Lyndon Johnson became president, the subject of Quebec came up in conversation in Washington. The occasion was Lester Pearson's ill-fated visit to the capital. Pearson, a Nobel Peace Prize-winning diplomat, began the meeting by eulogizing the late Kennedy. Johnson was not pleased; the new President was struggling to emerge from under the immense shadow of his predecessor. He was also trying to neutralize a second Kennedy brother, Robert, who was eyeing the Oval Office Johnson had so recently inherited.

Ambassador Charles Ritchie remembers that "the President appeared to be in a very unforthcoming mood" at the dinner at the Canadian embassy in Washington. He and the Canadian Prime Minister clearly did not speak the same language. According to Ritchie, "Pearson was very proper in his language; it was not for nothing that he was the son of a Methodist minister. But oh, with LBJ, every second word was 'fuck' and the rest of it, and a great deal of bourbon being consumed at odd hours. Not the Pearson style."

How did the conversation drift towards the topic of Quebec separatism? Neither Ambassador Ritchie nor Basil Robinson, the high-ranking civil servant who accompanied Pearson, remembers. According to Lady Bird Johnson, "This was a topic of discussion with the Pearsons," who were "excellent company." When she arrived home that night, she noted in her journal that just as the United States had problems with its black minority, "I gather they too in Canada have their difficulties with minority populations, with the French province actually talking of seceding from the Dominion. Certainly nothing could conceivably come of this. Could it?"

Two months later, the topic of Quebec separatism was almost unavoidable. *The New York Times* announced on its front page that "Secession of the French province is no longer merely a distant possibility." The newspaper quoted two senior ministers, René Lévesque and Eric Kierans, as well as an eminent political scientist, Léon Dion. All three thought that an independent Quebec would work. Seven months later, three important magazines discovered Quebec. *Harper's* ran "The Case for an Independent Quebec." Foreign Affairs offered a more scholarly approach in "Quebec in Revolt." And *The Atlantic Monthly* commissioned a dozen articles from Canadian writers in order to dedicate an issue entirely to the Quebec situation. Gérard Pelletier penned "The Trouble With Quebec" for the issue.

Early the following year, a group of researchers financed by the US Army became interested in the Quebec question. The group's mandate was to examine the phenomenon of uprisings. This larger, ambitious study, entitled Project Camelot, was designed to advise the Pentagon on how it might prevent or suppress social unrest in the Third World. One member of the team, a Franco-American named Normand Lacharité, convinced his superiors — with some difficulty — to include Quebec among the "test cases" to be used in preliminary research. He was passionately interested in the political turmoil in the province, and was sympathetic to the separatist movement. It was ironic then that he trained the Pentagon's rebellion-suppressing attention on Quebec. His was a theoretical suggestion, but suddenly Project Camelot loosed a political storm, first in Washington, then in Ottawa. The State Department, anxious to appease "ultra-sensitive" Canadians, ordered Lacharité to desist from his work. Canadian and Quebec political annals would forever be littered by the legend of the American army hatching plots to suppress the independence movement in Quebec.

## A Quebecker in America

The State Department had good reason to follow events in Quebec; the Québécois would soon be knocking on its door. In April of 1965, André Patry, international advisor to Premier Jean Lesage, went to Washington to meet with two officials from the State Department. The Canadian embassy was never informed of the meeting. Patry was deeply involved in the effort to gain international support for Quebec, and his separatist tendencies were no secret. The American consul general in Montreal, Richard Hawkins, played go-between.

Patry's mission was to find out whether the United States would grant the same tax advantages to the *Délégation générale du Québec* in New York that they granted to consulates. If not, Quebec planned to tax American consulates in Montreal and Quebec City. The request was not new: American Ambassador Butterworth had rejected it himself at a meeting with Lesage three months earlier. The irascible ambassador had warned Lesage that taxing the American offices "would not prove to be a lever for seeing any changes it desired but would merely constitute an irritation between Quebec and the United States." At any rate, Washington dealt only with sovereign states, not with mere provinces. In essence, Lesage was told to channel his requests through Ottawa.

Patry was presenting Quebec's request once again. Initially he spoke with Howard Brandon, head of the Bureau of Canadian Affairs; over lunch in the city, he raised the issue with Brandon and a Mr Harris, a State Department legal counsellor. Patry wanted to sound the Americans out: how did they regard the changes underway in Quebec? American diplomats posted in Quebec tended to be open-minded and well-informed, but did this reflect official attitudes in Washington or was it merely a question of personal sympathies? In October of 1964, consul general Hawkins had a lengthy discussion with Claude Morin, deputy minister of federal-provincial relations, on the direction and future of the Quiet Revolution. What did Washington readers think of his report?

Patry learned that "Washington was only beginning to discover Quebec's distinct character," and was preparing "to draw its conclusions in cultural and social domains." At least this was the official line. On his visit he would also find that "certain people even believe that the French language will disappear in Canada because of excessive urbanization in Quebec." In general, the State Department appeared not "yet ready to draw political conclusions about Quebec distinctiveness"; it certainly was not prepared to confer any sort of status on Quebec's diplomatic corps in New York.

The diplomats with whom Patry spoke showed absolutely no enthusiasm for the idea of independence. Brandon did let it be understood, however, that his government "would not worry about the Quebec situation until it posed a threat to the security of the continent." Patry used his visit to transmit a message to those officials he met in the administration; he "underlined" the "necessity for the United States to change its perspective on Quebec."

It would take much more than this short secret mission to shape America's conscience, however. While France was rapidly beginning to view Quebec sympathetically, the United States refused to budge. Their potential to determine Quebec's future was huge, but they remained disinterested. Diplomats posted in Quebec were in fact not the best barometer for their bosses' attitudes.

On his return, Patry prepared a report and a plan of action. He proposed a new strategy to settle the problem of taxing consulates, and stressed the huge importance of setting up "an information campaign directed at the United States government and at its electronic and print media, which would explain Quebec's unique character and the consequences flowing from this." Quebec must "try to educate people capable of extending aid when aid proved necessary." It "had become urgently necessary" and "essential" he added, "to develop a coherent, realistic policy regarding the United States."

When Lesage read the report, he asked Claude Morin to follow up on the suggestions regarding the taxation issue, but said nothing about Patry's more far-reaching recommendations. "The political will just wasn't there," according to Patry. Ottawa and Washington continued to thwart attempts to secure quasi-diplomatic status for the Quebec Delegation in New York. "It was clear we weren't going to create ties with the United States." In spite of the need to win over its nearest and most powerful neighbour, Quebec chose instead to pour most of its diplomatic time and energy into Paris and Africa. It would slowly grope its way along on the American front, guided by the often distorted impressions relayed by bilingual diplomats sent by Washington.

## Apocalypse Quebec

The lack of overall American interest in Quebec was made all the more frustrating when, several months after Patry's visit, one of the State Department's most respected strategists, George Ball, came up with a project for Quebec. Far from taking into account the province's distinctiveness, it placed North America's French-speaking minority in one of the worst scenarios imaginable.

Ironically, it was none other than Charles de Gaulle, Quebec separatists' greatest ally, who inspired Ball's grandiose and threatening ideas. Ball was right-hand man to Secretary of State Dean Rusk, and was known as the most European of his diplomats. He believed in the dream of a unified, reconstructed Europe and defended it with the passion of a Jean Monnet, father of the idea.

De Gaulle also had a vision of Europe reconstructed and unified, but unified under France, not under the United States or its perceived vassal, England. In 1963, the General slammed the door on England, who had wanted to join in the European Community. England was "insular and maritime," according to the General. It was not close to Europe, but had "economic relations with a host of other countries, most important of which was the United States." London, he mused loudly enough so that anyone could hear him, was the American Trojan Horse, sent to infiltrate the young European fortress. Open the door, he predicted in his clear, slow voice, and you lay the foundations for a "colossal Atlantic community under American direction."

By the end of 1965, Ball despaired of ever seeing England in the European Community, which he remained convinced was its proper place. It could provide a counter-balance for French and German powers, and play a "leading role" in Europe. Could America tolerate an England set adrift if the Continent persisted in its "narrow and petty policies"? The promising European Community refused to throw a life preserver to once-proud England, now flailing in the waters like a poor castaway. Washington spoke worriedly about "little England" and its sad decline.

There had to be, in Ball's mind, another community to which England could attach herself and regain the flower of her youth. Ball assigned a task of awesome proportions to his assistants: they were to study the possibility of a federation between the United States and the United Kingdom, they would "reverse the American Revolution." Ball's plan was bigger yet; his proposed "English-speaking Union" would encompass not only the USA and England, but also Canada, Australia and New Zealand. His was "an Anglo Saxon political confederation that might, over the years, transform itself into a federation." Ball wrote that with "common bonds of language and institutions and history, the building of Anglo Saxon political unity ought to be far easier than the construction of a political Europe," with its diverse languages and histories.

They could start with the "limited" proposal of huge joint meetings of the five national cabinets. These meetings would engender permanent sub-committees responsible for coordinating military policy; fusing the dollar and the pound sterling and setting up a common monetary reserve; and instituting free circulation of goods, people and capital. The modest project also proposed the founding of a "provisional legislative body" whose members would come from the parliaments of each member state. Ball's vision, of course, would have plunged Quebec's leaders into a state of panic. The Québécois people numbered five million and were threatened by assimilation when held up against 15 million English-speaking Canadians. Up the ante to 300 million English speakers — in which case they would represent less than two percent of the population — and the future looked bleak indeed.

The plan seemed all the more dangerous because, from a number of different angles, it was rational. England was indeed isolated. America and Australia were already at work establishing military and economic ties. It was highly possible that the smaller nations would be tempted to join a United States-England alliance more willingly than the United States alone. And the British would feel more confident with their loyal colonies of old at the confederate table, helping them control the arrogant grandchildren of George Washington's revolutionaries. The arguments fit together disturbingly well.

Once the London-Washington axis was established, Ball knew that Canada would have to be won over. But in Ball's mind that process was already begun. "Canada, I have long believed, is fighting a rearguard action against the inevitable," Ball wrote. Claims of independence, the maple leaf and beaver were all well and good, but "I cannot predict a long life expectancy for her present policies" of Canadianizing the country's economy. "The great land mass to the south exerts enormous gravitational attraction while at the same time tending to repel." It was the old Canadian-American love-hate relationship. "Even without the divisive element of a second culture in Quebec," Ball continued, "the resultant strains and pressure are hard to endure." Canada was already inexorably drawn to the United States: the day would eventually dawn when the free trade of goods, capital, services and people between the two countries would create "a progressively expanding area of common political decision." The Anglo Saxon Super State would, he concluded, "offer the best solution for neutralizing the conflicting pushes and pulls in Canadian life."

"Very likely," he continued, "the peoples of Britain and Canada and the United States would still be united if the policy of George III had been more soundly conceived and been executed with greater sensitivity for the feelings of the colonies."

Ball's document was circulated in the State Department, eliciting the wrath of many diplomats. John Leddy, assistant secretary of state in charge of European affairs, remembers: "I saw that thing. I thought it was absolute nonsense ... I certainly did my best to kill it." The idea of an Anglo Saxon community "would be considered in some parts of the world as an almost racist proposition."

Ball admits that by 1965 he felt it would be better if England joined the European community: his plan would ultimately "create more problems than it would solve." (Especially with the Canadians who, it has been noted, were so ultra-sensitive.) In the end, Ball decided not to submit his proposal to either the secretary of state or the President. It was shelved.

## Daniel, Lyndon, Elvis

There was at least one Quebecker who wanted to come and sound out the Americans himself. His name was Daniel Johnson. Elected premier of Quebec in June of 1966 on the deliberately ambiguous platform, "Equality or Independence," Johnson was considered by most American diplomats to be "pro-confederation and anti-separatist," even though he had "one avowed separatist in his cabinet [Cultural Minister Jean-Noel Tremblay]." According to Francis Cunningham, the consul general at Quebec City, Johnson was a pragmatist who "subscribed to the North American free market system." He ran his province with a "fundamentally American approach" to management. Cunningham boasted of having predicted Daniel Johnson's surprise victory in one of the electoral prediction competitions of which Butterworth and the White House were so fond.

During winter of 1966-1967, the White House received a curious request. Daniel Johnson wanted to be received by American President Lyndon Johnson. Did he want to visit Washington after a stop-over in New York planned for January 1967? Did he personally wish to invite the President to come and see Man And His World, Montreal's 1967 Worlds Fair? Did he want to speak with the American leader before visiting de Gaulle in May? In Quebec, no one — not Patry, not Morin, not even Cunningham — had got wind of his plans. According to George Springsteen of the State Department, "As far as I know, it might have come from the French embassy."

The request provoked some surprise at the White House. One diplomat ironically described the reactions of the President's advisors. "Who's this guy Johnson? Where's he from? Premier, that's like a governor, isn't it?" Eventually Johnson's request ended up on Springsteen's desk in the European Affairs Office, which included Canada due to some quirk in State Department logic. (The Department had been nicknamed "Foggy Bottom"; a reference to the bog on which the institution had been built.) Springsteen remembers that the request raised "a nasty little question: Should we receive the high Pope of free Quebec?"

Rufus Smith, the "Mr Canada" of the State Department, also remembers the petition, which came "at least orally." He interpreted it as a Quebec effort to get "some indication of the recognition of something special about Quebec." Smith advised the White House that "this wouldn't be considered appropriate." In any case, a provincial premier's place was not in the Oval Office. The decision was "one of those things you'd answer in five minutes," according to Springsteen.

LBJ, de Gaulle and other foreign leaders were due to meet at Man And His World in Montreal that year. It was a golden opportunity for LBJ to get an eyeful of Quebec society seething with unrest. Long before, LBJ had promised to inaugurate the stunning American pavilion — the metal and plastic ball called the "biosphere." But as the months passed, the Americans delayed fixing a date. Like de Gaulle, who did not initially see the point of visiting "this fair," LBJ wanted to cancel the trip. Early in May he scribbled on a memo, make "no travel plans. Rather doubt if I can come." His advisors convinced him otherwise; a promise was a promise.

On May 24 at three o'clock in the afternoon, Rufus Smith was informed that the President would leave for Expo the next morning. What? Tomorrow? "For God's sake, we can't do that!"

From the other end of the telephone line, Walt Rostow shot back, "Don't tell me what the President can do or can't do ... The President is going to wake up and early tomorrow morning he'll look at the intelligence reports on the Middle East situation, and if he thinks he can leave, he's going to leave."

The Middle East was the official explanation offered for the catastrophic planning of LBJ's 1967 Expo trip. Belligerent Arabs and Israelis were preparing for war.

"The danger implicit in every border incident in the Middle East," LBJ wrote in his memoirs, "was not merely war between Israelis and Arabs but an ultimate confrontation between the Soviet Union and the United States and its NATO allies." That was why he postponed his decision to send for the pilots of Air Force One until May 25, "when intelligence reports indicated that I could be reasonably sure the Middle East would not explode while I was gone ... The only explosion was in the White House Press Corps," he wrote. "The reporters resented being called on short notice early in the morning to go on a trip they insisted we had known about for two days. They did not realize that we were in the middle of a fast-moving crisis and it was impossible to have firm plans. Nor could we tell them."

Neither the journalists nor the Canadians knew that the President was planning to leave the morning of the twenty-fifth. Rostow gave Smith the official order: give them a few hours warning, just enough time for Pearson to change into a clean shirt. Rufus Smith recalls it was "the worst 36 hours in my life." Fate had willed him to invite Canadian Ambassador Ed Ritchie (the replacement for Charles Ritchie, and no relation) and his wife to celebrate Mrs Smith's birthday. Smith only arrived home at ten thirty, after organizing the President's schedules and speeches. His entire career revolved around managing bilateral Canadian-American relations. How on earth would he explain to his guests that routine matters had kept him late at the office? He gave in to the ridiculousness of the situation. In no time at all, Ritchie had informed Pearson of the impending visit.

In Montreal, however, the assistant to the American Expo commissioner, Roger Provencher, had been rehearsing for two weeks with secret servicemen in charge of the President's safety. He had long known the date of the visit: "I was not to tell the commissioner for Expo [Leonard Marx] or the ambassador anything or the consul general in Montreal anything," he admits. "The President himself says if Provencher leaks it in Montreal, he's fired," someone from Washington warned him.

What was the real reason for so much secrecy? According to LBJ's spokesman George Christien, it was a fear of demonstrators. Johnson hated the anti-American demonstrations that cropped up every time he left his fortified residence. As one State Department official put it, announcing his arrival too early "would have given all the Vietnam types an opportunity to warm up; that's what he wanted to avoid." Rusk had another explanation. "He was under great pressure from the Secret Service not to announce his travels in advance, to the greatest extent possible. They were still smarting from the assassination of President Kennedy." That was understandable, but announcing at six fifteen in the morning that you will be needing a foreign country's limousine services later that day is cutting it a bit close.

In the end, Johnson was not to avoid being haunted by Vietnam, regardless of the precautions he took. All eyes were fixed on the American flag, hoisted May 25 during "United States Day" Expo celebrations, in the presence of the President. As the star-spangled banner unfurled in the wind, people noticed a gaping hole, meticulously cut by a protestor to extinguish ten of the 50 stars. And it did not end there. As the President attempted to pronounce the names of Mayor Drapeau ("Drape-O") and Expo Commissioner Pierre Dupuy ("Doo-Pee"), the demonstrators cried out, "Assassin." Others took up the awful rhyme that was chanted nearly every night under the windows of the White House: "Hey, hey, LBJ, how many kids have you killed today?" Officers of the Royal Canadian Mounted Police quickly silenced the chant.

LBJ then had to cross the US pavilion and offer the Canadian government his gift, "The Great Canadian Ring," an impressive circle of cut glass engraved with the Canadian and ten provincial coats of arms. The State Department had even been so thorough as to consult experts to see if the first "e" in "Québec" should be accented. It should.

When the visit was decided only the night before, Charles Kiselyak, assistant to Rufus Smith, realized there was no alternative but to put the ring in his car and make the 12-hour drive that separates Washington and Montreal. After crossing the border and raising the eyebrows of more than one Canadian customs officer (What was this story about the president's gift being transported so late at night in a lowly station-wagon?), Kiselyak arrived at the pavilion and set about installing the thing on its ceremonial plinth.

Powered by a motorized table, the ring was designed to turn; a light installed inside would illuminate the intriguing sculpture. All LBJ had to do was flick on a switch and the majesty of the piece would be revealed. As he went to plug in the table, Kiselyak discovered, to his horror, that the outlet was too far away from the installation. And the President was due to arrive at any moment. Fortunately Kiselyak was an inventive fellow. He spotted an electric guitar that had once belonged to Elvis Presley hanging on a wall. He grabbed the sacred relic and cut the electrical cord with his penknife. He now had his extension. Legend has it that Kiselyak spent the entire ceremony holding the makeshift link together with his two, sweating hands.

In all, Lyndon Johnson spent only a couple of hours in Quebec territory. Legally, he never even set foot in it. He landed in the federal zone of Dorval Airport, took a helicopter to the international zone of Man And His World, and left immediately for Harrington Lake, Ontario, where the Pearsons had a summer residence. (Mrs Pearson was understandably furious at having been told so much at the last minute about the arrival of the presidential entourage. She needed to feed all these people!)

Discussions between Pearson and Johnson focussed on Vietnam. The President rarely inquired about Canada's domestic problems, although Canadian cabinet minister Paul Martin does remember LBJ sometimes asking "How's your problem coming with the French?" Walt Rostow, Johnson's advisor on international affairs, says that his boss became more and more aware of the Quebec problem. According to Rostow, who prepared his daily menu of information, "He was a junkie for news and intelligence." Johnson believed that the Quebec problem "would go away." If he did not bring it up with Pearson, Rostow claims, it was because "he was very careful asking about domestic issues just as Pearson was careful asking about [race riots in] Detroit."

In a letter of thanks to Pearson, the President lied. "I had a wonderful time at Expo," he wrote. He later refused "Drape-O" an audience at the Oval Office on two separate occasions. But Lyndon Johnson had not seen the last of Montreal, Expo and the province of Quebec. The huge American political apparatus was slowly waking to the changes taking place in the northeast corner of the continent. Charles de Gaulle's visit to Montreal, only two months after Johnson's trip, would ring out like a warning shot, shattering the deceptive tranquillity.

# 4

# The Insufferable
# de Gaulle

*With the unerring accuracy of a sadistic dentist, Charles de Gaulle has
drilled straight to the most sensitive nerve in Canada's anatomy and
proceeded to probe it gleefully.*
Editorial from the Washington *Evening Star*
the morning after "Vive le Québec libre!"

There are those who refuse to listen, those for whom reality is so unpleasant
that they proceed to block it out. Such had been Ottawa's attitude toward de
Gaulle. In spite of hundreds of warning signals, it took "Vive le Québec libre!"
("Long live free Quebec!") to convince the capital that the General actually and
truly supported sovereignty for the "French of Canada." Seated in the wagon
next to the Queen Elizabeth Hotel, federal headquarters for the famous visit,
External Affairs Minister Paul Martin "squirmed" when he heard those four
little words on the radio. He hastened to assure his assistants that the phrase was
not necessarily sinister. This was to be the last sign of this political deafness.

There are those who look ahead and anticipate danger, those who know the
slap in the face is on its way long before it arrives. This was Washington's
attitude toward de Gaulle.

In October of 1963, when French Minister of Culture André Malraux
visited Quebec, the American consul general in Montreal sent Washington —
as was standard procedure — a description of the visit. But why, of the
thousands of reports sent annually by Canadian diplomats to the State
Department, did this one end up in the "Canada" file of John F. Kennedy's
presidential archives? And why did Jerome Gaspard, the diplomat who wrote
it, send it by telex rather than air mail, which was procedure for routine
matters? Why did he stamp it "Priority"? Whatever the case, his readers in
Washington learned that Malraux "is inflaming French Canadian audiences
here with promises France and Quebec together will create a new mutual
future." Gaspard remarked that listening to Malraux, one "could not help but
infer ... [that the] destiny of France and Quebec ... would be replete with
political ties as well as economic and cultural ones."

Five months later, but still a full three years before de Gaulle's bombshell
would be dropped at Montreal City Hall, the Research and Information Bureau

(INR) of the State Department made the link between Quebec and de Gaulle. A memo of April 1964, part of a longer paper on French foreign policy, stated that "In the last 12 months de Gaulle has begun to assume the role of leader of the actual or potential 'third force' countries of Asia, Africa and Latin America. His name has become, more than ever, one to contend with in world affairs. Latin Americans vie for his visit; Cypriots seek his mediation; Panamanians look to him for assistance; Quebec separatists are inspired by French 'independence' from the 'Anglo Saxons'; and his very words have, or are believed or said to have, the weight, in distant areas, of gold and armies."

The General's trips abroad were aimed at increasing France's prestige. Prestige, as one INR analyst was to write, generated power. On a more prosaic note, the General wanted to remove certain countries, primarily under-developed ones, from the zones of influence of the two superpowers. De Gaulle called this procedure "neutralization."

The INR's linkage of de Gaulle and the separatists was still entirely theoretical. In September of 1963, as he was preparing to receive Lester Pearson, de Gaulle wrote, "French Canada will inevitably achieve statehood. We should act accordingly." The letter was addressed to his collaborators. It was the earliest and clearest testimony to de Gaulle's thoughts on Quebec, but not one agent of the CIA got wind of it.

## The Forecast: Scattered Gaulle-Storms

In broad daylight, to the horror of a stunned diplomatic community, de Gaulle publicly slapped Canada's face. In June of 1964, the new Canadian ambassador in Paris, Jules Léger, met with the General to present his credentials. He had prepared a mildly abrasive speech. Canada, he told de Gaulle, was undergoing an important social transformation. The country could very easily do without France, but it preferred to forge a partnership. It was a warning sent by Marcel Cadieux, Ottawa's deputy external affairs minister, who was more sensitive than most to the danger France posed. De Gaulle was put out by Léger's insolence; he banished the ambassador from the Elysée for having been overly frank. And he made his own views known.

"Without France," he said, Canada's equilibrium would be precarious indeed. He added that Ottawa should do more for its French-speaking minority, especially in economic matters. Then the General revealed a shade of his thoughts. "Many Canadians have French roots, speak the French language and share the French mentality. In short, they are French in every way excepting the matter of sovereignty."

In May of 1965, an American diplomat in France reported "a small but not insignificant episode" which suggested a link between de Gaulle and Quebec sovereignty. Well Stabler, the embassy's political advisor, was invited by the mayor of Cholet, a village in the Vendée region, to attend a presidential visit. The mayor, who knew Americans were not popular at the Elysée, neglected to tell the General that Stabler worked at the US embassy. When, however, he introduced a dozen Canadian students studying at the Ecole nationale d'administration, he made a point of indicating that most of them came from Quebec. According to Stabler, "De Gaulle raised his hands in a form of salute and said, 'Ah, le vrai Canada!'" ("Ah, the real Canada!").

The diplomat regarded the incident as "revealing of de Gaulle's attitude with respect to Canada and fits well into what is now a growing tendency amongst the government and the gaullists to draw a sharp distinction between French Canada and English-speaking Canada."

Where his words spoken in jest? Were they to be taken seriously? Ministerial visits back and forth between Quebec City and Paris were increasing with a frequency that did not escape the attention of the American embassy. Premier Jean Lesage was received in Paris with as much pomp as the American President. A general delegation from Quebec, endowed with the status of a quasi-embassy, was established. A cultural agreement with Quebec conferring "an exceptional measure of independent authority" on the province in matters of international affairs was signed with visible enthusiasm. The minister of education, Paul Gérin-Lajoie, suddenly took it into his head that he would like to meet one of the four most powerful men on the planet. He was ushered into the inner sanctum of French power without the slightest delay. Things were becoming serious.

One month after Stabler relayed his story to Washington, the INR added an essential ingredient to the file: the name of the French politician who was meddling in Quebec affairs. According to the memo, "it appears highly likely that the very responsive attitude that France has shown toward Quebec initiatives in regard both to the [cultural] entente and to Quebec House stems from a direct, personal interest in Quebec on the part of President de Gaulle." (More than a year later, Paul Martin still thought that "extremists in Quebec and France were using the President." In reality, de Gaulle was the foremost Quebec fan. Twenty-five years after the fact, senior civil servants in Ottawa admit they still do not know who "masterminded" the pro-Quebec policy.)

Given this state of affairs, the INR memo suggested, even Gérin-Lajoie's diplomatic exploit made sense. "A Quai d'Orsay [the French ministry of foreign affairs] official explained this unprecedented interest in a foreign, provincial minister of education with the extraordinary [if literally true] observation that President de Gaulle considered French Canadians to be Frenchmen and would probably receive any Quebec minister who asked for an appointment." The official was right. A whole slew of Quebec ministers — not to mention a delegation of Acadians who had a hard time getting invited to Ottawa — were welcomed at the Elysée. Federal minister Jean Marchand and Canadian Governor General Georges Vanier (an old friend of President de Gaulle's), on the other hand, could not seem to make it past the front door.

French diplomats at the Quai d'Orsay confided to the Americans that they did not share the General's infatuation with Quebec. According to one analyst at the INR, it made them "uneasy."

The memo attempted to identify de Gaulle's ulterior motive, his "political calculation." It speculated that Paris wanted "to acquire leverage on Ottawa and bilateral relations and in multilateral dealings involving France, Canada and other western nations." The Quebec-Paris link would, in fact, "oblige Ottawa to avoid becoming involved in any serious, and certainly any public, quarrel with France." On the other hand, the memo continued, Canada had been friendly with Paris for years, and often tried to play mediator between de Gaulle and Washington. The General's political motives remained an open question.

The State Department was less confused by the forces propelling the Quebec government. It felt Premier Jean Lesage had no choice but to deal with France. His actions were prompted by "an important body ... of opinion in Quebec [which] still harbors autonomist aspirations which the Lesage government (despite its record of achievement in this area) has not yet satisfied." According to the memo, what was needed was a "continued high level of statesmanship" in Ottawa as well as in Quebec, to "keep autonomist centrifugal tendencies in Quebec within manageable bounds."

In Paris, Stabler's boss, Richard Funkhouser, did not like questions left unanswered; having only recently come to work in Paris he wanted to make sure his analyses were airtight. "I read everything that the General had written that we could lay our hands on. One thing that I didn't want to have happen to me as the political consular was to be surprised, and General de Gaulle was a master of surprise." De Gaulle had already caused many a headache for the Americans in Indochina. He was the first western leader to recognize Mao's China. He was making eyes at Moscow and the Eastern bloc countries even as he cold-shouldered neighboring England. He refused to go along with the super powers and sign a nuclear nonproliferation treaty, which he felt would give Washington, London and Moscow an atomic monopoly.

Midway through 1965, Funkhouser asked his staff for a list of "surprises" that General de Gaulle might have up his sleeve. "What are the most damaging things that the General might pull with respect to American interests anywhere under the sun, across the globe?" he inquired. He instructed his staff to put themselves in the General's shoes, to think like de Gaulle and predict the future based on principles enunciated clearly by the French leader in the past. Funkhouser recalls that the list was not long, a page at most. One advisor wrote that France would intensify its criticism of American policy in Vietnam. One year later, de Gaulle went to Phnom Penh and denounced US military intervention. Another advisor predicted France would withdraw from NATO or would force the organization to transfer its quarters outside French territory. Ten months later, de Gaulle fulfilled both prophecies. A third staff member said that de Gaulle would put "the heaviest possible political pressure" to promote his " 'Québec libre' policy." The forecast came true one July day in Montreal, two years later.

The potentially explosive document was considered too "sensitive" to be transmitted via ordinary channels. According to Funkhouser, "if it ever got into the hands of some of our congressmen, they would have hopped on it and shown how little the State Department trusted General de Gaulle." After all, the General was still one of Washington's allies. The document, which would prove to be a weather forecast of gaullist storms to come, was dispatched with great care to high-ranking officials in the State Department.

By the summer of 1965, the American diplomatic community understood the essentials of Franco-Quebec intrigue. It had identified the chief player, de Gaulle, and was ready for his next coup: "Vive le Québec libre!" The American analyses were never shared with Canadian diplomats, however, even though the latter certainly could have used them. According to Allan Gotlieb, who was at the time working in External Affairs under Marcel Cadieux, "If the Americans knew whether there was a plot, whether there was a conspiracy, whether there was a design, whether there was a grand scheme, they sure as hell didn't tell us." Small wonder, since Canadian relations with the United States were not at their best during this period.

Early in 1965, while LBJ's "Rolling Thunder" operation was scattering bombs across North Vietnam, Pearson decided it was time to announce his disapprobation. He chose an American rostrum: Temple University in Philadelphia, which had invited him to receive its World Peace Award. LBJ was livid. The Canadian leader could say whatever he wanted in Canada, but he had broken a golden rule by criticizing the President on his own soil. LBJ summoned Pearson to Camp David and proceeded to fly into an uncontrollable rage.

The Canadian sat on the balustrade while the American President shouted for over an hour, scandalizing the senior civil servants in attendance. At one point, LBJ grabbed the Prime Minister by his shirt collar and lifted him as if he were about to thrash him. "You pissed on my rug," he told him. Ambassador Charles Ritchie, a helpless witness to the scene, recalls that Pearson was "quite shaken" by the incident. Never before had bilateral relations sunk to the level of hand-to-hand combat. The press did not immediately get wind of the affair. "It has been a very pleasant couple of hours," Pearson lied. A "friendly" meeting, Johnson smiled.

America's failure to warn Canada of the Paris-Quebec connection can also be explained by the fact that the men at Foggy Bottom had more important things on their minds. According to Funkhouser, "I assigned the Quebec problem a relatively low priority in my work. We had many far more crucial problems than we thought the Quebec effort was causing the United States."

## A Motive: Anti-Americanism

Washington approached the problem of de Gaulle from one angle only: possible damage to the United States. De Gaulle, for his part, was primarily motivated by advancing the interests of the one and only, irreplaceable, indispensable France: a nation that "was herself only at the head of the line." Since retaking the presidency in 1958, the hero of the Liberation had set himself one goal: re-establishing France's lost grandeur. One of his first political gestures revealed how loudly he intended to trumpet that resurrection. He proposed to President Eisenhower the founding of a tripartite directorate, to be composed of the United States, England and France, which would coordinate the western alliance. He would never allow Washington to slip into a position of supremacy; the army that fought under the tri-colored flag would never submit to any Yankee general. France must take its place at the summit, as an equal partner with other great nations. Otherwise it would seek its niche elsewhere. In short, it was equality or independence. Eisenhower did not even bother to anwer the bold request: there would be no directorate. There would be de Gaulle.

The resentment in the great man's attitude was palpable. In London during the war, he had been hostage to the English and the Americans. He could not swallow the notion that France's future would be decided by foreigners. He never forgot that President Roosevelt regarded him as "a narrow-minded French zealot with too much ambition for his own good and some rather dubious views on democracy." Nor did he forget the endless quarrels with Churchill, even though he was his closest ally. (Churchill joked that "De Gaulle considers himself to be Joan of Arc, but my bishop won't let me burn him.") What was more, the special relationship between Washington and London — the Anglo Saxon alliance — left a bitter taste in the General's mouth.

His persistence in formulating French policy uniquely according to national interests did not spring from rancour so much as from attempted far-sightedness. At a press conference in November of 1959, he revealed the scenario that both haunted and inspired him. "Who can say that in a completely transformed political universe of the future the two powers with a monopoly on nuclear arms will not get together and agree to divide up the world? It wouldn't be the first time in history such a thing had occurred. Who can say that western Europe won't be wiped out by Moscow, and central Europe by Washington? Who can swear that the two rivals, after some unimaginable socio-political upheaval, won't join forces?" The reversal of alliances among great powers was the historical rule rather than the exception. Hitler had fought Stalin. Hitler later allied himself with Stalin. Then, one final time, Hitler fought Stalin. All in less than a decade.

De Gaulle had no sympathy for the American presidents who dreamed of an Atlantic alliance where Europeans, meekly grouped behind the leader, harmoniously let others look out for their best interest. He told Eisenhower, "You personally would use nuclear warheads to defend Europe because you understand what's at stake. But as the Soviet Union develops its technology and the ability to strike American cities, the day will come when one of your successors will refuse to make nuclear war for fear of a nuclear counter-attack." In short, a future president would not risk Chicago to avenge Lyon. De Gaulle wanted his own atomic arsenal because, as he put it, "The Soviets know me." They had no doubt the proud Frenchman would defend his hexagonal land. They knew he would risk Paris to avenge Lyon. "I have to be insufferable all on my own." It was more than a resolution; it would dictate his conduct.

In response to Washington's rebuff over the tripartite directorate, de Gaulle began to dismantle every organizational tie binding France to the United States. Not only did he start stockpiling his own nuclear arsenal, he also developed a personal East-West dialogue. It could be summed up in one word: detente. Tensions polarized nations, cemented the blocs into place and eliminated the margin of manoeuvre. If the Gaullist republic wanted to lift itself to the summit, it would have to widen margins, open cracks in the foundations and, in general, ease tensions. De Gaulle would play the tightrope-walking neutralist. Better yet, he would play the game of keeping Washington and Moscow off balance. If either of them was on the verge of getting too strong, he would throw a little Camembert in the works.

The English-speaking world (the United States, England and, by extension, Canada) was riding an economic wave that had originated in Detroit and California. The Canadians brought up the rear of this Anglo Saxon battalion. They also refused to sell France the uranium it required for its bombs, while they were supplying Washington and London. Canada wanted to maintain close ties with the Americans and British — as well as with the French. Pearson, who liked to be on good terms with everyone, frankly told this to the General in Paris at the beginning of 1964. But because Canada had aligned itself with the Anglo Saxon camp, it became part of de Gaulle's target. Paris could use it in its strategy against the United States.

Pearson seriously misjudged the General. He returned from Paris believing de Gaulle to be "far more sympathetic" to Canada than he had expected. The General "really did not believe that we English-speaking Canadians had a chance to maintain our separateness against US pressures," but Pearson, confident that he had made an ally, vowed to "disabuse him on that score."

Funkhouser, who monitored French politics closely during the critical years, claims de Gaulle's "basic policy was to enhance the prestige of France globally in every possible way he could ... It was completely consistent with the building of a French enclave (which was already existent) in the Anglo Saxon world, and giving it as much prestige and importance as he possibly could. But as a corollary to building up French prestige globally it required diminishing, lowering, attacking and fragmenting the Anglo-American hegemony to which he always referred."

The Americans were not the only ones to interpret de Gaulle's interest in Quebec in this manner. The Canadian ambassador in Paris, Jules Léger, saw things similarly. The General's "anti-American bias," he wrote in the summer of 1965, "works to our disadvantage."

De Gaulle was determined to rain on the capitals of the English-speaking world, Funkhouser explained, because the Americans, "aided and abetted ... by our very close relations with our English brothers" Ottawa and London, had exerted "overwhelming control over international affairs ... since World War II." He would darken the skies over Phnom Penh or Montreal if need be, even reserving his warmth for the other bloc that had lost much of its haughtiness since the Cuban crisis. De Gaulle's flirtation with Moscow turned out merely to be tactical. In the last analysis he placed himself squarely in the western camp; if Moscow were to attack tomorrow, Paris and Washington would shoot in the same direction. The General would let circumstance dictate the obvious. He would not be content to plan only for his seven-year term; he would plan for the entire century. De Gaulle regarded Russia as an essentially European, stabilizing power. Bolshevism was the foreign, destabilizing force which would prove transitory. One of these days Mother Russia would either swallow it whole or spit it out. Then the old Franco-Russian alliance would be reborn and the real menace for both east and west, Germany, would be contained.

There was, however, a gaping hole in de Gaulle's international logic. France had been half-destroyed by the war. It had lost its reputation as a military power when the Germans crossed the Maginot Line. It had recently been defeated in Indochina, and things did not look good in Algeria. Its colonial empire was crumbling before its eyes. In short, France did not have the means to promote de Gaulle's policies of grandeur. The General turned that argument on its head. "Since we are no longer a great power," he stubbornly reasoned, "we need grand policies or we will be reduced to nothing."

## Kennedy and de Gaulle: A False Start

Washington did not know what to make of France's acrobatics. Kennedy had spent quite a bit of time with de Gaulle, whom he admired and whose counsel he had sought during a Paris meeting in May of 1961. He did not understand why their relations were deteriorating, why France insisted on playing off-beat in the pan-Atlantic concert. Kennedy was the first American president de Gaulle had ever respected. But personal affinity carries little weight when two nations choose to follow divergent paths.

In April 1963, Charles ("Chip") Bohlen, American ambassador in Paris, visited Palm Beach to explain de Gaulle's mindset to Kennedy. Having served as Roosevelt's advisor at Yalta, Bohlen had rubbed shoulders with de Gaulle on many occasions. He was a regular visitor at the Elysée, and even indulged in black humor from time to time in the General's presence. "I recall one conversation with de Gaulle in which he told me that he used to be a heavy smoker, but he had finally given it up as it was not particularly good for his health or his energy. He added, however, that 'if war ever breaks out, I will resume smoking.' With some imprudence I remarked with a smile, 'Well, General, you may not have time even to light your cigarette.'"

Bohlen was a distinguished figure, an aristocrat. American journalists called him "our Lord Mountbatten." He did not like the way Kennedy managed international affairs while lounging at the poolside. Their conversation at Palm Beach "was on the whole rather desultory and interrupted constantly by the arrival of children or Mrs Kennedy," he wrote. "Kennedy was actually having a manicure at the side of the pool as we conducted most of the conversation." Between splashes and nail clippings, the distinguished ambassador laid out his views on the workings of de Gaulle's mind. For that he usually resorted to metaphors of astronomy. "Every planet has its own gravitational pull," he explained. "A medium-sized planet has to stay out of the gravitational field of the larger planets or become a satellite. For exactly the same reason, France had to stay away from the United States."

According to Bohlen, "Kennedy seemed to me to be pretty much on the right track with regards to de Gaulle. He realized that very little, if anything, that the United States did could change any of de Gaulle's fundamental policy of the independence of France, and he felt, however, and in this I thoroughly agree, that the proper role of the United States was to play it in a relaxed, calm and cool manner, and not to allow ourselves to be irritated by the General unnecessarily."

Another Kennedy advisor in international matters, Walt Rostow, was less charitable in his description of the General's policies. "Since de Gaulle couldn't make much of a dent in the enemies of France, he asserted himself against its friends," he explained. Rostow adds that Kennedy's final comment on the subject was: "That's cheap."

While Kennedy's relationship with de Gaulle had started on the right foot only to falter with each passing day, Lyndon Johnson never got past the word go with the General. When de Gaulle arrived in Washington in November of 1963 to share the grief of a mourning nation, Lyndon Johnson learned, through an allied ambassador, that the General was wary of America. If the Soviets invade Europe, de Gaulle had said, we cannot count on Yankee help. They had to be dragged forcibly into the two world wars: had it not been for Pearl Harbor, they would have taken even longer. Now that the stakes are nuclear ...

LBJ said the report on de Gaulle's attitude was still "fresh in my mind" when he shook the General's hand. Once they had folded their long bodies into the chairs of the Oval Office, the two simulated dialogue. The General assured the American that disagreements between the two countries had been "greatly exaggerated ... the important thing was that Frenchmen knew perfectly well they could count on the United States if France were attacked," he continued, according to the memoirs of the indignant President.

LBJ "stared hard at the French President, suppressing a smile." Their conversation, which bears witness to the General's deviousness, would stay with Johnson for years. If the United States followed French advice and abandoned Vietnam, LBJ reflected, "I suspect he [de Gaulle] might have cited that as 'proof' of what he had been saying all along: that the United States could not be counted on in times of trouble."

Johnson had to stomach the Frenchman, just as Kennedy had before him. De Gaulle, who wanted to be "insufferable all alone," fostered all kinds of quarrels with the Americans. Had the President of the United States hit back, he would implicitly have recognized his opponent's calibre. It would have become a vicious circle. LBJ, echoing his predecessor's policy, said, "I made it a rule for myself and for the US government simply to ignore President de Gaulle's attacks on our policies." Several months before "Vive le Québec libre!" Pearson asked the American President how he managed to stay calm in the face of de Gaulle's exploits. The General had just withdrawn from NATO, so the question was especially apt. "When he winds up for one of his pitches, I step off the plate," LBJ had answered.

De Gaulle could throw whatever stones he pleased into Chinese, Vietnamese or Quebec ponds, but he never managed to wet the Americans. In 1966, when he announced his withdrawal from NATO (France refuses, he said, to play "humble auxiliary" to the United States any longer) and asked 60,000 American army personnel to pack up and go, LBJ called in his advisors. For one of the great western powers to fragment the defense network of the western alliance was the worst blow to America since the missile crisis.

Secretary of State Dean Rusk was unable to attend the meeting. His assistant, George Ball, an ardent anti-Gaullist, suggested that Johnson denounce the French leader, or at the very least try to reason with him. He urged immediate American action. LBJ answered, "George, when someone asks you to leave his house, you tip your hat and go." Then he turned to Defense Secretary Robert McNamara and asked, "How long did he give us? Three months? Well, I want you out of there in two months." He turned back to Ball. "George, your job is not to denounce de Gaulle, your job is to make sure that everyone [meaning all members of NATO] except France goes with us to Brussels," NATO's new headquarters.

According to Walt Rostow, who witnessed the exchanges between Ball and LBJ, these dodging manoeuvres "help account for the fact that we didn't get into a big flap" when the storm finally broke close to home, over Quebec.

## A General on the Balcony

Daniel Johnson, who had been snubbed in Washington when his request to talk with LBJ was turned down, was warmly welcomed in Paris. On May 17, 1967, "a bright red carpet" was rolled out for him, according to American Ambassador Bohlen in an 11-page report on the visit.

The Premier of Quebec had come to invite the French President to Expo. De Gaulle received him four times during his visit. Bohlen described one "particularly warm" toast in which the eloquent General "never once mentioned Canada or referred to Quebec as a province." De Gaulle also spoke of "the common destiny of all Frenchmen from wherever they come or wherever they are."

Johnson knew de Gaulle was not enthusiastic about going to Expo. But he found exactly the right words to entice him. "My General, Quebec needs you. It's now or never," he told him. The Québécois politician had touched every key on the gaullist organ. He had played de Gaulle's theme song, sounding allegiance ("My" General), need and urgency.

The Premier's visit had all the outward trappings of a success. In reality, however, the list of agreements signed was "long but somewhat thin," the American ambassador noted. Johnson left in a "euphoric" state, he added, and would certainly arrange a welcome for his host that was an "equally warm — if not warmer — reception."

In July de Gaulle finally headed for the shores of the St Lawrence. The General had long ago chosen his side; now he was being offered his hour. "I will be heard over there; it will make waves," he said as he boarded the *Colbert*, the French flagship that would take him to Quebec. "It's the last chance we have to make amends for France's cowardice," he added, referring to Paris's having abandoned Quebec to the British in centuries past.

On the night of the twenty-third, he gave a speech in Quebec City's Chateau Frontenac in which he revealed his thoughts. Not only must Quebec "have the right to self-determination in all areas," but the "French people living here" must refuse to "submit" any longer to "the preponderance of foreign influences" and must forge alliances with English Canada "to save their character and independence from contact with their colossal neighbour to the south ..."

De Gaulle had invented sovereignty association. The General would later allege he had dreamed up the concept in 1960 during a visit to Montreal, when he was shocked by the city's Americanization and the economic inferiority of the French-speaking majority. In his unfinished memoirs, drafted after his retirement from public life in 1969, de Gaulle wrote that the visit inspired him to imagine "a nation with French roots existing alongside one whose roots were British ... associating their mutual independence in order to safeguard it." The association would negate the "injustices of history." Both his biographer, Jean Lacouture, and Quebec historian Dale Thomson suspect de Gaulle of "historical superimposition."

Federal politicians at the Chateau Frontenac that evening refused to hear de Gaulle. Paul Martin applauded the speech — not with much vigour to be sure, but he did applaud. As one member of de Gaulle's entourage put it, that night "everything was made clear." But "for the deaf to hear, he would have to shout." The chance to shout arrived the following day, July 24, on a City Hall balcony where someone, in violation of the mayor's orders, had installed a microphone.

American Consul General Richard Hawkins wrote from Montreal that de Gaulle had stood on the balcony and "addressed an orderly five to six thousand among whom were 15 to 20 small groups of flag-bearing and placard-carrying nationalists who seemed to do all the booing of 'Oh Canada,' and to join lustily in the cheerings for de Gaulle." The famous microphone was bifurcated like a pair of handlebars. De Gaulle clung to it as if he were about to execute a perilous leap. After winning the crowd over with a few flattering remarks about Montreal — he compared his welcome to that he had received during France's Liberation — he clutched the microphone for his final message.

"Vive Montréal," he began.

He took his position, inhaled deeply and announced, "Vive le Québec ..." but a final word he was preparing to say was cut off by the crowd's applause. He checked himself, backed off a little and let the wave pass.

Again he advanced, leaning into the microphone. In a single breath he cried out, "Vive le Québec libre!" There was a moment of stupefied silence, then a delirium of applause. De Gaulle straightened his back, unclenched his fists and caught his breath again. It was done. The deaf would hear at last. "Vive le Canada français et Vive la France!" he shouted as a curtain call.

"He said it! He said it!" chuckled a young bespectacled Liberal with a future, Robert Bourassa. The General "went too far," said another MNA, René Lévesque. "There's going to be trouble," moaned the premier, Daniel Johnson.

His mission accomplished, de Gaulle walked through City Hall to the reception where 500 people awaited him, among them, the dumbfounded diplomatic community.

Hawkins later wrote, "This audience had been at first a bit bemused by the dramatics of de Gaulle's balcony scene ... Then quite shocked by his comparison of his journey to Montreal with the liberation of France and by his emphasis on such a separatist sort of catch phrase as 'a free Quebec.'"

When "the terrible phrase" rang out, Mrs Hawkins, widow of the consul general, recalls, "it was a terrible shock. That was hardly the thing to say ... We were all looking at one another saying how could this be? We were all buzzing around together."

At the reception, Hawkins thought the General looked tired. "The General's eyes were swollen and red, his voice slightly hoarse, and his interest in this audience not noticeable by the time the consuls came along" to shake his hand. The diplomats and dignitaries did not interest him. It was those in the streets who constituted his true audience.

De Gaulle was staying just a few doors away from Hawkins, who zealously reported that the General looked "rested and fresh" the next morning. He was thus in shape to receive the federal government's communiqué labelling his speech "unacceptable." The General had not really been keen to go to Ottawa; nonplussed, he prepared his departure for the twenty-sixth. But he did not leave Montreal without launching into a tirade directed at the United States. In a speech at the University of Montreal he warned that Quebec "lay beside a huge nation which by its very size could threaten your existence."

## Washington Analyses "Vive le Québec libre!"

The next morning at the White House, Walt Rostow read the dispatches from American diplomats in Paris. News of the de Gaulle initiative was very badly received there, they explained. Even television, which was state-controlled, "made no attempt to disguise overwhelmingly unfavorable press reactions." As for the politicians, radical Jacques Duhamel explained de Gaulle's "stupefying interference" by his "fixed idea of anti-Americanism." Socialist leader François Mitterrand kept his counsel, but two sources close to him openly asked whether the old General "possessed all his faculties." According to the embassy reports, "Even among totally commited gaullists, belief in de Gaulle's infallibility has been brutally shaken."

There were a few exceptions. Gaullist writer Pierre Charpy, for example, regarded the Quebec bombshell as one more manifestation of a coherent foreign policy that included such things as the withdrawal from NATO and strategy in the Middle East. The embassy gave a resumé of an article in *Paris-Presse*, in which Charpy explained de Gaulle's motives. World peace, he said, was threatened by the growing hegemony of the United States. De Gaulle was serving the cause of peace by encouraging French Canadian aspirations.

Part of Lyndon Johnson's daily routine was to glance through a brief synopsis of diplomatic texts sent to the White House and choose several pieces that interested him. On July 28, he asked to see the paper prepared by Charles Bohlen on the General's latest escapade.

The ambassador had never been so critical:

It has now become increasingly apparent that de Gaulle has lost [his] sense of timing and appropriateness and his public utterances and indeed actions have more and more taken on a purely willful and personal character. According to our information, de Gaulle conducts completely single-handedly French foreign policy and is more and more neglecting other aspects of government activities. His statements on Vietnam, which have tended more and more to free himself from the normal restraints, his action on the common market, and finally, most incredible of all, his recent behavior in Canada, have all reflected this tendency. It would seem that de Gaulle is suffering from two aspects of old age: (1) a progressive hardening of prejudices — of which he has plenty; and (2) a growing indifference and even unconcern with the effect of his words on international and French public opinion. The fixation which he has always had in regard to the power and size of the United States has grown into a compulsive obsession. [...]

We have noted that along with his powerful intrusion into Canadian domestic affairs in favor of the French Canadians, de Gaulle found two occasions to make relatively mild cracks about the United States and its size. I feel, however, that now we must definitely recognize that one of the motivating forces of de Gaulle's conduct of foreign policy is his anti-American obsession and I believe we can expect that almost anything he says in the future will contain some uncomplimentary references to the United States. [...]

It is perhaps too soon to state that de Gaulle is becoming 'senile,' but certainly the restraint that used to accompany his actions and characterize his words seems to be slipping very badly.

The dispatch was on LBJ's table, along with many others, at eight o'clock in the morning. But Detroit was going up in flames; race riots were tearing the social fabric of America's cities to shreds. The gunfire, pillaging and conflagration in the American automobile capital — transformed that day into the capital of hatred — left Johnson no time to think about de Gaulle. At 11:30 he handed Rostow the document and asked him to "analyze this and give it to me in four sentences." At 12:35 the following paragraph was returned to him: "(1) De Gaulle is increasingly operating a personal rather than governmental foreign policy; (2) His anti-Americanism grows worse as he estimates US power and influence expand; (3) The French press is almost universally against him on his Canadian performance; (4) The Canadian performance has hurt him politically but how much, we can't say — notably because it's vacation time in France." LBJ read this short memo at 12:50.

If he was at all angered by de Gaulle's latest pirouette, Johnson did not show it. He had at least one good reason to be relieved. Barely two weeks before, a French dignitary had suggested the Americans arrange a meeting between Johnson and de Gaulle, since they would be on the same side of the Atlantic. Nothing was done about it. It would certainly have put Pearson's nose out of joint if Johnson had indeed met with the man who had been chased out of Ottawa. A CIA official rememebers that "everybody howled with glee" at the sight of these Canadian moralists wallowing in the Gaullist molasses.

Analysts at the INR went into high gear, inundating the State Department with papers on the Ottawa-Paris-Quebec triangle. As far as domestic French politics went, they felt the Quebec affair "undermined the General's prestige" and might cost him his parliamentary majority in the next election.

Two days after the balcony incident, the INR sent Secretary of State Rusk a paper on "de Gaulle's stepped-up anti-Americanism." Anton DePorte, the INR's senior analyst, felt the Quebec bombshell was the French strategist's reprisal for the defeats he had suffered since June on the scene of world affairs. Forty-one days before "Vive le Québec libre!" the Israelis had thrashed the Arabs in the Six Day War. The General had been "profoundly disturbed." Not that he was anti-Israeli, but the Soviets had penetrated the region via Syria. The Americans, who supported Tel Aviv, were occupying a political area that had formerly been under the unique control of the French and British. De Gaulle proposed a "four-power" conference, including France, to attempt to resolve the conflict. But Moscow, which was on shaky ground after the latest round of fighting, and Washington, which was flushed with victory, came to a private agreement. The war brought the logic of blocs into the region. For de Gaulle and for France, it was a defeat.

Thirty-one days before "Vive le Québec libre!" Soviet Premier Aleksei Kosygin met with President Johnson. The two great men seemed to want to agree to stabilize spheres of influence and strike a balance. The Frenchman, who made progress only in troubled waters, was very upset. According to DePorte, "consolidation of the east-west status quo" especially in Europe "would be check mate to de Gaulle's policy."

In the summer of 1967 it was almost possible to imagine the scenario de Gaulle had painted early in 1959: a tragic turn of events which concluded with the "two rivals" uniting. DePorte wrote that if "de Gaulle fails now" he might consider himself "as far as ever" from his goal of "weakening the hold of the two super powers on two halves of" the European continent.

It was no wonder that the General set upon the United States with such fury, denouncing the "American hegemony, a danger which he sees threatened by Soviet weakness."

According to another of DePorte's analyses, "It is not fanciful to speculate that his politically pointless behavior in Quebec can be traced to the sense of impotence and defeat which events of that summer laid on him." Taking aim at Ottawa in order to strike Washington was "foolish. That was not the right target; it didn't bother us at all."

If the American analyst's words are true and "Vive le Québec libre!" was simply a reprisal — the last-ditch effort of a frustrated loser — then the bold phrase, which raised both cheers and chills, gains a pitiful, mean-sounding resonance.

## The Two Johnsons

American diplomats in Paris were news-starved. Had de Gaulle simply blundered? Would he repent? Was it capriciousness or premeditated strategy? Support for de Gaulle's actions varied from one floor to another at the Quai d'Orsay. Whether they agreed with it or not, French diplomats were certain that the General's course would not waver; he would be very aggressive in the future with his Quebec policy.

George Springsteen, a State Department official, happened to be in Paris. He made a courtesy visit to Hervé Alphand, right-hand man to the minister of foreign affairs, where he was treated to a little joke. There are two Johnsons on the American continent, the diplomat explained. The good one is in Quebec, the bad one in Washington. When Springsteen related the comment to Ambassador Bohlen, the latter was furious. "That was not the kind of remark to be made by the number two in the French Foreign Office about the President of the United States." They could heap all kinds of invective on us, but Good Lord, a little politesse was in order.

Far from repenting his speech, de Gaulle called his ministers together to force them, despite their disapproving glances to suggest new avenues of cooperation with Quebec. New joint projects were announced, but as the INR noted the following day, "since French assistance to Quebec has been minimal and insignificant to date, any increase would be 'considerable,' but not necessarily either substantial or significant." In the long run, the insubstantiality of monies invested would lead Quebeckers to realize that "France really provides no alternative to Quebec's role and participation in the Canadian and North American economy." The State Department was convinced that the citizens of Quebec saw their future "lying with Canada [...] although this realization can be clouded from time to time by sentiment."

According to the INR, the "good" Johnson was going to "reap all the political benefits" from French initiatives. Yet, high-ranking Quebec civil servants had told Consul General Cunningham that France was "long on 'belles paroles' — fair words — but short on performance [...] Quebec would pay for most of the French educational and cultural cooperation it received."

In December, Paris increased its Quebec budget five-fold; it swelled to five million dollars. According to "a source" who relayed the information to an American diplomat, the finance committee at the Quai soon realized that Quebec wasn't a Third World country. In fact, the province was capable of injecting some much-needed North American capital into France's old world veins. "In many important sectors," said the informant, "France can benefit more from Quebec aid than vice versa." This posed a structural problem, of course; French aid programs usually went one way, in the opposite direction.

Jean Drapeau, while seeking a loan for Montreal, was not overly dazzled by the promise of French loans. According to an American diplomatic dispatch, he told Parisian financiers, "I can do better elsewhere, including Canada and Wall Street."

Meanwhile, Cunningham diagnosed the effect of de Gaulle's trip on Quebec's citizens. They were "extensively irritated" by de Gaulle's use of the term "the French of Canada." But this was overshadowed by the "wonderful attention de Gaulle drew to Quebec's aspirations," not to mention "the boost it gave to Quebec's self-respect and self-confidence." "Vive le Québec libre!" was a "jab at what Quebeckers called Ottawa's stuffiness." The people were applauding loudly because this type of exercise was "of course, a favorite sport here."

Cunningham also relayed the phrase that INR analysts would make popular in future texts. De Gaulle's visit, according to a Quebec civil servant, meant that from that day on "every Quebecker is a separatist at least one hour a day."

In November, while speaking in Paris, de Gaulle upped the ante. In the past he had said Quebec should be "free." Now he wanted it to become a "sovereign state." He began to refer to his Quebec policy as "a great and necessary French task of the century." Walt Rostow misread this and wrote LBJ that this policy was "the major French task of our century." The American President was scheduled to see Bohlen that very day in Washington. They discussed in detail the press conference full of anti-American venom de Gaulle had just given, and pondered his appeal for the establishment of "a sovereign Quebec closely linked to France." Rostow called it "his most extreme statement."

Rostow suggested his boss ask Bohlen about the effect of the "Quebec fiasco (now repeated)" on the leader's already faltering political health. He wanted to know if they should maintain dodging and ducking manoeuvres or "begin to take active counter-measures." Johnson's determination not to provoke the Frenchman was unshakable; he chose to duck. That summer, LBJ had received the head of state for the French Ivory Coast, Houmphouet-Boigny, en route to Man And His World. LBJ's speech writers suggested he embellish his toast with a "very light thrust" directed at de Gaulle. Speaking of his own visit to Expo he could add, "I have noticed that French-speaking leaders have an especially lively time up there." Despite the supplications of one advisor who told him, "The public would enjoy hearing you make at least this easy reference to him [the General]," LBJ had the passage removed. Not a single word nor smile would upset his strategy of avoidance. The aging de Gaulle, who had just celebrated his seventy-seventh birthday, would not live forever, he thought. His successor would likely be more pleasant.

The French diplomatic community in Washington wanted to know how the Americans were reacting to the General's latest initiatives. André Baeyens, advisor to the ambassador, attempted to grill Rufus Smith on the subject. He asked if "possible constitutional changes in Canada would present difficulties for the US in its relations with Ottawa." Baeyens asserted with a straight face that the General's statements in Montreal "had in no sense sought to stimulate a secessionist movement in Quebec." Rufus Smith remained silent as the grave, and Baeyens returned empty-handed from his visit to Foggy Bottom. The Frenchman found Smith's reticence regrettable. He was responsible for keeping an eye on relations between Ottawa and Washington, and the Quai d'Orsay "had complained that it receives reams of reports from the French embassy in Ottawa but virtually nothing from the embassy in Washington on this subject."

The Americans, as well-informed as they were mute, still did not have any clue about one of the most important elements in de Gaulle's Quebec initiative — a handwritten letter sent to Daniel Johnson in mid-September. "There is no longer any doubt that Quebec will eventually assert its autonomy in every area," de Gaulle wrote, confident that he himself had given Quebec the determinant push. "Don't you think the moment has arrived to accentuate that which has already been started?" he added, putting pressure on Johnson, who was too slow and cautious for his taste. "Solutions are needed," he wrote, offering French support for the "huge national undertaking of Quebec's advent."

On the balcony he had "turned on the ignition," to use his own expression. With the letter, he now wanted to switch into high gear; instead, Daniel Johnson slammed on the brakes. In a written reply that was to disappoint the General, he repeated his willingness to "reintegrate French Canada to a certain degree into the universe of French-speaking nations." But, he added, "I have to be realistic." Economic problems were weighing him down. There were reports that the province was being drained of capital. Quebec was experiencing insecure times economically, due in no small measure to constitutional upheavals and the gaullist outbursts. "My first duty is to act responsibly," he concluded. The words had the finality of a slammed door.

## A French Cuba?

Up until now, historians have viewed General de Gaulle's Quebec policy as an operation involving France and Canada alone. The General, ever-anxious to extend the influence of France and French culture, answered the call of its old colony in need. In his remarkable book, *Vive le Québec Libre*, Montreal historian Dale Thomson asserts that "de Gaulle had an interest in Quebec quite apart from his relations with the United States." Jean Lacouture, in his biography of the French leader, writes that de Gaulle's actions in Quebec were prompted by "decisions made, whether rightly or wrongly, on the basis of specific circumstances and interests pertaining primarily to France." As a footnote he adds, "and peripherally to the United States."

Washington read these events quite differently. It did not take mental gymnastics for its analysts, diplomats and decision-makers to link goings-on in Quebec to de Gaulle's world plan. The General himself had made the connection, unsolicited, before, during and after his visit. During a televised speech upon his return from Quebec, he listed initiatives that formed part of his general policy: the Middle East, Europe, NATO, Quebec. Again in November, he brought up the policy in a press conference, explaining that he had to intervene in Quebec because "United States expansionism threatened to engulf the economy, character and language of this country."

He did not invent this logic; from Quebec and Quebeckers he heard little else. As early as 1961, on a trip to Paris, Jean Lesage declared that his government wanted "to get closer to the united states of Europe in order to free itself from the stranglehold of the United States of America." Lesage mentioned to the mayor of Paris "the exceptional danger" that the American "cultural invasion" represented for Quebec. (The father of the Quiet Revolution strayed from de Gaulle's logic when he added that Canadian confederation was "the antidote to the americanization of our culture.")

Many Frenchmen believed that de Gaulle's antics in Quebec were motivated by anti-American sentiment. In a poll conducted after the balcony speech, more than half of those questioned explained the gesture as an attempt to fight American influence. Another 16 percent thought de Gaulle was preparing to reunite France and French Canada. French Communists initially applauded the anti-American move and supported the idea of "a national state of the French Canadian people" established in "joint opposition to Yankee imperialism." But Soviet policy called for more subtlety. The French communist daily, *L'Humanité*, had to retract earlier statements and print that "no one would venture to say that" Quebeckers were not "Canadian." *L'Humanité* condemned de Gaulle for having supported "reactionary" Quebec politicians like Johnson and Lesage.

When Mitterrand finally handed down his verdict on the balcony scene two weeks after its occurrence, he also spoke in geopolitical terms. The French in Canada, he said, were "first of all Americans." The dissolution of Canada would not "neutralize the power of attraction of the United States of America"; on the contrary, it would be to the "superpowerful neighbor's" advantage. And it certainly would do nothing for faraway France.

The border separating de Gaulle's international policy from strategies in Quebec was thus far from impenetrable.

American governmental analysts did not view the two theses as mutually exclusive. They believed that de Gaulle's policy to promote French prestige and his anti-American obsession were two sides of the same coin. After all, they wrote, didn't prestige generate power?

In de Gaulle's eyes, Quebec was on the front line in the fight against Americanization. His francophile and americophobe concerns resounded in Quebec's battle. He once flattered a Quebec diplomat by calling Quebec's awakening "one of the most significant facts of our period." — he meant significant for France and against the United States.

How far was he prepared to go? American advisor Funkhouser believes he would have gone to the limit. But de Gaulle was "a realist" and it was hard to judge "how much he felt he could accomplish." The General would have taken it "step by step," aiming for the distant goal of setting up "a Cuba in the western hemisphere." Not that he would have wanted to install his *force de frappe* (the name he gave his nuclear missiles), but it was "a geopolitical move." Funkhouser thinks de Gaulle foresaw a sovereign Quebec having "the closest possible relations with France," perhaps entailing the presence "of Québécois in the French government." Perhaps, Funkhouser speculates, de Gaulle wanted Quebec to play a role "not dissimilar to the role of the French colonies," where a French official lurked "behind every African minister." Ambassador Bohlen's right-hand man, Woodruf Wallner, raised the possibility of a "transatlantic French community."

It should be noted that de Gaulle never once spoke of the Quebeckers as a nation. As a people, yes. But his irritating phrase, "the French of Canada," exposed his belief that the Quebeckers "were still as French as ever," and were not collectively a nation of their own. Mistaking his own wishes for reality, he declared it was "well-known" that the Quebeckers "not only remember the mother country with considerable affection, they view her as a nation with the same blood, heart and spirit as their own." When he spoke of "the huge national undertaking" in his handwritten letter to Daniel Johnson, he meant undertaking of the French nation to which the Quebeckers belonged, much like the Normans or the Savoyards.

De Gaulle did not manipulate the term "nation" unthinkingly. Bohlen writes that the General "once told the Belgian representative to NATO that Belgium was an artificial country created by France for foreign policy reasons and therefore had no legitimate right to exist as a nation." He also claimed that Italy was not a nation; it was a "conglomeration of cities and provinces." Germany was merely "in the process of becoming a nation." De Gaulle, according to Bohlen, saw "France, England, Spain and Russia as the only genuine nations of Europe."

An artificial country created by France for foreign policy reasons. An interesting concept. Didn't de Gaulle explain how much a sovereign Quebec "would bring France in terms of progress and influence?"

One March day in 1969, Charles de Gaulle spoke some last words about his Quebec interest. He welcomed the new occupant of the White House, Richard Nixon, along with his national security advisor, Henry Kissinger, and their entourage to the Elysée. Spirits were high. Nixon and Kissinger regarded de Gaulle's politics as a reinforcement to western power. It was better to have two planets — rather than a single one and its moon — in the battle against the Soviet solar system.

Nixon was a great fan of the Frenchman. One of his advisors wrote that he "patterned himself on Charles de Gaulle above all others." "Read de Gaulle on the mystery of power, the power of mystery," Nixon said, before closing himself up in his fortress of power, mystery and paranoia.

One evening during a reception under the wainscotting of the French presidential palace, de Gaulle found himself chatting with William Safire, Nixon's erudite speech writer. Safire did not speak a word of French, but he knew de Gaulle understood English well. In London during the war he had spoken it fluently, and he had conversed at length with Canadian Prime Minister Mackenzie King in the language of Canada's majority. His linguistic abilities had been dulled by a lack of practice, by pride, and by his use of interpreters to slow down dialogue to give him time to think.

Safire was nervous. Amidst the normal run of cocktail chatter, de Gaulle had managed, with one typically mordant phrase, to cow Henry Kissinger into silence. Kissinger had asked the General what means he would use to contain Germany if the latter aggressively reasserted itself. De Gaulle responded with one word. "War."

At the side of one of the great leaders of the century, Nixon's chief scribe did not want to remain silent. He seized his opportunity. "You created quite a stir," he said in English, "with what you said about Québec *libre*."

The balcony speech was already a year and a half old. Daniel Johnson, who had dragged his feet over "the huge national undertaking" was no longer of this world. His successor, Jean-Jacques Bertrand, was trying to extirpate any trace of separatism in the Quebec government. Would de Gaulle relinquish the dream?

From his great height, the General looked at Safire with sudden interest. In English he declared: "One day Quebec will be French!"

"Not free, French!" Safire was struck by de Gaulle's distinction. He later related the exchange to Nixon and Kissinger, but the two new leaders of American foreign policy only gave him, he recalls, "a Gaelic shrug."

Two months later, a majority of the French electorate chased de Gaulle from the Elysée. It was the final expression of a disenchantment that had been growing for years, and in which "Vive le Québec libre!" had played an important role.

# 5
# The Spiral of Furor

*The tides of Quebec nationalism, and its extreme form, Quebec separatism,*
*have not yet been harnessed or contained, and it is doubtful*
*that there will ever be a calm sea with visibility unlimited.*
WALT BUTTERWORTH
American ambassador in Ottawa, October 1967

The man's hair was closely cropped; underneath was a fiercely logical mind, a mind full of ideas. They claimed he could come up with at least three possible solutions for any problem he encountered. They said he could improvise complex analyses, presenting them without notes and without losing his train of thought. That was why Walt Rostow sought him out at Columbia University in New York and made him part of the Policy Planning Council, the branch of the State Department responsible for formulating policy. The INR remunerated its personnel for their analyses. The Policy Planning Council paid its people for proposals.

They also said he was capricious, that he put on airs, that he stuck his nose into matters that did not concern him. They said he was a hawk, an alarmist, a nuisance. Furthermore, he had a name that every journalist and typographer on the planet would one day curse. His friends called him Zbig, as did his enemies, between themselves. His full name was Zbigniew Brzezinski.

One day Brzezinski called a meeting of all the officials from the Pentagon, the CIA and the State Department responsible for Canadian affairs. The group comprised fewer than ten experts. Strangely enough, one of the giants of domestic and foreign policy in the country sat amongst these galley slaves of the diplomatic corps. He had been governor of New York, a confidant of Roosevelt, a presidential candidate, ambassador to Moscow, special counsellor to the secretary of state and eminence grise to the Democratic Party, currently in office. His name was Averell Harriman, and he was listening carefully, in silence.

The date was October 5, 1967. On the table before Brzezinski was a several page memo he had written. It concerned Quebec; the separatists and their growing influence were worrying him. De Gaulle had already come and gone, setting off his fireworks. His actions, Ambassador Butterworth had written from Ottawa, ignited "a crisis over national unity." Of the two main Quebec provincial parties, one was demanding equality for Quebec, the other, special status. Even the federal Conservatives were espousing the "two nations" concept, which would give Quebec some special powers in Canada. Prime

Minister Pearson had not wholeheartedly embraced the idea, but he had not rejected it either. That was good news.

(False) rumor had it that the party currently in power in Quebec, the Union Nationale, had a five-year plan leading to independence. One of the most influential figures in the opposition Liberal Party, René Lévesque, had proposed a sovereign Quebec associated economically with the Dominion. If he were able to convince his party to go along with him at the Liberal convention that October, the entire political spectrum in Quebec might soon seek to sever connections with confederation.

Out of all this activity — this "spiral of furor," as Butterworth called it — Zbig zeroed in on Lévesque's sovereignty association idea. That concept combined with the man promoting it could turn everything on its head.

Brzezinski did not care for the analyses of US diplomats. He did not believe that anyone in the country knew Quebec the way he did. As the son of the Polish consul in Montreal, he had grown up on the West Island, he had studied at McGill and knew the city's ethnic tensions. It was only at 25 that he crossed the American border and began his ascent in the spheres of scholarship and politics.

Brzezinski still kept in touch with Montreal through his family and friends there, who provided a constant stream of information about the political turmoil in Quebec. He understood the depth of resentment in the province, and he could predict the force of its undertow. He feared what a mixture of nationalism, neutrality and anti-Americanism would produce — he had seen the political slide to the left in his native Warsaw — and in his fertile mind he hatched catastrophic scenarios for Quebec. Had not radical separatist Pierre Bourgault after all promised that "the first thing a sovereign Quebec should do is sink a ship in the middle of the St Lawrence seaway?" It would cut off passage to Toronto, but also to Buffalo, Detroit and Chicago, the industrial heartland of the country.

It was a serious situation, Zbig explained to officials sitting around the table. Lévesque might well win over the Liberal Party. Who could say that eventually the US would not "have another Cuba across the St Lawrence, astride the St Lawrence?" Would there be violence? "We can't just sit here with this on our doorstep, jeopardizing our vital interests," was the essence of his warning, according to one participant at the meeting. They should "form a task force," and "really assess this and analyse it and get more information and examine carefully what the consequences might be."

Brzezinski was not the only one positing catastrophy for the northeastern part of the continent. In Ottawa, Butterworth thought the State of Quebec "might also be socialist, authoritarian and fair prey to cultivation by inimical foreign influence," notably that of France. The "nationalists-racists" of Quebec, as the ambassador called them, would quickly transform "the reservation" into an "egocentric" and "bitter" enclave. To say nothing of the "immediately apparent and dangerous ... gap" secession would make "in our northern defences."

But Butterworth was not in the little room in Foggy Bottom where the meeting was being held. When Brzezinski had finally finished terrorizing the group with his vision, another participant began to speak. Brzezinski's ominous predictions, "while within the realm of possibility, represented the extreme end of the spectrum of possibilities," protested Rufus Smith, director of Canadian affairs, who had spent six years posted in Canada. Smith did not think Lévesque's manifesto would be adopted at the Liberal convention. Quebec would not blow up, he said, contradicting each point in the aspiring strategist's agenda of catastrophes. What they were witnessing was, on the contrary, "a drawn-out process of political ferment and negotiations." In any event, Smith added, "the Canadian government had the situation in hand, was on top of it." Both Lester Pearson and the leader of the opposition, Robert Stanfield, were seasoned diplomats. Both promised reform. Butterworth was forever praising their leadership in his missives from Ottawa. There was that fellow in the Liberal Party, Pierre Trudeau, who treated the two nations concept as a "hoax" and who termed special status "a dirty word," but he was only minister of justice.

Furthermore, Brzezinski's ambitious study on Quebec separatism was "going to do ten times more harm than good." Smith did not believe that any major study "however classified it might be stamped, like that, could be undertaken by the United States government without it being picked up by the press." It could be disastrous if ever it were to fall into Canadian or Quebec hands. They were so ultra-sensitive! "It would be a great mistake for the US at this point to try to do anything other than keep ourselves informed," he concluded.

Brzezinski, the bold visionary, proposed action. Rufus, the pragmatic civil servant, favored discretion. Harriman — the founder of twentieth century American diplomacy, along with Chip Bohlen and a few others — finally broke his silence.

"I think Smith is right," he said, settling the matter. There is "no cause for alarm." Smith had presented his arguments with a certain degree of restraint. Harriman was far more blunt. "Forget it," he told Brzezinski, ordering him to stop distributing his alarmist memorandum; he left the meeting before it ended. And with him gone, the meeting had no purpose.

Twenty years later, a sibylline Brzezinski explained that "Discussions with the government don't always lead to specific actions ... At that time there were very few people who took Quebec nationalism very seriously. I think I made the top policy makers aware of this issue."

But Walt Rostow, who was by that time the President's National Security Advisor, says he never heard of the scenarios painted by his protégé.

## The "Secret Committee" at Power Corp.

Barely ten days later, the first of Brzezinski's predictions proved false. The Liberal convention, which American diplomats in Montreal were following closely, rejected the ideas put forward by René Lévesque. According to one diplomat, prominent Liberal leader Pierre Laporte — "known for his political expediency" and the "heir apparent" to party chief Jean Lesage — joined forces with Lesage and Eric Kierans and used "pressure tactics" to orchestrate Lévesque's defeat. When Lévesque and 150 of his supporters left the hall, the Liberals the US diplomat chatted with were "in an almost exultant mood." They were convinced they had punctured the abscess, and they were thrilled.

The US diplomat remained perplexed, however. The special status concept adopted by the convention could mean anything, including "de facto separatism." And he was sure the party would pay dearly for Lévesque's expulsion. "The image of ideological innovation which the Party has reflected since 1960, the image of Lesage, the master politician presiding over a team of brilliantly clashing and mutually stimulating intellects, has now been blurred by the rather brutally executed removal of Lévesque," he wrote. Lévesque had always been in "the ideological forefront" of the Quiet Revolution, "providing the reformist dynamism which has irrevocably changed the province."

The men who had ousted him were probably "settling old scores" with him as well as rejecting his separatist ideas. These just "served as a convenient pretext," the diplomat alleged.

The Americans also received other reassuring news from Premier Daniel Johnson. In the autumn of 1967, Daniel Johnson lay on a beach in Hawaii, exhausted from his intense political activity of the previous few months. Unfortunately for the Premier, Quebec's turmoil hounded him even as he reclined beneath the coconut trees. Rumors of the Union Nationale's sovereignty plan and the economic uncertainty that had St. James Street (Montreal's business center) in its grip combined to ruin Johnson's holiday.

Montreal businessman Paul Desmarais and financier Marcel Faribault dropped in unexpectedly on the premier, disturbing his rest with slightly embellished stories of capital pouring out of the province. Johnson fell victim to the urgency he heard in his guests' voices, and issued a statement that would forever be known as the "Hawaii Declaration." In it he seemed to turn his back on the dream of separatism. He said he did not want to "build a Great Wall of China around Quebec."

In Ottawa, Butterworth noted that Johnson still kept up his tightrope act with the theme song, "Equality or independence." But Bryce Mackasey, at that time parliamentary secretary to the federal minister of labour, claimed the nationalist Premier surrendered unconditionally. At a reception in Chicoutimi he explained to Consul General Francis Cunningham that "When Johnson had his breakdown," the federalist Montreal financiers who dropped in on him took complete control. According to Mackasey, "This meant that while Johnson did and said a certain number of things to keep the separatists in their place, he was actually working hand in glove with Ottawa on everything." In an attempt to bolster his argument, Mackasey told Cunningham that Johnson "doesn't even go to the toilet without telephoning Ottawa." The American diplomat, who knew Johnson well and admired him, had some difficulty swallowing this. The minister's account "seemed both oversimplistic and inaccurate to me," he wrote in a dispatch.

But Cunningham was convinced separatism held no attraction for Johnson. And that was the important thing. Early in 1968, Johnson had told *Washington Post* reporter Robert Estabrook and a German colleague visiting Quebec that "Vive le Québec libre!" and de Gaulle's subsequent sovereignty statements put him in an awkward spot. The remarks were made "off the record," but Estabrook immediately repeated them to Cunningham, who reported them to Washington, journalistic ethics notwithstanding.

Regardless of how reform-minded they were, provincial Liberals and Union Nationale members had once again professed their faith in federalism. The only question was what the more dedicated separatists would do. The federal government took care of them in two ways.

Lester Pearson initiated constitutional reforms which, he claimed, would give French Canadians the equality they demanded. At the end of December

1967, Pearson gave a detailed account of his plans before a learned assembly in Washington. Secretary of State Dean Rusk had called to his dinner table Walt Rostow, John Leddy, Rufus Smith and other high ranking civil servants for the occasion. The entire hierarchy of officials responsible for US-Canada relations was there: everybody, that is, except the President. The assembled crew wanted to know when the storms brewing in Quebec would settle; chill winds were beginning to upset bilateral ties.

Relations between France and Canada had been frozen since September by de Gaulle. Canadian diplomats were describing Canada's woes and weeping on American shoulders in NATO's new Brussels headquarters, in Ottawa as well as in Washington. An INR memo reported one official from the Department of External Affairs as saying, "The Canadian government was no longer able to speak with confidence in its foreign relations because everything that it said or did was in some way affected by the division in Canada itself." American diplomats in Ottawa predicted that the United States "may encounter perplexing difficulties in dealing with Canada even on the most trivial matters whenever the Quebec issue and the question of Ottawa's authority are involved." According to the State Department, Canadian foreign policy, which provided important support for American initiatives in many regions, had been reduced to "immobility."

Pearson reassured the diplomats over dinner and gave them "a guardedly optimistic assessment of the likely outcome" of his constitutional reforms. Canadian Ambassador Ed Ritchie, who attended the meeting, wrote that it "may have improved the perspective" of those present.

American diplomats stumbled across less publicized plans devised by the Liberals to put a check on separatism. In January 1968, the economic advisor to the American embassy, Edward Bittner, organized a series of interviews on the possible economic impact of separatism. He questioned Quebec civil servants and American businessmen and met with Claude Frénette, one of Power Corporation's executives, who offered surprising revelations.

According to Frénette, right-hand man to Paul Desmarais and a Liberal with close ties to Trudeau, "the threat of separatism is serious but no longer irreversible. Within the [federal] Liberal Party," he explained, "a secret committee has been established whose object is to defeat separatism in Quebec. The committee, which includes Quebec federal ministers such as [Jean] Marchand, [Pierre Elliott] Trudeau and [Maurice] Sauvé, has adopted a several-pronged plan which thus far has been going according to schedule." Before he was recruited by Paul Desmarais, Frénette had been assistant to minister Sauvé.

Phase One of the plan concerned October's Liberal convention. According to Frénette, "The committee has encouraged René Lévesque and his sympathizers within and without the Quebec Liberal Party to establish a separate party which would be roundly defeated in an election show-down; the theory being that Lévesque would be less dangerous operating outside the Liberal Party than within."

In November, Phase Two was initiated. The setting was a meeting of the *Etats généraux du Canada français*, a conservative, nationalist organization. "In order to discredit the separatist inclinations of the Etats généraux which is heavily influenced by the St Jean Baptiste Society of Quebec, the committee infiltrated the recent conference of the Etats généraux and it encouraged it to take a position so radical with regards to the issue of separatism as to be incredible," Frénette explained to Bittner.

The Etats généraux, whose president was university professor Jacques-Yvan Morin, did, in fact, attract a good deal of attention by adopting an instransigent separatist stance. The editor of Montreal's daily *Le Devoir*, Claude Ryan, condemned the group's "strong-armed tactics:" their debates were too heatedly radical and they marginalized French-speaking delegations from outside Quebec. Regardless of whether they were manipulated, it was far from clear if their actions discredited the separatist cause. The INR felt the group's promotion of separatism "added to the momentum of the separatist cause," especially in the "lower middle class" where they recruited members.

"The Power Corporation intends to use the network of television and press which it controls in Quebec to help defeat separatism through subtle propaganda operations," continued the diplomat in his resumé of Frénette's Phase Three. "Another keystone in the committee's plan includes using the constitutional conference scheduled" for February 1968, to "achieve sufficient reform of the federal system to take the wind out of demands by separatists for an independent Quebec."

The committee had no power to do this, of course, and the constitutional conference designed to revamp the federal system failed. But why quibble? "The committee" met its objectives in both the Liberal Party and in the Etats généraux. All that remained was its list of "subtle propaganda operations."

Twenty years later, Frénette confirms "about 90 percent" of what the diplomat recorded. He remarks, however, that "the committee wasn't much of a secret." Primarily a think tank of federal reformists, it soon became a discussion center where Pierre Trudeau's team was formed. Members met every Friday night in Frénette's office at Power Corporation. Frénette confirms the existence of the strategy to polarize political debate in Quebec and corroborates the committee's intervention in affairs of both the Liberal Party and the Etats généraux.

On the other hand, he denies the use of propaganda in newspapers owned by Paul Desmarais (Montreal's *La Presse*, Sherbrooke's *La Tribune*, Trois Rivières's *Le Nouvelliste*). "We focussed much more on Radio-Canada," where the nationalist message was evident "even in the choice of drama." The only efficient strategy, Frénette claimed, was "to promote and make place for a strong federal presence, and the press would quite simply have to take notice of it."

## "René" and the Yankees

American diplomats and analysts sported superlatives whenever they described Lévesque. He has "the broadest appeal of any 'independentiste' politician to date." He is "especially effective in winning the support of labour people" and is known as "the working man's friend," Consul Harrison Burgess wrote from Montreal. In Quebec City, Cunningham praised "his formidable charisma." In Washington, an analyst at the INR regarded him as an "articulate and influential" leader offering "imagination and inspiration," and lending the separatist ideal "a new respectability." Furthermore, he had nothing but "disdain for violence."

What about Lévesque's theory of sovereignty association? "Ostensibly an appeal to common sense," wrote one analyst at the INR, it "shows little of the rancour and xenophobia often displayed by the more extreme separatists." While it was true that "like most Quebec nationalists," Lévesque "resents the pervasiveness of American culture in Quebec and the province's great dependence on US capital," the same could be said for "many other Canadians as well," including members of the Pearson cabinet. Once in power, Lévesque would probably exercise "greater control of foreign investments." He did, however, recently announce to the American press that he would not attempt to halt the "spillover" of American capital into Quebec.

Labels like "dangerous" or "radical" were never applied. On the contrary, explained Burgess, who had met him a few times, "We felt that René was a moderating influence" on the separatist movement. He had a "settling effect in a difficult situation." (The INR went so far as to call Pierre Bourgault "pragmatic" for pushing his followers to join with Lévesque's new movement Souveraineté-Association, or MSA.)

As soon as the MSA was established, Lévesque knocked on the door of American diplomacy. He asked Claude Morin, one of Johnson's advisors at the time, to arrange a private meeting with Francis Cunningham. In February of 1968, the two men met over dinner in Quebec City. Lévesque had no particular message for the Americans other than to reiterate his political position. In the course of his long political career, Lévesque did not hold back at such meetings. He did just the opposite, in fact, sharpening his words, embellishing and elaborating on his political views and speaking forthrightly about colleagues, enemies and future elections.

He explained sovereignty association to Cunningham, lining up arguments which he had himself put together only months before, but which he would stand by from that day on. He did not mention US investment in Quebec to the American; nor did he reassure him that a sovereign Quebec would keep its membership in military alliances like NATO or NORAD. "He told me that he felt his views ought not to frighten the Americans," Cunningham explained. Lévesque was so certain that the Washington representative was open-minded that he shared his impressions of a meeting he had held with young English businessmen in Montreal two days before. After speaking for fifteen minutes, Lévesque said, he had felt "a sullen hatred" fill his audience. There certainly was nothing of the kind in this Quebec city house, where Cunningham conversed with Lévesque in a beautiful French, warming a cognac with the palm of his hand.

The American asked about Trudeau, who had vaulted into the federal Liberal leadership as if dropped by the Holy Ghost or the stars. Unwittingly, he had touched a tender nerve. Lévesque drew a frank portrait of Trudeau, with whom he had spent considerable time. The two men addressed each other with the informal pronoun "tu," which was rare for both of them. Trudeau possessed a terrific intellect, Lévesque admitted. He was refined and spoke an excellent French. But Trudeau was fundamentally British, Lévesque explained, partly due to his mother, Mrs Elliott, partly because of his studies at Oxford. One only had to read the famous omnibus bill on judicial reform presented by Justice Minister Trudeau to understand. It was a superb bill. But it was also an exact replica of a bill voted a year before in London.

Lévesque explained that "despite his French culture and language, the English components of Trudeau's background make him a spokesman for English rather than French ideas." It was no surprise that Ontario Liberals "had fallen in love" with him. "The reason was simple. Trudeau appeared to them to be the kind of French Canadian they had always yearned for, that is to say, one who advocated ideas that were basically English."

Then Lévesque made a prediction which proved to be another example of his unfailing optimism: Trudeau would never get a majority of Quebeckers to support him. He would fail to win a majority of seats in Quebec and his election would speed up the process leading to independence. Four months later, Pierre Elliott Trudeau's Liberals took 56 of Quebec's 74 seats, and 54 percent of the votes. As for speeding up independence, Lévesque had another think coming.

In the autumn of 1968, the consul general in Montreal, Richard Hawkins, invited René Lévesque to his opulent residence on Redpath Avenue. Hawkins had also invited Edward Doherty of the Planning Council for a "familiarization visit." Once again, Lévesque had no qualms about revealing his plans. The sovereignty movement had only, he said, shaken up the "bloody English establishment" until now. French voters had to be educated. The leader of the MSA claimed he was annoyed with Pierre Bourgault for unilaterally breaking up the RIN. He wished Bourgault "had waited at least six months, so that the RIN could continue to provide a rallying point for more radical separatist elements." As for his old friends Trudeau, Gérard Pelletier and Jean Marchand — the three doves sitting in Ottawa — Lévesque predicted inaccurately that if it came down to a choice between Quebec and Ottawa, Pelletier and Marchand would choose Quebec.

The Americans asked what role the United States should play. Lévesque answered unequivocally that they should keep out of it all. The memorandum prepared later reported that "He expected the US to watch and wait with no action, as long as separatism was achieved through regular political processes." Burgess, who attended the dinner, remembers the conversation as being very cordial.

René Lévesque's propensity to offer unsolicited, exclusive and often explosive information to the Americans was a surprisingly common phenomenon. Quebec and Canadian politicians, and important figures like Bryce Mackasey and Claude Frénette, treated American diplomats like priests at confession. They talked for hours, laying out their plans and fears and giving their game away.

American diplomatic dispatches concealed scoops which, had they been leaked, would have made front page copy in Canada and seriously embarrassed many high-ranking officials. What inspired Canadians to offer their secrets to the first American to pass their way? Quebec separatist leaders likely wanted absolution. Getting acquainted with Washington's representative was a start. Being invited to dine with him was akin to promotion from the status of local player to participant in the continental games. It was more difficult to explain the Canadian federalists' attitude, caught up as they were in the struggle for national identity. They had just endowed the country with a flag and they were involved in a permanent campaign to prove that Ottawa, not Washington, was the center of the Canadian universe. Were they trying to let the US know that things were under control in Quebec? Were they sending messages to calm Washington's frayed nerves?

The hemorrhage of information could not have come at a better time for Americans charged with gauging Canada's pulse during the political crisis. The fact that Edward Doherty of Planning was so eager to meet Lévesque demonstrated the extent to which a renewed interest in Quebec was sweeping through State Department corridors. The INR was issuing lengthy analyses at a steady pace. At Planning, Doherty was directing a work group whose members came from various government agencies and whose aim was to prepare a national policy paper on Canada, including a section on Quebec. The ghost of Brzezinski, who had long since quit Planning, still haunted its halls. In October, Robert Beaudry, an official from European affairs at the State Department, asked Rufus Smith whether "contingency planning" should be instituted to prepare for a possible separatist victory. Smith seized his diplomatic extinguisher one more time and put out the fire that was smoldering anew. The necessity for an exercise of this kind, he wrote, was "considerably reduced" by Trudeau's victory in the June federal elections and by dissension in separatist party ranks. What was more, Smith indicated that he had already asked the Treasury and Revenue departments to "come up with a realistic appraisal of the extent and nature of US private investment in the province of Quebec." The request was never met.

Two days later the Parti Québecois held its founding convention, boasting 25,000 members and adopting a platform which, the INR noted with interest, defined the party as "neutralist, pacifist and non-nuclear." Diplomatic personnel put the thing in context. "Neutralist, pacifist and non-nuclear" was almost identical to the platform of the new prime minister in Ottawa, Pierre Elliott Trudeau.

## Nixon and Trudeau

The changing of the guard was complete. In Quebec, Daniel Johnson was gone, replaced by Jean-Jacques Bertrand. In Ottawa, Lester Pearson had ceded his chair to Pierre Trudeau. And in Washington, Lyndon Johnson passed the White House to Richard Nixon.

American diplomats closely scrutinized events in Quebec. Rumors of Canada's eventual dissolution were discussed at the consul's home in Quebec City, at the secretary of state's table and in conversations reported from Brussels, Paris, Ottawa and Chicoutimi.

At the end of January 1969, only a few days after President Nixon's inauguration, the new National Security Advisor, Henry Kissinger, ordered a general survey of the world's hot spots. The memorandum was not destined for just anyone. For the first time, the Quebec file was presented before the National Security Council (NSC), the elite team of American politics. The select club met in the legendary "situation room" of the White House basement. Its leader was President Richard Nixon. At his side were Vice President Spiro Agnew, a corrupt political dinosaur whom Nixon had drawn from anonymity; Secretary of State William Rogers, a sad bit-player; Defense Secretary Melvin Laird; and National Security Advisor Henry Kissinger.

Important decisions were taken at the NSC, where cold, rational analyses mattered most. Lévesque's charm held no sway in such a room. Pearson, Trudeau and the strategies of the federal government as well as the young Parti Québécois were examined without an ounce of emotion. The intent was to probe the Quebec issue from the point of view of America's best interests.

Each member of the NSC received a National Security Special Memorandum (NSSM) at the beginning of February. It was the ninth such document prepared for the new administration and was blandly titled, "A Review of the International Situation." The paper contained a section on Canada with a sub-section on "Canadian Separatism." The NSC wanted to know: "What is the present strength of the Quebec separatist movement? Is it likely to increase over the next one-three-five years? What factors will affect its strength?"

The answers filled three pages. For the moment, Lévesque's Parti Québécois was a "success story" in unity, membership recruitment and grass roots organization. Separatist ideas, however, had not made much headway among the electorate. In a poll conducted in November 1968, 11 percent favored sovereignty, compared with the nine percent who had voted for separatist candidates in 1966. Lévesque was encountering the "basic conservatism of many Quebeckers," who feared "the likely economic consequences of secession." According to the INR, which prepared the report, the Parti Québécois would likely gain strength one to three years hence, especially as younger people acquired the right to vote. "Unless the Party scores a significant breakthrough in the next provincial election," the paper predicted, "its future seems dim." Indeed, according to American analysts, "If the P.Q. offers no more hope of ultimate success in five years than it does today — and we are inclined to doubt that it will — its appeal will probably recede."

Two factors could influence the future strength of the movement. Proposals of renewed federalism and special status were in the works, both of which promised to be less risky than independence. And in Ottawa, Pierre Trudeau was mixing "firmness with flexibility" and attempting to make the entire country bilingual.

In short, according to the answer to Question #2 in NSSM#9, there was no need to panic. "There is much hope in Quebec, as well as in the rest of Canada, that Quebec's aspirations can be reconciled with the need to preserve 'one Canada.'"

The terrorist "Front de libération du Québec" (FLQ) was dismissed parenthetically. It was described in the memorandum as a "mere handful of tiny extremist groups who are willing to resort to violence but who have become less and less significant in recent years."

Henry Kissinger and Richard Nixon could sleep soundly. Or at least they could restrict their nightmares to Vietnam, Cambodia and Italian communists; there would be no Cuba or Chile on the banks of the St Lawrence. The separatists would not step into power, and there would be no more upsurges of violence.

The NSC members had barely finished reading their memoranda when the FLQ returned to the scene with one of the most barbaric acts in its sad history. An explosion at the Montreal Stock Exchange injured 20 people in February of 1969. It was one of six bombs announcing a return of Quebec terrorism that year. FLQ explosives were detonated again in May, June, July, August, September, November and December. The Front even hijacked a plane from New York to Cuba, striking "in the belly of the beast" as Che put it. And more was yet to come.

The new American ambassador to Ottawa, Adolph Schmidt, smelled a rat. He predicted that in the upcoming April 1970 election the Parti Québécois would win between 25 and 30 percent of the vote (it won 26) but would take "only 5 to 10 seats in the 108-seat Assembly" (it took 7). Schmidt saw a danger in this discrepancy, and predicted that "Extremists" in the separatist movement "already skeptical of the electoral process, will repudiate election results and return to violence and terror."

# 6
# Snoopy Smells an Apprehended Insurrection

*It was a case of six kids trying to make a revolution.*
JAMES RICHARD CROSS,
moments after his rescue.

American diplomats excel at gathering information, analysing it and forecasting danger. For the men and women posted in Canada, Quebec nationalism was a goldmine. Most had chosen careers in diplomacy to observe the workings of history first-hand. When they were transferred north of the border, to a country reputed to be one of the most boring on the globe, they invariably embraced the outbreak of Quebec nationalism and even terrorism as a rare blessing.

"It was as fascinating a subject there for us as apartheid was in South Africa. You talked about it every night," recalls Mac Johnson, a specialist in Canadian affairs who worked first in Ottawa, then in Washington. David Macuk, political advisor to the embassy, agrees. "It was the most exciting political thing floating around ... We might have been tempted in our youthful enthusiasm for political movement, things happening, to think, Gee whiz, this is going to be something exciting." This, meaning the Parti Québécois, independence, and the Front de Libération du Québec (FLQ).

In their delight at having found some interesting instability, the Americans forgot that they themselves might become targets. Since 1964, when the two brains behind Quebec terrorism, Pierre Vallières and Charles Gagnon, announced that "The number one enemy is no longer Ottawa but Washington," the FLQ never missed a chance to aim at the Yankees.

On the night of May 1, 1965, the FLQ planted a bomb that shattered 78 windows in the three-storeyed American consulate on McGregor Avenue in Montreal. It made the front page of *The New York Times*. "American buildings have been frequently attacked in countries such as the Soviet Union, Indonesia and Egypt, but yesterday, for the first time, a similar incident occurred across the border in Canada," the New York *Herald Tribune* noted. Federal Minister of External Affairs Paul Martin had to apologize to the American embassy and offer to pay for the damage.

In July 1965, the police surprised an FLQ commando unit planning to attack a military base equipped with American nuclear warheads. The Macaza base near Mont Laurier in the Laurentians was part of the North American defence system, NORAD. The cause of so much acrimony between Kennedy and Diefenbaker, the famous ground-to-air Bomarc missiles were based there. The terrorists took refuge in the forested area around Macaza, dragging a policeman along as hostage, and were only found after a four-day search. They had over 200 detailed military maps in their bags.

In 1966, a time bomb was found and dismantled in the American consulate in Montreal; in October 1967, a molotov cocktail was thrown through one of its windows. The FLQ was not content simply to attack buildings; it soon began to train its sights on human targets. In November 1968, bombs were planted near the residences of American United Aircraft Company executives, whose products contributed to the war effort in Vietnam.

In spite of all these attempts, American officials in Montreal took no particular precautions. There was so little security at the home of the American consul general that a burglar easily broke into the house on Redpath Avenue one day while its inhabitants were away. His exploit was nothing compared to that of a mental patient of St Jean de Dieu Hospital, who escaped in April 1969, entered the residence and took a nap on the diplomat's bed while Madame and the maids went about their business on the first floor.

It was only after the night of October 7, 1969, when rioters took advantage of a police strike to ransack Montreal's financial district and — once again — smash the windowed door of the American consulate, that diplomat Howard Burgess requested police protection. Burgess, who was in charge of the consulate only until a replacement could be found for Consul General Hawkins, reported that "my request to RCMP for protection made early in the evening was turned down with regrets. Explication was [police] jurisdictional sensitivity involved."

Yet Burgess was in dire need of protection. A cell of the FLQ was preparing to kidnap him.

## Kidnapping: Bungled Beginnings

In the spring of 1970, about 20 or so members of the FLQ paced the cells of Quebec prisons. Their comrades on the outside were disgusted by the outcome of the provincial elections and the injustice separatist candidates had suffered; they also longed to concretize their identification with foreign revolutionary groups with an act of violence. In Europe, Latin America, the Middle East, Ireland, even in the United States, expressions of political violence made the FLQ bombings look tame by comparison. Quebec terrorists saw that in Brazil, the kidnapping of a German diplomat had led to the freeing of 40 political prisoners. A half a planet away, the FLQ realized that kidnapping paid off — a pretty piece of evidence of the danger of caving in to terrorist demands.

In June they prepared their plan of action and wrote the communiqué announcing Burgess's abduction; they rented a Montreal apartment and a chalet north of Montreal near St Jérome where they would hide their prey. Their list of demands included the liberation of "political prisoners" and safe passage to

Cuba; the reinstatement of the "Lapalme boys," 450 truckers laid off by Canada Post, who had become a sad symbol of Quebec labour unrest; a half a million dollar ransom to be paid to the FLQ and diffusion of the FLQ manifesto by the media.

The incident might have entered the annals of Quebec history as the "Events of June 1970," if RCMP officers investigating a bank robbery by the FLQ in May had not traced the network through to the chalet, where they nabbed six conspirators and enough evidence to convict them. The FLQ was experiencing great difficulty launching its kidnapping career. In May, two kidnappers on their way to seize the Israeli consul in Montreal, Moshe Golan, were stopped by police because the rear lights on their truck were out. The police did not immediately make the connection between the gigantic wicker basket found in the van, a piece of paper with the name "Golan" scribbled on it and the sawed-off shotgun. The two men in question — one of whom, Jacques Lanctot, was later implicated in the Burgess affair — were released on bail before the RCMP discovered they had inadvertently foiled a political kidnapping.

When Burgess was informed of his selection by the terrorists, he was finally able to obtain police protection. In the ranks of the FLQ, the botched kidnap attempt put an end to an old debate. The Lanctot cell, which was trying through political kidnappings to turn the FLQ into a North American version of Uruguay's Tupamaros, prevailed over the cell directed by the Rose brothers and Francis Simard. This latter cell had been content to limit itself to bank robberies (one a day, during this period) and the purchase of arms. The Rose brothers were inclined to regard the FLQ as ants or termites, quietly preparing the ground for the uprising to come. But the Golan and Burgess bungles convinced the FLQ to plan a feat that would not go unnoticed. According to Simard, "The project of abducting an American diplomat and demanding the liberation of political prisoners became top priority." But Burgess and his colleagues had woken from their stupor. They were taking precautions and, according to Simard, "couldn't be found."

Their caution was short-lived. When John L. Topping took over his functions as the new consul general in Montreal, he paid scant attention to security and the residence on Redpath Avenue was once again as accessible as ever. Simard and his associates wondered whether the new arrival was the target they had been waiting for; with Topping they would prove once and for all that Quebec terrorists were a force to be reckoned with. During the course of the summer of 1970, their comrades in Latin America more than showed them the way. In the space of a single week, the Tupamaros took four hostages, two of them American. They killed one. In neighboring Argentina, the Montoneros abducted and "executed" an ex-head of state, Pedro Aramburu. In Bolivia, guerrillas exchanged two West German hostages for the release of ten prisoners. The FLQ seemed way behind in the terrorist game.

At the end of that summer, Jacques Lanctot, Jacques Cossette-Trudel and Marc Carbonneau spent many weeks stalking Redpath Avenue and the neighborhood where, in Cossette-Trudel's words, "the houses were big hotels and the people were all rich." They couldn't decide between the American, Topping; his neighbor, British Trade Commissioner James Richard Cross; and a representative of the International Civil Aviation Organization, Charles Butler, who lived further up Redpath Avenue. The neighborhood was clearly not safe.

They finally settled on the American. They had followed his comings and goings, knew the hour of his departure in the morning and his return in the evening. They knew his complete itinerary, including when he took his walks.

But on October 4, 1970, the day before the abduction, the seven FLQ members responsible for what they called "Operation Freedom," revised their plans. "We figured the English in Quebec would never identify with an American," Cossette-Trudel explained. "But if we took the Englishman, we thought it would stir more hostility from the English in the province and across Canada and then the French people would realize the racism that existed." (!)

This was a different story from the one Cross heard from his abductors. During his captivity, cell members explained they had abandoned their target of preference, John Topping, because his house was so extravagant. The American's home was so big, they claimed, that Topping would have time to hide or flee, making the abduction too difficult. They liked the more modest house where Cross lived. It would be less problematic. It certainly paid to be rich!

The wife of the American consul, Doris Topping, stays convinced that the FLQ intended to abduct her husband until the very last moment. Ironically, the French language might have saved him. Every morning, she explains, Topping left the house at 8:50 AM to go to the office. That Monday, October 5, Mrs Topping was to go to her first French lesson. The consul general, ever the gallant husband, left a half hour earlier than usual, at 8:20 AM, to drive her. In all likelihood, their car crossed paths with the taxi stolen by the FLQ, which between 8:20 and 8:30 AM stopped at the Redpath Avenue home of James Richard Cross, interrupting his morning toiletry.

"I always have had excellent relations with the French in Quebec," the Englishman protested. "We have good relations with the English," the intruders shot back. "That's why we are taking you."

The whole operation only took minutes, but the abductors, it turned out, had all the time in the world. According to a dispatch sent by Topping, it took the police an entire hour to respond to the call from the Cross residence. Was there so much static on the line that the name "Cross" was transformed into "Greece"? The police first made a visit to the peaceful Greek consulate before they realized their error. A second call had to be made before they headed off towards Redpath Avenue.

In the first of many communiqués, the FLQ then made known its list of demands. These missives would become the best-read literature in Quebec in the fall and winter of 1970. The list was almost identical to that drawn up for the Burgess abduction.

After the kidnapping, the police finally offered the Topping residence round-the-clock protection. Black iron bars were installed over the windows, which made the place look like a prison. Rufus Smith, posted once again to Ottawa, in charge during the absence of Ambassador Schmidt, telexed Washington: "US Consul General Montreal is safe and alert."

## The White House Wants to Know

The Americans hardly needed to send a special team to Montreal to learn more about the first political hostage-taking in North America. Superior fact-finding machinery was already in place. All that was needed was to speed up the works.

Several times a day, Smith and his team of advisors sent telexes to keep the State Department informed of the latest events and news. In Montreal, Topping and Burgess did the same. For the most part, Washington would have learned just as much listening to Montreal's radio station CKAC. The diplomats could only re-transmit information that was altogether public, accompanied by the occasional commentary.

There was one exception. The under-secretary for external affairs and one-time Canadian ambassador in Washington, Ed Ritchie, met with Smith about once a week, to assess the situation. The American learned more from these exchanges than the best journalists could. Ritchie fed Smith detailed information on the progress of the inquiry, which put him in a privileged position. External Affairs was supervising the Cross investigation because a foreign diplomat was involved. "He probably wanted to forestall any pressure from Washington, for more information," according to one American diplomat privy to the Ritchie-Smith conversations. "Because of his own experience he had an appreciation of the concerns that Washington would be feeling and probably wanted to allay those concerns so far as he could." His main message was, "Look, this is in good hands." The underlying message was that Canada didn't need US interference.

The Americans learned, either from Ritchie or another source close to Minister of External Affairs Mitchell Sharp, that Trudeau's cabinet was not as united as it seemed regarding anti- FLQ strategy. According to one of Rufus Smith's dispatches, "Prime Minister Trudeau had angrily rejected Sharp's urgings that the 'FLQ Manifesto' be broadcast, and had reluctantly given in only when others, especially Marc Lalonde [Trudeau's top aide], supported Sharp's views." The dispatch continued, "Trudeau is prepared to tough it out right to the end, according to our source who nevertheless adds that some of those around him clearly favor letting the [political] prisoners go."

Washington also received its information on the crisis through FBI agents in Ottawa. Just as RCMP liaison agents could roam freely through FBI headquarters in Washington, their FBI counterparts enjoyed open access to the offices of the RCMP in the federal capital. Joseph Marion, FBI liaison agent in Ottawa, trekked back and forth between his office at the embassy and RCMP headquarters. He discussed the incident with officials in the Mounties' newly established G Branch, responsible for fighting Quebec terrorism and recovering the missing Cross. Marion "came over almost every day during the crisis, and he had a very good idea how things were developing," one of his contacts recalls. Marion confirms this. "If the Mounties knew," he says, then so did Washington.

The exchanges between the FBI and the RCMP intensified during the October Crisis, though they had long been routine. Ties between the FLQ and groups from the American left, most notably the Black Panthers and the Weathermen, the latter also great planters of bombs, gave rise to frequent information swaps.

Marion "arrived with answers to questions we'd submitted to him, and then he asked us things. The exchanges were open and we trusted him," the aforementioned RCMP contact remembers. He did not have direct access to files, but he hardly needed it, the contact continues. He learned enough through word-of-mouth to prepare the telex he sent daily to his headquarters.

This internaional police cooperation produced at least one result during the crisis. At Canada's request, American border guards were alerted to the possibility that FLQ members might seek refuge in the American republic. It would be ludicrous for them to entertain such a notion, but some Quebec revolutionaries had done it in1837 when defeated by British troops, and anything was possible. Washington journalists observed that security measures were being tightened at the White House as well as at diplomatic residences. The police maintained that this was unrelated to the FLQ; Secretary of Justice John Mitchell said he had heard that American terrorist groups were planning some abductions. Kidnapping is a contagious disease. It easily spreads across borders.

Copies of Joseph Marion's daily output as well as the collection of diplomatic dispatches were also sent to the INR, the State Department's analysts. Kenneth Thompson was in charge of the Canadian file; he also supervised the troubled situation in Malta.

"This was unique," Thompson recalls. "We had never had faced it so close to home." Thompson and his colleagues sifted through the mass of dispatches they received every day. "There was a lot of police-to-police and FBI-to-police cooperation," he says.

Several dispatches were sent from abroad. They came from Paris, for example, where the very "pro-separatist" views of the French press and the measured government reactions were analysed. Or from Algeria, where an informer reports meeting a representative from Ottawa. The latter had come to see if Algeria would harbour the terrorists if they accepted exile there in exchange for the freeing of their hostage. A local correspondent for *Le Monde* in Algiers confided to an American diplomat that the FLQ was planning to open an office there. (An "FLQ delegation" would exist in Algiers from December 1970 to the spring of 1972. The Black Panthers, among others, also had a base there.)

Thompson was asked to put together a brief daily summary, a page in length at the very most, for the secretary of state. As he put it, "Bureaucrats don't like to read more than that ... Assuming they even read that far." But Thompson sensed that there was a special interest in Quebec terrorism. "For a period during the crisis and on and off afterwards," he recalls "there was high level Secretary of State interest in this, the secretary of state [William Rogers] was following it." Thompson also remembers that curiosity over the Quebec crisis extended to the highest level. "We had feedback from meetings saying that the President has an interest in this."

Director of the INR (and former associate to the director of the CIA) Ray Cline briefed Secretary of State Rogers every morning. "Bill Rogers was a wonderful guy but not the most profound analyst of foreign affairs," he remembers. "He just wanted to know what he had to do." With Nixon and Kissinger monopolizing foreign policy this did not amount to much.

## The British: A Second Sight

Several obliging Americans offered their assistance to the RCMP detectives. A private eye from the state of Michigan volunteered his investigative services and was politely turned away. A young mystic from California happened to see Cross's photograph in the newspaper and told local police the hostage was in a wooden church near Quebec City. The RCMP followed up on the lead. They located a picturesque, albeit empty, wooden church near Stoneham.

A spy did finally arrive from Washington to meddle in the investigation, but he was of British origin. A liaison agent from MI-5, one of Her Majesty's secret services, he was sent from his base at the British embassy in Washington to lend the Mounties an unusual helping hand.

He discovered that an employee of the British High Commission in Ottawa, who knew Cross and had once lived in Montreal, also had the gift of second sight. By concentrating on a photograph of the hostage, she claimed to "see" him in a warehouse on Notre Dame Street just behind the Court House in Old Montreal. Donald McCleery and another RCMP agent immediately inspected the area, searching two warehouses to no avail. The clairvoyant tried again. The agent from MI-5 brought her to the bathroom in Cross's home where the abduction had taken place. She put her hands on his razor, his after-shave lotion, and pronounced her verdict anew. Cross was being sequestered on St Helen's Street in Old Montreal. She described the building. There was a staircase, she said. Halfway up towards the first floor there was a trapdoor in the wall. At the top of the stairs a man was standing guard in front of a door; behind the door they would find the British diplomat.

Once again McCleery was forced to follow a supernatural lead. He found the building, the staircase, the trapdoor. At the head of the stairs, a uniformed man was indeed standing watch. But he was a legitimate security guard, and behind the door there was no trace of Cross.

The RCMP agents had had enough of this nonsense. McCleery, who would eventually track down Cross's kidnappers, had better things to do with his time. How was he to rid himself of his bothersome colleague from MI-5? "I'll take care of it," promised John Starnes, director general of RCMP security services. Who knows what strings he pulled? In no time at all, the liaison agent was called away on urgent business to the Bahamas. Back in Ottawa after Cross's release, the agent was heard to say, "We were close!" Laughed one of the Mounties he had worked with: "He had us running all over Old Montreal while Cross lost weight in a house up in the north end."

It was not the first time the British had given some thought to Quebec affairs. According to a confidential report of the American government, "The Montreal police had been severely limited in their effectiveness after reorganization in 1966" when a group of consultants from Scotland Yard came to give Canadian police advice on anti-FLQ tactics. They proposed "doing away with the network of paid informers who were infiltrating terrorist groups." According to the report, the surprising decision to do away with the network was supposed to resolve jurisdictional problems between federal and Quebec police over the control of informants. By recommending the dismantling of the main source of police information (a recommendation which was only followed in part), Scotland Yard actually managed to help the FLQ abduct a British diplomat.

Canadian police authorities hardly needed British aid in dreaming up outlandish strategies and theories; they did very well on their own. Investigators found several books recounting the adventures of Winnie-the-Pooh, in all likelihood belonging to Cross's daughter, at the scene of the abduction. For some inexplicable reason, one official of the Montreal anti-terrorist squad deduced that Winnie-the-Pooh was the diplomat's bedside reading. He concluded from this superficial evaluation of Cross's intellectual abilities that the little bear's story contained keys to a code the hostage would use in handwritten letters to his wife throughout his captivity.

In actual fact, the only "code" Cross resorted to was far simpler: once, when his abductors dictated a missive to him, he deliberately inserted an extra "n" into the word "prisoner" to indicate that he was not the author of the message.

In Ottawa a team of analysts was established under the direction of Jim Bennett in the secret service department of the RCMP to deconstruct the "Cross – Winnie-the-Pooh" texts. They determined after careful analysis that Cross was being held in the fort on St Helen's Island, south of Montreal. Wrong again.

While the RCMP was busy with their wild imaginings in Ottawa, FLQ terrorists were preparing a second October attack. The Rose brothers and Francis Simard were in Texas at the time, trying to obtain financing and firearms in the trigger-happy American state. They heard and read about the Cross abduction in the news, and — afraid the balance of power was slipping dangerously toward the government — they immediately jumped into their car and drove non-stop to Quebec. They believed the choice of Cross as a hostage had been a mistake; his symbolic value was minimal. The government "wouldn't give two cents to save a British citizen" according to Simard. They began to search for an appropriate American victim to re-establish the equilibrium.

The first candidate they came up with was James H. DeCou. He had arrived the previous June as a representative of the United States Information Agency, an organization which distributed information on the United States and occasionally doubled as a front for the CIA. "We knew one of the diplomats from the American consulate in Montreal lived on Nuns' Island," Francis Simard wrote in reference to DeCou. "But the bridges were under constant surveillance," he added, and could become traps for getaway. "Another [American diplomat] lived in Montreal-north. But it was too far. We would have had to cross the entire city," Simard explained, which would have given the police time to spot the abductor's car.

Once again, the American option had to be abandoned. Then someone suggested the Labour Minister and Vice Premier, Pierre Laporte, who lived only a few minutes' drive from one FLQ hideout. Laporte was tossing a ball with a child on his front lawn when the group came to spirit him away on Saturday, October 10. The kidnapping, which had been planned only several hours previously, was effected without a hitch.

Laporte's abduction lent the October Crisis a new dimension. The FLQ had proved it could strike again despite a massive, round-the-clock police operation. "If they could kidnap Cross, if they can go around putting a chain around Laporte's neck," mused David Macuk, one of the political advisors at the American embassy, "they could be nutty enough to try and get the American ambassador."

Minister Laporte was strangled with his own gold chain. On October 18, when the terrible news of Laporte's murder reached René Lévesque, Lévesque burst into tears. An old companion in arms was dead, and a new, still fragile idea had been defiled.

## The Usefulness of Cowards

In Ottawa, Ambassador Schmidt was away. His stand-in, Rufus Smith, was in the United States at the bedside of his ailing father. The military attaché to the US Army in Ottawa was taking a tour of the Great North. In short, the Americans very nearly missed the War Measures Act. No one bothered to warn them in advance. Minister Sharp claims that the idea to inform them of the most important movement of Canadian troops ever to take place in peacetime "never entered my mind." In spite of this, the State Department managed to learn of the plan almost as soon as it was made public. They owed the intelligence to "Snoopy."

During the night of Thursday, October 15, in response to Laporte's kidnapping, the federal cabinet, at the behest of Robert Bourassa's government in Quebec, decided to suspend the civil rights of Canadian citizens. The army fortified a deployment of troops sent out the day before; the police were granted almost unlimited power.

Late that night, Rufus and Peggy Smith's dog, Snoopy, started to growl. He was "a real dumb dog but an attractive beast," recalled Peggy Smith, who awoke suddenly, afraid that burglars had broken in. Alone in the house, she turned on the television hoping to scare them off, and stumbled upon a public announcement at 5:15 AM that war measures were being instituted. She immediately phoned her husband in Illinois and woke him, then alerted his assistant, Emerson Brown, in Ottawa. He tuned in to the televised news and contacted the diplomat on call in Washington.

A minor crisis was thus avoided at the US State Department. It was always humiliating when the State Department learned of a major event in a foreign country from questions posed by journalists first thing in the morning. Diplomats hate surprises; Snoopy allowed them to save face. "Now I understand why Rufus is such a good political officer," Brown commented. "Even his dog has a political nose." Had Snoopy heard the tanks rolling in? Had he sensed tension in the air, or smelled the collective fear of 150 suspects pulled from their beds at dawn by police made bold by their new powers? Was it the noise of democracy aching from the blow it had received, or the sound of the social contract rending that made him startle?

It was nothing so grand, Peggy Smith admits. Her loyal Snoopy had taken fright because, like many Quebec politicians in this season of poltroons, he had glimpsed his own reflection in a mirror.

## The Two Faces of Nixon

In spite of a mutual aversion, as Kissinger noted in his memoirs, Richard Nixon and Pierre Trudeau "worked together without visible strain ... They settled the issues before them and did not revert to their less charitable comments until each was back in his own capital." The two could even show some humor; in fine form after a meeting with Nixon, the Prime Minister told the two delegations meeting behind closed doors, "We've just been having a very interesting discussion with my friend the President and I've been at some pains to let him know that what we Canadians really want from the United States is respect for our inferiority complex."

Nixon did find Trudeau's hair style too long for his taste, and his dress too flashy, but he was much too cunning to let personal antipathies of this nature affect foreign relations. Trudeau's policies, however, had begun to irritate him. Since a first uneventful meeting in 1969, the Canadian had undertaken an in-depth study of the country's foreign strategy and was questioning whether Canada should withdraw from NATO and NORAD. He had already announced his intention to "de-nuclearize" the nation, which would mean the Bomarc missiles would have to be moved. He denounced, like most Canadians, American nuclear tests in Alaska, and he had opened the door to draftdodgers from the war in Vietnam.

Much later, in 1973, Nixon would immortalize his sentiments about Pierre Elliott on a tape that recorded every word spoken in the presidential office. "That asshole Trudeau," he cursed. But even three years earlier the hostility he felt for the Canadian Prime Minister was palpable. In February, he sent Kissinger an "action memo" ordering his advisor to "find a way to attack Prime Minister Trudeau on an economic issue which involves his prestige."

The President had access to all information gathered by his administration, and in all probability the broad outlines of the October Crisis were succinctly presented to him during his morning briefings on international affairs with Henry Kissinger. The first thing that fell into the President's hands at the dawn of each new day was a document of 30 or so typed pages containing every interesting item from news programs televised the night before, and stories published in the morning papers. Current events, reports by influential editorialists and indications of the weight given to various news items were included. The President could learn all he needed to know about what every journalist was saying in less time than it took to read a single newspaper.

In the wake of the Cross abduction, for example, the summary announced on October 6 that "political kidnappings had moved to the North American continent." On both October 7 and 15, several items outlined recent Quebec developments. On October 16, however, the summary failed to mention the nighttime imposition of war measures.

Nixon seems to have learned about the extraordinary legislation on the morning of October 17, when he underlined the words "suspension of civil rights, government control over property, shipping, ports and transportation" in his copy of the summary. He wrote in the margin for the benefit of his chief of staff, Bob Haldeman, "H. — Watch the Press — they will defend their 'liberal' friend!"

The President did not mean "their friend from the Liberal Party." He meant that journalists, whom he considered a band of anti-establishment democratic leftists — thus "liberal" in the American sense of the term — would rally around one of their own, Trudeau, in spite of the terrible, anti-democratic measures he had so recently brought into force. Nixon was perfectly right. It was quite an about-face for a group which, five months earlier, forcefully denounced the actions of the National Guard at Kent State University. The Guard had killed four people when it opened fire on a crowd of protesting students; now the press rushed to Pierre Trudeau's defence, scrupulously avoiding any comparisons with Kent State and ignoring critics from the Canadian left denouncing the suspension of civil liberties.

For their part, American diplomats reacted to Trudeau's use of force with a satisfaction that grew proportionally with the distance between the official in question and the site of the drama.

At the National Security Council, Kissinger's staff thought that "given the festering issue of Quebec," Trudeau had acted with "firmness provoked by the events." According to Helmut Sonnenfeldt, the man in charge of Europe and Canada, not one tear was shed for the non-violent separatists arrested in the night. In Washington, he said, there was little "substantial sympathy for Quebec's independence, especially since it was fanned by the French who weren't popular in those days." The link between de Gaulle and the Quebec independence movement would die hard.

Officials at the State Department privately expressed their admiration for Trudeau's "gutsy" reaction. "When our diplomats get kidnapped," said one, "we go, 'cheep, cheep' and talk softly and the result is we're becoming hostages to any two-bit kidnapper overseas ... It's time someone took a leaf from Trudeau's book." Diplomats in Ottawa, on the other hand, reacted more negatively. "There is no question that we were — disappointed is too mild a word and repelled is too strong a word — we disliked the extraordinary, ruthless actions of the Quebec police," says Vladimir Toumanoff, then principal political advisor to Ambassador Schmidt. "They rounded people up and threw them in the slammer and they didn't do it gently. So this is a repugnant thing to see in any society at any time, anywhere."

Over 500 suspects were arrested, many in the early hours of the morning. The scenario was one that Quebec citizens — like all North Americans — had known only second hand, through movies in which the Gestapo or some Latin American police force called in the night to lock the unsuspecting in handcuffs without any explanation. The authorities also effected over 4600 searches and seizures, confiscating items such as books on Cubism, which they thought had something to do with Cuba. In the end, none of the charges brought against the October prisoners withstood even preliminary examination in the courts. The victims of October included not only a half thousand suspects, but faith in the protection of fundamental liberties.

Toumanoff remarks, however, that professionally "the fact that some foreign service officers' emotions may be jolted by the police action is utterly irrelevant." Their indignation barely showed in the dispatches they sent to Washington; what was demanded of them was analysis. "The issue is, what is the Canadian reaction going to be to this? What effect is it going to have on the crisis? What are the chances that it will help? Why was it done? Who is going to take advantage of it, for what purposes?"

Toumanoff and his colleagues did not think for one moment that there was any danger of an "apprehended insurrection," the legal pretext used by Ottawa to impose the measures. There wasn't the slightest possibility that terrorists would acquire political power or influence or anything else." According to the principal political advisor to the embassy, the FLQ abductions "did not threaten the stability of the government of Canada. It was an act of terrorism, and as such regrettable, but it was in its own way comparable to acts of terrorism elsewhere."

If this was the case, then why was Canada employing such extreme measures? Toumanoff uses an explanation Trudeau himself would resort to when the crisis had passed. Disproportionate as they seemed to the crisis at hand, war measures were necessary to allow the police the immediate powers necessary to track down the abductors.

"My hunch about the Prime Minister is that he really did this to save the man's life. He was willing to pay a high political price," Toumanoff concludes. Like all American diplomats questioned on the subject, he extolled Trudeau for his "firm, decisive action" — to use the words of his colleague Macuk — taken under trying circumstances.

## Detoxification Treatment

Throughout the crisis, American diplomats continued to reject the threat of an insurrection. Like the majority of Canadians, however, they were convinced that the FLQ was a vast and shadowy army. On October 18, when Pierre Trudeau gave his second televised speech about the kidnappings and warned, "Vicious men may attempt to shake our will in days ahead," the embassy pricked up its ears. They interpreted these words as meaning that "the threat posed by the FLQ is much greater than the government of Canada has yet revealed."

Intoxicated by exaggerated federal predictions, US diplomats sent Washington the following analysis. "The government of Canada evidently hopes that sweeping police dragnet, put in motion at four AM October 16 with invocation of the War Measures Act, will so decimate leadership and organization of FLQ that its capacity for organized terrorist action will be destroyed and FLQ will be broken. These would be far gladder tidings to announce to nation in a few days than would be disquieting description of extent of plot involving, according to [Jean] Marchand's statements in Commons, up to 3,000 terrorists armed with machine guns, rifles and dynamite, and FLQ infiltration of decision-making levels in Quebec and federal governments."

While faithfully relaying federal explanations to Washington, American diplomats also kept an ear to the ground for other, conflicting theories. On October 22, Rufus Smith reported that most Canadians still supported the Canadian government, but that contradictory stories about the strength of the FLQ were sowing "some seeds of confusion and doubt." On November 6, Ambassador Schmidt raised the issue of the New Democratic Party's opposition to war measures. "While history may support NDP claim that government of Canada overreacted to FLQ threat, at present NDP is far out on political limb which Liberals intend to saw off," he noted.

In Quebec City, new Consul General Everett Melby, who had barely had a chance to unpack his suitcases, analysed appeals made by editor-in-chief of *Le Devoir*, Claude Ryan, Parti Québécois chief René Lévesque and various union leaders for flexibility and negotiation. He refuted rumors circulating in Ottawa and printed on the first page of the *Toronto Star* to the effect that these leaders were plotting a "parallel government." Instead, he felt they were offering "constructive" criticism, and were motivated by "the leaders' legitimate concerns for the lives of both hostages and for the future of democracy in Quebec." Ryan, Lévesque and the others even showed a measure of political courage because their opinions "were seemingly not held by the vast majority of Quebecers." The polls proved it; the people of Quebec were solidly behind the hard line taken by the federal Prime Minister.

The hardest blow to strike the federal cabinet's beloved FLQ bugbear came from one of the terrorists, Bernard Lortie. He was arrested on November 5, in an apartment where two of Laporte's other abductors escaped police by hiding in a cupboard with a false back. Lortie spilled the beans, giving a detailed description of how amateur the hostage-taking operation had actually been. The entire operation had been planned in 48 hours and the kidnappers had not had a blessed cent with which to work.

On November 12, Consul General John Topping wrote, "The simple, capricious abduction of Pierre Laporte by four youthful 'losers' challenges the concept of the FLQ as an elaborate structure capable of bringing the Quebec government to its knees ... Unless the liberation cell (which is still detaining Cross) and other FLQ cells are found to be more sophisticated and better organized than were Lortie, *et al.*, second guesses about the necessity of imposing the War Measures Act are bound to increase."

The detoxification treatment had begun. On December 1, Schmidt wrote that "failure of government to produce convincing evidence of 'apprehended insurrection' and inability of combined efforts of Montreal, Quebec provincial and Royal Canadian Mounted Police to demonstrate by arrest or testimony existence of sophisticated or widespread terrorist organization has blunted government argument that it was forced to invoke War Measures Act by threat to established order in Quebec."

On November 20, Topping noted that in view of the lack of progress in the hunt for Cross's kidnappers, Quebec politicians were turning their attention to how the crisis had been managed. Questions were being asked about Ottawa's motives and the evident weakness of Quebec's premier, Robert Bourassa. The politicians were also wondering whether "The FLQ, horrendous as its behavior may have been in these instances, does embody some valid grievances of a considerable percentage of the population." This kind of questioning, Topping added without bothering to hide his sympathy, "portends continuation of social tensions and at least occasional extremism for some time to come."

By December 3, Cross's release was imminent. His abductors had reached an agreement with Ottawa: Cross's life in exchange for one-way tickets to Cuba. From that moment on, they would be known as the "exiles." As soon as he learned the terms of the agreement, Topping telephoned Washington. It was customary (and sometimes mandatory) for the State Department to alert the White House immediately to major developments in any one of a dozen hot files. (In the absence of an immediate alert, the events were summarized in documents sent to the President's office in the evening and again first thing in the morning.) As soon as it received Topping's call, the State Department prepared a memo for Henry Kissinger on the conditions of the hostage's release.

## The Lessons of October

The first political hostage-taking incident in North America yielded many useful lessons. In 1973, the State Department and the Pentagon ordered a series of studies on hostage-taking from the Rand Corporation. The aim was to offer American politicians, at the time buffeted by a growing tide of kidnapping attempts, "a better understanding of the theory and tactics of terrorism, particularly as these may affect US national security and the safety of US government officials and other US citizens abroad."

Researcher Eleanor Wainstein interviewed American personnel, studied diplomatic dispatches, and consulted newspapers of the period and the several books published since the incident. She spoke with reticent federal officials in Ottawa who prohibited her from continuing her inquiry in Quebec. Her main objectives were to analyse what had worked and might work elsewhere and what had failed and ought not to be repeated in terms of anti-terrorist action. She summarized her findings in a sixty-five page document produced on the October Crisis.

She wondered why Cross had survived rather than Laporte. John Topping, Cross's neighbor and friend, offered her the following explanation. "Cross was the traditional controlled Englishman to the core, who would bear up under the ordeal. Laporte, however, was no innocent in politics, and his captors might have had something on him: there were probably arguments and insults that ended in his death."

The Rand Report was referring to Laporte's alleged ties to the Montreal underworld, but calculated that the nationalistic politician had probably made his fatal mistake in reprimanding his jailors. "It would have been natural for him to carry on a spirited dialogue" on the future of Quebec. If truth be told, Cross had been much more verbose than the Québécois politican. In an attempt to sweet-talk his abductors, he condemned British policies in Northern Ireland. "He said things," Cossette-Trudel laughed, "that would make the Queen's crown fly off her head."

In contrast to the unflappable Cross, the more passionate Laporte had simply cracked under pressure. Initially convinced that his friend Bourassa would pay his ransom, he became increasingly depressed as he and his captors realized the government was not willing to bargain. Neither the future of Quebec nor the minister's mafia connections were touched upon.

If Simard's account is true, Laporte's only attempt to escape was more an excercise in desperation than in calculation. After managing to slip out of his handcuffs, he threw himself at a window without taking off the band that covered his eyes. He thereby doomed his escape plan to failure.

His "execution" the following day respected the senseless logic of terrorism. His abductors became automatons, according to Simard, relentlessly fulfilling their part of a hellish contract they themselves had drafted: if there would be no concessions from the government, there would be no pity for the hostage. Once the collective strangulation had taken place, the murderers denied the reality of their actions, wrapping the corpse in a blanket and placing a pillow beneath the head as if Laporte could still care for comfort (other theories about the execution abound).

For the analyst at the Rand Corporation, however, there was more to the death of the Quebec native and the survival of the Englishman than interactions between the hostages and their captors. The Rand Report commended the government's tactics in their dealings with the cell holding Cross. "Canadian federal and provincial authorities, using an effective balance of firmness and flexibility, were able to bring the Cross kidnapping to a successful conclusion." The Americans had a good deal to learn from Canadian methods and the manner in which the British government gave free rein to local authorities, Eleanor Wainstein wrote. In contrast, when Laporte was abducted, the heavy-handed use of war measures sowed widespread panic which was probably a contributing factor in the execution of the hostage.

Over 20 years later, she claims that the lesson to be gleaned from the war measures is: "try to find the size of the terrorist gangs before you get too excited. Find out that there are just a few people and keep the public from believing this is a big crisis."

Otherwise, as her report concluded, the government will not only "fail to obtain the hostage's release." "More was lost than the life of a French Canadian official," the report reads. "With the invoking of the War Measures Act — because the government overestimated the FLQ's strength and because the public, police and media overreacted to the FLQ threat — French Canada temporarily lost a part of its civil authority and all the Canadian people temporarily lost a number of their civil liberties."

There is one missing suggestion in the Rand Report, missing as well from the analyses of diplomats in Ottawa and at the INR: No one mentions the ever-popular notion of conspiracy. According to believers in this notion, the RCMP manipulated the FLQ or allowed the abductions to take place to discredit and eventually destroy the organization; Pierre Trudeau knowingly exaggerated the FLQ threat, not merely to justify war measures but also to strike a fatal blow to the entire independence movement. Clearly, according to this theory, Trudeau's real target — behind the Rose brothers, Lanctot and the rest — was René Lévesque. None of this was even suggested by the Americans.

True, not all the documentation has yet been made public, but the total absence of these ideas in analyses which were once labelled "confidential" and which claim to cover all the events in context, tends to validate the official version of the Crisis. This version was also supported by Jean-François Duchaine, Esq., who headed an inquiry into events at the behest of the Lévesque government.

Police wrongdoing after October, and the McDonald Commission's inquiry into illegal procedures used by the RCMP (notably the theft of a list of Parti Québécois members), leave no doubt that the Prime Minister and his entourage as well as the top brass at the RCMP wanted to infiltrate both the Parti Québécois and the Front de Libération du Québec and did not pause to distinguish the two. Since 1968, this monolithic "separatist threat" had officially been considered more dangerous to Canada than the Communists. That the October Crisis was deliberately orchestrated by the federal government to kill the separatist movement in Quebec remains in the realm of theory. The fact that the Americans, generally so well-informed and particularly well-researched on this subject, found no traces of a federal plot or even of political ulterior motives considerably weakens the seductive conspiracy theory.

# 7

# Our Friends at Langley

*In Quebec, there are no state secrets.*
*Because we have no state, and we have no secrets.*
YVES MICHAUD,
Friend and adviser to René Lévesque.

*Life in Canada wasn't exactly a bed of roses.*
CLEVELAND CRAM,
CIA Chief of Station in Ottawa, 1971-1975.

A winter morning in the woods of Langley, Virginia. In a small room in the Central Intelligence Agency building, a dozen or so CIA people await a representative from the RCMP's secret service. They are all impressively well-informed on the Quebec situation, eager to be brought up to date.

The meeting promises to be interesting. The October Crisis has ended a few weeks before and the "guest speaker" is Joseph Ferraris, one of the rare French Canadian senior officers in the Mounties. He had participated in the hunt for the FLQ kidnappers as director of G Branch (Quebec anti-terrorism) in the Canadian security service. The service was known among Mounties, without irony, as the SS.

One of the participants remembers that Ferraris was surprised by the number of CIA employees present for his talk. There were twice as many people present as had formed the entire G Branch complement at its creation in September of 1970. Since the end of the crisis, Ferraris and his superiors had been preparing briefs for friendly security services on FLQ strategy and tactics — referred to in the intelligence sphere as modus operandi, or MO. It was useful to know how communications were maintained between cells of the Front, how kidnappings were organized, communiqués drafted, decisions taken. Once catalogued, the FLQ's MO passed into the common information pool of western anti-terrorist organizations. The FBI and CIA had already received copies of the reports. There was thus no need to go over technical questions with Ferraris, a husky man who arrived in the company of the RCMP's liaison officer in Washington.

What the CIA men really wanted to know more about was the independence movement. They were curious about the philosophy, the strength, and the prospects of the PQ. They wondered about leftist groups as well, about the not-quite-marxists who lent occasional support to the FLQ networks. The trade union movement — and for that matter the whole of Quebec society — seemed to be entering a radical phase. What was behind it? Ferraris's surprise was visible when questions started coming from around the table in a French which was not half bad. Even in Ottawa, Ferraris was unused to conferring with colleagues and superiors in his native tongue (the exception was SS Director John Starnes, a relatively enlightened ex-diplomat).

These Americans did not just speak French, they read it, notably in *Le Devoir*. They wanted to know about Claude Ryan, editor-in-chief and editorialist, whose pronouncements were made with uncommon assurance. And what about the "provisional government" that Ryan, Lévesque and others were said to have suggested to replace the Bourassa government during the crisis? Was Ferraris also convinced it was really just a rumor? They had thought so.

The conference lasted more than two hours. The CIA's Quebec specialists asked no questions which suggested access to privileged information from covert sources within either the Canadian government or the independence movement. Rather, they gave the impression of being extraordinarily careful readers of *Le Devoir* and meticulous observers of Quebec. They said goodbye to Ferraris without indicating what conclusions they had come to, in the secrecy of their mythical Langley building, from the information which they had been collecting so feverishly.

## Two Quebec Scenarios

They offered their conclusions a few months later, in the spring of 1971, to an agency officer who had just been posted to replace the outgoing CIA operative at the American Embassy in Ottawa.

This was not the first contact with Canada for Cleveland Cram, the agency's new chief of station in Ottawa. On his return from the London station in 1958, he had for four years directed Langley's British Commonwealth division, of which Canada was a part. In 1971, in his fifties, Cram was thrilled to get a posting "in a nice place like Ottawa."

Before leaving, however, he had to brush up on his knowledge of Canada, now nine years out of date. The CIA's assistant director in charge of intelligence, Ed Procter, called him in for his initial briefing, a routine procedure for station chiefs on their way to new postings.

This was one of the moments when the two major branches of the CIA, the operations and intelligence directorates, meet. Cram and the Ottawa station answered to the Canadian desk, which was attached, in turn, to the British Commonwealth division, which formed part of the Europe division. The whole formed an element of the operations directorate (also known as "plans" or "clandestine"). These are the people whose job it is to infiltrate governments, to set traps for Soviet operatives or to maintain liaisons with friendly services like the RCMP or Britain's MI-5. In the other branch, the intelligence directorate, information is stored, managed and analysed; reports, biographies and psychological profiles of foreign leaders are produced; enemy troop strengths are evaluated; and the strategies of opponents, as well as of friends, are assessed.

It was with these intelligence specialists that Cram met before his departure. Procter introduced him to the two or three analysts best-informed on Canadian affairs. "Professionals," Cram remembers. Their understanding of the Quebec situation was "superb, superb. I wish I could have taken one of them with me" to Ottawa, he adds, because "in many respects, they were better than the people in the Embassy."

These Canada specialists advised Cram that Ottawa had not yet seen the end of its troubles and predicted that "a surge of separatist strength" was "coming along."

"The main thrust," Cram recalls, "was the fear that if Quebec separated, an independent Quebec would be a country which (a) might not be very stable; (b) would be prone to perhaps assert itself in various ways which would not be in the overall interest, in the long run, of the US government, as well as the rest of Canada — policies, foreign policy, maybe relations with the Soviets, all that sort of thing. There would be the temptation of a typical country which achieves sovereignty to begin to assert itself in various ways." The analysts' other worry, Cram continues, was that Quebec "might not be economically viable in the long run and therefore would weaken the general security of North America." The resulting economic chaos "would be susceptible, maybe, to subversion, perhaps by an even more extreme group inside, or to blandishments from the East bloc, the Soviets in particular," the CIA specialists reasoned.

That was the CIA's worst-case scenario. They had less bleak forecasts too, however: "They felt that, had there been a peaceful resolution and a separated Quebec which would have been stable," adds Cram, the emergence of a new country on the northern border would have been "a nuisance that should be accommodated," but "not a danger" for the United States.

The CIA's was a moderate view. It was not worried about the separatist forces themselves. There were no images of René Lévesque surrounded by Soviet double agents, or of a Parti Québécois whose left wing was under Havana's orders, or of an FLQ preparing an armed revolt with Colonel Khadaffi's assistance. No trace, in other words, of the McCarthyite paranoia which saw a red behind every reformer. The CIA took a clearer, and a longer, view. What it feared was that by a slippery-slope process — independence, an inexperienced and arrogant new government; economic, and then political, instability — the situation would become another worry in the turbulent geopolitics of the early 1970s. Better to keep a close eye on events.

On his arrival in Ottawa, Cram met with greater pessimism among his SS contacts, who were convinced that Quebec terrorism had not died with Laporte. Cram, who had written his doctoral thesis on the Irish rebellion, became himself convinced that "the worst aspects of separatism might win" in Quebec. He foresaw "a very radical kind of government, maybe pro-Soviet or excessively neutral," a situation which "would be damaging to Canada and, in the end, damaging to the welfare of the West."

In the spring of 1971, Cram was convinced that "blood, certain violence, might be on the way." His opinion tallied with the view submitted to the Prime Minister by the federal special committee which had been created in October, and which held that the FLQ was "undoubtedly more dangerous now than before the crisis."

## Eavesdropping on René Lévesque?

To follow events in Quebec, the Langley analysts had access to copies of all documents emanating from American diplomats in Quebec City, Montreal and Ottawa. Their foreign radio and television monitoring section could also provide them with the latest copy from the Télémédia news or from the TV magazine *Le 60*, even, for that matter, from the TV comedy *Symphorien*. Needless to say, they read everything. Occasionally they obtained a useful scrap of Quebec information from their wide network of unofficial American informants — businessmen of all sorts, zealous tourists, visiting academics or vacationing ex-policemen who, in the defence of the free world, called Langley to report an incident, a conversation, a rumor they had picked up by chance on a business trip or a guided tour. In the mountain of trivia lay occasional gems. Langley also had a direct line to the most secret intelligence agency in the world, the gigantic American electronic monitoring center known as the National Security Agency, or NSA (known also, because of its secrecy, as "No Such Agency").

Created in 1952, the agency's stated objective is "to intercept foreign communications, to obtain foreign intelligence necessary to the national defense, the national security and the conduct of the foreign affairs of the United States." Its budget is unofficially estimated at $10 billion, its staff at 100,000 employees. Its headquarters — within a kilometer of which cameras are forbidden — lies about 40 kilometers north of Washington, at Fort Meade, in Maryland.

The NSA is the hardware of the American intelligence apparatus. With its spy satellites, its dish antennas and its intelligence exchanges with parallel organizations like the Canadian CBNRC (Communications Branch of the National Research Council, renamed the Communications Security Establishment in 1975), the NSA can monitor just about any communication, involving anyone or anything, anywhere.

Not surprisingly, its data banks contained information on René Lévesque. How much? Why? On what topic? Dating from when? The NSA refuses to say. All it will confirm is that its information involves the monitoring of communications "relating to René Lévesque" which took place between 1963 and 1980. Does that mean communications by René Lévesque, or simply on the subject of René Lévesque? The NSA maintains that the publication of this information, classed SECRET and TOP SECRET, "could reasonably be expected to cause exceptionally grave damage to the national security" of the US. It also maintains that the publication of relevant documents in its possession would reveal confidential information on the data collected and on the means of collection.

On the subject matter: the information concerns "the national defense and foreign relations of the United States." On the means of collection: the documents carry indications on coding and decoding (which suggests that diplomatic communications or counter-espionage were involved) and on sources of the information or the method used to collect it. In the latter case, the NSA explains, any publication would compromise the source or the method and would be "extremely damaging to the Agency operations," which suggests that the source and/or the method involved are still in use today.

Langley had official access to NSA intelligence, and therefore to the information on Lévesque. But the CIA did not have — or at least did not legally have — any direct window on the internal workings of the FLQ or PQ, on their active strengths, the degree of police penetration, the morale of FLQ members or the extent of their networks of sympathizers. And this interested them greatly.

The intelligence specialists therefore asked Cram to keep an eye on the Quebec situation. "The appetite of Langley is insatiable," Cram comments. "It's a bureaucracy," he sighs. "The more paper they have, the happier they are." But if the CIA had agents operating in Quebec society (see below), it certainly was not the Ottawa station, with its five employees, that was pulling the strings. The chief of station, his assistant, the communications specialist for coded messages and the two agency secretaries in Ottawa were well-known to the Canadian police and diplomatic establishment, as well as to the East-bloc diplomatic contingent in Ottawa. Using Cram for illegal work would have been strictly bush-league. And the official structure provided for no permanent agency presence in Montreal or Quebec City.

There was, of course, another way to find out about the FLQ: ask the ones whose job it was to know, G Branch of the SS. After all, the CIA's Ottawa people could walk in and out of the tightly-guarded SS offices in Ottawa practically without showing their ID's, just as the RCMP's liaison staff in Washington had nearly complete access to the Langley center. Why not knock on the door of Ferraris and his assistants Don Cobb and Don McCleery and ask, "By the way, how many new informants did you recruit this week?"

"I know I could go to that division of the Mounties," Cram recalls, "and I could talk about all kinds of communist subversion — because you know, they also looked at communist subversion — but when I got around to the FLQ, the terrorist side of the Quebec situation, they didn't throw me out of the office, but they gave me a very polite, friendly brush-off." The American refused to be discouraged. "I kept probing and prodding over the occasional double martini." But he did so in vain; the members of G Branch were silent as the grave.

"It wasn't a matter of leverage," Cram explains. "I couldn't go into the front office of the RCMP and say, 'Look, if you don't tell us what you know about the FLQ, I'll shut off the flow of Soviet information.' That's not productive. It wasn't our business, and we were in a friendly neighbor's house." When Cram came back empty-handed, the Langley analysts hardly complained. "They understood. Canadians are not an easy group of people to deal with at any time. They're very prickly, a bit standoffish."

Someone, somewhere — Cram suspected Trudeau — had decided the Americans had no business knowing Canada's family secrets.

### In Search of a Conspiracy

Though the RCMP refused to open its Quebec files to the CIA representatives, it had no hesitation about asking for the agency's help.

In the Cold War atmosphere all intelligence services probed for telltale signs of a foreign enemy in every nook and cranny of domestic politics. And the RCMP, with the CIA, was eager to find traces of the hidden foreign hand which, it was convinced, was agitating the separatists. When Cram met his predecessor, Robert Jantzen, chief of station since 1968, Jantzen told him that the SS "will never stop beating you around the head on this one." The question, as Cram sums it up, was this: "Is this purely a Quebec terrorist problem, or is it part of a larger conspiracy funded perhaps by the Cubans or Soviets?" (In the United States, Richard Nixon was desperately searching for signs that Moscow and Hanoi were behind the American anti-Vietnam War movement; it seems the political leaders of North America had a low opinion of their populations' own capacity for rebellion.)

SS counter-espionage experts devoted much effort to surprising some Soviet or North Korean consular official in the act of passing an envelope to an FLQ leader. They were unsuccessful. And having been criticized by the Prime Minister's office for having come up with no meaningful clues during the October Crisis, the RCMP wanted more than ever to turn up some hard information. The force thus hoped that the CIA, through its international network of spies and sources, especially in the East bloc, would find the clue that proved a conspiracy.

The best way to go, Jantzen explained to Cram, "is to send a cable every week [to Langley] just to be sure someone doesn't doze off, and if there is something there, be sure and get it." Jantzen and Cram knew that in the ongoing CIA-RCMP liaison game, a single good Soviet source on the FLQ would earn Langley Ottawa's eternal gratitude. Unfortunately, nothing very interesting ever came to the American spies' attention, save for one Cuban defector who informed the CIA in the early 1970s that Cross's kidnappers, exiled in Havana, were living a quiet life in their hotel, and that one of them was showing all the symptoms of deep homesickness. SS agents met this Cuban in a safe house in the United States.

Three FLQ members eager to master guerilla techniques had already visited Cuba during an 18-month period prior to 1970. Langley had introduced SS representatives to another defector who told bewildering stories of the training that the three men received from the Cubans. The CIA set some store by the account, but in Ottawa the Mounties had their doubts. "We knew from people who had seen them that the FLQ people in Cuba hadn't had training. They'd played marbles in their hotel corridor," says one Canadian officer. In fact, it is now known that the instruction received by the three would-be Che Guevaras was purely theoretical.

The RCMP nonetheless asked the CIA to instruct its Havana sources — which were neither numerous nor well-informed — to keep an eye on the FLQ exiles. The force also asked Langley now and then to verify whether its files contained information on one individual or another. The procedure was routine when the individual was a newly-arrived employee in one of the East-bloc embassies and the Canadian authorities wanted to know whether he had been spotted photographing secret military installations on a previous posting. If there was no file on the name in the CIA computer, then Langley would open one, just in case.

But since the beginning of the 1960s, the RCMP had been asking for traces on individuals who had no apparent connection to the KGB or its satellites. "You could pretty well tell from what they gave you that it wasn't an espionage problem," comments one former American officer.

The Mounties would want to know if the Langley data banks held "any derogatory information on whoever," according to Seymour Young, then on the Canadian desk at Langley. Another CIA Canada-watcher on hand during the first half of the 1960s guesses that the RCMP made around 20 such requests. The force, which had no personnel abroad apart from a few liaison officers, also requested that CIA operatives keep certain French Canadians, FLQ members or not, under surveillance during their foreign travels, especially in Europe.

These requests had not always been looked upon favorably. An agency officer who was based in Canada for some time remembers occasionally responding to a Canadian request by saying that the CIA had no information on the person in question, even when that was not the case. He explains that he refused to cooperate "because that would have mixed us up in a domestic problem. Also, I guess I had some sympathy for these people. I mean, I have English friends, but I know a lot of French Canadians too, and as an American, I figured the French Canadians had been getting a raw deal long enough."

But as Quebec terrorism evolved from graffiti to explosives to assassination, this kind of reluctance gave way to cooperation at Langley. Under Jantzen and Cram, all requests for information received full attention.

Apart from some intelligence relayed by the Israeli security service, Mossad, on the training of two FLQ members in Jordan, and later on international contacts made by these same two *felquistes* based in Algiers (then the world capital of leftist extremism), Langley's pickings were generally slim. It seems not only to have been the fault of the intelligence community; while there is no doubt that the Quebec revolutionaries wanted nothing more than to be admitted into the world network of guerilias, particularly of the Cuban, Algerian and Palestinian sort, the attraction seems not to have been mutual. RCMP officials on hand during the October Crisis say they had to twist the Cubans' arms before they would accept Cross's kidnappers. Havana had feared acceptance would compromise their relations with Ottawa and limit the freedom of action of their diplomats and spies in Canada.

## The Cuban Lists

Only once were the intelligence services able to put their hands on documents proving that Cuba had taken an interest — and only an interest — in the separatists. Those documents had made their way into RCMP safes after much effort.

At a quarter to one in the morning of April 4, 1972, a powerful bomb was placed in the ceiling of an elevator at 3737 Crémazie Boulevard in Montreal. The elevator was then sent to the twelfth floor of the building, where it exploded, setting a fire and fatally wounding one security guard of the Cuban consulate. Within minutes police were on the scene. They ran straight into three Cubans armed with Belgian FN submachine guns, all of whom were staffers at the consulate. Despite the fire, the dying security guard and a second employee's critical injuries, the Cubans claimed to be defending the inviolability of their diplomatic territory. This was not wholly unreasonable, because an RCMP intelligence officer responsible for Cuban matters arrived, according to some of his colleagues, in less time than it should have taken for him to make the drive from his home in suburban Ste-Thérèse to the site of the explosion. Disarmed and arrested, the Cubans were brought to the police station. As soon as the Department of External Affairs advised the police that they could not detain diplomatic personnel, the Cubans returned to their building and, despite desultory resistance from the thoroughly confused police officers on hand, managed to retake their office by storm and barricade themselves inside, brandishing their arms at the officers outside.

The Cubans immediately emptied their files into the wastebaskets and tried to set fire to them. But the explosion had set off the sprinkler system and the soaked documents would not burn. Changing methods, the Cubans still had time to pour a little acid on the piles paper before police reinforcements showed up in bullet-proof vests and, with submachine guns, regained control of the area.

The official account attaches responsibility for the bombing to anti-Castro commandos from the United States, already responsible for a few minor attacks on Cuban diplomatic missions in Canada. But in 1975, a California Democrat in the US House of Representatives, also a member of the House Intelligence Committee, which supervises the activities of the CIA and other intelligence services, suggested that the bombing had been a planned diversion with the specific aim of obtaining documents for examination by the RCMP and CIA. The office of Congressman Ronald Dellums claimed to have written proof to back up its assertions. (Questioned on the point in 1980 by journalist and author John Sawatsky, Dellums' office refused to comment, invoking the confidential nature of the information. The RCMP denied any responsibility at the time. To this day both Cram, then the CIA chief of station in Ottawa, and a former senior officer in the SS deny having had a hand in the explosion.)

Since Cuba had no diplomatic mission in the United States apart from its UN delegation, it was generally acknowledged that its Montreal and Ottawa missions served as bridgeheads for its espionage operations on American territory. The Cuban representatives enjoyed considerable freedom of movement, being unaffected by the travel restrictions which applied to Soviet diplomats in Canada. This helps explain how the office building at the corner of Crémazie and St Michel boulevards, a stone's throw from the traffic jams of the Metropolitan Autoroute, came to contain one of the principal stations for Soviet espionage in the West.

Little surprise, then, that Langley had always insisted on cooperation between its Cuba specialists and the RCMP's Cuba desk in Montreal. It was important to keep the closest possible tabs on the activities of Fidel Castro's emissaries in Quebec. The intelligence establishments in Washington and Ottawa, knowing that Soviet officers directed operations from key posts within the Cuban espionage apparatus, took it for granted that Cuba was merely a pawn in the KGB's grander schemes.

When SS analysts began to sort through the harvest of documents and photographic negatives taken from the Cuban consulate, they found names. And lists. "They had extensive lists on who was in the separatist movement, complete with profiles and evaluations of whether those people could be used in some way," reveals a former SS officer. "They obviously had set themselves the task of being well-informed about the separatist movement, as such, and on the more active or militant elements in the movement," he adds. The SS also found the key to the code used by the Cuban mission in all the messages it had been sending, in particular to Havana. It would be child's play now to decipher the messages, which had been intercepted and filed without being read because they had until now been unintelligible. The Cubans would, needless to say, now be changing codes.

The lists, especially the evaluations of certain militants, made for significant circumstantial evidence of Cuba's interest in the separatists. But the true question was that of recruitment. Had the Cubans penetrated the independence movement? Had they turned one of its members, through ideology, blackmail or bribery, into an informer, or even an active *agent provocateur*? The consular documents provided no insight into this matter, or into the always-revealing one of secret financing. There was no trace at all of money having changed hands.

That may be because even slightly enterprising Cuban diplomats had no trouble introducing themselves into leftist, and even moderate, circles in Quebec in the early 1970s. The Cuban revolution was still wreathed in a rebel mist which intoxicated zealous reformers and hardened *felquistes* alike, blind at that date to its more repressive aspects. Even pop singer Robert Charlebois, who has no gift for political thought, recorded a hymn to the glory of *"mon ami Fidel"* in 1976, thus earning himself a personal audience with the *lider maximo*. In 1974, the social democratic separatist daily *Le Jour* would regularly print the "journalistic dispatches" on Latin America sent out of Havana by the Cuban government agency *Prensa Latina*. It would be another 15 years before the revolutionary's bushy beard would be found to hide the totalitarian intransigence of the last of the Stalinists. In the meantime, wherever separatists got together, the Cubans felt right at home.

Another SS member says the Mounties succeeded in identifying "one or two Cuban sources" within the independence movement in the early 1970s. Militants whose actions were "motivated by ideology" rather than greed or blackmail. But having made this revelation, the Canadian spy refused to say more and tried awkwardly to backtrack. "Let's just say the Cubans were, maybe not the most active, but in any case the most visible of the [East bloc] intelligence services in Quebec, no doubt because, being less professional in their work, they were easier to spot."

Were these valuable lists from the Cuban consulate shipped down to Langley? Cram says no. "The Mounties kept us pretty much out of it. We thought we were going to get more," he says. "Later we got some tidbits, but we didn't take part in the reviewing, we didn't get the hot stuff. There was a great deal of hush-hush. But not a thing about the FLQ."

In his well-informed book on the RCMP's security service, John Sawatsky claims, on the contrary, that "within hours, the entire body of documents, code book included, was on a desk at CIA headquarters in Langley, Virginia. In this case the Cuban desk of the RCMP had simply served as a messenger."

## Twinning the Ukraine and Quebec?

The Soviet espionage machine had a Quebec list as well; theirs was not a list of names, but a list of potential targets. The Soviet document called for the recruitment of Quebec journalists and politicians, initially as informants, then as sources of influence and action. This document held that Quebec, like any region in which two cultures meet in confrontation and conflict, was "a breeding ground for dissent and continuing problems between the two races. It therefore offers an ideal target for manipulation, provocation of strife and social conflict." A bargain, in "an industrial country which was democratic and opposed to the Soviet Union," reports the head of the Soviet desk of the RCMP, Jim Bennett, who saw the information.

Bennett obtained the document in 1968 or 1969 and was not surprised by it. "It was something we were always looking for, anyhow," he confesses, "since the Soviets had made an art of inciting ethnic hatred." Colleagues in the British intelligence service transmitted this treasure to Ottawa. But there was a slight problem. The document was more than 40 years old. Only when the British had been in the midst of a reorganization of their archives at the end of the 1960s did they pass this intelligence, gathered sometime between 1920 and 1925, on to the Canadians.

The Canadians were grateful all the same. The SS had been worried by the lack of interest the Soviets were showing in Quebec separatists. They did not believe the Soviets had grown wiser; rather, they thought KGB operatives working in Quebec were cleverly evading surveillance.

From 1954 to 1972, during the period in which Bennett observed Soviet comings and goings in Canada with the help of those he called "our friends at Langley," he never once saw a Soviet citizen posted to Canada after a stay of any duration in a French-speaking country. "This would obviously have tipped us off that the individual was coming over to make trouble on the French question," he comments. CIA agents responsible for Soviet "targets" in Ottawa from the beginning of the 1960s until the mid-1970s add that to their knowledge, no enemy agent was ever observed working on the independence movement.

The KGB did not ignore Quebec, however. Montreal was regularly chosen as the arrival point for Soviet "illegal agents," individuals who did not have the benefit of diplomatic status and who came under false names into Quebec, often in order to cross the border and establish themselves in the United States. Both Langley and the FBI took a very lively interest in such individuals. There was no doubt in SS minds that KGB officers were cultivating informants or controlling illegal agents in Quebec, with the classic espionage goals of obtaining military, scientific or economic intelligence.

Of course, if the KGB wanted to know about developments within the political left in Quebec, it did not need to waste these valuable resources. The small but loyal Communist Party of Canada and its adjunct, the Communist Party of Quebec, which maintained a presence on the campuses and in the major trade unions, could provide all the desired information. Relying on the Canadian Communist Party as an instrument of recruitment for the Soviet intelligence service was a practice which dated back to 1924, as the celebrated defector Igor Gouzenko had revealed at the end of the war.

The RCMP had in fact identified a leftist leader, not French Canadian and not a separatist, but active in Quebec since the end of the 1960s, whose activities were indirectly financed by the Soviets. In an interesting turn of events, this individual appeared on the list of people to be arrested during the October Crisis, but happened miraculously to be in Moscow at the time.

One should not seek a direct link between Soviet diplomatic strategy and its daily espionage practices. It was, for example, vital for the Soviets to maintain good relations with West Germany, but that in no way inhibited their intense espionage and subversive activities there. Moscow also had no qualms about recruiting agents from political movements it opposed. And so far as Quebec was concerned, it seemed clear that the Soviets were strategically opposed to independence.

"They saw Canada as a sort of balance in North America against the United States and a country which was not nearly so violently anti-Soviet as the US was at that time," explains Robert Ford, then Canadian ambassador in Moscow. "They obviously found that if Quebec became independent, Canada would fracture and eventually fall into the American empire, which they didn't look on with very much favor." If de Gaulle's anti-Americanism led him to favor the independence of Quebec, Brezhnev's anti-Americanism relied on a Canada which was "strong, stable and unified," in Ford's words.

In 1967, when de Gaulle shouted "Vive le Québec libre!" Moscow did not know quite how to react. According to one INR analysis which came to the attention of Walt Rostow, Lyndon Johnson's national security advisor, Tass tiptoed around the subject without ever informing its readers of the French President's choice of words. Readers were only told that, "according to Radio Ottawa," Prime Minister Pearson had accused de Gaulle of "encouraging Quebec nationalism."

The idea of meddling in Canada's troubles, as suggested by the 1920s document discovered by the British, was far from the intentions of Soviet Vice-Premier Dmitri Polianski, who arrived as his country's representative at Expo just after de Gaulle had rocked the political landscape.

Ambassador Ford accompanied Polianski on his rounds, which included a dinner in his honor hosted by Quebec Premier Daniel Johnson. In his memoirs, Ford describes the scene, which sounds surreal. In his welcoming address, Johnson

> ... at some length explained that he would like to see Quebec have the same position in the Canadian confederation as the Ukraine had in the Soviet Union.
>
> I was sitting next to the Minister of Justice, Jean-Jacques Bertrand. I told him the Premier was badly misinformed, and that even the worst enemy of Quebec would not wish on it the fate of the Ukraine. Officially, it had the status of a republic, with all the visible signs of independence: its own language, flag, constitution, foreign ministry, and a seat in the United Nations [...] but in practice it was [...] firmly under the thumb of the central government, which had not the slightest compunction in suppressing any sign of Ukrainian nationalist or religious feeling. Bertrand took it all in, said it was clear the analogy was wrong, and right after the banquet told Johnson.
>
> Polianski, with the example of de Gaulle before him, studiously ignored these remarks in his public reply. Later Johnson called on him in his hotel room. Polianski told him he would be happy to supply documentation on the Soviet constitution, but the Premier should understand that in practice, his country was a strongly centralized administration. Clearly, the Soviets did not want to get involved in the Quebec-Ottawa dispute; yet it would have been easy, if they had wished, to stir up more trouble.

In private, staffers at the Soviet consulate in Montreal were saying the same thing. On several occasions before and after the October Crisis, a Soviet consul confided with utter sincerity to Michel Vastel, who was then working for the

Conseil du Patronat (an employers' organization), "One Cuba in North America is enough, we don't need a second."

When Tass subsequently accused the Parti Québécois of being simply a "party of the little bourgeois," the insult provoked future Finance Minister Jacques Parizeau to react, "Why 'little'?" Sticking to the idea that Quebec independence would create conditions favorable to an expansion of American power, Tass would later accuse the PQ government in 1978 of being "infiltrated" by the CIA, which it claimed exerted "a certain influence over events in the province."

In sum, the Canadian security service and its friends at Langley always had suspicions — and in the Cuban case, at least a hint — that the East bloc had some informants, and maybe even a few agents, in the independence movement. But the absence of any sign of a pipeline for personnel, money or propaganda connecting Moscow to the separatists, violent or moderate, convinced the security people that East-bloc activity did not go beyond information gathering.

"Apart from the obvious help that they got when they left Canada," observes one high-ranking SS officer of the separatists, "It was a genuine home-grown independence movement," rather than the product of any Moscow plan. Coming from a specialist in hunting reds, this assessment has substantial weight.

In Quebec, then, Canada's enemies kept pretty much to themselves. The same cannot necessarily be said of Canada's friends, the French and the Americans.

## French Connection I: The President's Files

During the seven days it took the French ship *Le Colbert* to make the crossing between Le Havre and Quebec City, Charles de Gaulle, installed in the admiral's cabin which he had commandeered with royal aplomb, gave himself over to some interesting reading. Some of the files on Quebec which he consulted to polish his speeches were labelled "Secrétariat Général de la présidence de la République." This meant they had been relayed by the office of Jacques Foccart, de Gaulle's aide responsible for intelligence. The documents' true origin was the SDECE (Service de Documentation Extérieure et de Contre-Espionnage), France's CIA.

These files summarized the reports sent from Quebec or drafted on return from Quebec missions by SDECE operatives. It was de Gaulle — and not Foccart, as Ottawa believed — who digested and synthesized these reports and decided what action to take.

Two French sources confirm the SDECE presence in Quebec. Philippe de Vosjoli, SDECE representative in Washington until 1963, recalls that the order to begin a concentration of energies on Quebec dates from de Gaulle's return to power in 1958. The French spy says the Elysée had a double objective: to fan the separatist flame and thus annoy the Americans, and to keep track of the anti-Gaullist rebels who had fled to Canada after the Algerian war.

According to Vosjoli, the Quebec network was controlled from the French consulate in New York. When he decided to leave the SDECE in 1963 because of his growing suspicion that there were double agents among his superior officers, Vosjoli was certain he was being tracked by SDECE killers. The retired spy needed a secure refuge. "Canada was only a few hours away," he writes in his memoirs, "but I dismissed the idea of going there because of the presence of numerous gaullist agents sent to organize subversive activities in the French provinces. I decided to go to Mexico."

Authors Anne and Pierre Rouanet, in *Les Trois Derniers Chagrins du Général de Gaulle,* state that the two branches of the SDECE, the intelligence branch — which gathers information — and the action branch — which controls operations — were active in Quebec, at least during the first half of the 1960s. Questioned directly on the usefulness to the President of SDECE agents in Quebec, Michel Debré, de Gaulle's prime minister in the early 1960s, answers, "It was available to him; he would have been crazy not to use it."

Quebec journalist Louis Fournier offers corroborating information. He quotes one of the ex-FLQ members in Algiers as saying de Gaulle personally asked Algerian President Ben Bella to help the *felquistes* in their "struggle for national liberation." The source of this information is Ben Bella himself.

In Ottawa, the concern over covert French activities turned into a red alert at the end of the 1960s, when British intelligence informed the SS that "FLQ members are trained by the SDECE at a terrorist school in southern France." Pressed for further details, the British replied that the officer responsible "no longer has access to his source." More than a year later, however, a Canadian politician returned from Paris with the same rumor, which had been making the rounds on the cocktail circuit. The matter never progressed beyond these two scraps of information, and no FLQ member ever mentioned training sessions in the Midi. But the question still raised doubts in the minds of federal officials. When the October Crisis erupted, Ottawa and Quebec City, anxious to leave no stone unturned, jointly sent Quebec Delegate General Jean Chapdelaine and Canadian Ambassador to France Léo Cadieux to the Quai d'Orsay to ask whether there was any information in ministry files which might accelerate the liberation of the hostages. The two diplomats got as high as the office of the minister's principal assistant, Hervé Alphand, where they were received coldly. "We didn't get a thing," Chapdelaine remembers. "We were told to get lost."

Pierre Trudeau would state after the crisis that there was no reason to believe "French *agents provocateurs* could have played a role" in the kidnappings. This opinion is confirmed by a high-ranking SS officer.

In hindsight, one officer in G Branch admits unhesitatingly that at the turn of the decade and in the first few years of the 1970s, Ottawa was seized by "a kind of anti-French paranoia." At one point John Starnes, the director of the security service, went to Prime Minister Trudeau with the problem. The suspicions had grown so strong, Starnes explained, that it would be necessary to put several French diplomats under surveillance. Trudeau agreed but insisted on keeping an escape hatch of "plausible deniability"; if necessary, he wanted to be able to deny knowledge of the intelligence service's indiscretions. "If you're caught, I'll have to deny having been informed," the Prime Minister said.

The RCMP would tail, among others, the man whom Trudeau had denounced as France's "more or less secret agent." His name was Philippe Rossillon, and he was officially with the Haut Commissariat à la langue française, an organization attached to the French prime minister's office. "It was costing them a fortune," a Quebec intelligence officer remembers of the surveillance. Rossillon "would go

to Winnipeg, to Moncton, would come back to Montreal, would leave again [...]
It took an army to follow him!" And to plant microphones in his hotel rooms, to
record his love life — conducted, oddly, in Portuguese with at least one
knowledgeable Québécoise — and translate it all into English.

The extent of the RCMP's surveillance of French diplomats in Canada was
never revealed. Nor was the number of microphones planted in diplomatic
offices or residences. According to one source, the RCMP's interest extended to
the representatives of major French aviation and automobile companies in
Montreal.

With what result? Trudeau observed rightly in 1981 that "no French diplomat
has ever been declared *persona non grata* or asked to leave the country." The
Canadian Prime Minister, in his struggle to preserve Canadian unity in the
1970s, would certainly not have hesitated to point a finger at French diplomats
caught encouraging separatism behind the scenes. Anti-French sentiment, as
Trudeau well knew, is always popular among Quebec voters. If they had been
given proof that the "damned French" were sticking their noses into Quebec's
partisan politics, the PQ vote would undoubtedly have suffered. If Trudeau
never resorted to such political weapons, it is probably because, despite his best
efforts, he could not find them.

## French Connection II: The KGB Moles

Anatoly had waited long enough. What were those CIA idiots up to?
Couldn't they see he was ready to make the big jump, that he had compiled, in
the secrecy of number 2, Dzerzhinsky Square, Moscow, enough information on
Soviet espionage in the West to turn the KGB upside down? A major in the
Anglo-American section of the KGB's foreign directorate, Anatoly had studied
the reports of the best Soviet sources in the West. Their names did not appear on
the reports, but he had filled his memory with dates, codes and descriptions.
Transferred to Finland in the fall of 1961, he had told himself that the friends on
the other side would spot him easily as a recruitment target. With his superiority
complex and his troublesome wife, he had the ideal profile.

In early December, in a hurry to begin his new life in America, he arrived
unannounced at the office of the CIA chief of station in Helsinki with a sheaf of
papers under his arm. The spy world would never be the same. And the foreign
intelligence front in Quebec would take on an added dimension.

Anatoly Golytsin happily identified about a hundred Soviet agents in the
West. He took the CIA through the KGB's structure, its activities and its
agents, as well as the strategy of its directorates. Clues he provided helped
expose a British admiralty officer working for the Soviets, a US Army
sergeant who was turning over secrets on NATO's unified military strategy
and an ex-Canadian ambassador in Moscow, John Watkins, caught in a
homosexual honeytrap.

But Golytsin opened an enormous Pandora's box when he began to discuss
the agents recruited by the KGB within NATO's own espionage networks. Two
moles had already been found within Britain's MI-5. He said there were five.
Kim Philby and Anthony Blunt soon joined the list, leaving the fifth mole still at
large. Golytsin also said there was a mole at work somewhere at the highest level
of the CIA. His code name was Sacha, and his name started with K.

An entire generation of CIA professionals is still marked by the intelligence community's version of McCarthyism, known as "the great mole-hunt." There were hundreds of suspects and thousands of interrogations; careers were broken and operations crippled. The atmosphere of paranoia at Langley reached such a pitch that an order went out in the 1960s to stop recruiting new agents in the East bloc for fear that Moscow would learn of them immediately by means of the undiscovered mole. Golytsin, according to many participants and victims of the hunt, could not have wreaked more havoc if he had been sent by Moscow to do just that.

When, at the beginning of the 1970s, Golytsin was shown some of the Canadian file against Jim Bennett, head of the RCMP Soviet desk, Golytsin gave a considerable boost to Bennett's accusers by declaring that the file showed the characteristic signs of a Soviet mole's progress. Ironically, he had met with Bennett six times in the past to discuss Soviet agents in Canada.

While Anatoly Golytsin saw moles everywhere, he saw more in France than elsewhere. "He said that the KGB general in charge of the division that controlled western Europe and France [...] referred to his sources, his moles, so to speak, in the French services as the Sapphires, the jewels of the KGB," remembers a CIA officer. "They were that good, he said. Unfortunately the KGB had nothing comparable in Britain anymore." But now his Sapphires were French, recruited during and after the war."

When John Kennedy learned of this, he had a letter delivered directly to de Gaulle advising him of the danger. Golytsin said some of the Sapphires were at the very top: an ex-minister, two or three ranking civil servants or legislators, one advisor to General de Gaulle. The French mole-hunt got underway — it was now 1962 — and eventually claimed a few minor victims, among them a French officer in NATO.

Several important French ministers were suspected: their files, with nothing concealed, were spread out before Golytsin for his examination. Vosjoli, still the SDECE liaison in Washington, even mentioned a certain François Mitterrand. But most of the attention focussed on the man at the Elysée who supervised intelligence services: Jacques Foccart.

For the Americans, Foccart would have been the ideal culprit. In Africa, he had consistently managed to stay one up on them; they would have been happy to have been rid of him. But although Foccart's history was occasionally mysterious, it still did not match the career profile drawn by Golytsin for the Sapphire in the General's coterie. The gaullists, meanwhile, wondered understandably whether the Americans were using Golytsin as a pretext for undermining French intelligence. Years passed without the Sapphire network yielding up its secrets. Principal suspects within the SDECE found themselves on fast tracks to nowhere. Finally, in the early 1980s, a staffer from the early years of de Gaulle's presidency confessed to the French domestic security service (the DST) that he had been a Moscow informant. In return for his confession, he received immunity from prosecution, and his name is kept secret.

Only at the beginning of the 1970s, when anti-French paranoia had reached its height in Ottawa, did the RCMP realize the Quebec implications of the Sapphire network. What if it was Moscow, through its infiltrators at the top of the SDECE, or through the DST, or through Foccart, that was pulling the strings in the separatist movement? The two Canadian bogeymen, the Russians and the French, thus became intertwined at this strategic intersection.

The Canadian security service was not alone in spotting the connection. At Langley, one of the legendary figures in the annals of espionage was thinking the same thing.

## The Superspy and Quebec

James Jesus Angleton, a CIA stalwart since the agency's early days in the Second World War, specialized in the difficult art of counter-espionage. According to a colleague, Angleton came to possess "a better understanding of Soviet espionage operations than anyone in the West." As head of the ultrasecret, ultra-powerful counter-espionage division during the 1960s, Angleton moved through Langley with the air of a Spanish Inquisitor. He took Golytsin as his advisor and hung on his every word. The two were inseparable. When Angleton walked by an office at Langley, its occupants would stiffen, terrified that he would identify Sacha or some other treacherous infiltrator on the spot.

Angleton "had almost mesmerized the senior officers in the security service of the RCMP," one Langley witness declares. "And whenever Angleton spoke, his voice of God was Anatoly Golytsin. By the beginning of the 1970s, some were starting to doubt the reliability of this defector whose information was now ten years old. "But the Mounties, who were very much enamored of Angleton anyway, took this all in," recalls the American spy.

"I remember specifically during the crisis or after the crisis [of October 1970], the Mounties all wanted to talk to Golytsin," and check with him "about the possibility of the French, the SDECE, being influential in the crisis or trying to manipulate it or support it clandestinely."

For Angleton, it all fit together. The French service was "sick" (infiltrated) and thus subject "to the clandestine pressuring, manoeuvring of the KGB. And the KGB, wanting to weaken Canada and subsequently weaken the United States, would be pushing every way they could for an extreme separatist state. Not just a separatist state, but the most radical, extreme kind," recalls the CIA man. (Angleton, evidently, did not subscribe to the theory that Moscow feared Quebec independence like the plague; he went so far as to believe the KGB would be happy "to provoke a civil war in Canada.")

At least once between the October Crisis and 1972, Canadian security service officers made the trip to Washington. They were brought to a safe house where Golytsin was introduced to them in conditions of utmost secrecy, since there were still fears that the KGB would try to put an early end to the turncoat's career.

The RCMP specialists questioned Golytsin at length and shared with him the few pieces of evidence they had managed to garner against the French. Golytsin weighed their arguments, tried to establish connections between what he knew of Soviet intervention and penetration techniques and the situation which the visitors were describing. Not all of his knowledge was outdated; thanks to Angleton, he had had access to all files, including the French ones. But he had little more to offer the RCMP than his own speculations. Basically, he knew nothing. And the less he knew, the more he guessed. The idea of a Soviet plot to break Canada in two probably did not surprise him very much; he had already declared that China's split with the Soviet Union was really just a gigantic ploy to throw the West off guard.

The SS agents left Washington unenlightened. "No one would ever say, you know, the emperor had no clothes," remembers one officer at Langley. "They sort of said diplomatically, well, it was very helpful. 'Brilliant fellow, that Golytsin, very interesting.' But frankly, I think, there wasn't much."

## The CIA in Montreal

Russian moles, French agents, a Cuban control center: could the cloak-and-dagger cocktail that was brewing in Quebec around the independence movement have failed to attract a battalion of CIA officers to Montreal?

Even in Ottawa, senior officials could not resist toying with the idea. "If they've been fooling around in every country in the world, why would they ignore Canada?" wondered, the future ambassador to Washington, Allan Gotlieb.

In Quebec itself, there was little doubt. In the FLQ and in the PQ, in the provincial and federal police forces, it was taken for granted that CIA networks were at work in the shadows.

"I could tell the difference between an RCMP infiltrator and a CIA agent," says a former FLQ member with some pride. "The RCMP guy always went overboard, pushed the cells to take risks. The one from the CIA stuck with the majority. He was just there to get information." His conclusions, he admits, were based on unverified suspicions.

In 1969 SS officers following "subversive elements" infiltrating the protest movement became slowly convinced — erroneously, according to one CIA source — that Stanley Gray, a well-known FLQ sympathiser, was in fact a CIA agent. Gray, an American-born English speaker, very active in leftist separatist circles, was a lecturer in political science at McGill at the time. "He was our Cohn Bendit," remembers one of his militant friends at McGill, Michel Celemenski, referring to the turbulent Jewish German who had led the student uprising in Paris in May of 1968. "Gray was our imported Jewish revolutionary," he adds. Gray led the *Front de libération populaire*, a group which had split from the RIN and which wavered between legal protest and more seductive clandestine activities. Most significantly, Gray was the leader of the McGill Français movement, which deplored English domination in Montreal. During a demonstration by the movement in 1969, two SS agents in plain clothes confronted Gray and, without provocation, warned him to "stop working for the CIA." A report dated October 1969, probably from the RCMP, also identified Gray as a liaison with the Black Panthers. He was arrested during the massive 1969 demonstration which attracted 15,000 marchers in favor of a French McGill, and he was subsequently one of the October prisoners.

Quebec's intelligence service also came to the conclusion that Gray was working for Langley. The Centre d'analyse et documentation (CAD), created during Premier Robert Bourassa's first term to collect and organize information on persons identified as subversives, built up a file on Gray. In 1974, when CAD officers felt they had reached a "sufficient degree of reliability," they submitted the file to Bourassa. By then, however, Gray had left Quebec for Ontario and the file only had value as a "historical illustration" of CIA activity in Quebec.

A senior official in the Department of Justice, however, attaches little credence to the Gray story. "They were just over-excited police officers barking up the wrong tree." An American source with indirect access to Langley files was actually able to check whether a Stanley Gray had ever had one of the code numbers assigned to all CIA sources, informants or agents. "If there was someone like Gray, he didn't belong to us," the American declares.

Gray, now a union organizer in the Hamilton area in Ontario, believes these accusations were probably trumped up by the police to discredit his militant activities. "Come and see how I live," he says. "I worked in a factory for 11 years, which ex-agents don't do, you know. They get some kind of reward, they don't go work on the line." Gray remembers hearing at the time that the police were spreading "these dirty lies" about him, but he says the incident at the McGill demonstration never took place.

The Quebec intelligence service also compiled a list of all the possible covers behind which, in its view, CIA operatives might have concealed themselves: it included an American business, a research institute, a church. At one point, several police officers were convinced that a small leftist group, comprising in all half a dozen people, a telephone and an office, was actually Langley's Montreal outpost.

More interestng is the account of a well-known Montreal woman who was romantically involved from 1969 until after the October Crisis with an Israeli intelligence officer in Montreal, purporting to pursue his studies. One day when she was complaining to him about CIA activity in some distant part of the world, he answered, "I don't know why you're so aggressive. The CIA guys are pals. I meet them all the time in bars here." Throughout their relationship, he frequently bumped into his "pals," telling her about it on numerous occasions.

And then there is the English-Canadian researcher who swears that, in Montreal in the early 1970s, he met an American who claimed to work for Langley and to have at least one source within the FLQ. According to the account, the FLQ member had been recruited while working as an informant for the RCMP. His name was never mentioned by any of the commissions of inquiry. A G Branch senior officer confirms that some informants recruited at the time remain unknown to the public.

The researcher and a Quebec expert in intelligence matters both say, however, that the CIA presence in Montreal wound down after 1972, by which time FLQ cells became in effect meetings of only informants of G Branch and the Quebec provincial police. Certain members of the Lévesque government claimed airily to have talked to CIA agents after the 1976 election; they were referring, however, to diplomats posted in Montreal and Quebec City who looked after the regular flow of diplomatic information.

However, there is no direct, verifiable evidence of an ex-agent or ex-officer in the CIA who was involved in an operation targeted at the PQ or the FLQ. The statement most often quoted in the few existing Canadian articles on the CIA in Canada is that of a former senior officer at Langley, Victor Marchetti. Employed in the office of CIA Director Richard Helms from 1966 to 1969, Marchetti stated that he had sometimes heard his colleagues "mention the Montreal base." (A "base," sometimes consisting of a single officer, is a branch of a station.) Were these people tending to the FLQ or the Soviets? Were they present with

RCMP approval or in secret? He does not know. When pressed, he admits to being uncertain even as to whether or not he actually heard the word "base" used. But, he adds, "I can't believe there wasn't one."

## A Statue in Danger

The idea that the CIA was working covertly in Montreal seems to have been supported by the fact that American FBI officers and agents had infiltrated leftist organizations in Canada. A black agent, Warren Hart, was a mole in Toronto's militant black groups: one of his colleagues, Joseph Burton, infiltrated the Canadian marxist-leninists.

The FLQ was the target of a third such operation in 1965, the biggest joint RCMP-FBI endeavour undertaken. A black officer in the New York Police Force, Raymond Wood, had infiltrated a small New York group of black nationalists, the Black Liberation Front. He had helped if not slightly encouraged his comrades to embark on a project to blow up several symbols of white America, including the Statue of Liberty in New York, the Liberty Bell in Philadelphia and the Washington Monument in Washington, DC. Militant black groups "always had grandiose ideas, but lacked the organizational skills to put them in motion," explains Frank Donner, a longtime investigator into FBI techniques who has worked mostly for the American Civil Liberties Union. "So police infiltrators helped them organize better."

Was Agent Wood inciting the Black Liberation Front members to attack national monuments and supply themselves with dynamite provided by their FLQ comrades, experienced in the delicate art of explosives? That was the defence raised at trial by the black militants and their lawyer, who accused the law enforcement agencies of having furnished Wood and black leader Robert Collier with the car they used to visit Montreal. Wood also supplied the group with a US Army manual on explosives and detonators. The Black Liberation Front and the FLQ had been in contact the previous year in Cuba, where Collier had met an FLQ sympathizer, Michèle Saulnier. She was the first person he sought out when he and Wood travelled to Montreal. Local FLQ members supplied him with enough explosives, according to experts, to disfigure the Statue of Liberty's head, or to knock off the hand which proudly holds her torch. The RCMP handled surveillance of the suspects during their travels in Canada.

FBI Director J. Edgar Hoover personally announced on February 17, 1965, the arrest of the suspects: the story made the front pages of major American newspapers. Three black militants and three *felquistes* were imprisoned. One FLQ detainee committed suicide in Bordeaux Penitentiary before his trial.

For the law enforcement agencies, cooperation had paid off. A complicated sting had led to the dissolution of an American revolutionary group, diminishing the popular sympathy that other black organizations enjoyed. Canadian police were able to incarcerate three FLQ sympathizers and beef up their files considerably.

Still, Wood, like Burton and Hart, had acted with the RCMP's blessing, not behind its back. He had simply passed through Montreal; he had not established a network there. And the FBI was too closely allied to the RCMP, needed its cooperation too much in a host of criminal cases, to sneak around behind its back. While the presence of FBI undercover agents in Canada is certain, it sheds no light on Langley's secret activities.

## Expo: Spies and Their World

Actually, CIA agents did come to Montreal from time to time for brief or extended periods. Experts from Langley's Cuba desk often came to meet their Montreal counterparts in the RCMP. After 1958, two agency workers, one man and one woman, were assigned to the American Consulate in Montreal for 18 months to help spot potential East-bloc agents in the flood of Hungarian immigrants fleeing to Canada after the 1956 revolt.

In 1967, the CIA was quick to respond to an RCMP request for a Soviet affairs expert who spoke fluent Russian. Jeff Gould's assignment was to help the Mounties keep track of fifty presumed intelligence officers among the personnel sent by East-bloc countries during Expo 67. He was also to be ready to greet any defector, whether from the group of fifty or among the many visitors from the East. Shortly after the close of the exhibition, Gould was posted to Rome, an assignment which made him the envy of his colleagues.

That much was certain. The rest of the picture, however, is far from clear.

On May 9, 1968, a Canadian Press story datelined Ottawa quoted an official source within the Canadian government as saying the CIA had recruited students on university campuses in Montreal to gather information about the independence movement. The Consul General in Montreal, Richard Hawkins, gave a series of interviews to deny the report. In a letter written some time later to a friend in the US diplomatic corps, Hawkins mentioned that he had been obliged "to give interviews to CJAD and CTV, and be quoted by Canadian Press, all to deny the old saw that the CIA has spies in Montreal. That's how it goes."

This comment by the late Mr Hawkins, private and unsolicited, would tend to rule out the presence of Langley people in Montreal — at least with the knowledge of American diplomats — were it not for the disturbing reaction of Hawkins' assistant, Harrison Burgess, when interviewed. Burgess, in Montreal from 1966 to 1971 and the target of an FLQ kidnapping attempt in March of 1970, denies that the CIA participated in the police investigation during the October Crisis, claims not to recognize the name Stanley Gray, and confirms Gould's presence at Expo, as well as the existence of the Ottawa station. His statement thus matches the rest of the data on all points.

But when asked about other CIA activities in Montreal, he avoids the issue, saying, "I really don't want to talk about it." While most diplomats state categorically that they know of no CIA activities in Quebec, Burgess makes it clear that he has not said everything there is to say.

Cleveland Cram, who, as mentioned, was responsible for Ottawa in the early 1960s and was posted there from 1971 to 1975, says he has reviewed station files dating back to 1960 and talked to his successor Stacy Hulse (1975-1977). He never found a trace of an infiltration operation. A CIA senior officer who oversaw Canadian matters until 1968, several workers on the Canadian desk at Langley during the 1960s, and officers posted to the station during the mid-1960s and mid-1970s, all now retired and all speaking openly in separate statements, swear that the agency has perfectly clean hands. Two FBI agents posted to Ottawa between 1969 and 1979 confirm that they never caught Langley people with their hands in the cookie jar, a development they would have had to report to FBI director and CIA foe J. Edgar Hoover.

(Beginning in March 1977, President Jimmy Carter's new CIA director, Stansfield Turner, reduced to the point of near nonexistence the clandestine side of the agency. Hundreds of professionals lost their jobs and numerous covert activities were terminated. One worker in the Ottawa station, a veteran of some fairly exciting missions elsewhere, paid with his own job for his refusal to draw up a list of other expendable employees. That a secret Quebec operation could have survived this wholesale purge is unimaginable. It was only in the spring of 1981, a year after the referendum on independence, that Turner's successor, William Casey, enthusiastically set himself to the task of rebuilding the agency's capacity for covert operations.)

## Difficult Conditions

The conviction that American agents infiltrated Canada and Quebec dies hard. Numerous factors, however, make such an infiltration highly unlikely, even if they do not rule it out.

A CIA presence in Montreal would have required an operation conceived and managed by a section of Langley which was separate from the normal operational networks, and which kept the organization and the results of its mission a complete secret, even from close collaborators of the agency director. The operation would have had to have been undertaken without the knowledge of the Canadian law enforcement agencies, in contravention of the bilateral cooperation agreement and behind the backs of the staffers both at the Ottawa station and on the Canadian desk at Langley. The operation would have had to have been so successful that it would have had to have escaped detection by the FBI's representatives and the G Branch informants within the independence movement.

"That's a possibility," declares Victor Marchetti, who believes that in such a case, only a few individuals would have been informed. Technically it was possible; it had been done elsewhere. The decision to send a small covert team to Montreal could have been made without White House authorization and, according to Marchetti, without informing the State Department. Keeping the Ottawa station in the dark would then have been simply an additional guarantee of the operation's success.

But to believe that all these conditions could have been met requires a considerable leap of faith. One must accept the idea — denied by all the Americans interviewed in the course of this investigation — that someone very powerful at Langley considered Quebec a short-term strategic threat to Washington.

All the same, high Canadian government officials remain ready to make that leap of faith. Ivan Head, advisor to Pierre Elliott Trudeau on international affairs from 1968 to 1978, maintains he would be "very, very surprised" to learn that American intelligence was not at work in Quebec, at least during the October Crisis. "We were both grown-ups," he says, referring to himself and Prime Minister Trudeau. "We know this sort of thing goes on."

In becoming Langley's close partner in intelligence matters, Canada must always keep in mind the unsettling side effects. In Head's words: your partner "will share everything with you, except what they're doing to you or on you."

# Part Two

# The Involved Spectator

*When I was asked to participate in the program today, to give the US government perspective on the Quebec situation, my reaction was not unlike the reaction of the preacher who was asked by one of the Sunday school pupils where the wives of Cain and Abel came from. The preacher responded: 'Young man, it's questions like that which are hurting religion.'*

JOHN ROUSE
American diplomat, making public
his government's position
on Quebec's independence

# 8
# Anguish at 24 Sussex Drive

*Every American statesman covets Canada.*
JOHN A. MACDONALD
FIRST CANADIAN PRIME MINISTER

*The Americans? 'What they have, they keep,*
*and what they have not, they want.'*
WILFRID LAURIER
FIRST FRENCH-CANADIAN PRIME MINISTER

November 15, 1976. The event Pierre Elliott Trudeau had been working to prevent since his entry into politics had come to pass. Six months after he had proclaimed the "death of separatism," Quebec had thumbed its nose at him. His old fraternal enemy, René Lévesque, had been brought to power. The sense of surprise was almost universal. With it came its old companion: fear.

Trudeau and Lévesque, these two incarnations of Quebec's destiny, could feel that fear on their respective banks of the Ottawa River, today a little wider, a little less navigable than yesterday.

Just before he mounted the stage to tell his joyful troops that this was a victory "we all hoped for in our hearts but didn't expect like this, so soon," René Lévesque seemed stunned by the sheer weight of the process he had set in motion. For the briefest moment, according to journalist Joan Fraser, who was watching from a few steps away, his expression betrayed a real, profound and paralytic fear. In Ottawa, the day after the political earthquake in Quebec, an observer read a similar emotion on the face of Pierre Trudeau.

Trudeau was "anxious" and "concerned" according to this witness; he wondered whether the Americans would seize the PQ victory as an opportunity to "redraw the boundaries of North America." "Obviously, he was anxious to see if the United States in fact believed it had a stake in the unity of Canada," remembers this witness, the American ambassador in Ottawa, Thomas Enders.

If the Prime Minister of Canada had invited the representative of the neighboring superpower to his office so soon after the PQ victory, it was because he understood that he could only hope to regain the initiative stripped from him the day before if the secessionists, now masters of Quebec, were deprived of Uncle Sam's encouragement. He asked Enders directly if the United

States genuinely believed its interests to be best served if Canada remained united. Ambassador Enders, at 45 a golden boy of American diplomacy, could not answer the question. He promised to inform himself.

Pierre Trudeau was not the only federalist to fear the formation of a Washington-Quebec axis. In the days that followed the election, the two most powerful businessmen in Quebec, the president of Power Corporation, Paul Desmarais, and the president of Canadian Pacific (and a director of 23 other companies), Ian Sinclair, paid Trudeau a visit to share their grief. They were none too cheerful. They agreed with Trudeau that Washington must be prevailed upon to side with the federalists. The Prime Minister asked both men to drop in personally on the ambassador.

When they met Enders, Desmarais and Sinclair explained that the United States could not afford to be without a stable, strong, unified neighbour. The ambassador was a little surprised by this gambit. "I think there were a lot of Canadians who weren't sure how we would react." The visit by the two men "gave me a better sense of the views of the business community," he says, as if there had been the slightest doubt as to the federalist leanings of Canadian businessmen.

Like Trudeau, Desmarais and Sinclair came away from Enders empty-handed. The American administration, in this election month, was poised between the defeated incumbent, Gerald Ford, and the unknown Georgian who had just taken the country by storm, Jimmy Carter. Pretty well every four years, between a new president's November election and the January inauguration, the United States puts the world on hold. The fate of Canada would be no exception.

## Guatemala 1954, Canada 1976?

Trudeau feared that he knew all too well what the Americans had up their sleeves. He had himself turned Canadian foreign policy upside down since taking power eight years before; he had made Canadian "national interest" rather than existing military alliances and commercial relationships, the basis for the country's international outlook. And now that philosophy would come back to haunt him. After all, there was no reason to think American "national interest" required the permanence of the Canadian union. History taught the contrary, quite clearly.

Teddy Roosevelt, the last of ten successive White House occupants to gaze upon young Canada with frank territorial ambition, had only left office 68 years before. His successor, William Taft, had sought a commercial reciprocity treaty which he was convinced "would make Canada only an adjunct of the United States." Officially speaking, the doctrine of "Manifest Destiny," which demands that Washington's influence extend over the entire North American continent, had found no defenders among American heads of state over the past half-century. But less than thirty years before the election of Lévesque and the *péquistes,* the Canadian prime minister who had the most contact with American presidents, Mackenzie King, had declared to his cabinet that he believed "the long-range policy of the Americans is to control the continent," to turn Canada into "a part of the United States."

No more than ten years before 1976, George Ball, principal aide to the American secretary of state, had drawn up plans in his office for a single

English-language state which would embrace the entire continent and beyond. This brilliant, well-respected strategist continued in the mid-1970s to state in public forums that a North American union was as inevitable as it was desirable.

Pierre Trudeau and his colleagues wondered how many other George Balls lurked in America's corridors of power. And now that a real, immediate opportunity had arisen to render one final homage to Manifest Destiny, would America hesitate?

Furthermore, since the beginning of the decade, one word weighed heavily on all politics: oil. The fuel of America's gluttonous economy had just yesterday been in the hands of countries which, if they were not quite friends, were at least easy to push around. Now this fuel had become the instrument of an aggressive international cartel: OPEC. Washington, London and Tokyo, in a view from which racism was not wholly absent, had not believed the Arabs could pull it off.

For years, Ottawa and Washington had been wrangling over a thorny issue: the gas pipeline which would connect Alaska, via Canadian territory, with the other American states. The legal wrangling stemmed from one basic problem: the presence of a foreign country between Alaska and the Midwest. Trudeau had himself exacerbated this situation when he raised by 250% the price of natural gas sold south of the border and made cuts, two years earlier, in Canada's petroleum exports to the United States. Oil rich Albertans now wondered more than ever what they stood to gain from belonging to Canada's confederation. There was oil also in Saskatchewan, in the Canadian North, and off Newfoundland's shores.

Teddy Roosevelt had believed that the Canadian west "should lie wholly within our limits [...] less for our sake than for the sake of the men who live there." Such sham altruism was amusing in the world of OPEC: how long would it take the Americans to realize that to their north a negligible 20 million Canadians claimed title to the greatest resource potential in the Western world?

As a member of the Club of Rome, Trudeau had hammered away at the theme of resource exhaustion. He had dreamed of the day when the western world, and especially Americans, would wake up and face this terrible reality. They suddenly had. And now, from the shores of the St Lawrence, they were being offered the keys to the store.

Pierre Trudeau belonged to the class of statesmen who know that all alliances are tactical. The first president he had dealt with, Richard Nixon, had not hesitated to strike a staggering blow to the Canadian economy by slapping a tax on all imports, as he felt American national interest required. His successor, Gerald Ford, had prevailed on the French — still troublesome, nine years after de Gaulle's visit — to admit Canadian into the select Group of Seven summit club. His was an accommodating but also a self-serving gesture: it was in the American national interest to have Canada on hand as a "junior partner."

Had Trudeau had a change of heart since writing, thirteen years earlier, "What makes you think the United States would react differently to Canada than to Guatemala, when national interest requires it and circumstances permit it?" In 1954, the Americans had financed, armed and lent air support to the overthrow of a Guatemalan reformer who was elected with 65% of the vote, but who had had the bad taste to confiscate the assets of an influential American company, United Fruit.

Canada's situation could be dramatically influenced by much more subtle measures. A little nudge was all it would take to give René Lévesque a running start and set the disintegration of the country in motion. "It's easy," comments a member of Trudeau's inner circle, Allan Gotlieb, then deputy minister of external affairs. "It doesn't have to come from the White House. You don't have to authorize it, [...] it's easy to have a diplomat say a few words of encouragement." Everyone would get the message. "The Americans had a tremendous opportunity for mischief. Tremendous."

If the separatists could barnstorm Quebec with the promise that, whatever happened, Washington looked upon the creation of their new state with a friendly eye, then the wheels would soon start falling off the federalist wagon. The pro-Americanism of Quebec's conservative voters was no secret. The idea of leaving Canada scared them, but leaving with American endorsement would be easier.

The conditions laid down by Trudeau — "when national interest requires it and circumstances permit it" — seemed to have been met. "If one foreign country [France] wanted it and thought they would gain by the dismemberment of Canada, and were contributing to it, it's quite conceivable another one could, too," Gotlieb says. In Ottawa, other top foreign policymakers were considering that scenario. "This idea frequently crossed one's mind," confirms the ex-ambassador to the United States, Charles Ritchie. "One wonders if the Americans wouldn't say, 'Look here, it would be much easier to deal with this northern neighbor if it were broken up into bits. Then we could do a deal with Quebec.'" "I believed in my heart of hearts that there was a view in the United States that the United States would be the big winners from the break-up of Canada," Gotlieb concurs.

The temptation seemed all the stronger at a time when Canadian-American relations were leaving a bitter taste in American mouths. In 1975, minister Mitchell Sharp had declared the death of the "special relationship" between Canada and the United States. With his boss, the Prime Minister, he hoped, in a sense, to "separate" Canada from North America and switch it to a "third option" approach to relations with Europe and Japan. This strategic shift was not well received in the United States, where the New York financial weekly *Barron's* roundly condemned the "anti-Americanism" taking hold of Canada. Trudeau had also taken time out in 1976 to shout "Viva Castro!" in Havana, a statement that had done little to boost his popularity in rabidly anti-Castro America.

That same year, William Porter, Enders' predecessor as American ambassador in Ottawa, had celebrated his departure by offering a venomous toast to a small group of reporters assembled for a farewell cocktail party. Abandoning the traditional pleasantries, Porter had set about listing in less than diplomatic terms the grievances his country harbored against Canada: the energy policy, first and foremost; the modest but irksome screening of foreign (i.e., American) investment; legislation which prevented American television stations from maximizing their income from prospective Canadian advertisers. Porter's list had been vetted and approved by both the State Department and the White House; his tone had been particularly sharp because, contrary to standard practice, Trudeau and his ministers had refused to meet with him before his departure.

They hoped for a more conciliatory successor, but instead got Enders. In his first public appearance in March of 1976, Enders stated frankly, "People on my side of the border have felt that their interests were not being taken into account" when the Canadians made their decisions. In June, he elaborated. "Canada can't simply cut back unilaterally on its relations with the United States and expect that there won't be a reaction from us." Finally, in September, Enders denounced the "paranoid style" in which Canadians formulated their American policy.

Given the friction generated by Enders and Trudeau, "René Lévesque had," in the words of a top federal civil servant "a lot going for him." His team was conscious of this fact several months before the election: Daniel Latouche, a sympathetic observer, wrote that they "hope to make the most of the tense climate which prevails today in Canadian-American relations." Federal apprehension might have been less intense if "Manifest Destiny" had been nothing but an old Yankee pipedream. But from sea to sea, Canada's English provinces indulged in fantasies of belonging to the great American family. Even Her Majesty's most loyal subjects were not immune to the idea.

On a tour of the Maritimes in 1964, an American diplomat posted in Ottawa could not believe his ears when the lieutenant governor of one of the provinces said of Quebec, "Let the bastards go. After all, you can always take us on as the fifty-first state." In 1976, a political party had come into being with a platform promoting independence for Canada's western provinces: some of its members called on the American ambassador to ask for his support. (He refused.) The premier of Alberta, Peter Lougheed, had been accused of seeking allies in Washington against Ottawa's energy policy. In New Brunswick, an anonymous group of businessmen asked a consulting firm to study the feasibility of annexing their province to the United States in the event of Quebec's secession.

Pierre Trudeau could see the entire game plan crumbling. He had predicted an end to the separatist threat, and he had thought nothing could stop him from achieving the goal he had sought for the past two years — a divorce from the American giant. The November 15 election was a sudden reminder of how much he needed his southern neighbor.

Trudeau's lack of interest in America was long-standing. On this, as on a hundred other levels, he was the antithesis of René Lévesque. One of his most brilliant chroniclers in Ottawa, Richard Gwynn, had this to say about Trudeau's relationship with all things American: "Of all Canadian Prime Ministers since Mackenzie King, Trudeau understood Americans the least and made the least effort to understand them. Official trips aside, he scarcely knew the country other than for its ski slopes and its Manhattan discos. He himself, as Joe Clark once observed deftly, wasn't so much a North American as a European who happened to grow up in Canada. Put more straightforwardly, Trudeau was a snob about Americans."

This was an attitude he could no longer afford.

## The Intuition of Mr Vine

The election of the Parti Québécois might well have taken Lévesque and Trudeau by surprise. Not Washington. "As far as we were concerned, this was all anti-climax," reported Richard Vine, who had replaced Rufus Smith as head of Canadian affairs at the State Department. He greeted the election of the PQ as though it were a simple change of season. "I found one of the funniest things that Ottawa was apparently flabbergasted by the election," he comments, and recalls "smirking in the way that one does that Ottawa might have been surprised but we weren't."

Vine had known nothing about Canada two years earlier. An expert in German affairs, he had replaced Smith when Kissinger's men stormed the fortress at the State Department and followed up with a diplomatic house-cleaning. Smith, realizing that no one was going to name him ambassador to Canada, took advantage of an administrative technicality to secure a comfortable early retirement.

Besides being in his superiors' good books, Vine had a further advantage over Smith: he spoke French. After two years in France during the war (he had witnessed the liberation of Paris), three years on a posting in Switzerland and four in Belgium, he was bilingual and a promoter of bilingualism. Vine was still only vaguely aware of the separatist phenomenon at the end of September 1976, when he had his eyes opened at a conference on Canadian-American relations at Niagara-on-the-Lake, Ontario. After a long day of discussions of the troubles afflicting the ties between the two countries, Vine and several others went out for dinner. One particularly engaging personality dominated the evening's conversation: André Fortier, an under-secretary in the office of the Secretary of State, the oddly-named Canadian department which administers federal bilingualism.

People accustomed to this sort of conference would agree that the dinner group was a good one. Apart from Vine, the senior American official responsible for Quebec, the party included William Diebold, senior fellow at the Council on Foreign Relations of New York; Al Hero, of Harvard, one of the few American authorities on Quebec; a fourth American whose name can no longer be traced; Fortier and two or three English Canadians, including one self-styled expert in Quebec politics. The discussion is singular in that it took place entirely in French and strictly among the four Americans and Fortier, as the other diners were unilingual. The next day, one of the excluded English-speakers would let Vine know that he was offended at the ill manners demonstrated by the little band of bilingual Americans.

It may be inaccurate to claim that a "dialogue" took place that evening; an "interview" is perhaps closer to the mark. Vine was fascinated by this Québécois whom he considered "articulate and bright and politically sensitive." Fortier explained the rise of nationalism and the need for a distinct, particular status for Quebec, introducing Vine to the ideas of Lesage and Daniel Johnson. He was convinced that the Parti Québécois would win, if not this time around — election rumors were rife in Quebec — then the next. Victory was inevitable. He explained gradualism (*étapisme*), the process by which Quebec would turn not necessarily into a state but into a partner, distinct from the other members of the federation. He informed Vine that the time was ripe for a step as decisive as the election of the PQ, although he confessed that he, Fortier, was a federalist. This statement only lent credence to his arguments.

Did he also explain the scandals besetting the Liberal Party of Robert Bourassa? Or the unanimous opposition that the Liberal leader had managed to provoke to his policies on issues like labour relations, language and political morality? Vine's subsequent recollections on these points would be less precise, but he became aware, whether through Fortier or otherwise, that these, too, were factors in the PQ's favor.

When Richard Vine returned to Washington, he convened the weekly inter-agency group which, under his chairmanship, was responsible for coordinating Canadian-American relations. Representatives from the Pentagon, the CIA, the White House and other government departments were on hand.

"There is, in my opinion, an extremely good chance that the Parti Québécois will win the next election," he announced. He might as well have told them that California was going to slide into the ocean. The reaction among the twenty or so officials present was one of utter disbelief. Those who had access to diplomatic dispatches knew that as recently as the previous April, René Lévesque had admitted to two American consuls posted in Quebec that victory would elude him. Showing them the results of internal polls, he expressed a hope of winning at least 35 seats, or about a third of the National Assembly; he did not think he could form a minority government unless some "third force" intervened. If René Lévesque himself was predicting defeat, why worry?

Since the October Crisis in 1970, the problem of separatism had in any case lost its urgency for American diplomacy. In the fall of 1972, the INR had produced a long study of the Parti Québécois, decorating the front cover with a nice photo of René Lévesque. But the report only predicted that the PQ would form the official opposition after the next election. The study, like all others prepared by the INR on Quebec, avoided the question of where American interest might lie in the matter, except to note that PQ finance wizard Jacques "Parizeau told our Consulate General in Quebec that, in drawing up the [recent] manifesto, the party wished to reassure the US on the character of an ultimately independent Quebec. The PQ also wished to demonstrate unequivocally that an independent Quebec would not be another Cuba and that it would remain a safe place for existing and future US investment."

In March of 1973, the consul general in Quebec City, visibly impressed by the PQ, reported that their most recent convention had yielded what was "probably the most professional program of any of the Quebec parties." The PQ, he added, had "more brains per square head" than their opponents, though he doubted that the voters would identify with these university types.

In July of 1973, the INR turned out another 20-page analysis; it was titled "Separatism quiescent but not dead." The document came to the general conclusion that "the majority in Quebec does not feel sufficiently threatened to seek separatism actively." Following the October 1973 election, another INR study — this one by a Québécoise working in Washington, Line Robillard Rosen — predicted that despite the injustice of a seven percent rise in popular support for the PQ and a one-seat reduction in its caucus (the party now had five percent of the seats but 30% of the popular vote), "there is little reason to believe that it [violence] will make a comeback."

Since then, the American diplomatic apparatus in Quebec had been in low gear on the independence question. At the end of 1975, Claude Morin, the high-ranking civil servant who had rallied to Lévesque's cause, assured one diplomat that the PQ counted at the very most "400 Marxists" in its ranks. Lévesque also assured the American envoys that in these radical times, he preferred to avoid formal ties between his party and the trade unions. So far as the "Foggy Bottom" was concerned, there was nothing but comforting news.

In the autumn of 1976, skeptics about the possibility of a *péquiste* victory could find further reassurance in René Lévesque's confidential statements to the Americans who had met him. He had assured them, for example, that despite Bourassa's new language law, Bill 22, Quebec's English-speaking voters would follow their "herd instinct" and support the Liberals once again. (He was wrong.) He said as well that Trudeau and Bourassa hated each other enough that "the federal Liberals might well back a third party in Quebec as an alternative to Bourassa." (Wrong again.) But apart from a minor lapse on the part of the consul general in Quebec, Terry McNamara, who referred to the Bourassa government in one dispatch as the "Bokassa regime," no one sensed an imminent political sea-change.

Vine had no use for such outdated information. He could feel that Quebec's hibernation was about to come to an end. His discussion with Fortier had crystallized his own observations and strengthened his conviction. He repeated his prediction to the little group of specialists. "I think the Parti Québécois is going to win the election in Quebec in the fall, and if it does, we will be immediately confronted with a series of major policy choices. We should get to work right now."

The attitude of the group grew from one of incredulity to one of resistance. "Immediately, everybody objected. Everybody, *sans exceptions*," Vine recalls. Prepare for the election of the PQ? They had spent fifteen years going out of their way *not* to prepare for it, during which time a terror of leaks and of a hysterical Canadian reaction had paralysed American diplomatic thinking. There was no way they were now going to overturn a policy that had been carved in stone since the early 1960s.

"I'm afraid I'm a very strong chairman," admits Vine, who had not meant to consult the group so much as to impose a plan of action on it. He gave John Rouse, head of the Canadian desk at the State Department, the job of consulting each of the government agencies represented at the meeting and producing, in collaboration with CIA analysts, "a very detailed study of what our interests in Canada are, how they would be affected by [Quebec independence] and what our recommended policy line should be." His request was unheard of: to analyse events in Quebec was one thing, but to define a line of policy that took Quebec's independence into account was another.

The initial reluctance by the American diplomatic establishment even to consider this working hypothesis arose in part from a sensitivity about the press. If a study on Quebec independence fell into the hands of *The Globe and Mail* or some other media organization, the fallout would be considerable. This was especially true since the Canadian journalistic community was "very parochial and provincial in the worst possible sense," according to Vine, who condemns the "idiocies" they write. The publication by a Canadian news organization of a study on the consequences of annexing British Columbia or Alberta would have had terrifying political consequences. It was infinitely better not to touch the subject.

Rouse, however, belonged to the brilliant, industrious strain of American diplomats. Within weeks, working with a small team of assistants, he had identified the various problems, assimilated the relevant information and condensed his findings into a couple of dozen pages.

Trudeau, Desmarais, Sinclair, Gotlieb and Ritchie had been right. When the Americans actually sat down and weighed the pros and cons of Quebec independence, they understood that the virtual disintegration of Canada was very possible. They saw other provinces sailing out of the Canadian harbor. This worry held true "particularly for British Columbia," says Vine. But Trudeau and the others were also wrong about one thing: annexationist fever did not burn at the State Department. In fact, it was practically a taboo. The idea of annexing Alberta, for example, "was never a point that ever had any currency in my tenure. I don't think it was even mentioned as a realistic possibility," remembers Vine.

On the contrary, the prospect of two or three or more Canadas worried Rouse's team, which foresaw in particular a compromised North American Air Defence Command (NORAD). Canada's combat forces, which had already shrunk under Trudeau's defence policy, would be cut into even smaller pieces, they reasoned. The logistical problems alone would be gigantic. "We could not see how we could carry out all the defensive matters embodied in NORAD, for example," with a Canada in halves like Pakistan, Vine recalls. Pakistan was "a case that was often cited" during the discussion, he says. From this standpoint, the complete dissolution of Canada "would have been the worst possible outcome for American policy," Vine declares.

The American political establishment was no longer driven, as in Teddy Roosevelt's day, by a thirst for territory. Quite the opposite. After the admission of Alaska and Hawaii to the union in 1959, any further addition to the country was destined to come up against a huge political outcry. The odds, for instance, that the District of Columbia would ever be granted statehood are minimal. Since it is certain that the black voters of the area would unfailingly elect two Democratic senators to represent them — thus giving the Democrats a permanent advantage in the 100-seat Senate, where majorities are often razor-thin — the Republicans can be counted on to oppose with vehemence the creation of a "State of Columbia."

Following this same logic, as early as the 1960s, the ex-ambassador in Ottawa, Walton Butterworth, had declared the annexation of Canada unthinkable. Knowing that Canadians were more social-democratic in their political outlook than the majority of Americans, he explained to an aide why the two countries were destined to remain separate: "Think, if we had ten or more states, the ten provinces of Canada, all voting Democratic because of an admiration for Roosevelt and Kennedy [...] the twenty extra Democratic Senators would tip our domestic balance [...] We have enough on our plate already."

The internal political realities of the United States now counted for more than the old dream of adding new territories, today seen as just another headache. "Maybe," a State Department official would admit in 1979, "if we could pick and choose, we'd take British Columbia. Its lumber would come in handy. Or Alberta's oil." The rest was not worth the political trouble.

Americans were often irritated by Canadians' views on the subject. "I got knocked around one night by the wife of a very senior Canadian official," recalls a CIA officer. "She said 'You aren't going to make Canada a fifty-first state.' 'Why in the hell do you think we'd let you in?' I answered. Next thing I knew, she was trying to convince me we had to let them in."

With Rouse's study in hand, Vine reconvened the interdepartmental group. The thorny issue of defence was discussed. Vine recalls, "As far as we were concerned, we wanted to see Canada remain united." That said, however, if Quebec "wanted to break away, they could have, and we would have managed."

With the interests of the United States thus defined, actual policy remained to be determined. What was the American government going to do and say if, a few weeks later, the Parti Québécois was elected?

It was at this point that the American diplomatic establishment, after fifteen years of watching Quebec, opted for caution. Having served in countries like Belgium and Switzerland, where cultural and linguistic conflicts were a way of life, Vine was convinced that there was "not a damn thing that any external factor can do except make both parties be mad at you."

The choice of reactions was thus limited. But choosing the terminology for an American statement, as innocuous as it was meant to be, was no easy matter. The modest words chosen to relay American policy in fact contained not the substance, but the echo, of all past debates. One could read as much from what was missing as from what was there.

The American "line," in its initial presentation, consisted of two elements. First, the Quebec question was an internal problem for Canada, and the United States had full confidence in the ability of Canadians to deal with it. The key word here was "Canadians." Washington, unlike Paris, did not openly recognize the exclusive right of Quebeckers to determine the outcome. The State Department wanted above all to avoid getting mixed up in a debate on the right of self-determination. Second, the United States admired the strength and vigor of the Canadian confederation. It was "the best neighbor we could have." The endorsement of Canadian unity was clear but indirect; there was no grand declaration of solidarity with Ottawa, and no promise of involvement. Nor were there any apocalyptic warnings.

These few sentences were assembled into a brief memorandum of policy widely distributed within the administration. Rouse's study, on the other hand, was copied only a few times and remained in a drawer, far from prying eyes.

When the polls opened in Quebec on November 15, the US State Department was ready.

## Iron Fist, Velvet Glove

Clausewitz's rule applies to all emergency projects and to all contingency plans. "When war begins, reality takes over," the German strategist had said. When the Parti Québécois came to power, and when Pierre Trudeau met Tom Enders, the American ambassador took it for granted that — notwithstanding Vine's prescience and all the accompanying preparation — everything had changed. Yesterday the questions had been hypothetical; today, the future of a country was at stake. Now faced with a question put to him by the prime minister of a neighbor-state in grave danger, the ambassador refused to commit his government before consulting its leaders directly. Perhaps, as well, he thought that as the senior American representative in Canada, he ought properly to propose a policy himself.

His conclusions were not opposed to those in the memorandum of policy, but they differed on important details. And Enders would rely on his own reconnaissance work. Of the Rouse study he says: "I knew of it, but I don't know how widespread its effects were in the US government, and I can't recall its conclusions."

After his discussions with Trudeau, Desmarais and Sinclair, Enders left for Washington. That November he met Vine, who restated his views. He met Henry Kissinger, the outgoing secretary of state, and Brent Scowcroft, the President's national security advisor, also about to leave his post. He also met with members of Jimmy Carter's transition team. No one in this round of consultations saw American interests being served by the disintegration of Canada.

Enders proposed a two-track policy. First, for public purposes, a dead calm. "We didn't want to make any aggressive statements," he explained. "We could see no advantage at all in taking a public stand." It was to be stressed that this was a Canadian problem which the Canadians would solve. But some care was called for, because "it would be wrong for us to leave the impression that [...] if there were two Canadas that emerged, we'd say, 'Oh fine, we can accommodate ourselves with that.'" Which was in fact exactly what they would have said, but for the time being they were letting it be known that the United States was "not indifferent." It should be clear, as Pierre Trudeau was arguing, that the US had an interest in continued Canadian unity.

As for the private posture, a second track would be used. Here the US would make their presence more strongly felt. Enders and a few others, fearing an all-out campaign by the new Quebec government to win American support, set out to throw up some ideological barriers. They contacted the major newspapers in Washington, New York, Chicago and Boston, and outlined to the opinion-makers their freshly-minted policy: "The US government was not interested in seeing an even-handed approach to a newest independent state north of the border, and that should not be the result of a visit by Mr Lévesque to any part of the United States." Tom Enders remembers: "We were quite active in this regard."

Enders recruited *The New York Times,* an ally of invaluable influence in tilling the political soil. Political columnist James "Scotty" Reston, one of the heavyweights of American journalism, shared Enders' desire to make the going rough on René Lévesque's road through America. James Reston was a friend of Lester Pearson, whom he had met at the beginning of the 1950s, when the future prime minister was ambassador in Washington. Reston remained on hand to console Pearson in later years, when Lyndon B. Johnson was making his life miserable. One of the few Americans to take an interest in Canadian affairs, James Reston now became, after the PQ victory, one of the staunchest allies of Canadian federalism in the American press.

The most urgent item of business was to prepare René Lévesque's New York audience. In late 1976 and early 1977, there was much excitement about his upcoming appearance before an important Manhattan forum, the Economic Club. This speech was seen as the kick-off of the separatist effort to sway American opinion.

Enders, Reston and a few others "spent a considerable amount of time on the telephone," the ambassador remembers, contacting "important members of his audience, insurance companies, banks," and outlining for them the official American position. Enders undertook the job all the more willingly because the

Carter team had let it be known, even before the new President's inauguration, that it "agreed with the approach" he had put forward.

Between his numerous trips to Washington during the fall and winter, Ambassador Enders returned to see the Prime Minister and assured him of the favorable result of his efforts: "We handled it very much the way you think we should." The two men then discussed at length the extent to which the Americans ought to participate in the Canadian debate. "We thought that it would be destructive to have the United States appear to be the guarantors, in some sense, of Canadian unity," he remembers. Enders promised that his government would subtly see to it that between Quebec and the US, "no separate channels, separate commercial and investment arrangements and so forth, were opened up." If the *péquistes* came knocking on Washington's door, it would be slammed in their faces. Under no circumstances would the PQ be given the American card to play.

At the same time, it was important that American companies not adopt the defeatist attitude of the Montreal English business community by fleeing the province, as numerous English-speakers were already doing. Though the every-man-for-himself impulse was undoubtedly less strong among Americans than among native English Montrealers, Enders still participated in "a fairly large number of discussions with American corporations" to urge them to keep up their levels of activity in Quebec. For the most part, they did. Enders advised them as well to be good citizens and as such to respect the letter of Quebec's new language law, Bill 101. He repeated this advice in impeccable French during a speech to the Montreal Chamber of Commerce in March.

America's Quebec policy thus boiled down to the proverbial iron fist in a velvet glove.

If the need had arisen, Enders explains, Washington could have stripped off the glove and shown its metal. "If it had been necessary, we might have gone to the extreme" of an outspoken public stance. "If we had been asked by Canada in the early stages of the crisis to take a more forceful stance, I have no doubt that we would have." But, he adds, "we didn't think the situation was getting out of hand." And the Canadian Prime Minister thought intervention unwise.

In short, Trudeau and Enders were suddenly getting along like a house on fire. The two men nonetheless made an odd pair. "You couldn't say they liked each other very much," comments Enders' former principal assistant, Robert Duemling. A Dutch ambassador, called upon several months after his arrival in Canada to give his first impression of the country, observed the single quality which united and divided the two men: "The two most arrogant individuals in Canada are Pierre Trudeau and Tom Enders," he reported.

Still, from 1977 on, Trudeau and Enders' dealings were cordial. When Enders' controversial public utterances were criticized by government minister Eugene Whelan, Pierre Trudeau rallied to the ambassador's side, declaring that he "respected" this "gentleman" who was "doing his duty" in expressing his opinions without qualification.

Paul Desmarais and Ian Sinclair, previously busy recruiting Enders to the federalist cause, now became go-betweens for the new political duo. They were used, Enders explains, as "a way in which statements I could make to Trudeau directly and personally could also be sent through others. That was useful. I did not want to appear to be — and I'm sure Mr Trudeau didn't want me to appear to be — going over to see him all the time." Desmarais and Sinclair thus became the best-dressed messenger boys in the world. They saved Enders and Trudeau from having to meet alone more than "about once a month," according to Enders' guess, which was already quite a lot.

Pierre Trudeau had won an important battle in winning over Enders. He had not, he knew, entirely won the guerrilla war breaking out on the American front. What of the powerful American Congress, where some of Trudeau's most vociferous critics had their stronghold? And could Enders, who was associated with the Republicans through past service, really speak for the new Democratic administration, whose members — especially the intriguing "Georgia mafia" brought along by the President from his home state — were still an unknown quantity?

Trudeau wanted at all costs to avoid becoming the butt of Georgia's most famous line: "Frankly, my dear, I don't give a damn." As long as the new President had not declared from the presidential rostrum that he was in favor of a united Canada, Trudeau would only feel half reassured. He arranged to meet Carter on February 21, 1977. And he stopped provoking his new-found friend; Trudeau the traditional party-pooper, Trudeau the supercilious, gave way to the United States' most pleasant neighbour. It was now crucial not to give the Americans any reason for wishing Canada would go away. Soon the Foreign Investment Review Agency was being so soft on American companies that *Barron's* was led to proclaim: "The only foreign company that wouldn't be welcome in Canada is Murder Inc." Canadian advertisements reappeared on American television. "Third option" diplomacy evaporated. Ties with Washington were once again "the most important of all our foreign relations," according to Trudeau. Canadian energy policy was suddenly more flexible. In early 1977, when a cold wave swept across the continent, Trudeau opened the petroleum taps to a grateful America. And the Alaska pipeline would finally be built. Sensing an opening, the canny Enders even disinterred the old chestnut of free trade and began to talk of the "convergence" of North America's two economies. Times had changed.

Trudeau had good reason to move cautiously. The entire American diplomatic establishment had not fallen in line behind Enders. At the end of January, when John Rouse was sent to Chicago to inform a group of businessmen on the American policy in the Quebec matter, no fist was visible in the folds of the velvet glove.

"The US government does not have anything to say about Quebec and its future in Canada, except that this is uniquely and entirely a Canadian problem. It's a problem to be dealt with by Canadians, with Canadian interests in mind and without any meddling from the United States, well-intentioned, inadvertent or otherwise," Rouse declared.

His talk in Chicago had been planned primarily as a response to pronouncements made by one of the most pro-American members of the new PQ cabinet, Rodrigue Tremblay. The minister of industry and commerce, author in 1969 of a book advocating the formation of a Quebec-US common market, Tremblay was now telling whoever would listen to him that the *péquistes* enjoyed "good contacts within the American government," and that American officials supported Quebec independence because they considered the east-west orientation of the Canadian economy artificial. North-south connections, which favored a separate Quebec, would be more "natural."

The Parti Québécois "wanted to create the impression that they had some support from the United States. That was precisely the kind of problem we wanted to avoid," Vine recalls. So he sent Rouse to Chicago "with clear instructions to make sure that view was not maintained."

Rouse answered Tremblay with a statement that his government saw on its northern border a Canada that was "vigorous, self-confident, independent and actively engaged internationally." As far as Quebec contacts in Washington went, he resorted to the party line: "Ottawa still represents Quebec in Washington," a fact which was "a fundamental principle that the US government can be expected to continue to respect."

The head of the Canadian desk nonetheless complimented the new Quebec government by stating that the Quebec problem "is in the hands of responsible leadership on both sides."

Two months after the election of the Parti Québécois, the American diplomatic establishment resorted to two different strategies: the veiled interventionism of Enders and the more marked neutrality of Vine and Rouse. Not until the meeting between Pierre Trudeau and Jimmy Carter would this divergence be settled. In the meantime, the crucial absent figure from these discussions and decisions, the man who had caused the problem in the first place, René Lévesque, would make a spectacular entrance on the American scene.

# 9

# Roughed up
# on Wall Street

*Yeah, well, it won't be a cakewalk, eh?*
RENÉ LÉVESQUE,
after his speech in New York.

At two in the morning, the man walked alone in the cold New York night. Unaware of the sirens which tore through the city, he could only think of the disaster that had just taken place before his eyes. He did not care that he would be blamed for it; he had played the scapegoat often enough. Sucking on the pipe which never left him, Claude Morin could well have been a Broadway director waiting at the newsstand for the first editions to appear with the reviews that would make or break his show.

But Quebec's minister of intergovernmental affairs hardly needed to see the newspapers. He already knew that the star of the new Quebec government cast had just, as the *Baltimore Sun* would put it, "laid an egg" at his international debut. If he bothered to look at the front page of *The New York Times* arriving on the stands, Morin would see a memorable quotation from one member of the stony audience. "The man is seditious," the unidentified spectator had said. "He's got to be stopped."

The day before, Morin had known that Quebec diplomacy stood before the steep hill of American opinion. Tonight, faced with a wall, he was left with only one strategy: to get out his climbing gear.

## The Euphoria of Victory

The new Quebec premier had hardly recovered from his election-night emotions of November 15 when the invitation from the Economic Club arrived on his desk. It was a prestigious forum, to which only true heavyweights were invited. Anyone who wanted to compile a Who's Who of the American financial oligarchy only had to copy the diners' names at one of the club's annual meetings. Now these New York bigwigs wanted the little *Gaspésien* to be their guest of honor. What could be more flattering?

"PQ sources claim [former premier] Bourassa long sought the opportunity to address the prestigious Economic Club," reported Consul General Terry McNamara from Quebec City. "Lévesque, after only two months in office, has succeeded in breaking into this golden circle, they happily chirp. However, the same publicists neglect to mention that the reason for Lévesque's early invitation is the uncertainty which now exists in New York financial circles about a PQ-governed Quebec."

Lévesque did not hesitate to accept the invitation. Since the days of Jean Lesage, it had been traditional for Quebec's new leader to introduce himself to Manhattan shortly after his election. Even Claude Morin, who only learned in December that the invitation had been received and accepted, did not think for an instant about breaking the protocol with an initial excursion to Paris. The first pilgrimage would be southward. No one questioned, either, the choice of audience. Another forum, academic or diplomatic, would have offered a softer landing. But for the moment, the Lévesque team was still flying high on "the euphoria of victory," as principal secretary Louis Bernard notes. They had only just taken off, and nobody was thinking seriously about a crash.

And in any event, Lévesque would be in his element in the America he knew so well. "When we talked about it, he didn't see how the Americans would have any problem with an independent Quebec," remembers his old friend Yves Michaud. "There's no question he had faith in his ability to explain it to them," he adds.

On January 23, on the eve of their departure, Morin walked the few steps that separated his office from the premier's. It was a walk he made regularly toward six o'clock in the evening to exchange impressions and discuss strategy. Lévesque sat writing at his desk. A conversation took place which reveals much about the confusion that reigned in the premier's office.

"I don't want to bother you, you've got work to do," Morin said.

"No problem," the premier replied. "I'm writing the New York speech."

"What, the damn New York speech isn't already done?" exclaimed Morin, who knew Lévesque well enough not to mince words.

"Well, I'm doing it right now so it will be ready for translation."

The minister responsible for Quebec's foreign relations, a man whose speeches were always written a month in advance, was shocked.

"Are you telling me that with a day and a half to go, it isn't finished yet?"

It was not finished. It had only just begun.

First, there was the dress rehearsal. On the evening of January 24, the day before the big speech, Lévesque, his new Finance Minister Parizeau and several others went to the Links Club in New York to meet the twenty-five Americans who together wielded the greatest economic power over Quebec. They represented major investors like Prudential Insurance and Metropolitan Life, which held hundreds of millions of dollars' worth of bonds issued by Hydro Quebec or the Quebec Treasury. It was their money that was paying for thousands of workers to build the immense dams of James Bay; it was their money that was paying the salary increases wrung out of Robert Bourassa by the common front of public sector employees. Since November 15, these institutional lenders had been losing sleep. Tonight, they wanted the new leader of Quebec to calm their nerves. They had the wrong man.

How could one blame them? They were used to the little game played by Jean Lesage, Daniel Johnson and Robert Bourassa, who were fiery in Quebec but always turned down the heat when they came to New York. "We say things at home, but you shouldn't take us too literally," the premiers invariably explained, according to Claude Morin, who, as a civil servant, had always accompanied them south. "It wasn't a repudiation, it was just a soft-pedal," he says. But René Lévesque did not know — or did not yet know — how to play the keys softly. The further he got from home, the harder he hammered away.

Lévesque was by no means awed but certainly nervous when he fired his opening salvo. Independence, he said, was certain. "Quebec and Canada can't go on like two scorpions in a bottle," he told the assembled investors. Hearing this opening shot, Jacques Parizeau joined the fray: "For all practical purposes, the federal government doesn't exist anymore." To supporters of the status quo, these words came as a slap in the face. "What really bothered them," notes Morin, who was present, "was that for the first time they were meeting someone who told them, 'Listen, that's what I said in Quebec City and that's what I mean!'"

Their anxiety could not have been deeper. While Lévesque was talking to them about the blessings of independence they were seeing columns of figures in red ink and steepening downward curves on imaginary graphs. "There were some at the table," remembers Joe Wilson of the securities firm Merrill Lynch, "who thought an independent Quebec would default on its debts." That was a nightmarish scenario; at the time, Quebec and Hydro led the field as the biggest borrowers on the New York market. If it occurred, a default would be historic.

"How do you expect on this basis to repay your obligations?" one businessman asked in a tone that bordered on the offensive. But Lévesque hit back and spoke of the "absolute necessity" for Quebec to set out on the road to sovereignty. "It's fine for you to be saying you're going to be doing this for a whole lot of philosophical reasons," the listeners responded, according to Wilson, "but what about all the people who have loaned you money and are going to end up with bonds that may be worthless? You haven't thought about that."

Far from quivering ecstatically at the dawn of a new nation, they shook in fear for their investment, for the return on their portfolio, their end-of-year bonus, their photo in the financial press. They could hear the competition crowing, "You know, What's-his-name had two billion in James Bay. Poor guy. They transferred him to Bonn. Not Zurich, Bonn!" A guffaw and then, "One more martini for the road?"

The discussion took a hostile turn. Lévesque was not particularly surprised; he himself had no affection for the people around him. "It's clear he didn't like bankers," says Alex Tomlinson, who, at First Boston, coordinated Quebec's money-raising activities in New York. "He saw them as a sort of powerful elite from which he was excluded. For him, these people were the enemy because they incarnated capitalism." At one point he told them, "We don't ask you to sympathize with us. We ask you to understand us as we achieve the same the same kind of independence you did 200 years ago." A participant declared the comparison with American independence ridiculous. "You're not being subjected to abuses" like the thirteen colonies in 1776, whose economies had been deliberately throttled by London's taxes. "Canada has a history of good, stable government."

The portfolio manager sitting directly across from Lévesque got carried away and slammed his fist into the table. "I felt like telling him to shut up," Wilson recalls. Lévesque's response was along the lines of "You can't tell us what to do." He peppered his comments with "bloody hell" and "Goddammit," expressions he thought indispensable in English but which sat wrong with this rather proper group. In Washington, influential people swear like longshoremen. But among New Yorkers, the real swordplay lays in subtle, well-turned phrases. Wilson, who sold Quebec bonds at Merrill Lynch and whose job it was to establish connections between his client and the investors around the table, was naturally on edge.

"What we do with our political situation is our business and none of yours," René Lévesque announced. "What we do with our money is our business," a banker shot back, "and none of yours."

Excluded from the closed-door affair, a pack of journalists were waiting for the premier at his hotel. He announced that the encounter had been "a success" and added, with his flair for understatement: "What struck me — and those were prominent people — is that compared with their counterparts in Canada, the Americans have fewer hang-ups about the Quebec situation. If they have something to say, they just say it."

That evening, Claude Morin tried again, in vain, to get his hands on a copy of the big speech. He did not suspect that, with a few minor variations, he had just heard it.

## Watching the Avalanche

The next day, René Lévesque visited the economic stations of the cross. With Tomlinson as his guide, he met important investors, bankers and representatives of large insurance companies. In the afternoon he met David Rockefeller, president of the Chase Manhattan Bank, then the leading bank in America. Lévesque felt no more at home than he had the day before. "He had darkish beige suede Wallabee kind of things," which ruined the effect of his otherwise very proper suit, remembers Tomlinson, who, like everyone else on Wall Street, dressed according to the code of the Northeastern ruling class: not a hair out of place, no demeaning clodhoppers poking out from under the impeccable trouser-crease. And Lévesque, his sparse hair uncombed, went from appointment to appointment in a brown leather overcoat, "which isn't done on Wall Street, either," says Tomlinson, who still smiles at the memory.

That morning the premier's words were more sober. Tomlinson heard him talk about "getting a better deal with Canada" and listened to him soft-pedal the independence theme. "We're not crazy enough to ruin our economy and our ability to borrow by doing something that you people in the investment community wouldn't understand and appreciate," Tomlinson remembers him saying. The statement only made the shock that came a few hours later all the more stunning.

While Lévesque was visiting the nerve centres of capitalism, Morin, in a little conference room, had finally gotten his hands on a copy of his speech. It was a disaster, he saw immediately. "We could scrap this paragraph," he thought, "but then this one would have to go, too, and then the whole thing would have to be overhauled." The text, benignly entitled "Quebec: A Good Neighbor in Transition," had already been printed and was being distributed under embargo to journalists. At best, it would be possible to rearrange the punctuation and add a line or two. During a meeting called specifically to review the speech for the first and last time before it was delivered, a Hydro Quebec representative read the document. He did so, he remembers, "with a tight feeling." Quebec's image in

New York was largely built around Hydro Quebec. According to the representative, Hydro had issued "a whole lot of paper" (i.e., bonds) in New York, and its credibility was at stake. He proposed two additions to the speech, one on Hydro and one extolling Quebec's hospitality to foreign capital. Morin agreed. "Absolutely right, absolutely right, I'll tell Mr. Lévesque ..."

Morin then came across Claude Ryan, the "pope" of *Le Devoir.* He had read the speech; he feared it would not do. It was awkward, poorly thought-out, ill-adapted.

But the time had come to assemble in the grand ballroom of the Hilton. Lévesque was playing to a packed house; it had taken some effort to find room for the large Canadian journalistic contingent in the overstuffed balcony, not to mention the local media, more curious than impressed. Scribes and cameramen paced impatiently, shunted off to one side.

As Lévesque emerged from the guests' suite where he had just been greeted by executives of the Economic Club, a local television crew was waiting for him in a corridor supposedly off-limits to the press. A floodlight went on and the reporter — something of a celebrity on New York television — held out a microphone and began to ask a question. He did not have time to finish it.

"A guy who came out of nowhere intervened roughly, to say the least," remembers Robert Mackay, an advisor to the premier who was caught in the confusion. The unknown man, who was powerfully built and in black tie like everyone else, manhandled the journalist and sent the camera flying. There were shouts about "the freedom of the press," Mackay remembers. The videotape kept rolling and the scene was recorded; the clip would be replayed on television that night and during the days that followed, giving the impression of a politician who had unleashed his thugs on the press. Mackay suspected a set-up. Who had let the crew into the corridor? The journalist wanted to know who had attacked him. He complained about it in a New York tabloid.

The chain of events which unleashed the stranger in the tuxedo probably began in Dorval. There, on January 23, someone at the airport heard two individuals, one white, one black, threatening to kill the premier of Quebec during his visit to the Economic Club. Worried, the witness called the New York Police Department, which relayed the information to the local FBI office. But René Lévesque was not an American. He could not benefit from American police protection without being expressly designated an "official guest" of the government. The FBI threw the Lévesque ball into the State Department's court on January 24. Two days later, the chief of protocol, Shirley Temple Black — the same Shirley Temple who had starred in the early talkies — determined that "injury to the person or property of Mr René Lévesque may adversely affect the foreign relations of the US." The Quebec premier thus became an "official guest." In New York, his room and the grand ballroom were searched for explosives, and a member of the New York Police Department's intelligence service was assigned to cover his movements. When the plain-clothes policeman "on duty" for the evening saw the television crew approaching where they should not have been, he may have decided to play rough. In his report, at any rate, the camera-tossing did not merit even a passing mention. "At no time during Lévesque's visit to New York City were there any incidents involving the premier," declares an FBI memo.

Lévesque was already "visibly out of sorts," according to Mackay; he was irritated at having to put on a rented tuxedo, which he detested, and the incident in the corridor further spoiled his mood. "This speech was rough," Mackay concludes. "We were treated roughly in Quebec to get the speech written, and we were roughed up in New York before it was delivered."

Lévesque mounted the podium; the lights came up; his image was retransmitted live to the television screens of Quebec and Canada. "The primary objective" of his government was "the political sovereignty of Quebec," he began. Having repeated in New York what he had said in Quebec City, René Lévesque passed to the historical comparison that would take up the entire first part of his speech. Its aim was to set the listeners' patriotic hearts beating to Quebec's rhythm. "I can find nothing more striking, by the way, than the many analogies between the psychological climate felt in Quebec today" and "the American atmosphere of 200 years ago."

The room froze but the speaker did not; he went on to quote to the Americans the preamble, which they knew by heart, of their own Declaration of Independence. Grasping at this sacred text, he explained that the question "is not *whether* Quebec will become independent, nor indeed *when* it will happen, but rather *how,* in due time, Quebeckers can be expected to take full charge of their own political affairs."

He was halfway through the speech when he raised general economic questions. He promised to limit the growth of the Quebec deficit and made a brief reference to Hydro. Following the advice of First Boston, he confirmed in passing his support of the James Bay project, which he had once forcefully criticized. But he did not say, as First Boston had begged him to, that Hydro's purse would remain outside the government's greedy hands. "If the situation becomes delicate," he had said some weeks earlier in an imprudent admission to *Business Week,* "there is money on hand; Hydro Quebec has money." This little sentence of Lévesque's, this threat of an assault on Hydro funds by Quebec and of a consequent weakening of the world's most indebted power corporation, was what "most bothers the financial community" in New York, declared one club member in private that evening. But here again, the premier was only being candid; in the succeeding years, government encroachment on Hydro would indeed grow exponentially.

Coming next to the thorny issue of foreign investment, Lévesque gave mixed signals and succeeded only in creating a muddle. "There is one strange belief that we suffered from for too long, a sort of institutionalized belief that our economy could only be developed by outsiders," he said, hardly flattering his audience. But the PQ was "quite ready to accept" foreign investment, even more than was now the case with the federal government, he added hospitably. Next he threw open the gates of uncertainty by announcing to his hosts that he would establish an "investment code" to determine in which economic sectors foreign investment would be welcome and which sectors would be "completely or partly reserved for domestic ownership." With the investors waiting for an elaboration, Lévesque offered them vagueness: foreign capital would be excluded "in such sensitive sectors as banking institutions and things like mass media, publications, etc., that have a direct impact on cultural development." Just what did he mean by "such as," "things like," and "et cetera"?

Lévesque added to the confusion by stipulating that this system of sectors would "needless to say" be applied only when "independence gives us the full set of policy tools required." Obviously, he could not specify a date.

In the meantime, "we do not intend to launch any policy of nationalization" except in the case of one asbestos company. "So, in a nutshell, we are not against foreign investment as such." Had he added: "Unfortunately, it is sometimes a necessary evil," he would have completed his thought.

After some polite applause, the master of ceremonies thanked the speaker for "his informative and reassuring speech." That did it. The audience, until then attentive and on edge, broke into waves of laughter.

### In The Frog Pond

"We thought we were going to get assurances that our investments in Quebec are safe. Instead, he threw us a quote from our own Declaration of Independence," complained a vice president of a major bank, Manufacturers Hanover, to the first journalist he saw. The Quebec situation was not comparable to American independence, he added. "We see it more akin to our Civil War."

In private, things were even worse. Once the big show was over, Lévesque, Parizeau and a small group of others were received by the president of the club. The American businessmen on hand showed definite symptoms of ideological indigestion. A few steps from the premier, one captain of industry declared that he was not likely to invest in an expansion of his Quebec plants. Another senior executive likened Lévesque's ambitions to those of "Kenya or Ethiopia or some West African state." Another banker accused the premier of economic blindness.

Elizabeth Harper, the consul general in Montreal, had made the trip so she could take the pulse of the crowd herself. She diagnosed hypertension. One participant who had attended the performances at both the Links and Economic clubs called Lévesque "crazy" and, not wanting to be attired with the same epithet, swore to advise his company against buying Hydro Quebec bonds. The vice president of another firm admitted to Harper that "his company had previously thought Lévesque could be pushed around and made to respond to financial realities. After his speech and feedback from private meetings, he said that this was obviously not the case, and that Lévesque scared the hell out of them." Two other senior financial people told Harper that Lévesque had given the impression that "separation was the be-all and end-all of the PQ, a goal to be achieved regardless of costs."

On the emotional Richter scale, the English Canadians on hand registered the highest disturbance. The Consul General in Toronto, John Diggins, observed on his television screen "the obvious pent-up anger" of Bruce Phillips, who was reporting on the event in New York for CTV. Diggins heard reporters reciting long quotations from unnamed Canadians who spoke of "sedition and treason." One of these, seated at the head table not far from Parizeau, was the head of A.E. Ames, the Canadian brokerage firm which represented Quebec in the financial markets of Montreal, Toronto and Vancouver. He would later tell Diggins that "formerly, such folk as the premier would have been strung up by the neck for such insurrectionist statements." The man seemed to feel, says Diggins, "that perhaps Lévesque deserved the same, but current custom prevented it."

Peter C. Newman, editor of *Maclean's* and author of *The Canadian Establishment,* was "in a state of advanced frenzy," says Morin, who bore the brunt of his outrage after the speech. "He was beside himself. That a Canadian should say such things in the United States, he saw as treason against Canada." Like a jealous husband, English Canada was hurt enough when there was talk of divorce in the privacy of the bedroom. But when the Latin spouse started sharing the domestic problems with the people next door, that was too much. A few minutes later, Newman announced on the air that the speech marked "the beginning of the end" for Lévesque. In his editorial in the following issue of *Maclean's,* Newman threw his best punch: "The mask slips, and René Lévesque stands revealed as a fanatic in a rented tux, a wild faun caught eating broccoli." Knowing that Morin usually wrote the speeches for Quebec premiers in foreign countries, Newman held him personally responsible for Lévesque's disaster.

Not all of English Canada was quite so indignant. On the evening of the speech, Diggins called Marshall McLuhan, world guru on the media. The eminent Canadian termed Lévesque's speech "cool-headed" and was surprised to hear the press shouting about "extremism."

*Le Devoir*'s Claude Ryan, even more worked up than he had been during the afternoon, also sought out Morin. "It was a partisan speech," he said. "That wasn't the premier of Quebec talking, that was the leader of the PQ." Morin could hardly contradict him. Writing speeches for his bosses, he had always practised the delicate art of "distinguishing between premier and party leader." Now he himself thought that Lévesque had spoken not in the name of Quebec but rather, he believed, in the name of "those in Quebec who were supporters of the PQ."

Back at his hotel, Lévesque had no second thoughts. He was "glad he'd roughed them up," remembers Morin, who did not conceal his ill humor. "Lévesque had the attractive quality" of being thoroughly anti-establishment, his former minister says. When he could "heave a brick into the frog pond, offend the constipated diplomats, the businessmen, the establishment, he was tickled." He really did not want to hear Morin scold him for having managed all by himself, in twenty-hour hours, to build a wall of American moneymen opposed to Quebec. So he cut Morin short with the remark he often used when he was in a fix and out of arguments: "If they don't like it, let 'em eat shit. There." At times like this, "there was no point in talking, it was useless," says Morin, who, still upset, went out for a long walk to vent his anger.

The next day, the effects of the Economic Club fiasco began to be felt. The president of one investment bank ordered his people in Quebec to move to Toronto and to sell all the bank's Quebec assets. His executives in Toronto and Montreal managed to calm him down, telling him it was too soon to "cut and run."

On the stock market, shareholders in the American company Johns Manville, Quebec's largest asbestos producer, had heard Lévesque mention nationalization. They dumped half a million of their shares that day, knocking 14% off the company's total share value. Johns Manville was one of the 30 stocks on the Dow Jones Industrial Index, principal barometer of the New York Stock Exchange. The company's drop in share price was the principal reason for a downturn on the Dow Jones, which lost nearly 1% of its value, bringing the volatile index into what brokers called "resistance zone," below which the whole medium-term performance of the stock market could be jeopardized. Ironically, the shares of General Dynamics, the real target of nationalization, though it had not yet been designated so, only lost 4% of their value. Holders of Quebec and Hydro Quebec bonds stepped up their sell orders, but "the bottom didn't drop out of the market," according to one trader. The Canadian dollar lost nearly half a cent.

On his return to Quebec City, with the stock market still shuddering, René Lévesque changed his tune. Finally admitting his setback, he found someone to blame: English Canadian businessmen who had, he said, "peddled their outdated ideas about Quebec" in New York. This "fifth column," this "English Canadian mafia" of New York, as he called it, would always be responsible, in his view, for his failure in the city. In his memoirs, he rails against the "underhanded diaspora" which had "done its best to turn my first trip among our neighbors into a resounding disaster." Blinded by his love for America, René Lévesque refused to see that he had been rejected. "He couldn't understand that the Americans are a bunch of reactionaries," was the subsequent succinct assessment of an advisor, Daniel Latouche.

The US representative in Quebec City, Terry McNamara, took Lévesque at his word. Believing the premier to have said, as usual, exactly what he meant to say, he analysed the speech in a report sent to Washington. If Lévesque had limited himself to economic generalities and had hammered away at the theme of independence, it was because he "cannot afford to alienate" the "hardcore nationalists" of the party. But — and here was the catch according to McNamara — Lévesque would need the endorsement of the foreign and domestic business communities to "convince the mass of Francophone voters" that the economic consequences of independence "will not be disastrous."

There are two unanswered questions about René Lévesque's New York expedition.

Who, colleagues have been wondering since the evening of January 25, 1977, was responsible for the speech? Louis Bernard takes responsibility for the first draft, which was prepared from notes submitted by several government departments. The Finance Department had even asked First Boston for some suggestions, though the bulk of these wound up in the waste basket.

In the speech, "the political aspect came out very strongly," Bernard says, though in principle, "our plan had been to save the independence theme for later," after the Lévesque cabinet had proven its mettle as a "good government." Robert Mackay, Lévesque's advisor, had a look at the final version before it went to press. Lévesque also told Morin that "someone at Hydro Quebec" had seen the text and given it the seal of approval. Between the first and final drafts falls only the shadow of the separatist leader himself.

"Say, Lévesque, you speak pretty well, but I'm starting to wonder if you can write," the young and arrogant Pierre Trudeau had said by way of introduction in a Radio-Canada cafeteria in the early 1950s. Trudeau was looking for a new writer for *Cité Libre*. He soon learned that Lévesque excelled with a pen; by the time he had become a politician, the former journalist accepted having his speeches written for him, but he still took care of major rewrites if the speech was an important one. Claude Morin and his top aide Louise Beaudoin remember his speech to the French National Assembly, written in the night; Lévesque wanted to devote it to the subject of electoral financing reform — a subject which would have amused French politicians, great lovers of secret funds — rather than to Bill 101. Others remember Lévesque at the back of an airplane fiddling with his little sheets and creating in his masterful handwriting — the manuscript could have been printed — another hymn to nationhood.

For his first major international appearance, in the America he revered, would Lévesque have left the speech writing to subordinates? He says in his memoirs, written ten years later, that he did. "I had consented for the first and last time to deliver a text prepared by a team whose talents were unfortunately not on America's wavelength, and who had put into my mouth the sort of little inanities which grate on the ear."

Really? The leader's hand is visible everywhere in the New York speech. His faith in America, his certainty, expressed a few months earlier in *Foreign Affairs,* that the Americans had "no imaginable reason" to fear Quebec independence — "especially during a bicentennial year" — fill the pages of the speech. The idea of making the parallel, for that matter, between the United States in 1776 and Quebec in 1977 smacks of Lévesque.

Lévesque had clearly long been obsessed with that battle for independence: in July of 1976, he had sent a message of congratulations to President Gerald Ford on the occasion of the bicentennial of the American Revolution. The PQ leader included in his note a passage laden with meaning, in which he noted that 1776 remained "among us ... a powerful inspiration to all those who hope to attain, in turn, the same liberty and independence..." (Washington asked its consulate in Quebec City to inform Lévesque verbally that his message had been received; the White House dared not reply to the premier directly.)

At the Links Club, he spontaneously repeated this plausible but faulty reasoning, which he had tried out nine years before in an interview with Peter Desbarats. It was the argument of a man who felt too great an affinity with his American friend to see the distance that separated them; the argument of a neighbor too convinced he was part of the family to imagine for a moment that he might be rejected as an intruder. In comparing himself to the American founding fathers, he wanted to pay homage to George Washington. What he said came out closer to blasphemy.

Who would have had the gall to write for Lévesque the line that so well captures his delusion: "There is in Quebec this steadily rising movement of collective emancipation, comparable enough to your own beginnings that we naturally hope for and expect sympathy maybe, understanding certainly, in American opinion."

The second question pertains to the speech itself. Was it the wrong thing to say to the wrong people?

Certainly, "there was a general reaction that the comparison he made with the American Revolution was totally inappropriate," Tomlinson says. The Revolution, Joe Wilson adds, "is a shrine in this country," and the Americans in the audience found it "presumptuous that someone would use this icon for what some considered base political motives." The blunder was compounded, in the canny eyes of one American diplomat watching the Quebec situation, by the fact that "anyway, the people he was talking to would probably have sided with the British during the Revolutionary War."

Certainly the reference to Hydro in Lévesque's speech was too brief, and the vague discussion of foreign investment clarified nothing. If he had said, "We're going to become independent; here are the five sectors in which foreign investment will be prohibited and the three conditions which must be met by anyone setting up shop among us," he would have been speaking the language of his hosts. An ode to Quebec entrepreneurship, to the local Bombardier success story and the strong and popular Desjardins financial movement, would have reassured his audience of his capitalist allegiances.

Certainly Lévesque could have put a little less emphasis on his separatist beliefs. After all, he had used the words "independence" and "sovereignty" thirteen times — he had even used the hated term "separation" (which also appears in the Declaration of Independence) — and never once connected them to the word "association." It was a record. (It would not be until an interview in March of 1977 that he decided "sovereignty-association" did not require a "split with Canada." After this the word-games never ceased.)

But these gaffes were minor compared to the discovery made on January 25 by the heavy hitters of the US economy: René Lévesque genuinely wanted Quebec to be independent, and he had the stature of a nation-builder.

New York businessmen did not have a very high opinion of politicians. Washington, they grumbled, was a necessary nuisance. They believed neither in election promises nor in grandiose professions of faith. They had known and overcome enough foreign politicians to regard revolutionary programs as castles in the sand or as outright jokes. Many had thought Lévesque, like the rest of his kind, "would say and do anything to get elected," Wilson recalls. "Others considered him to be a self-proclaimed messiah with distorted views on things." They thought him someone, in short, who would trip over the first crisis he encountered.

To their surprise, they met a man who was sincere, solid, unflappable. The crowd of bankers and captains of industry, observed diplomat Harper, had a two-part reaction. "First, there was little appreciation before Lévesque's speech of the extent to which he is dedicated to separation. Second, Lévesque impressed people as being a highly articulate, persuasive politician, even upstaging [New York Governor Hugh] Carey, who spoke immediately before him. As a result, some who were not previously worried about the possibility of separation are now concerned about what Lévesque, with his political gifts, may be able to accomplish over the next several years in the way of gaining public support for the PQ's objectives." Tomlinson concurs. "He's really serious," he felt that night, "he could pull it off."

In short, Lévesque had shown himself to be so competent, so eloquent, so inspired, that he made Wall Street tremble.

# 10
# The New York Millstone

*Mr. Lévesque is a man of destiny.
But we as lenders will have to sit back and consider
whether we are to be a part of that destiny.*
The head of a major investment firm in New York,
the day after the Economic Club speech

Parades of PQ supporters intoxicated by their stunning victory still filled the streets of Montreal when the man of the hour, returning to his home after the delirious mob-scene at the Paul Sauvé center, heard his telephone ring. It was economic reality calling.

Roland Giroux, president of Hydro Quebec, wanted to see his new boss first thing tomorrow, November 16, 1976. The subject: the immense loans that Hydro was trying to obtain on international markets to finance the James Bay project. It would take $16 billion to turn the waters of the La Grande River into kilowatts. Hydro had only raised half that amount, which was not enough to finish the project, and too much to turn back. The election, Giroux knew, would cause a storm in the financial markets. It was necessary to ready the corporate flagship of the Quebec economy for the rough waters ahead.

Begun in 1971, the James Bay project was at once an economic engine, because of its spin-off effects, and a brake, because of the constraints it imposed. Did Bourassa set it up that way? By borrowing to the hilt from American lenders, he had increased ten-fold New York's influence over the management of Quebec; strewn more obstacles along the path to independence; and obliged the newly-elected separatist leader to bear the weight of a huge financial millstone.

That election night, sitting in a cafe in Old Montreal not far from the new premier's home, Fred Ferber was listening to the nationalist songs and watching the revellers wave their blue *fleur de lys* flags. The New Yorker did not understand the lyrics of the songs but the language of the flags was unmistakable. Ferber was one of the people Giroux and Lévesque would talk about; he managed the portfolio of the Prudential Insurance Company. It was he who had lent Hydro billions, accumulating more IOU's signed "Giroux" than anyone else but his counterpart at Metropolitan Life. Ferber, one of the participants that evening remembers, wanted to get a personal feeling for Quebec's emotions. Lending to governments was not an unreasonable risk, he felt, since "political entities are usually around." But this Lévesque was "talking about changing the political entity," shifting the points on Quebec's compass.

## The Cognoscenti and the Ignoramuses

Innocent politicians who expect to find all the tools of Quebec political power in the premier's bunker in Quebec City lose their innocence the day after their election. Two thirds of the buttons on the political instrument panel are commanded from across the Ottawa River in the federal capital. And on the wall marked "Loans," apart from the *Caisse des Dépôts* line, there is basically one telephone with two numbers to dial: one to Toronto and one to New York. René Lévesque and Jacques Parizeau, who had weathered one financial storm together during the nationalization of electric power in 1962, could not be numbered among the innocent. But they were among the stubborn.

Lévesque felt the weight of his millstone for the first time at a breakfast some days after the election. "Why the hell are you asking me to do this?" the premier çomplained, a cigarette between his lips. Joe Wilson, bearing bad news, belonged to the second category of New York money-men who mattered more to Quebec's finances than any Beauce chamber of commerce or Jonquière trade union. When the Ferbers signed the cheques, it was to the Wilsons that they handed them.

If Ferber and the others were lenders, Wilson, Merrill Lynch, First Boston, Salomon Brothers and the rest were the connections, the middlemen. Half-bookies and half-advisors, their own interests always came first. These investment banks never seemed quite sure who, between Quebec and the lenders, was the boss and who was the customer.

They were also trapeze artists. In this vertiginous business called bond-issues, there came a moment between heaven and earth when the investment banks bought Hydro's entire new debt, released their grip on Quebec and, after an agonizing pause, got hold of the lenders. If they misjudged the jump (by overestimating Hydro's market value, for example), the prevailing wind (fluctuations in the New York market) or their partner's strength (the lenders' available cash), then they tasted sawdust.

One typical example of the kind of wind blowing down the investment banks: one day, between the purchase of a Hydro bond issue and its resale to lenders, Paul Volcker, then chairman of the Federal Reserve Board, hinted that interest rates would be going up. If that was the case, investors reasoned, why buy Hydro bonds at the offered rate when other rates were about to rise? The investment bank in question was forced to promise to sell the Hydro debt at a higher interest than it had secured for itself. One banker says he lost $300,000 on that single transaction.

The investment banks competed fiercely with each other. Wanting the best contracts, they courted the biggest customers. The bigger the debt, the bigger the commission. Hydro and the Province of Quebec were among the most lucrative accounts. For some years — "since the dawn of time," in Parizeau's words — their interests in New York had been represented by one group, or syndicate, of investment banks, led by First Boston. This favored firm, whose biggest client was Quebec, was known as the lead manager. It took the biggest piece of the action. But it shared the job with four partners, called managers. They were, in order: Halsey Stuart, which had first offered its services in 1962; A.E. Ames, the firm which managed the Quebec and Hydro Canadian syndicate and which provided, in one banker's words, an invaluable Torontonian "mark of respectability" to the New York syndicate; Salomon Brothers, known in the community as Solly; and Merrill Lynch, represented by Joe Wilson.

Each, of course, coveted the lead manager's chair. And some had not been above courting Quebec's political opposition, on the off-chance that the PQ might someday take power in Quebec. All was fair when the prize was the summit of the James Bay debt mountain, which had been seen over the horizon since the early 1970s. "You couldn't be choosy or very selective if you wanted to guarantee that your name was at least going to be considered for leadership," explains one of the principal actors in this long-running drama, a manager at Solly, who admits to having "actively pursued" Lévesque and Parizeau during their years in opposition. There was more chance of winning the prize in courting the "potential radical elements, the new elements," than in "upsetting relationships that dated back to the Duplessis era," he explains.

But the cardinal rule in hunting the goose that lays the golden egg is to make sure the goose is in good health. And this was what worried Wilson at his breakfast with the premier. The Olympic flame had only gone out in Montreal three months before, and the final bill for the Games was huge. Montreal, unlike New York, was not on the edge of default. But its balance sheet — thanks to Mayor Jean Drapeau and his favorite French architect Roger Taillibert — was full of holes. Moody's (along with its counterpart, Standard & Poor's, the credit rating agencies which graded prospective borrowers and thus influenced lenders' inclinations) was threatening to drop Montreal's rating. If Montreal fell, Quebec would slide, and Hydro would shudder.

There was a solution, and Wilson proposed it to Lévesque: force Montreal to impose a special tax to wipe out the Olympic deficit. The city's accounts would be restored to order, Moody's would maintain its rating and there would be one less stumbling block for Hydro and Quebec on the money markets. "Son of a gun, Wilson, why are you doing this?" replied the new premier. "My strongest support is in Montreal!" What a way to thank the loyal voters, with a special tax.

"Mr Premier," answered Wilson, who had known him since the financial campaign of 1962, "maybe there's a time when you will have to stop being a politician and start being a statesman."

"I thought he was going to dump his coffee on my head," Wilson remembers. But he was safe; it was Montrealers who were about to be scalded.

Lévesque decided to pursue his old ally on another front. "Well, Joe, now that I run the government of Quebec, I presume you'll do something about your French. You know what our views are on language." Wilson, a Vancouver native who had lived in New York for a quarter-century, promised on the spot to double his French vocabulary. "Ah well, then that would bring you up to what? Maybe twelve, fifteen words?" Lévesque retorted playfully.

Wilson, Ferber and the people at Moody's were among the cognoscenti on the subject of Quebec. The provincial economy, the budget, the politicians and the backroom deals held no great mystery for them. For the moment, this knowledgeable handful was waiting. They were not about to dump the billions in bonds they already held. Nor were they about to commit themselves to billions more before the electoral dust settled, before the new government made its intentions clear.

Nevertheless, the president of Metropolitan Life took the bull by the horns and wrote to the Lévesque government, expressing his desire to schedule a meeting. In Quebec City, either thanks to a secretary who simply filed the letter away, an advisor who had never heard of Metropolitan Life (one of the world's biggest investors) or a minister who thought it was just another prospectus, the letter went unanswered. At the insurance company, Quebec's silence raised eyebrows. The insurer decided not to press the matter further. The lack of a reply was in line, anyway, with New York's impression of the new cabinet: "A combination of bureaucrats, academics and technocrats," in the tradition of "French socialism." In short, "a group of people who didn't understand business," one informed individual recalls.

They had admittedly heard good things as well as bad of Parizeau. He was thought of as a "liberal economist" of the sort one found by the dozen at Harvard, one acquaintance remembers. But the 1970s had sharpened the leftist views of this rising financial star. The same acquaintance recalls, still indignantly, a conference attended by Parizeau in 1974, barely two years before the election.

"A group of American economists and businessmen jumped on him and said, 'What are you guys going to do if you become independent about investments, about trade, about transfers of technology,' and a whole bunch of specifics. And here is an economist, full professor at l'Ecole des Hautes Etudes Commerciales and a PhD from the London School of Economics, likely to be handling Quebec foreign economic policy if it became independent, and his reply — and it absolutely floored the American audience — was: 'Well, economics, you know, is something like when you buy a house, and it's the plumbing. Economics is the plumbing. You go and you buy a house, you worry about the architecture, the quality of the school, the neighborhood, what it costs, the mortgage rates, and you worry about the plumbing after you buy the house and just before you move in.' Now, to tell a bunch of economists and businessmen this was his view on economic relations with the United States, the most fundamental foreign economic relation that Quebec was going to have [...] I can understand why, when they did come to power, some of these guys said, 'This is a bunch of madmen.'"

There was no doubt in New York that of Lévesque and Parizeau, the latter was more avid in his desire for independence. "Everything he said was colored by his goal" of independence, says one banker. But there was also a great fascination with him in the financial capital. Apart from the fact that he always seemed to have just walked out of a top London tailor's, "he had the look, he spoke and seemed to have ideas of this combination of intellectual, technocrat and bureaucrat, and often quite brilliantly phrased things, that one associates with some of the best French officials," says one of those who watched him.

In any case, several months later a medium-sized investment bank, Kidder Peabody, got wind of the breakdown in postal communication between Metropolitan Life and Quebec, and informed the Quebeckers. As soon as Hydro got the news, it sent the insurance company's president an invitation that was as courteous as it was late. The lines of communication were open again.

There were also some in New York who were proud ignoramuses. Frantic for news, they would reach out to William Diebold, senior fellow and economist of the Council on Foreign Relations, the prestigious New York organization, half economic and half diplomatic, to which influential foreigners come to speak behind closed doors. Bank representatives repeatedly asked Diebold about the ideology of this unheard-of party in Quebec. Diebold was stunned by "the level of ignorance" of the people calling him. "I said, 'Gee whiz, if the bank lent money without paying attention to political possibilities, what's the use of thinking about it now?'"

When the bond market opened, a clutch of smaller institutional investors — modest pension funds and minor insurance companies — dumped their Hydro and Quebec securities, fearing a sharp drop in value. Once can always resell its debt holdings. This secondary market had no direct effect on Hydro, but the amount investors are prepared to pay for the bonds gives an idea of the current confidence level in Hydro and its government. By selling off their holdings, these small investors drove down the market value of Hydro debt. A hundred dollars' worth of debt was now selling for, say, $98. But Hydro was still bound to pay 10% interest on the face value of a $100 bond. Since the new buyer had only paid $98 for it, he was in effect getting an annual return on his investment not of 10% but of 10.2% (and a capital gain of about 2% at maturity). The next time Hydro issued bonds, it would have to take this variation into account. Money it could have raised at 10% interest before the election of the PQ would now cost it around 10.2%, the price of lenders' nervousness. Lévesque found this unacceptable. "You scare the hell out of them," Wilson told him. "Why? What's the matter with them?" Lévesque replied. He would never get used to the market's jittery nature.

All government and major corporate bonds are affected by currents in the secondary market. Interest rates rise and fall for reasons that often have nothing to do with the soundness of the company, the stability of the government or the viability of the project. An oil shock, a volcanic eruption in Japan or an ill-timed presidential statement can make all bonds' rates, including Hydro Quebec's, soar or fall. For that reason Hydro Quebec's rate fluctuations have to be looked at in context: against the fluctuations of a major American company or of another Canadian power company like British Columbia Hydro.

On the morning of November 16, 1976, a gap opened between Hydro Quebec's rate and those of its counterparts in other Canadian provinces. This gap continued to widen until mid-December. By then, Hydro Quebec bonds were only finding takers at 0.5% — "50 basis points," in market jargon — higher than usual. This was the "spread." It gave a real measure of American anxiety in the face of Quebec's political upheaval. The wider it became, the more Quebeckers would have to pay, through their electric bills and taxes, for their decision to gamble with their future. The narrower it became, the more America was expressing its satisfaction with, or at least indifference about, the situation.

The PQ election had added 50 points to the spread. If Hydro Quebec had chosen to launch a $500 million bond issue over 30 years that December, the additional cost would have been $75 million.

## First Commandment, First Sinner

The new finance minister called his first American financial strategy session. The five members of the investment syndicate — led by Tomlinson of First Boston — assembled to listen to what their new partner had to say.

"It's understood, you look after the finance and I look after the politics, and we don't mix up the two," said the minister, his portly frame encased in a three-piece suit. "We'll get along fine," he said, citing Parizeau's First Commandment, "as long as you don't get involved in politics. I don't want any statements coming from you."

Parizeau knew the market was sensitive to the political situation. He knew his bankers would demand a premium rate to find a market for his borrowing and Hydro's. That was their right and their job. If they wanted to moan in the privacy of their office towers about the sudden pallor of their golden goose, that was their business. But in public or in front of investors, they were to act like the soldiers they were; they were to close ranks and rally around the Quebec flag.

The First Commandment was immediately adopted by the syndicate. "They swore to it — their mouths still watered over Hydro bonds," Parizeau recalls. " 'No, no, no, don't you worry, there'll be none of that...' " the minister remembers. "It went very well."

But the members of the syndicate took the fact that the minister bullied them badly. One of the participants described him as "abrasive." Tomlinson went away with the most unpleasant recollection of the occasion. "He met with us at his desk instead of sitting around a table, which is the normal thing to do. With all of us in a ring around one side, he sat there at his desk. I remembered him as a relatively short man, so I couldn't figure out why he was looking down on me until, as we were leaving, I snuck around and I discovered he had his chair all the way up as high as it could possibly go, so that he could look down on us, and kind of give himself a position of power." (Parizeau forcefully denies this, saying his chair had no such flexibility.)

For these conservative money-men, there was no shortage of reasons to worry. How were they supposed to stay calm when the new government was playing Santa Claus, passing a law before the holidays which established the highest minimum wage on the continent; when René Lévesque was calling himself a "socialist" in an interview with *Business Week,* using a term with Americans that he studiously avoided in Quebec? (He would go further in September 1977, informing the conservative readership of *US News and World Report* that he was not a "dogmatic socialist," but noting that there was a "long-term shift to the left in the world, including the United States, and that will continue." In December, he would tell *Newsweek* he wanted to create in Quebec a cooperative economic model like Scandinavia's, with, "eventually, labour and management as equal partners in the economy." Three months later, in *Time,* he came back to the same theme: "The absolute lordship of private interests has had its day and will have to adapt to a mixed system. That's eventually going to be true in the US as well as elsewhere.")

For the time being, in any case, the air was expectant. Neither Hydro nor the government of Quebec risked testing the New York market. People were waiting for January, for the Economic Club, for the avalanche.

Parizeau remembers the events surrounding Lévesque's speech with detachment. "What did they expect to hear, those people? That we were Cubans of the north? Well, they learned that we weren't Cubans of the north, but that on the other hand, we were people who would probably cause a pile of problems for Canada. And that didn't exactly thrill them!"

The day after the speech, Hydro bonds weakened. Initially, the spread went from 50 to 150 points — as ignoramuses dumped their holdings, again — but the bonds bounced back during the day to reach a steady level at about 70 points. A $500 million borrowing by Hydro over 30 years would now cost Quebeckers $100 million more than in November.

But Hydro would not even have a chance to pay this painful premium, because on the day after Lévesque's visit, New York was in no mood to lend. Since November, the Montreal and Toronto markets had closed their gates. Now New York was raising the drawbridge. There was no plot at work, no sinister Trilateral Commission meeting at midnight on the top floor of the Empire State Building to organize a financial blockade of Quebec. The system was simply driven by a combination of economic reality and political perception.

There were certainly those who believed, like the Links Club pessimists, that Quebec's bonds had just died. But this was a minority view. One investor to whom US consul general to Montreal Elizabeth Harper spoke after the speech said, on the contrary, that if it were up to him, he would buy all the Hydro Quebec bonds he could get his hands on because, Lévesque or no Lévesque, "it's the best utility in North America." But the smaller players were still driving the bonds' market value down, and it was this value which figured in investors' portfolio analyses. Prudential, for example, could be absolutely certain of getting the 8% promised by Hydro Quebec every year for 30 years, but when its directors looked at the books, they would see that Ferber had bought the bonds when they were issued at 100, and they were now trading on the market six months later at 94. Were the price to fall to 88, or even 85, the drop would be enough to bring about a decline in the company's share value.

It was therefore getting "difficult to explain to policy- and shareholders any new investments in Quebec," Harper was told by one portfolio manager. That manager was convinced all the same that, with or without the separatists, Quebec's rivers would keep flowing in the same direction: toward Hydro profits.

It stood to reason that as uncertainty grew, the spread would widen and Hydro would be forced to offer an ever higher rate of return on its borrowing. "Generally speaking," one investor notes, "you can finance anything at a cost." But there is a threshold beyond which the borrower offers so much that the investor starts asking questions; if the deal is too good, it starts to smell bad. After the Economic Club speech, investment bankers concluded that the threshold had been reached. They told Harper that "the issue of separation presented such a unique problem that it might well prove difficult to attract investors at any tolerable price."

The market was following, almost despite itself, a logic that would shut down the vital pipeline feeding US dollars to James Bay. Harper thus reported from New York a piece of news that would have made Parizeau fall from his chair: "Prudential and Metropolitan both said that a moratorium on Quebec investments was not yet company policy as boards had not yet met, but it was a foregone conclusion that a moratorium would become official." The American consul general in Toronto had only one word for it: boycott.

When the lenders closed their chequebooks, the investment bankers, caretakers of the Quebec goose, began to wonder whether it was time to leave the barnyard. The president of Merrill Lynch, Don Regan, who had heard Lévesque speak, asked Joe Wilson to "come up" and talk things over with the executive committee. The embodiment of the American dream, Don Regan was the son of an Irish immigrant, a self-made man who had largely built Merrill Lynch. He guided his employees, and his destiny, with a firm hand; he would only meet his match ten years later in the person of Nancy Reagan. (At the conclusion of a bitter and very public feud, Nancy succeeded in removing Regan from his job as White House chief of staff, the second most powerful job in the country. "It's him or me," she is reported to have told her husband.)

Don Regan knew that there were some risks which were simply not worth taking. "When you go around and sell bonds, you don't like to be in the position of having later to be reminded that you sold bonds that couldn't be repaid," says Tomlinson. In this line of work, credibility and reliability were the main selling points. In addition, if a business defaulted, the outraged investors could go so far as to sue. (In 1983 when the Washington Public Supply System — known as WOPPS! to its customers — was unable to make payments on 2.5 billion dollars in bonds, Merrill Lynch and Salomon Brothers were, among others, the targets of lawsuits by 22,000 bondholders.)

An independent Quebec, Wilson told Regan and a small group of Merrill Lynch executives, would pose a similar risk. But in his report of less than two pages — "operating on the basis that most executive committee members fall asleep by the time they reach the bottom of page two," he explains — the Vancouver native stated that the probability of Quebec independence was very low.

Don Regan read and reread Wilson's report. If he decided the risk was too great, he would pull Merrill out of the Quebec syndicate. This would be a worse blow for Quebec than the Economic Club; the spread on Hydro bonds would widen dramatically as a consequence. At the table, that day, the future of James Bay lay in the balance.

"There were moments," Parizeau admits today, "when it was uncertain whether Hydro would get its money." This was one of those moments. Would the people of Quebec have forgiven René Lévesque for turning Hydro Quebec into a historic failure? How could a government which had crippled the corporate symbol of the new Quebec claim the ability to lead its people to statehood? The effect of a work stoppage on the largest construction site in Quebec history would have had a staggering effect on an economy which, with a 10% unemployment rate, was already groggy.

For Don Regan, too, the stakes were high. If he was wrong, if he abandoned a ship that was not sinking, Merrill Lynch would probably be excluded for a generation from trading in lucrative Quebec bonds.

"Joe, why don't you just talk about this for a bit?" Regan finally said. Wilson set out his argument for a quarter of an hour. Under Canada's economic umbrella, Quebec bonds were "every bit as strong as before the election." "Why do you believe that there will not be an ultimate separation?" asked an executive. "If there were a separation, what do you think the result might be?" another wanted to know. Wilson knew Quebec, believed its people to possess "Common sense, logic and reason." Those three qualities would undoubtedly work, everyone at the table agreed, in favor of maintaining the federal union. Merrill, said Wilson, had no reason to pull out of the valuable trade in Hydro securities. Apart from the fact that no one wanted to buy them, he said, there was nothing wrong with them.

Don Regan made up his mind. "Well, what you say makes sense." The rest of the committee hastened to agree. It rarely did otherwise.

Another member of the syndicate, the Canadian firm A.E. Ames, had no thought of pulling out of the Hydro bond business. But at least one of its spokesmen broke Parizeau's First Commandment ("You look after the finance and I look after the politics, and we don't mix up the two.") and began to launch political barbs at the new government. This spokesman had already told the American consul general in Toronto that Lévesque's Economic Club speech should cost the seditious separatist his head; the boys at A.E. Ames did not stop there. They mouthed off in New York as well as Toronto. It was not long before the comments got back to Parizeau, who was none too pleased.

"It didn't help bond sales," Parizeau remembers, half-annoyed and half-amused, "to have people know that Quebec's traditional lead manager in Canada was running around the financial markets with a long face, saying, 'But you have no idea, it's dreadful, it's awful what's going on [...] we've got to be very careful.'"

To make matters worse, there was already bad blood between Parizeau and A.E. Ames. During the nationalization of the power companies in 1962 Parizeau was the young man in charge of financing. Under the guidance of two ministers, Eric Kierans and René Lévesque, Parizeau had discovered the virtues of competition and for the first time thrown open the question of whether the province's traditional money-raiser, Ames & Sons, should continue to hold the monopoly it had enjoyed since the 1920s. The manager of the Quebec account at Ames, an almost mythical figure named Doug Chapman, was outraged by such temerity and reacted by saying Parizeau was a "dirty little rat." That very expression, Parizeau remembers, had found its way into the pages of Montreal's daily *La Presse*.

While Chapman had long since left the scene by the mid-seventies, throwing Ames out of the syndicate once and for all would have been sweet revenge for Parizeau. It was too risky, though. "Changes like that are unheard of," Parizeau explains, they create disorder. It was necessary to "send out a signal," but at the same time to show a "certain tact." Parizeau kept A.E. Ames on as a minor member of the American syndicate — but removed the indiscreet bank from its long-standing role as lead manager of the Canadian syndicate. He replaced it by two co-leads, one French-speaking firm, Lévesque Beaubien, and one English, Wood Gundy. Let other loudmouths be warned!

There was some irony in the choice of Wood Gundy. Ten years earlier, during his first meeting with the American consul general in Quebec City, Lévesque had cited it as a prime example of an anti-Quebec English-speaking firm. Lévesque "predicted that if Quebec evolved towards his kind of separatism, the English-speaking Montreal financiers, such as Wood Gundy, would go all-out to wreck Quebec's credit," the consul, Francis Cunningham, had reported. When they were offered Ames' place at the table, the English-speakers at Wood Gundy worked hard and long to sell $200 million in Quebec bonds in a very unwilling Canadian market.

## The Providence of the Innocent

When they opened their newspapers on the morning of February 7, the New York money-men believed their Quebec nightmare was coming to a close. That weekend, René Lévesque had surely brought an end to his political career. Driving home at four in the morning from a party at the home of his friend Michaud, Lévesque had run over a tramp lying in the street. The man had died. Whether the premier was drunk remained an open question; the police officer dispatched to the scene had not dared take a breath sample from the unfortunate late-bedder. Investigators did note, however, that Lévesque had been driving without his glasses, a breach of the conditions of his license. Finally, the public learned — and this was the clincher in the New Yorkers' minds — that Lévesque, a married man, had been in the company of his secretary, with whom he had been having an affair for six years.

Death, adultery, breach of the Highway Code and questionable sobriety — clearly he was done for. Any American presidential candidate would have been, at any rate. When the markets opened, traders rubbed their hands and bought into Hydro. All was wonderful. Within fifteen days, the spread actually narrowed a little.

But the reprieve was short-lived, because René Lévesque's accident would prove as nothing had before the affection that Quebeckers had for him. In Quebec City, McNamara could hardly contain his sarcasm, so struck was he by the strange situation. In a telex entitled "Wasn't It Terrible What Happened to Poor René?" the diplomat noted that "Even some little old ladies of our acquaintance act almost as if Lévesque had somehow been the victim in the accident." In this affair, he explained, the fact that "the poor wretch who was killed was a known alcoholic has further tended to blur moral judgement." The consul mentioned also that Parizeau had "carefully explained to me recently that Lévesque is widely known as someone who is sparing in his use of alcohol." The Liberals' hope to turn the incident into a "major scandal," McNamara added, was "wishful thinking."

By the end of the winter, there were in fact signs of a financial thaw. Several developments helped lessen Quebec's headaches in New York. First, the firm of Kidder Peabody published a study which firmly stated that Hydro Quebec, far from being a risk, was "presently undervalued and offers attractive opportunities for capital gains." As for independence, who cared? Hydro Quebec "will be basically unaffected by the achievement of whichever form of political autonomy develops, that of premier Lévesque (a sovereign Quebec with a Canadian association) or as offered in 'accommodation' by Prime Minister Trudeau," who had made it clear in recent speeches, without committing himself explicitly, that if Quebec chose to remain Canadian it would somehow be rewarded.

The Kidder Peabody study recommended that agencies like Moody's and Standard & Poor's should give Hydro their highest rating, AAA, rather than the AA it now had. After all, the report's author, Ed Waters, wrote that Hydro's performance was the best among Canadian power companies. He placed Hydro on a par with "the highest-quality electric utilities, both public or private, in the United States."

The Waters study gave Hydro's credibility a big boost, but a few nasty tongues were quick to suggest that Waters' scholarship had its ulterior motive: It was no secret that Kidder longed to get into the Hydro syndicate. Waters did not immediately get what his competitor at Salomon Brothers, Richard Schmeelk, calls "the reward." Hydro knew the credibility of the report depended precisely on Kidder's "independence" of Quebec's fortunes. The most Hydro would do was pay for the doughnuts when Waters came to present his study in Montreal, where the first journalist to ask a question called out, "That's a heavy study. What's in it for you?"

"Hydro told me at the time, 'We can't take you on as manager, we don't want anyone to suggest that there was a quid pro quo,'" Waters recalls. Still, Quebec named Kidder as its advisor in the nationalization of the Asbestos Corporation, a Quebec subsidiary of General Dynamics.

At the same time, Moody's, only temporarily sobered by the Olympic tax, reexamined Quebec's rating. At First Boston, Tomlinson expected the worst. Hydro and the province could lose their AA ratings. Tomlinson presented the case before Moody's. First, Hydro's finances were sound. Second, if Quebec did become independent, it would necessarily make a considerable effort to maintain its capacity to pay. Third, by assembling all powers of taxation in Quebec City, it would increase its means. Fourth, Quebec, in any case, owned this magnificent company called Hydro. Tomlinson declares he was "reasonably convinced" of the validity of his arguments.

He could have added a fifth: his personal feeling that separatism had no future. This was in any event the feeling at Moody's: "So-called separatism as an issue is undefined and without a calendar," pronounced the analysts, who, like everyone else, were in the dark about when the PQ's promised referendum on independence would be held. The separatist project, "while introducing an element of market uncertainty," was nonetheless "vague," Moody's concluded, maintaining its AA rating for Hydro and, more surprisingly, for Quebec. The Canadian dollar rose half a cent. (In June, Standard & Poor's would follow Moody's lead, stating that Quebec's middle class would realize eventually that independence was not in its best interest, and would withdraw its support for separatism. Canada's Consulate General, as we will see, did play a part in these decisions.)

A few weeks later Parizeau managed to further relieve Quebec's headaches with its bankrollers in introducing a tough first budget. The social democratic minister put his redistributive impulses on hold and brought his tax collecting wiles to the fore in what became known overnight as "the banks' budget." "When there's no money," he said, "there are no miracles."

In New York, the combined effect of the Kidder report, the Moody's rating, the banks' budget and Trudeau's February 1977 pledge that Canada would survive, reduced the spread progressively. By mid-May, the post-election Hydro spread had shrunk from a high of 70 points after the Economic Club speech to only 40.

It was not a minute too soon: six months after the election, Hydro still had not raised a single dollar in new American loans. Such a situation would, under normal circumstances, have created great difficulties, but in this case Hydro had happily benefitted from what its treasurer called "the providence of the innocent."

From the beginning of the James Bay financing, Hydro had decided to bolster its liquidity — its rainy-day fund, so to speak, set aside against possible hard times ahead. From $25 million in 1972, this fund had risen to $500 million in 1975. The objective in 1976 had been to set aside another $300 million. But as the year began the major insurance companies found themselves flush with cash and were clamoring at the doors of big borrowers like Hydro Quebec. Why not take advantage of the situation? Thus Hydro had already realized its biggest private borrowing in New York, over a billion dollars, at a favorable rate. On November 15, 1976, before the vote-counting had begun, Hydro treasurer Georges Lafond was busy collecting another $50 million from the Equitable Life Insurance Company on the Avenue of the Americas in New York. By the time Radio-Canada announced "a majority Parti Québécois government" at eight-forty that evening, Hydro was sitting on a cosy $1.1 billion.

## The Snail Approach

Still, eight billion dollars had to be raised, and only the New York market could cover the enormous need of the James Bay project. but the road to New York was now littered with obstacles. Georges Lafond, Ed Lemieux, and the Hydro financial team were in no shape for a New York marathon. So they busied themselves on other, less threatening ground, training for the race, as Parizeau puts it, "far from the earthquake's epicenter."

Ten days after the election, Lafond set out on what he called "the snail approach." The road to New York was a long spiral. New York, Parizeau says, was at the center. The beginning of the road lay at the spiral's outer limit, in Zurich. The three biggest private banks in Switzerland lacked the ideological nervousness of their American counterparts. The question in New York was "Is your government socialist?" and the answer was either yes or no. In Zurich, they asked, "Your government is socialist, but what kind?" Swiss bankers knew well the range of differences which separated the rightist social democrat from the out-and-out socialist, and so they knew that between Lenin and Lévesque there was a world of difference. Each of the three banks took $100 million in bonds, denominated in Swiss francs, over five years. The deal was closed before Christmas, 1976.

The snail moved inward. German banks came in on the third turn with a comparable amount, reassured by the Swiss support for Hydro. What was good enough for the Swiss and the Germans soon attracted eurodollars; it was then no trouble to court the Japanese.

"Obviously, all this changed the atmosphere in Canada," Parizeau explains. "If we were borrowing without difficulty abroad," then bankers, brokers, agents and a host of other financial middlemen would realize that with "all their ill-humored reactions to us, the only thing they achieved was a loss of commissions."

Only then did the snail set its course for New York. For the crucial fifth turn, no expense was spared. Hydro and its managers put on what is known as a road show. This one lasted 168 hellish hours. One selling team hit the east flank: Boston, New York, Chicago, a few other cities. Another team, led by Lafond, started in the west: Seattle Monday, Los Angeles Tuesday, San Francisco Wednesday, Dallas Thursday, Atlanta Friday. It went like this: each morning, a private meeting with the two biggest institutions in the city. At noon, cocktails and lunch with the major institutional accounts: pension funds, insurance companies. Another private meeting in the afternoon. In the evening, discussions with local representatives of the managers' syndicate, followed by a review of the day's events and calls to the other team, to Quebec, and to the First Boston representative in New York who kept the "book" on the operation, a ledger of orders made for the recently unsaleable Hydro bonds. After another plane trip and a new hotel, the cycle began again.

"One election isn't going to change the course of Quebec's rivers," Lafond explained to local businessmen who, six hours by airplane from Montreal, had learned at the same time that some Canadians spoke French and that they were now speaking, in French, of breaking away. The Hydro team talked up its dams. Yes sir, these babies were pollution-proof, inflation-proof, time-proof, resource depletion-proof, politics-proof.

And this referendum, when was it going to happen, asked the Americans. "It never failed," Lafond says. "The Americans want a recipe for instant coffee... Their problems might take ten years to solve, but when it comes to other people's problems, they want an answer right away, solutions right away." When, Georges? When? When? "God knows when," Georges would reply, giving his audience a crash course on the French fact, national affirmation, the Quiet Revolution, the Parti Québécois. "It reduced them to a state of shock," he remembers. Then he would tell them that Canada and the United States were not cut from the same cloth, that Canadian links were looser, the provinces stronger and political instability as much a permanent condition as the snow, the Canadian Shield, the direction of those powerful rivers. And anyway, added one Quebec spokesman boldly during the road show, "If there's one province that's going to separate, it won't be Quebec first but British Columbia." In the American west, where no one had ever really grasped the difference between Seattle and Vancouver, this was an effective argument.

On the third day, the book had filled up to the point that First Boston suggested raising the stakes. Why borrow only $200 million? Why not 250? 300? The object of the operation, Lafond believed, was not to take the biggest possible helping, but simply to prove that Quebec was welcome at the table again. They would have time later for seconds.

On September 13, 1977, Hydro Quebec resurfaced in New York with a $200 million US bond issue. Sixty million was going to Prudential alone, the remainder was divided among 25 converts to the cause, from Connecticut to California. Of course, there had been a spread to pay. But it was now only 15 points; the additional cost to Quebec over the 13 years of the loan was barely $4 million. Three quarters of the Economic Club setback had been overcome. And Hydro had attained its financing objective for the year.

The shut-out had lasted ten months.

The market was now getting used to the idea of independence. Still, it comforted itself with the thought that Lévesque, despite his acknowledged "political gifts," had little chance of pulling separation off. Apart from their one obsession, the *péquistes* "aren't as wild and irresponsible as some people think," noted Richard Schmeelk of Salomon Brothers. And the referendum still seemed so far away. There was time to watch and wait.

## The Misfortunes of Solly

By the autumn of 1979, the troubles of 1977 seemed like ancient history. In June, Hydro had raised a further $200 million in New York and the spread had become too small to be of interest to anyone.

There was still trouble ahead, but not so much for Quebec as for its powerful New York bankers. For starters, First Boston's dominance would waver. One analyst among the fifty employed by the firm, an oil industry specialist, came up with a study in which he explained, according to Tomlinson, "that the separatist government was no good and was going to get thrown out, and this would have such and such an effect on something to do with oil." When Tomlinson saw the study, already in distribution, he "went into a tizzy." He remembered Parizeau's First Commandment, delivered from the heights of a boosted chair.

Someone suggested pretending that nothing had happened. It was an absurd idea; some competitor would be only too pleased to give the show away. There was one solution, Tomlinson decided: he must notify Parizeau directly, come clean and hope for forgiveness.

"We hadn't kept an eye on our analyst," — Parizeau here takes up the account — "it was a terrible mistake, they were truly sorry. I said, 'Okay, maybe you're sorry, but you'd better wait and see how things turn out.'" Current fashion favored co-lead managers, alternating in the management of the syndicate and competing with one another to stay in the good graces of clients who behaved more and more like outright bosses. Parizeau wanted someone established in the retail market, at the small-investor level, an area in which Merrill Lynch far outstripped its competition. So he asked Joe Wilson of Merrill Lynch to alternate with First Boston, apparently only half-forgiven. Solly (as Salomon Brothers is known), which had been hankering after the position of lead or co-lead for nearly ten years, was still a bridesmaid.

But this bridesmaid did have a second suitor: Ontario Hydro. And on that heavyweight account, Solly was the sole lead manager. (First Boston had tried in vain to be named a co-lead.) Among Solly's executives, Richard Schmeelk and John Wiley looked after Hydro Quebec and Peter Gordon looked after Ontario Hydro. Solly was thus at the height of its glory. The princess of Wall Street "surveyed Quebec from on high," one Quebec diplomat in New York remembers. But two misfortunes were to befall her.

In early 1980, Hydro Quebec was waiting for the right moment to raise new funds. The dates of bond issues are not decided long in advance. Whole months go by when investors do not have a penny. There are weeks when the market goes wild, when interest rates jump up and down, and then there are weeks when lenders have cash and the market is steady. That is when bonds issuers like to strike. In February, Hydro Quebec thought it saw its chance. Its financial people were known to be the fastest borrowers on the eastern seaboard. In three days, they could assemble their files, draft the prospectus, contact investors, negotiate interest rates, take the money and run. When a Hydro Quebec representative decided to cut short a European trip to strike the New York financial market while it was hot, he found a message waiting in his hotel room which maddened him. The message said Ontario Hydro was preparing its own bond issue and, worse, was doing so fully aware that Hydro Quebec was itself preparing to soak up the market.

First, such information is supposed to be confidential. The Hydro Quebec man learned that Peter Gordon, "the Canadian on lackey duty," he smirks, had given away the game to the Ontarians. Gordon confirmed as much but added that his colleagues on the Quebec account had been supposed to inform Hydro Quebec at the same time. It was, he protested, an honorable step, informing two ships that they were about to collide in the night.

Next, Ontario Hydro asked Hydro Quebec to delay its borrowing. "We've been getting ready for fifteen days," the Ontarians pleaded. When two borrowers arrive on the market within hours or a day of each other, the first one on the market tends to siphon off available funds and the second is often reduced to paying a slightly higher rate to get the dregs. Hydro Quebec and Ontario Hydro went head-to-head; the two issues came out almost simultaneously. Hydro Quebec suspected Toronto of having pushed forward its issue date, acting on Gordon's confidential information. One member of the Quebec syndicate claims to have taken a loss because of the interprovincial stand-off.

Back in Montreal, Hydro informed Parizeau's office of the New York mess. According to one version, which Parizeau contests, the minister ordered an outright dismissal of Solly. Would a representative of Parizeau's Finance Department deliver the bad news, Hydro wanted to know. Out of the question, said Parizeau; let Hydro strike the blow.

When two Hydro executives arrived to give Solly its notice, Richard Schmeelk and John Wiley pleaded for mercy. In the previous year alone, Hydro had added half a million dollars to Solly's revenues. And Hydro's loss would do serious damage to the firm's reputation. "We'll build a glass wall" between the Quebec and Ontario sections, they promised. But Hydro had its orders. The answer was no.

Parizeau tells the story differently: "I was convinced that it was no big deal. Fine, it was an accident, they shouldn't have done it [...] I asked for a hurried investigation." He was ready to forgive. But a second misfortune sealed Solly's fate. The press reported that Peter Gordon, in an interview, had cast serious doubt on Quebec's ability to finance its borrowings on Wall Street. "God bless him!" It was an "unutterably stupid" thing to say, says a competitor who gained from the blunder and who still laughs about it. Gordon claims heatedly that he was misquoted and that he only stated an obvious fact: that political instability had created a spread which damaged Hydro Quebec bonds. (In fact, it would have been ridiculous for him to have denied at the time that Hydro Quebec could raise money, since it was doing so without difficulty.) But for Parizeau, the mistake was unforgivable. "I had the deputy minister call them and say, 'Fine, you don't agree with us, well, we don't agree that you should make statements like that. So you're out!'"

It would be six years before Solly returned to Quebec's good books, and that, needless to say, would be after Parizeau's departure.

Parizeau's First Commandment created such anxiety among the investment banks that when a French-speaking analyst for Merrill Lynch in Montreal publicly criticized the Parti Québécois government, the president of Merrill

Lynch Canada lost no time in reassuring the minister: "Well, I'm not waiting until you get rid of me; I'll get rid of the analyst!"

"Basically, there's an impression," Parizeau says, "that small governments are necessarily under the thumbs" of the major financial houses. "We always forget," he adds with a wide smile, "that competition is a wonderful thing."

# 11
# The Southerner and the Secessionists

*Don't rely on subtlety.*
*Frighten them, or they won't see.*
Pharisees plotting against Jesus
in *Jesus Christ Superstar*

Jimmy Carter was thinking about oil, about oil and Canada, Canada and Quebec, Quebec and the United States, the United States and oil. He had occupied the Oval Office for only a few weeks, and was preparing for a visit from his Canadian neighbor, Pierre Elliott Trudeau. The Prime Minister of a country that might soon be two countries.

Jimmy Carter had never seen, read or heard so many facts about Canada and Quebec. During the long presidential campaign which had changed him from a politician unknown beyond Georgia's borders into a national figure, he had never once read about or spoken of the Canadian problem.

Now, in February 1977, this lover of details plunged into the Canadian file with a great thirst for information. That quality would stand him in good stead during delicate negotiations like those which would lead to the Camp David Accord, but would be his weakness when the time came to rise above the minutiae and make hard decisions.

Thomas Enders sat before Carter in an armchair. The problem was not strictly Canadian, the ambassador explained. One had to consider the impact on the United States of a possible Canadian split.

Enders remembers: "It was actually quite a full briefing, so he asked me in some detail my estimate of what might happen, what could go wrong, how strong the movement for independence was, possible compromises, how I thought the situation would evolve." Carter "knew a good deal about this already [...] but we went into a full analysis.

"I told him that it would be a very long crisis, that it was surely going to gain momentum from where it was, its ultimate outcome was unpredictable, and therefore we had to act with extreme prudence. [...] He thought of it as a slow-developing crisis. Not an acute one, but one which could have enormous consequences for the United States."

The consequences stemmed, of course, from this cursed oil. There was not enough of it, and it was costing America too much. This shortage drove the

President's reasoning on the Canadian crisis in a direction exactly opposite to that which Ottawa had feared.

"At the same time the United States was struggling with the consequences of the oil crisis," Enders continues, "and our country was showing strong divisions between producing areas [like Texas] and consuming areas [like the northeast]. The ability of governments to make policy and create a sense of community was being put through what turned out to be quite a severe test. So the idea that there might ultimately be some redrawing of the boundaries in North America was not an idea that was necessarily very congenial to the leader in Washington. [...] After all, at the same time you had western Canadian interests asserting rights on petroleum policy, combatting the views of the center.

"In the United States, a variety of very vigorous producer interests and consumer interests in the petroleum business were being asserted at that time. [...] What would it mean for the United States if the great federation to the north began to loosen? What kind of pattern would that be for the United States?

"It was a long-term question," Enders concludes, "but Carter saw it as a potential issue."

## Old Stitches

Could Quebec independence aggravate the tensions that threatened to tear America apart? That Quebec's struggle might find echoes in Corsica, in Scotland, in Brittany, the Basque region, even in the Ukraine — all this had been suggested. But that it might provide a spark for decentralization in the United States — either directly or through events in the Canadian west — was a question no one had looked at. Only an American leader alarmed by the cracks that were starting to appear in his own country would look at the Canadian crisis from this point of view, and only such a leader would let the dynamics of the ongoing confrontation between Dallas oilmen and shivering Bostonians tailor his Quebec policy.

Yet how could Carter fail to consider these factors? During the icy winter of 1977, no one talked about global warming. The US economy was suffering from the high cost of energy. The industrial north of the country, which was also coping with industrial decline, had been renamed the "rust belt," while the southern states, riding the wave of the oil boom, were calling themselves the "sun belt." It was a matter of salt rubbed in a wound: not only was heating oil practically free in New Orleans, it was hardly needed at all.

In the White House (which Carter the southerner barely heated), regional sensitivities were particularly intense. Was Carter himself not the first son of the Old South to be elected directly to the White House since the Civil War? (Lyndon Johnson, a Texan, had enjoyed the stepping-stone of the vice presidency.) "After a hundred years, [the US is] just beginning to go the other way and bring the American South into the Union under Jimmy Carter," wrote James Reston, for example, to illustrate how much the Quebec situation seemed "a little out of date and almost tragic." How could Carter, anxious to heal old wounds in his own country and to prevent the oil crisis from opening new ones, indifferently watch his neighbor's national fabric being torn apart?

Additionally, there were many reasons why a united Canada would be a valuable ally for Washington. Enders mentioned, of course, the matter of military alliances, from which the newly-elected Parti Québécois was promising to withdraw. He also mentioned the party's left wing, which was under-represented in the Quebec cabinet. But these, he said, were minor concerns.

"I said I thought there was a much larger issue here, that Canada was one of the most successful societies in the West, that it was one of the most successful multilingual societies in the West, as well as being a major international player and, of course, our most important trading partner. Its prosperity and strength were of enormous importance to us as well as its influence in the world.

"If it broke into pieces, its influence would be less than it was, it might well be less prosperous, which might be of concern to us, and further, I didn't see that we had any interest in seeing the boundaries redrawn on the North American continent."

The Democratic President was nonetheless "absolutely" in sympathy with some of the grievances expressed by French Canadians, Enders recalls, and "he wanted to be careful to avoid an anti-Quebec stance."

A second expert on Canadian affairs participated in Jimmy Carter's education on Quebec. Zbigniew Brzezinski, who had made his first appearance in the 1967 Planning Group and had sounded the alarm on the separatist threat, was now in the White House. As national security advisor, Brzezinski rehearsed his boss for Trudeau's arrival.

"We viewed Prime Minister Trudeau as a person who was, in effect, safeguarding Canada as a binational entity, who was preserving Canada as a viable state," Brzezinski remembers. If Quebec wanted a place for itself within Confederation, Trudeau was making one for it, believed Brzezinski, who says he stressed to Carter "the importance of the visit and the very special role that Pierre Trudeau was playing within the Canadian crisis."

Carter had done his homework. He had consulted Enders, one of the most respected diplomats in Washington. He had read the material sent from the State Department by Richard Vine and his team. He had made an effort to grasp some of Canada's finer points with the help of his close aide Brzezinski. Now he was waiting only for the chance to meet an actual Canadian. He had not, it should be said, heard, either directly or indirectly, Quebec's side of the story. Enders had not met the new representatives of the Quebec government before briefing Carter; Brzezinski had no sources within the independence movement; Vine had never engaged in direct dialogue with a separatist. American diplomats in Quebec City and Montreal represented the only point of contact between Quebec and Washington. And their presence was felt only through their dispatches, in the reviews and analyses being prepared in Washington.

Subsequently, the *péquistes* and their small team of diplomats would rail that they had never had a chance to put their case directly to American decision-makers, that they had never presented the arguments which held independence to be an advantage to Washington rather than a thorn in its side. "The American government, before taking any position, should have the elementary common sense to inform itself on all facets of the question," Quebec's chief diplomat, Claude Morin, would fulminate. "But there is one facet it has never seen, and that's ours." It is highly unlikely that the *péquistes* could have changed the American view. But they would try in a hundred ways, as we shall see, to make it clear they wanted to be heard.

## The "Plausible Denial"

In the rarified stratosphere of American power, as in diplomacy, there is a world of difference between what people think, what they want and what they say. Jimmy Carter thought the jolt of Quebec independence would widen the cracks in the American union. He wanted to avoid this troublesome turn of events without stumbling into the sort of interventionism he had so eloquently denounced during the primary campaign. And he wanted to say as much to Canadians in an interview he had agreed to give the CTV television network.

He was briefed with material sent by Vine — undoubtedly a version of the memorandum of policy — and by Robert Hunter, the National Security Council advisor responsible for Canadian affairs and Europe. After a page of the usual platitudes on mutual admiration and justice and peace, Hunter gave his boss precise instructions, underlining key words:

Quebec: It is important not to get involved in any discussion of Quebec politics, on the grounds that, "I don't think I should comment on what is happening in your country, particularly on an issue where people feel so deeply." However, carefully put, you can indicate how much we here admire the "strong, vigorous Canadian confederation" — which gets the idea across, without stumbling on the buzz word "unity."

"The problem with presidents is that they don't always follow the script," comments Robert Duemling, American diplomat in Ottawa, who heard Jimmy Carter stray considerably beyond Hunter's limits.

Carter had an excuse; between getting his instructions and giving the interview, he met Trudeau, first at an official ceremony and later in private with Brzezinski and the pro-Canadian Vice President, Walter Mondale. "The personal friendship was almost instantaneous when I met Pierre Trudeau this afternoon," Carter would say; Brzezinski confirmed as much the same day. Nothing had actually happened during this first contact, but Duemling infers that "coming out of his meeting with Trudeau," Carter "felt moved to be more outspoken about it than his own advisors would have liked him to be."

Only a few minutes passed between this meeting and the interview which Carter gave Bruce Phillips of CTV. The President did not use the word "unity." He went far further.

"The stability there in Canada is of crucial importance to us," he said, taking up Pierre Trudeau's refrain more strongly than it had ever been heard in the United States. This stability "is an integral part of our lives," he added, as though breaking up Canada would somehow shatter America's own unity.

"If I were the one to make the decision, the confederation would be my preference," he went on, trampling Hunter's instructions with each word. "But that is a decision for the Canadian people to make," he added, coming back on track and stating that it was up to "Canadians," not just up to Quebeckers, to decide. The English-speaking Phillips, who followed up on the topic with some tenacity, had neither the presence of mind nor the inclination to underline the distinction.

Would Washington recognize a sovereign Quebec? he asked. "I don't know. We'll cross that bridge when we come to it," Carter replied.

Phillips asked next whether the American government possessed, was preparing or would prepare a study of Quebec.

"No," said Carter, adding that he obtained his information on the Canadian crisis from "routine briefings, newspapers, television."

Did the absence of a study, Phillips persisted, "imply a judgment on your part that nothing very serious is likely to happen?"

"That is my judgment," answered the President.


With these answers, the American government lied.

There was, in fact, already one study in existence — Rouse's — and a second was in progress. Ordered the previous December 9 with the approval of Henry Kissinger, then still in office, the study would cover all aspects of the election of the PQ: its domestic and international effects. Diplomats and civil servants had been called upon to submit preliminary contributions by January 15 so that Rouse could write a first draft by January 30, listing possible scenarios for the five years ahead and evaluating the possibility of a *péquiste* victory in the referendum. (Terry McNamara, consul general in Quebec City, had predicted that Quebec would attain independence after a "rather messy" period.) Rouse's first draft should thus already have been somewhere in the files of the President's advisors; as Carter spoke to Phillips, the second stage of the study was already in progress. That stage evaluated the impacts of the various scenarios on the future of Canada and the United States and proposed a specific policy for Washington.

Yet no one took the trouble to correct the President by mentioning these studies. Nothing proves that he himself knew of their existence. Enders, Vine and Hunter did, however.

"There is no reason that he [Carter] should have known" there were studies in existence, Richard Vine explains. "I think, as a matter of fact, it's fine that senior people should be in a position to deny that plausibly."

Be that as it may, in diplomatic terms, Jimmy Carter had overstepped a significant boundary on the Quebec question. He had expressed a preference in a foreign national debate, and he had associated Canada's future with the well-being of his own country.

At the American Embassy in Ottawa, "we considered it a mistake," Duemling remembers. "It takes great subtlety to say at the same time that we support something [confederation] and that we are hands off, that we won't interfere in the internal matters of another country [Canada]."

## A "Crime Against the History of Mankind"

For Trudeau, the White House visit had paid off. In the American rink, the score was now Trudeau 2, Lévesque 0. In Ottawa the expectation had been that Lévesque would come out of his New York trip a winner. "It was a surprise that Lévesque had proclaimed himself to be something of an economic radical and just a separatist," remembers Allan Gotlieb. "It was a rather unsophisticated speech, and the feeling was that he blew it."

The Canadian Prime Minister would score a third goal — a hat-trick, in hockey parlance — and take a decisive lead the day after the Carter interview, when he gave a well-received speech before a joint session of Congress.

It was the first time a Canadian prime minister was addressing America's legislators, whereas it was customary for the American president to deliver a speech in the Commons. And Trudeau had chosen the occasion to confront head-on the Canadian political problem which obsessed him, the Quebec question. He was speaking, as well, on live television to the people of Canada. Delivered one month after Lévesque's address to the Economic Club, his speech was seen as a rebuttal. It disturbed many Canadians to see the two most important politicians in Canada speaking to them, and quarreling with each other, from podiums in the United States.

More numerous, however, were the Canadians who now approved of their national leader, whose sagging popularity had been in need of a boost. The reaction to what some commentators called "the best speech of his career" was immediate: the Prime Minister's switchboard in Ottawa was swamped, and there were suggestions that an election should be called immediately to take advantage of the sudden wave of support.

"I say to you with all the certainty I can command that Canada's unity will not be fractured," he told the 200 American legislators who had come to hear him speak. He accused the Parti Québécois of representing only a "minority view," and of having no mandate to break up the country. But he admitted that French-speaking Canadians had reason not to feel "completely equal" in the present Confederation.

In terms as ambiguous as those he would use during the referendum campaign, Trudeau promised that "provisions will take place, accommodations will be made, so that the Canadian confederation can be seen by six and a half million French-speaking Canadians to be the strongest bulwark against submersion by 220 million English-speaking North Americans." Having established the PQ's bad faith — its lack of a mandate — and his own good will, Trudeau went on to describe the stakes of the contest. A breaking of the federal bond, he said, "would create shockwaves of disbelief among those all over the world who are committed to the proposition that among man's noblest endeavors are communities in which people of diverse origins live, love, work and find mutual benefit."

Then came the key sentence: "Most Canadians understand that the rupture of their country would be an aberrant departure from the norms they themselves have set, a crime against the history of mankind."

The assembled lawmakers applauded wildly. Trudeau was compared to Churchill; his speech was described as the best heard in that chamber in 20 years. (A comment regularly made after a speech by a foreign statesman.) Edmund Muskie, a former presidential candidate and an influential senator from Maine, called Trudeau "eloquent" and said that following the Canadian crisis was a little like learning that "neighbors for whom one has affection are planning a divorce."

Revealing the monumental ignorance which sometimes reigns in Congress, one Wisconsin representative remarked that some of his colleagues "didn't know a Canadian could speak English so well."

Trudeau's was not a reassuring speech. He could have weighed his words and calmed the legislators, spoken of the economic, monetary, perhaps even military and diplomatic association which the separatists were proposing. He could have told them that the damage, if there was to be any, would be limited; he could have said the Americans had no reason to get worried, or to get involved. Editorialist Claude Ryan, among others, noted this "oversight."

But Pierre Elliott Trudeau had not come to tell Americans things would be okay. He had come to tell them their own future was at stake. He had come to recruit them to Canada's cause. The next day, before the assembled journalists of the National Press Club, he declared that Quebec's secession would be, for the United States, "much more grave than the Cuban missile crisis." This equation of Quebec's entry into the United Nations with the threat, in 1963, of nuclear conflict between the USA and the USSR caused some jaws to drop, in Washington as well as Ottawa. But the Prime Minister's verbal inflation followed a strategy fed by fear; he worried that the Americans, despite their rhetoric, would choose the wrong side.

For the journalists on *Meet the Press*, who found the Cuban comparison a bit far-fetched and who asked why America should fear a split which would push Canada's provinces closer to its sphere of influence, Trudeau calmly trotted out his pat explanation: "If the country that is north of you breaks up, it seems to me that it will send shockwaves through a lot of world capitals. I would be very surprised if Washington were not somewhat concerned."

In fact Trudeau's efforts seemed to sow enough concern that Carter was prompted to make one last pro-Canadian gesture. After his address to Congress, Trudeau spoke with Carter and Secretary of State Cyrus Vance for a little over ten minutes in the privacy of the Oval Office. Carter first congratulated his guest on his excellent performance in Congress. But would Quebec separate? the President asked. In politics, nothing is inevitable, Trudeau responded, saying he was nonetheless convinced that in the end, Canada would remain intact. Pleased that he had sensitized Carter — who, according to James Reston, was "impressed by Mr Trudeau's private candor and public caution" — the Prime Minister did not want to overdo it. He wanted the Americans to be federalists but not open interventionists. America's friendship, he knew, was sometimes intrusive.

Carter understood. He would not step onto the field unless asked. The President described to the Prime Minister how he planned to raise the Quebec question himself at his televised press conference the following day. The Prime Minister was very pleased. The two men were on the same wavelength. Pierre Trudeau had never been so happy to be in the Oval Office.

The next day, Jimmy Carter modified his position slightly. Whereas he had assured Bruce Phillips three times that he was "not concerned" at all about the Quebec situation, at the press conference he declared, "There is a great deal of concern in this country about the future of Canada." This was just the message Trudeau wanted conveyed.

But Carter also made a promise which gave Quebec nationalists some solace: "I would certainly make no private or public move to try to determine the outcome of that great debate. I promise you that."

In fact, he had already made moves, in private and in public, which would influence the debate. Even beyond his statements adhering to Trudeau's line, the manner in which he had received the Prime Minister was implicit proof of his sympathies. "Having the Prime Minister here and showering him with praise, talking about the things that Canada means to us," explains Bob Hunter, all amounted to a boost given for the federalist cause. A week earlier, the Mexican president, Lopez Portillo, had been greeted by a meager crowd at the White House. For Trudeau, an enthusiastic crowd of 3,000, mostly civil servants, had been assembled on a cold, wet day. The speaker of the House, Tip O'Neill, had opposed the Prime Minister's address to Congress on the grounds that the last head of state to speak there, the unfortunate Lopez Portillo, had only drawn a handful of legislators. The White House nonetheless prevailed on O'Neill to invite Trudeau and then twisted congressional arms to be sure the speech was well attended.

The Washington summit, enhanced by this bit of stage craft, had thus provided Trudeau with a break in the cloudy Canadian political weather. For this he owed much to the President's men.

## The True Nature of Brzezinski

The picture was still not entirely clear at the White House. Ivan Head, Trudeau's advisor in international affairs, a sort of Canadian Kissinger, returned from the summit without gaining any final insight into his American counterpart, Brzezinski. Head and his boss Trudeau would have been furious if they had known that shortly after his arrival in the White House, Brzezinski had asked his assistants to draw him a singular map.

"I remember at one point, [there was some] particular hook, some intelligence item or some report from our embassy in Ottawa or the consulate in Montreal," recalls Gregory Treverton, an assistant to Brzezinski. "Zbig asked for a map of what would happen if Canada disintegrated. [...] It raised the question of whether, if Quebec left, Canada would come apart politically, prairie provinces would want to join the United States, what would happen to the Maritimes."

Treverton remembers thinking that this was "mischief, Zbig at his irrepressible best," toying with ideas as though he had still been in university. Brzezinski denies having asked for the map, and no one knows who finally saw it. But Bob Hunter confirms that discussions did take place within the National Security Council (NSC), which was Brzezinski's foreign policy unit at the White House, "in terms of possible scenarios." It amounted to a guessing game with speculative questions like "Would the Maritimes stay with the rest of Canada or would there be three countries?" Treverton says no one suggested out loud that the separation of the western provinces would serve certain American interests, but he notes that "it was an undertone." No one saw the western provinces actually becoming American states, but "left to their own devices, Albertans and others would make more sensible, from our point of view, arrangements with the United States."

These discussions and the preparation of the map are important clues, since the personal convictions of the national security advisor about Quebec's future remain unknown to this day. If he believed in 1977 that Canadian federalism was a good cause but a lost one, he had the influence to "position" Washington for the post-Confederation period: the influence to abandon the Canadian ship before it went down. In Canada, some found this worrisome.

"Zbig thought Canada was a goner," reports one high Canadian official, who claims that he heard that opinion stated by the man himself at the time. "Brzezinski was a man who thought that Canada was breaking up. He thought it was terminal. Brzezinski had sources in Quebec, and I think he was one who believed that it was very, very serious and could go all the way, [...] that it was irreversible, and I think he may not want to say that." (Indeed Brzezinski denies ever having held this view.)

As it happened, Brzezinski the strategist had already expounded, in his most widely-read book, a theory that nationalist movements like Quebec's were a normal, even desirable, counterweight to the advent of the global village. Like the Flemish and the Scots, he explained in *Between Two Ages,* "The French and English Canadians in Canada [...] are claiming that their particular nation-state no longer corresponds to historical needs. On a higher plane, it has been rendered superfluous by [...] regional arrangements, while on the lower plane, a more intimate linguistic and religious community is required to overcome the impact of the implosion-explosion characteristic of the global metropolis." This reaction, Brzezinski added, entering into direct conflict with the ideas of Pierre Trudeau, "is thus not a return to the emotions or to the ecstatic style of 19th Century nationalism." On the contrary, this nationalism was modern, he wrote, adding that such nationalism "accepts as an ideal the functional integration of regions and even of whole continents [a view borne out by the fact that the people of Quebec were later the most enthusiastic supporters of North American free trade.] It is a reflection of the desire for a more defined sense of personality in an increasingly impersonal world."

Having identified this historical tendency, did Brzezinski believe Canada could resist it? On two occasions, he gave Ottawa reason to fear he did not.

In September of 1977, in an interview with the CTV network, Brzezinski used his own Montreal origins to illustrate his understanding of the conflict. "I grew up in Westmount, and in a way, my childhood makes me understand the nature of the problem. When I went to prep school, which was a very good prep school, and then later on to other schools, I never dated French Canadian girls. It just wasn't considered the thing to do. We lived really in a little British compartment. And there was definitely among my friends not only a sense of separate identities, British and French, but a real sense of hierarchy.

"And therefore I am very sensitive today to French Canadian grievances, or if you like, to Québécois grievances, and I do have a feeling that in a historical sense, there's something to be redressed."

English speakers, he went on, had not shown enough flexibility, but he added that it was "terribly important that the Québécois community doesn't overcompensate historically for that neglect."

Brzezinski had not told all to the cameras. He himself had not simply been an observer of this "hierarchy" in which French Canadians were at the very bottom. As a Pole in Westmount, he too had been a victim of the ethnic pecking order. When Canada's ambassador to Moscow, Robert Ford, met him in April 1978 to prepare a common position on East-West relations for the upcoming Group of Seven summit, he heard Brzezinski make some astounding comments. "He went to private schools in Montreal and he sensed the arrogance of the English-speaking students at the schools, vis-a-vis not only French Canadians but also people like himself," Ford recalls. "He was just completely turned against the English Quebeckers as a result of that, and this sort of rankled with him. It was a curious kind of thing."

The discussion gravitated naturally to the political problem of independence. Brzezinski "showed considerable, considerable sympathy for the point of view of the Quebec separatists at the time — I wouldn't say separatists, necessarily, but certainly nationalists," adds Ford, who refuses to say more on the subject.

On his return to Ottawa, Ford reported these perceptions to a "somewhat worried" Trudeau. After weighing them at length, Trudeau and Ford concluded that they were "a personal opinion, a view of Brzezinski, that wouldn't necessarily affect US policy."

Ford's report is all the more surprising because Ivan Head, Trudeau's advisor, had inferred from his own conversations with Brzezinski that the American national security advisor was, in fact, deeply disturbed by the separatist threat.

During the Washington Summit, Head remembers having "crossed intellectual swords pretty crisply on this issue" with Brzezinski. The ex-Montrealer claimed to have a better understanding of Quebec than the Canadian delegation. Emerging from a meeting with Carter and Trudeau, Brzezinski did not pass up an opportunity to tell Head — who had been excluded from the meeting — that Trudeau "didn't seem to agree with his projections or his appreciation of the scene" in Quebec. Head took this to mean that Carter, influenced by Brzezinski's views, had asked a question or made a remark to Trudeau which had provoked a disagreement.

Head was nonplussed. He found it a bit much, he told Brzezinski, "that a New York City law professor now residing in Washington, DC, should presume to have a better analysis and a better sense of events in the province of Quebec than did Pierre Elliott Trudeau, who continued to be a Quebecker."

"Nothing could stop Brzezinski in full flight," Head adds. "'Of course,' he said, 'when one is too close to the scene, one sometimes gets confused. One has to remove oneself some distance and look at it from afar.'"

Head was all the more irritated because Brzezinski did not base his ideas on reports from the embassy or the consulates. He derived his opinions "from his Canadian background, his Polish sense of nationalist urgency," and he even mentioned, without revealing its contents, the memo drafted in 1967. Brzezinski, Head says, "indicated that whatever it was in his previous paper was now coming to fulfillment, and this was going to be a major problem." (Brzezinski contests the accuracy of this part of Head's account.)

His comments did not lead Head to the conclusion that Brzezinski was sympathetic to the Quebec nationalists, in any event. "If Brzezinski was of the opinion that there was going to be some sort of schism in Canada, and that this schism was not in the interest of the United States, and that there was such a thing as the International Seaway, and there were defence agreements, and there were other things that would impact upon United States national security, what kind of contingency planning was he entering into?" Head wondered.

"Brzezinski, in that very sensitive position" in the White House, the Prime Minister's advisor adds, "could, for all we knew, be sending signals that would not be acceptable to us to the United States military establishment about what role should or should not be played."

Head was particularly worried that the Pentagon or the White House would publicly discuss military scenarios. "This could be so misunderstood in Canada, there could be a backlash that would develop of very unfortunate proportions," he adds.

Since that time, Head has asked Brzezinski about those scenarios. "He pretends not to remember."

In conversation, Brzezinski now says that no emergency plan was ever ordered. Only a few theoretical discussions on different scenarios took place, much like those described by Hunter and Treverton. And in fact, nothing suggests otherwise.

But there are hints that Brzezinski, apart from his animosity toward English Montrealers, saw Quebec's secession as a serious strategic problem. At the time, in his CTV interview, he used the expression "apocalyptic outcomes" to describe independence. And in conversation now, though he refuses to discuss anything which touches on "national security," he does not reject the notion that such a turn of events could have represented "a threat" for the United States.

It was perhaps the collision of his own contradictory intuitions that worried him so much at the time: convinced that Canada was being pulled apart by the centrifugal forces of modern history, forces which fed on the ethnic rivalry still fresh in his personal memories, Brzezinski feared more than anyone else the strategic turbulence which could result.

But if Brzezinski was an alarmist, no one in the American diplomatic establishment shared his views. When the State Department re-examined the Quebec question with more care than ever, it certainly saw problems on the horizon, but it glimpsed no monster looming in the waters of the St Lawrence.

## "It is therefore in our interest ..."

The document was stamped SECRET and dated August 1977. The twenty-two pages of dense print were the result of the study commissioned in December by Kissinger; it bore the title "The Quebec Situation: Outlook and Implications." The document reviewed the historical and current situations, defined the interests and preferences of the American government, raised hypotheses and proposed steps to be taken.

Jean Lesage would have been pleased. The Americans supported the idea of a special status for Quebec.

In the two central paragraphs of the summary, American policy became clear:

"The US preference, as stated by the President, is for a united Canada. This is clearly in our national interest, given the importance of Canada to the US in defence, trade, investments, environmental questions, and world affairs."

But the document continued, "As long as legitimate grievances remain unresolved, the Quebec situation will continue to be unstable, to the detriment of United States interests. It is therefore in our interest that this problem be resolved."

The document — whose high quality, according to Richard Vine, suggests that it was submitted to Secretary of State Cyrus Vance and to the President — examined five scenarios. The status quo, first of all, would present "the least problems" for the United States. The study, which declared "the failure of Trudeau's bilingualism policy," anticipated that a defeat of the separatists could provoke anti-US feelings in Quebec, give Ottawa greater freedom to manoeuvre in foreign affairs and make it "probably less accommodating to US interests." The study noted how friendly Pierre Trudeau had become to Washington now that he sought "expressions of US support for a united Canada." (In April, a memo on recent developments in bilateral relations had noted the state of "economic and political vulnerability" in Canada and the advantages the United States could draw from it.) The expectation that Trudeau's pro-Americanism would not survive his winning the referendum victory would prove accurate beyond anyone's predictions.

The second scenario was a devolution of powers to all the provinces. The State Department shuddered to consider the tangle of US-provincial relations which would result. "A transfer of power to the provinces could make it more cumbersome and time-consuming to deal with Canada because the Canadian federal government would have to consult with or obtain the agreement of the provinces to a greater extent than is now the case. [...] This could create differing and discriminatory rules between provinces in the conditions for US business operations, investment and ownerships. [...] Depending on the extent of the devolution of powers, the US could end up, as a practical matter, 'dealing' with eleven Canadian entities rather than one and could find itself indirectly involved in interprovincial issues and federal-provincial problems. Some of the provinces would probably seek closer practical ties with the US than with the rest of Canada in areas under their control, further complicating Canadian internal affairs and US-Canadian relations."

The third scenario convered the concept of a special status for Quebec. "It would be easier to deal with a Canada where only Quebec, rather than all the provinces, had a special status," the document noted. "In some ways, it might also be easier than the present situation because there would not be the uncertainty about the rules of the game that prevails now and will continue to exist until the Quebec issue is settled."

The United States' inclination toward a new Canadian constitution with special provisions for Quebec had existed before 1977. Ten years earlier, in his long dispatches from Ottawa, American ambassador Walt Butterworth was already praising Conservative leader Robert Stanfield, who, he wrote, "sees the problem in its true perspective, and has pledged himself and his party to a 'deux nations' concept." And when Butterworth quoted Jean Lesage's statement that "it may very well be, thanks to Quebec's obtaining a special status, that Canada will truly survive," he was expressing approval for the father of the Quiet Revolution. To the ambassador, the bilingualism program in the federal civil service and the promise of French schools for French Canadians outside Quebec were "starters at best and superficialities at worst."

One of his successors in Ottawa, Tom Enders, along with McNamara in Quebec City, also favored a more flexible formula, supporting the desire of Quebec for greater autonomy. "The best solution to the separatist threat," they wrote, "may ultimately be found in a formula which Quebec could call sovereignty and which the rest of Canada could call confederation."

But Enders felt that this ideal solution could not fly in the Canadian sky. "It is not clear whether any federal government could give Quebec 'special status' and survive the ensuing anglo backlash," he wrote.

"The Quebec Situation" then considered a fourth scenario: sovereignty-association.

Obviously, the document explained, everything depended on the ability and willingness of the two sides to come to terms on the nature of the association. Washington hoped the federal government would retain control "over defence, foreign policy and monetary affairs." Certainly US-Canada relations would have to be redefined. "In any case," the document continued, "in the event that the two, Ottawa and Quebec, can reach an amicable settlement on this basis, it should be possible for the US to work out acceptable solutions to problems with both or jointly, even though the process would necessarily be more complicated and cumbersome."

The fifth and final possibility: a unilateral declaration of independence, which the document referred to as a UDI. This would result if, after a referendum in which the PQ government won "the mandate to negotiate sovereignty-association" (the document accurately guessed the wording of the referendum question two and a half years in advance), Ottawa refused to negotiate, forcing Quebec to declare its independence, perhaps after a second referendum.

A UDI was by far the most problematic scenario. First, it threw Washington into the quagmire of deciding whether to recognize the new state. The problem was a complicated one; Washington would base its decision in part on Ottawa's reaction, on the reactions of other countries and on Quebec's attitude toward the United States, particularly on defence questions. But withholding recognition would be hard to justify, because "Quebec does meet generally accepted criteria for national self-determination in the sense of ethnic distinctiveness in a clearly defined geographic area with an existing separate legal and governmental system." The new country would perhaps be less well-off than the old province, the document noted, but it added, "There is also no question regarding the basic long-term viability of an independent Quebec in an economic sense or in regards to its ability to be a responsible member of the family of nations." In fact, the document observed, "Quebec would certainly be a more viable state than most UN members."

What kind of country would the new Quebec be? "We see a possibility that either an independent Quebec or the remaining Canada would become more anti-US than is the case for Canada today," since both states would want to preserve their fragile identities. This was, however, only a possibility. In fact, the State Department study believed that "it is likely that an independent Quebec would at least attempt to establish good relations with the US." The study saw the transition period between provincial status and independence as possibly "a period where skillful efforts to ameliorate tensions could bring long-term benefits to the US." For that matter, "having established once and for all the supremacy of its French character in language and culture, Quebec might well become less xenophobic. This could permit the strong North American elements in Quebec society to be brought to bear on policy formulation."

So it would not be so awful to have Quebec on its own. The real problem was with Canada. "We have serious doubts about whether the rest of Canada could stay united if Quebec separated," the authors wrote, "Strong regional divergencies, the natural North-South pull, and the exposed situation for the maritime provinces would probably inexorably in time lead to one or more of the provinces or regions breaking away from Ontario-Ottawa domination. Once started, it is questionable whether the process could be stopped. Some of the provinces or regions would try it alone, some would seek some form of association with the US. The effect would be that the US would be faced with either new responsibilities and/or opportunities, or a number of small and weak, although probably friendly, countries to the North." This, they continued, would be "less desirable than the present situation. The possibility that one or several Canadian provinces would seek to join the US raises prospects that we have not contemplated. They could be negative or positive, but probably difficult to resolve."

In its concluding section, the document stated that "the present situation also is not to our benefit. As long as the legitimate grievances and aspirations for safeguarding their ethnic identity are not resolved in a manner satisfactory to the francophone majority in Quebec, an unstable situation will continue that could result in damage to US interests, increasing Canadian impotence, and even a resumption of terrorism and violence in Quebec."

The State Department thus favored a constitutional accommodation for Quebec alone. It had heard Trudeau's occasional references to "provisions." The study wondered how long Trudeau — "a committed federalist and central power advocate" who would not abandon his position except as "a last resort" — "can get away with enticing his audiences with vague references to new approaches to federal-provincial relations, without being willing to clarify his position with specifics."

## Uncle Sam's Vote

The final page of the State Department study set forth American policy for "the next two years — a time frame that could be considered a transition period since no decisive action on Quebec is expected during it."

The policy involved four points:

1.  The President in February 1977 stated that:
a.  The US considers the Quebec situation to be one for the Canadians themselves to resolve;
b.  The US considers Canadians completely capable of resolving the question; and
c.  The US prefers confederation.

2.  In public statements, US Government representatives will not go beyond the position detailed in point 1.

3.  In private communication with the Government of Canada, the US Government will reiterate its expressed willingness to consider ways we might be helpful on the Quebec question, if the Government of Canada should conclude the United States Government could play a useful role.

4.  US Government representatives will conduct relations with Canadian provincial authorities, including those of Quebec, in the same manner as has been the practice heretofore.

At the same time, the US Government will closely follow and analyze developments in Canada and Quebec on a continuing basis and will review its policy periodically as developments warrant.

Everything would turn on point three. Washington was not promising to act on all requests it received from Ottawa, notes Richard Vine, in charge of the file at the State Department. Washington was only promising to "consider" such requests. Still, the State Department already knew what to expect. As the referendum approached, "it would not be surprising for Ottawa to ask the US Government to take a stand much more unequivocally in favor of a united Canada." Specifically, Canada could want the US to declare "out of the question" any "special US trade arrangements" with the new country. This was because "the threat of economic isolation and difficulties is Ottawa's strongest argument in persuading the Quebecois to stay with Canada." If Washington intervened in such a fashion it would undermine the theory often advanced by Lévesque that in the absence of association with the rest of Canada, the United States would open its arms to Quebec. The document also predicted that Quebec would try "to persuade the US to adopt a neutral position" in the referendum campaign.

The document came to no decision, because the problem still lay, at the time, outside the two-year "transition period." (It also violated — though no one seemed to care — Carter's promise not to intervene.) The authors of the study had made it clear that the time would eventually come to reconsider the question and opt, perhaps, for a change of approach.

For the Lévesque team, a vigorous US intervention just before the referendum would have been a nightmare. "Strategically, the feds weren't wrong to seek open American sympathy for Trudeau's positions," explains Claude Morin. As the referendum drew near, if American favor for the "NO" side "had been the slightest bit vocal, popular support for sovereignty-association would, in my opinion, have fallen dramatically." Lévesque and Morin had always thought that even in a best-case scenario, they would win the referendum by a slender margin. Uncle Sam's vote, they believed, would annihilate that margin.

"Let's assume," speculates Richard Pouliot, one of the architects of Quebec diplomacy under Lévesque, "that there had come a day when a president of the United States declared in public, during the referendum campaign, that Americans didn't agree with the idea of sovereignty-association, that if the people of Quebec voted "YES," they could expect retribution [...] the result would have been very different."

In numerical terms, how afraid were the Quebeckers of the Americans? Would one percent or two percent of the ballots be lost in a close vote?

"It could have reached 20%," says Pouliot, who does not underestimate the voters' conservative reaction if Quebec had found itself faced with a monolithic North American "NO."

From that moment, the absolute foreign priority of Lévesque's strategists was to neutralize Washington, to keep the Americans out of their contest. Their entire political project hung in the balance.

But in early 1977, Quebec's US diplomacy had yet to exist.

# 12

# A Voiceless Quebec

*[Quebec] having sung its song*
*[In Paris] all summer long,*
*Found itself hungry and alone*
*As [America's] winds began to moan.*
LA FONTAINE [as amended]

Like Hollywood, Washington is a company town, a city dominated by a single industry. And like Hollywood, Washington has a trade paper, a daily newspaper which, with breakfast, gets every day off to the right start. *Variety* does for one town what the *Washington Post* does for the other.

Two pages are crucial in the *Post*. One is the front page, which decides the subject of conversation for the day at the White House and in Congress. The second is the op-ed page, in which the big names of past and future governments, along with hardnosed columnists and a few lucky academics, air their views. A sort of intellectual grab bag, this is the page that often gets clipped by the administration and the White House so that its suggestions or points of view may be borrowed.

On Sundays the op-ed page expands. An entire section, entitled "Outlook" and nicknamed "the brains section" by its creator, Ben Bradlee, treats the *Post*'s Sunday readership (which is most of the city), to a smorgasbord of fresh ideas and brand-new viewpoints.

On Sunday, April 17, 1977, the "Outlook" offerings consisted of predictions from a professor at Duke University of Brezhnev's probable successors; an update from a specialist on the MTS epidemic (AIDS had not yet been invented); and the eloquent account of a "young French-Canadian journalist" on "What It Means to Be French in Canada."

Never before had Quebec been discussed in so august a forum. Two columns on the front page of the section and an entire inside page were devoted to the piece. Never before had so many congressmen, lobbyists, diplomats, journalists and senior civil servants all simultaneously been offered so detailed a description of contemporary Quebec in so weighty a publication. It would be another three years before the *Post* revisited the subject in depth; in the meantime, Washington's vast ignorance of Quebec would be shrouded in a veil of facts, impressions and colours generated by the "Outlook" article.

That veil was anxiety-producing. Tom Enders, would state during a meeting with *péquiste* minister Robert Burns in Quebec City the following week that the article had "created quite a stir" in Washington. He was almost apologetic. The article, he said, presented "A lugubrious view of Quebec." The civil servant who took notes at the meeting was under the impression that that was the title of the article.

Robert Guy Scully, the 27-year-old author of the fiery article, had written an indictment of the French Québécois nation, a society which he called incurably "sick." "No one would want to live there who doesn't have to," he wrote. "There isn't a single material or spiritual advantage to it which can't be had, in an even better form, on the English side of Montreal."

Scully seemed to draw on family recollections for the portrait he drew of Montreal's Hochelaga-Maisonneuve district, one of the "Harlems," he claimed, of French Montreal:

> ...the kids are fed sweets and fats, they are made to eat at every opportunity, as if the food supply were to stop tomorrow. Their teeth and their health are shot by the time they are ten. Later, at forty, when the first pains start, from decades of bad eating habits, of alcohol, of stale air and no exercise, the people are afraid to see a doctor, or to even call one. They might try the left-over pills from the neighbor's old prescription. But they would be terrified of stepping out of their dark, greasy kitchens into bright, clean hospitals.
>
> Because they might learn that they are really sick, that they must be committed. Then they could no longer sleep two or three to a bed as widowed mothers or grandmothers often do with their grown sons and daughters who do not marry. Some of the mothers will even keep their youngest at home, afraid of losing the last one to the world outside. So this child will grow up illiterate, and the grown-ups will be afraid to answer the phone, in case the school board calls.

*Washington Post* readers learned also that "the Quebec civil service, in many instances, [is] a corrupt banana-republic bureaucracy," and that the people of Quebec were urged "never to buy Heinz ketchup or other such 'foreign' products."

Unable to explain the vitality of Quebec society in the 1970s, Scully dismissed it succinctly as an "extraordinary neurotic creativity," which, in his view, "means nothing." He summarized his argument — strongly tinged with regret that French Canadians had never been assimilated into English Canada — in a few words: "Quebec is small and isolated. That will never change: a cripple could no more grow his legs back." Any left-leaning Democrats who had sensed some kinship between Quebec's struggle and the American fight for social progress and civil rights would have been convinced by Scully's article — as gripping as it was shocking — that the people of Quebec wanted only to remain enclosed in their miserable, xenophobic and corrupt society. One would be doing them a favor in preventing them from governing themselves.

(In several letters to Quebec newspapers a contrite Scully tried to explain that his *Post* article was meant to have had the opposite effect, that it had been intended "to hit hard, to sting, to rub their noses in our misery," to break, "violently, if need be, the wall of indifference separating Quebec from the United States." He believed he had succeeded and claimed that "now, the men and women of Maryland and Virginia have sympathy for this bit of island called Hochelaga-Maisonneuve.")

The decision by the *Post* to grant such prominence to so singular and unrepresentative a view of Quebec society — otherwise ignored by the newspaper — reflected a more serious problem. A dozen years after the fact, John Anderson, the *Post* editorialist who had introduced Scully to the "Outlook" staff, offers this candid explanation: "It was something that explained the life of a city that was not far from us but that we didn't know much about." Today, as then, Anderson believes the article offered a journalistically accurate view of Quebec. Al Horne, editor-in-chief of "Outlook," who commissioned the article from Scully (he had first presented his ideas in a speech to a Washington symposium), remembers that the article struck him as "provocative and controversial," exactly the kind of material he was looking for. He claims never to have heard at the time that this description was far removed from the mainstream of discourse about modern Quebec, even in anti-nationalist circles. The editorialist and editor-in-chief's reactions highlight the perfect absence of a Quebec voice in North America's news services, and the frightening degree of ignorance in the American press on the subject of Quebec.

Horne explains that he would probably have printed a second piece on Quebec in response to Scully's article, if anyone had given him one. But no one took the trouble to repair the considerable damage that had been done, and he himself never commissioned a rebuttal.

## A Sea of Black Ink

Claude Ryan of *Le Devoir* took the trouble to read a hundred American editorials published in the wake of the PQ victory and found only two which suggested some understanding of the separatist ideal. One of those was in a daily in Richmond, Virginia, the old Confederate capital. The paper's editorialist, "relying on the experience of the Southern States, claimed to understand the aspirations that had created the Quebec separatists' desire to secede," Ryan reported.

But this was nothing beside the negative reactions which appeared. Many denounced the "unspeakable folly" of the separatist project. *The Los Angeles Times,* one of the country's major dailies, compared the election of René Lévesque to that of Hitler in 1933. Los Angeles was very far away, indeed.

Nor was there any suggestion of giving the new government the benefit of the doubt. The day after the Economic Club speech, the *Wall Street Journal*'s editorialist was skeptical about Lévesque's promise that there would be only one nationalization. "Even Fidel Castro promised similar things on one of his early journeys to the US," the *Journal* wrote.

To get a clearer picture, the American media's instinctive reaction was to call upon colleagues in English Canada, which explains how the influential financial weekly *Barron's* came to ask John Harbron, of Canada's Thomson newspaper chain, to write a long economic article on Quebec. Harbron, too, compared Lévesque to Castro. "Socialism, not separatism, triumphed in Quebec," the weekly wailed.

*Foreign Policy,* aimed at American foreign affairs specialists, also weighed in at the end of 1977 with articles by two English-Canadian writers. F.S. Manor, editorial page editor of the *Winnipeg Free Press,* declared that in the event of independence, "the third-world option of inviting Soviet help could become attractive to a beleaguered Quebec regime, an option that would be highly palatable to the influential Marxist wing of the Parti Québécois." Manor concluded that "since the most vital interests of the United States are at stake, Washington cannot afford to hide behind the excuse of non-interference in the affairs of others." The next step, of course, would be to call for the Marines to be sent in. Manor refrained.

His colleague Nicholas Stethem, assistant editor-in-chief of the *Canadian Defence Quarterly,* author of the second article, had no such scruples. To counter the "fanatics" and particularly the left wing of the PQ, which was riddled with "extreme Marxist- Leninists," and in light of the violence which now seemed "inevitable in the province, or the republic, of Quebec," Stethem sounded the call to Washington's decision-makers: "Strategic reality demands that any attempt to make that change be thwarted — if not by Canada, then by the United States."

These alarmists had no impact on America's Quebec specialists. The State Department's August 1977 study explained clearly that within the PQ, "the radicals are too few in numbers and lacking in general support for them to gain power in Quebec in the foreseeable future, even under a scenario where it would be clear that the independence drive had failed and radical solutions might have some greater appeal." But the inflammatory articles were read in Washington by members of Congress, Pentagon staff and academics. Like Scully's article, they were the first items to fill the information vacuum in the capital; they thus framed the debate in terms which made the whole picture more ominous.

American intellectuals who wanted to know more about Quebec could also refer to a long article which appeared that December in the widely-read *Atlantic Monthly.* Its editors called on an occasional contributor, Mordecai Richler. Author of the exquisitely sensitive *The Apprenticeship of Duddy Kravitz,* Richler is one of the important literary figures in Montreal's English-speaking community and one of the most prominent writers Quebec has produced. In a long cover story, Richler offered a considerably more sophisticated view of Quebec than had Scully. From his standpoint in a minority within a minority (Richler spoke from the Jewish community, which represented a little more than 10% of the English minority in Quebec), Richler distributed criticisms with humor and style, condemning on one hand "the infuriating refusal of so many Anglos in high influential places to learn French," and on the other "the antiquated, church-ridden educational system" which Quebec politicians had imposed on their citizens until 1960.

The aspect of Richler's articles (there would be others) that set René Lévesque to "grinding his teeth," according to a friend of his, was the suggestion that Quebec was heading inexorably toward totalitarianism. "So far, it is not an offense to think in English here," Richler wrote, but he had no doubt that the current "cultural paranoia" would soon drive Quebec's officials in linguistic matters — whom he accused of "zealotry or corruption" — to "disqualify a Greek restaurant if they hear a scalded Greek kitchen-hand curse in his native tongue."

As writers, Richler, Scully and the others were fulfilling an obligation to describe precisely what they saw, thought and felt. But *The Atlantic Monthly*, having published this view of the situation, felt no need to return to the Quebec question before 1983. And when they did, it would be again and only with Mordecai Richler.

The natural crossover between the American and English Canadian journalistic communities played the Quebec government yet another nasty turn. In the autumn of 1977, one government department invited five major periodicals *(Time,* the *Boston Globe,* the *Chicago Tribune,* the *San Francisco Chronicle* and the *Fort Worth Tribune)* each to send an economic reporter to the province. What the PQ government hoped for was a group of journalists who did not have to make a tremendous effort to be impartial. They were hoping for reporters like Henry Giniger, who had been assigned by *The New York Times* to cover the referendum campaign.

"I have fewer hang-ups as a foreigner than if I were part of the struggle," Giniger explained. "I didn't start off with the deep prejudices that the English Canadian community is apt to have. I could move from one world to the other. I can understand both — but I'm not involved in the damn thing. If Quebec wants to be independent, it's okay with me."

At the other end of the spectrum, an editor at the esteemed *Globe and Mail* told his Montreal correspondent, "On this question, I'm a Canadian first and a journalist second." A policy memo at *Maclean's* advised a reporter not to give an inch to this "government not like the others," and especially not to waste articles on the "fake alternative of sovereignty-association."

The editors-in-chief of the five American publications contacted in 1977 — and the dozens of others who would later find themselves in the same position — approached the Quebec problem in an utterly casual manner. These editors, who would never for an instant have considered assigning the coverage of a labour dispute to a union member, invariably chose for the Quebec issue the staff member who knew the most about Canada, generally an English-Canadian living temporarily or permanently in the States. Four of the five journalists sent to Quebec by the dailies in question fitted this description. As professionals accustomed to the exacting standards of American journalism, these reporters were all capable of coming up with well-balanced accounts. But none could say, as Giniger could, "I'm not involved."

All of which explains why the American media did not give Quebec an objective chance. The emotional overtones — not to mention the personal connections and linguistic barriers which naturally favored English Canadian points of view — seemed unavoidable.

## René Lévesque's Greatest Sorrow

Nothing that appeared in the American press upset René Lévesque so much, or wounded him so deeply, as the accusation of anti-Semitism brought against the Parti Québécois.

The charge was made in September of 1977 by the New York monthly *Commentary,* widely read by Jewish academics and journalists. Its readership represented an important element in the American left, since the traditionally liberal Jewish community had always been in the front line of the fight for social change and formed one of the pillars of the Democratic Party. In short, the *Commentary* readership was a target audience for the separatists in their search for southern allies.

In the article in question, two respected Montreal Jewish academics, Ruth Wisse and Irwin Cotler, summarized the concerns of their community with this then popular joke: "How does a smart Montreal Jew talk to a dumb Montreal Jew? Long distance."

"The Jews, of course, are haunted by a national memory that interprets current events in an ominous light," wrote the authors, who followed up with a long text in which they themselves interpreted recent developments in an ominous light. Though they admitted that Quebec society was superior to many in its treatment of its Jewish minority, they were still worried by the government's moves to make bilingual government-funded schools French-only — schools in which English- and French-speaking Jewish students studied side by side, a unique situation in the province. The separatist government was reluctant to subsidize schools which, it believed, anglicized French-speaking Jews. The authors of the article saw this desire for linguistic protection as "a veiled policy of intimidation" toward Jews.

Apart from this specific practical problem in the Jewish community, the authors found — in five pages of alarming hypotheses — only one other documented occurrence to criticize: the pro-Palestinian stance adopted by certain leftist leaders in Quebec, including René Lévesque. Lévesque was "honest and fair," they said, but he had also shown doubtful judgment when he had written, after the massacre of Israeli athletes at the Munich Olympics in 1972, an article in which he deplored both the "most senseless of extremisms" of the terrorists and "Israel's imperial intransigence, which leaves Palestinian activists no other recourse" but murderous folly. (Senior Quebec official Richard Pouliot, on the other hand, remembers a private discussion in which Lévesque defended a strongly pro-Israeli position.)

"The ethnic and religious pluralism which was so hospitable to Jewish creativity and self-determination seems to be giving way to a unidimensional nationalism that eschews minority distinctiveness," concluded Wisse and Cotler.

Unlike these writers, Richler had the good sense to point out that, apart from some anti-Semitic speeches and articles connected with pre-war Quebec nationalism, the real discrimination suffered by Jewish Montrealers had traditionally been inflicted by the English-speaking minority, which, Richler noted, imposed a quota on Jewish students at McGill and refused Jews entry into its country clubs or into the Montreal Stock Exchange. All of these offenses had occurred, needless to say, during the period of "hospitable pluralism."

Richler also observed that there were grievances on both sides. He noted that just before Lévesque's election, the influential Charles Bronfman had, in an address to 400 leaders of the community, said of the PQ, "Make no mistake, those bastards are out to kill us." Bronfman, owner of the Montreal Expos and a major investor in the province, subsequently threatened to pull out his money in the event of a PQ victory.

It was inevitable that the Montreal Jewish community, with its links to the English minority and its hypersensitivity to any form of fervent nationalism — except Israel's — would feel uneasy during the PQ years. It was inevitable, too, that despite large French-speaking and bilingual contingents within the Jewish community, the leaders and the press of Quebec's French majority, obsessed with their sense of themselves as a minority in English Canada, would never quite figure out how to approach this internal minority.

But beyond the bleak outlooks and mutual misunderstandings, the situation was decidedly uneventful. A professor at the State University of New York, Martin Lubin, himself originally a Jewish Montrealer, noted that during this entire period, the two North American Jewish organizations based in New York, the World Jewish Congress and the American Jewish Congress, received "no complaints from Montreal Jewry about anti-Semitism, discrimination against them for jobs, or other maltreatment by the Quebec majority." The person responsible for Canadian affairs within the World Jewish Congress, Lubin writes, "argued that developments relative to Jews in other parts of the world had overshadowed any 'Quebec question,' if indeed either PQ governmental policies or relations with the Francophone majority in general really posed any significant problems at all to Jewish well-being." A third organization, the Anti-Defamation League, informed Lubin that it had never considered Quebec as one of the numerous "problem environments" for Jews.

But in the absence of proof of anti-Semitism, Richler, Wisse and Cotler relied on another argument. It was damaging, offensive and utterly false.

"When the jubilant mass of Parti Québécois supporters at the victory rally of November 15 sang a French version of 'Tomorrow Belongs To Me,' the Nazi Party song from *Cabaret* that has unfortunately been adopted as a French Canadian nationalist hymn, it triggered in countless Jewish minds fresh images of storm troopers and jack boots in the night," wrote Wisse and Cotler, in language almost identical to that chosen by Richler.

The fact was — and the three writers would subsequently admit as much — that Stéphanne Venne's song "Demain nous appartient" bore no resemblance to the Nazi song, either in its French lyrics or in its melody. Nor was it the "nationalist hymn of French Canada." That honor belonged, as all Quebeckers knew, to Gilles Vigneault's "Gens du pays."

But in the descriptions which appeared in both respected magazines was an inkling of Lévesque, Parizeau and Venne in some basement on a winter night, asking themselves, "What Nazi song could we translate and turn into a hymn for ourselves?" In response to Venne, who protested his good faith in the pages of both periodicals, Richler conceded that the song "was not a wilful provocation, it was merely insensitive." It did not occur to him that accusing the supporters and leadership of the Parti Québécois of knowingly singing a Nazi song (which had in fact been written in 1972, for *Cabaret*) might represent, on his part, a certain insensitivity. Wisse and Cotler, for their part, showed no hint of regret in their reply to Venne.

These articles did considerable harm to Quebec's image on intellectual circles, particularly on the east coast. "It always came up, it was in the files of people we spoke to," remembers Evelyn Dumas, who served as information officer for Quebec's delegation in Boston starting in 1978. When René Lévesque came to speak at Harvard in April of 1978, he was, according to his host, Elliott Feldman, "obsessed with the question." All day long, recalls Feldman, who directed a research program on Canada and Quebec at the prestigious university, Lévesque asked, "Why do you suppose we are anti-Semitic? Look at all the things we're doing that suggest the contrary." In private and in public — and so often that an American journalist remarked to Dumas that the premier protested too much — Lévesque defended himself against an accusation which offended him deeply. As a war correspondent, Lévesque had been one of the first North Americans to discover the horrors of the concentration camps and to describe them to a disbelieving world. He resented the doubts being cast on his good faith now.

Feldman would have liked to see Lévesque attack the issue head-on, to discuss it before an audience at Brandeis University, a predominantly Jewish school. But, Feldman says, the president of Brandeis, Marver Bernstein, influenced by the *Commentary* and *Atlantic* articles, refused to invite the separatist premier and presumed anti-Semite onto his campus.

## The Palestinian Party

The term that did the premier justice was not "anti-Semite." It was "tactless."

At Harvard, for example, he had tried to put things right by speaking of the "special financial assistance" his government had provided to French Jewish schools. But that was not the problem. The Jewish community considered that, since it belonged to the North American diaspora, English was part of its basic culture. The more Lévesque talked of gallicizing them, the more their hackles rose.

At the same time, in an effort to improve his image, the premier ordered the purchase of a half-page advertisement in an "Israel Section" of the New York daily *Newsday*. Instead of dealing only with "the spirit of cooperation always found in the Jewish community in Montreal" as it would exist in the future Quebec, open to "the contribution of each," the text, signed by Lévesque, dove into the thorny Palestinian question and managed to associate the notion of Palestinian self-determination — anathema to many Jews — with that of Quebec's self-determination. René Lévesque was allowed to have views about a solution to the Middle East crisis, but those ruined his PR effort.

The existence of a "Palestinian party" within Quebec's mini- diplomatic corps was doubly offensive to the Jewish community and highly noticeable, as Quebec had little other foreign policy. Apart from the occasional obligatory statement of sympathy for earthquake victims, the Department of Intergovernmental Affairs almost never took a position on international questions except when they concerned the Middle East, and then it was invariably to support the Arab side. "It was a strange foreign policy," remembers Evelyn Dumas, one of the few *péquistes* who knew what was going on in the Quebec English-speaking community, who served as a liaison with Montreal's Jewish minority.

One of the forces behind these statements was Louise Beaudoin, chief of staff to minister Claude Morin. On Arab questions, she restated positions which had been adopted now and again at party meetings. Beaudoin took particular exception to the openly pro-Israeli position of the Conservative government of Joe Clark, elected in 1979. But she ran up against the opposition of Morin, who advocated a moderate approach. "I was pushing one way, he was pushing the other, and since he was the minister, in the end not a whole lot got done!" she explains.

Still, the pro-Arab stance was fairly consistent. The White Paper on sovereignty-association, published in 1979, was to give an idea of which countries would receive diplomatic delegations from an independent Quebec. In May, an initial draft of the text did not mention a single new Arab country, since Quebec had a mission in Beirut at the time. But in October, Algeria, Iraq and Saudi Arabia were added to the list. Iraq was subsequently struck, but Quebec would have had a total of four delegations in lands hostile to Israel — and none in the Jewish state.

This whole debate was somewhat rough-hewn and never went beyond a small group of individuals. "But if you didn't know that," Feldman explains, "this was an official very close to the powers of the government making statements about how a separatist state would have a different policy in the Middle East. That was very disturbing to people." Apparently no one realized that the internal realities of Montreal politics and the external realities of US politics meant the development of a full-scale Quebec policy on the Middle East might have to wait. This short-sightedness spoke volumes on the confusion and inexperience which reigned on the subject in Quebec City.

Minister Bernard Landry was dispatched to New York on "a very important pilgrimage," as he called it, to visit former Montrealer Edgar Bronfman, Sr., president of Seagram's (and brother to Charles). Prominent in the North American Jewish community, Edgar Bronfman chaired the World Jewish Congress and contributed generously to the well-being of the Jewish community as, occasionally, to Democratic presidential candidates. In September of 1977, in *Newsweek,* this naturalized American offered his own solution to the Canadian crisis: a strong central government, American-style, "rather than to backslide further into provincialism."

Landry had two aims: to tell this leader of the Jewish community that "the extreme right is the very opposite of what we represent," and that the Parti Québécois "recognizes Israel's right to exist." There was no need to worry about those pro-Palestinian policies, which came from "the union movement," he explained. In front of the Rodin which graces the front hall of the Bronfman residence, Landry reminded his "very courteous" host of Lévesque's wartime experiences and of the presence of Henry Milner, a Jew, on the PQ's national executive. Landry left without knowing whether he had convinced Bronfman: he was satisfied to have been heard.

Lévesque never shed the anti-Semitic label. Feldman remembers a much later occasion when the premier stumbled again over the Jewish question. At the end of his mandate, in the spring of 1985, he paid a visit to Governor Michael Dukakis in Boston. It was during the time when Americans were divided over President Ronald Reagan's decision to visit Bitburg, a German cemetery in which SS officers were buried.

Lévesque commented on "how we can all be friends, because if the President could go to Bitburg, that proves how even enemies can become friends." After this "spectacularly dumb" comment, according to Feldman, murmurs of disapproval rippled through his audience. The blunder was compounded by the fact that Kitty Dukakis, the governor's wife, was not only Jewish herself but a member of the National Holocaust Commission. She was highly offended by the presidential visit. Lévesque "was obviously unaware of what he'd said,"

Feldman remarks. He suggests that Lévesque, mired in his own good intentions and still haunted by the accusations of anti-Semitism seven years later, wanted to heal a wound but only ever succeeded in rubbing it raw.

## "Anyway, we don't trust you!"

In the eighteen months following the election of the PQ, the American press failed, on the whole, in its central task, indeed, in its function: it proved unable to present both sides of the complicated and emotional Quebec debate. (The two notable exceptions were Stanley Meisler of *The Los Angeles Times* and Henry Giniger of *The New York Times*; a Canadian diplomat in Ottawa even complained, in a December 1977 note, that Giniger was "more and more understanding toward the Lévesque government.")

But the press was not the only force at work in the US blackening Quebec's name. Wild rumors, originating in Montreal and Toronto, flew about as well. Bernard Landry remembers that after a speech he gave in Manhattan, someone asked him, "Why have you closed McGill University?" McGill, one of the proudest symbols of Montreal's English community, was doing just fine. All the same there were rumors in Toronto that English courses had been banned at McGill and that cinemas were no longer allowed to show films in English.

"What's the fine if the French language police catch a citizen speaking English in Quebec?" another American listener asked an incredulous Claude Morin.

Even the chairman of the New York Cultural Affairs Commission, former dance star Edward Villela, declared that if he had to direct a ballet in Montreal, he would hesitate. "I'd have to ask, 'What is the prevailing political wind? Would I have to employ French-speaking artists only?' If so, I'd certainly think twice."

One day in Austin, Texas, an audience member asked Morin about a simple matter. Morin cleared up the man's confusion and explained his government's true position, pleased to be able to discuss a subject on which he and the listener seemed to be on the same wavelength. Louise Beaudoin, who was on hand, remembers the reaction of the Texan, who, having run out of arguments, stood up and declared, "Anyway, we don't trust you!"

"Claude and I said, that's the core of the problem. We could say anything we wanted, in the end it was a question of confidence. 'We don't trust you!' "

"There was," says Beaudoin, who accompanied the minister on many of his speaking trips, "often a sort of dam of suspicion, a kind of indifference, in any case, that we had to get through[...] 'Who are these loonies, these oddballs who want to change the strategic balance in North America?' "

Morin remembers spending most of his time explaining the basics of the Canadian situation, the existence of French-speaking Quebec, the difference between French Canadians and immigrants, between provinces and states, between French Canadians and Cajuns. "There were times when the point of my speeches, my whole message, was to get those facts across," Morin says. He adds that he made between fifteen and twenty such visits to the US, usually to address local chapters of the Council on Foreign Relations, small meetings at which elected officials, academics, business people and interested journalists came to take the pulse of the planet. Morin never invited the Quebec press or even informed it of these excursions, knowing the destructive effect a single hostile question, usually asked, Morin felt, by a local English Canadian, could have once related by the French-language press.

"At least," shrugs Beaudoin, "we managed to diffuse some hostility."

"It was tough."

## Canadian Diplomats: The Indispensable Foes

The PQ leadership has always accused Canadian diplomats in the United States of having raised the spectre of an evil Quebec. But there is no evidence to support this claim. Canadian diplomats undoubtedly sinned by omission, failing to correct the untruths and exaggerations which were published now and then. And certainly they tried to prevent direct contacts between Quebec and Washington.

But the efforts of staffers in Quebec's Intergovernmental Affairs Department to find evidence of federal "sabotage" were unsuccessful. The texts of speeches obtained from various Canadian ambassadors and consuls in the USA, for example, were masterpieces of restraint and fairness, sometimes affirming the legitimacy of French-Canadian claims before expressing the certainty that a united Canada could address them.

In practice, relations between Quebecois and Canadian diplomats ran hot and cold. In New York, for example, the Quebec Delegation accused the Canadian consulate of dragging its feet on the question of representing Quebec at the UN — a grey area in international representation where Ottawa had every motive to rein in Quebec's ambitions — and of poorly explaining the new Bill 101, which made French the predominant language of Quebec. (Adding to Robert Bourassa's legislation that made French the only official language of the province, the new law basically made unilingual French commercial signs obligatory; restricted access to the well-established English public school system to English-Quebeckers only; established French as the primary language of the workplace, of the courts and of the government; and obliged the extensive English hospital system to offer French-language services to patients who requested them.)

In New York, Quebec's complaints against the Canadians were unfounded, since, where immigration was concerned, the consulate took great care to assign only French-Canadian staff to answer the questions of people who wanted to move to Quebec. Dealing with businessmen, however, consular employees originally from Brandon or Moose Jaw probably had trouble justifying the finer points of the language law.

More worryingly, Quebec delegate general Marcel Bergeron found Canadian economic counsellors more effective at promoting Ontario products: "One can't blame them. It's natural for them to sell what they know best." Canada's Consul General Barry Steers took this as a personal insult, since he believed his team was largely responsible for the Montreal textile industry's success in exporting to the US market.

In fact, the Quebec government owed a debt of gratitude to the Canadian diplomatic staff in New York. The explanations offered by First Boston and Hydro Quebec had been insufficient to convince the Standard & Poor's and Moody's rating agencies not to lower the ratings on Quebec and Hydro bonds in

1977. Detailed briefings from the consulate had provided the credibility which soothed the firms' nerves. Investors, frightened by what they were reading, were more inclined to contact representatives of Canada than of a Quebec that was so unflatteringly portrayed in the financial press. A major Virginia investor who had read that Quebec bonds might be redeemed in the worthless Quebec currency of the future (*Fortune* wondered whether it would be called "le franc") had his worries put to rest by a Canadian diplomat. The important Teachers Pension Fund, reluctant to buy more Quebec bonds, was eventually prevailed upon to buy $40 million worth after Canadian counsellors in New York reviewed the situation with them and set up meetings in Ottawa and Montreal.

Canada's economic interest, as Consul General Steers saw it, lay in keeping things calm, so as to "promote the idea of stability and continuity in Canada," rather than scaring away potential investors. Besides, it was tough to attract Americans to New Brunswick while talking about a revolution in Quebec. "There's no bad-mouthing of Quebec around here, and if there was, I'd be pretty bloody mad," Steers thundered.

On the other hand, direct personal contacts between influential English Canadians and Americans were often coloured by the panic that had seized some in Toronto and the West Island of Montreal. Willis Armstrong, who spent a career in and out of American administrations as a member of the influential Atlantic Council and as an advisor, in his time, to the CIA, remembers that as the referendum approached, "senior businesspeople" whom he refuses to name buttonholed him in the elegant surroundings of a private club in Toronto.

"We are worried stiff. You ought to be as worried as we are," they told him. "If we had a civil war, would you help us?" Armstrong remained cool: "I'm not going to be as scared as you want me to be. I've been in Quebec and I'm comfortable with them."

Bernard Landry claims to have surprised a Canadian general in the act of drawing an alarming scenario for an American diplomat. "They're all socialists, leftists, dangerous people," the general said, describing the *péquistes*. The minister subsequently accosted the diplomat with his ideological reply. "But," sighs Landry, "what credibility has a 'pinko communist' got, faced with a general?"

## Bourassa: The speaking Tourist

And then there was Robert Bourassa.

After his defeat at the hands of the PQ in 1976, the premier went into self-imposed exile, to Belgium and to the US. He lived briefly in Washington, where he was a guest professor at Johns Hopkins University's Center for Canadian Studies. The center is a sounding board and meeting place for America's Canadian specialists, a place where the administration, the academic world and the nearby Canadian Embassy could exchange views.

When Claude Morin came to speak to students at Johns Hopkins in April of 1978, he faced an audience which was well-prepared by their professor. When Bernard Landry went to Chicago to address a university audience, he ran into young people already under the influence of the pro-federalist arguments made by Robert Bourassa the week before. For the *péquistes* who made their way through the United States, Bourassa was a curse that did not want to go away.

The former premier was not, however, leading any anti-Quebec campaign during his stay in the US. John Anderson, the *Post* editorialist whom Bourassa invited over one day for a chat, had often met "the guy who had lost the election and went around screaming, 'Watch out, these guys [the winners] are a bunch of communists.' " But Bourassa, says Anderson, "was not, as I recall, very vehement." What did he say? Nothing very memorable. "It was one more conversation with someone who had lost an election."

There was great nostalgia in Robert Bourassa's years in the wilderness. Perhaps it was the distance from home, the itch to be back in the saddle, or the reappearance of an old separatist virus he had caught ten years earlier through contact with Lévesque (it was in Bourassa's living room that Lévesque and his friends had cooked up the idea of sovereignty-association in 1967) but since kept latent for career reasons. Whatever his motive, the fact remains that at one point, Bourassa toyed with the idea of supporting the project of sovereignty-association.

He talked about it with Claude Morin and Louise Beaudoin, with whom he crossed paths in Brussels, Paris, Washington and Montreal. But there was one condition. For him, the association aspect would have to include some sort of common federal parliament, made up of members who were elected and endowed with certain powers. Faced with such a proposition, he said, "80% of Quebec would vote yes," as would he. Morin, a long-time participant in the process of softening the separatist line, found, however, that Bourassa's suggestion took the heart out of sovereignty. Morin was also suspicious of this man who had so recently been a political rival; he decided not to follow up on the offer.

Bourassa's gesture proved, if proof was necessary, that the former Liberal leader was dying to get back into the game. He lived only for Quebec politics and, even when abroad, closely followed the situation at home. Knowing that Morin was coming to Washington, Bourassa called and asked him as an old colleague (Morin had also been Bourassa's constitutional expert) to bring along newspapers and copies of *Argus,* the Quebec government's daily press review.

After a long conversation in the minister's Washington hotel room, Morin watched from his window as the former leader of Quebec departed. "Watching him go into the street with his bundle of newspapers, looking for a taxi, was both sad and symbolic," Morin remembers. "He was really all alone."

## A Strategic Blunder

The media powers and the networks of personal connections that were marshalled after November 15, 1976, to build a wall of anti-separatist ideology around Quebec had an impact all the more striking because Quebec, as a state, and the separatists, as a party, had made the mistake of doing nothing to prepare their ground.

Twenty-two years had passed since André Patry had noted the "urgency" of making a "real effort to educate the groups that will be able to come to our aid when we need it." Nobody, since then, had bothered to sow any seeds of sympathy in America. And now that Quebec needed informed listeners, if not allies, in America, all it found were stony or disbelieving faces.

The Parti Québécois had not been unaware of the stakes from the very start. As early as 1969, René Lévesque had known what his party had to do: "Set up offices in New York and at the United Nations, in Washington and Boston." When the PQ came to power, it would "reap the dividends of this effort," in the form of "a far greater understanding in America than anyone could have hoped for." Having been a conscious architect of its own American isolation, the Parti Québécois, once in power, paid the price of its strategic blunder.

If the PQ wanted to keep America on the sidelines as the referendum approached — a condition it considered necessary for victory — then it would have to effect a turnaround in that part of American public opinion which could influence the government's position: members of the Councils on Foreign Relations, readers of the *Washington Post,* the *Atlantic* and *Commentary,* senior civil servants and congressional advisors. For the moment, drinking exclusively from streams of negativism and paranoia, these people gave every sign of being committed partisans of the "NO" side.

# 13

# Operation America

*Nine-tenths of diplomacy is being there.*
Diplomatic saying

There was a strong temptation, in Quebec government circles, to dismiss the Americans, to place them definitively in the "enemies" column, to write them off as too much trouble.

The supreme weapon, the pro-American leader of the PQ himself, had not managed to put a chink in the United States armor after all. Why waste energy on a lost cause when there were a hundred matters to occupy the frantic government: abolishing the system of shadowy electoral funds, reinventing automobile insurance, dusting off agricultural zoning, francizing the linguistic landscape, raising the minimum wage, and protecting strikers from scabs as did no other government on the continent. On top of all that, the population had to be prepared for the great referendum challenge.

The day after Jimmy Carter's statement at the summit with Trudeau in February of 1977, René Lévesque, whose dreams for American "sympathy and understanding" had perished a month earlier in New York, shrugged and commented, "We'll live with it." The President's little promise not to interfere, his insistence on the fact that it was "up to Canadians to decide" their future, seemed at least to skirt the worst.

Apart from the feeling that Quebec could not match the strength of the federal diplomatic machine on American terrain, four arguments militated in favour of a policy of immobility. First, Quebec officials worried about waking the sleeping giant. Fear of the mammoth United States stopped them dead in their tracks. Quebec was also remarkably ignorant of the reality of American power. The impression was that Washington was a mysterious monolith — organized, efficient, implacable — which would as soon cut off one's hand as shake it. In fact, power in Washington, much more than in Paris, is fluid, divided, constantly changing, and eminently permeable to foreign influences.

This misapprehension had a corollary: since Washington formed a cohesive unit, there was no reason to take its pulse. "It has not been demonstrated that having someone with an office in a city will provide us with better information," explains Claude Morin, who usually had better intuition. In fact, Washington, more than Quebec City or Ottawa, is such a complex city that it can be read correctly only from within. Even from New York, it is difficult to sort out the essential from the secondary or the insignificant; what is true last week and false this week can be judged unconstitutional next week and obligatory next month.

Third, the legal screen blocked the view of Quebec diplomats. For a province to open a diplomatic office in Washington — or Kalamazoo — it must in theory have the approval of both Washington and Ottawa. The State Department had firmly decided to recognize only one kind of Canadian in the capital: the federal kind. To Quebec's chagrin, the Department even refused to forward to its general delegation in New York copies of public official documents that could be handed out to any passerby. "Speak to your ambassador," the Quebeckers were told.

American diplomatic personnel in Quebec City, Montreal, and Ottawa, finally, played their role of killjoy to perfection. Quebec diplomats recall that they were told by US envoys "to keep a low profile," not to make waves, to stay quietly at home. US consuls were there for two reasons: to relay instructions sent from Washington, and to ensure the supremacy of their own role. As the sole guardians of this unique communication channel, they had influence in Quebec and the ear of Washington. If they allowed themselves to be bypassed or overwhelmed by their Quebec "clients," they were to be no more than mailboxes.

Ironically, the Americans and Trudeau's staff had expected the new Quebec government to quickly launch an aggressive and, they felt, potentially fruitful campaign to establish its credibility and seek allies to the south. Ambassador Enders wore himself out on the telephone to try to prevent a PQ assault. The State Department's August 1977 study, "The Quebec Situation," informed its very select group of readers that Quebec would "try to involve the US on its side" and to enlist, among others, Franco-Americans, "who may try to influence the US government and Congress."

When it was later explained to American officials that Quebec did not feel legally authorized to set foot in Washington, they broke out in smiles. Ontario had long had its own lobbyist, under a transparent disguise. There were a hundred ways to break into the American capital if one really wanted to. A Quebec-US friendship committee would be an expedient way to put out feelers. Hydro Quebec could happen to open an office there. The Montreal separatist daily *Le Jour*, which had gone weekly at the beginning of the Lévesque mandate, could send a pseudo-correspondent. Perhaps there could be a press outlet for the Parti Québécois. After all, even *Pravda* had an office!

In fact, Washington awaited the Quebeckers. Washington was eager for the Quebeckers to arrive. It was a test of will, and of skill.

## Through the Keyhole

Lévesque's government had two friends in the United States: Elliott Feldman and Alfred Hero. These two comprised the entire American wing of the "Quebec Mafia." They organized conferences, facilitated contacts, passed on messages.

Hero, a brilliant academic from Louisiana, was one of the very few Americans who was truly expert on Quebec affairs. He was the director of the World Peace Foundation in Boston, and had studied Quebec since the sixties. He was unavoidable. This was what made him useful.

At the beginning of 1977, the State Department organized a two-day conference on separatist movements: Quebec, the Basque, Scotland, and a few others. Under the cover of a Washington think tank, some twenty government experts on Canada and Europe, including representatives from the Treasury and Commerce departments, the Pentagon, and the National Security Council, met in secret at Airlie House, in a suburb of Washington. A representative from the CIA's analysis division, economy section, also attended. There were no secretaries or under-secretaries, but those middle-level officials who actually managed dossiers and wrote recommendations.

Hero was asked to prepare one of the two presentations on Quebec. He had initially suggested that the organizers invite a Quebec nationalist, a Scot, and so on, but he was told that only Americans were invited. If that was so, Hero responded, he would present his text to his Quebec nationalist friends for comments first. He needed no opinions "from the federalist side," he explained, "I knew what those were."

Yet Hero, who favored sovereignty, was the most critical of advocates. He protested that the new government had not sufficiently prepared itself to deal with the United States, and deplored its amateurism and naiveté. He even had some doubts about its competence. His twenty-four page document strongly criticized the new government on this point, a position that would not reassure his audience. But when he distributed copies of his draft in Quebec, some readers close to the PQ cooled his ardor. One of them was Richard Pouliot, Claude Morin's choice as the organizer of Quebec diplomacy in the United States and later a deputy minister.

"I don't think they changed the overall thrust of the paper," said Hero. Guided by his intellectual honesty rather than by his sympathies, he told the American officials, "It is difficult to imagine how an independent Quebec could either directly or indirectly advance the long-term interests of the US" He explained, however, that since the PQ had not completed "the business of just sorting out their policy toward the US, I just, across the board, toned all of this down." In fact, his readers, including Pouliot, felt that the PQ just "didn't think they were going to get in, however they did these [ambiguous electoral platforms] to get elected." Given a little time, they pleaded, they would be more specific.

If these comments weakened his thesis, it would have been interesting to see the original draft. Hero told the American officials:

> It is still too early after its election to estimate how, in fact, the PQ government will behave in respect to these economic issues of concern to Americans. Off the record, private discussions with pertinent PQ leaders over nearly a decade since Lévesque established the sovereignty movement suggest they have not examined empirically, or even thought systematically, about economic (or other) relations with the US Other issues, more directly related to winning the next election and negotiating with the federal government have monopolized their attention. Much of their perception of probable reactions of interested élites in pertinent US governmental and private decision-making roles has been rather vague, undifferentiated, and naive, including a good deal of wishful thinking.

This perception was widespread, since at this meeting and in the following months Hero was repeatedly asked regarding the PQ, "Are they just naive, or have they something up their sleeves they don't want to talk about? If it's the latter, then we ought to really be alarmed."

The main points of Hero's analysis were similar to those put forth in "The Quebec Situation" six months later. His contribution to the discussion and debate at Airlie House served to calm the nerves of the officials regarding the PQ's ideology. These officials tended to put the PQ "much further to the left than any characters I knew," Hero says. The representative from the Commerce Department had been particularly alarmed. There were questions about Parizeau and some of his past statements, as well as about the "investment code" in an independent Quebec. But Lévesque's pro-Americanism was reassuring and clear.

"You couldn't go beyond a point, because, I thought that some of the stance of the PQ was counterproductive to their own interest up to that point, myself," says Hero. Another difficulty was fear of violence. A number of speakers, including Hero, doubted that the process of independence could unfold without some spontaneous acts of violence between the two involved ethnic groups.

Still, Hero's main recommendation to the group of American bureaucrats gave Pouliot and his team reason to be happy: "The practice of shying from opportunities for frank contact with talented observers sympathetic to, or part of, the independentist leadership which seemed to prevail prior to November 15th, need be rapidly remedied." The serious gaps in the Americans' knowledge about the Quebec reality were attributable, he said, to the monopoly held by "Canadian Anglophones and bilingual Francophones in the business and professional communities of relatively conservative, federalist views" in the network of contacts between the United States and Canada.

Pouliot could not have known how much Hero's document shared with State Department reasoning. It gave him a view of the problem from inside the United States, however, which was a thousand times more pertinent than the analyses blindly concocted in Quebec City living rooms. In Boston, barely days after the closed-door conference ended, Hero gave Pouliot a scandalized description of the meeting, notably of the ignorance that some officials had shown of Quebec.

The image of the American monolith began to crumble in Pouliot's mind. He remembered having met John Rouse, director of the Canada Desk at the State Department, at some Quebec-Canada committee meeting in 1975. (At the time Pouliot was a high-ranking civil servant in the ministry of industry and not politically linked to the PQ.) Now in charge of Quebec diplomacy in the United States, he decided to see whether he and Rouse could not get together for lunch.

A dozen times between 1977 and 1981, Pouliot thus had a direct contact with the kingpin of the Canadian dossier at the State Department, Rouse, with his successor Richard Smith, and with some others. Often they met at a Washington restaurant; a few times at the State Department itself. Nothing particularly momentous happened during these encounters, except that Rouse had access to a bona fide Quebec official who could explain the policies and philosophy of his government. Pouliot also verified the quality of information that Rouse was obtaining from his diplomats in Quebec City and Montreal; conversely, he compared what Rouse said to positions taken by his consuls in Canada.

Pouliot and Rouse got along well. They were both self-assured and energetic and in the prime of their careers. In diplomatic terms, their friendship was a revolution. For the State Department, Quebec amounted to more than simply telegrams or bits of paper sent by airplane. For Morin's advisor, the "Foggy Bottom" was no longer a black hole.

In the spring of 1978, a meeting was arranged for Claude Morin, John Rouse, Rouse's assistant Carl Clement, and Canadian ambassador Peter Towe, on the neutral territory of Washington's Capitol Hilton Hotel. On another occasion, Pouliot met with State Department staff in the presence of a federal official, Jacques Cousineau. A Radio-Canada reporter ambushed them as they left the building, and the affair was the source of a few indignant questions in the House of Commons. It was ironic, as this was the only time that a federal representative was present at one of Pouliot's little sessions.

## Our Man in Washington

Quebec was best known and understood at the State Department. Elsewhere — in the the administration, in Congress, the institutions, and the press — people remained totally ignorant about Canada and Quebec. During his brief visits to Washington, Pouliot could not possibly spread himself thin enough to see and impress everyone with his calm regard and his quiet strength. And the idea of establishing a Quebec delegation in Washington was pitilessly torpedoed by Ottawa — which had done the same to an Ontario project some years before — and by the "Foggy Bottom." The legal screen was working perfectly.

Yet in Ottawa, the legality of a Quebec diplomatic offensive on Washington was investigated. The conclusion was that it had a good chance at success: "Quebec could put an information officer in Washington without the American administration indicating its approval or intervening in any way," wrote the general director of coordination at the Department of External Affairs, James Hyndman. In fact, Quebec had a clear field, he added, "given that when it registered its Quebec office in New York with the American Justice Department, it mentioned 'financial, trade, touristic, and cultural' interests and that other Quebec offices in the US were considered as extensions of the New York office."

In Washington, Gilles Mathieu, the Canadian ambassador's right-hand man, added that aggressive Quebec lobbying in Congress would certainly contravene some American law, but on the whole, he wrote, "The symbolic political presence of the Quebec government in Washington could become significant in the long run." Quebec's "contacts with Congress could influence some important members."

Due either to defeatism or to a lack of means, the Quebeckers did not bother to analyse the holes in Ottawa's legal blockade closely. Not only did they too quickly reach the conclusion that Washington was impenetrable, but months went by before they began to explore the many roundabout ways they might break in.

What if Quebec opened a tourism bureau to solicit clients from among national associations based in the American capital for the new Palais des Congrès de Montréal? And what if the bureau consisted of an office for an "information officer"? For Quebec City's anemic "United States" team (which at first comprised only two experts to cover "from the Arctic to the Antarctic"), this notion was bold to the point of foolhardiness. "I believe that the risk of inconveniencing the American authorities is too high," wrote a senior official in June of 1977. His reaction was typical.

In December, the announcement was made that the much-discussed bureau would open in February of 1978, some 15 months after the PQ came to power. René Lévesque confided, with a big smile, that someone there would be able to dispense political information on Quebec to anyone who wanted it.

When the minister of tourism, Yves Duhaime, presented promotional material to the press at the bureau's official opening, it was obvious that the bureau's designers had taken some liberties. On the map of Canada, Quebec appeared in relief. It occupied a disproportionately large area, and there was no trace on its northeast border of Labrador (which Quebec never recognized). The event was the subject of newspaper articles, call-in shows, and debates in the Quebec National Assembly, all proving that the operation was essentially political.

Once this little tempest had subsided, the PQ government finally had its bureau in Washington. It had paid the political price for its presence in the capital and many commentators assumed that a political beachhead had been established. In fact the bureau was occupied only by a tourism officer surrounded by his interesting maps. There was no "information officer" in sight. The Quebec underdog had braved the elements and survived the storms, and returned home without making any territorial gains.

Starting in the fall of 1978, however, a Quebecker occasionally occupied the office that had been reserved for the "information officer." Jean-Marc Blondeau, political advisor to the delegation in New York, where he served as a liaison with the United Nations, several universities, and others, travelled to Washington about every three weeks. He was there to prepare for René Lévesque's visit to the capital in January of 1979, but also to forge links with the local political fauna to the extent that his quick trips permitted.

At the State Department, where introductions had already been made, access was easy. Blondeau met with a Canada Desk official during each of his visits, most of the time in a restaurant, but once in the hallowed building itself. Regarding the most timely dossiers — environment and energy — he was sometimes able to arrange a meeting with a senator's assistant or a government agency specialist. This inch-by-inch progress required patience, but its promise still failed to convince Quebec that with a more continuous presence the province would gain ground more quickly. When Blondeau left his position in New York, in the summer of 1979, the office in Washington was again empty until February of 1980, three months before the referendum.

The new Quebec representative assigned to the New York–Washington beat was Peter Dunn, an official at the US desk in Quebec City. He was perfectly bilingual — he came from an eminent Quebec Anglophone family — and looked more youthful than his thirty-four years. He took up Blondeau's contacts, and frequented restaurants with the men from "Foggy Bottom."

"The person they chose was quite junior," explained a civil servant, speaking of Dunn. "No one wanted to make waves. No one wanted to draw attention to the advisor."

Despite this almost pathological timidity, Quebec did succeed in opening two doors at the White House. One was thanks to a slow and persistent presence in Washington. Jean Chapdelaine, a long-time delegate general in Paris, had been the third secretary at the Canadian embassy in Washington in 1940. One of his young friends at the time, Hedley Donovan, had since gone on to be the publisher of *Time*. The two men never completely lost touch, and when Donovan became a senior advisor to Jimmy Carter, in 1979, Chapdelaine met with him a couple of times in Washington and in New York. "We didn't talk in depth about Quebec," Chapdelaine recalled, but this personal conduit to one of the three people who had direct access to the American President was a precious thing. Foreign countries paid millions to local lobbyists for the privilege. In emergency situations, messages could flow in both directions.

Evelyn Dumas opened the second door, which let into Zbigniew Brzezinski's office at the National Security Council. This was where recommendations from "Foggy Bottom," the Pentagon, and the CIA underwent a final synthesis before being relayed to the President. Dumas established communication with a high-ranking NSC official via a common friend. She met him in 1978, when she and Blondeau were preparing for Lévesque's visit to Washington. She saw her contact — whom she prefers not to name — a few times, once during a week when a magazine had published a report on a "CIA emergency plan" to go into effect if Quebec separated. "The last time we had an emergency plan," her contact told Dumas, "was for the Berlin crisis, and when the crisis started, no one even looked at the plan." The collapse of American policy in Iran, in the news at the time, was one illustration of this situation. Dumas and her contact agreed to stay in touch as needed.

They had almost become regulars at "Foggy Bottom," they gained access to a presidential advisor and a National Security Council staffer, they knew, through Hero, what was being said about them behind closed doors. Not bad for or a bunch of rank amateurs.

## Inventing Policy

Quebec's timid efforts to gain a permanent foothold in Washington did not fairly reflect the feverish activity of the United States division's small team. They stumbled, trembling, toward the heart of the beast, but they devoted great energy and considerable talent to other parts of its anatomy. Over a year and a half, from the beginning of 1977 to the middle of 1978, twenty-five ministerial visits to the United States were organized; according to Ottawa's Department of External Affairs, Quebec government envoys participated in more than 100 conferences.

Operation America had a budget of $1.5 million to concentrate Quebec resources and energy on the United States over the 18 months from mid-1978 to 1980. Five ministries were asked to contribute, and ministers poured over the border as never before. The goal, as it was expressed in an internal document, was to:

> Get the United States to <u>manifest, at all levels, an attitude of benign neutrality</u> with regard to Quebec's political and social process and, <u>in certain sectors</u> (economic, for example), to <u>take an attitude of active and cooperative sympathy</u>.

The document explained that the operation must "reassure the business world," "spread Quebec culture," "counter the influence of truncated information," "project the image of a modern, dynamic, civilized Quebec," and "create a permanent interest in Quebec in all of the circles that count in the United States." "The primary audience is the business world," stated the document; this sector could, according to the defined goal, offer "active sympathy." The operation would "not rule out actions with regard to decision makers in the areas of education, culture, communications, and the economy." This list, made at the first meeting of the interministerial committee for the operation in August of 1978, left out politicians and journalists. That fall the operation adjusted its objective to include "opinion-making circles and people." Thus, journalists, academics, and "politicians at all levels" now figured among the "primary audience," alongside business people. (The "secondary audience" comprised "the Quebec population" and "the civil service." These groups had to be made aware of the importance of staying on good terms with the United States. After Bill 101 was passed, increasing numbers of Americans complained about the drop in courtesy at tourist establishments in Quebec City and Montreal.)

The notion of concentrating specifically on the "economic sector" arose from the logic of political returns. Quebeckers dreaded the potential negative economic fallout of sovereignty. The PQ scored a point every time an important American business person expressed confidence in the bright economic future of Quebec. In January of 1977, for example, the vice-president of Imperial Oil (the Canadian subsidiary of Exxon) stated that a future State of Quebec "would offer foreign investors a viable and healthy economy."

The designers of Operation America were right to think that some in the American business world would find an independent Quebec interesting. Americans in New York and Washington who supported official US policy recalled that they had to intervene often not with industrialists who wanted to send in the Marines, but with those who were thinking of ways to profit from an independent Quebec. Heads of companies on occasion stated intentions of this sort to George Vest, undersecretary of state for european affairs. "After all, businessmen are very venal," comments Vest, who had a strict policy of trying to convince CEOs that long-term American interests militated for a united Canada. This generally was enough to dampen their separatist fervor, Vest says.

In New York, Alex Tomlinson of First Boston also recalled these rebel voices. "There were always people saying, 'Gee, maybe if they separated we could snap up Quebec or our next-door neighbor would be weakened and maybe this would be good for us [...] Maybe we ought to encourage these people instead of being neutral.'" Tom Enders, recalled Tomlinson, "was quite clear" in dealing with these hot-heads. "Whenever anybody said that, the answer was 'Forget it, this is not our business at all, our relations with Canada are more important, our own interest clearly is in Canada remaining strong and united.'"

On the other hand, Vest said that in the case of heads of American companies who wanted to promote a united Canada, "I wouldn't have done other than say 'Be careful.'" He would simply warn them, "Don't extend your activities to the point that Canadians feel you're intervening with their internal policies." The economic ground was thus fertile for Operation America, perhaps precisely because it played on pecuniary interest and not on the ideology of the Americans concerned.

With such a profusion of targets, the Operation made up a list of some fifty projects to complete during the eighteen months, with descriptions, schedules, distribution of responsibilities, and budgets. The United States division shifted into high gear. Its staff in Quebec City more than doubled, new information directors were sent to New York and to Boston, and staff in the Quebec network in the United States rose to 68, from 48 the previous summer.

Still, the Operation America document was taken with a large grain of salt by a number of Quebec diplomats posted to the United States. "When we received it, we put it in a drawer," commented Rénald Savoie, communications director in New York. Yet the spirit of Operation America, if not the letter, kicked Quebec diplomacy out of its lethargy.

## Charming the Media

A media campaign began, in which journalists who had written pieces deemed offensive were contacted. One early Operation America memo suggested that a list of American journalists and their political biases be compiled but the suggestion, of great scandal-value, was never implemented. In every city they visited, Quebec ministers and staff systematically met with editors of the big newspapers and tried to explain the difference between "sovereignty-association" and "separatism" — always an intellectual challenge. René Lévesque's speech at the Economic Club was cited as an example of what not to say. When Lévesque visited Boston in the spring of 1978, he was asked if he would again talk about American independence. "I won't go into any parallels today," he answered. "Last year I tried ... and it wasn't a roaring success."

When Bernard Landry was preparing to visit New York in 1979, the Quebec delegation gave him a short list of discussion points: "1. Prove that Quebec is not socialist; 2. Demonstrate that Quebec is not anti-American." As well, "it would be excellent if the minister could develop the idea of the government's proposed [Canada–Quebec] common market."

One of the most widely read journalists on the Quebec question was William Safire, once Nixon's speechwriter, now a columnist at the *The New York Times*. His interest in Quebec separatism had persisted since his brief conversation on the subject with de Gaulle. In his futuristic political novel, *Full Disclosure*, published in 1977, he described a world in which the strategic equilibrium had changed. One of his characters, the secretary of state, made a status report to the president, who had been blinded after an attack in the USSR:

> We have an immediate problem on our borders, as you know: both the Québécois and the Mexicans are aligned against us, leading the Fourth World, along with Nigeria [the Fourth World also included the poor African and Latin American countries]. That makes all the more necessary a solid Soviet-American alliance to keep the world from flying apart.

It was Safire's ultra-conservative columns, syndicated in dozens of the country's largest newspapers, rather than his fiction that gave René Lévesque the impression that Safire was "Strangelovian" (a reference to the title character in a Kubrick film who inadvertently leads the world into nuclear war). In a column published just before Lévesque visited Washington in 1979, Safire called attention to "the potential Balkanization of Canada," which separated "the land mass of the Soviet Union from the half-continent that is the United States." He reprimanded "Foggy Bottom" for its timid approach to the subject of Quebec, and wrote that Pierre Trudeau had "neither the stature nor the gumption to rally all Canadians" to the cause. Mr. Safire certainly knew how to make friends.

But Safire had the courage of his convictions and walked up to Lévesque when the Premier visited Washington. The Quebec leader told Safire that he had read his most recent column twice and — flashing his sly smile — that he had liked it even less the second time. Lévesque's advisors jumped on the opportunity to arrange a second meeting for the two men soon after. Safire was influential enough that Quebec and Canadian diplomats in New York felt the impact each time he pointed his pen — one of the sharpest in the country — toward Quebec. Nixon's ex-speechwriter had decided to make Quebec secession a personal crusade.

"I just don't want us to get caught in Canada as we did in Iran," where the Shah had just fallen, he said, "wondering how all this could have happened." Safire hoped that Washington would warn Quebec before the referendum that the US would look very dimly on any attempt to dismember Canada, and that an independent Quebec would pay dearly, economically and politically, for such impudence. This tirade was more vitriolic than Claude Morin's most pessimistic imaginings.

In April, Safire and Lévesque talked in Montreal. "It seems that Mr Safire returned home," wrote a civil servant after the interview, with "respect and admiration" for Lévesque, but still with the same "obsession with destabilization" of the continent. In fact, one week after their meeting, Safire wrote in the *New York Times* that "Mr Lévesque is surely the world's most likeable revolutionary leader." He found him "personally" and "intellectually honest" and predicted that he "is likely to win" the referendum. Lévesque had explained that he was pro-American, that his socialism was based on the moderate Scandinavian model, and that the economy would remain sound, since even Saudi Arabia was contemplating investing in Quebec. From this Safire concluded that after independence, "when the engaging founder [of the new Quebec state] steps aside, the rest of Canada and the United States face the unknown, except that our St Lawrence Seaway partner will be socialist, Arab-influenced, and its friendship a question mark."

Neutralizing American journalists was no easy feat.

## The Return of René Lévesque

In spite of his previous setback in New York, René Lévesque remained convinced that his persuasive powers could make a difference in the United States. In his next American speech, before a thousand students and professors in Boston in April of 1978, his preoccupation with anti-Semitism did not entirely drain his power over his audience. He succeeded in making them laugh, and he won several warm rounds of applause. (Among the admirers who went to meet him after the speech was one Armand Morissette.) At Harvard he would not, as he did in New York, revel in the word "independence." Here, the term was "sovereignty-association" and Lévesque did appear to have made some conquests; three weeks later, when the Canadian Secretary of State, John Roberts, spoke before the same audience, a few students used the premier's points to argue against the minister's federalist option.

The trip to Boston was only a rehearsal, however; it was in New York the following month that Lévesque was to make his true comeback. His audience was the Council on Foreign Relations: ambassadors, bankers, and past and future political heavyweights.

The Council hosted its meeting according to strict and rigorously observed rules. The speech was to start around 5:20 PM, and to last exactly 20 minutes. The next half-hour was reserved for questions. At 6:30 PM, everyone stood up and made for limousines or commuter trains. René Lévesque knew this, since he had broken the cardinal rule when he had last been invited: in 1972 he had arrived late. Many members of the audience, offended by this impropriety, had left before he made his speech.

This time, Lévesque was on time. But the importance of this event had made him nervous. The moment he started his speech he sounded a false note by scolding the master of ceremonies, the president of the Bank of Montreal, William Mulholland, for having presented him as "Prime Minister." In English, he said, the term was "premier" for provincial heads; there was "only one prime minister in Canada," Pierre Trudeau. Why Lévesque made this awkward opening remark remains a mystery.

René Lévesque talked. His audience was eager to hear about his plans for sovereignty, his intentions regarding foreign policy, his centre-left leanings. He talked about automobile insurance for fifteen minutes. In detail. Then about the asbestos industry. In detail.

It was now 6:00 PM Protocol dictated that this next half-hour was reserved for questions; Lévesque continued talking. Mulholland placed his watch on the lectern, where another watch was already ticking away. Lévesque proved indefatigable. At 6:08, Mulholland passed him a note indicating that he had gone over his time limit. Lévesque wouldn't stop. At 6:18, a senior staffer of the Council, Zygmunt Nagorski, stood up and whispered in the Quebecker's ear that it was time for questions. Lévesque talked for several more minutes, his audience clearly aware of the drama unfolding at the head table. By the time Lévesque made his final point, it was 6:22.

Lévesque spoke on the first question — on the "exodus" of English Canadians from Quebec — for six minutes. A second question, regarding the average Quebecker's interest in independence, took him to the end of the session. "The group's frustration was visible," noted Nagorski to the New York delegate general in a letter in which he listed the temporal transgressions of the premier's address.

Jean-Marc Blondeau, a Quebec diplomat in New York, thought that "Mr Lévesque's speech went well in general," in spite of the hitches. Other witnesses were less complimentary. "He laid the biggest egg I've ever seen at a Council meeting," said one. "He was bush league. He could have been the mayor of Albany attempting to address the United Nations — way out of his depth."

"Maybe Quebeckers are gullible," said another. "We're not. He'll never be invited again."

During a reception the next day, René Lévesque asked Nagorski if it was true that the Council had not been pleased with his performance. Nagorski confirmed his fears. According to a Canadian diplomat, "Lévesque's response was to stick out his tongue" at Nagorski. A few days later, Nagorski wrote Lévesque. He emphasized that "reports on no-fault insurance and the asbestos industry and other topics could perhaps have been left out," of Lévesque's address. The premier's message, he added "was somewhat blurred by our inability to engage in a dialogue, something we are accustomed to at our gatherings with heads of state and other important visitors." Nagorski was tactful enough not to mention that other recent visitors, notably Pierre Trudeau and Claude Ryan, had been more respectful of the rules of the Council. Trudeau had talked for only ten minutes, opening the remainder of his time to questions.

Lévesque continued his New York visit with a stop at the morning program *The Today Show*, where Tom Brokaw bombarded him with questions on sovereignty. For five million viewers Lévesque tried to defend the ideological Maginot line that distinguished "separatism" from "sovereignty-association" but it collapsed. "You can call it 'separation,' since we want our own constitution," he admitted. "We want to get out of the Canadian federal system, which means separation." All the same, an NBC producer judged that Lévesque had done well. "There's something winning about him," he said.

Lévesque also wanted to meet Kurt Waldheim, then secretary-general of the United Nations. The federal blockade applied here as elsewhere, and Ottawa informed the Quebec diplomats that it would allow the meeting only under the condition that Waldheim and Lévesque discussed matters of provincial jurisdiction only — there could be no talk of international questions. As it turned out Waldheim was away during Lévesque's visit, and so Lévesque did not have the luxury of holding forth on problems of roadworks at Trois-Rivières or of sewage in Paspébiac with him. But he did have someone much more important to meet in New York than a mere UN secretary-general.

## The Rockefeller Case

The premier met at Rockefeller Plaza with the man whose name was synonymous with American capitalism: David Rockefeller, president of the Chase Manhattan Bank, leader of the American financial intelligentsia, and founder of the Trilateral, the high-flying think tank that addressed geopolitical and economic questions regarding North America, Europe and Asia. Hundreds of authors and left-wing journalists (including Pierre Vallières in Quebec) were convinced that this eminent group was in effect the disguised embryo of a directorate that could make and break foreign governments.

Three men on the rise — Zbigniew Brzezinski, Cyrus Vance, and Jimmy Carter — actually met at the Trilateral Commission and Rockefeller thus had even more influence at the White House than was customary. He used it, among other things, to convince the President to allow Rockefeller's old friend, the Shah of Iran, to come to America for medical treatment for his cancer. This decision ended up serving as a pretext for the siezing of the American embassy in Teheran by Iranian "revolutionary students."

Rockefeller's record on Quebec was not completely blank. Ten years earlier, in the wake of "Vive le Québec libre!" Rockefeller had told a French reporter that he would react to Quebec's independence calmly and tactfully and would treat the new state as he would any other borrower. The separatist leader had often cited this sentence, since as evidence that the top financiers were not panicking. The day of his speech at the Economic Club, Lévesque went to see the banker, to tell him how highly he thought of his moderate attitude, and to acknowledge how much "Quebeckers appreciated his understanding of their objectives." But Rockefeller was a touch offended by this boldness. "It seems to me that it is rather a weak straw to be grasping at — something I said ten years ago," he complained to a reporter.

In fact, Rockefeller was financially, personally and emotionally attached to Canadian unity. Mackenzie King, the prime minister during the war, had made an important impression on his life. Hired as a lawyer in 1914 by David's father, John Jr., King had invented the concept of "shop unions" for the Rockefellers. The young David became very fond of the impressive Canadian, who became a sort of adoptive uncle. When Rockefeller finished his university studies at Harvard in 1936, he travelled by train to Ottawa to discuss his future with King. The prime minister of Canada was waiting for him in the Ottawa train station; the two spent a friendly weekend together. Much later, Rockefeller funded a chair for Canadian studies at Harvard which he named the William Lyon Mackenzie King Chair.

At the beginning of 1978, months before he would see Lévesque in New York, David Rockefeller decided to spend a little time in Canada. The Canadian consul general in New York, Barry Steers, passed on to Rockefeller Ottawa's request that he avoid making statements that could in any way be construed "as a source of solace or strength for the forces of Canadian disunity." The banker acquiesced, confirming his understanding that "separatists could derive considerable stature if they could be seen to have even tacit support from an international figure such as himself."

Rockefeller delivered his message to the Toronto business community at the Canadian Club. Yes, he declared, "I said ten years ago, and I reiterated earlier, that I do not believe it the proper role of outsiders to tell Canadians what to do about their own affairs. I think this is especially true with respect to the Quebec question." Having said this, Rockefeller went on to tell Canadians what to do about their own affairs: "It is my opinion that Canada, as a united nation for more than a century, has served as a strong and important partner of the United States. I believe it is absolutely essential — to the US and to the world — that that partnership be perpetuated, without interruption, in the difficult months and years ahead."

During his stay in Canada, a Radio-Canada reporter, Gilles-André Gosselin, button holed Rockefeller and asked him if American financiers would invest in an independent Quebec. The banker decided to take advantage of the opportunity to counter the words that had stuck to him like glue since 1967. "Uncertainty weighs against investment," he notably answered, in hesitant French. Pleased with himself, Rockefeller moved on. But the banker may have been too subtle, for Gosselin drew a surprising conclusion. Rockefeller, he reported, had said that "investors are not at all worried about the result of the referendum, whether it is decided in favor of the sovereignty option or the federalist option; for the president of the Chase Manhattan Bank, money has no political allegiance, nor does he feel that a sovereign Quebec would have problems attracting investment as long as the investors know what to expect."

The next day, when Rockefeller went to see Pierre Trudeau, he was not a little surprised that the Prime Minister had taken umbrage at the "support" that the eminent New Yorker "had given the separatist movement on Radio-Canada." Rockefeller sheepishly pleaded "not guilty" and convinced Trudeau that his intent had been quite the opposite.

Lévesque could not ignore the fact that Rockefeller had spoken from the heart at the Canadian Club — that he wished to distance himself from Quebec's plans. In New York in April of 1978, the PQ leader undertook to persuade the eminent billionaire that his government was not against private enterprise. During their 45-minute meeting, he cited an uncharacteristic speech given by the head of Canadian affairs of Prudential Life, an English Canadian named Lewis, who had praised the Quebec government's budget, its automobile-insurance legislation, the principle behind its Bill 101, and the economic summit it had organized in May of 1977. Prudential's assets in Quebec amounted to more than a billion dollars — much more than those of Chase Manhattan — yet Lewis had declared that "there was no scenario, including independence or separation of Quebec, to which Prudential could not accommodate, provided only that the general political orientation of the Parti Québécois permitted private enterprise to continue to operate in a reasonable way," which Lewis said was not in doubt. Soon after, Lévesque sent a copy of the complete speech to Rockefeller.

The banker did not really need a briefing; he was one of the best-informed people in the world. Still, he asked for news about the Quebec economy, about which he had heard bad things, discussed Prime Minister Trudeau's chances of being re-elected — about which he had also heard bad things — and asked Lévesque his opinion on the new federal banking law. Finally, smiling, he let Lévesque off the hook. According to Blondeau, who took notes, "Mr Rockefeller assured Mr Lévesque that, although he had indicated in his Toronto speech that he would prefer a federalist system for Canada, he had no problem with a new political régime for Quebec if the people of Quebec decided that that was what they wanted in the referendum."

David Rockefeller probably, as a foresighted businessman, decided to play both sides of the game. There was another indication that he was not that jittery about Quebec separation: he helped to finance the University Consortium for Research on North America, at Harvard University. The consortium, directed by Elliott Feldman, also received funding from the Quebec government and dealt largely with Quebec questions. It was on occasion even seen as a platform for the dissemination of the sovereignty message. Rockefeller was well aware of all this. "In an area in which he could have had, in one way or another, I suppose, an influence," says Feldman, "he certainly never tried to exercise it."

In the fall of 1978, the premier left for a week of US lobbying which took him to Chicago, San Francisco, and Los Angeles. He had refined his message since New York. As well, he could finally respond more precisely to questions on sovereignty-association, since his team — two years after the PQ came to power and ten years after the party was born — had now reached agreement on the principle of a monetary and customs union with Canada.

On every rostrum in the Midwest and the West, Lévesque sang three refrains: 1. We are North Americans; 2. We are a good government; 3. Stop being so nervous about the risk of Canada splitting up once Quebec leaves; Canada will end up stronger for the test.

This time, the Lévesque show was no flop. The local critics raved: "A terrific speaker," "a skilled advocate," "an impressive performer." Lévesque was always interesting, sometimes reassuring, almost never persuasive. He himself accurately described the atmosphere during this trip as a "genial skepticism" on the part of the Americans. "They've got their doubts that it'll come out the way we think," he added.

Lévesque made only one false move in his visit to the West. During an hour-long appearance on a local public-broadcasting station in San Francisco, he monopolized the airwaves with interminable responses, perhaps irked because one of the reporters had asked "Why are Quebec's Jews leaving the province?" Voices were raised as the reporters tried, without great success, to interrupt the voluble Quebecker. Viewers called the station to complain about the interviewers' tactlessness. After the verbal duel, a reporter confided that he had been tempted to say to Lévesque, "Obviously, you have no intention of answering our questions, so why don't you just go on talking for the remaining 40 minutes?" Lévesque admitted that the San Francisco broadcast, his chance to get his message across to a huge number of Californians, had been "catastrophic."

Ottawa seemed to feel that the trip had been something of a success — the score now stood at 3 to 1, Trudeau to Lévesque — since federal minister Marc Lalonde soon made an appearance before the World Affairs Council, one of the important forums Lévesque had addressed in San Francisco. "Perhaps we may even see the spectacle of a Canadian 'truth squad' following Lévesque as he stumps the US," wrote the consul general in Quebec City, Terry McNamara.

## "Dreams of Oval Room"

With his political show relatively well rehearsed in the West and after a year of planning, René Lévesque was ready for the command performance, in Washington, scheduled for January of 1979. The premier's advisor on international affairs, Yves Michaud, asked McNamara if a meeting with Jimmy Carter could be arranged. If not, Michaud was prepared to settle for Vice-President Walter Mondale. When he heard about it, John Rouse, in Washington, hastened to discourage the idea and reproached McNamara for not having done so himself. "Impression conveyed may have been more positive than situation warrants," he wrote. The absence of historical precedent and the extremely high value of these men's time must immediately be cited to stop this affair in its tracks. As well, Rouse noted, such a meeting could possibly "encourage plans to be made for Washington trip for Lévesque," which "Foggy Bottom" would have preferred to have avoided altogether. McNamara passed the message to Michaud and reassured Rouse: "Dreams of Oval Room exorcised."

Quebec leaders had always made every possible effort to meet with America's statesmen. Daniel Johnson's request, in 1967, had not had a ghost of a chance; Robert Bourassa had not managed to meet with Nelson Rockefeller, Gerald Ford's vice-president, in 1975. At the end of 1977, René Lévesque had asked to meet with see Walter Mondale, who had stopped off in Ottawa before setting off to meet with Peter Lougheed, premier of Alberta. Unfortunately, Ottawa responded, "the Vice-President's very full schedule during his short stay in Ottawa precluded accommodating the Premier of Quebec's request." And Lougheed? He was almost Mondale's neighbour, came the official response, since the Vice-President was from Minnesota. Over time, it became standard procedure. Every time an important United States government official arrived in Ottawa, Quebec asked to meet with him. Each time, Ottawa took note of the request, and then consigned it to the trash.

In Washington, where she was preparing for René Lévesque's arrival, Evelyn Dumas was having some trouble. Senator Frank Church, famous for having uncovered CIA scandals, would have been happy to meet with Lévesque during his visit. But now that the senator was chairman of the powerful Senate Foreign Affairs Committee, he had a quasi-official position and could not receive provincial premiers without approval from the Canadian embassy. Ted Kennedy, who was happy to discuss the successful Quebec medical insurance plan with senior officials, refused to be seen with the separatist leader. Only Edmund Muskie, senator from Maine, who had so loudly applauded Pierre Trudeau's speech, agreed to receive René Lévesque. He was not a bad man to visit; he was a very senior and very powerful senator.

A request was made directly to "Foggy Bottom" for Lévesque to meet with Secretary of State Cyrus Vance or some other high-ranking person. "Speak to the embassy," responded the department, following protocol. Secretly American diplomats crossed their fingers; if the embassy were to say yes, they would be quite put out. They heard no more about it. (Retrospectively, Ivan Head admitted that he would have given his approval: "I would have said, 'Get your own sense of this guy.'")

The most important forum René Lévesque addressed was the National Press Club, whose lunch-meetings were broadcast by dozens of American cable-network stations. Slowly, the Club filled its long head table. Invitations were issued to Canadian Ambassador Peter Towe, who accepted, and to a State Department representative, who also accepted, though only with the embassy's nod. Rouse's successor, Richard Smith, condescended to be seen in public with the Quebec separatist leader. The French embassy's chargé d'affaires rounded off the guest list. The French embassy also lent a hand to the team organizing the visit.

Dumas also succeeded in opening a door for Lévesque at the Center for Strategic and International Studies (CSIS), a Washington think tank where the upper crust of the foreign affairs community gathered. But the ex-journalist first had to pass muster herself by bearing up under aggressive questioning by six experts who, over dinner, grilled her on the PQ's strategic policy and raised the rarely discussed question of the Arctic border which an independent Quebec would share with the USSR. Dumas stood the test well.

When Lévesque presented himself at the National Press Club on January 25, 350 journalists, lobbyists, diplomats and high-ranking civil servants were there to hear him. A dozen reporters even asked for his autograph, a rarity at such events. Lévesque spoke reassuringly, promising that Quebec would "remain a staunch partner in North America and a member in good standing of the Western world." His speech, rambling as usual, captivated the crowd.

In spite of his staff's admonitions, Lévesque talked for fifteen minutes longer than he was scheduled to, which obliged the master of ceremonies to extend the question period by fifteen minutes. This time, no one fretted. The questions were precise and pointed, revealing a knowledge of Quebec that would have been unthinkable two years earlier. When someone mentioned the parallel with the American Civil War, Lévesque thundered, "That's a sick analogy that some people like to push around because they are panicking."

When he finished, there was warm applause. *The New York Times* even reported a standing ovation, which Quebec witnesses denied. "I thought he was an entertaining, forceful, and intelligent speaker," said the president of the Press Club, Arthur Wiesse, of the *Houston Post*. "Still," he added, "the prospect of an autonomous Quebec is something else altogether." This was apparently the most that a separatist speaker could hope for in the American capital. Richard Zimmerman, of the *Cleveland Plain Dealer*, summed up the situation thus: "He's an awfully good speaker. He's impassioned, yet appears reasonable at the same time. But that's not to say that he's changed me around." This was an improvement over what Zimmerman heard when he returned to Ohio, where people "have the impression that you've got some kind of screwy government up there that's run by crazy frogs who want to go off on their own."

As he left the Press Club, Lévesque was jostled by a group of ten Anglophone demonstrators who had come from Quebec to protest his language policy. Their placards, tangible proof of the acuteness of the problem, read "*En bas* [sic] *la loi 101!*" and "*Movement* [sic] *de la liberté.*" Their English was no better: "Second Class Citicens [sic again]."

Lévesque continued on to the Senate, where his meeting with Muskie was delayed for an hour, since the latter was in the middle of budget talks with President Carter. When Muskie returned from the White House, he briefly discussed sovereignty-association with Lévesque, then moved on to energy and potential electricity purchases by his state, Maine. Lévesque asked for no more.

But in leaving, Muskie astonished and delighted the premier by saying, on the record, what had never been heard from a highly placed American politician: "There seems to have been something of a panic among non-French-speaking Montrealers, and a lot of our feeling here has been a reflection of this. It seems that separatism is not a very precise word to describe what Mr Lévesque is talking about. My impression is that his aim is not separatism in the sense of isolation, but a new relationship that would bring a fresh dimension to Canada." Muskie's support was unexpected. "It was the icing on the cake," recalls Dumas. In Quebec, McNamara reckoned that the senator had succumbed "after a half-hour of concentrated exposure to Lévesque's disarming charm."

Lévesque then gave a long interview on the *McNeil-Lehrer News Hour*, the highbrow news dear to political junkies in the capital and to 10 million influential viewers. That evening, the entire program was dedicated to the premier. Perhaps buoyed up by Muskie's words, Lévesque was in good form: he did not get carried away, and he presented his political plans clearly and firmly.

He then left for CSIS, where some twenty guests awaited him for a closed-door dinner. Dumas was furious that the gathered guests were not of the caliber promised by the organizers. When it wanted to, the CSIS could seat at its table the Washington foreign policy establishment, including cabinet members. That evening, some senior officials were present, but there were no impressive figures. Lévesque's words for Washington should have reached journalists at the Press Club, politicians in general through *McNeil-Lehrer*, and decision makers through CSIS. One member of the troika had missed the call. "I took note of this duplicity" by CSIS organizers, Dumas wrote.

Rufus Smith, the former "Mr Canada" at "Foggy Bottom," was also among the guests. He did not let an allusion the premier made to "assistance from other governments" go by unnoticed; anxious to clear up any misapprehension regarding possible American involvement, Smith asked Lévesque what support he was talking about. The Quebecker evaded the question. Smith asked again. It was clear that Lévesque "didn't like the tone of my question," Smith recalls, but Lévesque finally let drop that "there is a great deal of sympathy in France," before rapidly turning to another subject.

Lévesque did manage to impress an important official, James Timberlake, Canada Desk Director at the Pentagon, to whom he had been introduced at the beginning of the evening. Lévesque later returned to the military expert, called him by his name, and asked him a question. "I was bowled over," recalled Timberlake, who also stated, "I was greatly impressed by him. I mean, I liked him. I didn't agree with his ideas, perhaps" — this seemed to be the new standard reaction to Lévesque's position. "A very good speaker, and a certain charm," he added.

The next day, the premier met with the editorial committee of the *Washington Post*. He was received glacially. The argument, always the same, was summarized by one of the participants: "What Lévesque doesn't seem to understand is that Americans don't care about a new constitutional arrangement Canadians may want to make among themselves. But they would be concerned about a subarctic Central America with fragments of states up there, each going its own way in a mixture of politics that could become everything from revolutionary to dictatorship." The nationalization of the potash industry in Saskatchewan, the election of a New Democratic government in British Columbia, and the separatist aspirations of Albertans gave the *Post* experts reason to feel that if Quebec separated, English Canadians would not be quite as boring as they once were.

In Quebec, McNamara wondered if the success of Lévesque's visit and, by extension, of Operation America, truly served Quebec's interests. "Lévesque had hoped, at worst, to neutralize American opinion by his soothing assurances. On the contrary, he may have aroused many complacent Americans to the realization that the erstwhile unthinkable threat to Canadian unity is after all to be taken seriously, and that it is being mounted not by a handful of crazies, but by sane, committed, determined people who potentially could succeed."

But Lévesque's visit was totally eclipsed, even in American newspapers such as *The New York Times*, by the publication of the long-awaited Pépin-Robarts federal report on Canadian unity. The report recommended, among other things, that responsibility for linguistic questions and protection of minorities be relegated to the provinces. This Pierre Trudeau categorically rejected the next day, proving, if there was need to, that the entire exercise had been a gigantic and costly smoke-screen.

## Allies Within Reach

If Robert Bourassa had hung a financial millstone around René Lévesque's neck with the James Bay project, he had at the same time granted Lévesque his best selling point for the United States.

The Quebec delegate in Boston, Jacques Vallée, realized at the October 1979 Conference of New England Governors, to which he was the only Quebecker invited, that the gigantic hydro-electric project "holds a true fascination for Americans in the Northeast, who are obsessed, to a degree that it is hard for us to imagine, with the energy crisis." The governors and their advisors, some of whom had visited the La Grande River where the finishing touches were being put to the turbines, were indefatigable on the subject.

Vallée discerned "a sort of admiration for Quebeckers' enterprising 'new frontier' spirit, and some envy, since they seemed to be able to solve their energy problems." Returning from the meeting dumbfounded that such good things were being said about his province in the United States, Vallée pushed the Operation America team to pursue this angle, which generated, he said, "a climate of sympathy and admiration for the successes of modern Quebec, the political consequences of which should not be underestimated."

Whole planeloads of Americans flew north to admire the artificial lake that was "as big as Switzerland," to walk on the gargantuan dam, to swoon before the "giant's steps" of the overflow sluices. Given such evidence of ingenuity and engineering prowess, American investors and diplomats (there were forty-three on one flight, in June of 1978) were discovering an aspect of Quebec that was difficult to reconcile with the image of incompetent Marxist bureaucrats whose children slept three to a bed, never went to school, and were forbidden to eat "foreign" Heinz ketchup.

Quebec was late in waking up to the local geopolitical scene. At first relations with the New England states were reduced and the eastern governors and premiers conferences were moribund. Daniel Latouche, the premier's advisor on constitutional questions, who also dipped a finger or two into American waters, considered these governors to be like "presidents of Richelieu Clubs." But in the process of negotiating for electricity sales, it slowly became obvious that potential allies and a source of political and economic goodwill were to be found much closer to home than in San Francisco. It was possible that Muskie, for example, was friendlier because Maine had a large Franco-American population. In any case, Richard Snelling, who had won the gubernatorial race in Vermont some days before Lévesque's electoral victory, ogled James Bay energy with an interest that increased proportionally to the cost of heating oil. His attention soon went beyond this single aspect; he ended up establishing long-standing amicable relations with Lévesque. The governors also provided a means to intercede with senators, to facilitate meetings, and to pass on information. These relations, a memo noted, were "hard to criticize on the constitutional level" from Ottawa's standpoint. It was in the Northeast that Operation America — a year old in the middle of 1979 — had the most success.

In Quebec, it was time for reports. These emphasized "the measurable improvement in the perception of Quebec in political and para-political circles. Important steps have been taken. The image of a radical society no longer holds. Premier Lévesque has gained the respect of his interlocutors and, in certain cases, their confidence." Efforts had also paid off with the press, noted the department of intergovernmental affairs. "The main prejudices have been considerably reduced. There is no more talk of tribal war or a fleeting phenomenon." (The Canadian embassy in Washington also noted that "the perception of the problem is deepening, at least in the big newspapers.") Quebec civil servants applauded the arrival of a larger number of dyed-in-the-wool American correspondents in Canada to cover Quebec and the "clear retreat" of English Canadian stringers. Who was responsible for this change? "Us," answered Roger Cyr, coordinator of the operation. "The quality and objectivity of articles published in the American press are in direct relation to the time invested to familiarize their writers with the reality of Quebec," he underlined, literally, in a document.

The universities, once the preserve of the Association of Canadian Studies in the United States (ACSUS), closely tied to the Canadian embassy in Washington, now offered programs in Quebec Studies. Even within ACSUS, a small pro-Quebec "opposition" reared its head. Academic circles "have developed a curiosity regarding Quebec that is almost insatiable," noted Roger Cyr in a memo. "This is undoubtedly the sector that best displays the attitude of benign neutrality that we were looking for to start with."

Quebec's active relations with the American Association of Teachers of French — an important market for Francophone products — offered Operation America one of its most satisfying small victories. The president of the association, Anne Slack, stated in an interview with Keith Spicer on the CBC network that her group had decided to hold its first conference outside the United States in Quebec in 1980 mainly because of Quebec's awareness campaigns aimed at its members.

Although this was an uplifting moment, Quebec could not mistake "this normalization for a favorable indication," warned the ministry. In fact, Quebeckers had simply "reduced alarmism." During the first year of the operation, Cyr noted, "we did not have a crisis or a period of real tension. The machine is in place, but nothing has occurred that would enable us to confirm that it will be really efficient in a period of crisis." He spoke, of course, of the approaching referendum campaign.

But a comparison between the state of affairs at the beginning of 1977 and that of mid-1979 was impressive. Information networks that had been invisible were now known. Computer printouts of subscribers to the information bulletin *Quebec Update* were lengthening; they now numbered in the thousands. The list of approachable senators was growing, and the quantity and quality of contacts, as much among Republicans as among Democrats, was increasing. Quebec diplomacy in the United States had risen, in record time, from nothing to the establishment of a wide and promising base, all in spite of misfires, slow fuses, and the smoke bombs of ignorance and timidity.

Still, there would have to be a crisis to see if the Operation America team had constructed a dam or a sand castle. And there was one brewing on the horizon.

# 14

# The Pentagon: Quebec, How Many Divisions?

*As a general rule, a newcomer should not make a noisy entrance.*

Louis Balthazar
United States specialist at the Université Laval,
consultant to Quebec on military policy

SCENARIO NO. 1: Civil war rages in Canada. The federal army, sent in to prevent the Francophone province from seceding, and to save the besieged Anglophone minority, meets lively resistance from the new Quebec patriots. On the CBS evening news, Dan Rather reports that Beaconsfield has been taken by troops loyal to René Lévesque, but that federal paratroopers landed in downtown Sherbrooke and managed to throw a battalion of Beauce separatists in the Saint-François River. Their ranks had been decimated as much by the pollution as by the December ice. A third of the Francophone soldiers of the 22nd Regiment, whose loyalty to the Queen is in doubt, are still under arrest in their barracks. Claude Morin has rushed to Paris but has not succeeded in his attempt to convince France to send its navy to dislodge the Canadian fleet deployed on the St Lawrence River at Montreal and Quebec City. Meanwhile, an "international brigade," composed mainly of troops from Breton and Gabon, is on its way. "Given the US interest in a united Canada, Washington would find itself in the position of continuing normal relations with Canada — including the provision of arms under the Defence Production Sharing Agreement — while preventing the use of American territory bordering Quebec from being used either as a sanctuary or as a point of access to Quebec." The American position is difficult, since "improbable as it is that Quebec would win a civil war, it is equally improbable that Canada could sustain a long war."

SCENARIO NO. 2: On the night of June 24, the Quebec armed forces, brandishing their fleur-de-lis flags and chanting "Tomorrow Belongs to Us," launch a blitz on two fronts: Labrador and Acadia (northern New Brunswick). The "recuperation–liberation" operation is deemed a glorious success except in Moncton, where the Anglophone population, mistaking the soldiers for participants in a St Jean Baptiste Day parade, try to cut them off at the pass. "Because the Canadian Maritimes are important to the security of the North Atlantic, any doubt about Canada's ability to provide protection for this area would lead quickly to an American response. Annexation would be one solution."

SCENARIO NO. 3: The government of René Lévesque, President of the Republic of Quebec, is overrun by its "Marxist-Leninist wing," which opens the door to international terrorist rabble. The new Soviet embassy houses no fewer than 850 diplomats; an additional 75 cadres are installed at the Rock Island consulate manning the parabolic antennas that hug the American border, guarded now by armed patrols. Soviet submarines anchor with impunity at Sorel, not far from the joint Cuba–PLO training camp. The "French socialist-communist coalition" exercises "considerable influence over a turbulent Quebec, where squads from metropolitan France might one day play the role of the Cubans in Angola."

SCENARIO NO. 4: Three days after the Minister of Peace of the State of Quebec, Reggie Chartrand, cuts the electricity supply to five Pinetree radar stations located in Quebec, Soviet supersonic Backfire bombers carrying cruise missiles armed with nuclear warheads leave their base on the Kola Peninsula. They swoop over the Arctic into Quebec airspace. "The weapons [are] released at a point smack in the middle of Quebec," then the bombers make a U-turn, neither seen nor recognized. The medium-range missiles are detected at the American border, minutes before they reach their targets — military bases and large cities in the American Northeast. Through the heroic efforts of the US Air Force's "top guns" the last missile is destroyed in flight before it hits Washington, but nuclear fallout, carried by the wind, soon forces all inhabitants of the capital underground, to shelters or to graves. Boston and New York are atomized. Thanks to the hole punched by Quebec in the West's strategic defences, the Soviet Union has finally initiated World War Three.

Apart from the local color added here in the interest, so to speak, of realism, these scenarios were presented in all seriousness, in 1977 and 1978, in publications intended for the eyes of American defence experts and think-tank members. The specialists in military affairs who wrote them, an American and a Canadian, wanted to alert their target audience at the Pentagon to this potential threat to the United States' "vital interests." "Each of the scenarios sketched above is a serious possibility," warned Howard Lentner, a professor at New York University, who proposed the hypotheses of civil war and what he called "Quebec imperialism" in the Maritimes. His ruminations were published in *Orbis, a Journal of World Affairs*. The theories of the left running rampant in Quebec and of Soviet bombers flying over its territory were put forth by F.S. Manor, of the *Winnipeg Free Press*, and Nicholas Stethem, assistant editor of a Canadian defence journal; their alarmist articles were published in *Foreign Policy*. Other versions of these four apocalyptic visions appeared in short pieces published on both sides of the border.

What did James Timberlake, who coordinated the Pentagon's Canada Desk from 1974 to 1980, think of this? "It's all bull," he says disdainfully. Not one of the scenarios drew his approbation. Joseph Jockel, a professor at Johns Hopkins University's Center for Canadian Studies, in Washington, DC, interviewed Timberlake and his colleagues at the time to write his own analysis of the military aspects of a sovereign Quebec. Jockel confirms that the Pentagon considered these scenarios "hopeless trash."

## The Pentagon's Slender Dossier

The Quebec separatist movement certainly had the potential to alter the Pentagon's ideas about defence of the continent. No one in the military was happy about the complications, at least administrative, that a separatist victory would create. However, from 1960 to the time of the referendum, the top American brass uncharacteristically adopted a detached, laisser-faire posture toward the turbulence in Quebec.

The tone seems to have been set by Paul Warnke on a winter day in 1968. Later a negotiator for SALT II, Warnke was then an assistant secretary of defense handling affairs that overlapped political and military concerns. A news item from Quebec — a terrorist action or an important political episode, such as René Lévesque's defection from the Liberal Party — caught Warnke's attention, and he put the Quebec question on the agenda of one of his regular Thursday-morning meetings with the most powerful military officer in the United States, General Earl G. Wheeler, Chairman of the Joint Chiefs of Staff.

The two men pondered whether the separatist movement and its terrorist faction seriously threatened Canadian unity and, hence, American military interests. Warnke and Wheeler rapidly reached agreement; it did not. "There was sort of a general feeling this was a Canadian problem and not a particular threat to US security interests," recalled Warnke. "There was never any discussion of any US use of military force in this situation."

Warnke and his successors had two reasons not to be concerned about Quebec. First, they felt that Canada had things well in hand, and that Quebec would wisely choose to stay within the federal framework. Predictions by the State Department and the CIA regarding the Quebec sovereignty movement's chances for success changed regularly. But at the Pentagon — that monument to the glory of the status quo — the permanence of the bonds of Confederation was taken for granted.

Second, the men at the Pentagon did not accord a high strategic value to Quebec. Starting in the mid-1960s, the Soviet threat was posed more by intercontinental nuclear missiles than by bombers that would have to fly over Canada to hit the United States.

In fact, Quebec played no part in the detection of Soviet missiles. The Canada-US North American Air Defence Command (NORAD) military installations located in Quebec were part of the bomber detection and interception system, which was declining in importance; personnel manning the early-warning stations were reduced by 75% between 1960 and 1980. NORAD had five Pinetree radar bases in Quebec — at Lac Saint-Denis, Senneterre, Chibougamau, Mont Apica, and Moisie — primed to spot approaching Soviet planes. The Alouettes, Squadron 425 of the Royal Canadian Air Force, were based at Bagotville and charged with interception, or in-flight reconnaissance, of these intruders. The radar stations and the squadron took their orders from a control center situated in North Bay, Ontario.

Warnke felt that if Quebec were to want this matériel off its territory, the Pentagon could easily do without it. "It would not have been that difficult," since there was "still lots of territory left" elsewhere in North America, he explained. "Alternate arrangements could have been made that would not necessarily have involved the use of territory in Quebec." Other Pentagon experts felt, however, that if the radar stations and the base for the Canadian squadron were moved, use of Quebec airspace, landing rights and refueling privileges would still be required.

A successor of Warnke's, Robert F. Ellsworth, in the office of the Secretary of Defense from 1974 to 1977, stated that in terms of Western defence a neutral Quebec "wouldn't have been anywhere near as disruptive as the departure of France from the Integrated Military Command in 1966, and while that was disruptive, it certainly didn't destroy NATO, or come anywhere close to it." According to Warnke, Ellsworth, Timberlake and all of the other former high-ranking Pentagon civil servants interviewed for this book, the notion that the loss of Quebec could be strategically significant for Washington was not seriously discussed. Warnke added that the Pentagon would have been irritated, but not tempted to intervene, if a French military base had been established in Quebec territory.

The American military's evaluation of the disturbances that Quebec's separation could create was vital. If the military had judged participation of the province to be indispensable to continental defence, they could have insisted that the State Department or the White House intervene in the referendum debate in a more aggressive fashion. But since Quebec was an unimportant pawn in the strategic chess game, such intervention was not necessary. The only concession Warnke made to the "threat" was to advise Americans who handled various tasks with the Canadian army to redouble their vigilance around military installations to guard against FLQ attacks.

In October of 1969, one of very few exchanges took place between a Pentagon officer and a member of the Parti Québécois. At a conference on Canada–US affairs in Racine, Wisconsin, Jacques Parizeau was a speaker; the officer asked Parizeau what an independent Quebec's policy would be regarding two military alliances, NATO and NORAD, which link Canada and the United States. Parizeau softly replied that Quebec would be willing to work with the United States to resolve military questions in a mutually satisfactory manner.

In 1969 the Parti Québécois had not yet started to formulate its military policy. By 1970 the PQ announced that an independent Quebec would withdraw from NATO and NORAD. This neutralist position set off no alarms in Washington, particularly because the PQ position was hardly more clear-cut than that of the federal government. Pierre Trudeau was toying with the idea of pulling Canada out of NATO. "We've had no defence policy, so to speak, except that of NATO," Trudeau declared in April 1969. "It is a false perspective to have a military alliance determine your foreign policy. It should be your foreign policy which determines your military policy." That September, Trudeau decided to reduce Canada's participation in NATO from 10,000 to 5,000 troops. In this context, the pacifist position of a political party that was celebrating its third birthday was not hard news.

The PQ reversed itself in 1975, adopting a Gaullist approach: Quebec, like France, would be a member of NATO but not of its military structure. During this period, from 1973 to 1976, René Lévesque told anyone who would listen that he would maintain ties to the alliances if Washington would foot the bill. The separatist leader did not seem disturbed by the idea that the armed forces of a newborn country would thus be under the effective control of another nation — precisely the opposite of the Gaullist position.

In 1976, however, the Parti Québécois's platform made no mention of Gaullism. It proposed a pacifistic foreign policy, disarmament, withdrawal from the alliances, and a substantial reduction in Quebec's military expenditures.

But the opposition parties' political programs — except for that of the communists — are not as a rule taken seriously by the Pentagon. "When they were outside of power they might say one thing, when they succeed to power then they see a different line of wisdom," says, for example, George Bader, the official in charge of NATO and Canada at the Secretary of Defense's office starting in 1978. "You can never accept this kind of a hypothetical plea before the fact." The certainty that acquisition of power would have the effect of moderating opposition to defence was entirely ingrained at the Pentagon. A report drafted in the winter of 1976 on the military aspects of a sovereign Quebec suggested, as if it were a given, that a PQ government would remain in NORAD and NATO no matter what the claims of its electoral program.

Staff Colonel Charles Roades decided to produce a short document to sum up the situation. Roades, one of the American members of the Permanent Joint Board of Defence, the official Canada-US military body, requested that the US Air Force, the US Army, and the US Navy each conduct a bit of research. The US Air Force, by far the most important participant because of Squadron 425 and the Pinetree radar system, concluded that there would be no major changes in the arrangements between Quebec and the Pentagon, notably because "there would be the soundness of residual political logic that would say, 'Hey, don't do some strange things' " — for example, disturbing the NORAD agreement, recalls Roades, himself an Air Force man.

Roades encountered major difficulties in his research when he tried to describe a future Quebec military force created from Francophone members of the Canadian army. How many Quebeckers were in the Canadian Air Force? How many were officers? Were there training bases in Quebec to serve the future army? Did they meet NATO standards? Roades established that the Pentagon did not possess this type of information; the only solution would be to ask the Canadian military. This was out of the question, since it would confirm that the Pentagon was seriously studying the possibility of Quebec's independence. Roades was therefore unable to complete his modest study. The Navy, which should have been anxious about detection of enemy submarines along the Quebec coast, never even submitted a report. (In fact, this task was not performed from Quebec.)

The incomplete working document, less than six pages in length, circulated among lower-level staff dealing with Canada–US relations. Their reaction, according to Roades: "Nothing major here, it doesn't seem like it's really going to become an issue, so let's just drop it ..." Since the Air Force had answered the essential question — NORAD would not suffer were Quebec to separate — the Pentagon could rest easy. No other document was ever produced on the Quebec question; the Pentagon files are empty.

(With one exception: in May 1977 the US Army Corps of Engineers, the branch of the armed forces that manages and constructs large dams and canals, cited "political developments in Quebec" to justify a study on expanding the Hudson River and the Erie Canal to open an all-American passage through to the Great Lakes for ocean-going merchant ships. The project would completely bypass the St Lawrence River maritime lane, situated in Quebec. Ships would come to New York, travel up the Hudson River past Albany, sail up the Erie Canal — totally reconstructed — and dock at Buffalo, on Lake Erie. The $1.5 million study was commissioned by a Congressional committee more concerned with the regional economy around Buffalo and the prospect of transporting coal by water than with the marine geopolitical situation. The Corps of Engineers concluded in 1980 that construction of this artificial St Lawrence River would cost between $37 billion and $54 billion. The case was closed.)

In 1976, Lévesque announced that Quebec would be prepared to defend its borders with an army of 14,000 troops — the number of Canadian soldiers based in Quebec. PQ thinker Jacques-Yvan Morin confirmed that defence of Quebec territory, notably the Arctic, would be one of this army's priorities. Quebec's neighbors would accept the new state's neutrality, he said, but they would not tolerate a military void at their borders. Lévesque had a different role in mind for his army: intervention in the case of police strikes or natural disasters and participation with the UN peace-keeping forces, the latter a traditional task of the Canadian Armed Forces.

At the time of Lévesque's speech, General René Gutknecht, commander of the 22nd Regiment based at Quebec City, passed on the following curious statistic to the consul general at Quebec City: 13,800 of the above-mentioned 14,000 soldiers would refuse to serve in a Quebec army.

## Soviets in Distress

Even if it were not crucial to the maintenance of the American strategic network, Quebec's attachment to NATO and NORAD had symbolic value. Strategic experts, members of Congress, and journalists on the military beat were quick to bestow ideological labels upon political parties or governments on the basis of their position on such alliances.

American foreign policy reacted to issues as one would to fires. As long as the house of Quebec wasn't burning, it received little attention. But the day after a positive vote on the referendum, members of Congress, think tanks, and the Pentagon would suddenly wake up. The scenarios presented at the beginning of this chapter would "find counterparts among similar-thinking Americans — some of whom are bound to be in positions of influence," particularly among conservatives, who are often preoccupied with military matters, stated two Ontario political scientists who studied the question. The writings of columnist William Safire between 1976 and 1980 certainly presaged this type of debate.

While Lévesque quietly prepared the ground for the referendum campaign, political debate in the United States grew passionate over the issue of the Panama Canal, control of which President Carter proposed to return to local authority. Fear of a strategic void — even an imaginary one — in the Northeast could very well have sparked a controversy on the same order, and be seen by Quebec voters as a very worrisome show of discontent from the all-too-powerful neighbour.

In the United States, where the other NATO allies were generally felt not to be supporting their share of the Western arsenal and to be relying on large Pentagon budgets, pacifism drew three reactions: impatience with such naiveté, suspicion that sinister forces lurked behind that idealism, and accusations that these disloyal allies wanted shelter under the American umbrella without paying their way in.

After the November 1976 election, foreign diplomats who filed through Claude Morin's office asked him how serious the PQ position was on NATO. Germans and Britons, among others, told the minister that he must be blind to the Soviet threat, which the Europeans felt so strongly, to consider thus weakening the Western alliance.

Morin, who had never been very concerned about this aspect of things, was particularly struck by the reaction of the Soviet consul, Vladimir Gavryushkin, who loudly confirmed what Canadian diplomats had perceived to be Moscow's fears about Quebec independence. "The Soviets were against Quebec sovereignty," Morin recalls. "The reason was that if we became an independent state — at the time the PQ's program had a pacifist policy, so we would have disarmed — we would create a hole in the shield protecting the United States from the USSR. This would force the Americans to defend Quebec in spite of itself, and thus to draw nearer geographically to the Soviet Union." Moscow, like Washington, feared that Canada would not survive Quebec's departure, and Moscow would rather be neighbors with a moderate ally of the United States than with the capitalist enemy itself. Paradoxically, the fact that Canada belonged to American-dominated military alliances was seen as a strategic shield as much for Moscow as for Washington. This surprising Soviet reaction and the fears expressed by European diplomats, more than the comments of their American counterparts, convinced Morin that the Parti Québécois position was untenable.

In May 1977 despite protest from the party's radical militants, the PQ convention agreed to withdraw the positions regarding NATO and NORAD from its program. The party therefore had no official policy on this issue. But Morin and Lévesque, in conversations and interviews, began to let it be known that an independent Quebec would continue to belong to both alliances. "It would be completely nutty not to keep the normal, basic Western ties, including NATO," the premier told *Time* in February 1978. American diplomats were convinced as early as 1977 that the Quebec government's position would rapidly align itself with Washington's defence priorities, which explains why "The Quebec Situation," produced in August of that year, barely touched on the subject.

Finally, at the 1979 PQ convention, Morin — through the interventions of other ministers — led the party into adopting a new resolution; it provided that a sovereign Quebec would accept "to establish jointly with Canada and the other implicated partners the modalities of its participation in security agencies such as NATO and NORAD."

This complete about-face took three years.

Morin recalled that he was tempted to phone Gavryushkin after the vote to tell him the good news: he would not "have to worry about Quebec's defence policy anymore. Inspired by his convincing remarks on the 'hole' that a disarmed and vulnerable Quebec would create in North America, we have resolved to protect ourselves by remaining in NATO and NORAD."

But Morin never made the call. Something in the Soviet consul's general demeanor made Morin worry that "Providence has not distributed enough sense of humor to go around."

# 15
# The Busybodies

*There are many ambassadors and foreign representatives
who are literally busybodies —
excuse the expression — in Quebec.
[They] find Quebec incredibly interesting these days.*
RENÉ LÉVESQUE
at the National Assembly

*The government of Quebec is
substantially more transparent than an iceberg.
[Its] number-one leaker, albeit sometimes
inadvertently, appears to be Lévesque himself.*
FRANCIS TERRY MCNAMARA
US Consul General at Quebec City

It was visceral; he could not stand him. The premier of Quebec was almost ill in the presence of the US ambassador to Ottawa, Thomas Enders. "Lévesque was physically incapable of seeing him, meeting him, being near him," recalls a senior official. "When he did, it was by gathering all his energy to perform his duty of office."

Lévesque's revulsion was aimed at Enders' role in the Vietnam conflict. As an assistant to the American ambassador to Cambodia from 1970 to 1974, Enders' task was approving the air raids on Cambodian territory near Vietnam. On at least two occasions, American bombers dropped their load on civilian targets by mistake. Later, a Congressional committee accused Enders of hiding the truth regarding these controversial bombings from Senate investigators who questioned him in 1973. His great intellectual capacity — everyone agreed that he was "brilliant" — more than Henry Kissinger's patronage, assured his climb through the ranks of the diplomatic world. (He would have liked to have been an army man, but his size — he was six feet, eight inches — and bad eyesight prevented this.) His diplomatic rise was stopped when he was considered too moderate to play on Ronald Reagan's team.

There is no indication that anyone in Quebec City was aware of all these details. But the Vietnam association automatically triggered a negative reaction in René Lévesque. In Enders he saw the "establishment" — the schemes and abuses of power of which Lévesque had always accused the Americans in Vietnam. In one of his spicier outbursts, as reported by his chief of staff Jean-Roch Boivin,

Lévesque railed against this personification of the dark side of his otherwise beloved United States: "He's the bum who launched the bombs in Vietnam. He's a damned spy — he must be working for the CIA."

## The Emperor and the Rebel

When the two men met, in April of 1977 in Quebec City, Lévesque hid his revulsion behind his best smile. "Both charming and wary," says Enders, "he treated me with much hospitality."

The ambassador himself presented a charming if skeptical face. During his previous visit to Quebec City, he had been more brusque. His host at the time was Robert Bourassa, whose government was lurching from disaster to disaster. The meeting took an interrogatory turn. Enders was "very imperious, informing himself on what was happening in the farther reaches of the empire," according to a witness. He coldly rattled off his questions: Will you be re-elected? What are your chances? What will you do between now and then? When Bourassa bit the dust on November 15, Enders shed no tears. He lumped Bourassa and Nixon together. "Both creeps," he said.

One year later, the ambassador approached the Quebec rebel with a great deal more courtesy. Enders, speaking his cultured French, was "discreet, distant," almost circumspect, while Lévesque — as always — controlled the conversation. In his colorful English, he presented his political plans, saying that Quebec's self-determination was "historically inevitable." "It is not in the United States' interest to appear to be lagging and appear to be unresponsive," he told the American most eager to create obstacles to separatism.

Enders asked a few questions and repeated Washington's position as stated by President Carter a few months before. Like everyone else, the ambassador wanted to know when the referendum would be held. At a second meeting, in April of 1978, he asked the question. "What we have obtained after ten years of constant work," answered Lévesque, "is the right to determine the date of the referendum."

Nor did the premier mince his words when, in private, he deplored the "political" decisions made by certain companies, notably Sun Life, which noisily left Montreal because of Bill 101. "That company will pay, and it has already started," he dryly told the ambassador. (He was even harsher in public, denouncing in an interview in *Time* magazine the "blackmail by those bastards.") Enders assured him that "if any [American] companies consider leaving Quebec, we will urge them to think hard before making such a move."

Lévesque mischievously insisted on being photographed standing beside Enders, to emphasize the marked constrast between the giant American and the little Quebecker: Caesar and Astérix.

## Like A Sporting Competition

Essentially, Enders was concerned with the federal aspect of the Canadian crisis. His visits to Quebec City, during which he could be seen jogging on the Plains of Abraham, were mainly symbolic. Another American was in the Quebec capital full time: the consul general. Unlike other American consuls in Canada, tightly controlled by the ambassador, since 1975 the consul in Quebec City usually took his orders directly from Washington.

Few Quebeckers knew his name. He appeared only rarely in official photographs or in the press. Yet, he was part of the local political fauna, at the same level as a deputy minister, a columnist, or an election organizer; he was present, active, well-known, impeccably well-informed, often respected, sometimes feared. He always spoke French.

The consul general was above all an intermediary between Washington and Quebec City. With the election of the PQ, his job was to say no, to cool the PQ government's ardor for the United States. He dedicated most of his time to information gathering, since he had to explain the bizarre Quebec reality to his superiors at "Foggy Bottom." In this respect, he was a glorified reporter. Several times a week he produced summaries of the local political situation and reports on specific subjects of interest to his government. His output, which contained secrets, big or small, confided to him by his sources in the government or the opposition, was distributed to only a handful of readers. The consul general was sometimes suspected of leaking confidential information to political adversaries of the government, but never to the press. In Quebec, he was among the few who knew how to hold their tongues.

He was backstage at important events. He was particularly interested in political conventions and in meetings of the national council of the Parti Québécois. These were good times to extend his network: to buttonhole a minister in a corridor or to get a feel for the ideological currents in which the PQ's famous "base" and its much-maligned "left wing" were swimming. One time, in his zeal, the consul sent to Washington the complete list of all the candidates for positions on the PQ national executive committee, their biographies, and their photos.

American diplomats in Lévesque's Quebec City were so diligent that Ottawa wanted to know if something was going on behind its back. Peter Dunn, the intermittent envoy from Quebec City to Washington, reported that an assistant to the Canadian ambassador frankly asked him to "transmit different political information from what we might obtain from our colleagues at the American consulate in Quebec City."

The importance of the consul general derived essentially from the personality of the diplomat chosen by Washington. From 1965 to 1969, Francis Cunningham had shown the most interest in Quebec. After that, and particularly following the October Crisis, the State Department assumed that the province had dozed off. Diplomatic "stars" did not seek the Quebec City post.

That is why, in November of 1975, the position was offered to Francis Terry McNamara, a fiftyish diplomat who had recently returned from a particularly trying mission to Can Tho, in the Mekong Delta. Quebec City was presented to him as an oasis of tranquillity, a place to recharge his battery. "Before I left Washington, they told me that not much was happening, that there was a separatist movement, not very important, which I shouldn't take seriously." Since he lived in Vermont, and his mother was ensconced nearby, McNamara regarded Quebec City almost as a vacation, just several hours' drive from his home and family. He was an expert on political and diplomatic issues, equipped for any political adventure that might come his way. After the Vietnam conflict, the American defeat, and the stress of evacuation, the political storm in Quebec seemed like a picnic.

Serious and reserved in his contacts with government members, McNamara unleashed his sense of irony at his typewriter. He approached the political game from the perspective of a half-serious, half-amused sports commentator, as evidenced by the titles of his diplomatic dispatches: on Lévesque and his left wing, "Rene the juggler"; on Trudeau, "Let's be serious, Pierre"; on Lévesque and business leaders, "Rene is having trouble keeping his pants up while juggling three balls"; on Lévesque and the "Canada Clause" of Bill 101, "Levesque plays Let's Make a Deal," then "Levesque turns the dagger." McNamara was particularly inspired by Lévesque's trip to Paris: "How ya gonna keep Rene on the farm after he's seen Paree?"

McNamara's information was always correct, his analyses pertinent, his approach reasoned. He explained that "the PQ is not an ordinary North American political party, it is a nationalist movement based, to a large extent, on the idealistic fervor of its members," notably those in the radical wing, who were "likely to rebel against anything they regarded as soiling the purity of their crusade." He liked the cabinet: "Aglitter with unusual talent, [it] includes the best and the brightest of Quebec's vital post-Quiet Revolution society." It was a team that had "no peer in Canada." However, he considered certain provisions of the French-language charter to be "blatantly vengeful."

But overall, in a cable entitled "PQ government appears to have completed toilette training," McNamara gave the Lévesque team a good grade after its first two years in power. "The consensus, to which we subscribe, is that the PQ has fulfilled its promise of giving Quebec 'good government'."

When Lévesque and Claude Morin talked about a "radically decentralized federalism" as a "serious alternative" to sovereignty at a first ministers' conference in Regina in 1978, McNamara kept calm. "Those who listened carefully with their Péquistes decoding devices understood," he wrote, and noted that the two champions of gradualism "were scrupulous in adding caveats to all statements that the Government of Quebec continues to pursue its sovereignist goals." This "pair of sleight-of-hand artists" would make cosmetic changes in the formulation of their separatist option, only to quietly move "two steps closer when the electorate is less alert." McNamara titled another of his dispatches "Hyphens are still a separatist's best friend"; even the semantical shifts regarding sovereignty-association were not lost on him.

Commenting on the internal dissent stirred up by the addition of another step to the process — a second referendum to decide about true independence — McNamara wrote that "hard-line separatist sentiment is vigorously alive within the PQ," and that "while many may trust Levesque and retain confidence in his good intentions, they are all too aware that he is a mortal, and a paunchy, chain-smoking, middle-aged one at that."

## Scoops Falling Like Rain

Washington's man in Quebec City had privileged access to confidential information — enough to make him the envy of every red-blooded parliamentary journalist. For him Quebec was indeed more transparent than an iceberg.

"We had an open-door policy with the Americans," recalls Louis Bernard, a close Lévesque advisor. Government officials met with them whenever they expressed the need. Responses were forthcoming to their questions "on goings-on in the party, on finances, on a multitude of things." "We took the chance of never concealing our intentions" from the consul general, Bernard continues, "because we thought it was the only way to keep them from being nervous."

At the top of the list of American "sources" was René Lévesque. In private meetings with the ambassador and the consul general, he laid out his latest strategic information as if it were yesterday's news. Prognoses for the referendum, comments on his political adversaries, his plan to nationalize the asbestos industry — nothing was taboo. It should be said, however, that the geopolitical value of this information was tempered by the fact that the premier changed his mind almost every month. All the same, his American interlocutors had, on average, thirty days' head start on the public — and on most of the ministers in his cabinet.

Among Lévesque's top staff, Louis Bernard, first the chief of staff then the government's secretary-general, was also a prime source. While the press was bursting with conjectures regarding the referendum question, Bernard let the American know where the debate stood. As well, he reported, "We always gave him the results of our internal polls" on government actions, the popularity of the premier, the constitutional question, or anything else.

Jean-Roch Boivin, who succeeded Bernard as chief of staff, was no less talkative. "You know, a lot of things were said over drinks," he recalls. And the consul general's bar was often open. Daniel Latouche, Lévesque's constitutional advisor, offered another view to Americans who wanted to get a peek at the premier's disorganized office. "Me, I had the reputation of saying anything," admits Latouche candidly. "I was not seen as a party militant, so I talked quite freely and, basically, they liked to have meetings with me."

No member of the Lévesque government was more open or eloquent than Claude Morin. In his position as minister of intergovernmental affairs, liaison with diplomats was part of his duties. He played the transparency card with a calculated zeal. When the Parti Québécois, after a crucial strategy meeting, decided to reveal that sovereignty-association would involve, among other things, monetary and customs unions with Canada, as well as a common central bank and passports, Claude Morin gave McNamara the scoop in a morning briefing. McNamara transmitted his summary of the strategy to Washington before Lévesque had had the time to announce it to the public and the press. One month before publication of the top-secret white paper on sovereignty-association — about which Latouche had divulged various details to McNamara, Morin offered the consul a detailed explanation of its not-yet-finalized contents. When the document was ready, Morin handed a copy to the consul one day before it was distributed to journalists. Regarding the exact date of the referendum, Lévesque, at dinner at the consulate, confided three months in advance that he was seriously considering May 26, 1980. (He finally decided on May 20.)

There was, however, no subject on which the Lévesque government was more open with American diplomats than its desire to nationalize Asbestos Corporation, a subsidiary of the giant American firm General Dynamics. The Americans' position on nationalizations was clear. First, they were entirely against it. Second, they would not lift a finger if three conditions were met for compensation of the shareholders. Three words were recited by each diplomat as if they were the first tenet in the State Department's catechism: compensation must be "prompt, adequate, and effective." The United States would be furious if, as had happened in Salvador Allende's Chile, expropriation was made without compensation.

But in Quebec, as had been the case with nationalization of the electricity companies 15 years earlier, it seemed that the conditions could quickly be met, as Enders explained later to General Dynamics representatives who came to ask him for help, in vain. The State Department's legal eagles went through the expropriation law with a fine-toothed comb and gave it, on the whole, their approval. Was clarification needed on any point? The consul general at Quebec City presented Louis Bernard with an amendment to be inserted in the text of the law concerning "the character of the indemnity that must be determined by the tribunal." "We felt all right with it, accepted it," remembers Bernard.

When the Saskatchewan government had nationalized its potash industry in 1975, Washington had officially declared its "concern." In the case of asbestos, Washington said nothing at all. State Department internal documents showed that General Dynamics' position was far from pristine since, of all the asbestos companies, it had "the worst record in the industry for compliance with regulations" in terms of "environmental and safety regulations." But not all members of the Quebec government understood that the State Department's three words were a catchphrase. Claude Morin, for example, saw in the US's line a serious warning: "It wasn't extortion, but they wanted to shake us up." René Lévesque asked a diplomat, "We're really scaring you with our expropriations, aren't we?"

Pushing transparency to its limit, even taking the risk that privileged information would leak to the enemy camp, Lévesque, Parizeau, and the others decided to inform the consul general in Quebec City of every chapter in the long political-economic-jurisdictional saga of expropriation. When Minister of Finance Parizeau decided to give General Dynamics an ultimatum, a senior official told the consul general — George Jaeger, who replaced McNamara in 1979 — twenty-four hours in advance the price Quebec would be willing to pay for the expropriation: $42 per share. (This information would have made stockbrokers jump for joy. Insider trading could have occurred on Asbestos Corporation shares on the Montreal market, and on General Dynamics US shares on the New York market, although not on General Dynamics Canada — the real target of the nationalization — which was a wholly owned subsidiary of its American parent corporation.)

When the cabinet approved the wording of the notice of expropriation of Asbestos Corporation, Jaeger obtained a copy some months before its publication. When Parizeau wrote to General Dynamics in a last effort to negotiate before expropriation, a copy of the letter was sent to Jaeger even before the American company received it and 24 hours before it was distributed to the press. When the expropriation was finally imminent, the consul general was assured that the Cabinet decision would be communicated to him the moment it was made.

With such quantity and quality of information, it was understandable that Washington had no need for CIA agents in Quebec.

American diplomats were not the only ones to benefit from Quebeckers' candor. At a cocktail party attended by the American consul, Jaeger, and the Soviet consul, Vladimir Gavryushkin, Morin decided to kill two birds with one stone and make friends all around. Knowing that *Pravda* was accusing the PQ of being manipulated by the CIA and that certain Americans saw the hand of the KGB behind René Lévesque, Morin said to his fellow guests, "Let's be frank: Jaeger will tell you that it's not the CIA, and you [the Soviet] will tell him that it's not the KGB. If the French consul were here, I'd ask him to tell you it's not the SDECE either." Leaving them to ponder his words, the minister concluded, "So, good luck!"

Some time later, after Soviet troops invaded Afghanistan and Ottawa had suspended all economic ties with the USSR, the new Soviet consul, Alexander Ereskovsky, came to ask Morin if he could not find a way to be a little more understanding. Ottawa and Quebec were on bad terms, the Soviet must have reasoned, so why not profit from the federal-provincial schism? "I have a solution, there definitely is a way," Morin replied. The consul took out his pencil, ready to take notes. "I recommend just one thing to make everything go smoothly," Morin continued. "Get out of Afghanistan."

## The French Connection Returns

In both Quebec City and Paris, American diplomats put their old Quebec City–Paris–Ottawa surveillance system back into action.

The election of the PQ drew a reaction of "pure joy" in the French press, reported an American diplomat in Paris. The big newspapers regretted having previously published criticisms of General de Gaulle, who had had the merit, *France-Soir* wrote, of having expressed before anyone else what since had become obvious. *Le Quotidien de Paris* called upon France to throw its support squarely behind the Quebec government.

The Americans looked to the Quai d'Orsay for reassurance regarding the French government's intentions. The election of the PQ was a surprise, said the chief of the North American desk at the Quai, who gave his word that President Valéry Giscard d'Estaing and his advisors would "resist all pressures from French public opinion to become involved in a problem that concerns Quebec and Ottawa."

Two days after the election, however, the French pro-independence network was preparing for battle. French parliamentarian Xavier Deniau visited Lévesque, then McNamara. Deniau, a "self-appointed advocate for the Québécois cause," wrote the consul general, "was clearly making an appeal for American understanding of René Lévesque." The Frenchman described the new head of the Quebec government as "a great admirer of the United States and a dedicated democrat." "Lévesque's feelings toward France, Deniau parenthetically commented, are less warm," McNamara noted.

Deniau then travelled to Washington to deliver the same pro-Lévesque speech to McNamara's superiors, including Richard Vine. A true believer in the cause, Deniau again brought the good word to the American capital in the fall of 1977.

In September of 1977, another member of the Quebec Mafia, Bernard Dorin, director of Francophone Affairs at the Quai, travelled to Quebec with French government minister Alain Peyrefitte, who delivered the new slogan on French policy regarding Quebec: "No interference but no indifference." Dorin, wrote McNamara, "seemed to take inordinate interest in the operations of this consulate general." As for Peyrefitte, he spent a day hunting in the rain on Anticosti Island, "but," McNamara noted, "the island's 70,000 deer managed to keep successfully out of his range."

Peyrefitte had come to Quebec to lay the foundations for the big event of that fall: Lévesque's visit to Paris. The Americans, like senior Canadian officials, were a little anxious about the rumors circulating that an invitation had been extended to the separatist premier to address the French National Assembly, a move that McNamara likened to General de Gaulle's "Vive le Québec libre!" "Comparisons cannot help but be made with PM Trudeau's trip to Washington last spring, during which he addressed a joint session of Congress," he noted. Even Winston Churchill had not received this honour after the war; the last foreign leader to address the French parliamentarians in their august chamber had been Woodrow Wilson, American president during the First World War.

In Paris, a source at the Elysée soothed American fears: "Giscard's firm personal policy [is] not to foster Quebec separatism." The American ambassador to France was convinced that "the French government, at the highest level, is alert to the psychological pitfalls involved." However, in a letter that Giscard sent to René Lévesque just after the PQ victory, the Frenchman sketched out a more flexible political picture: "We [France] respect the choice of the people of Quebec and remain, more than ever, ready to support any efforts they make to preserve their identity and ensure their future." More than ever? This was much indeed from a man who had expressed doubts about General de Gaulle's intellectual capacity ten years earlier.

The Giscard team was preparing for Lévesque a spectacle of sound and light to eclipse the reception given Trudeau in Washington at the beginning of the year. But first France had to do Ottawa a favour that the latter was to regret having asked. Under intense federal pressure, Paris modified its invitation, offering to have Lévesque speak before the parliamentarians but not at the Assembly. This satisfied Trudeau.

Lévesque would, however, speak in the "Salle des fêtes" in the Bourbon palace, that is, in the building where the Assembly sat. The parliamentarians adjourned their session during his visit, but not before having applauded, from their benches, the arrival of the premier within the walls of the palace via a door that had not been opened for 150 years. This was not just *one* enormous statement but a number of protocol statements in quick succession, all of which added up to a welcome even more stunning than had originally been planned, before Ottawa's intervention. It was an illustration, if ever there was one, of the agility of French diplomacy.

In Paris, dignitaries and the press accorded Lévesque a royal welcome. In Quebec City, his visit was seen as "a major personal triumph for Lévesque and a very significant boost to the separatist cause," according to McNamara, a verdict shared "even in the Anglophone press." "Only a tightly played Stanley Cup victory by the Montreal Canadiens could have rivalled public interest and the enthusiasm in Lévesque's triumphal march through France," he wrote in a dispatch entitled "Rene returns from Wonderland."

Giscard was swept up in the whirlwind of this spontaneous "emotional intensity," according to an American source at the Elysée. Prodded by Peyrefitte, who urged him to "take off the brakes" according to a source at the Quai d'Orsay, he poured on the hospitality and fell headlong into the "psychological pitfalls" that he had supposedly wanted so desperately to avoid. He presented Lévesque with the Legion of Honor, an unexpected gesture — and one that was, *dixit* Ottawa, illegal, since the awarding of any foreign decoration must first be approved by federal authorities.

The French president also launched the tradition of annual visits by premiers, thus creating between Paris and Quebec City an "almost organic relation," wrote an American diplomat. Giscard talked of the "Quebec" spring and pronounced the following sentence, negotiated word by word and written jointly by Louise Beaudoin and Bernard Dorin: "What you want from France is our understanding, our confidence, and our support. You can be sure that these will not be withheld no matter what path you decide to follow."

It was a poetic way to express Quebeckers' right to self-determination; Giscard bestowed upon Quebec, rather than upon Canada, responsibility for the province's future. The American ambassador commented, "Giscard had indeed distributed just enough manna for the Québécois to satisfy their views." McNamara commented, "Short of recognition of the province's independence, it is hard to see how France could have gone further." A cartoon in the *Washington Post* portrayed Giscard pinning a "self-determination medal" on Lévesque, while in the background protesters demonstrated for a "free" Corsica, Bretagne, and Basque. Enders' comment was that this was all very well, but, "The Québécois cannot eat medals."

While these events were unfolding and being closely reported by the American press, the State Department was telling its Ottawa and Paris press agents what they should say if journalists asked questions about Washington's position: "The question of Quebec is for the Canadian people themselves to decide." However, this response omitted the usual line on the "preference" for Canadian unity; it failed to mention that Canada was a "strong and beautiful country." Had the pro-Quebec deluge orchestrated by the French temporarily doused the American ardor for federalism? More likely, Washington, whose relations with Paris were looking up — Carter was in awe of Giscard's intellect — did not want to stress any difference of opinion on this question. René Lévesque played on precisely this point by expressing, on French television, the hope that the welcome he had received in Paris would have some impact on President Carter's federalist leanings.

But the American position was elastic — and pragmatic. Two and a half years later, when a *Washington Post* reader protested against the presence of the consul general at a meeting with Lévesque in Quebec City since he felt this lent legitimacy to the separatists — the State Department prepared another press release in which the sentence "We hope it [Canada] remains strong and united" was reinserted. When Giscard expressed his pro-Quebec leanings, the blade was dulled; when anti-Quebec sentiments arose, the knife could be sharpened. An illustration of the agility of American diplomacy.

However, these little pirouettes had little effect on the internal Quebec politics of the premier's trip to France. "No matter how carefully his image-handlers work on tidying up Lévesque's ruffled casualness, he still looks charmingly out of place reviewing the Garde Républicaine," commented the consul general to Quebec City, who then offered this analysis: "The act of acceptance with full honors of little René from the Gaspé into the most revered precincts of French political and cultural life has a symbolic meaning which only a people with as profound a lack of self-confidence as the Québécois could fully appreciate."

The only thing missing from the rosy picture in France, according to diplomatic wags in Paris, was the absence of any show of interest, spontaneous or forced, on the part of left-wing opposition leader François Mitterrand. Mitterrand had visited Quebec at the end of 1978 and had essentially adopted the Giscardian position — he would accept any decision by Quebeckers "as the affirmation of a brother people." But he refused to express any preferences or to endorse the separatist option. McNamara's perception was that Mitterrand had gone to Quebec only to gain a foothold in the pro-Quebec camp otherwise occupied by his more openly pro-independence rival in the Socialist Party, Michel Rocard.

At a private event with some twenty guests from Quebec, among them government minister Denis Vaugeois and Lévesque advisor Yves Michaud, Mitterrand did display an admiring and sympathetic comprehension of the PQ's theories. According to one witness who took notes that day, the future French president issued the following pro-independence statement, the most forthright he would make:

> What you are undertaking is courageous. I hope that you will succeed in ways that are not for me to define for you, whether you choose sovereignty, sovereignty-association — which I am trying to understand — or another type of arrangement with Canada. France is in a situation somewhat like yours, since we are being asked to become part of a larger entity, the European community, without, however, giving up our own identity. Quebec is in the same position. One cannot be part of a larger whole without first knowing who one is.

Trudeau received an icy reception in Paris the following month. Giscard seemed to want to leave no doubt that his attitude during Lévesque's visit had been neither fortuitous nor temporary. To create the appropriate atmosphere of hostility, the French president let it be known on the eve of Trudeau's arrival that Canada would not be invited to the summit Giscard was preparing in Guadeloupe for President Carter and the European heads of state. With Trudeau in Paris, Giscard announced that France would attend no Francophone summit at which Quebec did not have the seat, the flag, and the label that satisfied Lévesque. To make things even clearer, a rumor taken up by American diplomats, despite Canadian denials, claimed that Giscard had cut short a lunch with Trudeau — a stiff insult in diplomatic terms.

Trudeau got his revenge three months later by stating a few days before French Prime Minister Raymond Barre arrived in Canada that it was a mistake for the French to "toy with" separatism and that they simply failed to understand the reality of Canadian federalism. If Quebec separated, Trudeau told French journalists, Canada would crumble and the United States would occupy the entire continent, except for Mexico and "perhaps" Quebec. Then France would have been well served indeed.

# 16
# Waiting for Cyrus

*Even paranoids have enemies.*
Popular American saying

The hour of truth was drawing nigh. Soon, two little words, YES, NO, would capture billboards, air time, headlines, jacket backs, apartment balconies. They would be insinuated into conversations, would punctuate speeches, would bear promises and blackmail. They would take the guise of advertising against alcohol (*"No, thanks!"*) and for the spirit of enterprise (*OSE*, French for "Dare"). They would even try to co-opt the other's meaning (*Un NON au référendum sera un OUI pour le renouvellement* — A NO in the referendum will be a YES for renewal).

Soon, Washington would have to make a choice. The "transition period" between the election of the Parti Québécois and the referendum campaign, as defined in the internal policy document "The Quebec Situation: Outlook and Implications" in August of 1977, was drawing to a close. "Before a referendum," the document explained, "it would not be surprising for Ottawa to ask the US government to take a stand much more unequivocally in favor of a united Canada," while Quebec would "try to counteract Ottawa's moves by trying to persuade the US to adopt a neutral position." According to the schedule drawn up at the time, Washington must now "review its policy," "as developments warrant."

The numbers Ottawa was coming up with were frightening. In February of 1980, when Pierre Trudeau re-entered the Prime Minister's office after a year off, he found a copy of a poll commissioned by the outgoing Conservative government. For the first time, the "YES" side was clearly ahead, 52% to 36%. The shattering of Canada, the nightmare of a lifetime, seemed entirely possible. In March, then in April, new internal polls confirmed the more or less steady advance of the "YES" side. The prime minister's staff heard the footsteps in their sleep.

The evidence said that the Quebec Liberal "NO" team, directed by the respected but non-telegenic Claude Ryan, was headed for defeat. Trudeau sounded the charge. "The formidable Liberal machine geared up for an all-or-nothing rampage into Quebec politics," noted two *Globe and Mail* reporters, Robert Sheppard and Michael Valpy, in a book that recorded the federal side of this battle. "Not since the provincial election of 1939, when the federal liberals swarmed into Quebec to defeat the anti-war policies of Maurice Duplessis and elect Adelard Godbout and his Liberals, had the party obtruded itself so boldly in the Province's affairs."

Ministerial committees, committees of members of parliament, and committees of senior officials organized a last-ditch campaign. Against Quebec's attempt to associate pride and progress with sovereignty (and to denigrate the Anglophone heritage of Pierre *Elliott* Trudeau), the federal message was based on the grandeur of Canada, the economic unknowns of separation, and also on the threat of losing old-age pensions, family allowances, and unemployment insurance. "It was the politics of fear," noted Sheppard and Valpy, "performed extravagantly, with the premiers of English Canada playing key supporting roles."

Defeat for the federalists was so plausible at this point that Trudeau's right-hand man, Michael Pitfield, dusted off an old bill which would give the federal government the right to hold a counter-referendum after May 20, only in Quebec if need be, to reshuffle the cards.

Pitfield's Quebec counterpart, Daniel Latouche, was working with a group to put together a post-victory strategy for the "YES" side. To kick off negotiations on sovereignty-association, why not take an American detour? "The idea was to announce Quebec's negotiating points at a conference of Eastern premiers and New England governors," Latouche explains. "We would first address the Maritimes, which felt the most threatened by sovereignty, and were thus the most vulnerable, but we would do this in the presence of the Americans, who could say to them, 'You see, it's reasonable, there is no reason to worry.' That was, we would play the New England card."

But Ottawa also had an American card to play before the referendum: the "NO"s from the south. That could easily tip the undecided onto the "NO" side. First, Jimmy Carter himself was expected to visit Ottawa in late 1979, but this trip was cancelled. Then, secretary of state, Cyrus Vance, announced he would be coming up in April of 1980.

And so they were waiting. Waiting for Cyrus.

## The List: Summit Neutralization

Starting in the middle of 1979, the Quebec helmsmen of the great operation to neutralize the United States prodded themselves to greater speed. Operation America had pieced together new networks of Quebec affinity in the United States, but what about the opinion-makers, those who could influence the entire nation, the politicians whose glorious past or promising future drew an audience?

In August of 1979, they prepared a list of leaders who must be contacted and given the good word on sovereignty-association — or, at least, arguments militating in favour of a position of strict neutrality. James Donovan, the methodical director of the United States division at Quebec's Department of Intergovernmental Affairs, sorted potentially useful American politicians according to two criteria: "advisable" and "possible." Operation America's meagre resources must not be wasted on has-beens such as ex-president Gerald Ford ("less advisable," wrote Donovan) and Richard Nixon's ex-chief of staff, Alexander Haig (noted as "less advisable," he went on to become secretary of state under Reagan); nor could they afford to spread themselves thin aiming at unattainable targets. President Carter, for example, was not on the list. He was not considered important, since Donovan and a number of other political observers felt (wrongly) that Senator Ted Kennedy was on his way to victory in the Democratic leadership race and could be the next president. Unfortunately, Kennedy had to be designated "more difficult," although Quebec did send him "information" via one of his assistants.

Vice-President Walter Mondale, with strong federalist connections, was the booby prize on the list of twenty-two Americans: he was "not advisable and difficult." All the same, Claude Morin sent him a communiqué via an academic who was meeting with him. From one person to the next, the message was always the same, according to Morin: "Before you state your opinion on anything, it is perhaps important to hear what we have to say, and it wouldn't be a terrible thing to contact us if you are thinking of making a [pre-referendum] decision."

The others on the list, all "advisable and possible," ranged from ex-secretary of state Henry Kissinger to Zbigniew Brzezinski, and included a number of senators and well-known social activists such as consumer advocate Ralph Nader, farm-union leader Cesar Chavez and feminist Gloria Steinem. The most interesting prospect was the oldest person on the list, an ex-governor of California whom few wanted to believe had a political future: Ronald Reagan.

## Ronald and René

How Premier Lévesque's office came to believe, in July of 1979, that Ronald Reagan was coming to Canada and that a meeting with Lévesque could be arranged, was and remains a mystery. The ex-actor was considered the favorite in the Republican leadership race. He had lost to Gerald Ford in 1976, but this time his only serious adversary was George Bush, who was not having a particularly easy time. In 1978 and 1979, Reagan was attempting to redress his reputation for being ignorant of foreign affairs by taking more trips abroad, hence the hypothetical Canadian sojourn.

Reagan's advisors of the time are certain of one thing: never, at any point, had a stop in Quebec been considered. "It would have been inserting Ronald Reagan gratuitously in a highly controversial Canadian issue that had no direct bearing in the United States," recalls his campaign organizer, Paul Hannaford. "He'd get nothing but criticism." But, as Hannaford and Michael Deaver, another Reagan advisor, point out, a presidential campaign, especially in its early stages, is surrounded by a multitude of hangers-on eager to lend a hand — even where they are not mandated to — in hope of future favors.

The fact remains: René Lévesque had been informed of a possible Reagan visit. He had to respond. But Reagan was typical of the kind of American whom Lévesque abhorred; for the premier, Reagan represented the extreme right, on top of which he was an intellectual idiot. "For Lévesque, Reagan was the equivalent of Jean-Marie Le Pen in French politics," recalls a senior official. "He had little respect for his intellectual stature, and little sympathy for and no symbiotic relationship with Reagan's ideological or social positions."

His advisors were concerned. "Mr Lévesque, stop! This isn't possible," they pleaded. "In international affairs, you cannot make value or morality judgments on the world, or you won't do business with anyone on this planet."

This was not the only time this issue had arisen. "However much he wished to succeed in politics, he was not ready to do so by any means," explains Morin, himself sometimes defeated by his leader's uncompromising side. "If, to help Quebec, he had had to kiss the feet of Khomeini, Qaddafi, or Pinochet, he wouldn't have done so." This was the anti-establishment Lévesque, all of a piece, honest at all costs. He also had a childish, almost mischievous, side. He refused to see "certain European politicians whom he didn't like," Morin explained, "sometimes because of the way they looked." When a certain French minister was passing through Quebec, Lévesque balked at meeting him, though he came from the only country that supported the separatists: "Oh well, I don't want to see him, he's a fool." He could prove unyielding as well with journalists; when one well-known writer requested an interview, Lévesque's response was, "He's boring, he thinks he's a big shot, he's not going to get ahead by seeing me."

But refusing to meet one of the two men who might soon be at the head of the free world was a luxury that Quebec could not afford. "Quebec's interests demand that you see him," he was solemnly notified. And it worked! "I'll drink to the dregs," Lévesque responded in the same tone of voice. However, this sacrifice proved unnecessary; Reagan was not to make the trip quite yet.

## Neutrality and Goodwill

The failure of the "American opinion-makers" operation was not dwelt on since, at the beginning of 1980, a few months before the referendum, Quebec diplomats thought they had triumphed. They had wanted the United States to take a position of "benign neutrality." They felt that they had obtained neutrality almost everywhere and even secured goodwill in certain spots.

This was the result of feverish fieldwork. Since 1976, ministers had been to the United States 38 times (four times more than had Bourassa's ministers); in addition, in 1979 alone, 60 Quebec lecturers and academics had paid visits. Conferences on Quebec proliferated. "For academics, people dealing with Canada, those were golden years," recalled one of the rare Americans who fit this description, Joseph Jockel. "There were grants and conferences and money, and we were flying all around and had to explain everything."

Quebec's delegate in Boston, Jacques Vallée, recalled that business circles in the Massachusetts capital were, on the whole, hostile to the "YES" side, academic circles were divided, and support by Franco-Americans for the "YES" side grew in inverse proportion to their age. But decision-makers in the Northeast — politicians — were particularly impressed by Quebec's audacity, as much in terms of James Bay as of the national question.

Vallée sent the following report:

> Political circles in New England with which we are in constant contact (state houses, New England Regional Commission, elected officials at various levels, and civil servants) show much interest and a degree of sympathy for developments in Quebec. Paradoxically, it is in these circles (and the sample on which I base myself is wide) that I encounter the least negative attitude. The hostility quotient is at zero. In contrast to university circles, they never claim to know better than we. They do not identify with

English Canadians. They express a sort of very amiable neutrality regarding Quebec, which is relatively familiar to them even though it is not a major preoccupation. A sort of admiration for the political professionalism in the current Quebec government has surfaced. "You got leadership. They have guts." Sentiments are the least divided in [political circles], and there is a sort of diffuse but unanimous sympathy.

The sparks of panic that had flown in 1976 and 1977 seemed to have been completely extinguished, even among the mass of Americans who otherwise knew little about the country to the north (a new poll had revealed that a vast majority of them could not name the capital of Canada). Tour packagers were planning jaunts to Quebec for the 1980–1981 season, without regard for the effect the referendum result could have on their customers. In Washington, a Canadian diplomat reported that there was a "dead calm." He chalked up the mood to internal American politics, not to Quebec's efforts. The Carter administration was preoccupied with the interminable hostage crisis at the American embassy in Teheran and caught up with the new presidential campaign. As the days and the polls rolled by, the Canadian diplomat warned that "the increased possibility of a YES will tend to raise the real or perceived level of nervousness."

But this nervousness was, for the moment, imperceptible. In April, Claude Morin made a last pre-referendum trip to meet with the Council on Foreign Relations in New York. "In contrast to the 1977 meetings," wrote Donovan, "there was absolutely no animosity in this audience."

As the referendum approached, Quebec's actions on the American front were quiet ones. Vallée proposed to organize a large Quebec reception on the occasion of festivities for Boston's 350th birthday in May, but deputy minister Robert Normand put on the brakes. "It's too risky," he said; from now on moderation must be practiced regarding the United States, so as not to awake what Operation America had gently lulled to sleep. Normand was in fact following the advice he had received from the American consul general at the beginning of the year: "Don't make a lot of noise in the United States before the referendum, keep ministerial visits to a minimum, reach the public indirectly through university and cultural contacts."

In New York, at both the Quebec delegation and the Canadian consulate, briefings of business people turned around a single theme: the referendum was a non-event, with no importance or immediate impact. At the consulate, despite contradictory polls, the happy prediction was for a victory for the "NO" side. That both offices were toeing the same line can be explained by the fact that the Quebeckers, of course, wanted to keep things calm, while the Canadians, whose role was to attract investors, did not want to frighten anyone.

Many swallowed this jointly-administered sleeping pill. In a memo to her bond salespeople, a vice-president of E.F. Hutton, Ruth Corson, explained that even a victory for the "YES" side, which she felt improbable, would signify nothing but the start of constitutional negotiations aimed at "a looser federal system with greater autonomy for the individual provinces." It would take at least five years for Quebec to gain "separate special status"; thus, there would not be "any near-term change occurring in Quebec's existing structure and/or inherent creditworthiness."

The manager of a large investment portfolio in New York agreed: "The PQ has done a good job putting its story forward the way it wants it. It hasn't done badly with the press." The effect on his firm? "My company's view is no view whatsoever," this anonymous source said. Was this not the precise definition of neutrality?

## "Nudge the Americans Lightly Without Pushing Too Hard"

The great unknown quantity in the American political system was Congress. In this political ocean, a tidal wave could surge from what had, the previous day, seemed a dead calm. However, the Quebec question raised neither waves nor eddies. A poll conducted among one hundred of the 535 members of Congress indicated that 71% of the respondents wanted the American government to "take no action" on this "Canadian internal matter." Among the 12% who felt the opposite, half of them wanted the United States to publicly state its preference for a united Canada, one-third (or four respondents) proposed to "discourage separatist leaders with American economic pressure." One respondent squarely called for "trade embargo; sequester foreign (US) assets in Quebec." The result could not have been more reassuring.

Even among the small group of elected officials who were knowledgeable about Canada there was a flagrant lack of interest in the Quebec question. Although the "Canadian caucus," formed of members of Congress from states bordering on Canada, met frequently, the separatist issue claimed little attention. Richard Vine, the State Department's representative at these meetings, reported that the discussions always revolved around issues concerning pork, salmon, wood shingles, the subsidization of potato farmers, and the like.

The Quebec minister of industry and commerce, Yves Duhaime, was charged with administering a final tranquilizer to Washington. For his appearance at the Johns Hopkins Center for Canadian Studies before a hundred American experts on Quebec, including a CIA economist, Eleanor Lowenkron, his advisors prepared a speech chock-full of encouraging statistics, enitled "Toward the Year 2000: Quebec and the North American Economy." As Duhaime's advisors wrote in a memo, the speech sought:

1.　to sell the political point of view without being too insistent;
2.　to nudge the Americans lightly without pushing too hard;
3.　to avoid being too open about internal questions with foreigners;
4.　to be careful not to insist too strongly on the importance of the public sector in the Quebec economy, nor on protectionist policies (purchasing policy), nor on our intention to break into the American market (*Société d'exportation*) to win away their customers, nor on our future weaknesses (population decrease) ...

Duhaime followed these instructions to the letter, casting doubt on Anglophone Montreal's catastrophic economic pronouncements by citing an article culled from the best possible source, Toronto's *Financial Times*: "It is a fact, for example, that the Quebec economy has grown faster than the Ontario economy, in the past years since the November, 1976, election victory of the Parti Québécois." In contrast to the unemployment rate in Ontario, the *Times* admitted, the unemployment rate in Quebec had fallen almost one percent in three years. (The false perception of a weakening Quebec economy during the first Lévesque mandate stems from the very real degradation in Montreal's economy, due notably to the end of the construction boom created by the 1976 Olympic installations. This decline, however, was more than compensated for by rapid expansion of numerous and vigorous small and medium-sized businesses in other regions and by the continuing work on James Bay sites. State Department analyses of the Quebec economy during these years noted the migration of head offices from Montreal to Toronto, but ascribed this phenomenon primarily to historical and economic reasons, rather than to PQ policy. English business people in Montreal who were living through the economic crisis of their city were not well placed to transmit these nuances to their American colleagues.)

After fifteen pages of good economic news, Duhaime dealt with the referendum question — in one sentence. "Very soon we will ask our people through a referendum a mandate to negotiate with the rest of Canada a new agreement, based upon the principle of equality between our two nations living in Canada." As if the goal of the process was not, precisely, to live outside Canada. This type of prose was a world away from the "inevitability of independence" proclaimed three years earlier at the Economic Club.

Commerce Department officials who had been so concerned about the PQ's socialist leanings during the closed-door meeting at Airlie House at the beginning of 1977 welcomed the news of the Quebec referendum. The house organ *Business America* dedicated its March issue to Canada. One article gaily announced to business people that "in Quebec, several major projects should provide opportunities for aggressive US suppliers. The Quebec referendum on separation or 'sovereignty-association' with Canada is to be held this spring. Capital investment is still hesitant, but investment intentions indicate that confidence is returning. The resolution of political uncertainty should be helpful in this regard as a sense of direction emerges." Either result — a "YES" or a "NO" — would be welcome, the author suggested. In another article, an economic officer at the Montreal consulate warned his readers that three elements would disrupt the Quebec economy that year. Listed in descending order of importance he cited: "The expected recession in the United States, important negotiations in the labor sector, and the referendum."

## A Very Foggy Bottom

The State Department was also nodding off, very gradually.

In January of 1977, McNamara had asserted that Quebec was well on the road toward independence. "We believe the most likely outcome will be a rather messy period leading to an eventual assumption of independence after a referendum or referenda," he wrote. He then acknowledged a peculiar phenomenon: in spite of the PQ victory and the concomitant healthy serving of national pride, in spite of the extraordinary support from France and the high degree of satisfaction with the government, the sovereignty option was barely holding its own in the polls.

In 1978, he adjusted his view: "All available indicators now seem to cast doubt on the possibility for a successful referendum vote on any question which would give legitimacy to a Quebec movement toward political sovereignty." Pointing to "the likelihood of a referendum defeat," he wrote: "The PQ government's chances of winning the next provincial election expected for 1980 are not bright."

Thomas Enders was slower than McNamara to embrace this view. In December of 1978, he still announced that "in the absence of a visible, determined federal effort to redistribute powers between the federal government and the provinces, including some recognition of the unique status of Quebec, it looks like Lévesque can win a mandate to negotiate sovereignty-association."

Enders thus thought Washington would be well-advised to hedge its bets, stating that Canada would be preserved — "with the implication that it need not necessarily be preserved in its present form." "At the same time," he wrote, "we should seize every opportunity consistent with correct Canadian federalism to extend our contacts with Quebec." Six months later, Enders would nonetheless follow McNamara's lead and forecast a separatist defeat if the referendum.

In April of 1979, an analyst from the State Department's Bureau of Intelligence and Research announced that Liberal leader Claude Ryan — whom he praised highly — had "a good chance to succeed in polarizing Quebec opinion and winning the referendum." Ryan, whom the analyst seemed to have met, viewed himself "not as a sprinter but as a marathon runner. In the past he has always outhustled, outproduced, outlasted his rivals."

The following month, Pierre Trudeau lost the federal election to Conservative leader Joe Clark. McNamara then slightly modified his prognosis: "With an inexperienced, virtually all-Anglophone government in Ottawa, this may not be as long a gamble as it appears." At any rate, this was just a different shade of grey since, he added, "portents for referendum success are not now bright."

One of the principal American diplomats working the Quebec file went even further. "We could see the whole picture. They were going to hold a referendum, they were going to lose. They were going to hold an election, they were going to win. And the question of independence would disappear for one generation."

Up to the fall of 1979 these analyses were similar to those of local observers of the political scene. But from then on, there began to be indications that the "YES" side could win. By the beginning of 1980 there was a possibility. The possibility became a probability. Then, according to federal polls, a strong probability. While the Canadian body politic closely followed this swing, the Americans, usually on top of this type of information, turned away.

In September of 1979, a new INR analysis presented the situation in Canada as if the referendum question were no longer pertinent. The sovereignty option was faded, finished, forgotten — it had "faltered." The order of the day was now a "fundamental restructuring of federal and provincial relations." This new document was consistent with the 1977 analysis "The Quebec Situation," which supported the "special status" option. It enthusiastically echoed the Pépin-Robarts report, which advocated giving more power to Quebec, notably with regard to culture, communications, family law, foreign policy, and taxation. Trudeau had dismissed this report the moment it appeared, but the INR hoped that its recommendations would succeed. It warned, "if Canadian unity is to be preserved [...] English Canada's glacial apathy and indifference to Quebec's demands for autonomy must begin to thaw."

Ambassador Enders left his post in October of 1979, but not before meeting with Lévesque one last time and hearing him predict, with figures to back him up, a slim referendum victory. Enders rendered his verdict: "When I left, I left confident that although the issue would persist for a long time, that Canada was not going to break." The probability of a victory for the "YES" side, he declared, was "quite low. Not zero."

At the end of the month, Ambassador Enders's successor, Kenneth Curtis, an ex-governor of Maine and a discreet and unpretentious man, met with a relaxed Lévesque. The two got along well. Lévesque and Curtis "very quickly found the affinities that bring two men who have spent their careers in politics together," noted Jean Chapdelaine, who was present at the encounter. The premier told the American that the referendum question would be lengthy and would deal with the "mandate to negotiate," since internal polls had indicated that this wording would garner 54% of the vote. Disheartened by a recent transportation strike, the separatist leader showed himself to be ambivalent, admitting that nothing had yet been won. He might reap only between 40% and 44% of the vote, a majority of Francophones. This would throw blame for the defeat back on the Anglophones, which could create a "very touchy situations," he emphasized.

Morin later met with Curtis, and underlined that nothing Quebec was doing was hostile to the United States. Consul General Jaeger, McNamara's successor, reported on the exchange, noting that the PQ politician did "not expect US support, but hopes US government will not undercut PQ plan."

By December, Jaeger had been in Quebec five months. In his capacity as consul he had quickly inserted himself in the information pipeline. Almost every evening he had guests from political, economic, and social circles over to his house. He even admitted to regularly inviting "a group of ordinary people" so that he could take the pulse of the population at large.

He sent his first firm prognosis to the State Department: "We think Lévesque, however persuasive, will no longer be able to make up the ground he has lost." Jaeger was particularly struck by the PQ defeats in three November by-elections, which had brought to six out of six the number of by-elections lost by the government.

The new consul general was sketching a portrait of the end of a régime. PQ politicians confided to him that they were looking for "new careers." Since the electoral reverses, "Lévesque has been in severe depression, hectoring his staff and vituperating his left-wing PQ 'enemies,' like [Louise] Harel and [Pierre] Bourgault in Montreal, to whose lack of discipline he attributes much of the disaster." He concluded, "If we were forced to bet now, we would say that Lévesque would indeed do well to get 44%" in the referendum.

Three factors, however, changed the rules of the game and erased the feeling of defeat created by the by-elections. First, the publication of the referendum question on the "mandate to negotiate," on December 20, pointed the debate toward the future, not the past. Then, in February of 1980, the extraordinary return to power of Pierre Trudeau, with massive electoral support from Quebec, revived the old Trudeau/Lévesque stand-off. The new polarization raised intentions to vote "YES." Finally, in March, the viewer ratings for National Assembly coverage reached new heights, thanks to the impeccable performance of PQ speakers in the debate on the referendum question, compared to a Liberal opposition that was disorganized and slow off the mark. In Ottawa, nothing was being taken for granted anymore.

At the end of March, Jaeger invited Lévesque to dinner. As was his custom, the PQ leader let drop a number of confidences. First came the upbeat news. The premier told Jaeger that "if he won the referendum, or even if he only got something above 45%, he might call snap elections." Jaeger reported, "In the first case [a victory], to drive home his advantage; in second [45%], to settle issue with Ryan before confusion and tensions increase. In both cases, he thought he had excellent chance to win."

Then came the sadder thoughts. If the result was between 40% and 44% — thus if a majority of Francophones had voted "YES" but the government still could not claim a moral victory (a PQ specialty) — "Lévesque again expressed his fears that there could be new violence in Quebec, 'like in Ireland.'" But at the consul general's very well laid-out table the separatist leader did not brood. He stated that, "for first time in months, he again felt he had some chance to win." Private polls and a public poll backed him up.

Jaeger was not unaware of the dissension that was tearing up the federalist camp. He knew that relations between Trudeau and Ryan were at their worst; his sources close to the Quebec Liberal leader confirmed this. However, his faith was imperturbable. His money was on the "NO" side. "Chances are Ryan will succeed, at least to extent of keeping "YES" vote in the middle 40%," he wrote to his superiors.

Claude Morin was delighted with the strategic lassitude of the Americans: certain that the separatist threat would melt away, they would find no reason to become involved in the Quebec quandary. But things were less serene at the tactical level, for two reasons. First, if the "YES" side won — which Morin also thought was possible — the giant to the south might react excessively, since it was poorly prepared for this eventuality: "I told myself that if we won by 51%, there must not be a disaster." Second, Jaeger knew everyone. If he let slip to other PQ members or to reporters that ministers such as Morin had not contradicted him when he predicted a federalist victory, morale among the troops would suffer. So the minister reached into his bag of secrets one more time and showed the consul general Parti Québécois internal polls proving that the "YES" side was shooting up while the "NO" side was going nowhere.

Jaeger sent only calming dispatches to Washington all the same. In fact, he advised "Foggy Bottom" on April 14 that "the most likely result is a rather narrow defeat of the Lévesque forces with the "YES" getting between 43-47%." These notes had an effect. The new head of the Canadian desk, Richard Smith, confirms that the possibility of a "YES" victory had never been seriously considered. In the higher ranks, Sharon Ahmad had replaced Richard Vine as deputy assistant secretary of state, the highest cadre involved with the Canadian dossier. "The discussion was murky enough and the choice if you were a Quebec voter must have been murky enough that the wording of the referendum and the discussion of it, it was just not clear," she said, a little confused herself. She had apparently never been informed of the possibility that the "YES" side could win.

At any rate, she added, this "would not mean the end" of Canada. To sum it up, she didn't "feel that the vibes, as far as they reach senior levels in the Department and elsewhere, were yet at the point of alarm."

## The Squaring of the Quebec Circle

Surely someone, somewhere in the United States would wake up and see that the gradualist logic that might be set in motion on May 20 would in fact lead to a redrawing of lines on the political map of North America. It would mean that, in spite of all the promised links between the two new sovereign states, Quebec would acquire the power, as Morin explained, "to define the conditions of its interdependence for itself"; that, despite all the soothing  packaging, a "YES" victory on May 20 would set a machine in motion; that the starting line was more of a determining factor than the finish line.

There would be someone: Karl Meyer of *The New York Times* editorial board, with whom Claude Morin met in New York. The wording of the referendum question had been public since the end of December, but Meyer had not yet read it. Morin showed him a copy:

The Government of Québec has made public its proposal to negotiate a new agreement with the rest of Canada, based on the equality of nations; this agreement would enable Québec to acquire the exclusive power to make its laws, levy its taxes and establish relations abroad — in other words, sovereignty — and at the same time, to maintain with Canada an economic association including a common currency; no change in political status resulting from these negotiations will be effected without approval by the people through another referendum; on these terms, do you give the Government of Québec the mandate to negotiate the proposed agreement between Québec and Canada?

YES                                    NO

When he finished reading, Meyer asked the minister, "Explain to me how this won't lead to separation."

Morin then explained how the procedure would lead, in effect, to independence. For the constitutional expert who had advised Jean Lesage, Daniel Johnson, Robert Bourassa, and René Lévesque, this was the climax of an entire political career — the squaring of the Quebec circle, a vicious circle that consisted, for a majority of citizens, of wanting to repatriate to Quebec enough power to make Canadian confederation hollow while insisting on maintaining its links with the federal government at any cost. If the "YES" side won a majority, negotiations would start, explained Morin, who had been assured of this in private by provincial premiers. The results of these discussions, a sort of agreement in principle, would be the subject of a second referendum in two or three years. A sovereign and associated Quebec would be born. If the negotiations failed — and Ottawa would be blaimed for this failure — the second referendum would deal with sovereignty itself rather than with a mandate to negotiate. In the interval, a provincial election would permit the Quebec government to renew its mandate with the electorate.

These steps did not lead inexorably to independence. Between the two referendums, the federal counter-strategists could advance powerful pawns. But the logic of the process obliged the players to make their moves on the separatist chess board.

Surely someone, somewhere in the United States government would also perceive that, against all expectations, the sovereignty side had a good chance of winning the referendum.

A federal source could have put a flea in their ear.

Could have asked them to do a little favour.

To say a few words.

Or just one.

No.

## The Shadow of Cyrus Vance

The American cavalry charge into the referendum debate came 29 days before the vote. George Jaeger passed the word on to Richard Pouliot, Claude Morin's assistant deputy minister, then to Morin himself.

An insidious wind of panic suddenly swept in; all the soporifics so cleverly administered to the lower strata of American politics had been of no use. The decisions were made at the top, among a handful of wide-awake decision-makers, and often for reasons that had little to do with the subject at hand.

Cyrus Vance would be in Ottawa on April 23, 1980. He would hold a press conference. There would be a question on the referendum. There would be, Jaeger announced, a response. And this response could be harder, clearer, than all others that had been given up to then.

Jaeger himself was mortified. Pouliot reported:

> [Jaeger] stated again that the American government understood Quebec's position much better today, but he also told me that the United States had global interests and that it could very well happen that the American government would practice "realpolitik." He continued by telling me that the Secretary of State had received an in-depth briefing on the whole Canadian situation before his visit to Ottawa this week. He also indicated that their recommendation to the Secretary of State leaned toward abstention. [...] He added that, as a civil servant, he could only make recommendations to the State Department, but he could not assure me that these recommendations would be followed by the Secretary of State, who was generally recognized as a "conservative" on foreign policy. The qualifier is his and not mine. Under the present circumstances, he added, [...] it was not at all unthinkable that the Secretary of State would "have his arm twisted" by Prime Minister Trudeau. Once again, the wording is his and not mine. [...] He then said that it was important for the United States to obtain Canada's support in the boycott of the Moscow Olympic Games [to protest the Soviet invasion of Afghanistan].
>
> I concluded, as I told the minister after my meeting with Mr Jaeger, that it could very well happen that Mr Vance could swap a declaration on Canadian unity for assurance of Ottawa's support for his policy regarding the boycott of the Olympic Games in Moscow.

A few hours later, Jaeger painted the same picture for Morin. "I remember it, of course! He told me that there was lots of federal pressure," says Morin. "The federal government was not happy about the Americans' nuances and their kind of silence, and wanted it made very clear that the Americans were against the idea of sovereignty and were hoping for a 'NO.'" Ottawa wanted the Americans to say, "Hey, it's time to stop the nonsense!" Jaeger said that the Secretary of State boasted that he knew Canada well and that he could make this decision himself. He talked of debates among American advisors in Quebec, Ottawa, and Washington.

The threat of Vance's intervention, the thought that — in spite of Operation America, in spite of the delivery of reams of confidential information to the door of the consulate general, in spite of the change in position regarding NATO and NORAD, in spite, briefly, of three years of careful stroking — the American superpower had still decided to strike a mortal blow and hand victory to the "NO" side was shocking.

No later than August of 1979, Jaeger, newly settled in Quebec City, had had to put out a similar fire, lit in Washington by a member of the National Security Council (NSC). According to the *Globe and Mail*, one of Zbigniew Brzezinski's advisors confided in private that the American administration was anxious about the way in which the Quebec government was organizing the referendum. If the vote was not democratic, he declared twice in his conversation with journalist Lawrence Martin, Washington would have to intervene by denouncing the procedure. "He thought he was a big shooter, he thought he had all the power, he gave the impression that he had access to all the things, that it was not just himself talking but a decision of the Administration," recalls Martin.

A rain of official denials started falling the next day. In Quebec City, George Jaeger met with Louis Bernard and hastened to tell him that he "had received written confirmation from Washington that very morning," wrote Bernard in a note to Lévesque, assuring him that any threat of "a possible intervention by the White House during the referendum was absolutely without foundation."

## Paying Off Abraham Lincoln's Debt

Perhaps Vance's intrusion into internal Canadian politics was a delayed reaction to the NSC official's indiscretion. And if it fit Ottawa's appeal — or the "Olympic boycott"/"Stop the nonsense!" swap — could it also have been the result of pressure by a small group of Americans who were anxious about the referendum, among them the influential *New York Times* columnist James Reston? Reston had lent a strong hand to Enders when René Lévesque visited the Economic Club by writing that Washington saw Quebec's secession as "the worst proposition put to the US government since Nikita Khrushchev invited us to accept the emplacement of Soviet nuclear missiles in Cuba." This time he had given Cyrus Vance some advice three days before his visit to Ottawa: "There is nothing in the US or Canadian constitutions that forbids [us]," he wrote, "from sending a few affectionate remarks to our friends above the Canadian border." "Canada is, in a way, 'our business,'" he continued, since it was "our strategic shield," "our most important trading partner," and "our dearest friend."

Like his colleague Karl Meyer, Reston did not see how a referendum could lead to anything but separation. Supporting the federal position would be a good way to pay off an old debt, he thought; after all, "Canada wasn't indifferent when Mr Lincoln said that he would preserve the union of the United States even at the risk of war between the states." How could Vance keep from saying something in Ottawa? History demanded it, the boycott of the Olympic Games begged for it, simple decency required it. Had Canada not, some weeks before, saved six American hostages in Teheran, at the peril of the lives of Canadian diplomats involved in the escape? The operation had taken place under Joe Clark and the pro-Canadian sentiment that had since swept through America was well worth "a few affectionate remarks to our friends" up north.

In a way, Cyrus Vance would only be repeating himself. He had already, in November of 1978, made a diplomatic trip to state in Canada what Carter had said the year before in Washington. Claude Morin and Louise Beaudoin had warned McNamara that "it would still be better if he didn't meddle in our affairs." The message would be transmitted, McNamara promised. But "All Americans," Vance intoned in a speech that had been carefully crafted long before, "hope that this great, rich country will remain united." He used the words "united Canada" a second time in his speech, twice more the next day in his press conference.

In Quebec City, his statement was not well received. A high-ranking official deemed that such insistence represented "interference in our internal affairs" and that it must not be repeated: "It would have a pernicious effect on public opinion," since "it would fear American 'reprisals.'" He proposed to send a diplomatic note of protest in good and due form. The note would first state Quebec's "surprise" regarding such bold words. Then it would squarely dot the i's:

The Quebec people would find it hard to understand that pressure could come from the outside regarding decisions that they will be called upon to make in conformity with rights which are universally recognized and of which the American government declares itself to be an ardent defender.

Such misunderstandings are perhaps explained by the fact that American authorities have, up until now, had the opportunity to hear only the federal government's version.

Yves Michaud transmitted a draft of the note to René Lévesque, with his commentary. "I wonder if this intervention will raise too many eyebrows, if it will be difficult to catch it later." A civil servant worried that if the note was leaked the headlines would read "Quebec Declares War on the United States." "*Le Devoir* might just do that," he wrote.

Michaud left the handling of this affair to Lévesque, who had, as he wrote to the premier, an "intimate and precise knowledge of American society and politicians." In the margin of Michaud's memo, Lévesque wrote: "Completely in agreement — stop this 'note' please."

Claude Morin decided to turn Cyrus Vance's diplomatic rebuff to Quebec's political profit. A Radio-Canada journalist was able to report that the "surprise" caused by Vance's statement "was equalled only by the lack of importance that seems to have been accorded to him by the government of Quebec." On television, an affable Morin explained that it was "normal, when a foreign visitor goes to Ottawa, that we don't expect him to say 'Vive le Québec libre!'" In fact, the minister emphasized, Vance had repeatedly indicated that the affair was for Canadians to decide. "We feel that this is progress compared to the impression that existed several years ago here in Canada and in the United States," he added. He acted as if he were about to send a thank-you note to the State Department.

## The Anti-American Straw Man

Vance's 1978 visit to Ottawa was gone from everyone's mind. Vance's visit to Ottawa on April 23, 1980, could yield lasting damage to the PQ.

Much was at stake: the votes of the undecided, that mass of Quebeckers who had not yet chosen between their two heroes, Lévesque and Trudeau, and their two landscapes, the Rockies and the Gaspé. Without Vance, the referendum could be won. With him, the fleur-de-lis would undoubtedly be lowered and the maple leaf run up the flagpole.

Morin and Pouliot grabbed onto Jaeger as if to a lifeboat. They had another 48 hours before Vance's arrival; there was still time to act. "Jaeger seemed, at that moment, to be taking our side," recalls Morin. The consul was seemingly skirting the hornet's nest that Vance's statement would stir up. Anticipating the wishes of the Quebeckers, he argued that he himself would prefer the United States to remain mute. He asked if he could, please, warn Washington that Quebec was not taking this American intervention kindly.

"I said yes," remembers Morin, "and then I piled up the arguments."

Their trump card was that any interference in the debate at this time would provoke an anti-American tidal wave among Quebeckers such as had never been seen. "It was very curious, they were scared of this," the minister says. The Americans mistrusted these unpredictable "Frenchies" and their reactions "as if we weren't true Americans, in the sense that we were Francophones, linked to France."

The anti-American straw man had been used before. Lévesque had warned in *The New York Times* a year earlier that if the Americans "became stupidly negative," this would "create a virulent anti-Americanism, which does not now exist in Quebec." The premier emphasized that intervention would have a second negative effect: "The giant next door could create fear. Like all colonized people, Quebeckers have complexes. It is always easy to appeal to one of these complexes, fear. That's what our adversaries in Canada always do. They would love to see Washington say, 'No way.'" Anti-American sentiment would be the price to pay but the US could succeed in "delaying" independence, Lévesque admitted.

Some people in Washington were at that very moment coming to the same conclusion. According to an INR analysis, "The US could arouse Quebec nationalistic pride if it too publicly espoused the Canadian union," thus helping the "YES" side.

For what it was worth, Pouliot and Morin hammered away on the anti-American theme. They had a good argument: when French socialist Michel Rocard had quietly confirmed in a letter that he approved of the logic of the sovereignty option, he had drawn howls of indignation from the press and the opposition for his "interference" in internal affairs. (Later, Morin would accuse Bourassa of leaking this confidential letter to a journalist, but it now turned out to be helpful ammunition.)

"Rocard didn't even intervene [officially], and you see the result!" Morin insisted to Jaeger. "Imagine what would happen with the United States, which is right next door!"

Did the top separatist strategist, who knew Quebeckers better than anyone, believe a single word of what he told the American with so much urgency? "Not at all," he now confesses. "I mean, come on!"

There was never any fertile ground for anti-American sentiment in Quebec, Morin knew.

## Cyrus and the Painful Question

April 23, 1980, began badly for the separatists. In the papers and on the radio, the news was that Mark MacGuigan, the secretary of state for external affairs, had announced that Canada would join the American boycott of the Moscow Olympic games. Had a bargain already taken place? Cyrus Vance talked with his counterpart MacGuigan all day. He lunched with Pierre Trudeau. When the time came for the press conference, MacGuigan warned him — as if he didn't know already — that he would be asked about Quebec.

The large press conference room in Ottawa was packed. Cameras and tape recorders rolled. Pens scratched away frantically.

In Quebec City, Louis Bernard, Claude Morin, Richard Pouliot and James Donovan had an aide rummage through the files for all major statements that members of the American administration had made regarding Quebec in the previous two years. Every word counted.

A reporter, leaving nothing to chance, asked the first question: "As you know, the people of Quebec are voting in a historic referendum on May 20th on a question relating to Quebec's place in the Confederation. In 1977, when Prime Minister Trudeau was in Washington, President Carter said in a television interview that if he were making his own preference, it would be that the Confederation continue. Is that still the clear view of the Administration in Washington?"

Cyrus Vance responded, "Our view is that this is an issue which should be decided by the Canadian people, and will be decided by the Canadian people."

Journalists waited for the other shoe to drop. Nothing happened.

After a few questions on other matters, a reporter returned to the subject from a different angle: "If Quebec decides to become independent, is the United States prepared to recognize its right to self-determination?"

The secretary of state: "That is a speculative question on which I do not wish to comment. I have already stated that this is a question for the people of Canada to decide. This is all I wish to say."

This was all Vance had to say? The reporters clearly felt that the secretary's answers were incomplete; what about the American preference for confederation? One journalist tried a final tack on the top American diplomat: "I'd like to come back to this referendum question. You don't seem to be prepared to go as far on this subject as President Carter. In his interview in 1977, he said he recognized the distinct American national interest in the outcome of this referendum, and that he felt it was in the interest of the United States that Canada stay together. Are you now saying you're not prepared to endorse that statement?"

Now Vance was annoyed. He responded dryly: "I am not repudiating anything the President said. I'm saying that this is a question for the Canadian people to decide."

Vance had provided nothing for the television news, nothing for the next day's papers, and nothing to feed Quebec's fears.

The press conference ended. The earthquake never took place; the United States had spoiled its ballot.

## Sad, Nervous, Bitter

Far from coming to the rescue of the "NO" side, Cyrus Vance had retreated. For the first time, "an attitude of strict neutrality" had truly been adopted, exulted a telex sent by Quebec to all its American delegations. "Mr Vance retreated from previous statements [in 1977 and 1978] by American leaders, including Mr Vance himself and President Carter, who, while refraining from actively meddling in Canada's affairs, wanted to indicate their preference for federalism and a united Canada."

Why had the American cavalry done an about-face within sight of the finish line?

"That's easy," says an exultant Claude Morin, "we won." The anti-American gambit, he believes, had paid off.

"I saved the day," George Jaeger told a reporter, explaining that he had had to intervene, in spite of the reticence of his diplomatic colleagues in Ottawa and Washington, to dampen the federalist ardor of the secretary of state.

In PQ headquarters, the troops gleefully envisioned the rage that must be engulfing the federalist enemies. Pierre Trudeau, with Marc Lalonde and Michael Pitfield, must be fuming about the treachery of the Americans, they thought; we saved their hostages, we supported their boycotts, and they turn away or, worse, stab us in the back in our hour of great distress! The separatists would have liked to see MacGuigan's face after the disastrous press conference.

But Trudeau did not rage, and a MacGuigan was not concerned. Everyone gaily waved goodbye to Vance, who was returning home that evening to ominous events. In Ottawa, no one had been waiting for cavalry. "There was no feeling of disappointment," reports a senior Canadian official who organized the visit. A major statement on Quebec had never been discussed. Even MacGuigan was surprised to learn that Quebec had been worried about this visit; no one had informed him that Vance was supposed to play some role in the national drama. Allan Gotlieb, undersecretary of state for external affairs and a Trudeau advisor, present at all meetings, did not bat an eyelash. The visit had gone as planned.

All indications are that in 1980, Pierre Trudeau wanted to lead the federalist charge with his own arsenal and was satisfied for Washington to watch silently from the sidelines. In spite of the polls and the feeling of panic around him, the Canadian prime minister believed that the country's future must depend on its own strengths and not on shock tactics by Uncle Sam, to whom, sooner or later, the favor would have to be returned. The outcome of the battle was a toss-up, but Pierre Trudeau wanted to be known for posterity as the man who had tamed the beast, all alone.

Ambassador Kenneth Curtis vaguely remembers having mentioned in a dispatch that Ottawa had been expecting a repetition of the usual political line on Quebec. But he does not remember even noticing during the visit that Vance's statement had omitted the "preference for a united Canada" line. In any case, he adds, no debate preceded or followed the secretary of state's visit. His right-hand man, Robert Duemling, offers the same account.

George Vest, Vance's assistant for European (thus Canadian) affairs, who had accompanied him on the trip, was amused to learn, nine years later, that his boss had been the cause of such nervousness in Quebec. He had absolutely no memory of any debates, strategies, swaps, or pressure from Ottawa or Quebec. Was he hugging the shore? On the contrary. "We never had any instructions from on high which said, 'Now we clamp down and don't say anything,'" he stated. "On high," at the White House, Zbigniew Brzezinski firmly states that there had been no pressure, federal or provincial, and that he had never veered off course. Richard Smith, director of the Canada Desk at the State Department, and his assistant, Wingate Lloyd, also state that they had had no inkling that there had been an internal debate on what Cyrus Vance was or was not supposed to do.

On the other hand, everyone well knew how nervous and sad, if not bitter, Vance had been on April 23, 1980. It was his last day on the job. He had submitted his letter of resignation a week earlier in protest of the military plan to save the American hostages in Iran. The elements of the operation were in place, on ships on the Red Sea and in the deserts of the Middle East, as Vance was answering questions from Canadian reporters. While they were concerned about their Quebec mini-crisis, he was anxious about the huge drama underway halfway around the globe.

Vance "may have had many other things on his mind" besides Quebec, Vest says. But it was difficult to believe that Vance, a professional, would have "forgotten" to say the key Quebec words, surely inscribed in his briefing book.

## In Cyrus' Plane

In reality, Cyrus Vance's interest in the Quebec question had been overestimated. He simply did not care for it. On December 30, 1976, a month and a half after the PQ was elected, the Canadian ambassador in Washington, Jake Warren, returned in surprise from his first meeting with the new chief of American diplomacy. He informed Ottawa that Vance "did not, repeat, not mention Quebec."

Vance got along famously with Don Jamieson, his Canadian counterpart, whom he met with regularly, notably for international negotiations on Namibia. According to an assistant who accompanied Jamieson to all his meetings, Vance never broached the subject of the crisis in Quebec. In fact, noted someone close to the minister, "Jamieson would have been the last to know" about developments in the Quebec dossier. With Flora MacDonald, the Conservative who replaced Jamieson, then with MacGuigan, it was the same: Vance did not inform himself either of the situation or of how the polls were developing, nor did he offer information, warning, or advice. He was absolutely indifferent.

"Vance is a very, very nice person, and he just doesn't like to put his nose into somebody else's business," explains Richard Vine. It was an unusual description for a head of American diplomacy, but it was true that Vance was considered a "dove" in Washington, especially when compared to the "hawkish" Brzezinski.

Even his statements of November 1978 came close to not being made. Richard Vine had prepared the speech, integrating sentences similar to those that had been pronounced by Carter. This was routine. But in the government plane carrying Vance and Vine to Ottawa, the secretary of state bridled.

"He said, 'I won't do it,'" recalled Vine. He wouldn't use the speech as drafted.

"The [Canadian] Foreign Office expects you to do it," Vine insisted. "The absence of that statement will be considered a change in our policy."

But Vance wanted nothing of it. He did not want to meddle in Canadian affairs, he insisted. The text as written, with its support of a united Canada, "smacked of American interference," he said again. He turned to an assistant, Lloyd Cutler, and asked him to rewrite the offending paragraph to soften the position.

"I pointed out that this was only a statement of our preference," Vine said, "that I knew categorically that Ottawa wanted to hear." And then he emphasized to Vance, as their plane approached Ottawa, that the text was already so timid that they could not say any less and still say something. After they arrived, Tom Enders got involved in the matter and supported Vine. Cyrus Vance finally yielded to the pressure of his two advisors. He would read the text as it stood.

After seeing the beaming faces of the Canadian politicians after the speech, then reading the local dailies which picked this paragraph out of the speech the next day, Vance admitted to Vine that he had perhaps been right.

But two years later, Vine was no longer there to insist on inclusion of such lines; nor was Enders. And Curtis was not the kind of man to bother his boss about the issue. "Whatever happens," he had already said to Lévesque, "we will remain neighbors, and people from Maine will continue to marry Quebeckers across the border."

On April 23, 1980, Vance did not even have a text of a speech to pick apart. There was only a briefing book — which predicted a "NO" victory from all of the evidence — and a press conference. Vance had no reason, this time, to hide his neutralist convictions. The next day he would resign on a question of principle; there was no reason now to make a useless compromise.

Cyrus Vance was thus the only member of the American administration who truly stood in agreement with Operation America, which advocating a policy of neutrality for the United States.

## After Cyrus

Why did the American consul general in Quebec City plunge his "clients" into such turmoil? Did George Jaeger truly believe that Vance would gum up the referendum works, or was he playing on the paranoia of the PQ to raise his stature in their eyes?

The Vance episode, explained one of his Quebec contacts, proved that "the consular network could have a certain amount of influence" on Washington. That is, Quebec's interests were in good hands with the local representative of the neighboring power.

This conclusion had to have pleased Jaeger since, in April of 1980, he was in a "truly foul mood," noted a civil servant, and angry at Claude Morin and his team. In an interview in an American university publication much read in foreign affairs circles, *The Fletcher Forum*, Morin had lashed out at the refusal of American leaders to meet any member of the PQ government. "We believe that we have a right to be heard by the government of the United States," the minister stated. "Yet up to now the American government has turned for explanations of the evolution of Quebec's internal political situation to the central government, which is opposed to our ideas!"

"What about me?" Jaeger seemed to be protesting. He was "offended" that in the interview, Morin "did not mention the activities of the United States consul general in Quebec City." Jaeger also suspected that the minister's assistants had circulated excerpts from the article, some portions of which appeared on the front page of the April 17 edition of *The Gazette*. He manifested his displeasure that day to a protocol official, to Pouliot on the twenty-first. The consul general "complained about the fact that he was little used, that generally when there was a question about the United States, it was he who had to take the initiative to ask for meetings." He felt that Morin had shown his ingratitude in the *Fletcher Forum* interview. Pouliot wrote that Jaeger "had taken as an example the secretary of state's visit to Ottawa, indicating to me that he did not want to lecture me, but that no one in the government had called him to discuss it."

The psychodrama of Vance's visit focussed the spotlight, as never before, on the consul general's influence. Once Vance had returned home, Jaeger confided to a senior official that he had "succeeded in making sure that Vance did not come out as strong" as planned, that he "wouldn't antagonize the political debate that was taking place here."

Beyond this bizarre episode, the question of American intervention remains. Why did Washington not feel the need to reiterate its position — if not via Vance then with another of its many spokespersons — in the weeks leading up to the referendum? The lulling of "Foggy Bottom" into the certainty that the "NO" side would win had something to do with it, as did the reluctance of Prime Minister Trudeau to ask the Americans for help at the end of the race.

On the top floor of the State Department, Operation America's existence was not ignored. "The Quebec provincial government simply tried to use all the levers of influence which they could," George Vest calmly states. "We, at the time, certainly recognized it and thought, 'Well, it's their business' — but it never influenced us," he added. "We saw it, but never felt any pressure stemming from" areas where Quebec was intervening. It was more difficult, however, to gauge to what extent the Quebec actions forestalled pro-federalist pressure.

Nothing, however, was more decisive in the American inclination toward indifference to the referendum campaign than the premise that René Lévesque was not, or was no longer, a separatist.

## Respect and Incredulity

"Lévesque is not truly a separatist, not at all. He never intended to arrive at independence as such," then reported an American diplomat, who wants to remain anonymous, charged with following the Quebec dossier. According to him, Lévesque "was politically obliged to hold the referendum, but he knew that it would fail." His goal was to "give Canadians a scare so that he could obtain more autonomy for Quebec." The entire referendum strategy — the whole separatist plan — was thus just a lever to serve René Lévesque's true objective: decentralized federalism and a special status for Quebec.

This would have meant that René Lévesque, a man who did not know how to hold his tongue behind closed doors, would have been living an immense lie. The Americans believed him capable of it — and regarded this as a compliment. This analysis, which the diplomat in question had been developing since 1978, was soon to become the dominant theory in Washington and in certain economic circles in New York. It had a variation. There were also those who believed that although Lévesque had wanted independence, he had finally admitted that it was unattainable.

Lévesque's best friend in the United States, Vermont governor Richard Snelling, was in the first group. "Separatism and an eventual [referendum] and a whole bunch of things were, at least in part, staged business, when the real theatre was not separatism, it was equality, or even superiority, of French-speaking people in Quebec and an end to the domination of management and professions by Anglophones." He felt that Lévesque, of whom he was a "great admirer," never "believed that it [independence] would occur." His Quebec friend had never been totally frank on this point, but Snelling was convinced that the PQ leader wanted social justice rather than sovereignty.

Richard Vine, at the State Department, was in the second group. "Sometime in the time frame [of 1978–1979], we became convinced that Lévesque no longer had the option to go" toward independence. "I think as he pushed, prodded, molded, tried to move things in terms of separatism, he became increasingly aware that it was a good slogan but it was never something that he could bring about. I think by the time of the '78–'79 time frame, it became perfectly plain that he could not pull it off." According to Vine, the problem of constitutional reform that would replace that of Quebec's secession was "very interesting but no longer of grave concern to us." Since the referendum was only an expedient, an internal political ruse, even a "YES" victory had no importance. In fact, Lévesque, says Vine, "couldn't have gone any place with it." His assistant, Richard Smith, says something similar: "It was less than completely clear what his [Lévesque's] long-range objective was."

In New York, these theories circulated as well in business circles. As early as the fall of 1977, the editors of the foreign pages of *The Wall Street Journal* confided to the Canadian consul general in New York that they "doubted the Quebec government was bent on full separation," that, in their opinion, "Lévesque would be willing to settle for constitutional concessions by the federal government." Three months later, this version of things appeared in black and white in the pages of the financial daily.

There are signs that the Quebec government is backing away from actual separation from Canada. A source close to the provincial government in Quebec City argues that "all that talk by Lévesque of sovereignty and economic association with the rest of Canada and about a referendum on independence is designed to keep Trudeau and the English [Canadians] off balance." It's realized, he says, that outright independence is unworkable and that Quebec can "get more power" while staying in Canada.

A partner in Salomon Brothers — thus a member of the syndicate representing Hydro Quebec on the financial market — made the following remark in May of 1978: "As for Quebec, we note a renewal of interest attributable to the Lévesque government's abandonment of a separatist strategy." These money men, who had had the shock of their lives at the Economic Club listening to someone who seemed truly to believe in his campaign promises, latched onto any moderate economic measure taken by the Lévesque government, such as the "bank's budget," to push this fleeting revelation deep into the back of their minds.

This tenacious refusal to believe in the possibility of an independent Quebec rose from a collective self-hypnosis. Robert Duemling, assistant to Enders and Curtis, best expressed this half-conscious reflex on the part of these sons of the Civil War: "I just had this visceral feeling that it was just not in the cards — and I could not even explain that to you very rationally." Quebec, of course, fed into this American incredulity. The denial of the word "separatism," the insistence on "association," the fiction that separation would not provoke "the rupture of Canada," all this sleight-of-hand performed by Lévesque and Morin fed a thousand false hopes. Daniel Latouche added a floor to this giant house of cards when he explained to Americans that the negotiations following the referendum could, given the balance of power, produce a diluted sovereignty-association, a "veritable confederation in which Quebec would have wide areas of responsibility."

## René Lévesque, Federalist?

Were the Americans right?

Close associates of René Lévesque's, people he had rubbed shoulders with for many years, deny these allegations. Yves Michaud, Claude Morin, Louis Bernard, Jean-Roch Boivin and Louise Beaudoin all swear on a stack of Bibles that his fundamental goal was sovereignty. "René Lévesque's constitutional thought had not changed much since *Option Québec*," his 1968 book in which he revealed his principles for sovereignty-association, Boivin states. "It was absolutely clear," Bernard adds. "I knew Mr Lévesque intimately, and the theory that he publicly defended was the theory which he fought for and which he believed in." The PQ leader had submitted to a multitude of compromises on currency and passports, Morin explains, but he had not sacrificed the "critical mass" of powers stated in the referendum question: the exclusive power to make laws, levy taxes, establish relations abroad — in other words, sovereignty.

Did he think he could carry it off? Here opinions diverged, as Lévesque's own must have. Jean-Roch Boivin and Yves Michaud felt — without really knowing, they say, since Lévesque did not confide in them about it — that their leader had always been pessimistic about his chances for victory. He had, as we know, been pessimistic about getting elected in the first place. Louis Bernard said, however, that Lévesque had told him that he felt "that there was a reasonable chance of winning the referendum." And Corine Côté-Lévesque, his wife and perhaps his only true confidante, said that in March of 1980, when a poll showed the "YES" side just four points away from 50%, "René always thought that with a good campaign he could catch that up. He was aiming for a clear majority among Francophones, something like 75%" (or 60% of the total vote).

What would he have done with the victory in the end? Lévesque knew that "the balance of power at the time would have much more influence on [Quebec's] status than any abstract definition," states Boivin. With from 51% to 55% of the vote, Lévesque would have taken a direct road to sovereignty-association, say the people close to him. With between 44% and 50% — the "moral victory" of which he spoke to Jaeger — he would have undoubtedly used this "very strong power of negotiation," but "not necessarily for a separation," which would have been out of reach, Boivin suggested. His "critical mass" would have escaped him, at least temporarily.

The Americans were familiar with all of these calculations, since Lévesque made them in front of them, in private. In fact, with Jaeger, whom he liked, and McNamara, whom he respected, Lévesque unabashedly made use of the word "independence." Even in public, when he was pressed, as he had been by Tom Brokaw on NBC in 1978, he admitted seeking "separation."

The Americans were not the only ones to want to turn their own desires into reality. Trudeau had announced the decline of separatism in 1964, its death in 1976. The premiers, gathered for dinner at 24 Sussex Drive shortly after the PQ victory and meeting with René Lévesque for the first time, asked him outright what his real intentions were for Quebec and Canada. "I want out," responded Lévesque, direct as always. This was a great shock to his counterparts, who had been sure that independence was merely a ruse to win the election and gain more power. One of them, Alex Campbell from Prince Edward Island, scribbled on a bit of paper in letters an inch high the word "OUT." Trudeau and the English Canadians stayed awake from this moment on. But the Americans took their turn at having a mental block from 1978 on.

The Americans' self-hypnosis grew deeper in direct proportion to the PQ government's improving reputation for moderation and good management in the United States and to rising respect for its leader. The more Snelling and the diplomats admired Lévesque's political flair and nose for strategy, the less it was believed that he was a separatist. The Americans felt in their hearts that an intelligent man, a man they respected, simply could not harbor such a repugnant notion as the splitting up of Canada. A CIA official expressed it best: "I have never talked to an intelligent French Canadian who fundamentally believed in separation."

The Americans' blindness served the interests of the Parti Québécois well. If they thought that the separatist leader was a disguised federalist, there was no need to trip him up.

## Countdown

Twenty-three days before the referendum, President Carter announced the nomination of his new secretary of state: Edmund Muskie, senator from Maine. In Quebec, René Lévesque grinned. The only American politician who had kind things to say about sovereignty-association had just taken over US diplomacy. It was a gift from heaven. The next day, the premier took his best pen in hand to remind Muskie of their meeting in Washington in January of 1979. "Please feel welcome to Quebec City at any time, Mr Secretary," Lévesque wrote, "should you wish to pick up on some of the issues we discussed last year." The relationship between Maine and Quebec, Lévesque continued, without daring to add that it did not pass through the intermediary of Ottawa, was "a very positive example" of the type of relations that "should exist between neighbor states, and is an asset in the furthering of our mutual relationships in the future."

The American secretary of state responded to the Quebec premier on May 12. In an unprecedented gesture, Muskie sent a polite little note in which he talked of "cooperation and friendship between the United States and Canada" and stated that "We will continue to work together in facing the difficult challenges of the future."

It was now Ottawa's turn to worry a little about the State Department boss's affection for Quebec. The day after Muskie's nomination, a senior official in foreign affairs close to Trudeau, de Montigny Marchand, asked his American desk if Muskie was worth Canada's confidence. The diplomatic services were put on alert to dig up the ex-senator's past statements. "This is urgent," a civil servant noted in a memo. Happily, the Canadian embassy in Washington indicated that several months after his meeting with Lévesque Muskie had professed, in a senate committee meeting, his faith in federalism. It had passed unnoticed at the time, but a copy of the statement existed. Ottawa drew a deep breath.

Eight days before the referendum, members of Quebec delegations in the United States felt out the country. From Chicago, one of them reported that the local media understood well "the truly democratic character of the referendum process." From New York, another announced that business people knew that "changes would not occur the day after May 20." The notion of sovereignty "no longer raised hostility," he wrote, because "they do not believe that it will happen or, if it does happen, they will be able to adjust." The closest, in Boston, gave the most positive report; but from the farthest-flung, sour notes were heard. People in Los Angeles felt that "Quebec looks like a spoilsport"; they were worried about separatist movements that were beginning to spring up in western Canada. They held "Quebec, more than Ottawa, responsible for this situation." In Atlanta, the average American told himself that "it would be so easy to follow the example of the US, the 'American melting-pot.'" For some, "the safeguarding of our language and our culture," the delegate wrote, "is an indication of a lack of the evolution that goes with progress."

Four days before the referendum, Ottawa sent its American consulates and its embassies around the world a long memo outlining official responses for the day after the vote. There were two pages of instructions for the case of a "decisive victory for NO (55% or more)" or for a "small NO victory (51%)"; twelve pages for the case of a "YES" victory.

On that day, on the New York bond market, American investors showed their characteristic sensitivity. The spread between Hydro Quebec stock and that of other Canadian energy companies reached a pre-referendum high: 100 points. Earlier, the spread had disappeared.

One day before the referendum, Canadian diplomats compiled articles and commentaries from the American national press. Of 38 articles analysed, 15 supported the "NO" side (39%), 19 were neutral (50%), and four leaned toward "YES." (This totalled 11%, or five times more than the 2% pro-separatist comments Claude Ryan found the day after the November 15 election.)

On May 20, 1980, referendum day, the Quebec delegations in New York, Boston, Chicago, Los Angeles, Atlanta, Dallas, and Lafayette readied themselves, with a budget of $20,520, to receive hundreds of guests for the evening. In New England, five PBS stations prepared to cover the vote live. At the State Department, Richard Smith made sure that the results were routed to him as quickly as possible.

*6:00 PM.* At the Canadian Press/*Presse canadienne* office in Montreal, the only spot in the country where Francophone and Anglophone journalists worked shoulder-to-shoulder, an official demanded silence in the noisy newsroom. He implored both sides not to make an outburst, not to manifest any joy or disappointment, when the result was announced.

*6:30 PM.* About three hundred people had accepted the New York general delegation's invitation. A large contingent of professors of French from the area and a good number of representatives from the business community, notably from the financial syndicate representing Quebec on Wall Street, mingled with Quebeckers from the city and the delegation.

*7:00 PM.* The polls closed. About 4.4 million Quebeckers, 85.6% of the eligible voters, had cast ballots.

*7:15 PM.* At the New York reception, reported a Canadian diplomat in a telex, "from first moments of coverage, when "NO" vote took lead, mood of fairly friendly gathering was one of controlled excitement and growing optimism on the one hand, and increasing resignation on the other. Despite free-flowing bars, very few overt expressions of emotion."

*7:55 PM.* Radio-Canada announced the victory of the "NO" side. "It's a disaster," a New York delegation member stated, as the three televisions carrying CBC and the two carrying Radio-Canada showed close-ups of "YES" supporters in tears. "Majority of guests appeared to view the results positively, with businessmen expressing highest satisfaction."

*8:15 PM.* At Canadian Press/*Presse canadienne*, in spite of the fact that the newsroom was functioning at full throttle, the sound level was uncommonly low.

*8:30 PM.* The PQ leader prepared himself to confront his supporters. Jean-Roch Boivin was with René Lévesque when he discovered the depth of the defeat. The "YES" side was on the way to a meager 40% of the vote; the "NO" side to a massive 60%. "Then, his face changed," Boivin recalls. "We knew that we wouldn't win," sighed Lévesque, who had lived with this feeling since the end of April. "But, damn it, we didn't even have a majority of Francophones!"

At the White House, the results were communicated to Zbigniew Brzezinski, who could compare them to the prognoses he had made in 1967. He transmitted the news of the "NO" side's victory to Jimmy Carter, who learned of it before he went to sleep, certain that the integrity of the continent was saved, that the regional tensions in his own country would not be amplified by a bad example to the north.

*9:31 PM.* René Lévesque arrived on the stage of the Paul Sauvé Arena. George Jaeger reported the scene. "Lévesque, close to tears, acknowledged defeat to roaring stadium full of cheering, weeping supporters." The Quebec electorate "had denied Lévesque, by a hair, the Francophone majority he would have needed to claim moral victory." Lévesque "ended what he called most difficult speech of his career by telling his Péquistes to keep up hope."

"We have a meeting with history, a meeting that Quebec will keep," Lévesque said. "This evening, I can't tell you when or how, but I believe it." He left the crowd intoning a song that was threadbare, bruised: Gilles Vigneault's "Gens du pays."

May 21, 1980. A dispatch from George Jaeger: "On the morning after the 'NO' victory it was clear that sovereignty-association, the dream of some and nightmare of others, was no longer an option — at least for the time being."

Analysts of all stripes monopolized the media to dissect the Quebec vote, paying little attention to what Washington's position had been. The little Operation America team had one consolation: "Perhaps we lost the referendum," sighs Louis Bernard, "but at least it wasn't the Americans' fault."

At Harvard, the day after the defeat, Daniel Latouche explained that, beyond the statistics and the strategies, "the party of the poets — of the singers, of the *chansonniers* — has lost." "That is what really worries me a great deal," he concluded.

And the poet of independence, the incarnation of his land and his people, on that day entered a long period of silence. When he broke it two years later, Gilles Vigneault offered in a few words a definitive explanation for the referendum result: "I was not numerous enough to think as I did."

# Part Three

# The Belated Allies

*It's not how you speak French
that's important, but how well
you understand the culture.
Ever since Jacques Cartier told me that,
I've been a great admirer of all
that is French Canadian.*

RONALD REAGAN
President of the United States
Quebec Summit, March 1985

# 17

# President Reagan's Smiles

*They were anxious for him to become a separatist again ...*
*[They] were supporting him as insurgencies, I'd say.*
*Like the contras.*
ALLAN GOTLIEB
Canadian ambassador in Washington

Ronald Reagan did not like to read. Rather than peruse briefing books on the summits in which he was to participate, he viewed briefing videos on the places and people he was to meet. When he felt compelled to read, he preferred letters from his fans, which the White House received by the thousand. He leafed through them almost every day, giving long responses to the most complimentary. He also liked fiction. To prepare himself for his first visit to the Soviet Union, he read a political novel on a third world war launched by Moscow. And the most powerful man in the world spent at least half an hour each day reading the three pages of comics in *The Washington Post*.

Comics or political fiction were an apt description for the magazine article that caught the President's attention one June day in 1982. A picture of the Canadian prime minister adorned the cover of one of Ronald Reagan's favorite publications, the ultra-conservative *National Review*. Written by a *Toronto Sun* political columnist, Lubor Zink, the article strangely implied that Pierre Elliott Trudeau was a Soviet mole who had tunneled to the top of the Canadian government. Zink selected and arranged his material to support his "penetration" thesis (the title of the article was "The Unpenetrated Problem of Pierre Trudeau"); any John Le Carré fan could easily draw the obvious conclusion. Trudeau's flirtation with Marxism after the Second World War "obviously wasn't lost on the talent scouts in Moscow," he wrote. "Evidence of Soviet interest in Trudeau came in 1952," when the Montreal intellectual led a delegation of five Communists to Moscow, "although he himself was not a regular Communist Party member." An irregular member then? Follow my pen, Zink seemed to say. Had Trudeau not written, in 1956, that he had to enter "one of the old parties and chang[e] them from the inside"? How had this tourist in China in 1960 managed to have "private talks with Chou En Lai and Mao himself" if he was not part of the invisible army of the enemy? And why, when the word "Canada" was whispered to a moribund Leonid Brezhnev, had he managed to smile and pronounce the syllables "Tru-deau"?

Once in power in 1968 with his "Quebec socialist troika" (the other members being, of course, Gérard Pelletier and Jean Marchand), the camouflaged Marxist got down to work, Zink explained: he weakened the Canadian army and its contribution to NATO, delivered secrets to the USSR, "supported Marxist 'liberation wars.'" He had only praise for the crushing of Poland.

Since the end of his nine months in the wilderness and his return to power in February of 1980, Trudeau had launched an all-out effort to attain the objective that had never left his mind: "a sweeping transformation of Canada from a liberal parliamentary democracy into a centrally planned state — a fundamental reshaping of political, economic, and social structures to codify the invisible revolution." This offensive would be launched on the economic and constitutional fronts; at this late date, Trudeau's aims were "marred only by Quebec's refusal to fit in."

Ronald Reagan was "impressed" by this article, confided a close advisor. In fact, this was not the first time that Trudeau had been associated with the hammer and sickle. Conservative Alabama governor George Wallace had stated back in 1971 that the United States had a "crypto-Communist premier in Canada just above us. He's got a worse background and record than Cuban premier Castro himself."

Reagan already had a few quibbles with the Canadian and now the Toronto writer had provided the background for him. The American administration was in an almost open war with this arrogant Prime Minister, who intended not only to put a brake on American investments in Canada, but also to oust a number of American companies from its oil industry.

The "Canadianization" of the economy to the north announced by Trudeau and his two accomplices, Energy Minister Marc Lalonde and Industry Minister Herb Gray, directly defied the Reagan team's desire to make the world a safer place for American industry. On top of this, Trudeau was dragging his feet in the great enterprise of reconstruction of the "arsenal of democracy." With his stinginess regarding NATO (why "waste all that dough?" Trudeau had said in the 1980 campaign), his criticism of Reagan's cold-war rhetoric, and his lack of interest in supporting American policy on Nicaragua, Trudeau contradicted the President more often and with more ardor than the declared socialist, French leader François Mitterrand, who had four Communists in his cabinet, and an ex-guerrilla, Régis Debray at the Elysée. Although Mitterrand was also engaged in a wide-ranging nationalization program, he limited himself only to French firms.

Trudeau wanted to reduce the American presence in his country, increase the state's role in the economy, centralize power in Ottawa. Who better fit the definition of a Soviet mole?

## Changing Partners

It was as if someone had unearthed the anti-Parti Québécois propaganda booklet from the back of a drawer, dusted it off, expanded it, and used it to fire red bullets at Pierre Trudeau.

Trudeau's two projects, the National Energy Program (or NEP, which aimed to put 50% of the oil industry under Canadian control) and his strengthening of the Foreign Investment Review Agency (or FIRA, which existed essentially to prevent the purchase of large Canadian companies by American firms) aroused the most ire. Trudeau's big offensive took place just after the referendum. "Trudeau was very expedient," Allan Gotlieb explains. "He followed a very cautious policy vis-à-vis the Americans, and then, the referendum was in May

[...] the NEP and the move to strengthen FIRA came after, damned soon after."

This new orientation amounted to a "xenophobic" policy, wrote *The Wall Street Journal*. It bespoke a desire for "withdrawal from the world," thundered a senior official in Washington. The nationalization of the asbestos industry complied with the rules, but one of the provisions of the NEP gave off an unbearable odor of "expropriation without compensation," wrote an assistant to the American ambassador in Ottawa.

Once, Lévesque had been accused of being a "Castro of the North," but it was now Trudeau's turn to appear as a red. When the premier of New Brunswick, Richard Hatfield, was in Texas to try to sell provincial bonds, he was asked during a meeting with investors, "Didn't your prime minister once paddle to Cuba?" Just as Carter had feared the precedent that an independent Quebec would create, Reagan's men now feared the repercussions of Trudeau's politics. "If the US allows Canada to get away with its new policies," said a member of the administration, "What about Mexico? It's not something we can just sit by and not fight." "When Chile nationalized our copper," sighed an official, "we could cut off our aid. But we don't give aid to Canada." It was a thorny problem indeed. So what could they do? "If we pass the word to Wall Street that Canada is not a good place to invest," continued this official, "the Canadian dollar will fall, inflation rates will rise, and the standard of living will decline." Ontario and Quebec, two Liberal strongholds, would withdraw their support from Trudeau. A very highly placed American official attached to the White House trade office, David Macdonald, was candid with Canadian diplomats: his government "may have an obligation to publicize the risks of investment in Canada."

This kind of language had never been used to block the advance of Quebec separatism. No American official had ever made such heavy threats to a Quebec representative. But against the socialist Trudeau, the Americans marched full steam ahead.

## Congratulations, Ronald!

The day after the referendum, the Quebec dossier was summarily tossed into the "resolved crises" basket. On the university circuit, interest in Quebec affairs plummeted. "I have never forgiven Quebeckers for voting 'NO,'" jokingly comments an American expert on the subject, Joseph Jockel, for whom a healthy source of revenue was suddenly cut off.

Even William Casey, the new CIA director whose mandate was to rebuild the clandestine branch of the agency and to keep an eye on future hot spots around the globe, showed no interest in the dossier. "I had a lot of contact with Casey. I never heard anything about the issue, and I talked Canada with him," states one of his advisors, an expert on Canadian affairs. Casey had eyes only for the red menace, notably in Central America and Africa. He knew that there was "a long way from Moscow to Trois-Rivières."

René Lévesque did not want to take any chances. The day after Reagan was elected, he set pen to paper. If Quebec had become independent under Reagan, he was later to say to Latouche, "what would we have done with the Marines in Montreal in December at 40 below?" For the moment, the man who had confessed to being a "socialist" in the foremost American weeklies had no more pressing task than to reassure the conservative leader of world capitalism of their compatibility.

"In the political area, we share the same democratic ideals," wrote the Quebecker. "We in Quebec are determined to assume fully the obligations we share with the Western countries and the Free World." From an ex-socialist and pacifist, this prose fairly rang out with Reaganisms. And did this "We, in Quebec" denote a contrast with "Them, in Ottawa"?

"In the cultural area," Lévesque continued, "we fully participate in the major currents of thought which originate in your country." Was he alluding to neo-conservatism, the principal "current of thought" in vogue in the United States? "We can be North Americans while retaining French as our language," he ended, adding his congratulations and warm regards.

When the letter was delivered to the consul general in Quebec City, George Jaeger, it burned his hands. He conferred with his colleagues in Ottawa and Washington. In the end, only when Robert Normand, deputy minister of intergovernmental affairs, promised that "the existence of this letter and its transmission via this channel would not be publicized," did Jaeger finally agree to send it.

There was one chance in a million that René Lévesque's message would land on the desk of the president-elect. The Reagan response, signed by a computer, was in fact written at the State Department by a junior official, approved by two superiors, and transmitted through Jaeger. Though the wording was banal — "I highly value the close traditional ties which have long existed between Canadians and Americans, and I look forward to strengthening these bonds" — the note established an interesting precedent. Never before had an American president (or his computer, or his junior official) responded to a letter from a Quebec premier. Daniel Johnson's condolences to Lyndon Johnson after John Kennedy's death had been worth only a verbal thank-you from the American embassy.

In March of 1981, while the Ottawa-Washington crisis was escalating seriously, Ronald Reagan was injured in an assassination attempt. René Lévesque, as an old and faithful correspondent, wrote that he was "dismayed" by this horrible event. For a change, it was a junior White House official rather than a junior state department official who penned the response. "Nancy and I" were "deeply touched" by the premier's concern. "We very much appreciate knowing that you are thinking of us and that I have your wishes for a speedy recovery. During my convalescence, my administration will continue to advance the policies and goals which both our countries share," continued the letter, deadpan. "Sincerely, Ronald Reagan."

This time, secrecy was not necessary. The State Department indicated, above Alexander Haig's signature, that there was "no release intended, but no objection if recipient wishes to do so."

Indefatigable, Lévesque wrote a third time to his friend Reagan on July 4, 1982, on the occasion of the American national holiday. Jaeger suggested that Washington offer only a verbal thank-you this time. But the White House computer acknowledged receipt of the letter: Ronald "deeply appreciated" the Quebecker's gesture and granted him the liberty to make this latest missive public.

## What Can We Do for You?

"Since the referendum, we have noticed a greater openness among State Department officials regarding their Quebec contacts," wrote Peter Dunn, who regularly rode the New York-Washington shuttle to ensure a Quebec presence in the capital. This was even truer after April of 1981 and the surprise re-election of the Parti Québécois. Dozens of doors that had been closed to Quebec diplomats now began to open.

Richard Pouliot, New York delegate general at the time, could see that the ideological universe had shifted. In August of 1981, he lunched in Washington with William Desrochers, a high-ranking civil servant in the Commerce Department, which was at sword's-points with Ottawa. Desrochers did not hesitate to air the bilateral dirty laundry before the separatist representative. "We must shoot Canada," he told him, discussing possible American reprisals against the NEP and FIRA.

Sensing an opening, Pouliot asked him "what the United States would ideally like from us," Quebec, in this skirmish. The answer was nothing in particular, but Desrochers emphasized that "in the conflict with Canada," the United States "wanted to" target the provinces that have political weight in Ottawa." From this conversation and the rest of his visit to Washington, Pouliot got the impression that "the Reagan administration is looking for a way to counter-attack Ottawa and that one of the ways would be to annoy the Canadian government for a little while by lending an open ear to the 'language' of the provinces."

A White House trade official mentioned to Pouliot the bad "example" set by Canada for other American trading partners. In the presence of a Canadian diplomat, Pouliot was also introduced to Thomas Niles, assistant secretary of state for European affairs and the future ambassador to Canada. This was a precedent: never had a Quebec representative been received at such a high level in the State Department. Niles, George Vest's successor, took his orders directly from Secretary of State Alexander Haig. And he hoped — it was too good to be true! — to tour James Bay.

The delegate general also visited James Edward, secretary of energy, with whom he spent an hour discussing hydro-electricity. A member of the American cabinet and a Quebec delegate, meeting without a Canadian escort? It was unheard of. The meeting had been organized through the good graces of Vermont Republican governor Richard Snelling. Clearly it had been a mistake for the Parti Québécois to have spent so much time looking for friends among the Democrats; the Republicans were decidedly more welcoming.

All was not well, however. Quebec was the subject of a whole new wave of gloomy press coverage. The Operation America network was unable to stanch the tide. The occasion was the taking effect, at the beginning of 1981, of the Bill 101 provisions barring the use of English on most commercial signs. Some typical headlines: San Francisco — "Quebec should be ashamed"; Atlanta — "Don't Widen the Gap"; Detroit — "*Sacre bleu! S'il vous plaît*, enough is enough, Québec!"

But in Washington, the left-wing threat from Ottawa was bigger news than Quebec's crime against the melting-pot. And the farther Quebec diplomats steered toward the right, the more open doors they found. James Lucier was their guide. Principal aide, man-Friday, and spiritual advisor to North Carolina senator Jesse Helms, Lucier was politically situated far to the right of Ronald Reagan. He remained faithful to the spirit, if not the letter, of what he had written in his youth: on South Africa, "Three and a half million civilized men surrounded by nine million aboriginal invaders"; on socialism in Africa, "It is easy to convince cannibals and savages that socialism will supply abundance without necessitating the earning of it"; on racial segregation in the United States, it "springs from the highest motives of Christian charity." This good Christian was attached to one of the most powerful men in Congress. He helped his boss fight moderates in the State Department — Helms had been the only senator to vote against confirmation of Edmund Muskie as secretary of state in April of 1980 — to promote the extreme-right Salvadoran political party ARENA, and, of course, to support the Contras in Nicaragua. Helms was a senior member of the powerful Senate Foreign Relations Committee, he chaired the sub-committee on Latin America, and he led a permanent war on State Department "liberals." secretaries of state move on, Jesse Helms stay put.

It was logical that James Lucier and his boss should have little enthusiasm for Pierre Trudeau's "Canadianization" programs, and they went out of their way to make his life difficult. In the fall of 1981, they invited Alberta premier Peter Lougheed, a major opponent of Ottawa's energy policy, to speak before a group of senators. The invitation was not sent via the good offices of the Canadian embassy, and Lougheed's speech was delivered behind closed-doors. Why not raise the ante by inviting Pierre Trudeau's worst enemy, René Lévesque?

Lucier had gone to Quebec in the summer of 1980 to meet with the director of the Department's United States division, James Donovan. In November of 1981, he contacted Peter Dunn in Washington to inquire if the separatist leader would accept Jesse Helms' invitation. Lucier took along a reinforcement: Peter Brimelow, editor-in-chief of *Barron's*, the economic weekly, which had never missed an opportunity to link the names of René Lévesque and Fidel Castro. The paper was now anchored firmly in Reaganite ideology. Born in England, Brimelow had made his career in the Toronto press corps, where he had contracted an allergy of rare virulence to Canadian nationalism. It was he who had first put Lucier in contact with Dunn.

Now Brimelow was offering to publish a long interview with René Lévesque, to pave the way for his visit to Washington. This was no coincidence: Peter Lougheed had received almost the same treatment in *Barron's*. The difference was that Lougheed had had to go to New York for the interview, whereas Brimelow was willing to go to Quebec City to see Lévesque.

## A Marriage of Convenience

If it had arrived a few months earlier, the invitation probably would not have tempted Lévesque. He "was no fonder than he had to be of Helms," said a Quebec civil servant delicately. Lévesque had had to be strongly coaxed to meet Lucier, who came in person with Helms' invitation in the spring of 1982. Among other things, Lévesque did not understand why, as a premier, he must receive a mere congressional aide. It was explained to him that this underling was more powerful than most members of Reagan's cabinet.

The invitation turned out to be well-timed. René Lévesque had been simmering for months, since November 5, 1981, in fact. On that night, while he was asleep in a Hull hotel room, representatives from the other nine provinces and the federal government had prepared a constitutional accord on the other side of the Ottawa River. Seven of these provinces had previously formed a "common front" with Quebec. Their premiers had sworn, before the cameras, that they would stand together come what may. On the morning after this "night of the long knives," as it is forever known in Quebec, English Canada had a new constitution.

The reform process had begun the day after the referendum, in conformity with Pierre Trudeau's promise to Quebec to renovate the constitution if Quebeckers voted "NO." Without being specific, Trudeau had let it be known that if the referendum failed to pass Quebec would be better accommodated by the constitution. As early as 1977, in Washington, he had pledged that his "revisions" would make the constitution "the strongest bulwark [for French Canadians] against submersion by 240 million English-speaking North Americans."

But the "revisions" adopted in November of 1981 weakened Quebec's powers and left Bill 101, considered by Francophone Quebeckers to be their "strongest bulwark against submersion," open to challenge through the federal courts. The treason perpetrated by his English-Canadian allies pushed Lévesque toward radicalism. Two years after the referendum defeat, he decided to take up the separatist battle once again, to forget about association if necessary, to fight the next election on the single theme of sovereignty. Claude Morin, whose referendum and constitutional strategies had melted in contact with reality, had bowed out. This was Lévesque's state of mind when the invitation from Helms arrived.

A Quebec diplomat summarized what he called this "marriage of convenience": "It was a game that was being played for Trudeau's benefit, to bother the people we despised and the institutions we despised."

Lévesque's alliance with American ultra-conservatives was, however, not purely tactical. Jesse Helms and René Lévesque had a common ideological thread, tenuous but fundamental: regionalism. One plank in Ronald Reagan's program was the theme of American "new federalism," with decentralization of powers. His promise, which he never kept, was to provide a new and improved version of the old concept of the "states' rights," once used by the Southern states to defend what they saw as their fundamental right to oppress American blacks.

And Helms was very much a Southerner. His advisor, Lucier, also supported decentralization, in the United States as well as in Canada, since recent history had shown that central governments were always more left-leaning than were local governments. Lucier used this argument in a discussion with Dunn, citing a famous example, the favorite of Quebec separatist theoreticians: that of the democratic process that had made Norway, once a Swedish province, an independent state.

Brimelow, for his part, believed in the ineluctability of Quebec's independence and felt that this schism would enable the Canadian right to vanquish the left-wing nationalists who, in his opinion, were ruining English

Canada. The junction of interests between Lévesque and Helms thus seemed obvious to him. (He advanced this thesis four years later in a controversial book, *The Patriot Game*.)

In June of 1982, René Lévesque gave the American right new reason to believe that they were all part of one happy ideological family. In an interview in *Barron's*, aptly entitled "No Castro of the North?," the premier hammered away at Trudeau's economic policy. FIRA was "poisonous," and the federal energy strategy, which was "rampaging all over the industry [was] even crazier," he said. He criticized the NEP provision that Washington considered to be expropriation without compensation. Actually, Lévesque was moving toward the ideological center. Although he still defined himself as a "social democrat," his description of a mixed economy was now based more on the predominance of private enterprise. He expressed his desire — part of the credo of any self-respecting Reaganite — to reduce taxes. "People always say 'big business can take it,' but there is a limit," he insisted, largely for the benefit of readers who ran or owned big business. He announced straight out that the central issue of the next Quebec election would be sovereignty and mentioned that this time he would hesitate to propose a common currency with Canada. Quebec would be independent by the end of the decade, he predicted, and he himself would realize his old dream: to be ambassador to Washington.

Peter Brimelow, who wrote the introduction to the interview, noted that members of Lévesque's cabinet stressed "their interest in economic links with all of North America in a way that paradoxically puts them close to the 'continentalist' pro-US free trade faction that still exists, mutely, in English Canada."

## The New Triangle

In the summer of 1982, the new Washington-Quebec-Ottawa triangle was drawn along the lines of the Paris-Quebec-Ottawa one. The rules were well known. The foreign capital had to show Quebec every courtesy. Relations between Quebec and Ottawa must — this was the easy part — be at their worst. Finally, the foreign capital must remain on bad terms with Ottawa.

So far as Washington-Quebec was concerned, doors in the American capital were continuing to open. The Quebec delegate general in New York, Raymond Gosselin (who had replaced Pouliot), visited American government agencies in Washington in May. The presence of a Canadian diplomat was required, but the delegate had no complaints, since he was meeting with very highly placed officials, aides, and assistants to cabinet members at the State, Energy, and Commerce departments, the White House trade office, and the Environmental Protection Agency.

Between Quebec and Ottawa there was nothing but friction. The new minister of intergovernmental affairs, Jacques-Yvan Morin (no relation to Claude Morin), loudly criticized Canadian diplomats' lack of enthusiasm for promoting Quebec's business in the United States. In private he warned his federal counterpart, Mark MacGuigan, before he went on to attack the Canadian trade service in public in San Francisco. Morin was particularly outraged by a speech given in Chicago by the new Canadian ambassador to Washington, Allan Gotlieb, in which Gotlieb held that Francophones would eventually fall in line and support the new constitution. (Jacques-Yvan was in tune with his colleague Bernard Landry, who, at that moment in Paris, clearly implied in a speech that Ottawa Francophones were "collaborators.") Federal minister Serge Joyal, also travelling in the United States, denounced Morin's tirade.

The new minister searched high and low for proof that the Canadian diplomatic service was demonstrating "pro-Ontario favoritism." He publicly declared his indignation that there was only one Quebecker among 150 consular officers in the western United States. Then he had a list of employees at the Canadian embassy in Washington drawn up so that he could make a count of Quebeckers and Ontarians (not that provincial origins were easy to distinguish among Anglophone names). This turned up a total of 40 Francophone names out of 326, only seven of which were in management positions. The minister also asked his delegations to take a census of all Canadian consular employees. And when Gotlieb wanted to come to Quebec that fall to light the peace pipe, Morin disappeared in a puff of smoke.

The State Department was not happy to see Canadians bickering on American territory, and warned them to keep their quarrels north of the 49th parallel. But the State Department had lost much of its power with regard to foreign affairs during the first Reagan mandate, and the right wing was in power in Congress. On the Washington-Ottawa side of the triangle, the Americans had no scruples about playing tricks on Trudeau and his advisor and ambassador, Allan Gotlieb. James Lucier did not advise the embassy of René Lévesque's impending arrival in Washington on July 14. Nor did Quebec, of course, which was awaiting a propitious moment to "leak" the news. But Jaeger was sitting beside René Lévesque at an official dinner at the beginning of June; he thus learned of the travel plans and informed Washington, which cooperated by not breathing a word to the Canadian embassy. Gotlieb learned by accident, from a *Chicago Tribune* reporter, that the premier would be arriving in the capital in eight days. Lévesque would be meeting not only with Helms, the reporter told Gotlieb, but with some twenty conservative and moderate Republican senators. "I thought unthinkable for a group of senators of this kind to receive the premier without the presence of the ambassador," Gotlieb thunders. Furious, he called Lucier, who told the Canadian diplomat to "go to hell." Gotlieb then proffered his services to the Quebec government to organize the visit, suggesting that he himself meet with Lévesque. He was not told to go to hell, but close.

The Canadian ambassador, one of the people on the Trudeau team who had reshaped Canadian foreign policy along centrist and center-left lines, thus had to watch, powerless, from his office in the most important foreign capital as a senator from the far right lent credibility and visibility to the man who wanted to break up Canada.

## Half a President

July 14 began with a solid testimony to the cohesiveness of the right: Helms convinced the ultra-conservative Washington newspaper, the *Washington Times* — financed by Sun Myung Moon — to print large extracts of the interview Lévesque had given to *Barron's*. But René Lévesque wanted to balance his visit by meeting as well with some star Democrats. Contacts established in New England, and locally maintained by Peter Dunn, opened doors that had been closed to the PQ leader before the referendum. He had appointments with the Speaker of the House of Representatives, Thomas "Tip" O'Neill, the true leader of the Democratic opposition, and with the prestigious, left-leaning senator, Ted Kennedy. Both men represented Massachusetts. O'Neill, an expansive and monumental Irishman, spent half an hour spinning out anecdotes of his political life for Lévesque and reminiscing about his visits to Quebec. Kennedy avoided discussing sovereignty-association like the plague.

Then came the meeting with Jesse Helms, at noon. Helms was held up in the Senate by an unforeseen debate, and sent word he would be able to spend only a few minutes with the premier. Lévesque marked time in the sumptuous office of the Vice-President of the United States, George Bush, situated at the entrance to the Senate. To meet with Kennedy, O'Neill, and Helms in one day was a superb political hat trick, since these legislators were among the six most powerful men in Congress; given that Congress has as much power as the White House, together this trio amounted to half a president.

The regionalist ideological thread that tied Helms and Lévesque together was very fragile. The hierarchy of their political values was in complete opposition. For Helms, there were "values that are more basic to human dignity than democratic values. Our democratic values are intended to support these more basic values, and in that sense are subsidiary to more fundamental human rights." "The right to property" was "one of the most fundamental of human values," along with "an orientation toward a spiritual outlook, and understanding for tradition." In the Chile of his friend Augusto Pinochet, for example, "such benefits have been restored, even though some lesser rights — that of a free press, or democratic processes — have been suspended." This position made the PQ founder squirm, since he had dedicated his life to the democratization of Quebec society — he regarded the cleansing of election financing as his greatest achievement — and considered the right to vote and freedom of the press infinitely more important than the right to property or an understanding, in itself, for tradition.

When Helms finally arrived in the Vice-President's office, about forty-five minutes late, he made Lévesque an extraordinary proposal: Come with me and I'll introduce you to my colleagues *on the floor of the Senate.* Helms had in effect obtained the unanimous consent of the senators present for Lévesque to come to meet them, perhaps even to say a word or two. (Technically, that meant that no Senator had objected to Helmes' proposal.) After having been denied entry into the French National Assembly, he was being invited into the temple of American legislative power.

Did Lévesque imagine the scandalized headlines in English-Canadian newspapers and news broadcasts, all of which would leap to draw a slightly crooked parallel with Trudeau's visit to Congress in 1977? Did he taste the revenge he could have on the instigator of the War Measures Act, the winner of the referendum, the nocturnal constitutional schemer? It was 1:00 PM on July 14, and Helms was offering him the Bastille.

René Lévesque took fewer than five minutes to say thank you no, however. He did not explain why he was refusing the honor. Perhaps it was because he would be tarred by the ideological brush of his escort; when one wants to get into heaven, one does not take the arm of Lucifer. But Jesse Helms was determined to mark the passage of Lévesque at the Capitol for posterity. He had inscribed in the *Congressional Record* a dithyrambic text on Lévesque, "a leader of stature and distinction," an "advocate of using private enterprise," who "has invited American investors to continue to participate" in Quebec's economy. The senator also included a biography in which Lévesque's role as a war correspondent in the American army was duly noted, but in which the referendum episode did not appear at all. "Canada wasn't mentioned," noted Ambassador Gotlieb. "Jesse told about how pro-American he was, how pro-foreign investment [...] It was written by a pure Gaullist."

## Canadian Apoplexy

Lévesque then went to the Republican luncheon. The twenty-one senators who heard him speak behind closed doors constituted the nucleus of the Republican majority in the Senate. After a few mouthfuls of roast chicken, Lévesque delivered a five-minute speech on his desire to increase Quebec economic ties with the United States. Breaking a personal record for brevity, he actually shut-up, and answered questions for the rest of the hour.

Lévesque told the Republicans what they wanted to hear: FIRA was "absurd," the NEP "idiotic." And he told them what he wanted them to hear: the Quebec sovereignty plan was "compatible with maintaining, if not increasing, strategic and economic ties to the US" These right-wing senators were obsessed with the Soviet threat and questioned him closely on the place of an independent Quebec in NATO and NORAD. The ex-pacifist answered: "We're part of the Alliance one way or the other, and we don't intend to drift away."

When the hour was up, Lévesque was warmly applauded. "I found him very pro-American," commented one of the conservative senators, Charles Grassley, as he left. "Every senator was very impressed with his presentation and his attitude toward our country, with his independent spirit, and with the independent direction in which he wants to lead his province." (The word "independent" seemed to have stuck in the senator's mind.)

A reporter asked, "How would you react if Quebec suddenly became an independent socialist country?" The right-wing senator did not rise to this provocative bait. "Whatever happens, we'll continue to have friendly relations," he answered, without expressing a preference for a united Canada. A little later, in an interview on CBC Radio, Grassley added that Lévesque had promised to fully support the NATO and NORAD agreements.

An American diplomat who heard the Grassley interview in Montreal advised his superiors that "his favorable impression of Lévesque could be used to convey the conclusion that the US need not be overly concerned about the prospect of an independent Quebec." Diplomats at the Canadian embassy had an apoplectic fit, and duly expressed their indignation to Helms' office. They were just as furious at "Foggy Bottom" for its silence.

"The embassy insisted that reporters question the State Department on the Reagan administration's official policy concerning Canadian unity," wrote a Canadian Press correspondent in Washington. The Canadians "let it be known that if this position wasn't enthusiastic, it would signify a retreat from the Carter administration's position."

In fact, two days before Lévesque arrived the State Department had prepared a memo for its press agents, listing the two specific positions defined under Carter: a preference for a "strong and united" Canada, and non-interference in a "clearly internal Canadian question." But no one called the State Department during Lévesque's visit. An American diplomat in Quebec City (not Jaeger) tried to convince Washington to distribute the memo to "set the record straight." The Department refused, perhaps out of political bad will: Ottawa was not as vilified at the State Department as it was in Helms' office, but it was not well liked either. Simple incompetence may have been at the bottom of things too: the new head of Canadian Affairs had started his job on the same day as Lévesque's visit. Yet another concern might have been how the powerful senator would react. In fact, an official in Helms' office explained having invited Lévesque precisely because "State Department officials had their information [on Canada] filtered through such a strongly pro-federalist screen that it was useful to hear directly what Lévesque had to say."

At any rate, the notion that Washington was considering a separatist victory serenely was etched in Quebec minds, at least for a few days. "In the overall guerrilla war, it's another point," commented a Quebec official. The point was all the more important because the extreme right could have roused an anti-Quebec backlash if the province separated. For the Quebec separatists, this tactical alliance served as a primary insurance policy against potential political backsliding.

Allan Gotlieb thought that deep down ultra-conservatives had reason to hope for Quebec's secession. Jesse Helms and his allies "hated Trudeau so much" that they "were anxious for [Lévesque] to become a separatist again." "I think there was a very strong undercurrent there, that if Quebec left Canada it would be a great thing, great thing. Because Trudeau was a Communist anyway."

# 18

# The Consul's Act

GEORGE JAEGER: *Your book covers what period?*
AUTHOR: *Right up until the referendum.*
JAEGER: *But many things happened*
*after the referendum.*
AUTHOR: *Such as?*
JAEGER: *No comment.*

He invited them to the University Circle, the Canadian Club, the Garrison Club, the classiest restaurants in the Old City. Invitations went out to ministers, members of the National Assembly, advisors to the government and the opposition, reporters, local economic and political commentators. Everyone responded as if he were the Pope offering an opportunity to confess. The luckiest, the most powerful, and the best-informed even had access to the consular residence, the windows of which pierced the old, solid-stone walls to provide a view facing the Seaway, Lévis, and, much farther south, the United States of America.

Everyone was impressed by a phone call from the American consulate. "It was very flattering," admits then PQ minister Gérald Godin, who was as sensitive as anyone to the attraction of "associating with the greats of this world."

George Jaeger brought an international flavor to Quebec City. His predecessor, McNamara, had been no novice; Jaeger was a high-calibre professional. And if his guests didn't get the picture, he told them outright, "They don't waste politicos like me on ordinary postings."

Born in Vienna, speaking German and Serbo-Croatian, Jaeger was a cold-war diplomat. He was the State Department's eye on the enemy camp, first in Yugoslavia, that strangely neutral country, then on the central front of West Germany. Later, when the socialist-communist coalition was about to come to power in Paris, he headed up the large contingent of advisors and political analysts at the American embassy there. In the fall of 1977, he kept tabs on a little man from the Gaspé who was being greeted in Paris as if he were the new Messiah.

To some, the transfer to Quebec seemed to be the opposite of a promotion. Rubbish, replied Jaeger, the Quebec posting had been promoted to match its new consul. Not that the 52-year-old diplomat had been overly eager to survey the Plains of Abraham. Richard Vine, his superior in Washington, had had to insist on the posting. Jaeger had considered the offer for a few days, read up on Quebec for two weeks, then packed his bags. He arrived nine months before the referendum. He found the local political fauna interesting, but he complained to Jean Chapdelaine that the city was far too provincial. He was shocked at having a hard time finding *The New York Times*.

Jaeger's European veneer, the elegance of his manners (despite the poor cut of his suits), his Harvard degree, and the depth of his knowledge, even the quality of his table, were impressive. "He was not like the other Americans," the loud and uncultivated boors, said one of his guests. Although he trusted no one, especially not journalists, the beetle-browed man whose French was not entirely fluent knew how to act warm and friendly. He quickly charmed his "clients." After an initial meeting with Lévesque, which the latter deliberately stretched out, Jean Chapdelaine noted that there was "good reason to get to know and understand Mr Jaeger — whose sympathy is obviously developing." With two other PQ ministers, he later showed himself to be "particularly open and receptive to Quebec positions," noted an aide. Jaeger was "endowed with a personality that seems to make it easy for him to establish cordial relations with his contacts."

Before the referendum, all regular Quebec visitors to the consulate found that Jaeger had a pleasant personality. Afterward, they discovered that he had two.

## "To the Rescue!"

"The United States consul general's attitudes and actions in Quebec are becoming less and less acceptable. We have reached the point where dear Mr Jaeger is dictating what we can and cannot do here," wrote James Donovan, of the United States division, in December of 1980.

The first skid came in protocol. Jaeger had organized a Quebec tour for American political experts for which he made appointments directly with the Liberal opposition, as was his prerogative. But during one meeting he insisted that the provincial protocol-service representative, whose function was to escort foreign representatives on their rounds, leave the room. Quite an initiative, since the Liberal leader himself had invited the protocol service representative to the meetings.

Then Jaeger advised the protocol people that he did not want them at meetings between the American ambassador in Ottawa and PQ ministers. "This perpetual bullying has its limits," Donovan wrote to his superiors. He concluded, "To the rescue!"

In fact, George Jaeger was ready — ready for post-sovereignty, for the new government, for premier Claude Ryan. All his networks in the Liberal opposition were in place, he already knew the members of the future cabinet, and he could not wait for the new play to begin.

"I will always remember one conversation," says Claude Morin. "It was like, 'Okay, listen, it's been very nice to know you, your government was not acceptable, so Mr Ryan will be arriving, and things will be more rational.'" "I'm simplifying," Morin adds, but for Jaeger, the PQ was "a government that should have the basic decency to leave as quickly as possible because we were delaying the reconstruction Quebec needed."

In contrast to McNamara, always an amused spectator at Quebec City, Jaeger was exhilarated by the local political whirlwind: he took positions, issued warnings, and waited impatiently for the Liberals to be elected. Good riddance to this "overactive social-democratic government," he wrote to the State Department. Clearly, the "sensibly appealing, moderately conservative program of less government" that Ryan was proposing was "a skillful blend which should succeed." He had trouble hiding his displeasure when, in the spring of 1981, Claude Morin showed him internal polls which predicted — correctly — the re-election of the Parti Québécois.

Jaeger gave Richard Pouliot to understand that Washington had instructed him to take a harder line. "Jaeger told me, before the referendum, in fact several times — more than twice, perhaps three times — that Washington considered him to be quite close to the [PQ] government, a little bit too pro-Quebec," and that the State Department "had reproached him for being a little too open and sympathetic."

According to his old colleagues and superiors, however, Jaeger was never accused of clientelism, a syndrome characterized by diplomats espousing the positions of their clients rather than those of their bosses. "I didn't get the impression that this came from Washington," stated another of Jaeger's Quebec contacts. "I had the impression that he had his own agenda and that he had a kind of plan, a script [for Quebec], and it deviated, perforce ..."

For whatever reason, the consul's confessing to Pouliot cleverly increased his value: you see, I'm taking risks for you, so trust me.

It was difficult to read Jaeger. "It was part of the whole act Jaeger concocted," recalls one of his main contacts. "In fact, I found it difficult, in our conversations, to distinguish between Jaeger's views, his acts, and reality."

## Veering Toward Reaganism

At the beginning of 1981, George Jaeger took a turn that went beyond local political debate.

It was as if, under Jimmy Carter's Democratic administration, Jaeger had had to muzzle himself and repress his personal ideological inclinations. With the arrival in Washington of the Reaganite hawks, George Jaeger was suddenly in his element. He filed his eye-teeth and sharpened his claws. Right-wing senators in Washington might be playing geopolitical ping-pong with Ottawa and Quebec; Jaeger would hold the hard line all the same.

Before the referendum, he had assured René Lévesque that Washington would respect the democratic decision of Quebeckers, whatever it was. As the Reagan years dawned, he told all and sundry that sovereignty was out of the question. "Do you think that we would permit a sovereign country to exist on the American border that would serve as an entry point for Soviet spies?" he rhetorically asked Gérald Godin at a cocktail party.

One day in September 1981, Claude Morin's cabinet chief, Louise Beaudoin, was "summoned" to a one-on-one breakfast at the consulate. She was to act as a lightning rod for the American. Jaeger told her that it was "troubling for the Americans to have a so-called social-democratic government beside them." "I couldn't believe my ears," Beaudoin wrote in a memo. Jaeger then criticized, specifically, the Lévesque government's desire to take control of companies — such plans were in the works for the Domtar paper mill and Québecair — and evoked "the danger that a new Cuba or El Salvador would represent to the United States"! Without wanting to "make any threat," the consul general added that the State Department "does not laugh at this kind of thing." As for sovereignty, declared the diplomat, Quebec "has no need for it." He regretted that the Parti Québécois wanted to import "European models" such as this upsetting concept of "nation"; he worried about the PQ's increasing links with the new French socialist government, which had four Communist ministers. The Reagan administration was livid over it.

Given the amount of pro-American sentiment on the PQ team, why had Jaeger chosen Louise Beaudoin, in her own words a "convinced anti-American," for this warning? Beaudoin, in any case, returned the favor: "The American tragedy since the last war," she told him, "is that they have always refused to comprehend what was happening around them in time. By attempting to block normal changes and natural evolution, all they have done has been to radicalize positions on both sides." Washington would have to learn one day, she added, "to accept that not everything that is good for them is necessarily good to export to the rest of humanity."

As for the consul's opinion regarding sovereignty and the course of nationalism — Beaudoin retorted: "Quebeckers were the first white North Americans," This fact might not empower them, but it was worth a little consideration.

Jaeger quickly found reinforcements for his aggressive new anti-PQ demeanor. That fall, Ronald Reagan named a new ambassador to Ottawa. Paul Robinson, a 51-year-old conservative business leader and important Republican fund-raiser from Chicago, the grandson of a Canadian to boot, established his presence within a few months by suggesting that Canada spend less on social programs and more on defence, calling the metricization program "rubbish," and telling the assistant chief editor of the *Toronto Star* to "shove off, kid," as was reported in the paper the next day. (Robinson protested that the reporter had not introduced himself.)

In Quebec City, in November, the ambassador had breakfast with Jacques-Yvan Morin, then vice-premier, and a few others, including Richard Pouliot. According to the latter, Robinson pulled no punches when he squarely told everyone that "sovereignty-association was a furious folly."

Robinson's memory of the event is less dramatic. He remembers having advised his guests that independence was an internal Canadian question and that the United States would prefer a strong and united Canada. "This was not very well received," he recalls. Thinking that he had invented this formula, he wrote it down so that, he said, the State Department could adopt it. Each new ambassador seemed to want to reinvent the Quebec wheel. In any case, it always rolled in the same direction.

Unlike Jesse Helms, the ambassador detested the separatist leader. "I didn't think that a man that wouldn't fight for his own country was a man that I would have any respect for," he states.

## The Slap to the Free Trade Advocate

"They were the pioneers of Quebec's liberation," declared a delegate to the Parti Québécois convention in December of 1981. At the microphone was

Jacques Rose, a member of the FLQ cell that had assassinated Pierre Laporte. The delegates had regressed to political adolescence since the nocturnal constitutional coup, one month before, and the apparent radicalization of their leader. The chairman of the convention explained his suspension of the time limit on speeches for the ex-detainee by saying, "Where you have been [in prison], you didn't have the right to speak." In the wings, George Jaeger was furious. He was not alone; that evening René Lévesque threatened to quit. If his advisors had not restrained him, he would have walked out the door.

Jaeger's anger was also fed by another aspect of the convention: the presence, among the international attendees, of two representatives from the Palestine Liberation Organization. Jaeger grabbed Louise Beaudoin in a corridor. "Jaeger really made a scene," she recalls. The American snarled, "You people are completely off your rocker!"

He continued on this theme a few days later, at a meeting with Claude Morin. He spoke of the US "government's very great concern about the turning of events in the last Parti Québécois convention." He was particularly upset by the presence of "terrorist organizations" such as the PLO and by Rose's speech. In addition to the PLO, there had been representatives from the Chilean extreme left-wing party MIR, the Salvadoran guerrilla movement FDR-FMLN, and the *Front Polisario*; Kurdish rebels also shared the benches with envoys from the French Socialist Party. The Franco-American visitors from New England no doubt suffered from a slight case of vertigo.

This bizarre assembly would have been lost in a crowd of moderate invitees, Morin responded, had not Ottawa so pointedly dissuaded representatives from democratic parties from coming. For the rest, he placed the blame on "members of the Parti Québécois whose education in international politics isn't as developed as it should be." As for the welcome accorded Rose, this must be chalked up to the PQ's radical wing, which had formed the majority of delegates at the convention, Morin said.

Jaeger, accompanied by his colleague, the consul general at Montreal, then asked "if the Parti Québécois wasn't becoming more and more socialist." Morin took umbrage. Washington should not interpret what was happening in Quebec "through the prism of economic nationalism as it was championed by the government in Ottawa."

Then there was the new Parti Québécois position on a sovereign Quebec's association with Canada. This shocked the American. Ever since the English-Canadian constitutional insult, association had not had good press in the PQ. In his opening speech at the convention, René Lévesque proposed, Let's first establish sovereignty, then we'll talk about associating with Canada and with "other countries."

This was not a new notion; it had often been raised during the first PQ mandate by Lévesque's ministers. Rodrigue Tremblay had written a book on the subject. Bernard Landry had stated in 1978 that "the day after [independence] we would begin to explore association with the south." Far from condemning this idea, Lévesque had added, "If Canada says no, I know of Americans who would not ask for more than to fill the gaps. They have rarely refused clients."

If the Americans had been irritated by these statements, they had not said so. When the theme was taken up again in 1981, Ambassador Robinson, in Ottawa, says he felt that these proposals "must not be given the dignity of a response." But Jaeger — the second Jaeger, the post-referendum one — would have nothing of this. The PQ, he grumbled, "continually" tried to distort the American position, to give the impression that Washington would welcome a separate Quebec with open arms. He sent out warnings to his Quebec contacts.

Bernard Landry did not hear Jaeger, or chose to ignore him, and took up his old North-South refrain again at the end of January 1983. He told a reporter, "An economic association with Canada proposed by the Parti Québécois remains interesting for reasons of history and convenience, but becomes less vital in the hypothesis or context of the continent moving toward a more integrated economy [...] when the common market extends from the Rio Grande to La Grande River," in northern Quebec.

The American consul general's cup was overflowing. He had to lash out, to tell these trouble makers, for once and for all, to keep their political baggage to themselves. He convinced the State Department to issue, from Washington, a communiqué that would keep the minister quiet:

> We have noted recent remarks by a Quebec provincial minister proposing a Quebec-US-Canadian common market and suggesting that an independent Quebec might be "associated" with the United States and Canada. [...]
>
> It would not be appropriate for the US government to enter into special trading relationship with provincial governments as distinct from Canada as a whole. [...]
>
> Americans care about what happens in Canada. They hope that Canada will remain strong and united. We do not intend to involve ourselves in internal Canadian issues.
>
> We would expect this reserve to be respected by all Canadians.

In diplomatic terms this was not a rebuff, it was a veritable thrashing; the American diplomatic note that had toppled John Diefenbaker's government in 1963 had not been more biting. This statement "came as a complete surprise to us," admitted Canadian diplomats in Ottawa and Washington, who had not dared to hope for this gift from heaven seven months after the lavish anti-federalist show put on by Helms and Lévesque.

Landry was devastated by this unexpected attack, which came just before a long-planned visit to Washington (he and ministers from other provinces were to meet with the Secretary of Commerce to talk about sales of Canadian wood). Shamefacedly, he showed Lévesque the inflammatory message. The separatist leader was philosophical: "Finally the Americans are paying attention to us," he said.

## The Franco-American Stake, 30 Years Later

If the threats Jaegar saw had been all — the "overactive social-democrats," the invitation to the PLO, the annoying will to associate with the US — then the consulate could still rest easy. But there was more. Clearly there was a Quebec conspiracy aimed at rending the very fiber of American society, its founding principle, its very definition: the melting-pot.

Jaeger complained to everyone: Jacques-Yvan Morin, Landry, Godin, Beaudoin, journalist Lise Bissonnette. Everyone looked at him, incredulous. But he was serious. If the American consul general had an act going, this was his Academy Award-winning performance. According to him the PQ government wanted to penetrate, organize, finance, and manipulate Franco-Americans in New England to fashion a political lever in the United States.

Under Carter, cultural minorities had been appreciated and the teaching of second languages had been in vogue. But the budget-cutting Reagan administration was attacking bilingualism of any sort, particularly the growth of Spanish in the South and New York. It carried in its wake a lobby that wanted to make English the only official language of the states and the nation. Americans did not want a Spanish Florida or California. Jaeger told a Quebec diplomat that this problem was "of the same stature as that of slavery in the last century."

Was a Francophone New Hampshire as deeply feared? Jaeger seemed to think so. He wanted his position to be well understood: "Any Quebec movement aimed at encouraging development of the French language among this ethnic group [Franco-Americans] would be frowned upon by the Reagan Administration."

In fact, Quebec was interested in Franco-Americans. When Operation America was conceived, Quebec's ex-delegate in Louisiana, Léo Leblanc, produced twenty-two tomes of text and notes on the situation of these several million descendants of French Canadians. The idea of supporting the "Quebec diaspora" had crossed many minds. For many, including Claude Morin, this would consist essentially of lending a hand to struggling minorities in the South and West for whom Quebec had a "moral responsibility." For others, including his deputy minister, Robert Normand, the Franco-American market could become an outlet for exportation of Quebec cultural products.

Quebec opened its portfolio to Francophone organizations. The number of its interventions — grants, colloquia, book donations, exchanges — rose above 30 every year starting in 1977. In 1978, at René Lévesque's instigation, Quebec organized the *Retour aux sources* (Return to the Roots), a politico-folkloric gathering, half conference, half-picnic, which some one hundred and fifty Franco-Americans attended. (Among the guests was Wilfrid Beaulieu, ex-editor of the newspaper *Le Travailleur*.) It was suggested that an association be created to group together all Franco-Americans; Quebec could serve as "neutral territory," one official suggested. In April of 1980, twelve representatives from various regions met with the minister of intergovernmental affairs to discuss their needs and decided to form precisely such an association: *Action pour les Franco-Américains*, or ActFA.

The representatives then visited an enthusiastic René Lévesque and a coterie of ministers and high-ranking officials. The result was a $25,000 grant to open a permanent office for this first American pan-Francophone organization. As well, the ministry's judicial service translated the group's constitution into French, since it had been written, in conformity with American law, in English only. For 1983-1984, the total budget for aid to Franco-Americans amounted to $150,000.

At one point, Canadian diplomats were concerned about these Franco-American activities as well. A political advisor to the ambassador visited Maine, in 1979, to see how the effort was going. When he advised one of his contacts of his visit, the latter warned Quebec. "What do you want me to do?" he wrote. "I'll tell them whatever you want."

There was nothing to hide, however. No one was inciting the Franco-Americans to political activism; even in Quebec, opinion was divided on the "political potential" of these groups. There was, on the other hand, no doubt about their number. In New England, Louisiana, California, and New York State, almost two million people stated that their "mother tongue" was French. Depending on the region, 37% to 61% of them had adopted English as their "language of usage." But even 30% of these two million was enough to create a lobby, and among the others, a fondness for the mother tongue frequently survived.

Strategically, Quebec (or the PQ) could assign two functions to this lobby. The first one was defensive: it would act to ensure that local elected officials, especially senators and members of Congress, knew that part of their electoral base supported Quebec's right to self-determination (not necessarily independence) and wanted the United States to remain strictly neutral. If the American administration put together an anti-sovereignty cabal, if a Canadian prime minister was looking for support for federalism at the White House, or if Quebec learned that the secretary of state was planning to enter the national debate, the lobby would go into action. In practice, this would mean two or three meetings with the local Congressmen, perhaps some twenty telephone calls and a few dozen telegrams. The Congressmen would then call the State Department or the White House to emphasize that there would be a political price to pay for taking such a position in the Canadian debate. If a certain number — say three senators or eight representatives — took this step, activists within the Administration would have to present sufficiently convincing arguments to overcome the inertia it would create. Nothing, in American politics, was as easily applied as the brakes.

The lobby's other function could be offensive. The distribution of French Canadians in the various states made for some interesting possibilities. French was, for example, the mother tongue among more than 15% of New Hampshire's population, the state on the cutting edge of the presidential primary process. Every four years, unknown hopefuls trudged through the February snow desperately searching for convention delegates; since the primary system had come into existence, no candidate had won the presidency without first winning New Hampshire. If the Franco-Americans in this state — twenty or so militants would suffice — gave political organizers the impression that some percentage of the vote would hinge on whether a candidate was for or against Quebec's right to self-determination and the principle of strict American neutrality in this debate, a number of candidates would surely pronounce, in some campaign rally in a church basement, the magic words.[*]

The Quebec government would then publicize these positions among its own electorate and keep these promises in its records. It would be relatively easy, later, to bring into play another twenty or so sympathizers in Louisiana (where another 15% claimed French as mother tongue); the lobby could even try its luck, if the race was very tight, in the last primary race, in California (where 1% of the population was originally Francophone). Later, after independence, when

* See the "List of Questions Affecting Minorities in the United States," used in 1952 by John F. Kennedy, in Chapter 2.

action would have to be taken to shape the definition of American policy toward the new Quebec state, the lobby's range of potential influence could widen.

That is what any American political consultants paid upwards of $200 an hour would explain. Paul Hannaford agrees; as Ronald Reagan's campaign organizer, he had twice guided his candidate along the backroads of New Hampshire: "If they could make them a voting bloc, they would force the US candidates to take a stand of some kind which might enhance the separatists' position within Canada," he explains.

## An Obsession, a Threat

Given their lack of sophistication regarding American politics, no one in Quebec City dealing with the American dossier had noticed how close were the dates of the primary, in February of 1980, and the referendum, in May of 1980. The notion that three months before the referendum vote, in an extremely tight 1980 presidential race, Quebeckers might read the headline "Jimmy Carter (and/or) Ted Kennedy (and/or) Ronald Reagan (and/or) George Bush recognize Quebec's right to independence" did not occur to anyone.

Except for Evelyn Dumas: in 1977, as Lévesque's advisor, she had visited Franco-American associations to test the political waters. She examined the possibilities, and had not found them promising. "They were interested in receiving operating grants, but looking at New England, or even Louisiana, where I also went, people were not ready to mount a political campaign of that nature."

Creating even an appearance of pressure in New Hampshire at the right moment seemed impossible to her. "I visited all the organizations, particularly in New Hampshire," she recalls. Nothing doing. For an "Operation Primary" "I couldn't find even one willing franco!" The reason was that these were tiny, divided groups, dominated by a conservative old guard concerned mostly with "the decline in religious practice in Quebec," she then noted. Many expressed the kind of feeling for Quebec that Quebec had for France: attraction-repulsion and an unwillingness to be dictated to. In 1978, Dumas stated categorically to Yves Michaud, "If we can help the Franco-Americans, it would be an illusion to wait for help from them for one of our projects."

The coordinator of Operation America, Roger Cyr, felt the same way. He identified other difficulties: "All in all, the Franco-American collectivity considers politics as dirty and degrading. Thus, it is completely absent from the American political scene," he wrote in October of 1979. He concluded that it was impossible "for Quebec to use the Franco-American milieu as a political lobby in the sense that Israel uses the American Jewish community." (A Committee for the Advancement of French in America, based in Manchester, New Hampshire, did produce a two-page ad to explain its support for the "YES" side in May of 1980, however — three months too late for the primary.)

Franco-Americans did not play, and were not invited to play, any political role. "We were perfectly aware of this interaction" between Quebec and American Francophones, George Vest, Vance's deputy at the State Department at the time, notes. "We never bothered with it," he says. And if there was a campaign, "it did not translate into any political pressure" at the national level. Thomas Enders, ambassador to Ottawa under Carter, was also very aware of the burgeoning links between Quebec and Franco-Americans. Was he upset? "No, no, no, no, no, not at all. [...] My own reaction to that, on the contrary, is that that was one of the really useful things" that Quebec did. "There was such a full relationship between French-speaking or formerly French-speaking communities in the United States of Quebec origin and Quebec, I thought that was the strong point, not the other way around." Paul Robinson, ambassador under Reagan, also stated that these stories about Franco-Americans "didn't bother us" in 1981 and 1982. He did not recall that George Jaeger, in whom he had complete confidence, had ever raised the question with him.

However, in Quebec City, Jaeger was making a veritable crusade of the matter. He officially expressed his irritation to Jacques-Yvan Morin when the latter took over the reins from Claude Morin. He asked Gérald Godin, minister of cultural communities, not to attend a meeting of Franco-Americans in Lowell. (Godin went anyway, although he did not inform the press.) Above all, Jaeger let it be known that continued Quebec efforts could provoke reprisals.

The threat, veiled though it was, was made on November 28, 1981, to civil servant François Bouvier, who swore in a memo that "the consul's comments were in no way solicited by myself — on the contrary — and I still wonder why he chose me to confide in." The occasion was the opening of the secretariat of the *Corporation des rencontres francophones* (Corporation of Francophone Meetings). Bouvier, a member of the corporation's board of directors, reported to James Donovan in a memo:

> The consul was worried about our activities with regard to Francophone Americans. He said he was astounded that we were inviting him to the opening of a secretariat whose activities will be directed in part toward American minorities, without having advised him in advance of the extent and the nature of this new operation.
>
> According to him, the American government is very sensitive to everything that touches on actions concerning linguistic minorities and, if the extent of our operations in this area were brought to light, the reaction could be very negative and could result in the closing of certain of our delegations.

In Washington, Wingate Lloyd, head of the Canadian desk at the State Department during this period, thus Jaeger's boss, was stunned when informed about this warning. "I am surprised at that, frankly. Look at AIPAC [the powerful Israeli lobby], France-États-Unis, the English-Speaking Union, the Polish groups, there are dozens and dozens of groups that are often funded from abroad. There's no law against that in the United States." It was not "at all surprising or bothersome" that Quebeckers wanted to organize their own support group. "They're trying to build a constituency in the United States, and this seems quite common." What difference did one lobby more or less make?

What about reprisals, shutting down delegations? Lloyd has never heard of any such thing. Could Jaeger have undertaken this huge initiative all alone, could he have invented his government's "anxieties" from whole cloth? Did he, as a Quebec deputy minister who knew him suggested cynically, want to "manifestly use his position to demonstrate his political importance and thus give his own career a boost?" Was this, in fact, "an act"?

Jaeger's ex-boss would not skate on this thin ice. "That's up to you to decide," Lloyd responds.

## John Paul II, Pierre-Marc, Jacques, and the Gang

Nevertheless, René Lévesque continued to confide in George Jaeger. He had many long and frighteningly frank conversations with the consul.

In June of 1982, he had ridden out the turbulent PQ convention. A plebiscite dubbed a *Renérendum*) had reaffirmed his authority over the party's radical wing. Lévesque was thought to have settled down. However, he announced to the American that he remained firmly convinced that "the Canadian system, which is structurally unworkable and flawed, first simply has to be broken down."

The Quebecker, said Jaeger, was "in top-notch form." Lévesque talked about not just two but many new countries arising from the provinces — the scenario that Washington feared most. He said that the confederation must be "cracked and stripped down to its component parts" and that in the end an agreement, something like the European Economic Community, would group together the "cooperating sovereign entities." According to Jaeger's report to Washington, the premier said that he "understood our [the United States'] current reserve vis-à-vis profound changes taking place to our north, but thought that, with rapidly developing pattern of North-South cooperation, we would come to find post-independence Canadian patterns stable and really in United States' interest."

And if a more accommodating prime minister were to replace Trudeau in Ottawa, would the separatist be ready to make a compromise that would not sound Canada's death knell, asked the consul general? "In his present mood," he wrote, "the answer was clearly no."

The American predicted that, in this new order, Quebec would want to increase its economic ties to the United States in the months and years to come. Jacques-Yvan Morin, the new minister, was militantly pursuing this very effort. (In a subsequent conversation, Lévesque would clearly indicate to Jaeger that this strategy was in fact aimed at creating a margin for manoeuvre, in case a Canadian association foundered.)

Lévesque also doubted that Quebec would necessarily continue to use Canadian currency. At any rate, Canada was in such confusion, he explained, that nothing would be served by attempting new constitutional reform. He was saying this as the rest of Canada was preparing celebrations for its new constitution, two weeks later. The Queen herself was to join her subjects for the festivities.

Lévesque was not talking about the distant future. He insisted that "things in Quebec were so far advanced" that with "one more hard push" independence would carry a majority. This lack of realism perhaps could be explained by Lévesque's abiding anger over the constitutional coup. Clearly he had not yet comprehended the breadth of the 1982 economic crisis that was decimating jobs all over the province, nor anticipated the harshness of the upcoming battle that would pit him against public-sector unions.

Seven months later, in January of 1983, in the middle of the worst economic crisis yet and at loggerheads with the unions, Lévesque's separatist fervor remained unmitigated. The conversation was "long" and "exceptionally frank," wrote Jaeger in an eleven page dispatch addressed to the State Department.

Consul general asked if Lévesque really could not visualize any deal with Ottawa with [Trudeau or his successor].

Lévesque emphatically said "no." The present system, he said, was "an abortion." French Quebec was entitled to a national identity like every other people [...] which meant "to get completely out of the Canadian system."

Lévesque said he would launch his new independence drive next fall [1983] — to culminate in elections on independence theme in 1984, if opportunity presents itself, or 1985, when Trudeau will have left the scene and been succeeded by an Anglophone. [...] Asked whether he really thought such an independence campaign had a chance to succeed, Lévesque said serenely he knew he "could not be elected dog-catcher today." [...] From then on, he said, he would "intensively exploit every opportunity" to again pump up independence [...] like the massive hooplah planned around the 450th anniversary of the arrival of Jacques Cartier in 1984 and the possible visit by pope (whom Lévesque surprisingly called "a hard-nosed trouble-maker" — perhaps an allusion to the undoubtedly unwelcome recent local appeal by the apostolic nuncio for greater "charity and mutual understanding between federal and provincial governments." "If the pope's visit cannot be avoided," Lévesque commented, "we'll still get the best out of it for our ends.") [...]

While thus surprisingly optimistic given present climate [recession, social problems, PQ's drop in polls], Lévesque did recognize that he might miss magic figure of 51%, which he had told PQ last February was minimum which could constitute democratic mandate for independence. In private he said that even a 48% or 49% third-term victory would represent a "massive endorsement" which "Canada could not ignore" — although in any such case he would probably call quick subsequent second referendum to drive point home beyond any further doubt. Canada would then have no choice but to go along: adding, in response to further questions, that he "could at this point care less about implications, i.e., for future of Atlantic provinces." [...]

Lévesque said, in unsentimental comment which may go to the heart of the matter, "I will at least have tried and left the party in good hands." "There will be Pierre-Marc Johnson [here a sentence in the cable has been blacked out by the State Department], Bernard Landry, or Parizeau to take over while they are in opposition." [...]

As regards the US [...] Lévesque maintained that any adverse US statements on Canadian unity would only "solidify Quebec" and "help the independence cause."

Beyond that, Lévesque said "Reagan's Republicans, who are ideologically opposed to Quebec independence, will in any case get voted out in 1984," [and that the Americans, enmeshed in their own transition] would "hardly notice" Quebec's independence drive and would not pose a problem.

Jaeger responded strongly to this, but without convincing his interlocutor, who replied that he had "no alternative but to go ahead."

Seven months later, in August of 1983, Jaeger packed his bags. He was going to Ottawa, where he would defend Reagan policy, particularly concerning NATO, with a zeal that would create some enemies among his Canadian interlocutors. Before leaving, he went to see the separatist leader, whose social and electoral problems (only 23% intended to vote for him) were even worse than at their last visit. Things were a shade better on the economic front. All the same, Lévesque was sticking to his schedule for separation. He still had time, he said, to climb "out of the pits," especially since Robert Bourassa would probably be returning to lead the Liberals. Bourassa was "a man we know well," Lévesque confided, whom he would "know how to handle."

"Lévesque went on, with more passion than we have seen for years, that the next election represented Quebec's last chance to break out of the Canadian confinement," wrote Jaeger.

But there was this fateful figure of 51% of the votes, in an election or in a second referendum, which he himself set and which seemed more far off than ever. Lévesque agreed, but added, "with an odd smile," that "perhaps something less than 51% could, after all, be viewed as an interim or provisional independence mandate." The PQ leader, the American commented, was toying with the idea of "compromising on this fundamental and potentially very explosive point."

Jaeger noted another change since January. Lévesque was suddenly concerned about the American reaction and expressed, in 1983 terms, an idea that he had mentioned to a reporter fourteen years earlier and had subsequently forgotten. Lévesque

said emphatically that he also intends to launch "major new efforts in the next two years" to break the "vicious circle of disinformation and blockage of Quebec's interest" in the US [...]

To begin to dispel these entrenched misconceptions, Lévesque said, he now planned to authorize a "systematic campaign" in Washington and elsewhere in the US focussed not so much on the Administration, "whose mind was made up," but on US senators, congressmen, and governors, and of course the media to create better understanding of Quebec's cause which he hoped, "in time," would also affect US official policy. In the process, Lévesque said, he would not challenge Ottawa's official diplomatic status, although he expected that the new campaign [...] would undoubtedly "make waves." However, Lévesque said, he thought making a "little fuss" was preferable to the present situation — in which (independentist) Quebec was basically not heard in Washington and officially did not exist.

Aware of the gap between his dreams and reality — the American campaign, which his advisors had not been privy to, was never launched — Lévesque raised the question of his successor. This time, he focussed the discussion on his favorite, Jacques Parizeau, whom Jaeger described as the "powerful, experienced, and loyal finance minister." In fact, Parizeau's loyalty was debatable, since he had come very close to joining the radical wing during the notorious December 1981 convention. But Lévesque had nothing but praise for the minister.

> "Ten years younger [than Lévesque], brilliant, disciplined, and a convinced independentist," Parizeau, Lévesque mused, would be a "very credible leader" to take the separatist cause through its "second phase." The unstated implication was that, unlike many senior PQ gradualists, Parizeau is perhaps the only top PQ leader personally strong enough and with good enough radical independentist credentials to have a chance, after Lévesque leaves the scene, to keep disillusioned PQ radicals in line and prevent PQ's disintegration.

Lévesque more or less continued to state his strategy of increasing the stakes with Jaeger's successor, Lionel Rosenblatt. But as time passed, he felt that his "double or nothing" gamble on independence risked ending with, as he said in February of 1984, "hara-kiri" for the PQ. The electorate, disgusted with 25 years of constitutional debates, wanted to forget the federalist and separatist issues and focus on the economy, leisure, and individualism.

He himself was aware that he was getting old and he told the Americans: "If I can stay the course," I will do this or that. Pierre Trudeau, "a flirt to the end," as his old and familiar enemy noted, announced his retirement on a February 29. Was this a sign? For the first time in his life, Lévesque began to keep a journal. He had "the feeling of perhaps starting the final countdown." After a meeting with Rosenblatt, he made this entry: "If the Americans have such substantial presence in the provincial capital, it is because our provincialism no doubt seems to them to be a bit fragile and, despite the referendum, perhaps quite transitory. At any rate, we are being watched by Uncle Sam."

When Brian Mulroney was elected prime minister, in September of 1984, his arms full of olive branches and his cabinet full of former PQ members, Lévesque understood that counting on the electorate to support separatism now amounted to political suicide. If Quebec "provincialism" was transitory, the transition would take longer than predicted.

Lévesque made an about-face. He invented the "noble risk," a new "last chance" that he had no choice but to offer to federalist renovators. His political turnaround, however, engendered a crisis in the Parti Québécois that had been brewing since May 20, 1980. Jacques Parizeau marched out of the cabinet, along with a large contingent of opponents to Lévesque's "noble risk." The Parti Québécois was in tatters.

To make matters worse, Mulroney dismantled FIRA and the NEP and aligned himself with Ronald Reagan and his administration. Lévesque's hope of conserving his tenuous connection with the extreme right was dashed; there was no longer any question of playing the provinces against Ottawa in Washington. Reagan never even responded to René's congratulations on his re-election in November of 1984.

In March of 1985, Reagan hastened to Quebec City to seal the new friendship between Canada and the United States in the shadow of the Château Frontenac. At first, Lévesque refused to show his face at this political fête for two Irish conservative politicians. Above all, he did not want to attend the huge gala that Mulroney was throwing in Reagan's honor. He finally yielded to pressure from his advisors, including Bernard Landry; he donned the hated tuxedo and listened to the two new pals sing an Irish ballad. But Lévesque failed to turn up for a lunch at which a place had been reserved for him not far from the future cold-war conqueror. He was represented by a minister, and he made it known that he had better things to do.

"Since we couldn't find one damned drop of that noble Irish blood anywhere," he said bitterly the next day, "we were made to feel a bit like *muzhiks*," Russian peasants.

Quebeckers deserved better, he seemed to be saying, forty years after he had turned in his US Army uniform. "There are no truer friends, I think, there are no better North Americans than us," he declared during question period at the National Assembly. "There are no truer friends of the Americans than Quebeckers."

Lévesque bowed out of political life, in June of 1985, after a short "farewell visit" to the United States, during which he met with governors and senators. It was the American consul general Rosenblatt who wrote his political epitaph for the State Department's files; his dispatch to Washington included this paragraph, which Lévesque would have cherished.

> The referendum illustrates most clearly Mr Lévesque's commitment to democratic principles. He never tried to sneak sovereignty across but played openly for public support on the issue. From the time separatism emerged, Lévesque is given high marks for his restrained and sober public rhetoric at times when he could have inflamed the public to rioting.

Harvard professor Elliott Feldman, one of Lévesque's two true American allies, had a last word for the post-referendum René Lévesque: "In the last years of his life, he was persuaded that he wouldn't get there. In him, there was a touch of Moses."

## An Epilogue

One morning in November of 1987, the *La Presse* reporter in Washington received an order from his editors: "Gather American reactions to René Lévesque's death." The task seemed neither pleasant nor difficult; there were only a few cognoscenti in the United States, so the list would quickly be exhausted.

In New England, the harvest was good. Vermont governor Madeleine Kunin, travelling in Italy, had her secretary pass on her condolences over "this true tragedy." An ex-governor of Maine called in person to say that "René was the pride of the people of Quebec." And an advisor to Michael Dukakis, governor of Massachusetts and presidential aspirant, composed a short condolence note on the spot, in which he spoke of Lévesque as a "source of pride and unity" for his people.

The reporter then tried his luck in Washington, among politicians concerned with international affairs. He called the press agent at the State Department's Canada Desk; he was asked to spell Lévesque. All day, the reporter was asked to spell out the unfamiliar name and patiently to explain who Lévesque was. At the

White House the question was, "Do we know him?" Of course, Reagan had even met Lévesque briefly, had shaken his hand at the Quebec summit in 1985. The journalist's call might be returned.

Senator Ted Kennedy's political advisor proved equally unforthcoming. Aides to Senator Patrick Moynihan, who had met with Lévesque in the summer of 1985, reacted as if the reporter were talking about a Serbo-Croatian leader.

The Quebec reporter grew impatient, almost angry. In Quebec City, messages of condolence from European and African politicians were pouring in. What was wrong with Washington? With aides of three other senators he played his best card. "Look, for Quebec, it's as if Martin Luther King had died. Your boss knows him, has talked to him. For goodness sake, give him the message. I would be surprised if he didn't want to at least be polite."

The office of Vice-President George Bush was indeed polite — or idle. An aide called the reporter back. He would be informed should Bush express an opinion.

But the reporters' phone would not ring. Washington had no time to waste on dead has-beens.

# Conclusion and Outlook

*There is no question regarding the long-term viability*
*of an independent Quebec in the economic sense*
*or in regard to its ability to be a responsible member of*
*the family of nations. The unresolved and determining factor*
*is and must be the will of the people of Quebec.*
US State Department, August 1977

The answer is yes. The question, which has long haunted Canadian living rooms, both separatist and federalist, is and has been, Would the United States allow Quebec to separate?

It has been asked of presidential advisors: of Walt Rostow and Dean Rusk for Lyndon Johnson; of Helmut Sonnenfeldt for Richard Nixon; of Zbigniew Brzezinski and Robert Hunter for Jimmy Carter. It has been asked of the military strategists at the Pentagon: of Warnke, Ellsworth, Bader. It has been asked of planners and staffers at the CIA. It has been asked of Wall Street bankers.

Everywhere, every time, the response has been two part. One: we do not want Quebec to separate. Two: we would accommodate ourselves. The US would, as they say, "live with it."

In all strata of the diplomatic service, in Congress, in the academe, in newsrooms, the Americans have expressed their anxiety over the idea that Canada aches. They hope that things will get better. They are so civilized, those Canadians. They set an example: they know how to take care of their poor and their sick and are dignified actors on the international scene. If only they were not so boring, we would want to be like them. Knowing that a minority, which must surely be well-treated, wants to cut this great country in two makes the Americans sad. It is "a tragedy," they say.

All the strategists, even the Quebec sympathizers like Al Hero, conclude that American interests call for permanent Canadian unity. In international debates, Canada is the best of allies; it is close enough to lean on, distinct enough to maintain its credibility. Without Quebec, how would the Americans justify keeping Canada within the group of the seven most industrialized nations, at the exclusion of Australia, Spain, or South Korea?

Economically, the large country to the north is often a little troublesome, but at least it is only one country. How many national energy policies, how many FIRAs, would there be in a future association of ex-provinces, not to mention among an unassociated group? How many new protectionist customs tariffs would there be at four, six, or ten borders? How many new embassies with which to negotiate agreements? Then there is the issue of political uncertainty. In Canada as a whole, it matters relatively little if a New Democratic government is elected in a province. But would the nation of British Columbia, under socialist Dave Barrett, make its contributions to NATO and NORAD?

When Americans talk about Quebec independence, they think primarily about the separation of British Columbia and Alberta, the bankruptcy of New Brunswick and Prince Edward Island, the drifting off of Newfoundland. "It's as if you're saying that Canada's unity rests on Quebec's shoulders," an exasperated separatist exclaimed one day to a New York newspaperman.

That is exactly what they are saying.

The whole American position is summed up in the following metaphor:

"Madam, you may be unhappy in your marriage, but if you get a divorce your husband will start to drink. Please don't leave him under any circumstances."

"And if I leave him anyway?"

"Oh, well, too bad then. It's your decision."

The Americans would find the situation regrettable, really, but they would not budge.

One word comes up again and again to describe what an independent Quebec represents for the United States: it is "nuisance." It is annoying; it makes everything complicated. But, as a military man said about the Quebec issue, "We don't always get what we want." The US would, as they say, "live with it."

What, in the end, did the American pressure to prevent this nuisance amount to between 1976 and 1980? Telephone calls from Thomas Enders to editors and financiers in New York to get them to temper their hospitality to René Lévesque in 1977 (he tempered it all by himself). Interventions by George Vest, Alexander Tomlinson, and, once again, Enders so that business people would not say out loud that they thought they could profit from a separate Quebec. Statements by Jimmy Carter, Walter Mondale, and — once — Cyrus Vance stressing their country's preference for "a strong and united Canada." How many Chiles, Dominican Republics, Greeces, would have prayed for such restraint, such timidity?

"We didn't have the feeling that the United States was trying to manipulate events here," concluded Louis Bernard, Lévesque's advisor. "We found that the Americans acted well in this whole thing. They acted well."

The day after independence, on the other hand, Quebec would have felt the southern presence. The weight of American inertia would finally have shifted. Until the referendum, the US wish for stability would have supported a united Canada. After a separatist victory, the same desire for stability would have demanded an agreement between the two new capitals, the greatest possible cohesion in their policies, the preservation of English Canada's unity.

The United States' interest would therefore have crystallized in one word — association — and Washington would have pressed Ottawa to negotiate with Quebec. Even the New York bankers' and investors' interests would have been served by successful negotiations between Canada and Quebec. The course of the Canadian dollar and the federal treasury bonds would have followed the progression of such talks. They would have risen with every agreement or handshake, fallen with every pounded-upon table or slammed door.

Perhaps the referendum exercise was a prologue, a dress rehearsal. George Jaeger, who had so correctly predicted the outcome of the referendum, wrote six months before the "NO" victory that the affair would not end there: "We have no doubts that in the longer term the referendum will be seen, not as the end, but only as a way-station in a continuing process involving an increasingly precise definition and delineation of Quebec's identity."

The day after the referendum he warned the State Department that sovereignty-association was no longer an option — "at least for the time being." The federalists had only a few years left, he also wrote, to rebuild the Canadian edifice to please Quebec. Without this, Jaeger warned, the separatist movement would rise again. "Even a massive Liberal referendum victory may give [...] Canada only a relatively brief respite" — to bring about constitutional reform, which, Jaeger wrote, would "provide sufficient emotional outlets for the Quebec nationals who do want change." Barring that, he warned, "the Quebec nationalists can regroup and the Quebec tide would turn again."

Were Quebec to once again embark on the path to independence, the conditions to the south will have changed. But only slightly. The United States' attachment to Canada is a lasting habit. True, Quebec separatism has grown more respectable since 1980. And the simple fact that Washington and Wall Street have already been through this turbulence once means that reactions will be calmer if history does repeat itself on this issue. The lack of reaction of the markets on June 26, 1990, after the collapse of the Meech Lake Accord, to Premier Bourassa's promise to "never" return to the constitutional table with other provinces, and to the largest nationalist demonstration in the history of Quebec (a quarter of a million people chanting "Quebec to Quebeckers"), speaks volumes on this new restraint. In fact, the Canadian dollar rose the next day on Wall Street.

New York now knows that the Quebec separatists are not Marxists; that they do not dream of massive nationalizations, are not colluding with the KGB, do not persecute Jews. They are capable of managing a government, presenting budgets, taming unions.

The texture of the Quebec nationalist forces is also changing, in a way that can only allay fears down south. Back in 1979, Jaeger had predicted as much: "Quebec is rapidly producing a new, growing francophone technological elite, which has already taken over government and public services and is now moving into other areas, including business," he wrote. "While these successes may over time blunt the radicalism of Quebec's demands," he added, "there is also little question that the emergence of this new elite is making Quebec more intensely francophone than it has ever been. The challenge to English Canada is therefore not likely to abate."

The former Canadian expert at the Council on Foreign Relations, William Diebold, has noted that Quebec business people are not now a rarity in New York, although — with the possible exception of Paul Desmarais — not a single one was known before 1976. These personal contacts with Quebeckers, even federalist ones, have been worth a thousand Operation Americas. If the PQ were re-elected today, Diebold declares, Wall Street would be "much, much, much more informed" and more sophisticated in its analysis of Quebec reality. One sign of the times: in 1977 Merrill Lynch was considering pulling out of the syndicate of investment banks representing Quebec in New York because it was concerned by the prospect of an independent Quebec. In March of 1990, it spontaneously advised its clients that Quebec's independence should not be any reason for investors to shy away from the new country.

In this year of the rebirth of the Quebec independence movement, the American press has also been surprisingly soft on the separatists. *Time* magazine and the *Washington Post* have published columns and editorials to the effect that a Canadian fragmentation might not be so bad after all. Peter Brimelow and Pat Buchanan have gone on writing and saying that a Quebec secession would be in the interest of the United States. Even William Safire, in a stunning reversal, forgot about his "Cuba to the North" and wrote that the US might gain in swallowing some parts of a divided Canada. *Et tu*, Bill. . . .

More importantly, Washington, which admittedly has a short memory, can take advantage of a platoon of diplomats and analysts who have already accumulated a body of knowledge — and a rather impressive one — on the Quebec problem. For a quarter of a century, they had been telling the White House that a solution to the Quebec problem would only come if English Canada granted some form of special status to the French province, thus satisfying what they called "the legitimate grievances of Quebec." Are these analysts and diplomats now explaining to the secretary of state and the President that the separatist renaissance has come on the heels of a decade of unkept constitutional promises, after a refusal to adapt the structure of Canada to the specific needs of Quebec?

The end of the cold war, of course, makes the question of military alliances, and the necessity for the Americans to have a solid buffer to their north, even less imperative than before.

The free-trade agreement, which will soon be irreversible (if it is not already so), is on the way to creating the north-south economic corridor of which Lévesque had dreamed. It amounts, in effect, to the gradual economic "de-Canadianization" of Quebec.

Since the separatists were driven from power, in 1985, Quebec has kept up its contacts with authorities in New England and New York, thus maintaining and increasing an extended network of relationships that may be useful in the future. Mario Cuomo, governor of New York, is waiting in the wings for the White House. George Mitchell, senator from Maine, has become the most powerful man in the Senate. John Sununu, the former governor of New Hampshire, is now George Bush's cabinet chief.

None of them is pro-separatist. But all understand the question well enough not to be led astray by the first prophet of doom that comes along. In a time of trouble they would probably take the call of the Quebec premier.

In addition, the English-Canadian nationalist reaction during the free-trade debate, as well as those nationalists' resistance to the concept of a distinct society for Quebec, may indicate a greater sense of solidarity among the nine other provinces. Perhaps one can conclude that the fear of being absorbed by the United States will guarantee the survival of English Canada; perhaps, paradoxically, it will prevent the split-up of English Canada so much feared in

Washington.

And if tomorrow Ottawa attempted to shut an independent Quebec out of the Canada-US free-trade agreement, American interests would oppose this fragmentation of the large continental market. A White House aide told a Canadian reporter in the spring of 1990 that Washington would hope and expect Quebec will remain party to the Free Trade Agreement if it is to secede. Senator Patrick D. Moynihan, one of the key congressional cheerleaders of the Agreement, repeated the same stance in July.

All of these developments point to the fact that Quebec's independence would be less a "nuisance" today for the Americans than it was ten years ago.

But a nuisance all the same.

New secret studies completed by the CIA and the State Department in late June of 1990, as separatist fervor rose again in Quebec, point to the disruption that Quebec separation would mean for "a broad range of security, trade and environment ties between Washington and Ottawa." Still, the studies of 1990, reported by *The New York Times,* as that of 1977 and all other administration analyses quoted in this book, indicate frustration at the prospect of a more complicated relationship, but no alarm. "In none of these projections do American officials view a potentially independent Quebec as hostile to Washington," the *Times* reported

On the contrary, the current handlers of the Canadian file at the CIA and "Foggy Bottom" regard the current Quebec premier, Robert Bourassa, "as a moderate whose views on politics, economics and Canada's involvement in NATO would be palatable to Washington if he were to lead the province to independence or greater autonomy." A likely prospect, as a sizable majority of Quebeckers (never less than 60%, an all-time record) express in poll after poll their willingness to dramatically loosen ties with English Canada.

George Bush promised to "courageously sit on the sidelines" of the Canadian debate. Pressed by Ottawa during the next and possibly imminent endgame for Canadian unity, it is a likely bet that the President will say two things.

"It's up to Canadians to decide. But we prefer a strong and united Canada."

"And if I leave him anyway?"

"Oh, well, too bad then. It's your decision."

# Appendices

## Letter from Franklin Roosevelt to Mackenzie King on the assimilation of French Canadians, May 18, 1942.

Source: Franklin D. Roosevelt Library

Canada Folder
1-42

18
May ~~11,~~ 1942.
~~Hyde Park,~~ Washington

Dear Mackenzie:

I had to forego Hyde Park ten days ago because the visit of President Prado of Peru was postponed, but he has come and gone and is a really delightful fellow -- the first civilian President of Peru for ten or fifteen years, a professor at the University of Lima which anti-dates Harvard by nearly a hundred years.

So here I am at Hyde Park again for three days on just the right weekend for the dogwood and the apple trees. I think that on the whole your election was not only perfectly timed and excellently conceived, but the result as a whole was better than I had hoped outside of Quebec.

That brings many thoughts to mind in terms of the future -- thoughts which may sound to you a bit amateurish but which may have some merit in these days of national planning, so I know you will forgive me if I put them down very roughly on paper.

When I was a boy in the"nineties" I used to see a good many French Canadians who had rather recently come into the New Bedford area near the old Delano place at Fair Haven. They seemed very much out of place in what was still an old New England community. They segregated themselves in the mill towns and had little to do with their neighbors. I can remember that the old generation shook their heads and used to say, "This is a new element which will never be assimilated. We are assimilating the Irish but these Quebec people won't even speak English. Their bodies are here but their hearts and minds are in Quebec."

Today, forty or fifty years later, the French Canadian elements in Maine, New Hampshire, Massachusetts and Rhode Island are at last becoming a part of the American melting pot. They no longer vote as their churches and their societies tell them to. They are inter-marrying with the original Anglo-Saxon stock; they are good, peaceful citizens and most of them are speaking English in their homes.

At a guess, I should say that in another two generations they will be completely Americanized and will have begun to distribute their stock into the Middle West states, into the Middle states. and into the Far West.

- 2 -

All of this leads me to wonder whether by some sort of planning Canada and the United States, working toward the same end, cannot do some planning -- perhaps unwritten planning which need not even be a public policy -- by which we can hasten the objective of assimilating the New England French Canadians and Canada's French Canadians into the whole of our respective bodies politic. There are, of course, many methods of doing this which depend on local circumstances. Wider opportunities can perhaps be given to them in other parts of Canada and the U.S.; and at the same time, certain opportunities can probably be given to non-French Canadian stock to mingle more greatly with them in their own centers.

In other words, after nearly two hundred years with you and after seventy-five years with us, there would seem to be no good reason for great differentials between the French Canadian population elements and the rest of the racial stocks.

It is on the same basis that I am trying to work out post-war plans for the encouragement of the distribution of certain other nationalities in our large congested centers. There ought not to be such a concentration of Italians and of Jews, and even of Germans as we have today in New York City. I have started my National Resources Planning Commission to work on a survey of this kind.

I am still without final news on the naval battle in the Southwest Pacific. I am inclined to think, however, that the result on the whole is definitely on the right side of the ledger. Apparently, the large scale attack on Port Moresby in New Guinea has been called off by the Japanese for the time being; and apparently we have sunk and damaged more of their ships and planes than they have of ours. As you have seen by the press, Curtin and MacArthur are obtaining most of the publicity. The fact remains, however, that the naval operations were conducted solely through the Hawaii command! I am not forgetting the possibility of coming to Ottawa but things are happening so fast, I dare not make anything definite for more than a few days ahead.

As ever yours,

Honorable Mackenzie King,
Prime Minister of Canada,
Laurier House,
Ottawa.

# Memo from Walt Rostow to Lyndon Johnson on de Gaulle and Quebec, November 27, 1967.

Source: *Lyndon B. Johnson Library*

Monday, November 27, 1967

MEMORANDUM FOR THE PRESIDENT

SUBJECT: DeGaulle's Press Conference and Your Meeting with
Ambassador Bohlen, Tuesday, November 28, 11:15 a.m.

Monday's Press Conference

DeGaulle pushed his regular themes further than he has before:

-- There is an American takeover of our businesses, but
this does not come as much from the structural superiority
of the United States as it does from the exportation of
inflated dollars." (Here deGaulle takes aim at the argument advanced in a new French best seller, The American
Challenge, which says that to compete with US industry,
Europeans must do hard things such as reforming their
educational and legal systems.) DeGaulle insists the US
balance of payments deficit must be ended so that it should
not continue to be a means of taking over European industry.

-- British entry into Europe is still out of the question. If the
other Five insist on negotiations with Britain now, they will
break up the Communities.

-- His most extreme statement was on Quebec: He called for
a sovereign Quebec closely linked to France. This is the
"major French task of our century."

-- Only Big-Four united action can bring peace to the Middle East.
US involvement in Vietnam makes such action impossible.

You may wish to get Bohlen's views on:

1. What deGaulle is trying to do:
-- is British entry dead?
-- how much trouble can he make on the NPT?

-- will he pull out of NATO in 1969?

-2-

2.   How strong is his position inside France in the wake of

     --   his unpopular Mid-East stand,

     --   the Quebec fiasco (now repeated),

     --   and discontent in Parliament over his domestic policies?

3.   What should we be doing:  avoid tangling with him or begin
     to take active countermeasures?

W. W. Rostow

RHU:mst

**Hand-written note by Richard Nixon on his morning news summary, during the October Crisis, October 17, 1970. His comment is "H [for his assistant, Haldeman] — Watch the press — they will defend their 'liberal' friend!"**

Source: Nixon Project

*10/17/70*

6

warrant. He acted on grounds of state of insurrection. Film pointed up the extent and swiftness of the operation as party members were herded aboard vans and police with army backup covered the whole province by daybreak. Some 250 FLQ members and sympathizers were arrested.

The networks emphasized the extraordinary powers -- which Trudeau says may not end until April 1971 -- which include the suspension of civil rights, government control over property, shipping, ports and transportation. Trudeau warned of insurrection as he invoked the powers with "deep regret."

The Interior Minister was on ABC attempting to show that the measures were not all that extreme. But on CBS, radical leader Le Mieux expressed considerable anger over the government's refusal to release the prisoners. CBS said there was some opposition to Trudeau moves but the country remained calm. Kidnapped victims believed still alive.

(CBS noted Attorney General Mitchell's comment that he sees no chance of the US taking such actions as have been taken in Canada. He said he was concerned with individual citizens taking vigilante actions to deal with terrorists.)

VIETNAM

NBC reported that bombs continue to "rain down" on the Ho Chi Minh Trail. Otherwise things have been so quiet that casualties are about

Document outlining American government policy regarding the Parti Québécois: *The Quebec Situation: Outlook and Implications*, August 1977.

Source: American State Department

**SECRET**

# THE QUEBEC SITUATION: OUTLOOK AND IMPLICATIONS*

* *Publisher's note*: Given the importance of this document, the author and the publisher had hoped to print a facsimile. Unfortunately, this proved to be impossible due to the poor condition of the origianl document. The following is a faithful transcription of the original version, along with a photographic reproduction of the first page of the abstract that preceded it.

X0082

BEST COPY AVAILABLE

SECRET                    069-2039

## THE QUEBEC SITUATION:  OUTLOOK AND IMPLICATIONS

Abstract.  This study analyzes the present situation in Quebec, the strategies of Trudeau and
Levesque, the likelihood of possible outcomes of
the power struggle, the impact on the U.S. of such
outcomes, the U.S. preference, and the parameters
for U.S. short-term policy.

Summary:

Background.  Quebec nationalism is older than Canadian
Confederation itself.  The francophone Quebecois (80% of the
Quebec population) have an ethnic identity and solidarity of
their own.  They have long standing grievances against English
Canada, among them a feeling of second class citizenship status
both in Canada as a whole, and, more importantly, in their
own province of Quebec.

The transformation of Quebec society in the last few
decades has brought with it rising expectations among the
majority francophones for expanded control of provincial
political and economic activities by them, rather than
Ottawa or the minority anglophones.  Handling their own
affairs is seen as a viable alternative and a cultural imperative.

Although the Parti Quebecois (PQ) government is committed
to independence, it was elected to provide good government.
The PQ has promised to hold a referendum on independence before November 1981.  Meanwhile, the contest for power continues
between Quebec and Ottawa.  This type of power struggle is not
peculiar to Quebec.  It is part of the Canadian system and engaged in by many provinces.

Significant changes are expected to take place in Canada
even if the Quebecois reject independence.  The effect on U.S.
interests depends on the form and manner these changes take.
Five billion dollars U.S. money is invested in Quebec.  It is
one of our larger trading partners -- about $7 billion annually.
Quebec forms an integral part of North American defense and
straddles the important St. Lawrence Seaway.

Quebec and Ottawa Strategies.  Quebec.  The PQ must demonstrate
it can provide good government.  At the same time it will
pursue its "educative" program on the desirability and viability
of an independent Quebec.

While offering to negotiate independence with continued
economic association with Canada, the PQ will continue to
confront Ottawa with further demands and assertions of

SECRET        *August 1977*

A.    *Quebec Situation*

*Quebec nationalism did not emerge with the establishment of the Parti Quebecois (PQ) ten years ago. It is a long term phenomenon dating back to before the formation of the Canadian Confederation in 1867. The five million francophone Quebecois, 80% of the Quebec population, have an ethnic identity and solidarity of their own. They have also had long standing grievances, real and perceived, against both English Canada — symbolized by Ottawa, and anglophones in Quebec — symbolized by West Montreal.*

*These grievances include such matters as a feeling of inferiority, second-class citizenship — both in Canada as a whole and, more importantly, in their own province of Quebec. The Quebecois have long felt that Ottawa: slighted Quebec when it came to developing Canada, did not look out for Quebec's interests in trade; interfered in and controlled economic, social, educational, and cultural affairs in ways detrimental to Quebecois values and aspirations; and did not properly represent Quebec francophones overseas. In Quebec itself, the complaint has been that the anglophones in Montreal controlled the Quebec economy and management positions, and that it was difficult for the French-speakers to get ahead because of poorer education and the need to know English. Studies have shown this to be true, and immigrants to Quebec have long realized it and have sought to assimilate themselves into the anglophone rather than the majority francophone community.*

*The grievances are deep-rooted, emotional and persistent. Societal and political changes have eliminated the causes of some of them, but the perceptions not only linger on but have become reinforced with social change and as the possibility to do something about them has grown. Quebec is no longer the backward area with uneducated farmers ruled by the church and corrupt politicians of a few decades ago — when the only chance for the best and the brightest was federal service or national politics. Over the past decades there has been a tremendous surge in industrialization, urbanization, education and opportunities for advancement in the province. To most active Quebecois in the 20-40 age group, Quebec is now where the action is. All this change and development has brought with it rising expectations for expanded control of political and economic activities in the province by the majority francophones, rather than Ottawa or minority anglophones. In short, handling their own affairs has come to be seen by an increasing number of Quebecois more and more as a viable alternative and cultural imperative.*

*The federalist affiliation has also been weakened by the perceived inability of Ottawa to take care of Quebec's problems—despite the fact there has been a francophone Prime Minister for eight years. The Quebecois are much more concerned with language questions in Quebec than in Canada as a whole, but see the failure of Trudeau's bi-lingualism policy as yet another indication that English Canada really is not concerned with the cultural aspirations of francophones.*

*Provincial aspirations for more local control, which have been pursued by all recent Quebec governments—whether Liberal, Union Nationale, or now Parti Quebecois, have clashed with the tendency by Ottawa to seek more and more centralization of power in the federal government. This basic contest for power will continue between Quebec and Ottawa, no matter who is in power in Quebec or, probably, Ottawa. This type of power struggle is not peculiar to Quebec, but rather typical of the Canadian system and engaged in by many provinces.*

*Although tremendous strides have been made in industrial development in Quebec over the past few decades, the Quebec economy is still not as developed as, and more dependent on tariff protection than some other parts of Canada. Quebec is heavily dependent on the Canadian and American markets. At this time, the Quebec economy is in difficulty even more so than the Canadian economy with unemployment at about 10 percent.*

*The PQ surprise victory at the polls in November 1976 has changed the basic situation of Ottawa-Quebec confrontation in that the people of Quebec will sometime before November 15  1981, be asked in a referendum to choose between independence and staying in Canada, and in that a group of people committed to independence are now in power in Quebec and have the opportunity to wield that power in pursuit of their goal.*

*The PQ was primarily elected to provide good government. It received 41 percent of the overall vote (but over half of the francophone votes). The number of Quebecois who support independence remains the same as before the PQ election victory, about 20 percent.*

*It is generally expected that some significant changes will take place in Canada, even if independence is rejected by the Quebecois; and U.S. interests will be affected to a greater or lesser degree depending on what form these changes take and the manner in which they unfold. Quebec is not only a place where $5 billion U.S. money is invested, but also one of our larger trading partners—about $7 billion worth each year. It is also an integral part of North American defense arrangements and it straddles the important St. Lawrence Seaway. There are over a million French Canadian descendents living in the United States.*

*Repetitions of the terrorism and violence that took place in Quebec in the early 1970s are not considered likely over the next few years. The whole issue of Quebec independence has entered democratic channels with the election of the PQ on the premise that independence would only come about on the basis of the will of the majority of the people expressed through a referendum. Isolated instances of violence cannot be completely ruled out, however. The possibility exists for anglophone violence in the Montreal area as a reaction to new restrictive language laws. Sustained terrorist activity is even more unlikely, but could possibly arise from a radical fringe element in or out of the PQ that felt completely frustrated as a result of: the PQ modifying its aims to something less than independence; the defeat of an independence referendum; or the defeat of the PQ in the next election. Violence would probably reduce support for independence. It would at the same time confront Ottawa with Hobson's choice of whether or not to again intervene with federal force, as was the case in the early 1970s — the psychological reverberations of which are still being felt. Terrorism would also raise the specter of outside terrorist organizations or radical third world forces entering the fray either directly or as financiers of terrorist activity. American nationals and property could become terrorist targets. Action against terrorists would, however, rest with Canadian authorities and there is no foreseeable set of circumstances that would call for direct U.S. action in dealing with a violence situation in Quebec.*

B.    *Quebec and Ottawa Strategies*

*1.   Quebec*

*The November 1976 election victory caught the PQ unprepared. Although it has fielded a provincial government composed of as able people as any before it, the PQ has had to concentrate simultaneously on mastering the task of governing — which it was primarily elected to do, and on formulating its strategy for reaching its goal of independence.*

*At this time the PQ strategy is still in flux, but there are certain trends or expectations. It can be expected that the PQ will concentrate on a) showing that it can provide good government; b) pursuing its program of "educating" the electorate concerning the desirability and viability of an independent Quebec; and c) confronting Ottawa with maximized demands while offering to negotiate. The PQ will take steps within the province to assert the primacy of the French language, such as passing new language legislation. It recently presented a White Paper on this question which would lead to French having the status of the only official language in the province, French becoming the language of the workplace, and children of future immigrants to Quebec being forced into French schools. This will create more tension between anglophones and francophones, especially in the Montreal area. Many anglophones can be expected to leave Quebec and their immigration into Quebec will slow down. There are also native peoples and other ethnic groups in Quebec — Italians, Greeks, Jews, ect. (sic), who have strong views on the language issue. Violence is not a PQ tool, but rash acts by radical factions on both sides cannot be ruled out. If a backlash develops on this or similar issues in English Canada, the PQ will try to use this to further whip up francophone emotions — which are already volatile.*

*The PQ can also be expected to try to gain more and more powers from Ottawa in other fields, such as French-language broadcasting and cultural activities. Each time it meets with resistance or is thwarted, the PQ will use this as further "proof" that Quebec's national affirmation cannot be accomplished within the federal structure.*

*In its "educative" campaign the PQ will attempt to underscore the need for Quebec to be able to make its own decisions. Preparations are already underway to show through a study of federal-provincial relations, on a sector by sector basis, that federalism places unacceptable constraints on the Government of Quebec to resolve Quebec's problems.*

*The PQ will on the one hand offer to negotiate independence, and continued economic association with Canada as part of it, and on the other hand continue to confront Ottawa with further demands and assertions of sovereignty. Examples of the latter can be found in the recent behavior of Quebec ministers at international meetings, where they have claimed to represent Quebec only, rather than Canada.*

*Compared with Ottawa, and Trudeau in particular, the PQ has time, nearly five years of it, to work on the Quebecois to bring them around to accepting independence. Both the PQ and Trudeau can try to outwait each other — but Trudeau only if he wins re-election in 1978, as he now seems likely to do. Each will hope that the other will stumble. The PQ has the advantage of deciding when to hold the referendum, choosing a propitious time when emotions are running high against English Canada. It can also control the pace at which it proceeds in challenging Ottawa, making sure that it is never too far ahead of public support for its actions. The PQ even has the choice of going slow, that is to seek a renewed mandate through re-election or by holding several referenda formulated in general terms — rather than a straight yes or no independence, thus gaining time for its "educative" campaign.*

*At the same time, the present moderate PQ leadership under party leader and Premier Rene Levesque is constrained by the fact that it must juggle the demands of several "constituencies". They must contend with their own PQ radical wing, which wants the party to push for independence now. They must seek to satisfy and enlarge the group of voters who are not party members but who voted for the PQ. They must build up general support for their goals, at least among the francophones in Quebec, in order to secure a sizeable majority support for the referendum. Finally, they must try to persuade Canadian and U.S. investors and lenders that the PQ program for independence poses no threat to their continued financial involvement in the Province.*

*Investors are not only concerned about the PQ drive for independence but also by the radical socialist orientation that they feel the party embodies. The more radical and socialist element of the PQ is relatively small in numbers, but has become entrenched in many party organs as the result of greater activism. As long as some chance remains that the PQ will succeed through democratic means, the present more moderate leadership of the party should be able to maintain control and contain the radicals. Indications are that Levesque would, if need be, let the radicals go rather than risking the general support — of a basically conservative electorate — that he has gained and hopes to expand. The radicals are too few in numbers and lacking in general support for them to gain power in Quebec in the foreseeable future, even under a scenario where it would be clear that the independence drive had failed and radical solutions might have some greater appeal.*

### 2. Ottawa

*Ottawa today means the federal government of Prime Minister Trudeau and his federal Liberal Party — which depends on its Members of Parliament from Quebec for staying in power. Trudeau will face an election within two years, and Quebec independence and what to do about it could well be the major issue.*

*So far Trudeau's policy toward the PQ has been low-key and somewhat passive. He has gone public pleading with the Quebecois: to stay in Canada; to remember their confreres outside of Quebec; to support bilingualism; to keep in mind that in an independent Quebec they would be an even smaller french entity in an english North America; and to consider the economic costs of separation. Trudeau, the Premier of Ontario, and four Western Premiers have threatened that economic association with Canada would not be possible for an independent Quebec. They probably consider this as English Canada's only real ace in the hole. At the same time, Trudeau has pleaded with English Canada for understanding of legitimate aspirations of Quebecois for cultural identity and equality.*

*So far, Trudeau's strategy otherwise has appeared to be a go slow one of conducting federal business as usual, even with the PQ government, to show that federalism does work and that the Quebecois can achieve their legitimate aspirations within the confederation. He has avoided confrontation with the PQ and has down-played challenges such as Quebec ministers claiming to represent Quebec rather than Canada at international meetings. He has taken some positive action, such as imposing textile quotas and providing dairy supports. Trudeau may be hoping that given time and room, Levesque and his relatively inexperienced government will trip itself up on Quebec's serious economic difficulties, or that schisms will develop within the PQ.*

*Taking the high road may seem like the safest thing to do for Trudeau but there are indications that he is not quite satisfied with the passivity of this approach. It is also questionable how long he can get away with enticing his audiences with vague references to new approaches to federal-provincial relations, without being willing to clarify his position with specifics. A good example of this was his masterful speech to the Congress in Washington in February 1977, which also served another aspect of his strategy, that of enlisting*

*U.S. support for a unified Canada. But there are limits to the effectiveness of the statesman-like stance, especially among the Quebecois.*

*Trudeau — unless he decides to leave politics altogether — must in the near future decide on some course of action in regard to Quebec. He can either "hang tough", basically letting matters proceed as they are — banking on the fact that, according to public opinion polls, support for independence has not grown in Quebec since the PQs electoral victory and is still a low 20 percent. It would not be unreasonable for Trudeau to count on the Quebecois rejecting independence on the basis that it would be too costly in economic terms. He may also believe that the PQ Government will in time succumb to internal rifts or the economic difficulties facing the province.*

*But Trudeau also knows that many of those Quebecois who do not support independence, do favor more control and power for the province. The question then becomes whether he feels that these aspirations must be satisfied, at least to a degree, and, if so, how and when.*

*There is some evidence that Trudeau may in time come to consider some formula that would transfer some powers to all the provinces, including Quebec. The mechanism for doing this could be: a) a unilateral transfer of powers to the provinces by the federal government; b) a joint parliamentary committee; c) a constituent assembly; d) a group of "wise men"; or e) a meeting with provincial premiers. The timing could be either soon or after a 1978 general election.*

*The fact nevertheless remains that Trudeau — although a francophone Quebecois — is a committed federalist and central power advocate. Giving up powers to the provinces therefore goes against his grain. It may well be that he feels a general shift in power to the provinces to be too high a price to pay is convinced that the other provinces would not agree to a special status for Quebec, and believes that Levesque and company will not be satisfied with anything that he could possibly offer them. If so, Trudeau may not be willing to use a transfer of powers approach to try to solve the problem. He could decide to try consensus building, co-opting opponents, and a direct effort to defeat the Quebec referendum. Although of lesser importance than the continued unity of Canada, it should be noted that a Canada without Quebec would also spell at least the temporary eclipse of the Liberal Party.*

*The other possibility as the representative of Ottawa is the opposition Progressive-Conservative (PC) Party, which could come into power within two years. The PC leader, Clark, has so far not offered any specific alternative program on Quebec, but the party is reportedly working on one. Clark has both attacked the Trudeau Government for its centralism and has given the broad outlines of a decentralization (he prefers the term flexibility) program involving devolution of some powers to the provinces. He has mentioned the areas of communications, cultural affairs, and immigration as possibilities.*

*Clark is also committed to a United Canada, but he and the PC may be able to contemplate a much greater degree of power for Quebec than Trudeau. He could be in a better position to speak for the rest of Canada to Quebec, since the PC's power base is in English Canada outside Quebec. He is also not handicapped by the long-standing personal rivalry between Trudeau and Levesque.*

### 3. *The Cost of Separation Issue*

*The battle has already been joined on the issue of the costs of separation. The PQ Government led off by releasing a study of their own which claimed that over the past fifteen years Ottawa had gained over $4 billion from its financial relationship with Quebec.*

*Ottawa has already attempted to rebut this claim, with some success. There are several other studies underway and the argument will continue. The availability of data is limited and the uses of it will vary from case to case. We are not in a position at this time to determine what the actual cost of separation would be for Quebec. What the actual facts may be is not as important, however, as what the Quebecois themselves come to believe. A certain economic cost will be acceptable to many Quebecois as compensation for the psychic benefit of being masters in their own house. Where the dividing line goes is impossible to determine, but a ten percent decrease in their standard of living would probably be more than what most Quebecois could be persuaded to accept.*

### 4. *Possible Foreign Intervention*

*The Soviet Union during the past few years has made a conscious effort to expand its relations with Canada and has attempted to capitalize on U.S. — Canadian disagreements — without success. There is no evidence that the USSR plans on trying to interject itself in the Ottawa-Quebec dispute, either directly or through a proxy such as Cuba, nor is there any indication that it would be welcomed by any Quebec group.*

*Unlikely as it seems, French intervention is a remote possibility. Quebec has maintained "special" relations with France since 1965, and Ottawa has remained suspicious of French intentions ever since DeGaulle's call in 1967 for a "Quebec Libre". During the past few years, however, France has pursued a very correct and careful policy vis a vis Canada and Quebec.*

*Quebec's Minister for Inter-governmental Affairs Claude Morin (de facto "Foreign Minister") recently visited Paris and was received by President Giscard d'Estaing, PM Barre, PM Guiringaud, as well as former PM Chirac. Only Chirac, the leader of the Gaullists, evoked echoes of DeGaulle's pro-independence sentiments. The French Government has extended invitations to both Levesque and Trudeau and it is expected that France, out of pure self-*

interest and lack of economic resources, will try to avoid being brought into the Canadian dispute. Any overt French stand or action in favor of Quebec independence would probably be counter-productive since the Quebecois do not have strong emotional ties to France, and this does not overly worry Ottawa. There have been reports of covert French activity in Quebec conducted by private French nationalists, but if true they are on such a limited scale as to be of no serious consequence and could prove even more counter-productive than overt action.

Attempts by radical third world countries to involve themselves in the Quebec situation are most unlikely and would in any case be ineffective since what is in question is a democratic resolution of a dispute rather than an armed insurrection or national liberation movement.

## C.   *Alternative Outcomes*

There are five possible alternative outcomes that need to be addressed. They are:

### 1.   *Maintenance of the Status Quo*

The underlying historical forces of nationalism and the process of societal change that continues unabated in Quebec make the maintenance of the status quo the least likely outcome in the struggle between the federalists and the separatists. All francophone Quebecois are nationalists to a degree, and many of those who are against independence favor more authority for the province. The PQ drive for independence cannot help but reinforce this predilection for greater provincial power to control at least its cultural and social affairs. Even if the PQ should be defeated, the next provincial government will have to keep on demanding concessions from Ottawa, though perhaps not such sweeping ones.

### 2.   *Devolution of Powers to All Provinces*

The alternative of transferring powers to all the provinces from the federal government is perhaps the only realistic way in the long term to keep Quebec in Canada. Just as Quebec, so the other provinces — with the possible exception of Ontario — are unhappy with the present federal / provincial power relationship. They would like to have greater taxing powers, more control over natural resources, revised transportation rate structures, more communications sovereignty, and an increased role in immigration. They do not, however, seek any significant degree of independence in defense, the conduct of foreign policy, or the management of a centralized monetary system. The question is therefore whether the federal government under Trudeau will be willing to give up powers generally and, even more importantly, whether this could be done to an extent that would persuade the majority of the Quebecois to stay with Canada without *seriously undermining the entire federal system. Trudeau probably is convinced that no amount of concessions would satisfy the PQ, and he may be right. A general devolution to all the provinces could therefore weaken Canada without achieving the desired result, that of keeping Canada united.*

### 3. Devolution of Powers to Quebec Only

*The alternative of giving Quebec special status of powers in certain fields considered important by the Quebecois above and beyond any possibly given to other provinces, would probably satisfy the majority of Quebecois, and possibly even the PQ. This course would meet any important provincial objectives with much less economic risk.*

*It is highly questionable, however, whether the other provinces would agree to this. They might, if most of their own desires were met, and if they were faced with the choice between a Quebec in Canada in a special status or an independent Quebec. Such an effort could be a principal objective of the Trudeau campaign already launched to gain a better understanding in anglophone Canada of the unique francophone problem; but, if so, he is keeping it to himself.*

*Whether Trudeau could envisage such a solution might partly depend on the price the other provinces would exact and the fields in which the special powers would be given Quebec. It would be difficult for Ottawa to give Quebec even a degree of independence in foreign affairs or in the management of a centralized monetary system. Short of that, it could be possible to give Quebec what would amount to a "two-nation" status, but still within Canada. This would mean giving French-Canada as close to co-equal status with English-Canada as possible—somewhat analogous with the Austro-Hungarian historical example.*

### 4. Political Sovereignty with Economic Association

*Levesque has argued for "political sovereignty with economic associa-tion" ever since he started his separatist movement, and is pushing it now. The PQ has offered to negotiate such an arrangement with Ottawa either before or after a referendum and / or independence. At the same time Levesque realizes that Ottawa is most unlikely to agree to any negotiations regarding economic association between Quebec and the rest of Canada before the people of Quebec choose independence, since holding out the threat of economic isolation and difficulties is Ottawa's strongest argument in persuading the Quebecois to stay with Canada. Levesque is also resigned to the likelihood that some time could pass after an independence referendum until Ottawa agreed to negotiate economic association; but he makes the argument that it is so much in the interest of both parties that eventually Ottawa would have to agree. There is no question but that such negotiations would be extremely difficult since they would involve such matters as a common market for trade and possibly energy, a monetary union, and control over foreign trade.*

*As to negotiations regarding "political sovereignty", Ottawa might be hard put to refuse if the PQ phrased its referendum so that it would ask the people for a mandate to negotiate this with Ottawa and the referendum passed with a clear majority.*

*If Ottawa refused to negotiate, the PQ would be in a much stronger position to ask the Quebecois to vote for outright independence in a second referendum. A negotiated settlement regarding "political sovereignty" that would still keep Quebec at least nominally in Canada, is difficult to envisage, but could be possible on the basis of a "two-nations" concept. This alternative does not seem overly likely, however, at least not under a Trudeau regime. How would one solve the questions of defense, foreign policy, foreign trade, monetary policy, national debt, etc. ad infinitum? Moreover, the PQ still has to bring about a major turn-around in public opinion before a sovereignty referendum can be expected to receive a majority vote.*

### 5.   *Unilateral Declaration of Independence (UDI)*

*If the Quebecois at some point in the future opt for independence in a referendum, the PQ can be expected unilaterally to declare Quebec independent and seek recognition from other countries. What would then unfold would depend on the basis for the UDI and how it came about. The size of the majority for independence in a referendum would perhaps be the most important factor. Quebec's willingness to assume international obligations, protect Canadian and foreign interests, and provide for minority rights would also weigh heavily in determining Canadian and foreign reactions. Other factors would involve the political climate in Canada, that is whether English Canada took a "good riddance" stance or attempted to overcome the UDI by further negotiations with Quebec. The deferal Canadian Government's position would determine what action, if any, it took to try to prevent other states from recognizing an independent Quebec.*

*Both Trudeau and Clark have said that they would not use force to keep Quebec in Canada if a clear majority of the Quebecois chose independence. Forceful federal intervention cannot be ruled out, however, in case the majority is not clear or if violence erupts.*

*The PQ clearly believes that declared independence if necessary will be followed by forms of association with Canada because this is in the strong interest of both. Thus UDI, for PQ, could be but a temporary means of working out associated status with "political sovereignty."*

### D.   *Most Likely Outcome*

*It should be recognized that the described alternative outcomes are first of all conceptualizations and secondly not exhaustive. Furthermore it is quite possible, and perhaps even likely, that there will be simultaneous and / or parallel developments in many areas.*

*It is likely that developments will be not only contradictory at times, but also take place in various stages. The first stage is that between now and a referendum. Since the referendum is not expected to be a yes or no on independence, but rather one asking for a mandate to negotiate with Ottawa, for "political sovereignty with economic association", the next stage would probably be from a referendum until negotiations either succeeded or broke down. If they broke down there would be a further stage before another referendum, this time for independence. If the referendum passed, there could be further negotiations or a UDI would follow, but this too could be just another stage, until negotiations for economic association started. The possibilities for scenarios seem endless.*

*Although any of the five alternative outcomes are entirely possible, some are more likely than others. The least plausible is the first — maintenance of the status quo. Alternatives two and three are variations on a theme, devolution of powers. Of these, a general devolution to all provinces is more likely than to Quebec only, at least as matters stand now. The last two are also variations on a theme, independence — either with or without economic association. Independance — UDI — is only expected to come about as the result of a clear majority choice in a referendum. Whether there would be economic association, and how soon, would depend on the approach to the question of the two parties at that time. It is therefore impossible to forecast now the likelihood of one outcome as against the other of these two alternatives.*

*What we end up with on the basis of this reasoning is that either Trudeau (or possibly Clark) can bring himself to agree to transfer powers to the provinces, in such a manner and to such an extent that the Quebecois will opt to stay with Canada, or developments will lead to a majority of the Quebecois coming to support independence — qualified or unqualified. The fact that support for independence has not grown appreciably in Quebec since the election of the PQ, and still amounts to only about 20%, would seen to augur well for Trudeau's chances. The whole question involves, however, so many imponderables, perceptions and emotions, that a swing in time among the Quebecois in favor of independence can be no means be ruled out. English Canadian actions and reactions will play an extremely important role in determining the attitudes of the Quebecois. Every time the Quebecois perceive actions by English Canada as either punishing Quebec, being a slur on the national pride of the Quebecois, or being an action designed to weaken the position of Quebec, the group favoring independence will gather strength.*

*At the same time, interplay between underlying historical forces of nationalism and economic determinism may be more important in determining the future of Quebec and Canada than the maneuverings of governments and political parties. Ultimately, the independence struggle may come to a decision* between heart and pocketbook. Outcome of such a choice could be greatly influenced by economic conditions in Quebec over the next two-three years. Much will depend on how the Quebecois perceive, or are led to perceive, the expected economic difficulties or, as they are called, the costs of separation. Should the PQ be able to convince the population, as they will try, that they can do as well or better than the Federal government or that Ottawa is responsible for much of their woes, then economic issues may tend to reinforce the already strong nationalist forces. Coversely, if the federalists could argue successfully that separatism and the economic uncertainty which it engenders are major factors in exacerbating economic difficulties, or that the costs of separation would be high, there would be a better than even chance that an already dubious majority in Quebec would sour on independence. If nationalist attitudes are reinforced, however, sagging economic conditions or expected economic costs of separation may not play as great a part as one might expect in defeating separatism. Emotions, possibly on both sides but certainly in Quebec, can be expected to be a key element in the decision-making process.

E.  *Impacts on the United States*

1.  *Short-term Impacts*

There are several likely short-term impacts on the U.S. growing out of the Ottawa-Quebec confrontation. By short-term is meant that time at least up to the Quebec referendum in about two-three years.

First of all it can be expected that the federal government in Ottawa will become increasingly preoccupied with domestic matters, reducing its ability to play a constructive role in international affairs. Because of this preoccupation and its desire to enlist U.S. public support for a united Canada, the Trudeau Government may become more accommodating to U.S. interests. There was some evidence of this during Trudeau's February 1977 visit to Washington — during which he was also very successful in gaining expressions of U.S. support for a united Canada. Whether the more accommodating approach can be translated into new cooperative ventures with the U.S. — such as in trade or energy questions is still not known. It would not be surprising for Ottawa to ask the U.S. Government to take a stand much more unequivocally in favor of a united Canada. And Ottawa might even at some point pressure the U.S. to make clear to Quebec, before a referendum, that any special U.S. trade arrangements with an independent Quebec would be out of the question.

The PQ, despite its radical and socialist elements, has so far been much less anti-U.S. than anti-English Canada and has assumed that it could always work things out with the U.S. The PQ will try to counteract Ottawa moves by trying to persuade the U.S. to adopt a neutral position in the Quebec-Ottawa confrontation. The PQ will also try to assure the U.S. Government and private American investors, as well as Ottawa and Canadian investors, that they have *nothing to fear from the PQ or an independent Quebec. The PQ might try to gain U.S. support, particularly after a successful referendum or while negotiating with Ottawa, by either threatening or holding out special consideration regarding American investments in Quebec, electric power swaps, trade, the St. Lawrence Seaway, and defense matters.*

*It is possible that Ottawa and / or Quebec will try to involve the U.S. on its side, especially as the time for the referendum draws nearer. U.S. involvement will be difficult to avoid, considering the extensive U.S. interests in both Canada and Quebec in the fields of investment, trade, and defense — just to name a few. There is likely to be demands from American business' for the U.S. Government to protect the interests of business in Canada, including Quebec. It is not known what position French-Canadian descendents in the U.S. will take, but they may try to influence the U.S. Government and Congress, as may other Americans in the U.S. or Canada. The possibility that U.S. or Canadian media attention will stir up interest and emotions cannot be ruled out.*

### 2. *Impacts of Alternative Outcomes*

*Given the many imponderables, such as how change comes about, what the changes are and the effect of possible U.S. involvement, any assessment of the impact of future developments in Canada on U.S. interests must necessarily be speculative and general.*

### a. *Impact on Maintenance of Status Quo*

*The effects of the first alternative — maintenance of the status quoi, i.e., that there are no significant changes to the present system, are probably clearest. U.S.–Canadian relations would then continue more or less as before. If it was clearly resolved through a referendum that Quebec would stay with Canada, and no serious outbreak of violence by discontented elements followed this, Ottawa would again become less preoccupied with internal matters — and probably less accommodating to U.S. interests. A defeat of the referendum would not necessarily lead to any lessening of pressures by Quebec to obtain more powers from Ottawa, or the permanent demise of separatist tendencies. One result could be a growing anti-U.S. sentiment in Quebec. Nevertheless, this alternative presents the least problems for the U.S.*

### b. *Impact of Devolution to All Provinces*

*Depending on which powers would be transferred from the federal government to the provinces, the second alternative — devolution of power to all provinces, could have a considerable impact on U.S. interests. These interests could come into play already in the informative stage, that is during the period when a transfer if powers would be negotiated between Ottawa and the provinces, or while Ottawa formulated the powers that it could possibly transfer uniltaterally to the provinces. A transfer of powers to the provinces could make it more cumbersome and time-consuming to deal with Canada because the Canadian federal government would have to consult with or obtain the agreement of the provinces to a greater extent than is now the case. If, as would be most likely, the provinces obtained greater powers of taxation, more control over natural resources, transport rate structures, communications, and / or immigration, this could create differing and discriminatory rules from between provinces in the conditions for U.S. business operations, investment and ownership, tariff and trade, resource extraction, transport rates (possibly including St.Lawrence Seaway), oil / gas exploration, fishing, and environmental questions — to mention a few areas.*

*Depending on the extent of the devolution of powers, the U.S. could end up, as a practical matter, "dealing" with eleven Canadian entities rather than one and could find itself indirectly involved in interprovincial issues and federal-provincial problems. Some of the provinces would probably seek closer practical ties with U.S. than with the rest of Canada in areas under their control, further complicating Canadian internal affairs and U.S.–Canadian relations.*

### c. Impact of Devolution to Quebec Only

*The effect of the third alternative — devolution of powers to Quebec only, would only differ in degree from that of the impact of the second alternative. Depending on how much power the other provinces also obtained and which special powers that would be given to Quebec, we would find that we were facing either an even more complicated situation or one where the new complications were primarily applicable only to U.S. interests in the province of Quebec. It would be easier to deal with a Canada where only Quebec, rather than all the provinces, had a special status. In some ways it might also be easier than the present situation because there would not be the uncertainty about the rules of the game that prevails now and will continue to exist until the Quebec issue is settled.*

### d. Impact of Political Sovereignty with Economic Association

*The effects of the fourth alternative — political sovereignty with economic association, would depend on the shape of the negotiated settlement, on how sovereign Quebec would be and what kind of approach the two economically associated entities would take toward other countries in trade and related matters. If the federal government retains control over defense, foreign policy, and monetary affairs, the impact would probably be manageable — since both Canada and Quebec need the U.S. as a trading partner and provider of investment funds or loans. Nevertheless, the U.S. would be presented with many different aspects and issues in its relations with this new Canada. In any case, in the event that the two, Ottawa and Quebec, can reach an amicable settlement on this basis, it should be possible for the U.S. to work out acceptable solutions to problems with both or jointly, even though the process would necessarily be more complicated and cumbersome. The situation could be further complicated by growing demands from other provinces for an equal degree of sovereignty.*

e. *Impact of Unilateral Declaration of Independence (UDI)*

*The impact of the fifth alternative — unilateral declaration of independence (UDI) by Quebec, would probably be the most severe on U.S. interests.*

*While Quebec would certainly be a more viable state than most UN members, it could well, to begin with, be less viable as an independent country than as a province. Canada, if it could survive at all, would be less viable as a country without Quebec.*

*In case of a UDI, the U.S. would first of all be confronted with the problem of whether to recognize Quebec. The U.S. position would have to be based in part on: the attitude of the federal Canadian government; the actions of other countries; the degree to which Quebec would provide adequate assurances that it would assume international obligations formerly carried out by Canada — including defense commitments; the best way to protect U.S. interests; and the danger of violence or armed conflict.*

*The reaction of the federal Canadian Government of major importance to the U.S., would depend on the size of the majority vote for independence, on the protection for minority rights that Quebec would be willing to extend, or whether there was widespread violence in Quebec as a result of a UDI, on the degree to which Quebec would be willing to assume its share of federal obligations — such as the national debt, and on the climate that prevailed at the time in the rest of Canada, i.e., either spitaful or a desire to salvage as much as possible — through negotiations for economic association and defense treaties.*

*The U.S. would have to work out a new basis for its relations with both Quebec and Canada. The North American situation would have changed from bilateral to trilateral with the possibility that in case of differences two would be aligned against one. Key areas of concern are defense, trade, investment, and transport, as well as the international role Canada and Quebec would play — including the question of NATO membership.*

*Much would depend on what kind of Quebec would emerge. The Quebecois feel that they must protect and assert their ethnic and cultural identity, but they also know that they need both Canada and the U.S. for their economic viability. Having established once and for all the supremacy of its French character in language and culture, Quebec might well become less xenephobic. This could permit the strong North American elements in Quebec society to be brought to bear on policy formulation.*

It can be expected that a realignment of political forces would take place in an independent Quebec, with the present split between federalists and separatists changing to a more normal left-right configuration. Ironical as it may seem, it is not at all sure that the PQ could survive as the leading party in any independent Quebec. Levesque and the PQ moderates would pursue Scandinavian-type social democratic policies. This would not satisfy many of the more radical-leftist PQ numbers who would probably bolt and form a new party. The PQ would also suffer losses of many of its present nationalist but conservative supporters, who would probably join a new right-of-center party composed of present Liberal Party and Union Nationale members.

The more advanced form of socialism or radical ideology that an independent Quebec Government would adopt, the more difficult it would be for the U.S. and Canada to deal with it. A Quebec that stayed out of NATO and North American defense, or pursued neutralist policies, would pose problems for the U.S. If it also, unlikely as it seems, would seek a special relationship with Russia or Cuba, U.S. security could be directly threatened.

Considering the apparent self-interest of Quebec, the basic conservative nature of much of the population, and the North American orientation that exists, it is likely than an independent Quebec would at least attempt to establish good relations with the U.S.

Although an independent Quebec would present new dimensions and likely problems of the U.S. — which it would be nice to be able to avoid — the likely impact that it would have on the rest of Canada is even more serious for the U.S.

The immediate aftermath of a Quebec UDI would probably be stormy and it might be difficult to avoid violence in Quebec. It would also be difficult for Ottawa and Quebec to negotiate or establish a new basis for relations in the acrimonious atmosphere that would prevail. This would be a difficult period for the U.S. as well, but also one where skillful efforts to ameliorate tensions could bring long-term benefits to the U.S.

The first flush of Quebec independence could bring about greater cohesion, at least temporarily, for the rest of Canada, and could result in an increase in anti-U.S. feelings as a means to preserve a separate Canadian identity deprived of the French peculiarity. Strong regional divergencies, the natural North-South pull, and the exposed situation for the maritime provinces would probably inexorably in time lead to one or more of the provinces or regions breaking away from Ontario/Ottawa domination. Once started, it is questionable whether the process could be stopped. Some of the provinces or regions would try it alone, some would seek some form of association with the U.S. The effect would be that the U.S. would be faced with either new responsibilities and/or opportunities, or a number of small and weak, although probably friendly, countries to the North.

F.    U.S. Preference

    The U.S. preference, as stated by the President, is a united Canada. This is clearly in our national interest, considering the importance of Canada to U.S. interests in defense, trade, investments, environmental questions, and world affairs. It is also understandable because we have developed a good system of managing our relations with the present Canada, a known quantity. We do not know what kind of neighbor an independent Quebec would be. We see a possibility that either an independent Quebec or the remaining Canada would become more anti-U.S. than is the case for Canada today. Quebec because of a shift in focus in defending its cultural identity against American rather than English Canadian encroachments, Canada without Quebec because of an increased need to emphasize a non-American identity, having lost its bicultural peculiarity. We would have to expect that both Quebec and Canada would try to involve us on their side, placing us squarely in the middle and in a no-win situation. We have serious doubts about whether the rest of Canada could stay united if Quebec separated, and see the alternatives of a smaller and weaker Canada or several mini-states to the North as less desirable than the present situation. The possibility that one or several Canadian provinces would seek to join the U.S. raises prospects that we have not contemplated. They could be negative or positive, but probably difficult to resolve.

    Nevertheless, the present situation also is not to our benefit. As long as the legitimate grievances and aspirations for safeguarding their ethnic identity are not resolved in a manner satisfactory to the francophone majority in Quebec, an unstable situation will continue that could result in damage to U.S. interests, increasing Canadian impotence, and even a resumption of terrorism and violence in Quebec.

    It is therefore in our interest that Canada resolve its internal problems. How this is done is of course primarily for the Canadians themselves to decide, but we have a legitimate interest in the result and must consider whether there is any positive policy in this regard that we can pursue.

    Our primary concern is the protection of over-all U.S. interests in Canada — including Quebec. A devolution of powers to Quebec only, particularly in cultural and social affairs — which have a human rights aspect, could well be less disruptive to U.S. interests than a general devolution of powers to all the provinces. At the present time English Canada does not support a Two-Nation approach, but this could change. It should also be kept in mind that Quebec does meet generally accepted criteria for national self-determination in the sense of ethnic distinctiveness in a clearly defined geographic area with an existing separate legal and governmental system. There is also no question regarding the basic long-term viability of an independent Quebec in the economic sense or in regards to its ability to be a responsible member of the family of nations. The unresolved and determing factor is and must be the will of the people of Quebec.

F.     <u>U.S. Policy During Transition</u>

*The U.S. Government policy for the next two years — a time frame that could be considered a transition period since no decisive action on Quebec is expected during it — should be based on the following positions:*

*1.  The President in February 1977 stated that:*

*a.  The U.S. considers the Quebec situation to be one for the Canadians themselves to resolve;*

*b.  The U.S. considers Canadians completely capable of resolving the question; and*

*c.  The U.S. prefers confederation.*

*2.  In public statements, U.S. Government representatives will not go beyond the position detailed in point 1.*

*3.  In private communication with the Government of Canada, the U.S. Government will reiterate its expressed willingness to consider ways we might be helpful on the Quebec question, if the Government of Canada should conclude the United States Government could play a useful role.*

*4.  U.S. Government representatives will conduct relations with Canadian provincial authorities, including those of Quebec, in the same manner as has been the practice heretofore.*

*At the same time, the U.S. Government will closely follow and analyze developments in Canada and Quebec on a continuing basis and will review its policy periodically as developments warrant.*

# Bibliography

## Books

Ball, George W. *The Discipline of Power—Essentials of a Modern World Structure*. Toronto: Bodley Head, 1968.

Bohlen, Charles E. *Witness to History*. New York: W.W. Norton & Co., 1973.

Bourgault, Pierre. *Écrits Polémiques 1960-1981; 1. La politique*. Montreal: VLB, 1982.

Bradlee, Benjamin B. *Conversations with Kennedy*. New York: W.W. Norton & Co., 1975.

Brimelow, Peter. *The Patriot Game—Canada and the Canadian Question Revisited*. Stanford: Hoover, 1986.

Brzezinski, Zbigniew. *Between Two Ages: America's Role in the Technocratic Era*. New York: Penguin, 1976.

Brzezinski, Zbigniew. *Power and Principle*. New York: Farrar Straus & Giroux, 1983.

Carter, Jimmy. *Public Papers of the President—Jimmy Carter, 1978*. Vol. 1. Washington, DC: USG Printing Office, 1979.

Clarkson, Stephen. *Canada and the Reagan Challenge: Crisis and Adjustment, 1981–85*. 2nd. ed. Toronto: Lorimer, 1985.

Collier, Peter, and Horowitz, David. *The Rockefellers—An American Dynasty*. New York: Henry Holt, 1976.

Daignault, Richard. *Lesage*. Montreal: Libre Expression, 1981.

Davis, John H. *The Bouviers—Portrait of an American Family*. New York: Farrar Straus & Giroux, 1969.

De Gaulle, Charles. *Discours et Messages*. Volume 3: *Avec le Renouveau, 1958–1962*. Paris: Plon, 1970.

DePorte, Anton W. *Europe Between The Superpowers: the Enduring Balance*. New Haven: Yale University Press, 1979.

Desbarats, Peter. *René, A Canadian in Search of a Country*. Toronto: McClelland, 1976.

Duchaîne, Jean-François. *Rapport sur les Événements d'octobre 1970*. Quebec City: Gouvernement du Québec, ministère de la Justice, 1981.

Faligot, Roger, and Krop, Pascal. *La Piscine—les services secrets français 1944-1984*. Paris: Seuil, 1985.

Ford, Robert A.D. *Our Man in Moscow—A diplomat's reflections on the Soviet Union*. Toronto: University of Toronto Press, 1989.

Fournier, Louis. *FLQ. Histoire d'un Mouvement Clandestin*. Montreal: Québec/Amérique, 1982.

Fournier, Louis, et al. *La police secrète au Québec—La tyrannie occulte de la police*. Montreal: Québec/Amérique, 1978.

Fraser, Graham. *P.Q.: René Lévesque and the Parti Québécois in Power.* Toronto: Macmillan, 1984.

Fraser, Graham. *Le Parti Québécois.* Montreal: Libre Expression, 1984.

Gillmor, Don. *I Swear by Apollo—Dr. Ewen Cameron and the CIA Brainwashing.* Toronto: McClelland, 1985.

Godin, Pierre. *Daniel Johnson.* Vol. 2.: Éditions de l'Homme, 1980.

Guertin, Pierre-Louis. *Et de Gaulle Vint ...* Montreal: Claude Langevin Éditeur, 1970.

Gwynn, Richard. *The 49th Paradox: Canada in North America.* Toronto, McClelland, 1985.

Gwynn, Richard. *The Northern Magus.* Toronto: McClelland, 1980.

Hero, Alfred O., Jr., and Balthazar, Louis. *Contemporary Quebec and the United States 1960-1986.* Cambridge University Press, 1988.

Horowitz, Irving Louis, et al. *The Rise and Fall of Project Camelot; Studies in the Relationship Between Social Science and Practical Politics.* Rev. ed. Cambridge: M.I.T. Press, 1974.

Johnson, Lady Bird. *A White House Diary.* New York: Holt Rinehart & Winston, 1970.

Kissinger, Henry. *White House Years.* Toronto: Little, 1979.

Lacouture, Jean. *De Gaulle.* Vol. 3: *Le souverain.* Paris: Seuil, 1986.

Lafond, Georges. "Hydro-Québec and the James Bay Project: The Financing Strategy." In Standbury, W.T., et al., *Financing Public Enterprises.* The Institute of Research and Policy, c. 1982.

Latouche, Daniel. "Quebec: One possible scenario." In Baker Fox, Annette, et al., *Canada and the United States: Transnational and Transgovernmental Relations.* New York: Columbia University Press, 1976.

Lavallée, Marc. *Adieu la France, Salut l'Amérique.* Montreal: Stanké, 1982.

Lee, Bruce. *Boys Life of John F. Kennedy.* New York: Bold Face Books, Memorial Edition, 1964.

Lescop, Renée. *Le Pari québécois du Général de Gaulle.* Montreal: Boréal Express, 1981.

Lévesque, René. *La Passion du Québec.* Montreal: Québec/Amérique, 1978.

Lévesque, René. *Attendez que je me rappelle ...* Montreal: Québec/Amérique, 1986.

Littleton, James. *Target Nation.* Toronto: Lester Orpen Dennys, 1986.

Lubin, Martin. "Quebec Non-Francophones and the United States." In Hero, Alfred, and Daneau, Marcel, *Problems and Opportunities in U.S.-Quebec Relations,* pp. 185-217. Boulder, CO: Westview, 1984.

Mallen, Pierre Louis. *Vivre le Québec Libre.* Paris: Plon, 1978.

Martin, Lawrence. *The Presidents and The Prime Ministers.* Toronto: Doubleday, 1982.

Martin, Paul. *A Very Public Life.* Vol. 2, *So Many Worlds.* Ottawa: Deneau, 1985.

McDonald, Donald C., et al. *Commission of Inquiry Concerning Certain Activities of the Royal Canadian Mounted Police.* Second Report, Vol. 1. Ottawa: Government of Canada, 1981.

Menthon, Pierre de. *Je Témoigne: Québec 1967, Chili 1973.* Paris: Cerf, 1979.

Michal, Bernard. *Le Destin Dramatique des Kennedy.* Geneva: Éditions de Crémille, 1972.

Morin, Claude. *L'Art de l'Impossible—la diplomatie québécoise depuis 1960.* Montreal: Boréal, 1987.

Newman, Peter C. *The Canadian Establishment.* Toronto: McClelland, 1975.

Nixon, Richard. *Public Papers of the President.* Washington, DC: USG Printing Office.

Patry, André. *Le Québec Dans le Monde.* Montreal: Leméac, 1980.

Pearson, Lester B. *Mike: the Memoirs of the Right Honorable Lester B. Pearson.* Vol. 3. Toronto: University of Toronto Press, 1975.

Pelletier, Gérard. *Les Années d'Impatience (1950-1960).* Montreal: Stanké, 1983.

Provencher, Jean. *René Lévesque, portrait d'un Québécois.* Montreal: Éditions La Presse, 1974.

Ranelagh, John. *The Agency—The Rise and Fall of the CIA.* New York: Simon and Schuster, 1986.

Rostow, Walt W. *The Diffusion of Power; an Essay in Recent History.* New York: Macmillan, 1972.

Rouannet, Anne, and Rouannet, Pierre. *Les Trois Derniers Chagrins du Général de Gaulle.* Paris: Grasset, 1980.

Safire, William. *Before the Fall.* New York: Doubleday, 1975.

Safire, William. *Full Disclosure.* New York: Ballantine Books, 1977.

Sawatsky, John. *For Services Rendered.* Toronto: Penguin, 1986.

Sawatsky, John. *Men in the Shadows—The RCMP Security Service.* Toronto: Doubleday, 1980.

Scully, Robert Guy, et al. *Morceaux du Grand Montréal.* Saint-Lambert: Noroit, 1978.

Sheppard, Robert Guy, and Valpy, Michael. *The National Deal — The Fight for a Canadian Constitution.* Toronto: Macmillan, 1982.

Simard, Francis. *Pour en finir avec octobre.* Montreal: Stanké, 1982.

Sorenson, Ted. *Kennedy.* New York: Harper and Row, 1965.

Stursberg, Peter. *Lester Pearson and the American Dilemma.* Toronto: Doubleday, 1980.

Thomson, Dale C. *Jean Lesage et la Révolution Tranquille.* Saint-Laurent: Éditions du Trécarré, 1984.

Thomson, Dale C. *Vive le Québec Libre.* Toronto: Deneau, 1988.

Thyraud de Vosjoli, P.L. *Lamia.* Toronto: Little, Brown and Co., 1970.

Vallières, Pierre. *L'Exécution de Pierre Laporte.* Montreal: Québec/Amérique, 1977.

Vallières, Pierre. *Un Québec Impossible.* Montreal: Québec/Amérique, 1977.

Vastel, Michel. *Trudeau, le Québécois.* Montreal: Éditions de l'Homme, 1989.

Wade, Mason. *Les Canadiens Français—de 1760 à nos jours.* Volume 2. Ottawa: Le Cercle du Livre de France, 1963.

Wolton, Thierry. *Le KGB en France.* Paris: Grasset, 1986.

# Articles

Alper, Donald. "Congressional attitudes toward Canada and Canada-United States relations." *American Review of Canadian Studies*, Vol. 10, No. 2 (Autumn 1980): 26-36.

Baker, Stephen. "How America Sees Québec." *International Perspectives* (Feb. 1983): 13-17.

Bissonette, Lise. "Quebec-Ottawa-Washington, the pre-referendum triangle." *The American Review of Canadian Studies*, Vol. 11, No. 1 (Spring 1981): 64-76.

Brimelow, Peter. "No Castro of the North?" *Barron's* (June 7, 1982).

Bronfman, Edgar M. "Cool it, Canada!" *Newsweek* (Sept. 26, 1977): 11.

Brouillet, Gilles. "Le Bilan de Georges Lafond, Financier." *Hydro-Presse* (mid-Sept., 1986): 7-9.

Byers, R.B., and Leyton-Brown, David. "The Strategic and Economic Implications for the United States of a Sovereign Quebec." *Canadian Public Policy/Analyse de Politiques* (Spring 1980): 325-341.

Clark, Gerald. "Levesque and the U.S.—MISSION IMPOSSIBLE." *The Montreal Star* (Feb. 12-15, 1979). Series of four articles.

Faribault, Marcel. "Can French Canada Stand Alone?" *The Atlantic Monthly* (Oct. 1964): 135-139.

Furgurson, Ernest B. "Ambassador Helms." *Common Cause*, Vol. 13, No. 2 (March 1987): 16-21.

Griffith, William E. "Quebec in Revolt." *Foreign Affairs* (Oct. 1964): 29-36.

Horowitz, Irving Louis. "The Life and Death of Project Camelot." *Trans-Action*, Vol. 3, No. 1 (Nov./Dec. 1965): 3-47.

Hutchison, Bruce. "Canada's Time of Troubles." *Foreign Affairs* (Oct. 1977): 175-189.

Jockel, Joseph T. "Un Québec Souverain et la Défense de l'Amérique du Nord Contre une Attaque Nucléaire." *Études Internationales*, Vol. 11, No. 2 (June 1980): 303-316.

Lentner, Howard H. "Canadian separatism and its implications for the United States." *Orbis, a Journal of World Affairs* (Summer 1978): 375-393.

Lévesque, René. "For an Independent Quebec." *Foreign Affairs*, Vol. 54, No. 4 (July 1976): 734-744.

Levine, Marc E. "Institution Design and the Separatist Impulse: Quebec and the Antebellum American South." *The Annals of the American Academy of Political and Social Science* (Sept. 1977): 60-72.

Long, Tania. "Quebec's Rising Nationalism a Problem in Canada." *The New York Times* (Feb. 24, 1964): 1.

Macadam, Bill, and Dubro, James. "How the CIA has us spooked." *Maclean's* (July 1974): 20-46.

Manor, F.S. "Canada's Crisis: The Causes" and Stethem, Nicholas. "The Dangers." *Foreign Policy*, No. 29 (Winter 1977-1978): 43-57.

Mayer, Herbert. "Business has the jitters in Québec." *Fortune* (Oct. 1977): 238-244.

Moore, Jacqueline. "The Case For an Independent Quebec." *Harpers* (Oct. 1964): 93-100.

Morin, Claude. "Morin: Quebec's Foreign Policy." *The Fletcher Forum*. Vol. 4, No. 1 (Winter 1980): 127-134.

Morin, Claude. *Études Internationales*. Vol. 20, No. 1 (March 1989): 236.

Pelletier, Gérard. "The Trouble with Quebec." *The Atlantic Monthly* (Oct. 1964): 115-117.

Richler, Mordecai. "Oh! Canada! Lament for a Divided Country." *The Atlantic Monthly* (Dec. 1977): 41-45.

Scully, Robert Guy. "What It Means to be French in Canada." *The Washington Post* (April 17, 1977): C1-C4.

Thomas, David. "The Winning of the World." *Maclean's* (May 15, 1978).

Trudeau, Pierre Elliott. "Pearson ou l'Abdication de l'Esprit." *Cité Libre* (April 1963): 7-12.

Wisse, Ruth R., and Cotler, Irwin. "Quebec's Jews: Caught in the Middle." *Commentary*, Vol. 64, No. 5 (Sept. 1977): 55-69.

Wolfe, Morris. "The other side of Bill 101—Read this before you believe the worst." *Saturday Night* (Jan.-Feb. 1979): 17-27.

Zink, Lubor J. "The Unpenetrated Problem of Pierre Trudeau." *National Review* (June 25, 1982): 751-756.

## Texts and Documents

Lévesque, René, et al. *René Lévesque à L'Economic Club*. Montreal: Éditions La Presse, c. Jan. 1977.

Provencher, Roger. *Québec Separatism: A Geopolitical Problem*. Washington: National War College, March 1970.

Sepenuk, Norman. *A Profile of Franco-American Political Attitudes in New England*. Cambridge: John F. Kennedy School of Government, Harvard University, c. 1968.

Wainstein, Eleanor S. *The Cross and Laporte Kidnappings, Montreal, October 1970*. A report prepared for the Department of State and Defense Advanced Research Projects Agency. Rand, 1977.

Waters, Ed., et al. *Hydro-Québec*. New York: Kidder, Peabody & Co., March 1977.

## Public Archives

Franklin D. Roosevelt Library, Hyde Park, NY.

John F. Kennedy Library, Boston, MA.

Lyndon B. Johnson Library, Austin, TX.

Nixon Project, Alexandria, VA.

Jimmy Carter Library, Atlanta, GA.

George Aiken Papers, University of Vermont in Burlington.

Washington University Archives, Washington.
National Archives of Canada, Ottawa.
Archives de l'Université de Montréal.
Library of Congress, Washington, DC.

## Personal Archives

Larry Black, New York.
Mrs Richard Hawkins, Washington.
Claude Malette, Montreal.
Lawrence Martin, Ottawa.
Mrs Doris Topping, Washington.
Theodore Valance, Penn State University.
André Patry, Montreal.

## Government Sources

Central Intelligence Agency, Langley, VA.
Defense Intelligence Agency, Washington, DC.
Department of Defense, Washington, DC.
Department of External Affairs, Ottawa.
Federal Bureau of Investigation, Washington, DC.
Ministère des Affaires internationales, Quebec City.
National Security Agency, Fort Meade, MD.
State Department, Washington, DC.
US Army Corps of Engineers, New York.

# Notes and References

*Nota Bene*:
Every source cited in this work is itemized below in the order of its appearance in the text. Key words at the start of a note allow the reader to link the text with the source or explanatory note. The keys can be found on the pages indicated in the margins. Since this narrative is based on a mass of documentation unavailable to researchers until now, it seemed preferable to err on the side of excess rather than inadequacy with regards to identifying sources.

American diplomatic documents quoted without a source reference were obtained from the State Department, which—after some pressure and legal action—declassified them in conformity with the American Freedom of Information Act (FOIA).

Documents declassified according to a similar procedure by the Canadian Department of External Affairs are identified by the notation EA. Those from Quebec's Ministère des Affaires Internationales use the notation MAIQ.

Documents issued from presidential archives, both public and private, are identified as such. French documents without any source indicated were obtained from individuals demanding anonymity.

The level of classification of each document is also indicated to give an idea of the State Department's thoughts on the quality and confidentiality of the information. The levels are as follows: UNCLASSIFIED, CONFIDENTIAL, LIMITED OFFICIAL USE (with two variants: NO FOREIGN DISSEM, and CONTROLLED DISSEM), SECRET, TOP SECRET.

The Canadian and Quebec authorities use these terms less rigorously, but levels of classification are noted whenever they appear on Canadian documents.

American diplomatic dispatches are grouped under two main headings: "Telegram," an often coded dispatch sent by telex; and "Airgram," a less urgent dispatch sent by diplomatic courier. In addition, many internal "memos," "notes" and "memoranda" of the American, Canadian and Quebec governments are quoted.

Oral sources are also indicated (excepting the few who wished to remain anonymous) on their first appearance in the text, along with the place and date of the interview, and the notation "tel." in reference to exchanges over the telephone. The word "Washington" has been abbreviated to "Wash." All dates are presented in the following order: day/month/year.

Any words underlined in the quotations were emphasized in the original texts. Additions to the quotations are signaled by brackets, "[ ]."

Chapter 1. Réne Lévesque and the Heart-Broken Lovers

1     [**Epigraph**] From René Lévesque, *Attendez que je me rappelle* ... Montréal, Québec/Amérique, 1986, p. 166.

1     [**Topping**] In a letter from John Topping to Rufus Smith, 31/5/72, CONFIDENTIAL.

2     [**CIA behind the scenes**] In Lévesque, op. cit., p. 485.

2     [**FLQ**] Pierre Vallières, former theoretician for the FLQ, wrote a book to defend this thesis: *Un Québec impossible*, Montréal, Québec/Amérique, p. 60-61.

2     [**Castonguay**] In an interview with *Le Devoir* on 20/11/73, quoted in Quebec Airgram A-40, *Criticism and Self-Criticism of the PQ*, 28/11/73, UNCLASSIFIED.

2     [**Joron**] Guy Joron, open letter to the author of *Un Québec impossible*: "You cannot change your model of development and scale of values as easily as you'd change your shirt." *Le Devoir* 12/12/77.

3     [**Lieutenant Lévesque**] From Jean Provencher, *René Lévesque, portrait d'un Québécois*, Montreal, Editions La Presse, 1974, p. 49-53.

4     [**Return from the war and FDR**] From Lévesque, op. cit., p. 163-167.

4     [**Empires**] From René Lévesque, *La Passion du Québec*, Montreal, Québec/Amérique, 1978, p. 202-203.

4     [**FDR**] Letters from King to FDR, 4/5/42 and 1/8/42; letter from Moffat to FDR, 26/8/42; letter from FDR to King 18/5/42; Franklin D. Roosevelt Library. These documents were first quoted by Lawrence Martin in his book, *The Presidents and the Prime Ministers*, Toronto, Doubleday, 1982.

6     [**Lavigne**] From Morris Wolfe, "The Other Side of Bill 101: Read This Before You Believe the Worst," *Saturday Night*, Jan./Feb. 1979, p. 17-27. At the time, Lavigne was vice president of the Office de la langue française.

6     [**Rostow**] Eugene Rostow, tel. interview, Wash., 7/2/89.

7     [**Grosvenor**] From *National Geographic Magazine*, 4/77.

7     [**Academy**] Marc E. Levine, "Institution, Design and the Separatist Impulse: Quebec and the Antebellum American South," *The Annals of the American Academy of Political and Social Science*, 9/77, p. 60-72. Another article compared ethnic violence on a country-to-country basis. Quebec had an average of .01 deaths per million citizens, the American black movement had .2 per million, Northern Ireland had 34.4 per million and—a record by any standards—the Arab minority in Zanzibar had 15,273 per million.

7     [**Balthazar**] From *Le Devoir*, 7/5/74.

7     [**Morin**] From *The New York Times*, 25/9/77.

7     [**Beaudoin**] Interview, Montreal, 1/6/89.

8     [**Clark**] From *The Montreal Star*, 13/2/79.

8     [**Desbarats**] From Peter Desbarats, *René: A Canadian in Search of a Country*, Toronto, McClelland, 1976, p. 214 and 221.

8     [**Curtis**] Tel. interview, Maine, 9/7/89.

8     [**Dispatches**] Louise Armstrong, interview, Wash., 2/3/89.

8     [**To delay independence**] From *The New York Times*, 25/1/79.


Chapter 2. The Irishman and the Franco-American

12     [**O'Neill**] "Tip" O'Neill was a colorful personality who dominated Democratic politics in the House of Representatives for the greater part of the 1970s and 1980s. Of Irish stock, he took over John F. Kennedy's old seat and was replaced in 1988 by Joseph Kennedy, Jr. The quotation, which has become part of American political vocabulary, signifies that to understand the real motives behind a politician's actions, you must study his local grassroots support.

12   [**Parker House: Morissette**] Unless otherwise indicated, anecdotes about Morissette derive from two interviews with the author, tel. Lowell 13/2/89, and Lowell 24/5/89.

12   [**De Gaulle's correspondence**] As reported by Morissette's former secretary, Abbot Richard Santerre. Tel. interview Dracut, Mass., 22/2/89.

13   [**very articulate**] A political rival, Richard Donohue, tel. interview Lowell, 16/2/89.

13   [**JFK Ottawa**] In *Journal des débats*, 18/5/61, Kennedy Archives, POF Box 103.

13   [**JFK in Paris**] From Bruce Lee, *Boy's Life of John F.Kennedy*, New York, Bold Face Books, Memorial Edition 1964, p. 63.

14   [**Wade, Laurentie and King**] From Mason Wade, *Les Canadiens français de 1760 a nos jours*, tome II, Ottawa, le Cercle du Livre de France, 1963, p. 341.

14   [**JFK at Mont Tremblant**] In a speech in 1952 designed for Franco American voters, Rose Kennedy stated, "Each year my children go skiing at Mont Tremblant" and "there is no longer time for Jack to ... go skiing in Canada." But in a speech delivered in December 1953 at the University of Montreal, JFK said, "This is my first journey to Canada." (JFK Library, Boston, Pre-Presidential Papers, Box 108, "French File")

14   [**Aiken**] The late George Aiken, who directed the Canadian-American Interparliamentary Committee for 20 years, told this story to William Armstrong, an American diplomat with extensive experience in Canadian affairs. According to Armstrong's version, Aiken was governor of Vermont when he met the premier (thus it was before June 1941) and during the war (so it was not earlier than 1939). This period corresponds to Liberal premier Adélard Godbout's term of office. He had ousted Maurice Duplessis for a short interval of four years. But Aiken's archives at the University of Vermont in Burlington mention only a "pilgrimage to Montreal" as evidence that he visited Quebec during this time. Governor Aiken's attendance at a "goodwill banquet" in Coaticook in June 1938 seems a more likely site for his meeting with the Quebec premier. This would mean his interlocutor was Maurice Duplessis. The quotation sounds more like him, at any rate, than like Godbout. When he said "during the war," Aiken was probably speaking loosely about the historical period.

14   [**JFK at Lowell**] Lowell's *L'Etoile*, 28/2/52.

14   [**Duplessis-Charbonneau**] Quoted by Dale C. Thomson, *Jean Lesage et la Révolution tranquille*, Saint-Laurent, Edition du Trécarré, 1984, p. 29.

14   [**JFK and Charbonneau**] Like Morissette, Frederick Holborn, Kennedy's advisor before and during the presidency, remembers JFK bringing up the Charbonneau affair. Tel. interview, Wash., 15/2/89.

15   [**Political situation in Mass.**] Larry O'Brien, organizer and later advisor under JFK, tel. interview, NY, 2/89.

15   [**Lodge-Kennedy Dynasty**] From Bernard Michal, *Le Destin dramatique des Kennedy*, Genève, Edition de Crémille, 1972, p. 92.

15   [**Donohue**] Interview, supra.

16   [**The Irish vs. the Franco-Americans**] Norman Sepenuk, *A Profile of Franco-American Political Attitudes in New England*, Cambridge, John F. Kennedy School of Government, Harvard University, circa 1968, p. 4.

16   [**Eunice and Wilfrid**] Tel interview. Josette Beaulieu, Wilfrid's daughter, Gulfport, Miss., 2/89.

17   [**Campaign memo 1952**] "List of Issues Which Affect Nationality Groups In The United States," undated, memo of Pauline B. 8/9/52, handwritten note by JFK with circumflex accents and the rough draft of Rose's speech, JFK Library, Box 108, supra.

17   [**JFK speaking French**] Quoted by Benjamin B. Bradlee, *Conversations with Kennedy*, New York, WW Norton and Co, 1975, p. 95.

17   [**Lodge in *Le Monde***] *Le Monde*, 11/7/52.

18   [**Jackie**] From John H. Davis, *The Bouviers - Portrait of an American Family*, New York, Farrar Straus and Giroux, 1969, p. 305-315.

18    [A "légion d'honneur" for Joe] From P.L. Thyraud de Vosjoli, *Lamia*, Toronto, Little, Brown and Co, 1970, p. 223-225.

18    [JFK in Montreal] At the ball, *La Presse*, 5/12/53, p. 29; at University of Montreal, *The Gazette*, 5/12/53, p. 21 and JFK Library supra; at the university, Jean Houpert and three other witnesses, tel. interviews, Montreal, 5/89.

20    [Faribault] Mason Wade (op.cit.) remarks that at the time, the University of Montreal was a beacon for ultranationalism. Faribault certainly does not fall into this category, but ten years later, in a respected American monthly, he denounced the injustices heaped upon the Québécois people. Marcel Faribault, "Can French Canada Stand Alone?" *The Atlantic Monthly*, 10/64, p. 135-139.

20    [Cardinal Léger] Salinger's letter of 6/3/61, JFK Library, WHCF Box 970. Salinger was not with JFK in 1953 and could not speak first-hand about the visit. The surviving files of the young senator only contain one document — the speech — concerning the visit in 1953. Salinger's letter, with its abundant expressions of courtesy, was probably dictated.

20    [JFK, Vietnam and Algeria] From Ted Sorenson, *Kennedy*, New York, Harper and Row, 1965, p. 65-66, and with Holborn, interview supra.

20    [Morissette in Washington] Morissette was occasionally called to Washington in his capacity as chaplain for French sailors stopping over in America, an honorary position he had enjoyed since the war. A secretary who wishes to remain anonymous and who accompanied Kennedy from Boston to Washington confirms Morissette's visits (tel. interview). Maurice Chateauneuf, one of Morissette's friends, also witnessed the two men conversing in Boston around 1959 or 1960 (tel. interview, Lowell, 22/12/89). They also corresponded over administrative matters, with Morissette asking the senator to intercede on behalf of a request from one of his parishioners. Santerre, interview, supra.

20    [Bohlen] From the rough draft of his book, *Witness to History*, Charles Bohlen Archives, Library of Congress, Washington, Container 12, p. 14.

20    [JFK Ireland] Bradlee, op.cit. p. 190; 1951 speech, JFK Library, Boston, Pre-Presidential Papers, Box 108, "Irish File."

22    [Arguin-Girard] Gérard Arguin used the pseudonym Roland Girard to cloak opinions that were often too abrasive for both secular and non-secular authorities of the period. Quotations from *Le Travailleur*, 11/7/57 and 18/8/60. Tipoff about the pseudonym: interview with Josette Beaulieu, supra; Roger Lacerte, who bought the newspaper printer, tel. interview, Manchester, N.H., 2/89, and Mme Gérard Arguin, tel. interview, Joliette, 2/89.

22    [Hardy] Jeanne Hardy, tel. interview, Lowell, 2/89.

22    [Santerre] Interview, supra.

23    [JFK foreign policy] Sorensen, op. cit., p. 538 et ss.

23    [Angolans at the White House] Ted Sorenson, correspondence with the author, 17/7/89, and Holborn, interview, supra.

23    [Bradlee and Cheysson] From Bradlee, op. cit., p. 97-99.

24    [De Gaulle] Message in Sorensen, op. cit., p. 231; "Bastard de Gaulle," experts on France and dinner with Malraux in Bradlee, op. cit., p. 104, 82-83 and 95; "trying to screw us" in Walt W. Rostow, *The Diffusion of Power;an Essay in Recent History*, New York, Macmillan, 1972, p. 367, and to the author, infra. Rostow was special assistant to the president in foreign affairs. For a more general discussion of de Gaulle and the United States, see chapter 4.

24    [JFK and Dief] From Lawrence Martin, *The Presidents and the Prime Ministers*, Toronto, Doubleday, 1982, chap. 12.

24    [JFK and Hirsh] JFK Library, Oral History of Jacqueline Hirsh, p. 13-18.

24    [S.O.B. and Canada] Quotation from Ted Sorensen, op.cit., p. 575.

24    [Scope Paper, memo] JFK Library, POF Canada, Rusk's Memo, dated 20/2/61 and classified as SECRET, was entitled "Memorandum for Meeting with Prime Minister Diefenbaker: Status and Atmosphere of US-Canadian Relations."

25    [**Québécois and Mulroney**] Letters from Quebeckers and letter from Mulroney to O'Brien dated 20/7/62. The manual was late. Mulroney sent a telegram on 17/8/62, and it was finally mailed to him 24/8/62. JFK Library, WHCF Box 43.

25    [**Trudeau**] From Pierre Elliott Trudeau, "Pearson ou l'abdication de l'esprit" ("Pearson's Mental Abdication"), *Cité Libre*, Montreal, April 1963, p. 9-10, p. 7-12. While Kennedy's desire to intervene in the campaign is common knowledge, his actual intervention is a subject of debate. In addition to the Bomarc affair, Kennedy was outraged at how long it took Diefenbaker to put the Canadian Armed Forces on alert during the Cuban Missile Crisis. Besides Norstad's visit and the State Department's communiqué, there are also rumors of a call made by Kennedy to Pearson, via an intermediary, offering to help him out with, for example, a public statement. "For God's sake, tell the President not to say anything," Pearson told one of his advisors. "I don't want help from him. This would be awful." The Liberal leader feared a boomerang effect. Kennedy's pollster and friend, Lou Harris, was hired by the Liberals during their campaign. The weekly magazine, *Newsweek*, considered by many to be an organ of the Kennedy fan club, was directed by Kennedy's buddy, Ben Bradlee. During the campaign he published an unflattering cover photo of Diefenbaker, which made him look slightly crazy. *Newsweek* was distributed widely across Canada. See Peter Strusberg, *Lester Pearson and the American Dilemma*, Toronto, Doubleday, 1980, p. 182-187.

25    [**Bundy**] Memo from Bundy to Lyndon Johnson, 1/5/64, quoted in Lawrence Martin, op. cit., intro.

26    [**Elections, Caouette**] Armstrong, interview, supra, and Memo for McGeorge Bundy, 5/4/63, entitled "Canadian Election Assessment," JFK Library, POF Box 113. Creditiste theory and quotation in Thomson, op. cit., p. 180. Quotation of a Social Credit farmer, Rodolphe "le cerf" Cloutier to the author, Weedon, circa 1965.

26    [**Wade, Churchill, Fisher**] From Wade, op. cit., p. 551-552.

26    [**Ireland and diversity**] From Sorensen, op.cit., p. 582.

27    [**CIA**] CIA official (1960-1968) to the author. He wished to remain anonymous.

27    [**Barbeau**] Raymond Barbeau, tel. interviews,Wash.-Montreal, 7 and 14/2/89, and Montreal 31/5/89. Quotations taken from *The Gazette*, 26 and 28/2/63, and from the *Montreal Star*,26/2/63. Strangely enough, neither *La Presse* nor *Le Devoir* picked up on the story. Canadian Press (CP) said they went to the source. In a paragraph published on 28/2/63 in *The Gazette*, an unnamed spokesperson for the White House called Barbeau's statements "ridiculous." The President "holds no such views;" it was "nonsense." The fact that a head of state's private opinions contradicted his public policy comes as no surprise. US reactions reported by CP make sense — the United States had nothing to gain by meddling in a question which, as de Gaulle put it, "was not yet ripe." But the archives of the Kennedy presidency and of his communications service contain no mention of an exchange between a CP reporter and a White House spokesperson. Neither Pierre Salinger nor Mac Kilduff, the two press attachés responsible for answering questions on foreign affairs in 1963, have any memory of such an query. It would have been especially surprising as Canadian-American relations were so strained at the time. The standard procedure for unexpected questions was to channel them to an advisor on foreign matters. Not one of the President's advisors of the time remembers having been asked about the Quebec question. If the question was asked, it was answered by some bureaucratic underling improvising to impress the journalist. JFK Library, and Pierre Salinger, interview, London, 17/2/89, Malcolm (Mac) Kilduff, interview, Kentucky, 17/2/89. Kennedy advisors: Sorensen's correspondence and interview with O'Brien, supra; McGeorge Bundy, tel. interview, New York, 2/89; Walt W. Rostow, special assistant to the President, tel.interview, Austin Tex., 13/4/89 and 24/4/89.

27    [**Holborn**] Interview, supra.

27    [**Cline**] Ray Cline, interview, Washington, 27/3/89. CIA official who requested anonymity.

28    [**Salinger, Bundy, Donohue**] Interview, supra.

28    [**Rusk and JFK**] Dean Rusk, tel. interview, Athens, Ga., 24/4/89. Hyannis Port is the coastal town in Cape Cod where the Kennedy family has a residence. West Palm Beach, Florida, is where JFK took his winter vacations. The Rose Garden is the garden outside the Oval Office where the president strolls, often in the company of distinguished guests. As for touch football, it was the Kennedy brothers' favorite, often roughly practiced, sport.

28    [**Sorensen**] Correspondence, supra.

28    [**O'Brien**] Interview, supra.
      The offices of Senator Edward Kennedy in Washington, and of Mrs Jacqueline Bouvier Kennedy Onassis in New York neither acknowledged the author's letters, nor returned his phone calls.
      **Ted Kennedy's** cameo appearances in this story will be dealt with in later chapters. However, a story told by Pierre Bourgault, then leader of the Rassemblement pour l'Independance Nationale, should be reported here. During a tour in France in the Fall of 1967, Bougault met with Pierre Salinger. According to Bourgault, Salinger promised to arrange a meeting between him and Robert Kennedy, "probably in the next few months." Bobby Kennedy's death in June of 1968, as he was campaigning to become democratic candidate for the presidency, would not let this happen, writes Bourgault. Pierre Trudeau, participating in a politcal rally in the Northern Quebec town of Rouyn shortly after the assassination, used the event against the separatists: "Like the assassins of Robert Kennedy, you are bearers of hatred." Pierre Bourgault, *Écrits Polémiques 1960-1981; 1. La politique*, p. 147.


Chapter 3. The Americans Discover Quebec


29    [**NIE**] JFK Library, POF Canada; NIE classified as SECRET/NOFORN (as in not for foreigners) is in POF box 113.

30    [**Martin**] Paul Martin, tel. interview, Windsor, 6/6/89.

30    [**Diplomat in Montreal**] Wished to remain anonymous, to the author.

30    [**Nationalization**] Willis C. Armstrong, interviews, Wash., 2/3/89, 8/3/89, and 16/7/89.

30    [**Dextraze**] Letter from Courtenaye to the embassy, 31/5/63, CONFIDENTIAL.

30    [**Armstrong**] Willis Armstrong, interview, supra. His feelings on the subjection of French Québécois were shared by a dozen or so diplomats interviewed by the author. Pierrepont Moffat, letter of 26/8/42, Roosevelt Library.

31    [**Butterworth**] His prejudices, reported by a diplomat who wished to remain anonymous. Quotations taken from Airgram Ottawa A-474, 24/10/67, CONFIDENTIAL.

32    [**LBJ Embassy**] Charles Ritchie and Basil Robinson, tel. interviews, Ottawa, 5/6/89. Extract from Lady Bird's journal in *Lady Bird Johnson: A White House Diary*, New York, Holt Rinehart & Winston, 1970, p. 59. Her explanation as to who among the Pearsons and the Johnsons first raised the issue, a letter from her assistant to the author, 18/4/89.

33    [**Autumn 1964**] Tania Long, "Quebec's Rising Nationalism a Problem in Canada," *The New York Times*, 24/2/64, p. 1; Jacqueline Moore, "The Case for an Independent Quebec," *Harper's*, 10/64, p. 93-100; William E. Griffith, "Quebec in Revolt," *Foreign Affairs*, 10/64, p. 29-36; Gérard Pelletier, "The Trouble With Quebec" and Marcel Faribault, "Can French Canada Stand Alone?" *The Atlantic Monthly*, 10/64, p. 115-117 and p. 135-139.

33    [**Patry in Washington**] This anecdote is taken primarily from Patry's report to Lesage entitled "Statut de la Délégation du Québec a New York" ("Status of the Quebec Delegation in New York"), 15/4/65, CONFIDENTIAL, from Patry's personal archives. The memo from Lesage to Morin also comes from these archives. The information was completed by tel. interview between Patry and the author, Montreal,12/6/89, and by his article, "La politique américaine du Québec" ("Quebec's American Policy") published in *Le Devoir*,14/12/76, p. 4. Butterworth's admonition to Lesage was quoted by the consul general in Quebec City,

Francis Cunningham, in Airgram Quebec A-176, 6/6/67, CONFIDENTIAL.

34    **[Europe]** Quoted in Lacouture, op. cit., p. 337.

35    **[Anglo Saxon federation]** From George W. Ball, *The Discipline of Power: Essentials of a Modern World Structure*, Toronto, Bodley Head, 1968, p. 110-117. Criticism of John Leddy, tel. interview, Wash., 17/5/89.

36    **[Daniel Johnson in Washington]** Thoughts on his ideology from Francis Cunningham, CONFIDENTIAL letter, 15/12/66, giving a political summary of the year in Quebec. George Springsteen, interview, Wash., 14/4/89, and Rufus Smith, Wash., 6 and 13/2/89. Also Francis T. Cunningham, tel. interview, Lincoln, Nebr., 12/3/89. Interviews Patry, supra, and Morin, infra.

37    **[LBJ memo]** On the memo from Rostow to LBJ, 3/5/67, TR CO43, LBJ Library, in Lawrence Martin's personal archives (hereinafter ALM).

37    **[Rostow and Smith]** Rufus Smith, interview, supra.

37    **[LBJ and the Middle East]** From Lyndon B. Johnson,*Vantage Point*, New York, Holt, 1971, p. 288-293.

38    **[Smith and Ritchie]** From Lawrence Martin, *The Presidents and the Prime Ministers*, Toronto, Doubleday, 1982, p. 233-234.

38    **[Provencher]** Roger Provencher, interview, Wash., 14/3/89.

38    **[Christien]** George Christien, interview, Austin, Tex., 8/89. Official, anonymously to the author. Rusk, interview, supra.

39    **[Kiselyak]** Rufus Smith, interview, supra.

39    **[Drape-O and LBJ]** Memo from James Jones (presidential advisor), 12/9/68, and from Joe Califano to LBJ 9/11/68, and letter from LBJ to Séguin 27/11/63, LBJ Library, ALM.

39    **[LBJ and Quebec]** Paul Martin, Rostow, interviews, supra.

Chapter 4. The Insufferable de Gaulle

40    **[Star]** *Washington Evening Star*, 25/7/67. During the 1960s, the *Star* was the biggest daily in the American capital. It was only supplanted by the *Washington Post* in the following decade.

40    **[Martin]** From Dale C. Thomson, *Vive le Québec Libre*, Toronto, Deneau, 1988, p. 209. The documentation and witness reports collected over the past 20 years (notably by Anne and Pierre Rouannet in *Les Trois derniers Chagrins du général de Gaulle* (Paris, Grasset, 1980), classified by Renée Lescop in *Le Pari québécois du général de Gaulle* (Montreal, Boréal Express, 1981), and by Jean Lacouture in *De Gaulle*, (vol.3,"Le souverain," chap. 19, Paris,Seuil,1986), should silence all those who thought *"Vive le Québec libre"* was simply a slip of the tongue. Thomson's book drives this point home in a definitive manner, puts forward new evidence and gives a thorough summary of de Gaulle's actions in Quebec, from the perspectives of Ottawa, Paris and Quebec. He also explains how badly Paul Martin and Lester Pearson wanted to give de Gaulle the benefit of the doubt. Marcel Cadieux, under-secretary at External Affairs, and Pierre Trudeau, elected in 1965, were more astute and refused to be reassured. Allan Gotlieb, Cadieux's assistant during this period, confirms this version of the facts and adds that English-speaking diplomats and officials in his ministry were the most hesitant to criticize Quebec's flirtation with Paris before *"Vive le Québec libre."* (hereafter, VLQL). They regarded the presence of a new international personality in Quebec as a good thing, a refreshing opening in a province that had always been too wrapped up in itself. Marcel Cadieux and Pierre Trudeau understood a little better the danger this Paris-Quebec waltz posed for Canada. Gotlieb, interview, Cambridge, 25/5/89, and tel. interview, Toronto, 13/7/89. According to Thomson, VLQL left Martin speechless, and outraged Pearson. He quotes Jean Marchand regarding Pearson's angry reaction. But Lacouture (op. cit., p. 125) quotes minister

Maurice Sauvé, who reports having spoken with a "phlegmatic" Pearson after VLQL. According to Sauvé, the Prime Minister didn't even plan to call an emergency cabinet meeting. It was Trudeau and Marchand who "mobilized Pearson with regards to the General's actions."

40  [**Malraux**] Telegram Montreal 9450, 11/10/63, in the JFK Library, NSC Files, Canada.

41  [**INR and de Gaulle**] Research Memorandum entitled "De Gaulle's Foreign Policy: 1964," INR, 20/4/64, p. ii and 14, for the Secretary of State, SECRET/NO FOREIGN DISSEM. This memo, available from the presidential archives of Lyndon Baines Johnson, has been reproduced on microfiche, "Declassified Documents" of University Microfilm I (hereinafter DD-UM).

41  [**De Gaulle-Pearson**] From Dale Thomson, in *Jean Lesage* ..., p. 528. The text was published 14 years later in *Le Quotidien de Paris*, 2/11/77.

41  [**Léger and de Gaulle**] De Gaulle's reply in a speech presenting his credentials, 1/6/89, quoted by Dale Thomson, *Jean Lesage* ..., p. 532.

41  [**Stabler, Vendée**] Airgram Paris A-2717, 27/5/65, CONFIDENTIAL, "Le vrai Canada" ("The Real Canada").

42  [**De Gaulle's interest**] Research memorandum entitled "Quebec's International Status-Seeking Provokes New Row with Ottawa," INR, 1/6/65, p. 4, 5 and 8, prepared for the Secretary of State, CONFIDENTIAL/NO FOREIGN DISSEM.

42  [**Martin, manipulation**] From Paul Martin, *A Very Public Life*, vol. II: "So Many Worlds," Ottawa, Deneau, 1985, p. 589.

43  [**Funkhouser, memo**] Richard Funkhouser, tel. interview, Wash., 23/3/89. Sent via a "back channel," the memo may have escaped classification as it does not appear in Franco-American documentation declassified by Washington.

43  [**Gotlieb**] Interview, supra.

44  [**Camp David**] From Lawrence Martin, *The Presidents...*, introduction and p. 225-226. "You pissed on my rug," confirmed by a high ranking American bureaucrat.

44  [**De Gaulle, great power**] Quoted in Lacouture, op. cit., p. 285.

44  [**Roosevelt**] Quoted in Thomson, *Vive le Québec Libre*, p. 71-72.

44  [**Churchill**] Quoted by Charles Bohlen in the rough draft of his book, *Witness to History*, Bohlen archives, supra.

44  [**De Gaulle and Eisenhower**] From Vernon Walters, *Services discrets*, Paris, Plon, 1979, quoted in Lacouture, op. cit., p. 352-353. Walters was an interpreter at the Franco-American and other summits.

45  [**Rivals unite**] From Charles de Gaulle, *Discours et Messages*, vol. III: "Avec le renouveau, 1958-1962" ("The Revival, 1958-1962"), Paris, Plon, 1970, p. 134; quoted in Walt Rostow, *Diffusion of Power*, p. 80.

46  [**French enclave**] Funkhouser, interview, supra.

46  [**Pearson and de Gaulle**] From Lester B. Pearson, *Mike: the Memoirs of the Right Honourable Lester B. Pearson*, vol. 3, Toronto, University of Toronto Press, 1975, p. 261, and from Dale Thomson, *Vive le...*, p. 120.

46  [**Léger and the US**] Léger's mid-1965 report in Dale Thomson's *Vive le...*, p. 163.

47  [**Bohlen**] De Gaulle the smoker and Palm Beach in rough draft of *Witness...*, Bohlen archives, supra. The anecdote about Palm Beach was toned down in the book's final version; "Lord Mountbatten," Joseph Kraft in Lacouture, op. cit., p. 344; de Gaulle as part of the stellar system: Charles E. Bohlen, *Witness to History*, New York, Norton, 1973, p. 511.

47  [**JFK, pettiness**] "That's cheap," in Walt Rostow, op. cit., p. 367, and to the author in interview, supra.

47  [**De Gaulle and LBJ**] From Lyndon B. Johnson, *Vantage Point*, p. 23.

48  [**LBJ's patience**] A high-level American bureaucrat, who wishes to remain anonymous, told the author he overheard LBJ say this to Pearson, either at their Lake Harrington meeting in May, or in Campobello in August 1966.

48  [**Auxiliary**] Speech 10/8/67, in Renée Lescop, op. cit., p. 180. De Gaulle withdrew France

from the military structure of the alliance, but remained within its political framework.

48  [Ball and LBJ] Walt Rostow, interview, supra.

48  [Daniel Johnson in Paris] Airgram Paris A-1873, 27/5/67, LIMITED OFFICIAL USE.

49  [July] Quotations from Lacouture, op. cit., p. 515-516.

49  [Chateau Frontenac] Quoted in Pierre-Louis Guertin, *Et de Gaulle vint...*, Montreal, Claude Langevin Editeur, 1970, p. 197-199.

49  [1960] From *Mémoires d'espoir*, Paris, Plon, 1970, p. 250; quoted in Thomson, *Vive le...*, p. 510.

49  [Deaf] Paul-Louis Mallen, quoted in Lacouture, op. cit., p. 523, and in Thomson, op. cit., p. 207. Mallen reports Bourassa's reaction, expressed in the presence of Jacques-Yvan Morin, and also Lévesque's reaction. (On September 29, Bourassa still did not know whether he'd vote for or against Lévesque's sovereignty association manifesto.) As for Johnson's words, they were noted by Claude Morin and passed along to Lacouture.

49  [Hawkins] Telegram Montreal 032, undated but obviously from 24/7/67, UNCLASSIFIED.

50  [VLQL] Audio-visual archives in the National Archives of Canada, Ottawa.

50  [Mrs Hawkins] Interview, Washington, 22/2/89.

50  [U of M] From Renée Lescop, op. cit., p. 169.

50  [Rostow] Note from the State Department to Rostow, 27/7/67, LBJ Library. Telegram Paris 1285, 27/7/67, LIMITED OFFICIAL USE. Charpy in Telegram Paris 1368, 29/7/67, UNCLASSIFIED.

51  [LBJ and Bohlen] Rostow, interview, supra. Note from Rostow to LBJ, 28/7/67, LBJ Library. Telegram Paris 1288, 27/7/67, SECRET. Note from LBJ to Rostow, and from Rostow to LBJ, 28/7/67, LBJ Library.

51  [LBJ and de Gaulle] Memorandum of conversation, de Gaulle's meeting with President Johnson, 13/7/67, CONFIDENTIAL.

52  [CIA] An official, who wishes to remain anonymous, to the author.

52  [INR and DePorte] Domestic Politics in Intelligence Note 638, 1/8/67, CONFIDENTIAL/NO FOREIGN DISSEM/CONTROLLED DISSEM. DePorte in "De Gaulle's Stepped-Up Anti-Americanism and the Crisis of French Foreign Policy," Research Memorandum, INR, 26/7/67, CONFIDENTIAL/NO FOREIGN DISSEM/CONTROLLED DISSEM, DD-UM. Like all INR analyses, this one was signed by Director Thomas Hughes, but DePorte was the real author. He draws from the text in his book, *Europe between the Superpowers: the Enduring Balance*, New Haven, Yale University Press, 1979, p. 241, in a paragraph on Quebec. His book is used in American universities as a reference for courses in international politics. The last comment made by DePorte from an interview with the author, Wash., 15/5/89.

53  [Paris, Quai] General commentary by John Hostie, principal analyst at the INR's French desk, who consulted dispatches from the period before an interview with the author, Wash., 17/2/89. Springsteen, interview, supra.

53  [French aid] In "De Gaulle to the Aid of Quebec," Intelligence Note 693, INR, 25/8/67, CONFIDENTIAL.

53  [Cunningham] Airgram Quebec A-62, 11/10/67, CONFIDENTIAL.

54  [Quai and Drapeau] Telegram Paris 7652, 8/12/67, LIMITED OFFICIAL USE.

54  [Rostow and LBJ] Memo from Rostow to LBJ, 27/11/67, LBJ Library.

54  [LBJ, sarcasm] Memo from Harry McPherson to LBJ, 16/8/67, copy of sample toast, and toast eventually delivered on 17/8/67, LBJ Library. LBJ appears to have consulted Rusk on the appropriateness of the joke.

54  [Baeyens] Memorandum of interview, State Department, 19/10/67, CONFIDENTIAL.

55  [De Gaulle's letter] Dated 8/9/67, reproduced in Renée Lescop, op. cit., p. 181-182. Johnson's answer quoted in Pierre Godin, *Daniel Johnson*, vol. II, Montreal, Editions de l'Homme, 1980, p. 259.

55  [Thomson, Lacouture] Dale Thomson, op. cit., p. 163. Jean Lacouture, op. cit., p. 345.

55    **[De Gaulle]** Speech 10/8/67, press conference 27/1/67 from which most of the de Gaulle quotations in the following paragraphs derive. Reproduced in Renée Lescop, op. cit., p. 179-189.

55    **[Lesage]** From Dale Thomson, op. cit., p. 97, 99 and 108.

55    **[Pearson]** Quoted in Telegram Ottawa 0506, 23/10/67, UNCLASSIFIED.

56    **[Poll,** *Humanité,* Mitterand] Quoted in Dale Thomson, op. cit., p. 224, 222, 231. The *Humanité's* reversal mentioned in "The Soviets Confused Over How To Play de Gaulle's Canada Trip," INR Intelligence Note 640, 2/8/67, LIMITED OFFICIAL USE. For a discussion of the Soviets' position on Quebec, see chapters 7 and 14.

56    **[De Gaulle, diplomat]** Jean Chapdelaine, who wrote Lesage 27/7/65, quoted in Dale Thomson, op. cit., p. 162.

56    **[Funkhouser]** Interview, supra.

56    **[Wallner]** Airgram Paris A-1107, 12/18/67, CONFIDENTIAL.

56    **[Bohlen]** From the rough draft of his book, p. 25 and 32, Bohlen archives, supra. On the concept of nation, *Witness to History*, p. 512.

57    **[Nixon]** Quotations in William Safire, *Before the Fall*, New York, Doubleday, 1975, p. 688.

57    **[Kissinger]** Account of his exchange with de Gaulle in his book, *The White House Years*, Toronto, Little, 1979. He explains his support for gaullist strategy on p. 106.

57    **[Safire]** Quotation of de Gaulle in *The Gazette*, 30/3/79, reactions of Nixon and Kissinger reported by William Safire in correspondence with the author, 13/4/89.

Chapter 5. The Spiral of Furor

59    **[Butterworth]** Author of a lengthy analysis, "Quebec - Separatism in Flood Tide," Ottawa A-474, 24/10/67, CONFIDENTIAL.

59    **[Zbig, Quebec]** Anecdote about meeting called by Brzezinski, and his ideas, from a letter Rufus Smith wrote to Walton Butterworth, 20/10/67, SECRET; from an interview between author and a participant who wishes to remain anonymous; and brief comments made by Brzezinski to author, Wash., 17/7/89. Brzezinski's memo dated 2/10/67, has to this day not been declassified by the State Department. Its author refused to summarize its contents for us on the pretext of "national security" considerations.

60    **[Bourgault, socialist]** Butterworth, Ottawa A-474, 24/10/67, CONFIDENTIAL.

61    **[Anger]** Butterworth, Telegram Ottawa 0347, 25/9/67, CONFIDENTIAL.

61    **[Trudeau, hoax]** Butterworth, Telegram Ottawa 0347, 25/9/67, CONFIDENTIAL.

61    **[Rostow]** Interview, supra.

61    **[Liberal convention]** Airgram Quebec A-64, 17/10/67, UNCLASSIFIED, signed by Frederick Quin, Cunningham's assistant. Quin attended the convention.

62    **[Mackasey, Post]** Letter from Cunningham to the embassy, 1/3/68, CONFIDENTIAL. Airgram Québec A-127, 6/2/68, CONFIDENTIAL.

62    **[Pearson, Rusk]** Telegram from Ed Ritchie, 29/12/67, National Archives in Ottawa (Acc 80-10/022, box 43, file 20-cda-9-Pearson, p. 9). Guest list in "Memo For the Prime Minister," 27/12/67, SECRET, Public Archives of Canada (MC 26, N4,Vol.119, File 313.4) in ALM.

63    **[Immobility]** In a 35-page INR analysis, "Quebec, Ottawa and Confederation - The 1968 Round Begins," Research memorandum, 2/2/68, SECRET/NO FOREIGN DISSEM/CONTROLLED DISSEM. Published after the meeting between Rusk and Pearson, but it draws its facts from embassy reports dating back to September 1967.

63    **[Power Corporation]** Airgram Ottawa A-843, 18/1/68, LIMITED OFFICIAL USE. Frenette explained that, given their number, nationalist and separatist groups monopolized the press. Federalists, who were few in number and largely inactive, seemed to be overwhelmed. He felt that promotion of the political polarization between separatists and

federalists would simplify and ultimately help to balance things. He also underlined the fact that in the beginning of 1968, Power Corp. abandoned its television and radio stations. Tel. interview, Montreal, 15/2/90.

In *The Canadian Establishment*, Peter C. Newman writes, "When Frenette, then a vice president of Power, won the presidency of the Quebec Liberal Federation [the provincial wing of the federal Party] by beating out an anti-reform candidate, Pierre Elliott Trudeau burst into his hotel room, hugged him, and said, 'We beat the bastards; now we can get something done.'" (Toronto, McClelland, 1975, p. 50, 57, 75).

63    [Etats généraux] INR on Etats généraux in "Quebec, Ottawa..." loc. cit.

64    [Lévesque] Burgess in Airgram Montreal A-124, 28/12/67, LIMITED OFFICIAL USE, Cunningham in "The View From Quebec in January 1968," Airgram Ottawa A-937, 6/2/68, CONFIDENTIAL. INR in "Quebec, Ottawa..." loc. cit.

64    [Lévesque, Cunningham] Letters from Cunningham to the embassy, 12/2/68, and 1/3/68, CONFIDENTIAL; interview with Francis Cunningham, supra, and with Claude Morin, infra; and tel. interview with Harrison Burgess, Wash.-Charlottesville, 23/7/89.

66    [Lévesque, Doherty] Airgram Montreal 4/10/68, LIMITED OFFICIAL USE.

67    [Beaudry, Smith] Quebec Contingency Planning, 11/10/68, SECRET.

67    [Pacifist] "Major Separatist Group Form single Party in Quebec," INR Intelligence note 857, 5/11/68, CONFIDENTIAL/NO FOREIGN DISSEM/CONTROLLED DISSEM.

67    [NSC] United States Government Memorandum, Information on Canadian Separatism for NSSM9, 30/1/69, SECRET. This reply may have been modified by NSC personnel prior to integration into the final NSSM.

69    [Schmidt, PQ] Telegram Ottawa 0543, "National Significance in April 29 Quebec Provincial Election," 23/4/70, CONFIDENTIAL.


Chapter 6. Snoopy Smells An Apprehended Insurrection

70    [Cross] The Englishman told this to Bernard Mergler, negotiator with the FLQ, when his four abductors and two of their wives handed him over to Cuba's Consul General on the Expo grounds. The quotation, published in the *Toronto Daily Star* 9/3/71, was repeated in an American report on the crisis. See infra.

70    [Johnson] William "Mac" Johnson, political advisor posted in Ottawa 1964-1969, director of Canadian Affairs at the State Department 1969-1973, assistant to the ambassador in Ottawa 1973-1976; interview, Wash., 14/3/89.

70    [Macuk] David Macuk, political advisor posted in Ottawa 1968-1972, interview, Wash. 7/3/89.

70    [Vallières] Quoted in Louis Fournier, *FLQ: Histoire d'un mouvement clandestin*, Montreal, Québec/Amérique, p. 92.

70    [Bombings] 1965 bombings, *The New York Times* and the *New York Herald Tribune*, 2/5/65; the Macaza and United Aircraft, Fournier, op. cit., p. 109-111 and p. 190; bomb and molotov cocktail, *The Gazette*, 30/10/67.

71    [Residence] *Dimanche Matin*, 13/4/69, and interview with Mrs Richard Hawkins, Wash., 22/2/89.

71    [Burgess, RCMP] Telex Montreal 0604, 8/10/69, UNCLASSIFIED.

72    [Simard] In 1982, Francis Simard wrote, in collaboration with cell members Paul and Jacques Rose and Bernard Lortie, *Pour en finir avec octobre* ("To Be Done With October") Montreal, Stanké, 1982, p. 28, 173.

72    [Burgess, Golan] Kidnappings in international context, in Fournier, op. cit., p. 267-270, 249-250 and 280, and interview, Burgess, supra. Unless otherwise indicated, Louis Fournier's book is used in this chapter as a fact source for the October Crisis.

72 [**Cross, Topping**] Jacques Cossette-Trudel quotations collected in Cuba by journalist Gérard Vallières and published in *Weekend Magazine*, 22/1/72, p. 6. Cross reported FLQ explanations to Topping, who in turn reported them in Airgram Montreal A-78, "Security in Montreal: United States Officials Likely Targets; Present Situation and Probable Developments," 11/12/70, CONFIDENTIAL. Cross confirmed it to the author, interview Montreal 27/8/90. Interview Mrs Doris Topping, Wash., 14/4/89.

73 [**Smith**] Telex Ottawa 1413, 5/10/70, UNCLASSIFIED. (Telexes show the hour of transmission.)

74 [**Ritchie**] An American diplomat, who wishes to remain anonymous, to the author.

74 [**Sharp, Trudeau**] Telex Ottawa 1492, 14/10/70, CONFIDENTIAL. The Manifesto was broadcast on Radio-Canada, October 8.

75 [**RCMP, Marion**] Tel. interview Joseph A. Marion, Wash.-New Jersey, 19/7/89. An RCMP official, who wishes to remain anonymous, to the author.

75 [**Border**] In State Department Telegram 171934, 19/10/70, UNCLASSIFIED.

75 [**Thompson**] W. Kenneth Thompson, tel. interview, Wash., 17/7/89.

75 [**Algiers**] Telex USINT Algiers 1572, 16/10/70, SECRET. In State Department Telegram 18999898, 19/11/70, CONFIDENTIAL, the Algiers desk was asked to ascertain whether the FLQ would open an office. Telex USINT Algiers, 20/11/70, CONFIDENTIAL, contained the reply.

75 [**Cline**] Interview, Cline, supra. William Rogers (like Henry Kissinger and Richard Nixon) refused to be interviewed for this book.

76 [**MI-5**] A member of the RCMP, who wishes to remain anonymous, to the author.

76 [**Scotland Yard**] Rand Report, infra.

77 [**Attachés**] Army attaché, Col. Richard H. Dolson, Sr, tel. interview, Wash.-Corpus Christi, 1/5/89. Chief military attaché, Col. Charles E. Taylor of the US Air Force, says he learned of the war measures in the press, tel. interview, Wash.-Ormand Beach, Fla., 1/5/89.

78 [**Snoopy**] Rufus and Peggy Smith, interview, supra.

78 [**Kissinger**] Henry Kissinger, *White House Years*, p. 383.

78 [**Inferiority complex**] A witness who wished to remain anonymous, to the author.

79 [**Nixon memo**] Memo, 6/2/70. Someone added in the words "Covered in the Canadian Oil Decision." The author was unable to find anyone who understood this reference. Nixon Archives, WHSF:WHCF CO28 Canada 60-70.

79 [**Nixon summary**] Nixon Archives, WHSF:POF October 1970. As was the custom, one of Nixon's staff, John Brown, reviewed the President's copy, and sent brief memos to interested parties. Haldeman was warned that the President "noted that you should watch the press; they are going to defend their 'liberal friends.'" (Brown had obviously had difficulty deciphering the President's scrawl.)

79 [**Nixon, Trudeau**] Interviews between Kissinger and Trudeau in the White House Telephone Log, 18/10/70, Grand Forks speech in Richard Nixon, *Public Papers of the President*, p. 882-889.

80 [**Sonnenfeldt**] Helmut Sonnenfeldt, director of Canadian Affairs at the NSC 1969-1974, interview, Wash., 16/3/89.

80 [**Toumanoff**] Vladimir Toumanoff, interview, Wash., 18/7/89. Interview Macuk, supra.

80 [**Proof**] Telex Ottawa 1524, 19/10/70, CONFIDENTIAL.

81 [**Doubt**] Telex Ottawa 1552, 22/10/70, LIMITED OFFICIAL USE.

81 [**Melby**] Airgram Quebec A-55, 12/11/70, UNCLASSIFIED.

82 [**FLQ, Topping**] Airgram Montreal A-68, 20/11/70, UNCLASSIFIED.

82 [**Kissinger memo**] Memo 16290, 3/12/70.

83 [**Rand**] Eleanor S. Wainstein, "The Cross and Laporte Kidnappings, Montreal, October 1970: A report prepared for Department of State and Defense Advanced Research Projects Agency," Rand, 1977, 65 pages. A lightly expurgated version of the 1974 report was made

public in February 1977. Mrs Wainstein gave to the author the contents of the missing passages. Wainstein, tel. interview, Wash., 17/7/89. The Rand Report mentions another channel of communication, or at least, another point of Canadian-American contact during the crisis. It speaks of "reports from Americans who have worked with the anti-terrorist squad" (composed of the RCMP, the Quebec provincial police and the Montreal Police Force). These Americans thought that the three police forces worked well together and commended their performance. This could be a reference to John Topping, who made comments of a similar nature in his Airgram A-78, loc. cit. Neither Marion of the FBI, nor Burgess, a diplomat in Montreal during the crisis, nor two of the RCMP officers involved in the FLQ hunt, nor Michel Coté, Esq. formerly head of litigation for the City and a regular at the squad's headquarters, has any idea who the mysterious Americans mentioned in the report might be. Wainstein herself has forgotten the source of this information. They are mentioned in the section of the Rand paper describing Scotland Yard's intervention in 1966. The reports cited could date back several years before the crisis. Interviews, supra, and tel. interview, Michel Coté, Wash.-Montreal.

83  [**Cross, verbosity**] From *Weekend*, op. cit.

84  [**Duchaine**] Jean-François Duchaine, Esq. *Rapport sur les événements d'octobre 1970*, Quebec government, ministère de la Justice, 1981. The conspiracy theory is particularly well-developed by Pierre Vallières in *L'Execution de Pierre Laporte*, Montreal, Québec/Amérique, 1977. He takes it up again, despite the publication of Simard's book, in his recent autobiography. Louis Fournier, who had access to FLQ and police sources for his book, *FLQ*, told the author that these theories were "spy novels" and that Duchaine had "done a very good job."


Chapter 7. Our Friends at Langley

For this chapter, more than a dozen members of the American, Canadian and Quebec intelligence services consented to speak to the author. Several were willing to be identified by name. Others insisted on anonymity. Some information is therefore not attributed, even vaguely, to any source.

85  [**Cram**] Cleveland Cram, interviews with the author, 17-18/3/89.

88  [**NSA**] The existence of information on René Lévesque at the NSA is revealed in a letter from the NSA dated 9/6/89, and in statements submitted by the NSA to the US District Court of the District of Columbia, dated 7/7/89 and 17/10/89. The author having requested, under the Freedom of Information Act, copies of all documents at the Agency concerning the independence movement between 1963 and 1980, the NSA was obliged to reveal the existence of the documents in its possession, but not necessarily to make them public. In response to a legal proceeding taken by the author, the NSA had to justify by affidavit its decision to maintain secrecy. The affidavit, itself secret, was to be submitted to a judge but not to the author's lawyer. As this book went to press, the wait had not ended. Normally, even documents classified TOP SECRET can be partially published after the confidential parts are deleted. The NSA maintains that not a line of its documents on René Lévesque can be published. For a discussion of the links between the NSA and the CBNRC/CSE, see James Littleton, *Target Nation*, Toronto, Lester, 1986, pp. 89-108. For a description of NSA activities, see James Banford, *The Puzzle Palace*, Boston, Houghton Mifflin, 1982.

188  [**FLQ**] From a document dated 10/12/70 of the Strategic Operations Center created in Ottawa during the crisis, quoted in Fournier, op. cit., p. 380; three FLQ members in Cuba, p.191.

90  [**Cuban defector**] Information on the kidnappers of Cross, tel. interview, Wash.-Australia 24/6/89, with Leslie James Bennett, ex-director of the Soviet office of B Section, later

responsible for security service surveillance until 1972, when he was forced to resign because he was suspected — without evidence — of being a Soviet mole. For more on Bennett see the excellent work of Sawatsky, *For Services Rendered*, Toronto, Penguin, 1986, 339 pages.

90   [**Young**] Seymour Young, tel. interview, Wash., 26/7/89.

91   [**Jordan**] The presence of two FLQ members in a Palestinian training camp in Jordan had been revealed by journalist Pierre Nadeau, who was preparing a report on the Palestinian resistance. He published this information in the magazine *Perspective* on 15/8/70. In *FLQ* (pp. 282-283) Fournier explains that the *felquistes* in Jordan and the ones in Algiers were the same ones, Normand Roy and Michel Lambert. Wanted by police after bomb attacks in 1969, they had hidden out with the Black Panthers in the United States before leaving for Paris, and then for Jordan and Algiers. For the American source in Algiers, see preceding chapter.

91   [**Cuban consulate**] See Bill Macadam and James Dubro, "How the CIA has us spooked," *Maclean's*, 7/74, pp. 20- 46. The description of the night of the bombing comes from John Sawatsky, *Men in the Shadows: The RCMP Security Service*, Toronto, Doubleday, 1980, pp. 1-8. These two sources also state that copies of Canadian observers' reports from Vietnam were given to the Americans.

95   [**Robert Ford**] Tel. interview Wash.-France, 17/4/89; and Robert A.D. Ford, *Our Man in Moscow: a diplomat's reflections on the Soviet Union*, Toronto, University of Toronto Press, 1989, pp. 101-103, 117.

95   [**De Gaulle-Tass**] "Soviets Confused Over How To Play De Gaulle's Canada Trip," INR Intelligence Note 640, 2/8/67, LIMITED OFFICIAL USE. The French comrades at the daily *L'Humanité*, initially enthusiastic about tweaking the Americans with a new country on their border, were immediately forced to backtrack. "Moscow's troubles with the coverage of de Gaulle's trip are of several types," stated the analysis submitted to the White House. "No report can avoid criticizing Canada (which is not now a target of Soviet propaganda) or suggesting that de Gaulle interfered clumsily in its internal affairs." The French press reaction having been most critical of de Gaulle's statement, Moscow could not comment on the event without offending either its tactical ally, de Gaulle, or one of its target audiences, the French journalistic and political class. "Consequently, though the USSR does not want to criticize de Gaulle, any coverage of his recent activities in Canada tends to offend someone important" in Moscow, the INR concluded.

95   [**Vastel**] Michel Vastel, interview, Ottawa, 6/6/89.

96   [**Tass-CIA**] Canadian Press and Reuters reports datelined Moscow and quoted in *The Gazette*, 20/2/78. Tass was answering allegations made the week before in the House of Commons by Conservative MP Tom Cossitt, that a French-Soviet espionage network was using Cuban ships to smuggle arms on a regular basis to terrorist groups working in Quebec. Tass declared that Cossitt was speaking "at the instigation of the American intelligence services." Hard to say which of the two statements was more ridiculous.

96   [**de Vosjoli**] In de Vosjoli, *Lamia*, p. 319 and in *The Telegram*, 12/9/68. De Vosjoli's superiors in Paris suspected him, in turn, of being a CIA double agent.

97   [**Debré**] In Dale Thomson, op. cit., p.159.

97   [**Ben Bella**] Louis Fournier, op. cit., p. 91.

97   [**Chapdelaine-Cadieux**] Interview with Chapdelaine, supra. Hervé Alphand would probably have been the last to know, since the SDECE networks were directly connected to the Elysée, and Quebec operatives would avoid the offices of Alphand and his minister by contacting the president's advisors without middlemen. The Trudeau quotation is taken from *Le Monde*, 30/8/81.

97   [**Starnes**] John Starnes revealed these details in 1981, during the McDonald Commission inquiry, presumably because he refused to be a scapegoat for all the excesses of the service while he directed it. Quotation from *Le Monde*, 31/8/81.

98   [Golytsin] Apart from the interviews granted the author, which reveal the RCMP-Golytsin-SDECE connection, general information was taken from John Ranelagh, *The Agency: The Rise and Decline of the CIA*, New York, Simon and Schuster, 1986, pp. 563 et seq.; from Thierry Wolton, *Le KGB en France*, Paris, Grasset, 1986, pp. 117 et seq.; and from Roger Faligot and Pascal Krop, *La Piscine*, p. 274 et seq.

101   [Gotlieb] Allan Gotlieb, interview, Cambridge, 25/5/89.

101   [Gray] General information on Gray in Louis Fournier, op. cit., and Stanley Gray, tel. interview, Montreal- Toronto, 15/2/90. Two plain-clothes policemen, perhaps the same ones, had been caught recording a meeting of the McGill Français movement. On this subject, see Louis Fournier and others, *La police secrète au Québec: la tyrranie occulte de la police*, Montreal, Québec/Amérique, 1978, p.17 (228 pages). One of the writers is future Montreal mayor Jean Doré.

102   [Marchetti] tel. interview, Wash., 13/8/89.

103   [Statue of Liberty] Frank Donner, tel. interview, Conn., 7/89; *The New York Times*, 17/2/65 and following, 3 and 11/6/65; also in Louis Fournier, *FLQ*, pp.101-103.

104   [Gould] On the Hungarians, interview with Ruth Joyner, assistant from 1956 to 1957 to the two first CIA chiefs of station in Ottawa — Andrew J. Steele and George MacMannus — later head of the Canadian office at Langley from 1958 to 1962. Interview, Wash., 18/5/89. On Gould, Cleveland Cram, interview, supra, and a second source.

104   [Hawkins] Letter of 14/7/68 to "Jeff," personal files, Mrs Richard Hawkins, Washington.

104   [Burgess] Harrison Burgess, tel. interview, Charlottesville, 23/8/89.

104   [Infiltration unlikely] Three factors make a covert CIA presence in Quebec unlikely:
First — and this is undoubtedly the least convincing and most often cited reason — the CIA and RCMP have concluded an agreement which prohibits both from sending spies to probe each other's national secrets. Together, they tracked the north-south movements of Cubans, Hungarians, Soviets and other suspicious- looking enemies. The intelligence section at Langley sends the Canadian Department of External Affairs mountains of documents on the political situation in Brazil, the dissident movement in Lithuania, the latest Chinese rice harvest and the movements of Soviet submarines in the Pacific. In short, nearly all of Langley's production, with only the sources and collection methods deleted, are passed along to Canadian analysts who lack comparable intelligence-gathering resources. In return, Canada's diplomatic service gives Langley confidential information which it has raised through its own contacts, notably in areas like the Caribbean and, presumably, French Africa, where it is better represented than the Americans. Many senior Canadian officials had so much faith in Langley's analyses — particularly the remarkable National Intelligence Estimates (NIE), which is a survey of one subject or a situation review for one country — that they participated voluntarily in the preparation of an NIE on Canada.
In 1964, the man in charge of NIE's, Sherman Kent, visited Ottawa to collect information for a major study of Canada. The CIA chief of station in the Canadian capital, Rolfe Kingsley, had assembled 20 of Canada's top decision-makers. "There was Bob Bryce [deputy minister of finance], Norman Robertson [under- secretary of state for external affairs] and Frank Miller, who was chairman of the Chiefs of Staff, along with [Robertson's assistant] Marcel Cadieux," in short, the keepers of the country's most important secrets, one participant remembers. "We all sat around until almost two o'clock in the morning and chatted about a whole variety of things," he adds. "This goes on between the United States and Canada all the time, and also with the Brits." The participant says those present could have had no doubt as to the reason for Kent's visit. But perhaps they wanted Langley to hear firsthand of the intentions of the Canadian government.
When the domestic situation in one of the two countries seems capable of producing repercussions in the other, a summary is prepared, like the FLQ report, to advise it of possible dangers.

When American spies are on the trail of a KGB agent who cross the northern border, they ask their SS (now CSIS) friends to handle surveillance, or they organize a joint operation. In this matter, according to Cram and all the CIA officers interviewed, the agreement was "scrupulously respected": hands off Canada. There were, of course, some problems.

If the suspect was military, agents of the Pentagon's Defense Intelligence Agency (DIA) could be dispatched. Two such agents in Montreal, in 1973, became embroiled in an affair which raised a considerable outcry but which, according to one participant, had no connection with the independence movement. It was an operation against an East-bloc target. "It was a good case," the intelligence agent recalls. But Canadian officers complain that Langley showed too much eagerness to use SS resources for its own benefit. "The Americans were always telling us what to do and how to do it. They'd ask us to plant a microphone or mount surveillance on a subject who was going through Canada, when we had other targets to worry about," one Mountie complains. "Sometimes they pressured us to put their jobs ahead of our own, and that created friction." Langley, on the other hand, believed that, in light of everything the American espionage apparatus had provided the Canadian authorities, a little enthusiasm for its targets would only be good manners. And the Canadians' reluctance prompted outbursts among the shorter tempers at Langley. "Sometimes a cowboy — we call them cowboys, the professionals in secret operations — a cowboy would say, 'Maybe we should send someone up there and get the information ourselves,'" Cram remembers. "If you want to operate," he would answer, "Go to the USSR or Ouagadougou or Bangkok."

At the end of the 1950s, agents from the CIA's scientific section came to Montreal to meet Dr Ewen Cameron of the Allan Memorial Institute, whom they provided with secret funding for bizarre experiments in "behavior modification" through brain-washing. Many unwilling guinea pigs still suffer from the consequences of those experiments. The presence of those science officers violated the CIA-RCMP agreement. See Don Gillmor, *I Swear by Apollo: Dr Ewen Cameron and the CIA Brainwashing Experiments*, Montreal, Eden Press, 1987, p. 97.

In the early 1960s, an American CIA agent became carried away and followed his subject to Toronto, where he was fingered by Canadian police. Cram had to endure the resulting fury of the External Affairs Department.

"We would go nuts in External Affairs if there was some evidence that they had interviewed somebody in Vancouver or Toronto, or some criminal or something, without going through us or the RCMP," remembers a senior official in the Department, Allan Gotlieb. Gotlieb, interview, supra.

Two months rarely go by without some MP or journalist making an accusation about the CIA in Canada, or some police force catching an odd bird and wanting an explanation. Normally these matters were settled in the RCMP's offices. Cram retains a vivid and uncomfortable memory of the day the under-secretary of state for external affairs, Ed Ritchie, summoned him to make a more serious allegation than usual, on a matter he can no longer recall. "I remember they brought me into his big office like they were bringing in a criminal," Cram says. "He didn't bother to say hello, hardly looked at me. Canadians love to treat us badly when they get a chance. And then he started his sermon: 'I will not tolerate this sort of American behavior...' I thought I was having a nightmare, and he still hadn't told me what we'd done wrong." An assistant on hand finally prodded Ritchie to give a few details, which Cram noted carefully. The chief of station sent an "Immediate Attention" cable to Langley, did some checking up and returned to see the assistant with a three- or four-page memo which exonerated the Agency of any untoward behavior. He wanted to put the document in Ritchie's hand personally and make him admit his mistake. At his strenuous insistence, he was admitted once again into the big office. Ritchie "read the whole memo, pushed it back along the table, got up and left the room without saying a thing." A few days later, the two men happened to meet in the Rideau Club bar. Cram saw his chance. "I'm happy we had an opportunity to sort out this little problem," he told Ritchie. "I don't know what you're talking about," the civil servant answered, turned his back once again and walked away. "A charming guy," Cram comments wryly. The federal bureaucracy was not alone in maintaining pressure on the CIA men in Ottawa to discourage interference. The press lent a helping hand. "This was fair game, I guess," admits Cram, who nonetheless bears a lasting grudge against one journalist in particular. "A real pest," he says, still incensed. "She was constantly calling me, often at eleven o'clock at night. I'd be in my pyjamas, getting ready for bed, and the phone would ring. It was her. 'Did you do this? Are you responsible for that?' She had no manners at all. Wait a second, her name will come to me. She was from Toronto. Just give me a second... Barbara Frum! She's the one. Any idea what she's up to now?" (Frum says she has no memory of ever having talked to Cram, interview tel. Toronto 12/4/90.)

The second reason why covert CIA action in Quebec was unlikely: the small benefits to be gained.

The RCMP link certainly did not satisfy the American analysts' appetite for a deep and detailed understanding of turbulence in Quebec during the key years of 1963-1972. But the availability of a good number of sources, RCMP reports, diplomatic dispatches and NSA listening meant that the CIA was still fairly well-informed.

Not to mention the fact that if the Americans were unsuccessful in getting the information they wanted at the highest levels of the police and intelligence pyramid through the RCMP-CIA link, they could still find it at the lower level of cop-to-cop cooperation.

The FBI and other American police forces had good reasons to wonder about the FLQ, because the Quebec extremists were forming numerous links with American terrorist organizations like the effective bomb-detonating Weathermen and the black nationalist Black Panthers.

Radical American groups occasionally wanted to ferry individuals in the United States to Canada via an underground railroad. The flow between Montreal and New York obliged investigators within G Branch to exchange information and leads with their FBI colleagues in Washington, and even more often with agents in Buffalo and Albany in New York State, and in Burlington, Vermont. In May of 1972, for instance, G Branch suspected that a group of FLQ members was preparing to hold a meeting with some Black Panthers in a barn in Ste-Anne-de-la-Rochelle, in the Eastern Townships. But the police officers did not have time to place a listening device on the site before the meeting, so they decided to burn down the barn, which was home to a jazz center, rather than let the meeting proceed without surveillance. This was one of a series of criminal acts by the SS which gave rise to the creation of commissions of inquiry into RCMP activities.

Interested as they were in the Panthers, the FBI agents were not only experts in political agitation. "One day, I called an agent in Burlington, but he was out working on a bank robbery," remembers a Canadian officer.

In principle, "we only gave them information that was relevant to their operations," he adds. "There had to be an American dimension. We wouldn't give them our list of FLQ prime suspects," the Canadian explains, adding, however, that it was "pretty easy to find an American dimension" in the FLQ's plans. Although the FBI did not have access to G Branch reports, a great deal of information was exchanged over a beer or during a planning session. In practice, "we told them everything," the Canadian intelligence agent says.

Except during the periods when FBI Director J. Edgar Hoover was in one of his rages against the rival CIA, Bureau reports on foreign terrorism were distributed to other members of what was known in Washington as the "intelligence community." After the Statue of Liberty operation, for instance, Hoover's office sent the INR (the State Department branch in charge of analysis) a report on "alleged French nationalist activity in Quebec." (Memo dated 15/11/65, CONFIDENTIAL.) A former FBI officer says this sort of information also went straight into the computers at Langley. While Cram was coming up empty in Ottawa, despite repeated requests from analysts who were better informed than he was, information on the FLQ was still piling up in the Agency's data banks. (FBI Headquarters in Washington says it has 1200 documents on the FLQ, 50 on the PQ and another 50 on the RIN, but it has only declassified a score of pages, after deleting any information that might not already be public. FBI 29/1/90 declaration to US District Court of DC.)

To make up the small blank spaces in the picture, the CIA would have had to send its own officers to recruit militant separatists on the scene, thus risking a grave political rift with Ottawa (those Canadians were so thin-skinned) and the possible loss of the RCMP's invaluable cooperation on Cuban and Soviet activities. (Not to mention the Canadian listening posts in the far north, which pick up the slightest Soviet movement.)

"We would be risking far, far more than any benefit we could derive from this," explains a senior officer at Langley. The difficulty in this kind of operation, he says, is that you always bump into the other side. "Look, the way you get caught is an accident. They decide to recruit the same guy. Why? Because he's in a position to know." And then one day, "the poor American arrives and there's a room full of Mounties waiting for him at the door. You don't risk that."

Which is not to say that the chief of station and his little team did not, as far as they were able, send to Langley any piece of information which fell into their hands. After all, the chief of station was a member of the fashionable Rideau Club, a favourite Ottawa haunt of the political and bureaucratic heavy hitters, who trade more government secrets over their scotches than in the minister's office. The same sort of thing goes on in the RCMP officers' mess, to which CIA and FBI people have open access. Whenever he caught a rumor by the tail, he ran it down with the embassy's political counsellors, like Rufus Smith, who were generally the best informed. At embassy political staff meetings, when opinion was canvassed around the table to prepare a report, the CIA representative, who always had a lot to say when the discussion was in Bangkok or in Santiago, maintained a bored silence in Ottawa. "In Canada, we were at the bottom of the league, we were way down, way off in the corner. We were of no importance, and we added nothing to the price," sighs Cram, who mentions in an almost wistful tone the exotic Middle Eastern and Asian capitals where the chief of station "is quite important, because he has secret sources and he may have the minister in charge of the secret service under his wing or something." The CIA station, like the analysts at Langley, had access to diplomatic dispatches. But the consuls sometimes kept to themselves an odd scrap of information or a half-rumor which was worth tracking down. Cram found that the consul general in Montreal, John Topping, had a repressed love of cloak-and-daggery. Topping would receive him joyfully and impart some tidbit about a Soviet or a Cuban he had met at an official or social gathering, without anything ever coming of it. Other diplomats, however, had less fondness for their spying countrymen. Cram remembers almost being ejected from the office of Topping's replacement, Elizabeth Harper. "A real anti-CIA fiend," Cram says. "She gave me this awful sermon," saying that "there will be a new attitude around here," and that she wanted nothing to do with the CIA. (Later, in Montreal during the 1976 Olympics, when the CIA came to the assistance of local security forces, Harper proved more cooperative. In an interview with the author on 15/3/89, Elizabeth Harper declared, however, that she did not know whether the CIA "had somebody in Ottawa.") But a wide gulf separated this mundane work and the clandestine infiltration of Quebec political organizations.

The third reason has to do with allocation of resources. During the 1960's, the CIA was stretched thin, particularly in Vietnam. The Quebec question, according to one Langley officer who then had authority over budget decisions, "was interesting enough that we wanted to know about it, but not enough to put people on it." "When you have 20 countries and 15 services to deal with, plus running operations against your main targets [...] it's of so little interest to us in terms of manpower, that the answer [to any request] would be no."

Especially, he adds, when one is convinced that "the Canadians can handle it."

These are the reasons why the CIA would have been reluctant in theory to get involved. There are also reasons for believing that in fact, there really was no CIA involvement.

First, in the past 20 years, the CIA has been the object of innumerable investigations, books and articles, in which hundreds of former Langley employees — especially victims of the Great Hunt or of the severe staff cuts during the Carter administration — have let most cats out of the bag. Yet not once has any of them, anywhere, made even a passing reference to illegal operations in Canada, French or English. Nothing, either, in the accountings rendered to numerous congressional inquiries.

There is a data bank in Washington which is claimed to be exhaustive on everything written, at least in English in the United States, about the CIA. The author consulted it, without success.

In addition, intelligence collected by CIA agents in the field is normally distributed, in a form that does not betray sources, to other members of the American intelligence community. The State Department's analysis branch, the INR, routinely receives reports from Langley. Several analysts interviewed said that though they had worked from CIA material when preparing notes on other countries, they had never had a scrap of CIA information which seemed to come from Quebec. (The only exception being reports from businessmen or academics returning from trips, along the lines described in the main text.) A diplomat specializing in Canadian affairs remembers reading a "rather pedestrian analysis" from the CIA on the Lévesque government, but which included nothing that could not have been taken from public or diplomatic sources.

All of which is to say that the product of some hypothetical covert CIA operation in Quebec would have had to be kept under lock and key, even in branches of the American government, like the INR, already subject to tight security.

105 **[Head]** Ivan Head, interview, Ottawa, 27/6/89.

**CIA October:** One quotation haunts the few Canadian writings on the CIA and Quebec. A sentence spoken by Jim Bennett in front of journalist — and, according to Sawatsky, sometime RCMP informer — Tom Hazlitt during a long discussion in 1973 in Johannesburg: "When the 1970 crisis erupted, someone down in Washington pushed the panic button and suddenly we had a full-scale infiltration of CIA agents on our hands." This quotation, along with another "revelation" concerning American troop movements on the border during October and Canadian forces' counter-movements to keep them at bay, was published in *The Toronto Star* of 22/9/73. Bennett immediately denied making the statement, a denial he has since repeated, including to the author. Beyond the fact that Hazlitt — now deceased — put quotation marks around a passage taken from a 14-hour interview during which, he stated, he had not used a recorder or taken notes, the use of the word "agent" is problematic. In espionage jargon, the "agent" is the recruit, the active field source of the "officer." "Agents" thus cannot be sent. In any event, an English-Canadian researcher who followed up the point and the author are both convinced that the quotation is a misunderstanding, if not a fabrication.

In addition, *The Montreal Star* of 24/9/71 published on its front page a TOP SECRET memo dated 16/10/70, the day war measures were imposed. The message is in a single sentence: "Sources advise that urgent action be taken to temporarily break contacts with the FLQ militants since the Canadian government's measures may have undesirable consequences." The *Star* explained that someone had slipped this memo into its Washington bureau's mail. A former Quebec intelligence officer is convinced of the authenticity of the document. Cleveland Cram, on the other hand, states that the note is one of a handful of documents circulating in Canada in the early 1970s, and which the CIA considered forgeries, produced by enemy intelligence services.

**CIA-Ottawa:** Here is a list, compiled by the author, of CIA chiefs of station from the opening of the station in 1956. The names are correct; dates followed by a "?" have a one-year margin of error. 1956 Andrew J. Steele; 1957? George MacMannus; 1960 Rolfe Kingsley; 1965 Sidney Stein; 1968? Robert Jantzen; 1971 Cleveland Cram; 1975 Walter McCabe (interim); 1976 Stacy B. Hulse; 1978 John K. Knaus, replaced in 1981. At Langley, the Canadian desk was headed by Ruth Joyner (1958-1962), then by Jim Smith (1962-1964), then by James Howley (?1968-1970), then by Philip Fendig (1970- 197?). The Canadian desk consisted, for most of the period in question, of a desk chief and an assistant. Because the desk only served as a liaison and rated low on the Agency's priority scale, there were periods when the post of desk chief or assistant went unfilled. One of the reasons for the weakness of the Canadian desk was that RCMP liaison officers in Washington had nearly unlimited access to many of the Agency's divisions and had no need to relay their intelligence requests through the desk. They dealt directly with the services concerned. A similar situation prevailed at the FBI.

## Chapter 8. Anguish at 24 Sussex Drive

107 **[Rouse preacher]** Speech given by John Rouse, 27/1/77, at a seminar at Northwestern University.

108 **[Macdonald-Laurier]** Both prime ministers quoted in Lawrence Martin, *The Presidents and the Prime Ministers*. This book is used for historical references throughout the chapter.

108 **[Lévesque frightened]** The eyewitness quoted by Graham Fraser in *Le Parti Québécois*, p. 13. Several members of the Lévesque government, when interviewed for this book, expressed great respect for Fraser's work. "It must be true if Fraser wrote it," remarks Claude Morin, for example, when his version contradicts Fraser's. Born in Ottawa, Fraser was the Montreal *Gazette's* Quebec correspondent beginning in 1979, suggesting that the PQ leadership knew how to distinguish between the general bias of the newspaper and the professionalism of several of its writers.

108 **[Enders]** Thomas Enders, tel. interviews, New York, 24/5/89, and 24/7/89. Pierre Elliott Trudeau refused to be interviewed by the author.

109 **[Desmarais-Sinclair]** In Peter C. Newman's *The Canadian Establishment* (pp. 57,194 and 198), he writes that "Desmarais genuinely believes that it is his mission to act as a broker between government and business on behalf of confederation."

109 **[Ball]** George Ball would only change his mind publicly on this subject in 1984, declaring that the annexation of Canada might not be desirable, "primarily because it would upset the political balance in a manner which would entail a complete change in American political life." Quoted in Richard Gwynn, *The 49th Paradox: Canada in North America*, Toronto, McClelland, 1985, p. 80.

111 **[Gotlieb]** Allan Gotlieb, interview, supra.

111 **[Ritchie]** Charles Ritchie, interview, supra.

111 **[Enders in 1976]** In *The New York Times*, 24/3/76 and 14/6/76, and *Toronto Star*, 9/11/76. A C.D. Howe and National Planning Association joint commission also stated in July that relations "are tense" and that it was "unlikely that there will be any improvement in the short term." Canadian Press report published in *Le Devoir*, 27/7/76.

112 **[Latouche]** Daniel Latouche, "Quebec: One Possible Scenario," in Annette Baker Fox et al., *Canada and the United States: Transnational and Transgovernmental Relations*, New York, Columbia University Press, 1976, pp. 336-366.

112 **[Separatist provinces]** Lieutenant-Governor: an American diplomat, who requested anonymity, to the author. The request for aid to the western separatist movement was made to a successor of Enders', Paul Robinson, after 1981: Robinson, interview, supra. Other examples taken from "Quebec Separatism: Is Canada Coming Apart?", a speech delivered on 1/2/77 by Canada's vice consul in Los Angeles, François Beaulne.

112 **[Gwynn]** In *The 49th...*, p. 130.

112 **[Vine]** Richard Vine, assistant under-secretary for Canadian affairs, 1974-1979, interview, Washington and Maryland, 13 and 20/4/89. During Rufus Smith's last months as head of Canadian affairs, Kissinger had tried to make him write a detailed report on Ottawa-Washington relations, an exercise which Mr Canada considered tedious and futile.

113 **[Fortier]** André Fortier, under-secretary of state, secretary of state's office, tel. interview, Ottawa, 24/7/89.

114 **[INR 72-73]** "The Parti Quebecois," INR Research Study, 19/10/72, 21 pages, SECRET/NO FOREIGN DISSEM/CONTROLLED DISSEM; and "Canada: Separatism quiescent but not dead," INR Research Study, 23/7/73, SECRET/NO FOREIGN DISSEM/CONTROLLED DISSEM.

114 **[PQ Convention]** Airgram Québec A-6, "An Unspectacular, Hard-Working PQ Congress," 1/3/73, UNCLASSIFIED.

114 **[INR election]** "Quebec election presages heated provincial-federal struggles," INR Intelligence Note, 15/11/73, 4 pages, CONFIDENTIAL/NO FOREIGN DISSEM.

114 **[Lévesque]** Airgram Montreal A-140, "Interview with René Lévesque," 5/11/75, 3 pages, LIMITED OFFICIAL USE. Lévesque spoke to the consul general in Montreal, Elizabeth Harper, and to her economic counsellor, Henry Lagassé.

115 **[Bokassa]** In Quebec Telegram 0245, 3/12/75.

116 **[Butterworth]** Reported by William Johnson, interview, supra.

116 **[British Columbia]** State Department source quoted by Gerald Clark, "Lévesque and the US: MISSION IMPOSSIBLE," *The Montreal Star*, 12 to 15/2/79 (series of four articles).

117 **[Enders]** Enders, interviews, supra. James Reston refused to be interviewed by the author and did not answer questions sent in writing.

119 **[Duemling]** Robert Duemling, deputy chief of mission at the embassy, 1976-1980, interview, Wash., 23/3/89.

120 **[*Barron's*]** Examples of the 1977 turnaround taken from Richard Gwynn, *The Northern Magus*, Toronto, McClelland, 1980, pp. 303-304 (399 pages). Trudeau quotation in *Maclean's*, 7/3/77, p. 18.

120 **[Trudeau defends Enders]** Quoted in *The New York Times*, 18/12/77.

120 **[Rouse in Chicago]** Speech by John Rouse, 27/1/77, at a seminar at Northwestern University entitled "The Business Significance of an Independent Quebec." Rodrigue Tremblay says he obtained his information from connections he maintained in Canada with top American State Department officials, and not from the White House, as was stated in a Canadian Press report picked up by *The Gazette*, 28/1/77. Rodrigue Tremblay, tel. interview, Montreal, 29/5/89. Vine, interview, supra.

Chapter 9. Roughed Up on Wall Street

122 **[Cakewalk]** Quoted by Louis Bernard, principal secretary to Lévesque, later secretary general of the government; interview with the author, Montreal, 12/6/89.

122 **[Morin in New York]** Except where otherwise indicated, the account of Morin's New York experience is taken from two interviews with the author, in Quebec City, 21 and 24/6/89.

122 **[Baltimore Sun]** Quoted by Graham Fraser, *Le Parti Québécois*, p.111.

122 **[New York Times]** *The New York Times*, 26/2/77, p. 1.

122 **[McNamara]** Quebec Telegram 021, 18/1/77, UNCLASSIFIED.

123 **[Michaud]** Yves Michaud, interview, Montreal, 1/6/89.

123 **[Links, Lévesque, Parizeau]** Quoted in *The Montreal Star*, 25/1/79.

124 **[Wilson at the Links]** Joe Wilson, tel. interviews, New York, 11 and 12/5/89, and telex from Canadian consul general in New York, "Lévesque visit to NYK: Postscript," 1/2/77, CONFIDENTIAL, EA.

124 [Lévesque's language] It happened that New York bigwigs took exception to Lévesque's profanity, according to a Quebec diplomat in New York who insists on anonymity.

125 [Tomlinson] Alexander Tomlinson, interview, Wash., 4/5/89.

125 [Hydro speech] Morin's additions and reaction, a former Hydro Quebec executive who insisted on anonymity, interview, Montreal, 6/89.

126 [Mackay] Robert Mackay, interview, Quebec City, 23/6/89.

126 [Threats] Telex from New York office of FBI dated 25/1/77, memo summing up the visit dated 31/1/77, FBI. State Department "Action Memorandum" 7701408, 26/1/77.

127 [The room froze] Fraser, English version of op. cit., *P.Q.: René Lévesque and the Parti Québécois in Power*, Toronto, Macmillan, 1984, p. 88.

127 [Speech] René Lévesque, "Quebec: A Good Neighbour in Transition", 23 pages, 25/1/77, as distributed to the press.

127 [Hydro] First Boston's suggestions, Tomlinson, interview, supra. *Business Week* interview entitled "Separatist Lévesque: Tougher on Foreigners," 20/12/76. "Bothered the most" quotation heard by the consul general in Montreal, then in New York, Montreal Telegram 0142, 28/1/77, CONFIDENTIAL. The anxiety stemming from the interview is confirmed by Tomlinson. In 1986, Georges Lafond summarized the manner in which Quebec did its skimming: "In 1978, Hydro Quebec paid about $40 million in property taxes and river use fees. In 1980 came the tax on gross revenue; in 1981, the tax on capital. In 1985, instead of the $40 million paid in 1978, the total was $246 million, and that doesn't count the sales tax which the company collected for the government." In Gilles Brouillet, "Le Bilan de Georges Lafond, financier," *Hydro-Presse*, Montreal, mid-September 1986, p. 9. Dividends should also be counted. Lafond said to the author, "It was done very discreetly, in any case, subtly," to cause the least possible stir in the financial markets. Interview, Montreal, 13/6/89.

128 [Laughter and public reactions] In *The Gazette*, 26/1/77.

128 [Private reactions] Montreal Telegram 0142, 28/1/77, CONFIDENTIAL. Toronto Telegram A-14, 1/2/77, LIMITED OFFICIAL USE. The American State Department inked out the portions of these texts in which quotations were attributed. In the case of A.E. Ames, only its director, Martin R. Hicks, was seated at the head table, not far from Parizeau. The president of the company, John Cook, was at a regular table. Newman is quoted by Diggins in Toronto Telegram 0295, 2/2/77, UNCLASSIFIED. Also, telex from Canadian consul general in New York, "Lévesque visit to NYK: Postscript," 1/2/77, CONFIDENTIAL, EA.

129 [Stock market] In *Wall Street Journal*, 27/1/77.

130 [Lévesque memoirs] In René Lévesque, *Attendez que je me rappelle...*, p. 392.

130 [Latouche] Daniel Latouche, interview, Montreal, 2/6/89.

130 [McNamara analysis] Quebec Telegram 031, 26/1/77, CONFIDENTIAL.

130 [Bernard] Interview, supra.

130 [Trudeau-Lévesque] Quoted in Gérard Pelletier, *Les Années d'impatience 1950-1960*, Montreal, Stanké, 1983.

131 [Beaudoin] Louise Beaudoin, interview, Montreal, 1/6/89.

131 [Lévesque consented] René Lévesque, "For an Independent Quebec," in *Foreign Affairs*, vol. 54, no. 4, July 1976, p. 744. Robert Mackay, supra, says he also had the "impression" that the historical parallel came entirely from Lévesque.

131 [Desbarats interview] Peter Desbarats, *René: a Canadian in Search of a Country*, op. cit., p. 220. In an interview in which he imagined himself in 1977 looking back on recent events, Lévesque said American reaction to Quebec independence was muted, "especially since the '76 election, with the Bicentennial year in the US." In 1969, he was surely the only person in Quebec thinking about this anniversary.

131 [Sympathy, understanding] René Lévesque, "Quebec: A Good Neighbor...", p. 22.

132 [Diplomat, revolution] An American diplomat who insists on anonymity, to the author.

132 [Harper] In Montreal Telegram 0142, 28/1/77.

Chapter 10. The New York Millstone

133   [**Lévesque destiny**] Quoted in *Wall Street Journal*, 27/1/77.

133   [**Giroux**] In Graham Fraser, *Le Parti Québécois*, p. 83.

133   [**Ferber in Montreal**] A participant who insists on anonymity, to the author.

134   [**Wilson-Lévesque**] Joe Wilson, interview, supra.

134   [**$300,000**] Ed Waters of Kidder Peabody, interview, New York, 10/5/89.

134   [**Parizeau, dawn of time**] Jacques Parizeau, interview, Montreal, 1/6/89.

135   [**Salomon Brothers executive**] an executive at Salomon Brothers who insists on anonymity, to the author. The courtship must have been too subtle, because Parizeau (interview, supra) does not remember being courted.

136   [**Met letter**] Ed Waters, interview, supra.

136   [**PQ, French socialism**] William Diebold, then Senior Fellow at the Council on Foreign Relations, tel. interview, New York, 23/5/89.

136   [**Parizeau intransigent**] A New York banker who insists on anonymity, to the author.

137   [**Some called Diebold**] Including "high government officials," William Diebold, interview, supra.

137   [**Spread during autumn 1976**] Using figures published by Kidder, Peabody & Co in its study on Hydro Quebec of March 1977. The calculations here are based on the Hydro Quebec/B.C. Hydro spread from November 22 to December 15, 1977. A spread of 27 basis points between B.C. and Hydro Quebec is considered normal. In the fall, it rose to 82 points, an increase of over 50. For our purposes, we will call "spread" this post-PQ-election variation. (Hence the potential additional cost of a new borrowing: $500 million times 0.5% times 30 years, equals $75 million.) In practice, the sum would be even higher because Canadian companies were also driven up by the PQ election. Bonds in the Maritimes suffered the most, because the market, which knew how to read a map, reasoned that the consequences of Quebec independence would be worse in the eastern provinces than in the west. If one calculated the additional cost from the spread with AT&T, 100 points in the autumn of 1977, it would be $150 million. But this was not a fair long-term standard, because Hydro's value was also affected by the market's assessment of the overall Canadian economy: poor results in Ontario, the election of the NDP in British Columbia, nationalization of potash in Saskatchewan and, after 1980, the Trudeau government's more aggressive stance on energy policy and foreign investments (FIRA). There is thus only one way to measure, if imperfectly, the variations due to the Quebec situation, and that is to use a spread with other Canadian companies, and to keep in mind that the result understates the spread somewhat.

138   [**Tomlinson, chair**] "Abrasive," a banker. Tomlinson, interview, supra.

138   [**Lévesque socialist**] In *Business Week*, loc. cit., p. 39; *US News & World Report*, 26/9/77, p. 72; *Newsweek*, 5/12/77; *Time*, 13/2/78, p. 36.

138   [**Parizeau Eco Club**] Parizeau, interview, supra.

139   [**Spread after Eco**] Calculated from the Kidder study, op. cit., p. 9, and from a B.C. Hydro bond (8 5/8 of 23/11/76). The spread, initially 27 points in mid-November, the starting point for the calculation, rose to 82 points by mid-December and 94.5 points on January 28. The raw data also come from figures provided by Merrill Lynch and Hydro Quebec. The calculations are the author's.

139   [**Harper**] Montreal Telex 0142, 28/1/77. "Boycott" in Toronto Telex 0334, 7/2/77.

140   [**Don Regan**] At the Economic Club, "Seating List," with Wilson, Wilson interview, supra.

141   [**Little rat**] Chapman told journalists Richard Daignault and Dominique Clift that in 1920, he had participated in a meeting of financiers at the Chateau Frontenac in Quebec City, and the result had been to oblige Premier Lomer Gouin to resign and be replaced by the candidate of their choice, Alexandre Taschereau. In Richard Daignault, *Lesage*, Montreal, Libre Expression, 1981; "Rat," p. 228; Gouin, p. 214. An ex-employee of Ames who insists

on anonymity also confirmed the anecdote about Parizeau. Parizeau told Black, supra, that *La Presse* had reported the insult.

141   **[Wood Gundy]** Letter from Cunningham to the embassy, 1/3/68, CONFIDENTIAL.

142   **[Accident-spread]** General information from Graham Fraser, *Le Parti Québécois*, pp.111-112. On the market, Ontario and B.C. Hydro bonds seemed also to benefit from the "good news." The spread between them and Hydro Quebec did not close. But from February 4 to 18, it narrowed 13 points between Hydro and a similar AT&T bond and 7 points between Hydro and an American Treasury bond, TSY 8 1/4, which First Boston used as a standard. Raw data furnished by Merrill Lynch and Hydro Quebec. Some would say the variations were not significant, but *The New York Times* decided at the time that the dealings following Lévesque's accident were worth reporting. The newspaper called them "macabre." (NY Times Services report published in the *Globe and Mail*, 21/2/77.)

142   **[Poor René]** Quebec Telegram 062, "Wasn't It Terrible What Happened to Poor René?", 10/2/77, LIMITED OFFICIAL USE.

143   **[Kidder, Waters]** Kidder study, op. cit.; Waters and Schmeelk interviews, supra.

143   **[Moody's]** Moody's, *The Gazette*, 12/3/77; Tomlinson interview, supra. Standard, *Globe and Mail*, 3/6/77. On the role of the Canadian Consulate in New York, see Chapter 12.

143   **[Budget]** In Fraser, op. cit., p.137.

143   **[Mid-May spread]** Calculated from a B.C. Hydro bond (8 5/8 of 23/11/76), the mid-November spread of 27 points, basis for the calculation, had widened to 70 points in mid-May 1977.

144   **[Hydro strategy]** Georges Lafond interview, supra. Figures also taken from Georges Lafond, "Hydro-Quebec and the James Bay Project: The Financing Strategy," in W.T. Standbury et al., *Financing Public Enterprises*, The Institute of Research and Policy, circa 1982, pp. 250-260.

145   **[September spread]** By the same calculation, the 27-point mid-November spread, basis for calculation, stood at 41 points on 9/9/77. Montreal brokers quoted in *The Gazette* of 14/9/77 also came up with a variation of about 15 points.

146   **[The Solly Affair]** No fewer than six sources spoke to the author on this subject; some openly (among them, Peter Gordon, tel. interview, New York, 16/2/90), and some under cover of anonymity. Each of the managers, including Salomon, received $421,269 in 1979 under the heading of "Discounts and Commissions" on the three borrowings of $200 million for the year. See Hydro prospectuses dated 30/1/79, 12/6/79 and 18/10/79.

Chapter 11. The Southerner and the Secessionists

149   **[Enders]** Thomas Enders, interviews, supra.

150   **[Reston]** *The New York Times*, 26/1/77.

151   **[Brzezinski]** Zbigniew Brzezinski, interview and correspondence, supra. See Chapter 5. For NATO, see Chapter 14.

151   **[Morin]** Claude Morin, "Morin: Quebec's Foreign Policy," *The Fletcher Forum*, vol. 4, no. 1, winter 1980, p. 129.

152   **[Hunter]** "Talking Points for President's Interview on AM-Canada", NSC, 19/2/77, and "Interview with the President by Bruce Phillips, Canada AM", 21/2/77, Jimmy Carter Library. Robert Hunter, interview, Wash. 26/4/89.

152   **[Carter-Zbig]** General information on the summit is taken from Lawrence Martin, *The Presidents...*, pp. 263- 267, from *Montreal Star* and *Southam News* reports of 22 to 26/2/77 and from *Maclean's*, 7/3/77.

152   **[Carter-Trudeau]** Emerging from the meeting, Cyrus Vance related the content of the discussion to Tom Enders, who conveyed it to the author. Interview, supra. The narration is

supplemented by James Reston, who saw Trudeau after his meeting with Carter, in *The New York Times*, 23/2/77. Carter press conference in *Congressional Quarterly*, 26/2/77, p. 367.

153 [**Kissinger study**] Launched in State Telex 303089, "Study of impacts of PQ election," 14/12/76, CONFIDENTIAL. The telex breaks up the research and analysis work among several participants. The text states that the decision to undertake the study was made at a State Department meeting on 9/12/76. The telegram was prepared by Carl Clement of the Canadian office and approved by John Rouse and Richard Vine, but bore Kissinger's signature. It is not certain, however, that Kissinger was aware of it, as the secretary of state's signature is often "delegated." Its presence nevertheless indicates the important nature of the project.

153 [**McNamara**] In Quebec Telegram 019, "Contribution to study of impacts of PQ election," 17/1/77, CONFIDENTIAL. "We believe the most likely outcome will be a period of disorder leading to an eventual declaration of independence following one or more referendums," the consul general wrote.

153 [**Vine**] Richard Vine, interview, supra. The concept of "plausible deniability" is often used in secret operations. The most recent example was in 1987, when Ronald Reagan's national security advisor, John Poindexter, declared that he had not informed his boss of the diversion of Iranian funds to the Contras, thus allowing Reagan to make a "plausible denial."

156 [**Treverton**] Gregory Treverton, interview, New York, 8/5/89.

156 [**Zbig nations**] In Zbigniew Brzezinski, *Between Two Ages: America's Role in the Technocratic Era*, New York, Penguin, 1976, p. 55. First published in 1970, this book was reprinted every year during Brzezinski's employment in the White House. Twenty years after writing it, Brzezinski states that such nationalism "does not always demand separate statehood, but normally requires a true sense of autonomy."

157 [**Zbig CTV**] Transcript of the program of September 30, 1977.

157 [**Zbig Ford**] Robert Ford, interview, supra.

158 [**Head**] Ivan Head and Zbigniew Brzezinski, interviews, supra.

159 [**Quebec study**] "The Quebec Situation: Outlook and Implications," 8/77, 22 pages, SECRET.

160 [**Canada vulnerable**] Memo by John Rouse, "Annual Review of US Policy Towards Canada," 14/4/77, SECRET. The memo states that Canadian vulnerability will "lead Canada to oppose the United States less often, and will, in fact, help restore certain aspects of the 'special relationship'" between the two countries, a relationship abandoned since Nixon's days.

160 [**Butterworth-Enders**] Butterworth, in his Ottawa Airgram A-474, "Quebec — Separatism in Flood Tide," 10 pages, 24/10/67, CONFIDENTIAL. Enders repeats a theme of McNamara's in his Ottawa Telegram 24732, "New Hope for preservation of Canadian unity," 6/6/77, CONFIDENTIAL, and Telegram Ottawa 9708, "How the National Unity Crisis may play out: an update," 12/12/78, SECRET, 17 pages.

163 [**Morin**] In Claude Morin, *L'Art de l'impossible*, pp. 264-265.

163 [**Pouliot**] Richard Pouliot, interview, Quebec City, 15/6/89.

Chapter 12. A Voiceless Quebec

164 [**Post**] Robert Scully, "What It Means to Be French in Canada," 17/4/77, p. C1-4. Letters to the Editor, 19 and 24/4/77. The only other substantial piece published by the paper, this time well-balanced, appeared on the eve of the referendum. (Was there a precedent? The *Post* had printed, in September of 1888, a report from a journalist sent to Nicolet, who wrote of "ignorant French Canadians": quoted in Martin, *The Presidents...*) By 1977, the *Washington Star* had lost much of its old glory. It ceased publication in August 1981.

165 [**Enders and Burns**] Notes taken during the meeting by Robert Trudel of the Quebec

Department of Intergovernmental Affairs, 28/4/77, MAIQ.

165 [**Scully**] In a letter to the author (7/6/89), Scully states that he has "nothing to add" to what he said at the time. He had offered lengthy explanations — and apologies — in *Le Journal de Montréal*, 10/5/77, and *Le Devoir*, 23/4/77. His *Post* article had been reproduced in its entirety in the *Montreal Star*, and extracts had been published in *La Presse* and *Dimanche Matin*. Scully stated that the *Post* had deleted, without his permission, "an extremely important paragraph at the beginning, which set the tone for the whole text. I said, 'I care only for my people,' and explained that I had a duty to say things painful to them." Scully explained also that he had expressed elsewhere the affection he felt for his city. In fact, in a short story dated October 1973 but published after the *Post* piece, Scully praised "Montreal, city of magic," to the skies. It was a "great city of America," which, he said, "draws its magic from the French presence in North America and the creative friction which results from that." In the same piece, he described the Hochelaga-Maisonneuve district warmly and spoke of a Montreal which, "like Miami or Vancouver or Chicago or Dallas or Detroit, explodes with motion, with discoveries, with violence, with new ideas, with contradictions." To live there, he wrote, was "a privilege." (In Robert Guy Scully and others, *Morceaux du Grand Montreal*, Saint-Lambert, Noroit, 1978, pp.10-13. In the same year, he helped Claude Ryan write his platform book, U*ne Société Stable*.) Scully, who calls himself "Franco-American," had lived in Ottawa until he was 14, then moved to Montreal. He was 27 when he wrote the *Post* article.

166 [**Anderson**] John Anderson, interview, Wash., 3/2/89. Al Horne, tel. interview, Wash., 8/11/89.

166 [**Ryan**] Claude Ryan, "La presse américaine et l'élection du 15 novembre," *Le Devoir*, 16/2/77.

166 [**Wall Street**] *The Wall Street Journal*, 2/2/77.

166 [**Barron's**] Quoted in *Le Devoir*, 16/2/77.

167 [**Foreign Policy**] F.S. Manor, "Canada's Crisis: The Causes" and Nicholas Stethem, "The Dangers," in *Foreign Policy*, no. 29, winter 77-78, pp. 43-57. Dumas, in a memo of 28/2/79, MAIQ State Department study, see Chapter 11. It must be noted that *Foreign Affairs*, a more influential rival of *Foreign Policy*, showed more care and balance in its treatment of the question. To an article by René Lévesque, "For an Independent Quebec," loc. cit., printed in July 1976, it carried, in October 1977, the measured federalist reply of Bruce Hutchison, historian and editorial page editor of the V*ancouver Sun*. Hutchison's article was entitled "Canada's Time of Troubles" (pp.175-189).

167 [**Atlantic**] Mordecai Richler, "Oh! Canada! Lament for a Divided Country," *The Atlantic Monthly*, 12/77, pp. 41- 55; letters in 3/78 edition, pp.107-109. Lévesque on Richler, to Yves Michaud, interview, supra. The Bronfman speech was given to a private gathering. Fraser, op. cit., p. 80, quotes other statements by the financier that evening. Electing the PQ would be "suicide, worse than a disaster, it would be a greater crime than stabbing ourselves in the backs. The election IS the referendum, [...] the referendum that decides whether we live or die, [...] because we are dealing with a bunch of thugs who want to destroy us." Richler's version of the "Nazi" song: "Nobody was reassured when joyous PQ members sang a French version of 'Tomorrow Belongs To Me,' the chilling Hitler Youth song from *Cabaret*, at their victory rally."

168 [**Journalists' visit**] In the *Montreal Star*, 25/10/77.

168 [**Giniger**] Quoted by Stephen Baker, American journalist in Washington, author of "How America Sees Quebec" in Alfred Hero and Marcel Daneau, *Problems and Opportunities in US-Quebec Relations*, Westview, Boulder CO, 1984, p.169. Baker notes: "Virtually everything the United States hears about French Canada comes from English Canadians. In US newspapers and magazines and on radio and television, Quebec news (on those rare occasions that it travels across the border) is gathered, edited and presented by Anglo-Canadians. The lack of Québécois voices might be expected because the linguistic barrier is

fundamental to the Canadian struggle. But that US news services have opted to let Canadians report the news for them instead of seeing for themselves is remarkable."

168 [Globe-Maclean's] In Fraser, op. cit., p.147.

168 [Commentary] Ruth R. Wisse and Irwin Cotler, "Quebec's Jews: Caught in the Middle," in *Commentary*, vol. 64, no. 5, 9/77, pp. 55-69. Letters in vol. 65, no. 1, 1/78, pp. 5-9.

170 [Lubin] Martin Lubin, "Quebec Non-Francophones and the United States," in Alfred Hero and Marcel Daneau, *Problems and Opportunities in US-Quebec Relations*, Boulder, CO, Westview, 1984, pp. 207-209.

170 [Feldman] Elliott Feldman was director of the University Consortium for Research on North America at Harvard from 1978 to 1988. Interview, Wash., 3/5/89. Journalist and Dumas, MAIQ.

171 [Newsday] *Newsday*, 14/5/78, p. 74. In interviews conducted on Wall Street and in Washington, the author never observed a hint of this notion of the PQ being accused of antisemitism.

171 [Beaudoin] Louise Beaudoin, interview, Montreal, 1/6/89.

171 [White paper] Comparison of first draft of 5/79, draft of 9/10/79 and published version. Claude Malette files.

172 [Newsweek] Edgar M. Bronfman, "Cool it, Canada!", *Newsweek*, 26/9/77, p.11.

172 [Landry] Bernard Landry, tel. interview, Montreal, 6/89.

173 [Diplomat, Giniger] Washington Telegram UNGR4671, 6/12/77, CONFIDENTIAL, EA.

173 [Rumors]See Morris Wolfe, "The Other Side of Bill 101. Read This Before You Believe the Worst," loc. cit., p. 17-27.

173 [Morin-police] In Claude Morin, *L'Art de l'impossible*, p. 270.

173 [Villella] Quoted in Gerald Clark, "Lévesque and the US: MISSION IMPOSSIBLE," loc. cit.

173 [Beaudoin, Morin in US] Beaudoin, interview, supra. Morin interview, and in *Etudes Internationales*, vol. XX, no. 1, 3/89, p. 236.

174 [New York] Memo from Barry Steers to Under-Secretary of State for External Affairs, NY #643, 6/10/77, CONFIDENTIAL, EA. Relations between Steers and Bergeron were less than perfect; Steers referred to him as "Guy" rather than Marcel in his memo. Jean-Marc Lajoie, interviews, supra. Other quotations taken from David Thomas, "The Winning of the World," *Maclean's*, 15/5/78. Reference to Quebec "franc" in Herbert Mayer, "Business Has the Jitters in Quebec," *Fortune*, 10/77, pp. 238-244.

175 [Armstrong] Willis Armstrong, interview, supra.

175 [Bourassa] Interviews, Beaudoin, Morin, supra.

175 [Patry] 15/4/65, see Chapter 3.

175 [1969] Peter Desbarats, *René: A Canadian in search of a Country*, op. cit., p. 214. See Morris Wolfe, "The Other Side of Bill 101. Read This Before You Believe the Worst," loc. cit., p. 17-27.

Chapter 13. Operation America

For this chapter, some ten Quebeckers, part of the diplomatic effort on the United States under René Lévesque, agreed to answer the author's questions. Some required anonymity; the others are named below.

178 [Dismiss the Americans] Strangely, noted a high MAIQ official who demanded anonymity, certain left-wing members of the cabinet, including Jacques Couture and Denis Lazure, supporters of immobility vis-à-vis the United States, felt that when the moment of truth arrived the United States would pronounce itself for independence.

178 [Lévesque] To Yves Michaud, interview, supra. Morin, interview, supra.

179 [The Quebec situation ] See chapter 10.

180 [Hero] His text entitled "Quebec Nationalism: Some Prognoses and Implications for the United States," 19/1/77. Hero, interviews, supra.

180 [Richard Pouliot] Interview, Quebec City, 15/6/89.

182 [Cousineau] Memo from François Beaulne, 13/4/78, DIFFUSION RESTREINTE, EA.

182 [Delegation] The evidence remains unclear on the first Quebec notions of opening a full-fledged delegation in Washington. Louise Beaudoin and some Americans, including ambassadorial diplomats Tom Enders and Robert Duemling, recalled that a request for a general delegation had already been made and rejected. A second request, for a simple delegation, met the same fate. Enders stated that Lévesque broached the subject during their first meeting. No available Quebec, American, or federal document corroborates these recollections. Richard Pouliot, who was in charge of this topic at the beginning of 1977, states categorically that the one and only intent was to open a tourism office. Interviews, supra.

182 [Ottawa] Memo James E. Hyndman FCP-120, 24/1/79, CONFIDENTIEL; letter from Gilles Mathieu in Washington, No. 11, 19/1/79, CONFIDENTIEL, EA.

183 [Inconveniencing the Americans] Internal memo, June 1977. Rhode Island, memo, July 1977. No Quebec Week, memo from Roger Cyr, July 1978. Dunn to the embassy, memo from Dunn, 25/3/80, MAIQ.

183 [Lévesque] In *The New York Times*, 22/12/77.

184 [Chapdelaine, Dumas] Interviews, supra.

184 [External Affairs accounting] Memo "'Meeting with Quebec Officials,' 23/8/78," FCO-1037, 21/8/78, CONFIDENTIAL, EA.

184 [Operation America] "Notes de la réunion de délégués," 19/6/78, New York; "Notes du comité interministériel" 16/8/78; *Opération Amérique: orientation et objectifs*, Oct. 1978, MAIQ.

185 [Imperial Oil] In *The Gazette*, 18/1/77.

185 [Vest-Tomlinson] George Vest, Undersecretary of State for European Affairs, 1977-1981, interview, Washington, 28/3/89, and tel interview, 12/7/89. Tomlinson, interview, supra.

186 [Savoie]According to Rénald Savoie, the delegate general in New York, Mario Gosselin, warned the Operation America coordinator, Roger Cyr, that he would coordinate nothing at all in terms of the delegation in New York. Cyr first occupied an office at the delegation in New York, then one in Boston. Savoie, tel interview, Montreal, 14/2/90.

186 [Lévesque in Boston] In *The Boston Globe*, 20/4/78.

186 [Safire] For de Gaulle, see chapter 4. Cited from William Safire, *Full Disclosure* (New York: Ballantine Books, 1977), p. 192 (orig. ed. Doubleday). In Safire's futuristic geopolitical world, the US and the USSR. formed the First World; Asia, dominated by the China-Japan alliance, formed the Second World; the Arab countries, allied with Israel (!) and India, formed the Third World, which was at this time under attack by the countries of the Fourth World, the poorest, headed by Quebec, as we have seen. Quite a scenario. (Europe does not enter this picture.) Meeting in Washington and Iran quotation, in Gerald Clark, "Lévesque and the US ..." loc. cit. In Montreal, memo from Normand Nadeau, 6/4/79, MAIQ. Safire's writings in *The New York Times*: "The Soft-Selling of Secession," 19/1/79; "Trudeau's Last Stand," 2/4/79; "Jefferson Davis Lives," 5/4/79. Among his many talents, William Safire is among the most-read linguists in the country. He proposed to use "Quebecker," as Lévesque pronounced it, rather than "Quebecer," as the *Times* "Style Book" prescribed. He also refused to write "Parti Québécois," another "Style Book" rule, though he translated names of other foreign political parties. He decided to "secede" from the "Style Book" and stated that, "as a reprisal against the elimination of English subtitles on road signs," he would henceforth call the PQ "the Quebecker Party." (See "Discourse," reprinted in the Los Angeles *Herald Examiner*, 15/3/79.)

187  [Boston] Southam News dispatch in *The Gazette*, 20/4/78. Report from Boston delegate 15/5/78, MAIQ. For anti-Semitism, see chapter 12.

188  [Council] Report by Jean-Marc Blondeau, 6/6/79, MAIQ. Letters from Nagorski to Lévesque, 18/5/79, and to Marcel Bergeron, 19/5/78. Dispatch from Canadian consulate at New York, "Rene Levesque Talk to Council on Foreign Relations," 19/5/78, RESTRICTED EA. Recollections in Gerald Clark, "Lévesque and the US ...," loc. cit., confirmed to the author by other witnesses. Brokaw in Southam News dispatch in *The Gazette,* 19/5/78.

190  [Rockefeller] Train anecdote told to Feldman by Rockefeller. Feldman, interview, supra. Toronto speech, "Canada-US Relations: A Solid, Working Partnership," 23/1/78. He also said that he understood "the depth of the cultural and economic concerns expressed by French Canadians." Speech by Mr Lewis, Canadian National Business Conference, 11/7/77. Notes by Jean-Marc Blondeau, 31/5/78, MAIQ. General information in Peter Collier and David Horowitz, *The Rockefellers: An American Dynasty* (New York: Holt, 1976), p. 122. Pierre Vallières, see *Québec impossible*, op cit.

192  [California] In Gerald Clark, "Lévesque and the US ..." and in Quebec Telegram 0350, "The missing drum beat: a lost week in California," 10/10/78, LIMITED OFFICIAL USE. On Lalonde, Quebec Telegram 020, "Levesque in Louisiana," 15/1/79, LIMITED OFFICIAL USE.

192  [Oval Office] State Department Telegram 083996, 1/4/78, CONFIDENTIAL. Quebec Telegram 0118, "Dreams of Oval Room Exorcised," 13/4/78, CONFIDENTIAL.

192  [Johnson and Bourassa, Washington] For Daniel Johnson, see chapter 4. Bourassa expressed this intention in a letter to the Canadian ambassador in Washington, Jake Warren, 21/7/75 (National Archives RG25, Acc 80-81/022, box 22, file 20-1-5, Wsh Pt 1). Lévesque and Mondale, memo R.H.G. Mitchell, "Visite du vice-président Mondale: requête québécois," 23/12/77, EA; "Demandes de rencontres," memo FCP-180, 3/10/78, CONFIDENTIEL, EA; memo, "Visite du président Carter: Intérêt du Québec," 18/9/79, EA.

193  [Visit to Washington] Lévesque to Washington, taken from Dumas, interview, supra; a note from Dumas to Donovan, 28/1/79, MAIQ; *La Presse*, 26/1/79; Quebec Telegram 036, "Mr Lévesque Goes to Washington: Much Ventured, Little Gained," 26/1/79, CONFIDENTIAL; Gerald Clark, "Lévesque and the US ..." loc. cit.; *The Gazette*, Jan. 26 and 27, 1979.

195  [Timberlake, Smith] James Timberlake, Canada Desk Director, International Security Affairs 1974-1980, interview, Washington, 24/4/89. Rufus Smith, interview, supra. Letter from Muskie to Vance, 29/1/79.

196  [Vallée] Jacques Vallée's report 29/10/79, MAIQ. Latouche, interview, supra.

196  [Reports] MAIQ memo, "La perception du Québec aux États-Unis," 3/3/79, unsigned; Roger Cyr, "Opération Amérique: évaluation de l'an 1," New York, 15/6/79; "Notre synthèse sur l'Opération Amérique," May 1979; "Compte Rendu de la septième réunion du comité interministériel de l'Opération Amérique tenue à Québec le 12 juin 1979," 12/7/79, DIFFUSION RESTREINTE; "Direction/États-Unis: Revue des opérations," Jan., 1980, unsigned. MAIQ. Washington dispatch UNGR4671, "Le 15 nov 76 plus un an: Impact," 6/12/77, Canadian embassy to Washington, CONFIDENTIEL, EA.

Chapter 14. The Pentagon: Quebec, How Many Divisions?

A total of 24 Pentagon officials, most of them retired, were interviewed for this chapter, including staff at the Canada Desk for the period 1967–1980, officers responsible for Canada and for NATO in the Joint Chiefs of Staff (Section J5), American military attachés in Ottawa, members of the Permanent Joint Board of Defence, and some others.

Background information was taken from R.B. Byers and David Leyton-Brown, "The Strategic and Economic Implications for the United States of a Sovereign Quebec,"

*Canadian Public Policy/Analyse de Politiques* (Spring 1980), pp. 325-341, and from Joseph T. Jockel, "Un Québec Souverain et la Défense de l'Amérique du Nord Contre une Attaque Nucléaire," *Études internationales*, Vol. 11, No. 2 (June 1980), pp. 303-316.

198 [Balthazar] Louis Balthazar, "Notes sur la politique d'un Québec souverain (et associé au Canada) à l'endroit des États-Unis," Dec., 1979, MAIQ.

198 [Scenarios] Quotations on the first two scenarios taken from Howard H. Lentner, "Canadian separatism and its implications for the United States," *Orbis, a Journal of World Affairs* (Foreign Policy Research Institute: Summer, 1978), pp. 375-393. Quotations on the third and fourth scenarios were taken from F.S. Manor and Nicholas Stethem, "Canada's Crisis," *Foreign Policy*, op. cit.

199 [Timberlake, Jockel] James Timberlake, Canada Desk Director at International Security Affairs, the Pentagon branch charged with politico-military affairs, interviews, Washington, 24/4/89 and 1/5/89. Joseph T. Jockel, Canada specialist at New York University at St. Lawrence, then at Johns Hopkins University in Washington, telephone interview, Washington-St. Lawrence Plattsburgh, 17/7/89.

200 [Warnke] Assistant Secretary of Defense for International Security Affairs 1967-1969, interview, Wash., 3/5/89.

201 [Ellsworth] Robert F. Ellsworth, Assistant Secretary of Defense for International Security Affairs, 1974-1975, Deputy Secretary responsible for information 1975-1977, tel. interview, Wash., 4/5/89.

201 [Parizeau] State Department memo, "Quebec Separatism," 23/10/69, LIMITED OFFICIAL USE.

201 [Trudeau] Quoted in James Littleton, op. cit., p. 69.

202 [Bader] Senior official in charge of NATO and Europe (thus Canada) at International Security Affairs since 1978. Interview, Wash., 12/5/89.

202 [Roades] Colonel Charles Roades, at Section J5 of the Joint Chiefs of Staff from 1973 to 1976. Tel. interview, Wash., 17/5/89.

202 [Documents] The American access-to-information law requires departments to reveal, on request, the existence of documents that are pertinent to that request, even if their classification prevents them from being divulged. Aside from a dozen unimportant dispatches, the Pentagon stated that it had no document bearing on the Quebec independence movement in the archives of the Joint Chiefs of Staff, International Security Affairs, or other sections responsible for defining military policy. The same response came from the Defense Intelligence Agency and from Army Intelligence, charged with military information.

203 [Erie Canal] Army Corps of Engineers documents, particularly a letter from Colonel Marven W. Rees dated 6/5/77, and "Public Information Brochure—Great Lakes–Hudson River Waterway (Great Lakes To Eastern Seaboard All-American Canal) Survey Study," Public Notice No. 10182, March 1980, p. 7 and table 3. As well, dispatches from EA dated 17/5/77, and Canadian Press dispatch in the *Montreal Star* dated 12/5/77. The Corps of Engineers study was later limited to renovation projects on the Erie Canal to improve barge transport.

203 [Quebec army] Quebec Airgram A-53, "Parti québécois Parliamentary Leader Discusses Foreign Policy of an 'Independent Quebec,'" 16/12/75, CONFIDENTIAL; Quebec Airgram A-39, "Parti québécois Leader Speaks on an Army for an Independent Quebec," 27/5/76, LIMITED OFFICIAL USE.

203 [Morin] In Claude Morin, *L'Art de l'impossible*, op. cit., pp. 280-283, and interview, supra.

203 [Political scientists] Byers and Leyton Brown, loc. cit., p. 328.

204 [Time] From 13/2/78, loc. cit., p. 36.

Other interviews for this chapter: Melvin Conant, American expert on Canadian-American defense relations, author of *The Long Polar Watch*, Frederick S. Wyle, assistant of Warnke 1966-1968; Brigadier General Rex H. Hampton, Regional Director Europe

International Security Affairs (ISA), 1968-1970; John H. Morse, Deputy Assistant Secretary, European and NATO Affairs, 1969-1973; Frank Tussing, American Secretary of the Permanent Joint Board of Defense, 1975-1979; Major General Richard C. Bowman, Regional Director, Europe, ISA, 1975-1981; Major General James C. Pfautz, executive officer of the Assistant Secretary for ISA, 1976-1977; David E. McGiffert, Assistant Secretary for ISA, 1977-1980; Rear Admiral S.H. Packer II, Assistant Deputy Director for Political Military Affairs, J5 Joint Chiefs of Staff (JCS), 1975; Brigadier General Robert W. Sennewald, Assistant Deputy Director for Political Military Affairs, J5, JCS, 1976-1978; Colonel Robert M. Lawson, Military Attaché Ottawa 1964-1968; Colonel Kenneth Lemley, Army Attaché, Ottawa 1968-1969; Colonel Charles E. Taylor, Assistant Air Attaché, Ottawa 1968-1971; Captain Bernard L. Garbow, Navy Attaché Ottawa 1968-1971; Colonel Richard H. Dolson Sr, Army Attaché Ottawa, 1969-1971

Chapter 15. The Busybodies

206   [Lévesque] Question period at the National Assembly, 24/5/79.

206   [McNamara] On iceberg, Quebec Telegram 304, "Levesque reaffirms 'unshakeable' commitment to sovereignty-association," 29/8/78, LIMITED OFFICIAL USE. On "chatterbox," Quebec Telegram 369, "Rene the fan dancer," 19/10/78, LIMITED OFFICIAL USE.

206   [Enders] On meeting with Lévesque, interviews with two senior Quebec officials who require anonymity, and with Jean-Roch Boivin, Lévesque's cabinet chief, tel. interview, Montreal, 31/5/89. "Summary of interview of American ambassador to Canada, Mr Thomas Ostrom Enders, with the prime minister, 27/4/78," 3/5/78, CONFIDENTIEL, MAIQ. Also Enders, interview, supra. *Time*, 13/2/78. On Enders's career, *The New York Times*, 26/3/82. On Nixon and Bourassa, in *Maclean's*, 29/11/76.

207   [Photos] Quebec Airgram "Biographies: Parti Québécois Executive Committee," 7/6/79, LIMITED OFFICIAL USE.

208   [Dunn] Memo dated 25/3/80, MAIQ. The ambassador's assistant was Gilles Mathieu.

208   [McNamara] Francis Terry McNamara, interview, Wash., 27/3/89.

208   [Dispatches] Quebec Telegram 356, "Let's be serious Pierre," 27/11/76, CONFIDENTIAL. Quebec Telegram 031, "Rene the juggler, "26/1/77, CONFIDENTIAL. Quebec Telegram 202, "Rene is having trouble keeping his pants up while juggling three balls," 26/5/77, CONFIDENTIAL. Quebec Telegram 278, "Levesque plays let's make a deal," 25/7/77, CONFIDENTIAL. Quebec Telegram 280, "Levesque turns the dagger, "26/7/77, CONFIDENTIAL. On visit to Paris, Quebec Telegram 435, "How ya gonna keep René down on the farm after he's seen Paree?," 14/11/77, LIMITED OFFICIAL USE.

209   [Quotations] On the PQ in "René the juggler," loc. cit. On Bill 101 in "Levesque turns the dagger," loc. cit. On the cabinet, in Quebec Telegram 339, "Quebec must decide between the heart and the pocketbook," 10/9/77, CONFIDENTIAL, and in Quebec Airgram A-04, "The Parti Quebecois: An Uneasy Blend of Idealism and Pragmatism," 19/5/78, CONFIDENTIAL; Telegram Quebec 430, "PQ government appears to have completed toilet training," 10 pages, CONFIDENTIAL. On PQ semantics, Quebec Telegram 275, "Fancy cape work at Regina," 15/8/78, LIMITED OFFICIAL USE. On paunchy Lévesque, Quebec Telegram 387, "René's fan slips a bit more," 31/10/78. On hyphens, Quebec Telegram 105, "Hyphens are still a separatist's best friend," 20/3/79, LIMITED OFFICIAL USE.

209   [Scoops] Interviews with Louis Bernard, Jean-Roch Boivin, Daniel Latouche, supra. On Morin and strategy, Quebec Telegram 364, "Curiouser and curiouser," 10/10/78, CONFIDENTIAL. On the white paper, Quebec Telegram 388, "Preview of a white paper for

'federalists who vote yes,'"2/10/79, CONFIDENTIAL, and Quebec Telegram 445, "Lévesque's white paper on sovereignty-association," 2/11/79, CONFIDENTIAL. On the referendum date, Quebec Telegram 122, "Quebec: three months before the referendum," 22/3/80, CONFIDENTIAL.

210 [Asbestos] Enders in Ottawa Telegram 149, "Quebec expropriation of Asbestos Corporation," 9/1/79, LIMITED OFFICIAL USE. Study in *Draft Possible Expropriation of Asbestos Corporation*, 2/1/79, then *Memorandum Quebec: Background on Possible Expropriation of Asbestos Corporation*, 6/7/79, CONFIDENTIAL. On health in *Notes on the Status of Other Pending Cases—Canada*, c. Sept. 1979. Morin, interview supra. In Quebec Telegram 373, "Asbestos Corporation," 21/9/79, CONFIDENTIAL, Quebec Telegram 428, "Asbestos Corporation: Quebec ministers approve notice of expropriation," 22/10/79, CONFIDENTIAL, and Quebec Telegram 107, "Asbestos expropriation: Text of Quebec letter to General Dynamics," 24/3/81, UNCLASSIFIED. On final decision, Quebec Telegram 386, "Asbestos expropriation imminent," 6/10/81, CONFIDENTIAL. On Ryan, Quebec telex 080, "Quebec appeals court lifts injunction against expropriation," 5/3/81, CONFIDENTIAL.

212 [Afghanistan] Claude Morin, interview, supra.

212 [French Connection] On the press in Paris Telegram 34346, "French reaction to Quebec election," 18/11/76, CONFIDENTIAL. Deniau in Quebec Telegram 341, "French parliamentarian's comments on Rene Levesque," 17/11/76, CONFIDENTIAL, and Paris Telegram 36819, "Levesque visit to France: tidying up," 16/1277, CONFIDENTIAL. On Dorin, Quebec Telegram 361, "Update on franco-quebecois relations," 23/9/77, LIMITED OFFICIAL USE. Quebec Telegram 383, "Levesque to address French national assembly," 7/10/77, LIMITED OFFICIAL USE, and Quebec Telegram 393, "Possible Levesque appearance before French national assembly," 18/10/77, CONFIDENTIAL. On Élysée reaction, Paris Telegram 30005, "Levesque visit to France," 13/10/77, CONFIDENTIAL. Letter from Giscard quoted in Claude Morin, *L'Art de l'impossible* ..., op. cit., p. 376. In Paris, Quebec Telegram 424, "Reactions to beginning of Levesque's visit to France," 3/11/77, LIMITED OFFICIAL USE, and Quebec Telegram 427, "Rene returns from wonderland with the looking glass," 7/11/77, CONFIDENTIAL. On Giscard sentence, Louise Beaudoin, interview, supra. On American reaction in Paris, Paris Telegram 32527, "Levesque's visit to France," 7/11/77, CONFIDENTIAL. This dispatch was nine pages long. According to the MAIQ, the American diplomat in charge of the visit in Paris was George Jaeger, later McNamara's successor in Quebec City. However, the dispatch was signed, as was usual, by Ambassador Hartman. On Enders, his Ottawa Telegram 9631, "Trudeau seeks to down-play significance of Levesque's trip to France," 9/11/77, CONFIDENTIAL. Cartoon in *The Washington Post*, 6/11/77. Lévesque on Carter in *The New York Times*, 7/11/77, p. A5.

214 [Press memos] Department's reaction to the press, State Department Telegram 264720, "Press guidance on Levesque visit to France," 4/11/77, UNCLASSIFIED, and State Department Telegram 42188, "Dept's press guidance Feb. 13," 15/2/80, LIMITED OFFICIAL USE. On Carter and Giscard, see Zbigniew Brzezinski, *Power and Principle* (New York: Farrar, Straus, Giroux 1983), pp. 24-25. He wrote, "I detected a touch of the country boy's awe for the elegance of the Parisian's intellect."

215 [Mitterrand] On the visit, Quebec Telegram 393, "French socialist leader finds nothing to smile about in Quebec," 6/11/78, LIMITED OFFICIAL USE. Mitterrand quotation, from notes taken by a witness who says that his transcription is "verbatim." On Trudeau-Giscard, Ottawa Telegram 6175, "Trudeau and Giscard at odds over Quebec," 15/12/78, LIMITED OFFICIAL USE. On Barre in Ottawa Telegram 693, "Trudeau criticizes France for 'playing around' with Quebec separatism and warns that Quebec independence would mean end of Canada," 6/2/79, LIMITED OFFICIAL USE.

Chapter 16. Waiting for Cyrus

217  [**Situation in Quebec**] "The Quebec Situation: Outlook and Implications," August 1977, SECRET. See summary end of chapter 11, "It was in the United States' interest ..." and entire text of document in the appendix.

217  [**Trudeau and polls**] Since April of 1979, the Clark government had been taking very sophisticated polls in Quebec. Trudeau continued with them, increasing their frequency. In March, a new poll showed 46% for "YES" and 43% for "NO." In his memoirs, Lévesque said that the same figures were on his desk at the beginning of April. Three weeks before the vote, Trudeau received a new crop of figures: "YES" 38%, "NO" 35%. The undecided had swollen to 26%. Starting in April, the PQ polls gave the "YES" side a lower percentage than did those of Trudeau. In mid-April, the figures were "YES" 48/"NO" 52; at the end of April, "YES" 45/"NO" 55, with the "YES" side rising by about a point a week from then on. Sources: Robert Sheppard and Michael Valpy, *The national deal—the fight for a Canadian constitution* (Toronto: Macmillan, 1982), pp. 26-30; René Lévesque, *Attendez que je me rappelle...*, op. cit., p. 407; Michel Vastel, *Trudeau, le Québécois* (Montreal: Éditions de l'Homme, 1989), p. 248; Graham Fraser, *Le Parti québécois*, op. cit., p. 259.

218  [**Latouche**] Interview, supra. He stated that this proposal had never been presented to Lévesque. Morin does not remember having known about it.

218  [**List**] Memo from James Donovan to Robert Normand, "Rencontres de certaines personnalités politiques," 6/8/79, CONFIDENTIEL, MAIQ. On Connally, *La Presse*, 18/11/76, p. A6. Also on the list were Howard Baker, Republican senator from Tennessee and minority leader; Jacob Javits, senator from New York; Charles Percy, senator from Illinois; Patrick Moynihan, senator from New York; and three senators from New England, William Cohen from Maine, Paul Tsongas from Massachusetts, and Patrick Leahy from Vermont. John Connally, ex-governor of Texas, was considered "advisable and possible," which was surprising since, on the day after the PQ was elected, he had proposed a freeze on American investment in Canada until René Lévesque specified his intentions. Claude Morin and Bernard Landry, interviews, supra.

219  [**Reagan**] Paul Hannaford, telephone interview, Wash., 28/7/89. Hannaford said that he verified this with his colleague at the time, Richard Allen, and in the Reagan campaign archives. Michael Deaver, in a telephone interview (Wash., 12/7/89), did not remember this episode. On Reagan 1979, a high-ranking Quebec official, who requested anonymity. Though candidate Reagan did not come to Quebec another presidential hopeful, less well known, did. Lyndon Larouche was the guru of a bizarre American political splinter group which mixed anti-Communism, anti-Semitism, and anti-British monarchism into a delirious cocktail that proposed that the Queen of England was conspiring with Henry Kissinger and Leonid Brezhnev to organize drug trafficking in order to weaken the West and pave the way for Bolshevism. There were two ways to save the Free World: nuclear energy and the Strategic Defense Initiative. This group also had an interesting fund-raising method: they would sell a book to an individual and then use his credit-card number to bilk him out of a few thousand dollars. Years later, Larouche would spend some time behind bars for this unorthodox method. At the time, however, he requested a meeting with an advisor to the premier. Larouche and Latouche? They were surely related, thought a secretary, and so the Quebec professor-turned-advisor met with the kook just down the hall from Lévesque's office. Larouche informed Latouche of the ins and outs of the warped conspiracy by the Jesuits and the British to plunge the West into chaos. The Parti Québécois, which seemed anti-British, and the Larouchians should make a common front to save the human race, he suggested. Daniel Latouche took stock of this "caveman," not knowing whether to laugh or cry. "I said, Look, in the government there are three Ph.D.s from Oxford and one from Cambridge, so I don't think that this government will be very anti-British." Daniel Latouche, interview, supra.

221 [**Soporific**] On the effect of Operation America, James Donovan's note, "Lysiane Gagnon's remarks on Seagram's advertising in the United States," 9/4/80, and Pierre Baillargeon's memo "Perceptions récentes du Québec aux États-Unis," 22/4/80, MAIQ. Joseph Jockel, interview, supra. Jockel added, jokingly, "I've never forgiven the people of Quebec for voting 'no' in the referendum, and I encourage all my Canadian friends to vote NDP, because an NDP government would bring back those golden years."

220 [**New England**] Telex from Jacques Vallée, "La Nouvelle-Angleterre et le référendum," 12/5/80, MAIQ.

221 [**Embassy**] Embassy telex WSHDC UNGR2266, "Référendum au Québec: réactions américaines," 22/4/80, CONFIDENTIEL ENTRE CDNS SEULEMENT, EA.

221 [**Normand-Vallée**] Summary of the meeting of 7/3/80, MAIQ.

221 [**Consul**] George Jaeger's suggestion was summarized by Jean Chapdelaine, who indicated that it "agrees with our point of view" in a note to Richard Pouliot, c. 15/1/80, MAIQ.

221 [**E.F. Hutton**] On the delegation and the consulate, Jean-Marc Lajoie, interview, supra. Inter-office memo from Ruth Corson, "The Quebec Referendum," 13/5/80. Investor quoted in *The Financial Post*, 5/4/80, pp. 1-2.

222 [**Congress**] In Donald Alper, "Congressional attitudes toward Canada and Canada-United States relations," *The American Review of Canadian Studies*, Vol. 10, No. 2 (autumn 1980), pp. 34-35. Richard Vine, interview, supra. On tourism, telex from J.M. Lepage, "Le pouls de la région de NY à une semaine du référendum," 12/5/80, MAIQ.

222 [**Duhaime**] Memo from Jacques Boucher, "Visite du Ministre à Washington," 11/3/80, and text of speech "Toward the Year 2000: Quebec in the North American Economy," 21/3/80. Duhaime quoted the *Financial Times*, 3/12/79, in which was written, "When the Parti Québécois took office, 9.8% of the work force was unemployed, compared with 6.2% in Ontario. Now unemployment is at 9.5% in Quebec and 6.7% in Ontario, a gap of 2.8 percentage points instead of 3.6." Economic analyses, see INR Report No. 1244, "Canada: Quebec separatist momentum falters," 26/10/79, CONFIDENTIAL NOT RELEASABLE TO FOREIGNERS. The author wrote, "Companies are reacting essentially to competitive stimulants and the appeal of population centres situated west of Quebec." US Department of Commerce, Business America, 24/3/80.

223 [**McNamara**] McNamara on independence, first in Quebec Telegram 019, "Contribution to study of impacts of PQ election," 17/1/77, CONFIDENTIAL, then in Quebec Airgram A-04, "The Parti Quebecois: An Uneasy Blend of Idealism and Pragmatism," 19/5/78, CONFIDENTIAL.

224 [**Enders**] The "YES" side won in Ottawa Telegram 6078, "How the national unity crisis may play out: an update,"12/12/78, SECRET. The "NO" side won in Ottawa Telegram 3673, "How the national unity crisis may play out: an update," 24/7/79, CONFIDENTIAL.

224 [**INR 1979**] INR Report No. 1668, by Mary Shoemaker, "Quebec: referendum battle lines begin to form," 26/4/79, CONFIDENTIAL—NOT RELEASABLE TO FOREIGN NATIONALS. McNamara on Clark's chances after the election in Quebec Telegram 210, "Little Rene rolls up his sleeves," 4/6/79, LIMITED OFFICIAL USE. Opinion varied on the strategic impact of having an Anglophone or a Francophone prime minister in Ottawa. In 1978, McNamara wrote, "As the PQ has found since coming into power, it is virtually impossible to arouse Québécois tribal animosities against a federal government with as prominent a Francophone contingent as the present Trudeau government now possesses." Quebec Telegram 380, "Bourgault urges militant not to change platform," 27/10/78, LIMITED OFFICIAL USE. After Trudeau returned to power, however, Lévesque told Jaeger that this would serve his interests (in fact, the "YES" side did rise in the polls after Trudeau was elected). Morin attempted to explain the phenomenon to Karl Meyer, of *The New York Times*: "With Clark, Quebeckers would have been scared to break up the system. With Trudeau, there would be a longer discussion. . . . To use an analogy, with Clark, Quebeckers

could compare themselves to an individual getting ready to jump into an empty swimming pool. With Trudeau, there was water in the pool." Memo "Transcription 'libérale' des propos échangés entre le ministre Claude Morin et Karl Meyer du *New York Times*," 3/4/80, MAIQ.

224 **[INR]** INR Report No. 1244, "Canada: Quebec separatist momentum falters," loc. cit. Enders, interview, supra, and Quebec Telegram 343, "Ambassador's farewell call on Levesque," 1/9/79, CONFIDENTIAL. On Curtis visit, Quebec Telegram 441, "Ambassador's visit to Quebec," 31/10/79, CONFIDENTIAL, and file memo "Entrevue du premier ministre, Monsieur René Lévesque, avec le nouvel Ambassadeur des États-Unis, Monsieur Kenneth Curtis, le mardi 30 octobre 1979, à 11 h 30," 31/10/79, MAIQ.

225 **[Jaeger]** In Quebec Telegram 497, "Quebec: six months before the referendum," 13/12/79, CONFIDENTIAL.

225 **[Lévesque-Jaeger]** In Quebec Telegram 122, "Quebec: three months before the referendum," 22/3/80, CONFIDENTIAL.

226 **[April 14]** Quebec Telegram 169, "Crystal-gazing some possible Quebec scenarios: Part I: analysis," 14/4/80, CONFIDENTIAL.

226 **[Smith-Ahmad]** Richard Smith, interview, Wash., 12/4/89. Sharon E. Ahmad, deputy assistant secretary of state 1979-1980, interview, Wash., 27/4/89.

228 **[Jaeger-Vance]** This narrative is taken from Richard Pouliot's memo "Entretien avec le Consul général des États-Unis," 22/4/80, CONFIDENTIAL, MAIQ, and from interviews with Richard Pouliot, Claude Morin, and some other Quebec diplomats, as well as with Lise Bissonnette, who discussed this subject in an interview with Jaeger after the referendum. Tel. interview, Montreal, 16/1/90. On lack of interviews with Jaeger, see Notes and References, chapter 18.

228 **[Jaeger-Advice]** In his defence, it must be noted that Jaeger effectively advised his superiors to follow a course of moderation. "For the present, it is important that we maintain our current posture unless we wish to become a referendum or election issue ourselves," he wrote, though he didn't allude to Vance's visit. Quebec Telegram 171, "Crystal-gazing some possible Quebec scenarios: summary, conclusions and some recommendations," 14/4/80, SECRET.

229 **[Globe]** In "Strange talk on Quebec," *Globe and Mail*, 18/8/79, memo "Rencontre avec le nouveau consul général des États-Unis, M. G.W. Jaeger," 24/8/79, MAIQ. Martin could not remember the name of his contact. However, when he attempted to verify the information at the State Department, Martin received a call from his source, who threatened never to speak to him again if his comment on Quebec was published. Martin chose to lose his source. Lawrence Martin, telephone interview, Washington-Ottawa, July 1989.

229 **[Reston]** In *The New York Times*, 23/2/77, and 4/4/80.

230 **[Vance 1978]** Transcript of the press conference and of Vance's speech, Nov. 21 and 22, 1978, EA. Note from Yves Michaud to Lévesque, "Projet d'intervention des Affaires intergouvernementales au sujet des déclarations de monsieur Cyrus Vance à Ottawa, le 21 novembre 1978," 30/11/78, note from Michel Chalout to Yves Michaud, "Déclaration de C. Vance," 30/11/78, and draft of diplomatic note, MAIQ. "Mémo du Service de Presse des Affaires extérieures Visite Vance—Commentaires par M. Claude Morin," 23/11/78, EA, and Beaudoin, interview, supra.

231 **[Lévesque scared]** In *The New York Times*, 25/1/79. INR, "Quebec: referendum battle lines ..." loc. cit.

231 **[Ottawa-Washington]** Senior official who requires anonymity; Mark MacGuigan, telephone interview, Ottawa, 5/6/89; interviews with Gotlieb, Curtis, Duemling, Vest, Smith, Brzezinski, supra; Wingate Lloyd, interview, Wash., 13/4/89. *La Presse*, 4/4/80.

232 **[Vance press conference]** Transcript, "Visit of Secretary Vance," in *Department of State Bulletin*, Vol. 80, No. 2039, June 1980, pp. 3-6.

234 **[Warren]** Telex WSHDC UNGR3028, "Mtg with Sec State designate Vance Dec 31," 31/12/76, CONFIDENTIAL CDN EYES ONLY, EA. Jamieson's assistant was David Elder, interview, supra; an associate of Jamieson's who requires anonymity; Flora MacDonald, and

David Elder, tel. interviews, Ottawa 5/6/89; Mark MacGuigan, interview, supra.

235 **[Airplane]** Richard Vine, interview, supra.

236 **[Fletcher]** "Quebec's Foreign Policy: An Interview with Claude Morin, Minister for Intergovernmental Affairs, Province of Québec," *The Fletcher Forum*, Vol. 4, No. 1, pp. 127-134; *The Gazette*, 17/4/80; note from Jacques Joli-Coeur to Richard Pouliot, 17/4/80; memo from Richard Pouliot, "Entretien avec le Consul général des États-Unis," loc. cit. MAIQ. In a rebuttal to the French edition of this book, George Jaeger, who refused to grant the author an interview, stated that the psychodrama of the Vance trip was not of his own making. He writes: "Someone had told me officially but very discreetly, less than one month before the referendum, that Secretary of State Cyrus Vance would perhaps part from the traditional American policy of strict non-intervention, pushed by high-level Canadian pressures, and that he would publicly support the "NO" forces during his visit. I was told that a document to that effect existed. It was suggested to me that I advise, at least, Claude Morin of that manifestly explosive possibility. As Lisée indicates, I did so. I then sent a personal, highly unusual and very urgent message to the Secretary of State, not only to convey Claude Morin's reaction but also my deep conviction that an American intervention three weeks before the referendum might provoke a violent counter-blow in Quebec, the consequences of which could be felt for years. I was later told that the Secretary of State had received my message on board the plane that brought him to Ottawa and that he felt the message was "useful." (*Le Soleil* of 13/6/90) Mr Jaeger's version of events is unfortunately supported by none of the other parties involved. The two documents he mentions were not declassified by the State Department nor do they fit, in their descriptions or dates, the summary of still classified documents on this subject filed by the State Department in the US District Court for DC on 25/4/90 (Civil action No. 89-1266).

236 **[Separatist Lévesque]** Diplomat who requires anonymity. Snelling, Vine, Smith, Duemling, interviews, supra. Letter from Barry Steers, No. 343, "Comments on Interview Given by Claude Morin to *The New York Times*," 6/10/77, CONFIDENTIAL, EA. *The Wall Street Journal*, 17/3/78. Salomon in *La Presse*, 20/5/78.

238 **[Lévesque's associates]** Michaud, Morin, Bernard, Boivin, Beaudoin, Latouche, interviews, supra. Corine Côté-Lévesque in Michel Vastel, *Trudeau le Québécois*, op. cit., p. 248.

239 **[Jaeger]** For example, Lévesque used the term "independence" with Jaeger in Quebec Telegram 416, "Talk with Levesque," 12/10/79, CONFIDENTIAL. See also chapter 18.

239 **[Trudeau]** In 1964, a reporter found that he was "serene in his conviction that separatist forces were in decline." Quoted in Peter Brimelow, *The Patriot Game—Canada and the Canadian Question Revisited* (Stanford: Hoover, 1986), p. 218. "My intentions are to get out," in Graham Fraser, *Le Parti québécois*, op. cit., p. 101. For Safire, see chapter 13.

240 **[Muskie]** Letter from Lévesque, 30/4/80, MAIQ. Letter from Muskie, 12/5/80. Memo from J.E. Hyndman No. FCP-169, "Déclarations passées de Muskie sur le Québec et la confédération,"1/5/80, CONFIDENTIEL, EA.

240 **[US regions]** Memo from Michel Brunet, "Perception américaine à la veille du référendum: Le Midwest," undated; telex from J.M. Lepage, "Le pouls de la région de NY à une semaine du référendum," 12/5/80; Telex from Yves Labonté, "Los Angeles: Opinion américaine à l'approche du référendum," 12/5/80; Atlanta, telex from Jean-Marc Roy, "Attitudes de l'Américain moyen du sud-est des États-Unis à l'égard du référendum du 20 mai," 12/5/80, MAIQ.

240 **[Questions and answers]** Message FCO-1003, "Referendum —Questions and Answers," 16/5/80, CONFIDENTIAL, EA.

240 **[Spread]** During the weeks leading up to the referendum, Hydro-Québec bonds sometimes showed a spread of only 20 base points from British Columbia Hydro, Manitoba Hydro, and Ontario Hydro bonds. They even overtook the value of the B.C. bonds twice, in the middle and at the end of April, erasing even the historic difference. Although Hydro-Québec was

100 points down on the eve of the referendum, this gap closed completely a month later. The trend is clearer if we compare the progress of a Hydro-Quebec bond to that of an American Treasury bill. The spread was the greatest after the Economic Club, one month before the referendum. After a precipitous drop of 70 points, it was back at its seasonal average three weeks after the vote. (The spread from B.C. Hydro of 16/5/80 was 130 points, less 30 "historic" points for a "supplementary post-PQ-election spread" of 100 points. In comparison to Treasury Bill TSY 8.25, used as a standard by First Boston, Hydro reached its minimum gross spread of 115 points from 15/11/76, on 12/8/78. The spread grew at the end of 1979 to reach its widest spread of 203 points on 18/4/80, then shrank to 177 points on 16/5/80, and to 130 points on 6/6/80.) Hydro-Québec and Merrill Lynch data.

240 [**Press**] Memo FCO-641, "Coverage of the Quebec Referendum Results and the Campaign in the American Press—May 1980," 5/6/80, UNCLASSIFIED, EA.

240 [**New York**] Telex CNGNY YICF0343, "Referendum night reception—Quebec house," 21/5/80, RESTRICTED, EA.

241 [**Boivin**] Jean-Roch Boivin, interview, supra. In his memoirs, Lévesque stated that at the beginning of April, due to a "heartening advance" of the "YES" side, victory "was not at all inconceivable. Have there not been examples around the world of people seized with unanimity, or almost, in comparable occasions?" Did he express the objective of 75% of Francophones reported by his spouse? "Near the end of April everyone knew," he wrote afterward, "that we would not attain our 62% [of Francophones necessary to a victory] and that we were no longer assured of even a simple majority in French Quebec." In René Lévesque, *Attendez que je me rappelle...*, op. cit., pp. 406-412.

242 [**Jaeger**] Quebec Telegram 231, "Quebec referendum: 'No' wins broad-based, decisive victory," 20/5/80, UNCLASSIFIED, and Quebec Telegram 233, "'No' wins but the game goes on," 21/5/80, CONFIDENTIAL. Brzezinski, interview, supra.

242 [**Bernard**] Interview, supra.

242 [**Latouche at Harvard**] In Elliott J. Feldman (ed.), *The Quebec Referendum: What Happened and What Next? A Dialogue the Day After with Claude Forget and Daniel Latouche May 21, 1980* (Cambridge: UCRNA, 1980), p. 40. Claude Forget indicated that in the Liberal Party's internal polls, "the 'YES' had a dominant position in January-February, up to the beginning of March."

242 [**Vigneault**] *Le Soleil*, 4/9/82. If it had wanted to influence the referendum result, American diplomacy had at its disposal a much more compromising tool than brute intervention by the Secretary of State. In mid-April, the consul general in Montreal, Lloyd Rives, obtained a copy of a PQ document on a future independent Quebec. Among the most controversial proposals were an increase in luxury taxes, the abolition of all corporate tax breaks except those for cooperatives, the creation of a Quebec economic plan and an industrial-reorganization agency, and total nationalization of the transport industry. If the Americans had leaked this information to the press, they would have put the "YES" forces on the defensive and given ammunition to the "NO" side. They chose to keep this document to themselves. It is summarized in Montreal Telegram 776, "Policy ideas from PQ for post referendum period," 17/4/80, CONFIDENTIAL.


Chapter 17. President Reagan's Smiles

244 [**Quotation**] Interview, Allan Gotlieb, supra.

244 [**Trudeau**] Lubor J. Zink, "The Unpenetrated Problem of Pierre Trudeau," *National Review*, 25/6/82, pp. 751-756. On the cover, the title was also translated: "Le problème non-pénétré de Pierre Trudeau," with the subtitle "He is a dogmatist/Il est dogmatiste." A Reagan "confidant" told Gotlieb that the President was "impressed" by the article. Michael Deaver,

Reagan's friend and advisor, confirmed that the latter devoured everything written in the *National Review*. Deaver, interview, supra.

245   **[Wallace]** Canadian Press dispatch in *The Globe and Mail*, 27/9/71.

245   **[Definition]** All American quotations are taken from Stephen Clarkson, *Canada and the Reagan Challenge: crisis and adjustment, 1981-85*, 2nd ed. (Toronto: Lorimer, 1985), pp. 23-49, except for the Hatfield anecdote, which was taken from Richard Gwynn, *The 49th Paradox ...*, op. cit., p. 26.

245   **[Trudeau the opportunist]** From Allan Gotlieb, interview, supra. Gotlieb was responsible for US policy at the Department of External Affairs in Ottawa until 1982, when he was named ambassador to Washington. The NEP and FIRA had been sketched out in Trudeau's April 1980 Speech from the Throne, thus before the referendum. But the true significance of the NEP was unveiled on 28/10/80. Tightening of FIRA's administrative regulations was accomplished gradually by Minister Gray; legislative reinforcement of FIRA was announced throughout 1980 and 1981, but was never accomplished.

246   **[Jockel-Casey]** Jockel, interview, supra. Willis Armstrong, who wrote the briefing book on Canada for the new Reagan team during the transitional period after the presidential election, reviewed some National Intelligence Estimates for Casey, to gauge their readability for non-specialists. Armstrong, interview, supra.

246   **[Lévesque-Reagan]** Letter from René Lévesque, 14/11/80, and memo from Robert Normand, 26/11/80, MAIQ. Also, Quebec Telegram 482, "Levesque letter of congratulations to president-elect Reagan," 26/11/80, UNCLASSIFIED. Response, State Telegram 331452, "Reply to Levesque letter of congratulations to President-elect Reagan," 15/12/80, UNCLASSIFIED. On Johnson, State Telegram 184338, 17/6/68, LIMITED OFFICIAL USE. Assassination attempt, State Telegram 105901, "Response to message to the President from premier Rene Levesque," 24/4/81, UNCLASSIFIED. National holiday, Quebec Telegram 307, "Fourth of July congratulatory message from premier Levesque," 6/7/82, UNCLASSIFIED, and State Telegram 183324, "Response to Fourth of July message to the President from Quebec premier Rene Levesque," 13/7/82, UNCLASSIFIED.

248   **[Dunn]** Dunn memo, May 1982, MAIQ.

248   **[Pouliot]** In Pouliot's telex "Visite à Washington 18-19 août," 21/8/81, and "*Département d'État*," 24/8/81, in memo from Lucien Vallières, "Réunion de réflexion de la direction États-Unis, les 26 et 27 août," 10/9/80, CONFIDENTIEL, MAIQ.

248   **[Bill 101]** "Sacre Bleu! S'il vous plaît! Enough is Enough, Quebec," *Detroit Free Press*, 5/1/81; "Don't Widen the Gap," *Atlanta Journal*, 9/1/81; "Quebec should be ashamed," *San Francisco Examiner*, 8/1/81. Speech by Godin, MAIQ.

249   **[Lucier]** References to Lucier and Helms's general policy are taken from Ernest B. Furgurson, "Ambassador Helms," *Common Cause*, Vol. 13, No. 2 (March 1987), pp. 16-21. (The original source is Furgurson's book *Hard Right: The Rise of Jesse Helms* [New York: W.W. Norton, 1986].) Report by Dunn, "Relations entre les États-Unis et le Québec," 25/11/81, CONFIDENTIEL, MAIQ.

250   **[Night of the long knives]** Lougheed was the most hesitant to sacrifice his ally Lévesque, notably on the question of linguistic rights. The argument that swayed him was presented by Jean Chrétien, Trudeau's minister of justice and the principal federal spokesperson in the referendum debate. The linguistic problem was "between us" French Canadians, Chrétien told Lougheed, to get him to drop his reservations. Lougheed was also the only premier who stayed to "discuss, plead, argue" with Lévesque for 20 minutes after the accord was announced to him. Though the seven had let Lévesque down (a Saskatchewan official participating in the negotiations went so far as to hide when he saw a Quebec representative in the small hours of the morning), it should be noted that the previous day Lévesque had opened a breach in the "common front" by accepting Trudeau's proposal to hold a national referendum on the constitution, a prospect that was detested by his Anglophone allies. There was even talk that

day of a new "Ottawa-Quebec axis." These details are drawn from the remarkable book by Robert Sheppard and Michael Valpy, *The National Deal* ..., op. cit., pp. 296-302.

250 [**Brimelow theory**] See *The Patriot Game*, op. cit.

251 [*Barron's*] Peter Brimelow, "No Castro of the North?," *Barron's*, 7/7/82.

251 [**Morin**] In memo by André Soucy, "Rencontre Morin/MacGuigan," 12/5/82, and memo by Claude Roquet, "Déclarations canadiennes et québécoises aux États-Unis," 18/6/82, MAIQ, and in *The Gazette*, July 10 and July 20, 1982, p. B-3.

252 [**Jaeger-visit**] Quebec Telegram 262, "Levesque to address senate republican caucus," 10/6/82, CONFIDENTIAL.

252 [**July 14**] State Telegram 192274, "Press guidance: Premier Levesque's Washington visit," 12/7/82, UNCLASSIFIED; Quebec Telegram 323, "Levesque's Washington visit receives heavy publicity in Quebec," 15/7/82, UNCLASSIFIED; Montreal Telegram 1552, "Senate interview on Levesque Washington visit," 15/7/82, LIMITED OFFICIAL USE; Quebec Telegram 325, "Press reaction: Levesque visit to Washington," 16/7/82; Ottawa Telegram 4944, "Levesque visit to Washington," 16/7/82, UNCLASSIFIED. Telex from Peter Dunn, "Visit PM Wash," 16/7/82; note from Peter Dunn, "Visite du Premier Ministre à Washington," undated, MAIQ. *The Gazette*, July 15 and July 20, 1982, *La Presse*, 15/7/82, Canadian Press dispatches, 14/7/82. *Congressional Record*, 14/7/82, p. S-8235. Gotlieb, interview, supra.

Jacques-Yvan Morin tried, in vain, to see American Education Secretary T.H. Bell during this visit. Morin felt that since education was under provincial jurisdiction, he could see Bell without a federal escort. But Bell asked for permission from the State Department, which advised the embassy, which required a federal presence. Jacques-Yvan Morin refused, and the meeting did not take place.

416 [**The Right-PQ**] Relatively little happened after 14/7/82, when Quebec separatism rubbed up against the Reagan right. When Morin returned to Washington in June of 1983, he stopped in on Helms and on two other important senators, Republican John Chaffee and Democrat Claiborne Pell. That month, the Quebec health minister and future premier, Pierre-Marc Johnson, met with Orrin Hatch, another ultraconservative, who had been at the lunch with Lévesque and who was also concerned with health questions. On 29/6/83, Quebec gave its first Washington reception to celebrate its national holiday. Among the guests were Helms's and Pell's congressional aides, those of two Republican senators, Richard Lugar and Lowell Weicker, and officials from four departments. This gathering would be deemed very creditable by local lobbyists, since it was held by a non-government.

In the fall of 1986, Peter Brimelow published his book *The Patriot Game* in Canada. The book was distributed in the United States in 1988. In the *Washington Times* and a number of other dailies, Patrick Buchanan, ultraconservative columnist and former director of communications for Ronald Reagan (a sort of ideological twin to William Safire), spokesperson for the radical right and briefly considered as a Republican presidential candidate, gave Brimelow's book and his conclusions a favorable, even approving, review. *Washington Times*, 20/1/80, p. F1. Buchanan went further and trumpeted this theory emphatically in two other *Washington Times* columns in April of 1990.


Chapter 18. The Consul's Act


256 [**Quotation**] Condensed extract of a brief conversation with Jaeger. In spite of many requests and two telephone conversations, George Jaeger refused, except for some brief comments, to give an interview to the author. He felt that it was not his place to give an "instant diplomatic history," and considered himself to be "still bound by confidentiality." Jaeger, telephone interviews, May 23 and June 27, 1989. In his rebuttal to *Le Soleil*, loc. cit., he surprisingly

avoids discussing the events covered in this chapter.

256 **[Godin]** Gérald Godin, tel. interview, Montreal, 29/1/90. Also interviews with Lise Bissonnette, Jean Chapdelaine, supra.

257 **[Lévesque meetings]** In note from Jean Chapdelaine, "Visite de monsieur Jaeger, Consul général des États-Unis, à monsieur Lévesque," 12/10/79, and note from André Soucy, "Entretiens Jaeger–Jacques-Yvan Morin Jaeger–Clément Richard," 13/12/79, MAIQ.

257 **[Protocol]** In note from Donovan, 9/12/80.

257 **[Morin-Pouliot]** Interviews supra, and with three Quebec officials. Curtis's successor at the American embassy in Ottawa, Paul Robinson, stated, however, that Jaeger had told him that he had been criticized by Canadians for his relations with the PQ. A senior federal official charged with American affairs does not remember this. Paul Robinson, tel. interview Chicago, 12/7/89. Also Quebec Telegram 057 "Quebec elections: a first look," 23/2/81, CONFIDENTIAL.

258 **[Godin-Beaudoin]** Interviews supra, and note from Louise Beaudoin, "Rencontre avec le Consul général des États-Unis," 25/9/81, CONFIDENTIEL, MAIQ.

259 **[Robinson]** Pouliot and Robinson, interviews, supra; *The New York Times*, 27/5/82; *Baltimore Sun*, 20/5/82.

260 **[PLO-PQ]** Beaudoin, interview, supra. Note from Robert Trudel, "Compte rendu de la visite officielle à Québec du Consul Général des États-Unis à Montréal, monsieur William D. Morgan, jeudi le 17 décembre 1981," 5/1/82. Jaeger was at this meeting and seemed, in fact, to monopolize the floor. MAIQ. List of guests in Montreal Telegram 2924, "PQ radicals begin to shift: international invitees to party congress," 10/12/81, UNCLASSIFIED.

260 **[Association-US]** Landry in *The Montreal Star*, 22/4/78, p. A2. Lévesque quoted in Linder, "Quebec's international personality," p. 31. Landry, interview, supra. Canadian Press dispatch, 2/2/83.

262 **[Franco-Spanish]** Note by André Soucy, "Rencontre avec le Consul Général des États-Unis," 31/7/81, MAIQ. Operation America, Notebook 5, *Actions gouvernementales répertoriées*, c. Dec. 1978, MAIQ. There were no more than 20 of these kinds of actions per year up to 1974, then 32 in 1975, then 21 in 1976, after which the number increased. On ActFa, memo "Rencontre du ministre des Affaires intergouvernementales du Québec et du Consul Général des États-Unis à Québec—Synthèse des principaux dossiers Québec/États-Unis," 28/7/81, MAIQ.

263 **[Defensive, offensive]** Statistics from "Percent French Mother Tongue Population for Selected States," US Bureau of the Census, Census of Population 1970, *General Social and Economic Characteristics*, Selected States, Table 49. Rate of decline in Clavin Veltman, "Le déclin de la francophonie aux États-Unis," *Le Devoir*, 28/3/80. Hannaford, interview, supra.

264 **[Dumas]** Interview, supra. Letters to Roger Cyr, 28/8/78, and Yves Michaud, 1/9/78, MAIQ. There was no way to know, in 1977, that the referendum would take place in May of 1980, but the New Hampshire scenario could have been useful under other circumstances.

264 **[Cyr]** In memo "Opération-Amérique—Programme de communications pour la Délégation du Québec en Nouvelle-Angleterre," Oct. 1979, MAIQ. Memo from Harvey, "Rencontre avec les leaders franco-américains," 18/5/77, and telex "La Nouvelle-Angleterre et le référendum," 12/5/80, MAIQ.

264 **[Vest-Enders]** Interviews, supra.

265 **[Bouvier]** Handwritten memo from Bouvier to Donovan, "Conversation du 28.10.81 avec M. Jaeger Consul général des États-Unis," 2/11/81.

265 **[Lloyd]** Tel. interview, Wash., 13/7/89.

265 **[Deputy minister]** Canadian Press dispatch in *La Presse*, 26/3/84.

The first French Canadian consul named to Boston, at the beginning of the 1960s, was Jean Lapierre. He recalled that Lester Pearson had personally given him the mandate to "convince the largest number of Franco-Americans" possible to come back to Quebec. But Lapierre quickly found that Franco-Americans he met were not interested, so he abandoned his efforts. In Peter Strusberg, *Lester Pearson and the American Dilemma* (Toronto: Doubleday, 1980).

266 [**Jaeger-Lévesque**] In Quebec Telegram 268, "A talk with Levesque: 'Canada must be broken down to its constituent parts,' " 11/6/82, CONFIDENTIAL; Quebec Telegram 27, "Levesque plans new fight for Quebec independence," 17/1/83, CONFIDENTIAL; Quebec Telegram 515, "Goodbye Call on Levesque," 22/8/83, SECRET; Quebec Telegram 624, "Call on Quebec premier Levesque," 19/10/83, CONFIDENTIAL; Quebec Telegram 045, "Call on Premier Levesque," 2/2/84, CONFIDENTIAL; Quebec Telegram 612, "Congratulatory message to the President from Quebec premier Levesque," 6/11/84, UNCLASSIFIED.

269 [**Lévesque-Uncle Sam**] René Lévesque, *Attendez que je me rappelle*, op. cit., p. 485.

269 [**Quebec summit**] On Reagan 1985, Evelyn Dumas and Bernard Landry, interviews, supra, and *Le Devoir*, 20/3/85, and *The Gazette*, 22/3/85. Joseph Jockel, who wrote Reagan's speeches for this visit, recalled that Reagan's toast at the breakfast included regards to Premier Lévesque and that the Americans had raised no objections to his coming to the meeting.

269 [**Rosenblatt**] In Quebec Telegram 308, "The Parti Quebecois in the wake of Levesque's departure," 26/6/85, LIMITED OFFICIAL USE.

270 [**Moses**] Feldman, interview, supra.

270 [**Spelling Lévesque**] Author's personal recollection.


Conclusion and Outlook


272 [**Quotation**] Last sentence of the analytical section of *The Quebec Situation*, loc. cit. See appendix.

272 [**Advisors**] All persons cited in the conclusion were seen by the author, and are identified supra.

273 [**Reporter**] Louise Beaudoin to Karl Meyer of *The New York Times*, in *Transcription "libérale" des propos échangés...*, loc. cit.

274 [**Jaeger**] In Quebec Telegram 497, "Quebec: six months before the referendum," 13/12/79, CONFIDENTIAL, and Quebec Telegram 169, "Crystal-gazing some possible Quebec scenarios: part 1: Analysis," 14/4/80, CONFIDENTIAL.

276 [**New York Times**] "US Sees Broad Effects in a Division of Canada," 30/6/90, p. A.2. *The Times* writes: "The [State Department] officials volunteered that they had great respect for Quebec's premier, Robert Bourassa."

# INDEX